PRINCIPLES OF PLEADING AND PRACTICE

AUSTRALIA
The Law Book Company Ltd.
Sydney : Melbourne : Brisbane

CANADA AND U.S.A.
The Carswell Company Ltd.
Agincourt, Ontario

INDIA
N. M. Tripathi Private Ltd.
Bombay

ISRAEL
Steimatzky's Agency Ltd.
Jerusalem : Tel Aviv : Haifa

MALAYSIA : SINGAPORE : BRUNEI
Malaysian Law Journal (Pte.) Ltd.
Singapore

NEW ZEALAND
Sweet & Maxwell (N.Z.) Ltd.
Wellington

PAKISTAN
Pakistan Law House
Karachi

ODGERS'

PRINCIPLES OF

PLEADING AND PRACTICE

IN CIVIL ACTIONS IN THE
HIGH COURT OF JUSTICE

TWENTIETH EDITION

BY

GILES FRANCIS HARWOOD, M.A.(OXON.)

Of the Inner Temple, Barrister-at-Law
Senior State Counsel (Republic of Kenya)

LONDON
STEVENS & SONS
1971

FIRST EDITION	(1891)	By WILLIAM BLAKE ODGERS.
SECOND EDITION	(1894)	By WILLIAM BLAKE ODGERS, Q.C.
THIRD EDITION	(1897)	
FOURTH EDITION	(1900)	
FIFTH EDITION	(1903)	
SIXTH EDITION	(1906)	
SEVENTH EDITION	(1912)	
EIGHTH EDITION	(1919)	
REVISED	(1922)	By WALTER BLAKE ODGERS.
NINTH EDITION	(1926)	
TENTH EDITION	(1930)	By WALTER BLAKE ODGERS and A. H. ARMSTRONG.
ELEVENTH EDITION	(1934)	By WALTER BLAKE ODGERS and B. A. HARWOOD.
TWELFTH EDITION	(1939)	By WALTER BLAKE ODGERS, K.C., and B. A. HARWOOD.
THIRTEENTH EDITION	(1946)	By WALTER BLAKE ODGERS, K.C., and LEWIS F. STURGE.
FOURTEENTH EDITION	(1952)	By LEWIS F. STURGE.
FIFTEENTH EDITION	(1955)	By MASTER B. A. HARWOOD.
SIXTEENTH EDITION	(1957)	
SEVENTEENTH EDITION	(1960)	By MASTER B. A. HARWOOD and G. F. HARWOOD.
EIGHTEENTH EDITION	(1963)	By G. F. HARWOOD.
NINETEENTH EDITION	(1966)	By G. F. HARWOOD.
TWENTIETH EDITION	(1971)	By G. F. HARWOOD.

SBN 420 42730 9

Published in 1971 by
Stevens & Sons Limited
of 11 New Fetter Lane, London
and printed in Great Britain
by The Eastern Press Ltd.
of London and Reading

©
Stevens & Sons Limited
1971

PREFACE

"Although a court cannot conduct its business without a code of procedure, the relation of the rules of practice to the work of justice is intended to be that of handmaid rather than mistress; and the court ought not to be so far bound and tied by rules, which are after all only intended as general rules of procedure, as to be compelled to do what will cause injustice in the particular case." (Lord Collins M.R. in Re Coles and Ravenshear [1907] 1 K.B. 1.)

SEVERAL enactments heralded the approach of this edition, more particularly the Civil Evidence Act 1968 and the Administration of Justice Act 1969, which have resulted in many new rules. And whilst these Acts are in their early childhood, the birth of others, expected shortly, will further affect parts of the text, *e.g.*, legislation resulting from the Report of the Committee on the Enforcement of Judgment Debts (an Attachment of Earnings Bill is already in print) and the Administration of Justice Act 1970, should soon be brought into effect. Thus the chapter on Execution and Enforcement of Judgments will almost certainly require considerable revision by the time of the next edition, and the accuracy of the sections dealing with committal and attachment of debts may even now be short-lived indeed. Changes in the organisation and administration of Assizes, following some of the recommendations of the "Beeching Report," cannot be far away.

Advantage has been taken of the permissiveness of section 12, Family Reform Act 1969 to avoid reference to "infants"; and since, by virtue of that Act, "minors" must be deemed to mature earlier, it will be found that the evergreen youth, who by one of the precedents in all previous editions has ever complained of breach of warranty on the sale of a mare, has become the more modern victim of an over-enthusiastic car salesman.

The procedure for appeals direct to the House of Lords is still very new; also the provisions for claiming interim payments in personal injury cases. And applications in interlocutory proceedings under Order 38, rr. 27 and 28, are still rather surprisingly rare. Therefore any comment on the practical utility of such matters would be premature and has been intentionally avoided.

Once again the two chapters on Chancery practice and procedure have been edited by Mr. Raymond Walton, Q.C., of Lincoln's Inn, thus perpetuating his valuable contribution of an essential part of this book.

v

Preface

It is sadly appropriate to record here the death in April 1969 of Walter Blake Odgers, Q.C., who not only assisted his father (William Blake Odgers, K.C.) with *Odgers on the Common Law* but became senior editor of *Odgers on Libel and Slander* (6th ed.) and also ensured that the family connection with this work remained unbroken for more than fifty years.

I am most grateful to Master Elton and to the publishers for advice and assistance readily given, and for undertaking the task of final revision at somewhat short notice owing to my retirement from practice in England soon after the preparation of the text for publication.

GILES HARWOOD.

March 1, 1971,
Attorney-General's Chambers,
Nairobi.

CONTENTS

vii

Contents

Contents

ix

Contents

Contents

Contents

Contents

Contents

TABLE OF CASES

Table of Cases

Table of Cases

Table of Cases

Table of Cases

Table of Cases

Table of Cases

Table of Cases

Table of Cases

Table of Cases

Table of Cases

Table of Cases

Table of Cases

Table of Cases

Table of Cases

TABLE OF STATUTES

Table of Statutes

Table of Statutes

Table of Statutes

Table of Statutes

TABLE OF RULES AND ORDERS

[The Rules will be found set out in full on the pages indicated by the figures in bolder type]

Table of Rules and Orders

CHAPTER 1

AN INTRODUCTORY SURVEY

THE SUPREME COURT

THE Supreme Court of Judicature was created by the Judicature Act, 1873, which came into force on November 1, 1875.[1] It is divided into two parts:

The Court of Appeal, and
The High Court of Justice.

As a rule proceedings are begun in the High Court of Justice and are only taken to the Court of Appeal subsequently. There are three divisions of the High Court of Justice:

The Chancery Division,
The Queen's Bench Division, and
The Family [1a] Division.

Proceedings in the High Court of Justice may broadly be divided into:

(1) Proceedings which do not arise from ordinary disputes between subjects or from claims by subjects against the Crown within the purview of the Crown Proceedings Act, 1947.

(2) Proceedings which do arise in either of the above ways.

The first class includes proceedings on the Crown side of the Queen's Bench Division whereby the High Court of Justice controls the activities of inferior courts and quasi-judicial tribunals by orders of mandamus, certiorari and prohibition; applications for writs of habeas corpus; proceedings to commit persons who are guilty of a contempt of court or to strike a solicitor off the rolls, and appeals by way of case stated from courts of summary jurisdiction or quarter sessions. Under this

---

[1] This Act and subsequent amending Acts are now merged in the Supreme Court of Judicature (Consolidation) Act, 1925, referred to throughout this work as the Judicature Act, 1925. It is nevertheless necessary to refer to the Act of 1873 when dealing with the history of modern pleading and practice.
[1a] Formerly the Probate, Divorce and Admiralty Division: see Administration of Justice Act, 1970, s. 1, Sched. 1. Probate business, except for non-contentious or common form probate business, is now assigned to the Chancery Division; Admiralty and prize court business is now assigned to the Q.B.D.

1

head there also falls the criminal jurisdiction of the High Court of Justice. There is also a special jurisdiction dealing with the revenue of the Crown, largely derived from the old Court of Exchequer. The High Court also has jurisdiction in bankruptcy.[2] These matters are wholly outside the scope of this book and no further mention will be made of them, save incidentally.

The second class includes actions [3] commenced by writ of summons [4] in the Queen's Bench Division or the Chancery Division, actions commenced by originating summons in the Chancery Division or (more rarely) in the Queen's Bench Division, petitions in the Chancery Division for the winding up of companies, actions and petitions in the Family [4a] Division and special cases stated by an arbitrator for the opinion of the Queen's Bench Division on a point of law. By the Crown Proceedings Act, 1947, the Crown for the first time in our legal history submitted itself to being sued as an ordinary litigant, subject to the limitations imposed by the Act (see *post*, p. 16).

The main purpose of this book is to describe the procedure in an action commenced by writ of summons in the Queen's Bench Division. The procedure in an action in the Chancery Division (which is dealt with in Chapter 22) is not now very different from that in the Queen's Bench Division, both Divisions having adopted with certain modifications the practice and procedure of discovery, which originated in the old Court of Chancery. There is, however, a difference in the interlocutory procedure in the two Divisions and there are also many matters commenced by originating summons and a few by petition which are peculiar to the Chancery Division. A brief description of these proceedings will be found in Chapter 23.

The remaining proceedings enumerated above have a procedure of their own and for information as to these special jurisdictions the student must consult the books which deal with their peculiar practice.

---

[2] See Bankruptcy Act, 1914, s. 98. The High Court jurisdiction is exercised by the judges of the Chancery Division, being assigned to Group B, and by the three Registrars in Bankruptcy. Outside London the jurisdiction is exercised by county courts.

[3] *i.e.*, civil proceedings commenced by writ or in other manner prescribed by Rules of Court (Judicature Act, 1925, s. 225). The various modes of beginning civil proceedings are dealt with in Ord. 5.

[4] Usually called simply a " Writ."

[4a] See note 1a, *ante*, p. 1.

Assizes

The Supreme Court of Judicature sits in London at the Royal Courts of Justice, Strand, London, W.C.2, but the judges of the Queen's Bench Division (and of the Family [4b] Division) also sit from time to time at various provincial towns throughout England and Wales at "Assizes." There the judges of the Queen's Bench Division try not only criminal cases (with which we are not concerned) but also civil actions and when so doing constitute a court of the High Court of Justice. The more important provincial towns (not always "Assize" towns) also have branch offices of the High Court for dealing with the procedural matters in an action. These branch offices are called district registries and cover the whole of the surrounding areas.[4c]

Minor Civil Courts

The minor courts having civil jurisdiction (county courts, borough courts, etc.) also have their own procedure which is not discussed in this book. In many respects, however, the procedure in an action in the county court (*e.g.*, in pleading and in conduct of the trial) is similar to that in a Queen's Bench action.

Court and Chambers in the Queen's Bench Division

Proceedings in the Queen's Bench Division are heard either in public by a judge sitting robed in open court,[5] or in private by a master (or district registrar) or a judge sitting in chambers and not robed. A master is an officer of the court who has power to decide, subject to a right of appeal to a judge, all, or nearly all, the preliminary questions which arise in an action before the trial. A district registrar has in any action proceeding in a district registry the same powers as a master and he exercises nearly the same jurisdiction in the area covered by his registry.[6] The masters sit every

---

[4b] See note 1a, *ante*, p. 1.

[4c] Certain changes are to be anticipated in the structure and administration of the Assize system following the Report of the Royal Commission on Assizes and Quarter Sessions under the Chairmanship of Lord Beeching (Cmnd. 4153). At the time of going to press many of these changes were embodied in a Courts Bill then before Parliament.

[5] See *post*, p. 309.

[6] Henceforth in this book the word "master" will include "district registrar." In effect a district registrar may not except by consent deal with cases in which the Crown is a party (see Ord. 77, r. 2); nor, save in Liverpool and Manchester, with originating summonses in Chancery proceedings (Ord. 7, r. 5 (2)); except that originating summonses (and writs) in mortgage actions may be issued out of the district registry of the district where the property is situated (Ord. 88, r. 3).

3

day in term time to hear lists of short non-counsel summonses in the morning and of counsel summonses at 1.30 and to deal with longer matters by special appointment. Lists of the more urgent cases are also taken in the vacation.

The administrative business of the Supreme Court, that is to say, such matters as the issue of writs, the entry of appearances and judgments, the issue of summonses and the drawing up of orders in the Queen's Bench Division, and the filing of affidavits and other documents, is performed by the " Central Office," [7] which is divided into various departments and is under the control and superintendence of the masters of the Queen's Bench Division. One of those masters in rotation sits as " Practice Master " and is always present to give any necessary directions to the staff, to help with any procedural difficulties encountered by litigants and their advisers, and to deal with the numerous and varied applications which are made " *ex parte,*" that is to say, without notice to the other side and usually by lodging an affidavit verifying the grounds of the application.

Orders made on these preliminary questions are called inter-locutory,[8] as opposed to final orders which are usually made at the trial of the action and which finally dispose of the dispute between the parties subject to any right of appeal.

The Rules of the Supreme Court

The procedure in actions in the Queen's Bench Division (as also in the Chancery Division and to some extent in the Family [8a] Division) is regulated by " Rules of the Supreme Court " [9] which are divided according to their subject-matter into " Orders." They have statutory effect, having been made by the Rule Committee under powers conferred on them by the Judicature Acts [10] and were completely revised in 1965. Those rules with which it is most necessary for the student to be familiar are set out in an Appendix to this volume. The remainder he must seek in

---

[7] See Judicature Act, 1925, ss. 104, 105; Ord. 63, rr. 1, 2.

[8] See *post,* p. 366n. The vast majority of interlocutory matters are dealt with by application in chambers but a few are heard on motion, that is to say, in open court. Occasionally, a summons which raises matter of general interest is adjourned into court for argument and decision.

[8a] See note 1a, *ante,* p. 1.

[9] See the quotation from *Re Coles and Ravenshear* [1907] 1 K.B. 1, at head of Preface.

[10] See Judicature Act, 1925, s. 99.

The Rules of the Supreme Court (*Revision*) *1965* as amended or in *The Supreme Court Practice* (usually called the " White Book ").

The rules provide, *inter alia*, how an action shall be commenced and how any application is to be made during the course of the action. An application may be made either in chambers (when it is made by a summons served on the other parties affected, unless the rules permit it to be made " *ex parte*," [11]) or in open court (when it is made by motion, notice of which must usually be given to the other parties affected).[12] A summons is a document calling upon the interested parties to attend. It is prepared by the applicant in proper form and taken to the summons room in the Central Office of the Royal Courts of Justice, where after payment of a fee it is sealed and is thereupon deemed to be issued. A return day is allotted according to the state of the list, and the summons is then served upon the opposite party.

In the rules before they were revised the expression " the court or a judge " constantly occurred and " the court " meant one or more judges sitting upon the bench in open court, and " a judge " meant a judge sitting in chambers. In the new rules the expression " the court " is constantly used. This includes, according to the context, the High Court, any one or more judges thereof whether sitting in court or in chambers, masters of the Queen's Bench and Chancery Divisions, registrars of the Family Division [12a] and district registrars.[13] The jurisdiction of these officers and what matters are reserved to the judges are defined in Order 32, rr. 11, 14 and 23. Interlocutory applications are now generally heard and disposed of by a master or registrar; in the Queen's Bench Division most of them only come before a judge on appeal from a master (see *post*, p. 367). Throughout this volume, therefore, " the master " is usually substituted for " the court." In the Chancery Division, as we shall see (*post*, p. 340), interlocutory matters are frequently referred by the master to the judge.

The Modes of Beginning Proceedings

Civil proceedings in the High Court may be begun by writ, originating summons, originating motion or petition.[14] More will be found about these in Chapters 3, 22 and 23. Most actions in the

---

[11] Ord. 32, r. 1.
[12a] See note 1a, *ante*, p. 1.
[13] Ord. 1, r. 4 (2).

[12] Ord. 8, r. 2.

[14] Ord. 5, r. 1·

Queen's Bench Division are begun by writ and it is with such actions that the rest of the book is mainly concerned. In some cases, however, an originating summons is appropriate. As its name indicates, this is a mode of actually commencing proceedings as opposed to an ordinary summons in a pending action.

The following proceedings by a plaintiff *must* ordinarily be begun by writ [15]:

(a) claims for any relief or remedy for a tort, other than trespass to land;

(b) claims based on an allegation of fraud;

(c) claims for damages for breach of duty (whether contractual, statutory or otherwise) resulting in death, personal injury, (including disease and mental impairment) or damage to property; and

(d) claims in respect of the infringement of a patent.

A claim for the possession of land in occupation by a trespasser may be begun by writ or by originating summons. It may be to the plaintiff's advantage to adopt the new summary procedure under Order 113 [16] in such a case by commencing proceedings with an originating summons (*post*, p. 14).

The following proceedings *must* be begun by originating summons, except where the application is expressly required or authorised by the rules or a statute to be made otherwise [17]:

Proceedings by which an application is to be made to the High Court or a judge thereof under any Act.

This does not apply to an application made in pending proceedings. Nor, for example, does it apply to proceedings under the Fatal Accidents Acts, for these must under paragraph (c) above be begun by writ. The commonest examples in the Family Division are summonses under the Married Women's Property Act, 1882, s. 17, concerning disputes between spouses as to the ownership or possession of property.[17a]

---

[15] Ord. 5, r. 2.
[16] Which took effect on July 20, 1970, see R.S.C. (Amendment No. 2) 1970: S.I. 1970, No. 944.
[17] Ord. 5, r. 3.
[17a] Such summonses were formerly heard in the Queen's Bench Division.

The following proceedings *may* be begun either by writ or originating summons,[18] except where the proceedings are by the rules or a statute required to be begun in one or the other manner or are authorised to be begun by motion or petition:

(a) Where the sole or principal question at issue is, or is likely to be, one of the construction of an Act or of any instrument made under an Act, or of any deed, will, contract or other document, or some other question of law, or

(b) in which there is unlikely to be any substantial dispute of fact.

These are both ordinarily appropriate to be begun by originating summons unless the plaintiff intends to apply for summary judgment under Order 14 or 86 (see Chapters 5 and 22).

The summons must include a statement of the questions on which the plaintiff seeks the determination or direction of the court or a concise statement of the relief or remedy claimed, with sufficient particulars to identify the cause or causes of action.[19] The procedure upon an originating summons is briefly described for the purpose of proceedings in the Queen's Bench Division at page 14. It is governed by Order 28, which applies irrespectively of the Division in which the proceedings are begun, and the reader is referred to Chapter 23 for further details.

Bodies corporate and the representatives of minors and patients must in all cases sue and defend through a solicitor and cannot act in person.[20]

AN ACTION IN THE QUEEN'S BENCH DIVISION

A preliminary outline of the more important steps in an ordinary Queen's Bench action may be of assistance to the student. In subsequent chapters the practice and procedure in such actions is considered in detail.

The Writ

A writ is a formal document by which the Queen commands the defendant to " enter an appearance " within so many days, if he wishes to dispute the plaintiff's claims; otherwise judgment may be signed against him. (See Precedent No. 3, in

[18] Ord. 5, r. 4.
[19] Ord. 7, r. 3.
[20] Ord. 5, r. 6; Ord. 80, r. 2.

the Appendix.) The writ states the name and address of the plaintiff and the name and usual or last known address of the defendant and it must be indorsed either with a full " statement of claim " (see *post,* pp. 45–46) or with a short indication of the general nature of the claim. The former used to be called a " special indorsement " and the latter a " general indorsement," but these expressions no longer appear in the rules. In appropriate cases the writ can be indorsed for an account.[21]

Issuing the Writ

As soon as the writ is prepared and its indorsement duly drafted, the next step is to " issue " it; that is, to make it an official document, emanating from the court. In former days, when everyone was less busy, issuing a writ was regarded as a judicial, not a ministerial act; the officer of the court drafted, or at all events settled, the plaintiff's writ for him, and would not allow any writ to issue which, in his opinion, was not in proper form. This often caused an eager litigant trouble and delay, though it might save him costs in the end. But there is no longer any difficulty of this kind. The plaintiff now settles his indorsement as he pleases; and the officers of the court raise no formal objection as to its sufficiency in law although it is within their discretion to call attention to any apparent defect. It is for the defendant to take objection subsequently, if it is not as it should be.

There are, however, some cases in which leave to issue a writ is still necessary, *e.g.,* where the defendant is beyond the jurisdiction of the court. No writ which the plaintiff intends to have served on any person outside England and Wales will be issued, unless the plaintiff first obtains the leave of a judge or master; and such leave will only be granted in the cases specified in Order 11 [22] (see *post,* pp. 37–39).

In ordinary cases issuing a writ is a very simple process. The plaintiff or his solicitor takes two copies of the proposed writ to the Writ Department of the Central Office of the High Court in London, or to a district registry, signs one copy, and pays the fee.[23] The officer impresses a stamp on the signed copy, and files it; he stamps the other with the official " seal," and hands it

---

[21] See *post,* p. 48.
[22] See also Ords. 73 and 76 dealing with arbitrations and probate actions respectively.
[23] £5. If the claim is solely for a liquidated sum not exceeding £100, the fee is £4.

back; this is referred to as the original writ. It is marked with a letter and number (thus " 1971—B.—No. 356 "), the letter being the initial of the first plaintiff's surname. If it is issued in an action in the Chancery Division, it will also be marked with the words " Group A " or " Group B " denoting the name of the group of judges of that Division to whom the action is thenceforth assigned, but this is not the practice in the Queen's Bench Division.

Service of the Writ

The plaintiff must next " serve " the writ on the defendant. The proper way to serve a writ is to show the defendant the original, if he asks to see it, and then to serve upon him and leave with him a correct copy of it (see Order 65, r. 2). This is called " personal service." But the defendant's solicitor often undertakes to accept service and enter an appearance for him. When neither of these courses is practicable the master may in certain circumstances make an order for what is called " substituted service." (See p. 52.)

Entering an Appearance

If the defendant wishes to defend the action, he must " enter an appearance," unless there is some irregularity in the issue or service of the writ, in which case he may with leave enter a " conditional appearance " and within fourteen days apply to set aside the writ or the service of it; he may indeed do so before entering an appearance. (Order 12, rr. 7, 8.) In early days the defendant had physically to appear before some court, and submit to or protest against its jurisdiction, and state publicly that he intended to defend the action and on what grounds. But now " entering an appearance " has become as formal a proceeding as issuing a writ, and merely entails lodging a memorandum in the office of the court. (See p. 53.) By so appearing the defendant submits to the jurisdiction of the court. If he objects to the jurisdiction, he may enter a conditional appearance, which is commonly called appearing " under protest." [24]

Default of Appearance

If the defendant does not enter an appearance within the period named in the writ (which is usually eight days after the service of the writ on him, inclusive of the day of such service), the plaintiff

---

[24] As to which, see *Keymer* v. *Reddy* [1912] 1 K.B. 215; 81 L.J.K.B. 266.

is, as a rule, entitled to judgment in default of appearance. Where the writ claims a liquidated, that is an ascertained, sum of money and the defendant does not appear, the plaintiff may enter *final* judgment for the amount claimed on the writ, interest and costs. (Order 13, r. 1.) If the action be for the recovery of land, the plaintiff is entitled to a judgment that the defendant do give him possession of the land. If the action be for unliquidated damages, the plaintiff is not entitled to final judgment; he can only have what is called an *interlocutory* judgment—a judgment, that is, in his favour but with no amount stated; the amount of damages must subsequently be assessed by a master unless another mode of assessment is ordered.[25] The defendant, although he has not appeared, may attend and argue and call evidence at the assessment. And then the plaintiff may enter final judgment for the amount assessed. (See *post*, p. 58.)

A judgment in default of appearance may, in the discretion of the court, be set aside upon terms. (See *post*, p. 58.)

Summary Judgment

After entry of appearance, Queen's Bench actions fall broadly into three classes: (a) those in which summary judgment is obtained under Order 14; (b) those which proceed to trial without pleadings; and (c) those which proceed to trial in the normal way. After the defendant has appeared, the plaintiff may apply by summons to a master for what is called " summary judgment." He or someone with knowledge of the facts swears an affidavit that he believes there is no defence to the whole or part of the plaintiff's claim. The defendant must then show by affidavit or otherwise satisfy the master that he has some genuine triable defence to raise. If he fails to do this, the plaintiff gets leave to sign judgment, either for the whole or part of his claim. A defendant may get leave to defend the whole or part of the case. (See Chapter 5.)

Pleadings

Either party may, after entry of appearance, apply for trial without further pleadings. In that case he must issue a summons (see *post*, p. 81). If summary judgment or trial without pleadings was

---

[25] *e.g.*, by an official referee (an officer of the court, who decides questions of accounts and tries actions which are unsuited for trial by judge alone or by judge and jury. See *post*, p. 264).

not asked for or has been refused wholly or in part, the next stage in the action will normally be the service of pleadings or further pleadings, as the case may be. Pleadings are statements in writing served by each party alternately on his opponent, stating what his contention will be at the trial, and giving all such details as his opponent needs to know in order to prepare his case in answer.[26] They are now served automatically under a time table prescribed by the rules: the usual pleadings in an action are:

(a) A Statement of Claim, in which the plaintiff sets out his cause of action with all necessary particulars as to his injuries and losses.

(b) A Defence, in which the defendant deals with every material fact alleged by the plaintiff in his statement of claim and also states any new facts on which he intends to rely. A defendant may also set up a cross-claim known as a Counterclaim.

(c) A Reply in which the plaintiff deals with fresh facts raised by the defendant in his defence. A reply is unusual except where the defendant sets up a counterclaim.

Although the plaintiff may have indorsed his statement of claim upon the writ, it sometimes happens, especially in apparently simple debt cases, that leave to defend is given upon an application for summary judgment and a fuller pleading is desirable. This the master may order to be served by way of amendment.

The nature and object of the various pleadings is explained in Chapters 12 to 15.

Summons for Directions

After the close of pleadings the parties must in many cases without order disclose to each other all relevant documents which they have (see Order 24, Chapter 16). Thereafter the plaintiff must take out a Summons for Directions before a master (Order 25) (see Chapter 18). But if he applies for summary judgment and fails to obtain it, the master proceeds then to give necessary directions just as though the summons had been taken out under Order 25.

The master has power to decide whether there shall, or shall not, be any further pleading or particulars served, whether any

[26] For a brief history of pleading see *post*, p. 78.

pleading should be amended, whether there shall be further discovery and inspection of documents, whether interrogatories shall be served and how certain facts, if not admitted, shall be proved at the trial, in which list [27] the action is to be entered, where it shall be tried, and whether by a judge alone or by a judge and jury or by an official referee; and practically all other questions which arise in the action before final judgment is entered, save only those that arise at the actual trial.[28] The decision of some of these matters may if necessary be postponed to an adjourned hearing of the summons.

Discovery

If either party has not yet, or not sufficiently, disclosed his documents, the master may order him to make an affidavit or a list of all documents which are or have been in his possession and are material to any question in issue in the action; and to permit his opponent to inspect and take copies of them before the trial. This process is technically known as " discovery of documents "; it often tends to save expense and shorten litigation. What is more, the master has power to order either party to answer on oath before the trial certain questions submitted by his opponent. These questions are called " interrogatories." The master goes through the proposed questions first to see if they ought to be allowed in the interests of justice. There are, of course, limits to the power of a party thus to extract evidence in his favour from his opponent before the trial (see Chapters 16 and 19).

Trial

After the order giving directions, the plaintiff (or in some cases the defendant) sets down the action for trial in the appropriate list at the Royal Courts of Justice, *i.e.*, " Jury," " Non-jury " or " Short cause," or for trial at assizes. In due course the name of an action tried in London appears in the " Week's List," and later in the " Day's List." Then the parties must attend in court with their counsel and witnesses, and bring with them all necessary books and papers. The procedure at an ordinary trial is described in Chapter 21. The plaintiff's counsel generally begins. He opens his case, calls his witnesses and examines them, and hands in his

[27] As to the different lists, see *post*, p. 273n.
[28] For the special procedure where the writ is indorsed for an account, see *post*, pp. 48 *et seq.*

documents to the officer of the court. The defendant's counsel cross-examines the plaintiff's witnesses, and then at the close of the evidence for the plaintiff, if there be any cause of action shown, he proceeds to meet it by stating what his defence is and, generally, but not always, by calling witnesses and putting in any documents upon which he relies. In a non-jury case the counsel then in turn address the judge who delivers a reasoned judgment. If there is a jury, counsel's speeches are addressed to them, the judge sums up and the jury return their verdict; and the judge orders the appropriate judgment to be entered thereupon. In either case the judge makes an order for costs.

Execution

After judgment has been entered there follows execution, that is, proceedings to enforce the judgment (see Chapter 25) unless the defendant pays up voluntarily; though execution is sometimes stayed pending an appeal.

The execution of High Court judgments is the responsibility of the sheriff of each county, though in practice the actual work is done by the under-sheriff and his servants. The High Court, unlike the county court, has never had officers of its own to serve process or to execute judgment; it merely issues at the request of the judgment creditor a command in the form of a writ directed to the sheriff of the county where the person or property of the judgment debtor may be. The most usual form of execution is that of fi. fa. (*fieri facias*) whereby the judgment debtor's goods are seized and sold (see Chapter 23). A High Court judgment may, however, be enforced in the county court.

Appeal

Either party may ordinarily appeal to the Court of Appeal against the decision on the law or the facts or both. The Court of Appeal studies the documents and reviews the oral evidence by reading the transcript. It does not, as a rule, see the actual witnesses but relies on the note of their evidence. Consequently it will seldom interfere with the judge's findings of fact so far as these depend on the credibility of the witnesses.[29] But with this important qualification the appeal is in name and in fact a rehearing. The powers of the court, which are freely exercised,

[29] See *post*, p. 378.

include those of varying or reversing the judgment or sending the case back for a new trial. It can, though it seldom does, hear fresh evidence.

From the Court of Appeal a further appeal lies to the House of Lords, but the appellant must have leave either of that House or of the Court of Appeal and such leave is somewhat sparingly given, sometimes on terms as to costs.

Originating Summons in the Queen's Bench Division

If the proceedings have been begun by originating summons (*ante*, pp. 6, 7) instead of by writ, it is likely in the Queen's Bench Division that the summons will be one to which no appearance need be entered, such as a summons under Order 113 (summary proceedings for the recovery of land).

A summons under Order 113 [30] claiming recovery only of possession of land from an unidentified trespasser should be served by affixing a copy of it to the main door or other conspicuous part of the premises at any reasonable time before the return day. A final order thereon can only be made by a judge and, except in case of urgency, not less than seven clear days after the date of service. Where the trespasser is identifiable he will normally be served personally (or by leaving a copy of the summons and supporting affidavit, or by sending them to him, at the premises) and unless he applies promptly to be joined as a defendant a final order may similarly be made against him.

For a fuller description of originating summons procedure the student is referred to Order 28 and Chapter 23.

[30] See *ante*, p. 6n.

CHAPTER 2

MATTERS TO BE CONSIDERED BEFORE WRIT

BEFORE beginning proceedings the plaintiff must decide whether he should issue a writ or an originating summons (see *ante*, pp. 5–7). The following matters may also arise for consideration:

    I.—Parties.

    II.—Joinder of Causes of Action.

    III.—Jurisdiction of the High Court of Justice.

    IV.—Whether Cause of Action fully accrued at date of Writ.

To make a false start in any of these respects will cause him trouble, expense and delay at some stage or other of the action.

I.—PARTIES

There must be set out at the head of every writ the name of every plaintiff and every defendant whom it is proposed to make a party to the proceedings. These names form the title of the action. And in the selection of these parties there is a twofold chance of error. A plaintiff may omit parties whose presence is essential; or he may add parties whose presence is improper. Hence you must learn what parties are necessary and what unnecessary, who *must* be joined, and who *may* be joined or not, as the plaintiff chooses. In the case of an originating summons the party taking it out will be plaintiff and the other parties defendants.[1]

Formerly the law and practice as to " parties " was of the utmost importance, misjoinder of a plaintiff being ground of non-suit, while non-joinder of a necessary plaintiff was the subject of a plea in abatement.[2] But now " no cause or matter shall be defeated by reason of the misjoinder or nonjoinder of any party; and the court may in any cause or matter determine the issues and questions in dispute so far as they affect the rights and interests of the persons who are parties to the cause or matter." (Order 15, r. 6 (1).) And " at any stage of the proceedings in any cause or matter

---

[1] Ord. 7, r. 2 (2).

[2] Pleas in abatement were abolished in 1875.

15

the court may on such terms as it thinks just and either of its own motion or on application:

(*a*) Order any person who has been improperly or unnecessarily made a party or who has for any reason ceased to be a proper or necessary party to cease to be a party; (*b*) order any person who ought to have been joined as a party or whose presence before the court is necessary to ensure that all matters in dispute in the cause or matter may be effectually and completely determined and adjudicated upon be added as a party." (Rule 6 (2).) [3] A plaintiff may be substituted although the original plaintiff had no cause of action.[4] But where an action is commenced in the name of a dead man, his representative cannot be substituted as plaintiff.[5] Nor will the court necessarily allow a person to be added as plaintiff to an action or to change the capacity in which he sues if thereby a defence under the Limitation Act would be defeated.[6] No one can appear on the record both as a plaintiff and as a defendant, even though he does so in different capacities.[7] All plaintiffs must appear by the same counsel, and cannot set up conflicting cases *inter se*.

It may be to the plaintiff's advantage to join a defendant—even though impecunious—in order to obtain discovery from him; but some substantial relief must be claimed against him or he may apply to be struck out.[8]

It is now possible, since the passing of the Crown Proceedings Act, 1947, to sue the Crown both in contract and in tort. The defendant will be the appropriate government department, *e.g.*, the *Department of the Environment* or *Home Office*; the writ is served upon the solicitor to the department or, in some cases, the Treasury Solicitor. The procedure differs from that in ordinary actions in certain respects. The department sued may, before appearance is entered, call upon the plaintiff to amplify the indorsement to the writ, which must state the circumstances in which the Crown's liability arises and the government department and officers of the Crown concerned.[9] Judgment in default of appearance or pleading cannot be entered without leave,[10] nor can summary

---

[3] See *Etablissement Baudelot* v. *R. S. Graham & Co., Ltd.* [1953] 2 Q.B. 271.
[4] *Hughes* v. *The Pump House Hotel Co., Ltd.* (*No. 2*) [1902] 2 K.B. 485.
[5] *Tetlow* v. *Orela, Ltd.* [1920] 2 Ch. 24; 89 L.J.Ch. 465.
[6] See Ord. 20, r. 5 (2) (*post*, p. 171).
[7] *Re Phillips, Public Trustee* v. *Meyer* (1931) 101 L.J.Ch. 338.
[8] *Wilson* v. *Church* (1878) 9 Ch.D. 552.
[9] Ord. 77, r. 3.   [10] Ord. 77, r. 9.

judgment be obtained under Order 14.[10a] Discovery of documents does not automatically follow the close of pleadings as in other actions but must be achieved as directed by the court (see *post* p. 237). The action cannot be ordered to be tried outside London except with consent of the Crown.[11] And, finally, execution cannot be levied against the Crown.[12] As to set-off and counterclaim against the Crown, see *post*, p. 215. There are other special rules, but these are the most important.

Foreign sovereigns and states,[13] Ambassadors and Ministers and their staff,[14] High Commissioners representing Commonwealth countries and the Republic of Ireland,[15] certain International Organisations and their representatives and officers,[16] and representatives and staff (included in an authorised list) of certain governments represented at conferences in the United Kingdom,[17] cannot be sued in the courts of this country unless they submit to the jurisdiction. The agent of a foreign government cannot be sued here without his principal.[18] Moreover, where a foreign government, though not a defendant, is indirectly impleaded because the action affects property to which it has some substantial claim, the action may be stayed.[19]

Contract

In actions founded on contract it is essential to state the parties correctly; a false start may not only entail delay and expense but may even be fatal in the sense that the remedy against the right party may be lost for ever.

The law relating to parties depends largely on whether the contract sued on be joint, or several, or joint and several. This is a question which turns primarily on the language of the contract

[10a] Ord. 77, r. 7.   [11] Ord. 77, r. 13.   [12] Ord. 77, rr. 16, 17.

[13] See from among many cases *Mighell* v. *Sultan of Johore* [1894] 1 Q.B. 149; *Duff Development Co., Ltd.* v. *Government of Kelantan* [1924] A.C. 797; *Compania Naviera Vascongado* v. *S.S. Cristina* [1938] A.C. 485; *Sultan of Johore* v. *Bendahar* [1952] A.C. 318; *Baccus S.R.L.* v. *Servicio Nacional del Trigo* [1957] 1 Q.B. 438.

[14] Diplomatic Privileges Act, 1964, ss. 1, 2, Sched. 1.

[15] Diplomatic Immunities (Commonwealth Countries and Republic of Ireland) Act, 1952.   [16] International Organisations Act, 1968.

[17] Diplomatic Immunities (Commonwealth Countries and Republic of Ireland) Act, 1961. And since Sierra Leone Independence Act, 1961, and any other particular Acts of a like nature which may from time to time be passed.

[18] *Twycross* v. *Dreyfus* (1877) 5 Ch.D. 605.

[19] *Juan Ysmael & Co.* v. *Govt. of Indonesia* [1955] A.C. 72; *Rahimtoola* v. *Nizam of Hyderabad* [1958] A.C. 379.

itself. Still, it is a question of the intention of the parties, and the judge will also have regard to all the surrounding circumstances, to the respective interests of the parties and to their conduct. Thus, a contract made by the executors of a will, the trustees of a settlement, or the partners in a firm, acting as such, will generally be construed a joint and not a several contract, unless there is something in the language of the contract which forbids this construction. The distinction is one of importance; as, on the death or bankruptcy of one joint contractor, his rights or liabilities pass to the others and not to his personal representatives or trustee (see section 118 of the Bankruptcy Act, 1914). Moreover, a judgment against one joint contractor, even though unsatisfied, is generally a bar to any action against the others, and a release given to one joint contractor releases all.[20]

In any action for breach of a contract made by or with several persons *jointly* all persons jointly entitled to relief who are alive must join as plaintiffs or, if they will not do so, be made defendants, unless the master gives leave to omit them.[21] Similarly all persons jointly, but not severally, liable should ordinarily be joined as defendants, otherwise the master may be asked to stay the proceedings until they have been added.[22] " A joint debtor has a right to demand, if he pleases, that he shall be sued at one and the same time with all his co-debtors." (*Per* Bowen L.J. in *Re Hodgson, Beckett* v. *Ramsdale* (1885) 31 Ch.D. at p. 188. And see *Norbury, Natzio & Co.* v. *Griffiths* [1918] 2 K.B. 369.) The personal representatives of a deceased joint creditor should not be joined as plaintiffs, nor should the representatives of a deceased joint debtor be joined as defendants; the right to sue and the liability on the contract vest in the survivors, and therefore only the survivors should be made parties. But if all the persons originally entitled to sue on such a joint contract be dead, the personal representatives of the last surviving creditor must sue; if all the persons originally liable on such a contract be dead, the personal representatives of the last surviving debtor must be sued.

---

[20] *Kendall* v. *Hamilton* (1879) 4 App.Cas. 504. But see *post*, pp. 56, 68–69.
[21] Ord. 15, r. 4 (2).
[22] *Ibid.* r. 4 (3).

If, however, a contract made by two or more persons be several as well as joint, the plaintiff may sue one or more or all of them in the same action.[23] If he joins them all, he can in the same action claim against all of them jointly, and also against each of them severally. If he does not join them all, then he can only rely on the several liability of those whom he has chosen to sue.

If the contract be several and not joint, the plaintiff may, at his option, join as parties to the same action all or any of the persons liable thereon, and a judgment against one of several persons *jointly and severally* liable on one contract is no bar to an action against the others.[24] If any of the persons originally liable on that contract be dead, he may also, if he chooses, add the executors or administrators of such deceased persons.

Again there may be a contract on which one or other of two persons is liable in the alternative, but not both. If judgment is taken against one of them, that is a conclusive and irrevocable election and a bar to further proceedings against the other.[25] Nor will it avail to set the judgment aside.[26]

If a necessary co-plaintiff refuses to join in the action, the proper course was formerly to tender him an indemnity against costs; and then, if he still refused to be joined as a co-plaintiff, to make him a defendant.[27] Now the master has a discretion to allow him to be left out. He can only be joined as a co-plaintiff if he gives his consent, which he must ordinarily do in writing by signing a consent himself though the master may authorise his solicitor to do so (see Order 15, s. 6 (2)).[28] If he be joined without such consent, his name will be struck out, and the solicitor who issued the writ will probably be ordered to pay his costs and also all costs occasioned to the defendant by such improper joinder.[29]

---

[23] *Ibid.* r. 4 (1) and (3).

[24] *Isaacs and Sons* v. *Salbstein* [1916] 2 K.B. at p. 151.

[25] *Morel Brothers* v. *Earl of Westmorland* [1904] A.C. 11.

[26] *Hammond* v. *Schofield* [1891] 1 Q.B. 453.

[27] *Cullen* v. *Knowles and Birks* [1898] 2 Q.B. 380; *Johnson* v. *Stephens and Carter* [1923] 2 K.B. 857.

[28] But an order can be made joining him subject to production of the consent (*Wootton* v. *Joel* [1920] W.N. 38).

[29] Order 62, r. 8. And see *Fricker* v. *Van Grutten* [1896] 2 Ch. 649.

Tort

In an action for a wrong arising out of a contract, the same persons must be joined as parties as are necessary in actions for breach of contract.

In actions of pure tort (*i.e.*, for wrongs independent of any contract), if several persons are joint-owners or joint-occupiers of any land or premises prejudicially affected by any trespass, nuisance or other wrongful act, or the joint-owners of any chattel which the defendant has taken, destroyed or injured, whether by negligence or design, they should all, as a rule, be joined as co-plaintiffs in the action. Where, however, premises are in lease, the tenant only should sue for trespass or nuisance; the landlord can only complain if there is damage to the reversion. But in actions for the prevention of waste or otherwise for the protection of property, one person may sue on behalf of himself and all persons having the same interest. (Order 15, r. 12.) And one of several co-owners of a patent may sue alone for an infringement of his right,[30] and so may one of several co-owners of a trade mark or copyright.[31] In an action for conversion one of several co-owners may sue alone but cannot recover more than his share of the value of the property converted.[32]

As to defendants in an action of tort, the plaintiff has a free hand. He is not now, and never was, obliged to join as a defendant every person who is liable to him for that tort. He may, if he prefers, sue only one or two; and the liability of the others will be no defence for those sued, and will not mitigate the damages recoverable, for all persons concerned in a common wrongful act are jointly and severally liable for all damage caused by it.[33] And a judgment against these is now no bar to a subsequent action for the same tort against anyone else who was jointly liable with them.[34] If, however, the plaintiff obtained

---

[30] *Sheehan* v. *G. E. Ry.* (1880) 16 Ch.D. 59.

[31] *Dent* v. *Turpin* (1861) 30 L.J.Ch. 495; *Cescinsky* v. *Routledge & Sons* [1916] 2 K.B. 325. As to proceedings for infringement of copyright where an exclusive licence has been granted see Copyright Act, 1956, s. 19.

[32] *Bloxam* v. *Hubbard* (1804) 5 East 407, 420; *Baker* v. *Barclays Bank, Ltd.* [1955] 1 W.L.R. 822.

[33] Co.Litt. 232 a; *Sutton* v. *Clarke* (1815) 6 Taunt. 29; *Greenlands, Ltd.* v. *Wilmshurst* [1913] 3 K.B. 507—reversed in the House of Lords on another point [1916] 2 A.C. 15.

[34] Law Reform (Married Women and Tortfeasors) Act, 1935, s. 6 (1); and see *post*, p. 200.

from the defendant the whole of the damages awarded, there would be no point in bringing another action against a different defendant, because the plaintiff could not recover further damages from the second defendant and would almost certainly be mulcted in costs. Where two or more tortfeasors are liable for the same tort, they can now claim contribution *inter se*.

Where special damage is essential to the cause of action, the plaintiff should be careful to sue only that person whose act caused him the special damage, unless he can prove that some other person instigated the act complained of. In that case the instigator and the actor would be jointly liable for all damage flowing from the act.

Recovery of Land

In this action the proper plaintiff is the person who is now entitled to immediate *possession* of the property. He may be the freeholder or only a tenant. If there be no tenancy created by, or otherwise binding on, the freeholder, then his ownership involves the right to present possession. And as between freeholders the first tenant for life is the proper plaintiff; there is no need to join any remaindermen or reversioners. All joint tenants must join; where there was originally a tenancy in common, which is now no longer possible, it is generally necessary for the trustees for sale to join.

Strictly, all persons who are actually in physical possession of the property should be made defendants. " In ejectment the tenant in possession *must* be sued." (*Per* Lord Tenterden C.J. in *Berkeley* v. *Dimery and Another* (1829) 10 B. & C. 113.) It is neither necessary nor proper to join any person who is merely in receipt of the rents and profits of the land. But where a large number of persons are in occupation of the premises who all claim title under the same lessor, the rule is relaxed and the plaintiff is allowed merely to make that lessor defendant.[35] By section 145 of the Law of Property Act, 1925, the tenant is bound, under penalty of three years' rent, " forthwith " to give notice to his landlord that a writ in ejectment has been served on him. And the landlord can then at once obtain leave to defend the action under Order 15, r. 10. The master will on an *ex parte*

[35] *Minet* v. *Johnson* (1890) 63 L.T. 507; *Geen* v. *Herring* [1905] 1 K.B. 152.

application grant such leave to any person who, by himself or his tenant, is in possession of the land sought to be recovered in the action, although he is not named on the writ.

Classes of Persons

A married woman may sue and be sued, either in contract or tort or otherwise, in all respects as if she were a *feme sole* (Law Reform (Married Women and Tortfeasors) Act, 1935, s. 1).[36] In this respect marriage or divorce now leaves a woman's position practically unaffected. But actions in tort between spouses may sometimes be stayed.[36a] A husband is no longer liable as such in respect of torts committed, or contracts entered into, by his wife unless she was acting as his agent; in the case of post-nuptial contracts, however, agency may in certain circumstances be implied from the fact of marriage, as in contracts for necessaries (see sections 3 and 4). The Act does not affect a husband's liability upon any joint contract or for any joint tort, and is retrospective.[37] If the husband has sustained any special damage, he should join as a co-plaintiff, so as to dispose of all the questions in one action. Although a plaintiff, who has a cause of action against a married woman on a contract entered into by her after her marriage, can still sue the husband on the ground that his wife made the contract as his agent, it is highly improbable that *both* husband and wife would be liable; for either the wife was agent for her husband to make that contract on his behalf, or she was not. If she was, then he alone is liable. If she was not, he cannot be liable, but she is.[38] The difficulty is frequently overcome by suing husband and wife in the alternative.

A minor sues by his next friend (see Precedent No. 34), who, though not a party to the action, is personally liable for the costs of the suit [39]; but the minor is prima facie liable to indemnify him against costs properly incurred in the interest of the minor.[40] The court has power to dismiss an action brought by a minor in his own name or to allow the proceedings to be amended by

[36] And see Married Women (Restraint upon Anticipation) Act, 1949.
[36a] See Law Reform (Husband and Wife) Act, 1962; Ord. 89, r. 2.
[37] *Barber* v. *Pigden* [1937] 1 K.B. 664.
[38] See *Morel Brothers* v. *Earl of Westmorland* [1904] A.C. 11, *ante*, p. 19.
[39] See *Masling* v. *Motor Hiring Co.* [1919] 2 K.B. 538.
[40] *Steeden* v. *Walden* [1910] 2 Ch. at p. 400.

adding the next friend.[41]   Any money recovered in an action by or on behalf of a minor must be paid into court to be held and applied for the benefit of the plaintiff, and no settlement of the action or acceptance of money paid into court is valid unless approved by the court.[41a]   A minor defends by a guardian *ad litem* [41b] who will not be held personally liable for costs unless he has been guilty of some misconduct.[41c]   A married woman is competent to act as guardian *ad litem*.

A person who, by reason of mental disorder, is incapable of managing his affairs (formerly termed a " lunatic " but now generally referred to as a " patient ") also sues by a next friend and defends by a guardian *ad litem*, who may be the receiver appointed pursuant to the Mental Health Act, 1959.   The title in the writ should be, " A.B. by C.D. of ——, his next friend [*or guardian ad litem*] (under Order 80, rule 2)."   The provisions of Order 80, rr. 10 and 12 (*ante*), apply also to patients.   Jurisdiction in the management of the property and affairs of such persons is ordinarily exercised by the master of the Court of Protection.

A person voluntarily resident in an enemy or enemy-controlled country cannot sue.[42]

Partners carrying on business within the jurisdiction may sue and be sued in the name of their firm; but if they sue in the firm name they can be compelled to disclose the name and address of every member of the firm.[42a]   If they are sued in the firm name they must enter an appearance in their own names individually, but the subsequent proceedings nevertheless continue in the name of the firm.[43]   An individual carrying on business within the jurisdiction under a trade name may be sued in that name as though he were a member of a firm.[43a]

A corporation and a company registered under the Companies Acts sue and are sued in their corporate name; they are legal

---

[41] *Cooper* v. *Dummett* [1930] W.N. 248.
[41a] Ord. 80, rr. 10, 12.
[41b] Ord. 80, r. 2.
[41c] *Hooper* v. *Mackenzie, The Times,* January 23, 1901.
[42] *Porter* v. *Freudenberg* [1915] 1 K.B. 857.   And see Trading with the Enemy Act, 1939, as to vesting of enemy property.
[42a] Ord. 81, rr. 1, 2.
[43] Ord. 81, r. 4 (1); and see *Ellis* v. *Wadeson* [1899] 1 Q.B. 714.
[43a] Ord. 81, r. 9.

persons. And a registered trade union, though not a legal person, may be sued in its registered name.[44]

In any action concerning trust property, all the trustees within the jurisdiction must as a rule be joined; in any action concerning the estate of a deceased person all administrators, or all executors who have proved the will, must be joined.[45] But in neither case is it necessary to add any of the persons beneficially interested in the trust or estate. (Order 15, r. 14.) Under the Law Reform (Miscellaneous Provisions) Act, 1934, many causes of action vested in or subsisting against a person who dies survive for the benefit of, or against, his estate. If there is no administrator, the court has power to appoint some person to represent the estate at the instance of a claimant under Order 15, r. 15 (1),[46] or a motion may be made in the Probate Division for the appointment of a nominee of the claimant as administrator.[47] In the event of the death or bankruptcy of a party after writ issued the action does not abate, if the cause of action is one that survives, and the personal representative may be made a party.[47a] But a writ issued after the death and before letters of administration are granted is a nullity.[48] The same principles apply where a party dies pending an appeal.[49] An action commenced by a trustee in bankruptcy must ordinarily be brought in the Chancery Division, unless it is of a kind specially assigned to one of the other Divisions.[50]

Where there are numerous persons having the same interest in proceedings, the proceedings may be begun, and, unless the master otherwise orders, continued, by or against any one or more

---

[44] *Taff Vale Ry.* v. *Amalgamated Society, etc.* [1901] A.C. 426; *Bonsor* v. *Musicians' Union* [1956] A.C. 104. (As to the procedure in the case of an unregistered trade union see the speech of Lord Lindley in the *Taff Vale* case at p. 443 and of Lord MacDermott in *Bonsor's* case at pp. 144–145.)

[45] See *Latch* v. *Latch* (1875) L.R. 10 Ch. 464.

[46] See *Lean* v. *Alston* [1947] K.B. 467 and cases there cited. The proposed representative must be willing to act, and if no other course can be adopted it may in rare cases be appropriate to institute proceedings against the President of the Probate, Divorce and Admiralty Division, in whom the deceased's estate vests under the Administration of Estates Act, 1925, s. 9.

[47] *In the Estates of Simpson and Gunning* [1936] P. 40; *In the goods of Knight* [1939] 3 All E.R. 928.

[47a] Ord. 15, r. 7.

[48] *Finnegan* v. *Cementation Co., Ltd.* [1953] 1 Q.B. 688.

[49] *Ranson* v. *Patton* (1881) 17 Ch.D. 767; *Smith* v. *Williams* [1922] 1 K.B. 158.

[50] Bankruptcy Rules, 1952, r. 121.

of them as representing all or as representing all except one or
more of them. (Order 15, r. 12 (1).) This is called a "representative action." Or after proceedings have been begun the master
may make an order under rule 12 (2) appointing or substituting a
representative defendant. All persons who have a common right
which is invaded by a common enemy are entitled to join in
attacking that common enemy in respect of that common right,
although they may have different rights *inter se*.[51] But while there
must be a common interest and a common grievance, it must also
be shown (if objection is taken to the form of the proceedings)
that the relief claimed is in its nature beneficial to all.[52]
A members' club is an association of persons, an unincorporated
body, which has no legal entity.[53] Named persons may be sued
on behalf of themselves and all other persons who were members
when the cause of action arose even in a case of tort, provided
that all such members have truly a common interest in defending
those proceedings.[54] It is otherwise where the members of the
committee are the persons primarily liable,[55] or where a libel has
been published by particular members or officers of the association.[56]

Special provision has been made to enable persons of small
means to bring or defend actions without incurring heavy
liability as to costs.[56a] This is achieved under the Legal Aid and
Advice Acts, 1949 and 1960. It would be beyond the scope of this
book to describe in detail the working of legal assistance under
these Acts. But, broadly speaking, persons whose " disposable "
income (*i.e.*, income as assessed by the Supplementary Benefits
Commission after making deductions for rent, taxes, maintenance of
dependants and other matters) does not exceed £700 a year and
whose " disposable " capital does not exceed £500 are eligible for
legal *aid*.[57] The applicant or his solicitor applies to a certifying

---

[51] Ord. 15, r . 12; *Duke of Bedford* v. *Ellis* [1901] A.C. 1; but see *Markt & Co., Ltd.*
v. *Knight Steamship Co., Ltd.* [1910] 2 K.B. 1021; and *Barker* v. *Allanson* [1937]
1 K.B. 463.

[52] *Smith* v. *Cardiff Corporation* [1954] 1 Q.B. 210.

[53] *Cf. Bloom* v. *National Federation, etc.* [1918] W.N. 337.

[54] See *Campbell* v. *Thompson* [1953] 1 Q.B. 445; *Winder* v. *Ward, The Times*, Feb.
27, 1957.

[55] *Brown* v. *Lewis* (1896) 12 T.L.R. 455.

[56] *Mercantile Marine Service Association* v. *Toms* [1916] 2 K.B. 243.

[56a] The former Poor Persons procedure has been abolished.

[57] In the case of claims not, or not yet, involving litigation the sums are less. Legal
advice is available under the Legal Advice Regulations, 1949 (as amended), from
solicitors on the panel. This is given free to persons receiving Supplementary Benefit

committee of practising lawyers who consider his case and, if they think he has a good cause of action or defence and that it is reasonable that he should be assisted, they may so certify and fix the amount he shall be required to contribute. Thereafter he employs his own solicitor and counsel and the case proceeds in most respects as though he were an ordinary litigant.[58] But an assisted person, even though unsuccessful, may be relieved wholly or partly from liability for his opponent's costs. (See *post*, p. 410.)

Illustrations

As a rule it is wrong to make the representative of a deceased trustee or executor a party to an action, if there be a surviving trustee or executor.

Re Harrison, Smith v. *Allen* [1891] 2 Ch. 349; 60 L.J.Ch. 287.

Where a legacy was bequeathed to A, in trust for X and Y, and A was made defendant, it was held unnecessary to join X and Y as parties to the action, as they were represented by their trustee.

Re Bowden, Andrew v. *Cooper* (1890) 45 Ch.D. 444; 59 L.J.Ch. 815.

Whiting v. *De Rutzen* [1905] 1 Ch. 96; 74 L.J.Ch. 207.

One shareholder in a company may sue " on behalf of himself and all other the shareholders " in that company for a declaration that the payment of a certain dividend was *ultra vires* and illegal.

Order 15, r. 12 (1).

Stroud v. *Lawson* [1898] 2 Q.B. 44; 67 L.J.Q.B. 718.

One of several joint contractors may on behalf and for the benefit of all his co-contractors sue the other parties to the contract.

Janson v. *Property Insce. Co.* (1913) 19 Com.Cas. 36; 30 T.L.R. 49.

Similarly the officers of an unincorporated society may be compelled against their will to defend an action on behalf of the society.

Wood v. *McCarthy* [1893] 1 Q.B. 775; 62 L.J.Q.B. 373.

Parr v. *Lancashire and Cheshire Miners' Federation* [1913] 1 Ch. 366; 82 L.J.Ch. 193.

But see *Walker* v. *Sur* [1914] 2 K.B. 930; 83 L.J.K.B. 1188.

If a surety sues his co-sureties for contribution, he must make the principal debtor a party to the action, unless the latter is insolvent and his insolvency is proved or can be reasonably inferred.

Hay v. *Carter* [1935] Ch. 397; 104 L.J.Ch. 220.

A mortgagor who is entitled for the time being to possession of the mortgaged property, or to receive the rents and profits of it, may sue for possession of it, or to recover such rents or profits, or to prevent, or recover damages in respect of, any trespass or other wrong done to it, without joining his mortgagee as a co-plaintiff.

---

and for 2s.6d. to persons whose capital does not exceed £125 and whose income for the previous week did not exceed £9 10s. The solicitor is remunerated out of public funds. In addition a voluntary scheme is in operation whereby anyone, whatever his means, may seek advice at one interview not exceeding half an hour for £2.

58 But he must serve on his opponent notice that he is an assisted person.

Law of Property Act, 1925, s. 98.

Turner v. *Walsh* [1909] 2 K.B. 484; 78 L.J.K.B. 753.

The assignee of any legal chose in action may sue for it without joining his assignor as a co-plaintiff, provided the assignment be absolute and in writing under the hand of the assignor, and provided notice in writing of the assignment has before action been given to the debtor or holder of the fund.

Law of Property Act, 1925, s. 136.

Hughes v. *Pump House Hotel Co.* (*No.* 1) [1902] 2 K.B. 190.

An equitable assignee cannot as a rule obtain more than interlocutory relief unless the assignor as legal owner is joined as a plaintiff. " No action can now be defeated by reason of the misjoinder or non-joinder of any party; but this does not mean that judgment can be obtained in the absence of a necessary party to the action, and the rule is satisfied by allowing the parties to be added at any stage of the case."

Performing Right Society, Ltd. v. *London Theatre of Varieties, Ltd.* [1924] A.C. 1, 14 (*per* Cave L.C.).

Where there is an equitable assignment by way of charge of part of a debt alleged to be owing, the assignor cannot recover either the whole debt or the excess over the part assigned unless the assignee is made a party.

Walter & Sullivan, Ltd. v. *J. Murphy & Sons, Ltd.* [1955] 2 Q.B. 584.

II.—JOINDER OF CAUSES OF ACTION

The Judicature Act gave a plaintiff a very extensive power of joining on one writ several different causes of action. And in a proper case the plaintiff should certainly avail himself of this power. For if he brings two actions where one would have sufficed he will probably have to pay the costs of one action. Section 43 provides that the court shall grant either absolutely or on just terms " all such remedies whatsoever as any of the parties thereto may appear to be entitled to in respect of any legal or equitable claim properly brought forward by them in the cause or matter, so that, as far as possible, all matters in controversy between the parties may be completely and finally determined, and all multiplicity of legal proceedings concerning any of those matters avoided." Rules of court have been made providing how the claims may be " properly brought forward," but the avoidance of unnecessary proceedings remains a cardinal principle in their application.

The key rules are Order 15, rr. 1, 4 (1) and 5 (1). By rule 1 it is provided that: " (1) Subject to rule 5 (1), a plaintiff may in one action claim relief against the same defendant in respect of more than one cause of action—(*a*) if the plaintiff claims. and the defendant is alleged to be liable, in the same capacity in respect of all the causes of action, or (*b*) if the plaintiff claims or the defendant is alleged to be liable in the capacity of executor or administrator of an estate in respect of one or more of the causes of action and in his personal capacity but with reference to the same estate in respect of all the others, or (*c*) with the leave of the court. (2) An application for leave under this rule must be made *ex parte* by affidavit before the issue of the writ or originating summons, as the case may be, and the affidavit must state the grounds of the application." Although rule 4 is headed " Joinder of Parties " it falls to be considered here in so far as the causes of action of the various parties may differ: " Subject to rule 5 (1), two or more persons may be joined together in one action as plaintiffs or as defendants with the leave of the court or where—(*a*) if separate actions were brought by or against each of them, as the case may be, some common question of law or fact would arise in all the actions, and (*b*) all rights to relief claimed in the action (whether they are joint, several or alternative) are in respect of or arise out of the same transaction or series of transactions." (Rule 4 (1).)   But, " If claims in respect of two or more causes of action are included by a plaintiff in the same action or by a defendant in a counter-claim, or if two or more plaintiffs or defendants are parties to the same action, and it appears to the court that the joinder of causes of action or of parties, as the case may be, may embarrass or delay the trial or is otherwise inconvenient, the court may order separate trials or make such other order as may be expedient." (Rule 5 (1).)

Sub-paragraphs (*a*) and (*b*) of rule 4 (1) are hereafter referred to as " the two conditions."

The master's discretion is exercised in *ex parte* applications for leave for joinder and in applications for severance. For although the joinder may be within the terms of the rules, or although he (or a different master) may on prima facie grounds have given leave for joinder on an *ex parte* application, he may, nevertheless, at a later stage order severance after hearing argument upon a summons, if it appears that embarrassment, delay or inconvenience may be caused by the joinder whether it be of causes of action or of parties.[58a]

The plaintiff's application for leave under rule 1 must, by the terms of the rule, be made *ex parte* by affidavit before the writ is

---

[58a] As expressed in a former rule, he might make " such order as may be just to prevent any defendant from being embarrassed or put to expense by being required to attend any proceeding in which he may have no interest."

issued; but it may be that an application to extend the time, so as to validate a subsequent application, could be entertained.[59] And if claims be improperly joined without leave, still this irregularity is waived if the defendant, without raising the objection, takes a step in the action which would be neither necessary nor useful if he intended to rely on that objection.[60] He is supposed to know the law, and thus has notice of the irregularity as soon as he sees the writ or pleading. As to what is a " step in the action," see *post*, pp. 192–193.

The expression " the same transaction or series of transactions " gives rise to difficulty, but was retained in the revised rules. " The language of this rule," said Lord Wright in *Bendir* v. *Anson* [1936] 3 All E.R. 326, " cannot be regarded as very well chosen. The phrase ' transaction or series of transactions ' is not a term of art, and I cannot find in the authorities any precise definition of the scope of these words. But it is quite clear that the tendency of the decisions has been to give a liberal interpretation to the rule. . . . The word ' transaction,' I think, necessarily means an act, the effect of which extends beyond the agent to other persons. For instance, to take this particular case, the building of the premises by the defendant is an act which from one point of view is limited to the builder and to the area covered by the premises; but its effects on other premises extend also to those premises in respect of which a nuisance or an interference with an easement may be created by the building. In that sense the building of the premises may be regarded as a transaction, and I find on the authorities that that view seems to have been taken." The court declined to decide whether the joinder of two plaintiffs occupying separate and not adjacent premises, each of whom complained of an interference with his right to light, was within the terms of the old rule, but refused to allow it as a matter of discretion.

The following sections show how joint, several or alternative claims may be included in the same writ and the principles on which the master's discretion may be likely to be exercised. In many of the old cases the joinder was permissible within the terms of the rules as they then stood, but nevertheless the court refused to allow it as a

---

[59] See *Lloyd* v. *Gt. W. Dairies Co.* [1907] 2 K.B. 727, decided under an old rule. See also Ord. 3, r. 5.
[60] *Per* Cave J. in *Rein* v. *Stein* (1892) 66 L.T. at p. 41.

matter of discretion. The principle of these cases presumably still holds good.

Take the simplest case first:

1. *Same plaintiff: same defendant*

Here the parties are the same in all the causes of action which it is sought to join.

The plaintiff may without leave join on one writ any number of different causes of action against the same person or persons provided that " the plaintiff claims, and the defendant is alleged to be liable, in the same capacity in respect of all the causes of action " (Order 15, r. 1 (1) (*a*)). To this proviso there is one exception, namely, that a person may sue or be sued both as executor or administrator and in his personal capacity if the personal claims have reference to the same estate. In all other cases leave is required. (Rule 1 (1) (*b*) and (*c*).)

Now we come to cases of more difficulty, where not every plaintiff, or not every defendant, is interested in every cause of action joined.

2. *Different plaintiffs: same defendant*

When may two or more plaintiffs join on one writ distinct and separate causes of action against the same defendant or defendants?

They may do so without leave on two conditions; first, that if each brought a separate action some common question of law or fact would arise in all the actions; and secondly, that all rights to relief claimed in the action (whether they are joint, several or alternative) are in respect of, or arise out of, the same transaction or series of transactions. In other cases leave is necessary. (Order 15, r. 4.) This will not be granted if the joinder may embarrass or delay the trial or is otherwise inconvenient; and even if the joinder has lawfully been made without leave, the master may on the same grounds order separate trials or make such other order as may be expedient (rule 5).

If the action goes to trial with the joinder undisturbed, and one plaintiff succeeds and the other fails, the defendant should ask the judge to make a special order as to his costs occasioned by joining the plaintiff who failed.[61]

---

[61] See for example *Keen* v. *Towler* (1924) 41 T.L.R. 86; *King* v. *Sunday Pictorial Newspapers (1920), Ltd.* (1925) 133 L.T. 397. The defendant was formerly entitled to these costs unless the judge otherwise directed, but the rule was altered with effect from January 1, 1960.

Joinder of Causes of Action

Illustrations

The owners and tenants of two or more adjoining houses may in some circumstances be allowed to join in one action to restrain, or to recover damages for, any nuisance or other injury which affects their respective properties, though to different extents, provided such nuisance or injury is caused by the same acts of the same person.

House Property & Investment Co., Ltd. v. *H.P. Horse Nail Co., Ltd.* (1885) 29 Ch.D. 190; 54 L.J.Ch. 715.
But see *Bendir* v. *Anson* [1936] 3 All E.R. 326, *ante*, p. 29.

If a committee, or trustees, or any other defined body of persons be libelled or slandered collectively as a body in respect of the performance of their official duties, they may all join in one action.

Booth v. *Briscoe* (1877) 2 Q.B.D. 496.

But where A defamed B on one occasion and C on another, it was held under the old rules that B and C could not join as co-plaintiffs in one action against A, and that consolidation would not have been ordered.

Sandes v. *Wildsmith* [1893] 1 Q.B. 771; 62 L.J.Q.B. 404.

And where X and Y were differently libelled in different portions of the same book an application to consolidate was refused on the ground of the grave embarrassment which would ensue.

Marchant v. *Ford* [1936] 3 All E.R. 104.

On the other hand, where A and B are defamed by the same publication of the same libel, they can join in one action; and if they do not do so, the court may order their actions to be consolidated, unless this would cause embarrassment.

Horwood v. *Statesman Publishing Co.* (1929) 98 L.J.K.B. 450.

The Universities of Oxford and Cambridge were allowed to join in one action to restrain a publisher from selling his books as " The Oxford and Cambridge Publications."

Universities of Oxford and Cambridge v. *Gill* [1899] 1 Ch. 55; 68 L.J.Ch. 34.

Four persons who have been separately induced to take debentures on the faith of erroneous statements contained in the same fraudulent prospectus may join as co-plaintiffs in an action against the directors. The claims to relief arise out of the same transaction.

Drincqbier v. *Wood* [1899] 1 Ch. 393; 68 L.J.Ch. 181.
And see the converse case of *Frankenburg* v. *Gt. Horseless Carriage Co.* [1900] 1 Q.B. 504, *post*, pp. 34–35.

So, several master builders can join in one action against the officials of various trade unions who had conspired to injure them in the way of their business.

Walters v. *Green* [1899] 2 Ch. 696; 68 L.J.Ch. 730.

But where a plaintiff claims certain relief in his personal capacity, and certain other relief on behalf of himself and all other the shareholders in a certain company, he cannot (without leave) join those two claims on one writ, unless the right to relief in each case arises out of the same transaction or series of transactions. It is not enough for him to show that a common question of law or fact will arise.

Stroud v. *Lawson* [1898] 2 Q.B. 44; 67 L.J.Q.B. 718.

31

3. *Same plaintiff: different defendants*

When may the same plaintiff or plaintiffs join on one writ separate and distinct causes of action against different defendants?

Here, too, Order 15, rules 4 and 5, apply and the joinder may be made without leave if the two conditions are satisfied. In other cases leave is necessary and the master has the same power to order severance or otherwise so as to avoid embarrassment, delay or inconvenience, as he has in the case of joint plaintiffs.

(i) *Claims in the Alternative*

Where a plaintiff has but one cause of action, which entitles him to judgment against either A or B but not against both, he may without leave join A and B on the same writ as defendants in the alternative, and so determine the question which of them is liable. In such a case he may have to pay the costs of the defendant who is held not liable; though he may recover them back again from the defendant who is liable, if he can satisfy the judge that it was a reasonable and proper course for him to join both defendants in the action (see *post*, p. 414). Although it is not necessary for the plaintiff to establish that the unsuccessful defendant had given him notice that he was going to throw the blame for what had happened on his co-defendant, or had been guilty of any misrepresentation or collusion or other misconduct in the matter,[62] it is desirable that the plaintiff should take reasonable steps to ascertain whether the one proposed defendant is going to blame the other or not.

Illustrations

A plaintiff may join in one action a claim against a principal on a contract made by his alleged agent, and an alternative claim against the alleged agent for contracting without authority.

    Bennetts v. *McIlwraith* [1896] 2 Q.B. 464; 65 L.J.Q.B. 632.

So where A has trespassed on B's land, and claims a right to do so under a grant of a right of way from B's landlord prior in date to B's lease, B may join a claim against A for trespass with an alternative claim against the landlord for damages in the event of A establishing his right.

    Child v. *Stenning* (1877) 5 Ch.D. 695; 46 L.J.Ch. 523.

---

[62] *Besterman* v. *British Motor Cab Co., Ltd.* [1914] 3 K.B. 181.

(ii) *Joint and Several Claims*

When a plaintiff alleges that two or more persons are *all* jointly liable to him on different causes of action, whether sounding in tort or contract, he may without leave join them all on one writ. This has always been so and is still so under the present rules, not necessarily by virtue of Order 15, r. 4 (for the claims may arise out of totally different transactions), but by virtue of Order 15, r. 1, " Subject to rule 5 (1), a plaintiff may in one action claim against the same defendant in respect of more than one cause of action . . . if the plaintiff claims and the defendant is alleged to be liable in the same capacity in respect of all the causes of action . . . ", so long as there is no change of capacity. (The Interpretation Act, 1889, applies for the interpretation of the rules [63] so that here " defendants " may be read for " defendant.") Where, however, the plaintiff wishes to add any separate cause of action against one or more of the defendants severally, he should first consider whether the two conditions laid down by Order 15, r. 4 (*ante*, p. 28) are satisfied. If they are, there is no difficulty and he may issue his writ without leave; if they are not, he would be wise to apply for leave, for it does not seem likely that an individual defendant would be held to be the " same defendant " as himself together with another or others jointly.

Illustrations

If A and B are both jointly liable to X on two different contracts, whether connected or unconnected in their subject-matter, X may without leave bring one action against them jointly on both contracts.

But if they are jointly and severally liable on unconnected contracts and he wishes to pursue his rights against them individually as well as jointly, he should seek leave for the joinder.

If they are jointly and severally liable on contracts so far connected that the two conditions are satisfied, leave is not necessary.

If A, B and C are all three liable to X on a bill of exchange, and A and B are also liable to X on a promissory note, and C alone on a cheque, and the transactions are unconnected, X will probably have to bring three actions; for, it may well be that leave for joinder would be refused if it would involve A and B in sitting idle in court while the claim on the cheque was being tried, and C would also be wasting his time while the claim on the promissory note was being considered.

Where several persons conspire to do the plaintiff an injury, and succeed, leave for joinder is probably unnecessary even though each may be concerned in different overt acts; for a common question of fact (*i.e.*, whether they conspired)

---

[63] See Ord. 1, r. 3.

33

arises, and the acts would be likely to form part of the same transaction or series of transactions.

> See *Walters* v. *Green* [1899] 2 Ch. 696; 68 L.J.Ch. 730.
> *O'Keefe* v. *Walsh* [1903] 2 I.R. 681.
> *Re Beck, Attia* v. *Seed* (1918) 87 L.J.Ch. 335.

The same considerations apply if certain of the overt acts themselves cause damage and claims are added against some of the conspirators individually in addition to the joint claim for conspiracy. Thus, under the former rules, where three persons conspired together to libel and slander the plaintiff, damages were claimed and recovered against all three defendants jointly for conspiracy, and also against each of them separately for libels or slanders published in pursuance of the conspiracy. But the master has a discretion to order severance.

> *Thomas* v. *Moore* [1918] 1 K.B. 555.

And the plaintiff could not under the old rules join in such an action separate claims against one or more of the defendants individually for torts independent of the alleged conspiracy. *Quaere*, whether leave would now be given.

> See *Pope* v. *Hawtrey* (1901) 85 L.T. 263; 17 T.L.R. 717.

(iii) *Separate Claims*

Where a plaintiff seeks to recover judgment against A on one cause of action and at the same time to recover judgment against B on a separate and distinct cause of action, he can only join the two on one writ if *some* common question of law or fact arises *and* the causes of action arise out of the same transaction or series of transactions. If these two conditions are fulfilled it matters not that the causes of action may not be identical or that the respective liabilities of the defendants may to some extent be based on different grounds.

Illustrations

If the same libel appear in seventeen newspapers, the person libelled could not formerly but may now be able to make the seventeen proprietors defendants to one suit, at any rate with leave.

> See *Colledge* v. *Pike* (1886) 56 L.T. 124; 3 T.L.R. 126.

But actions by the same plaintiff for substantially the same libel or slander can in any event be consolidated on the application of the defendants under the Law of Libel Amendment Act, 1888, s. 5, or the Defamation Act, 1952, s. 13, respectively.

> See *Stone* v. *Press Association, Ltd.* [1897] 2 Q.B. 159; 66 L.J.Q.B. 662.

A and B promoted a company, of which they and C became directors; the three then issued a misleading prospectus. *Held,* that the plaintiff, who had been thereby induced to take shares in the company, could not join in one action a claim against A and B for conspiracy, with a claim against A, B and C for fraudulent misrepresentation.

> *Gower* v. *Couldridge* [1898] 1 Q.B. 348; 67 L.J.Q.B. 251.

But where an action is brought by a shareholder against the company and its directors for relief in respect of an improperly issued prospectus, the fact that the relief claimed against the several defendants may differ in detail is no ground for objection that the action is bad as joining separate causes of action against separate defendants, for in substance there is only one cause of action, namely, the improper issue of the prospectus.

> *Frankenburg* v. *Great Horseless Carriage Co.* [1900] 1 Q.B. 504; 69 L.J.Q.B. 147.
>
> *Kent Coal Exploration Co., Ltd.* v. *Martin* (1900) 16 T.L.R. 486.

H. Brothers contracted to carry meat for the plaintiffs from Bahia to England; they employed for this purpose a ship called the *Devon*, which was unseaworthy. In an action brought by the plaintiffs for damage to the meat caused by the unseaworthiness of the *Devon*, it was held that the plaintiffs might join as defendants H. Brothers and the owners of the *Devon*, claiming against the former on the contract of carriage and against the latter on the bill of lading.

> *Compania Sansinena, etc.* v. *Houlder Brothers* [1910] 2 K.B. 354; 79 L.J.K.B. 1094.

An English company and a Scottish company joined in a policy of marine insurance, each making itself liable for half the amount of the policy. These companies had a common office in London, and a common secretary, who signed the policy for them both. The liability of each company depended upon precisely the same facts. *Held*, that both companies could be joined as defendants in one action on the policy.

> *Oesterreichische Export A.G.* v. *British Indemnity Insurance Co.* [1914] 2 K.B. 747; 83 L.J.K.B. 971.

The plaintiff contracted to supply B with cards printed in accordance with certain specimens. He engaged C to do the actual work for him; C did so and sent the cards to B. B refused to accept delivery on the ground that they were not in accordance with the specimen cards. The plaintiff brought an action against B and C, claiming against B the price of goods sold and delivered and against C in the alternative damages for breach of contract. *Held*, by the Court of Appeal that, as there was a common question of fact to be tried, namely, whether the cards were in accordance with the specimens, the plaintiff could join his two claims on one writ—subject, of course, to the discretion of the court to disallow the joinder.

> *Payne* v. *British Time Recorder Co.* [1921] 2 K.B. 1; 90 L.J.K.B. 445.
>
> And see *Green* v. *Berliner* [1936] 2 K.B. 477; 105 L.J.K.B. 662.

A widow agreed with the plaintiff that he should act as companion to her son (who was of age) in consideration of a salary and an allowance to cover travelling and other expenses. The plaintiff brought two actions, one against the widow for wrongful dismissal, and the other against her son for indemnity against liabilities incurred and for repayment of disbursements. *Held*, by the Court of Appeal, that an order consolidating the two actions was properly made and that the claims might have been joined on one writ.

> *Bailey* v. *Marchioness Curzon*; *Same* v. *Duggan* [1932] 2 K.B. 392; 101 L.J.K.B. 627.

4. *Different plaintiffs: different defendants*

It was formerly the law that separate causes of action with different plaintiffs and also different defendants could never be joined on the same writ. Thus if A had a cause of action against B, and X had a different cause of action against Y, A and X could not have united in bringing a single action against B and Y, even though their causes of action arose out of similar transactions and involved similar questions of law or fact. All that could be done was for the parties to agree that one should be taken as a " test action " and the other (or others, if there was a series of them) should be stayed until the first was tried, and then follow its event. Now, however, it seems that there might be cases in which such joinder would be permissible, provided always that the two conditions were satisfied. Thus if A and B each had a right of action both against X and against Y in respect of the same accident, it is conceivable (though perhaps unlikely) that A might wish to pursue his remedy against X alone and B against Y alone and that they should unite in bringing one action in order to get some point decided. For the present, however, it is best to refrain from speculation as to the proper construction of the rule in this respect.

III.—JURISDICTION OF THE HIGH COURT OF JUSTICE

The High Court of Justice has jurisdiction over the whole of England and Wales, but not over Scotland. The High Court has also a general jurisdiction to hear actions for all injuries done by one Englishman to another in any corner of the world, whether in the Commonwealth or in a foreign country,[64] and also for injuries done by one alien to another abroad, provided such injuries be actionable by the law of England and also wrongful by the law of the country where they were committed.[65] But the court will allow an unrestricted right of suit only in cases in which the defendant is within the jurisdiction at the time the writ is served.[65a] And, indeed, if the plaintiff induces the defendant by fraud to come within the jurisdiction so that he may be served with a writ, the court will set aside the service as an abuse of the process of the court.[66] If the defendant is out of the jurisdiction, no writ for service out of the jurisdiction can be issued except by leave or by virtue of an enactment giving the High Court power to hear the action (Order 6, r. 7 (1)), and such leave will only be granted

---

[64] *Scott* v. *Lord Seymour* (1862) 1 H. & C. 219; 32 L.J.Ex. 61.
[65] *Machado* v. *Fontes* [1897] 2 Q.B. 231; *Carr* v. *Fracis Times & Co.* [1902] A.C. 176; *Evans* v. *Stein & Co.* [1905] F. 65.
[65a] See *Colt Industries Inc.* v. *Sarlie* [1966] 1 W.L.R. 440.
[66] *Watkins* v. *North American, etc., Co.* (1904) 20 T.L.R. 534.

in the cases specified in Order 11 [67] subject to the discretion of the court.[68] Moreover, substituted service cannot be ordered in cases where personal service would not in law be permissible.[69] If service is to be effected outside Scotland, Northern Ireland, the Isle of Man and the Channel Islands, leave will only be granted to serve a notice of writ (Order 11, r. 3) and not the writ itself.

Under Order 11, rule 1 (1) (*a*) (*b*), leave is readily granted if the whole subject-matter of the action is land situate within the jurisdiction (with or without rents or profits) or if any act, deed, will, contract, obligation or liability affecting land within the jurisdiction [70] is to be construed, rectified, set aside or enforced. Such matters by international law belong to the *forum rei sitae.*

Again, under rule (1) (*f*), leave can be obtained to serve a writ or notice out of the jurisdiction upon a defendant not domiciled or ordinarily resident in Scotland, where the subject-matter of the action is a contract (i) made within the jurisdiction [71]; or (ii) made by an agent within the jurisdiction on behalf of a principal trading or residing out of the jurisdiction; or (iii) by its terms or by implication to be governed by English law. So, too, under rule (1) (*g*), where the action is brought against a defendant not domiciled or ordinarily resident in either Scotland or Northern Ireland for breach within the jurisdiction of a contract wherever made. It will be sufficient if a part of the contract has been broken, provided that that part was substantial and had to be performed within the jurisdiction.[72] And under the rule it matters not that the breach may have been preceded or accompanied by a breach committed out of the jurisdiction which rendered impossible the performance of so much of the contract as ought to have been performed within the jurisdiction.

In cases where a contract (wherever made and whatever its subject-matter) contains a term conferring jurisdiction on the

---

[67] *Re Eager, Eager* v. *Johnstone* (1882) 22 Ch.D. 86. The student will here observe how English law tends to develop substantive law (in this case important principles of English Private International law) under cover of forms of procedure. The notes to Ord. 11, r. 1, in the " Red Book " (that is the " Yearly Practice " defunct since 1940 but well worth studying in this and other matters) and in the " White Book " will repay careful study in this light.

[68] *Kroch* v. *Rossell et Compagnie, etc.* (1937) 156 L.T. 379.

[69] *Wilding* v. *Bean* [1891] 1 Q.B. 100; *Jay* v. *Budd* [1898] 1 Q.B. 12.

[70] An action for breach of a repairing covenant in a lease is within this sub-rule. *Tassell* v. *Hallen* [1892] 1 Q.B. 321.

[71] See *Bremer Oeltransport G.m.b.H.* v. *Drewry* [1933] 1 K.B. 753.

[72] *Hemelryck* v. *William Lyall Shipbuilding Co., Ltd.* [1921] 1 A.C. 698.

High Court, leave may be given although none of the provisions of rule 1 is satisfied (r. 2).

There is more difficulty in obtaining leave in an action of tort, except where the tort was committed within the jurisdiction (rule 1 (1) (*h*)).[73] It is possible, however, to bring an action of tort under rule 1 (1) (*c*), (*i*), (*j*) or (*l*). Thus it may be that the proposed defendant, though temporarily abroad, is "domiciled or ordinarily resident within the jurisdiction" (rule 1 (1) (*c*)). But the mere carrying on of business within the jurisdiction by an individual, whether in his own name or under any other style or firm, is not sufficient.[74] A foreign company will be deemed to be resident within the jurisdiction if it has conducted its business, or a material part of it (*e.g.*, either manufacture or sale), at some fixed place in this country for a substantial period of time.[75] It is not sufficient if the agent here of the corporation is carrying on a business merely ancillary to that of the corporation.[76] Every foreign company which establishes a place of business within the United Kingdom must within one month from so doing file with the Registrar of Companies the name and address of some person resident in the United Kingdom who is authorised " to accept on behalf of the company service of process and any notices required to be served on the company." (Companies Act, 1948, s. 407.)

The plaintiff may obtain leave under rule 1 (1) (*i*) if his writ includes a bona fide claim for an injunction as to anything to be done within the jurisdiction.[77] The claim for an injunction must be one of substance and not made speciously for the purpose of founding the jurisdiction of the court.[78] Under rule 1 (1) (*j*), where the writ has already been duly served on a defendant within the jurisdiction, leave will be given in a proper case to serve another defendant

---

73 It is not sufficient that the damage flowing from the tort should have taken place within the jurisdiction. The tortious act itself must have been committed therein (*George Monro, Ltd.* v. *The American Cyanamid, etc., Corp.* [1944] K.B. 432; *Cordova Land Co.* v. *Black Diamond Steamship Corporation* [1966] 1 W.L.R. 793).

74 *Field* v. *Bennett* (1886) 56 L.J.Q.B. 89; *MacIver* v. *Burns* [1895] 2 Ch. 630; and see *Hobbs* v. *Australian Press Association* [1933] 1 K.B. 1.

75 *La "Bourgogne"* [1899] A.C. 431; *Saccharin Corporation, Ltd.* v. *Chemische Fabrik Von Heyden* [1911] 2 K.B. 516, distinguished in *Okura & Co.* v. *Forsbacka* [1914] 1 K.B. 715.

76 *Actiesselskabet Dampskib "Hercules"* v. *Grand Trunk Pacific Ry.* [1912] 1 K.B. 222; *The Lalandia* [1933] P. 56.

77 *Tozier* v. *Hawkins* (1885) 15 Q.B.D. 650, 680; *Alexander* v. *Valentine* (1908) 25 T.L.R. 29.

78 *Watson & Sons* v. *Daily Record (Glasgow), Ltd.* [1907] 1 K.B. 853; *Rosler* v. *Hilbery* [1925] 1 Ch. 250.

who is outside the jurisdiction, provided he be a necessary and proper party to the action.[79] But where two defendants are out of the jurisdiction, one defendant cannot by submitting to the jurisdiction confer jurisdiction as against the other.[80] Leave may be given under rule 1 (1) (*l*) in actions under the Carriage by Air Act, 1961, the Carriage by Air (Supplementary Provisions) Act, 1962, the Carriage of Goods by Road Act, 1965, or the Nuclear Installations Act, 1965.

Leave can also be obtained to serve with the writ, or notice of the writ, notice of motion for an interlocutory injunction.[81] But, when once a plaintiff has obtained leave to serve out of the jurisdiction a writ indorsed with one cause of action, he cannot—even under Order 18, r. 15—afterwards add a second cause of action, for which no such leave would have been granted.[82]

There are three other classes of case in which leave is required to issue a writ:

(i) Proceedings in respect of an act specified in the Mental Health Act, 1959, s. 141.

(ii) Proceedings in respect of the breach of a repairing covenant within the Leasehold Property (Repairs) Act, 1938.

(iii) Where the proposed plaintiff has been declared to be a vexatious litigant. (Judicature Act, 1925, s. 51.)

There is one curious exception to the jurisdiction of the High Court. If the defendant be a member of the University of Oxford resident within its limits, he must be sued in the University Court, although the plaintiff be in no way connected with the University or resident within its limits, and although the cause of action did not arise within those limits.[83] In the University of Cambridge there is a similar rule, save that the privilege cannot be claimed if any person not a member of the University is a party to the action. (Cambridge Award Act, 1856, s. 18.)

---

[79] *Croft* v. *King* [1893] 1 Q.B. 419; *Duder* v. *Amsterdamsch Trustees Kantoor* [1902] 2 Ch. 132.

[80] *Russell & Co.* v. *Cayzer & Co.* [1916] 2 A.C. 298; 85 L.J.K.B. 1152.

[81] *Overton* v. *Burn* (1896) 74 L.T. 776.

[82] See *Waterhouse* v. *Reid* [1938] 1 K.B. 743; 107 L.J.K.B. 178.

[83] *Ginnett* v. *Whittingham* (1885) 16 Q.B.D. 761; 55 L.J.Q.B. 409.

The plaintiff will also have to consider in which Division of the High Court he will bring his action. At present, as we have seen (*ante*, p. 1), the business of the court is distributed among the three Divisions in accordance with section 56 of the Judicature Act, 1925; and although a judge of any Division has jurisdiction to hear any action properly brought in the High Court, he may order an action to be transferred from one Division to another, if the plaintiff has commenced his action in the wrong Division,[84] and the plaintiff may have to pay the costs occasioned by the transfer.

Although the High Court may have jurisdiction, the plaintiff may be unwise to commence proceedings there if the action is one which could be commenced in a county court; for in that case, as we shall see (*post*, pp. 406–407), he may run a serious risk as to costs. Apart from this, it has always been a matter of common prudence to count the cost before embarking on legal proceedings and to consider whether the defendant is worth powder and shot; and since the passing of the Legal Aid and Advice Act, 1949, under which the liability of an unsuccessful assisted party to pay costs may be limited (*post*, p. 410), such considerations loom even larger.

IV.—WHETHER CAUSE OF ACTION FULLY ACCRUED
AT DATE OF WRIT

An intending plaintiff will also do well to consider carefully whether his action is not premature. That is to say, whether he has a good cause of action fully accrued at the date of issuing his writ. Broadly speaking, subject to certain equitable exceptions which it will be beyond the scope of this work to consider, *e.g.*, the case of principal and surety, the action speaks from the date of writ and nothing occurring since writ can be used to eke out a cause of action that did not exist when the writ was issued.[85] Thus, if you seek to sue on the covenants in a lease, it is no use showing that the reversion was assigned to you the day after you issued your writ; or if you sue in detinue, that demand and refusal to return the goods were made after action brought.

It is, however, permissible to recover damages accruing after

---

[84] Ord. 4, r. 3; and see *Societa Anonima Morandi* v. *Horner* [1935] W.N. 105.
[85] See *Eshelby* v. *Federated European Bank* [1932] 1 K.B. 254; *Coutts & Co.* v. *Duntroon Investment Corpn., Ltd.* [1958] 1 W.L.R. 116.

writ from a cause of action existing before writ. This is because all the damages flowing from a single cause of action must ordinarily be assessed and recovered once and for all, whether they be past, present or future, certain or contingent.[86] Where the cause of action itself is continuing, in the sense that it arises from the repetition or continuance of the act complained of (*e.g.*, in trespass or nuisance),[87] the damages are, by virtue of Order 37, r. 6, assessed down to the time of assessment; but for that rule this would not be permissible save where damages are awarded in lieu of an injunction under the jurisdiction which originated under Lord Cairns' Act.[88] There may be continuing breaches of obligation in contract as well as tort (*e.g.*, in the case of a covenant not to carry on a particular business). But to be treated as such the breaches must not be intermittent, nor must the obligation be a recurring one, as in the case of a contract to pay by instalments.[89]

So far we have assumed that the proposed plaintiff has a legal cause of action. But in some cases it should be apparent from the outset that the defendant has, or may have, a perfectly good answer to it, as, for instance, that the contract is not in writing—as it should be under so much as remains of the Statute of Frauds, 1677, or Lord Tenterden's Act [90]—or that the action is commenced too late and is therefore barred by the Limitation Act, 1939.[91] If so, he had much better refrain from bringing an action, of which he will almost certainly have to pay the costs on both sides, unless there are facts which will take the case out of the statute. These statutory defences will be more fully considered hereafter, but they are matters which should be borne in mind before any writ is issued.

---

[86] *Darley Main Colliery Co.* v. *Mitchell* (1886) 11 App.Cas. 127; and see *post*, pp. 200, 329.

[87] See *Hole* v. *Chard Union* [1894] 1 Ch. 293.

[88] Chancery Amendment Act, 1858 (since repealed); and see *Fritz* v. *Hobson* (1880) 14 Ch.D. 542 at p. 556.

[89] *National Coal Board* v. *Galley* [1958] 1 W.L.R. 16.

[90] Statute of Frauds Amendment Act, 1828.

[91] Amended by the Law Reform (Limitation of Actions, etc.) Act, 1954; and the Limitation Act, 1963, under s. 1 of which certain personal injury claims may nevertheless succeed even though the period of limitation has expired, provided that the requirements of s. 1 can be satisfied. Application for leave to bring the action may be made before or after its commencement. The procedure is governed by the Act and by Ord. 110.

CHAPTER 3

THE WRIT AND ITS INDORSEMENT

HAVING carefully considered all the matters set out in the previous chapter and more particularly who are the proper parties to sue and be sued, the plaintiff will now be in a position to issue the writ of summons, commonly called " the writ," which begins the action. This is an important document and every detail of it must be carefully studied.

At the top of the writ the plaintiff must state the Division of the High Court in which he sues. On issuing his writ in that Division it is marked with the plaintiff's initial letter and a serial number for that year, thus " 1971 B. No. 540." The parties to the action must be correctly set out. If any of them sue or are sued in a representative capacity, in the Queen's Bench Division [1] this fact is commonly stated when setting out the parties at the head of the writ, *i.e.*, the " title " of the action. It *must* always be stated in the indorsement.[2] The body of the writ contains its date of issue which marks the commencement of the action. On the back of the writ are stated the name and address of the plaintiff's solicitor (if any) and also the plaintiff's place of residence. This is done for a variety of reasons: so that the defendant may know where to find his creditor and pay him, where to serve notices, summonses and other documents, and so that he may ask for security for costs (*post*, p. 266) if the plaintiff lives abroad. (See Precedents, Nos. 3, 20 and 22.) The plaintiff must also make on the writ before it is issued an " indorsement of claim." (Order 6, r. 2.)

THE INDORSEMENT OF CLAIM

Before a writ is issued it must be indorsed *either* with a full statement of the plaintiff's claim (formerly called a " special indorsement"), to which all the rules of pleading apply (*post*, pp. 84–125), *or* with a concise statement of the nature of the claim made, *or* with a concise statement of the relief or remedy required in the

---

[1] But not in the Chancery Division (*Practice Direction* [1959] 1 W.L.R. 743).
[2] Ord. 6, r. 3; *Bowler* v. *John Mowlem, Ltd.* [1954] 1 W.L.R. 1445.

action. (Order 6, r. 2 (1).) Despite the wording of this rule, however, the indorsement should state the nature of the claim made *and* the relief or remedy required.[2a] The purpose of this is to let the defendant know why he is sued. And if the claim is for a debt or liquidated demand only (see *post*, p. 44), the writ must further state the amount claimed in respect of the debt or demand and for costs and must inform the defendant that further proceedings will be stayed if within the time limited for appearing [3] he pays the whole amount.[4] Notwithstanding the stay, the defendant is entitled to have the costs taxed if he thinks that the claim for them is excessive.[5]

If the writ is indorsed merely with a concise statement as above (formerly called a " general indorsement ") the plaintiff must subsequently serve upon the defendant a full statement of claim because the former is intended merely as a label to show to what class of action the suit belongs and to let the defendant know in very general terms the reason why he is being sued. An indorsement merely claiming " damages for breach of contract " or " damages for negligence " is insufficient; the defendant should be given some indication of the contract which he is alleged to have broken or the duty which he failed to perform.[6] The defect may, however, be remedied by the service of a statement of claim.[7] In actions of libel the indorsement must state sufficient particulars of the publications in respect of which the action is brought to enable them to be identified (Order 82, r. 2); and in moneylenders' actions the indorsement must state that at the material time the lender was licensed as a moneylender (Order 83, r. 2 [8]) and, if the indorsement is in the form of a statement of claim, the details of the transaction required by rule 3. (See Precedents, Nos. 5, 6 and 14.) In certain hire-purchase actions the statement of claim must include particulars of the circumstances in which the claim arises (see Order 84, rr. 1 and 2). As to Crown Proceedings see *ante*, p. 16, and Order 77, r. 3.

The exact wording of the general indorsement may become important if the defendant does not appear. But if he does, a

---

[2a] *Sterman* v. *E. W. & W. J. Moore* [1970] 2 W.L.R. 386.
[3] Ordinarily eight days after service, including the day of service (see Ord. 12, r. 5).
[4] Ord. 6, r. 2. Where the Exchange Control Act, 1947, applies, the money must be paid into court.   [5] Ord. 62, r. 9.
[6] *Marshall* v. *L.P.T.B.* [1936] 3 All E.R. 83; *Batting* v. *L.P.T.B.* [1941] 1 All E.R. 228.
[7] *Hill* v. *Luton Corporation* [1951] 2 K.B. 387; *Grounsell* v. *Cuthell* [1952] 2 Q.B. 673.
[8] And see *Nihalchand Navalchand* v. *McMullan* [1934] 1 K.B. 171.

statement of claim will be served in due course, stating everything in proper form. The plaintiff may not introduce in his statement of claim a fresh cause of action distinct from anything
mentioned on his writ.[9] But apart from this the indorsement on
the writ in no way fetters or limits the statement of claim. For by
Order 18, r. 15 (2), " a plaintiff may in his statement of claim
alter, modify, or extend any claim made by him in the indorsement
of the writ without amending the indorsement." But this rule does
not apply where the defendant has not appeared.[10] Hence, in case
judgment goes by default, even a general indorsement should be
carefully prepared. (See Precedents, Nos. 4–8.)

Illustration

In an action for slander the writ will be indorsed with the words " The plaintiff's
claim is for damages for slander." In the statement of claim the plaintiff may
also claim " an injunction restraining the defendant from repeating the alleged
slander."

Whether the plaintiff's claim comes within the definition of
a " debt or liquidated demand " affects not only the question whether
the plaintiff should indorse his writ with a claim for fixed costs, but
also the form of judgment which can be obtained in default of
appearance or defence (see *post*, pp. 56–59). When the amount to
which the plaintiff is entitled can be ascertained by calculation, or
fixed by any scale of charges or other positive *data*,[11] it is said to
be " liquidated " or made clear. But when the amount to be recovered depends upon the circumstances of the case and is fixed by
opinion or by assessment or by what may be judged reasonable,
the claim is generally unliquidated. It has, however, been clearly
decided that a claim upon a *quantum meruit*, where the plaintiff
states the precise sum which he claims as the value of his services, is
a liquidated demand.[12] In such a case no question of damages arises
and the money could have been recovered under the old *indebitatus*
count. But if the claim is in its nature a claim for damages at large,
it is not in law treated as a " liquidated demand " even if the plaintiff
puts a figure on the damages which he is claiming. A contract may,
however, provide for the payment of a fixed sum by way of damages
in certain events; and if such a sum is a true pre-estimate of the

[9] Ord. 18, r. 15 (2); *Cave* v. *Crew* (1893) 62 L.J.Ch. 530; *Sterman* v. *E. W. & W. J.
Moore* [1970] 2 W.L.R. 386; and see, *post*, p. 175.
[10] *Gee* v. *Bell* (1887) 35 Ch.D. 160; *Kingdon* v. *Kirk* (1887) 37 Ch.D. 141.
[11] See, for example, *G. L. Baker, Ltd.* v. *Barclays Bank, Ltd.* [1956] 3 W.L.R. 1409 ;
[1956] 3 All E.R. 519. [12] *Lagos* v. *Grunwaldt* [1910] 1 K.B. 41.

damage likely to flow from the breach and is not a " penalty " [13] it may properly be claimed as liquidated damages.

Illustrations

When the price of a ship is made payable by instalments, a claim for each instalment as it becomes due is a liquidated demand.

> *Workman, Clark & Co., Ltd.* v. *Lloyd Brazileno* [1908] 1 K.B. 968; 77 L.J.K.B. 953.

Indorsement: " The plaintiff's claim is £50 under the defendant's undertaking in writing to repurchase from the plaintiff on the 1st of November, 1881, forty fully paid-up shares in Old Shepherds Mines, Limited, for £40 at a premium of 5s. per share:

1882. Feb. 3.	To forty fully paid-up shares ..	..	£40
	Premium ..	.. .. ..	£10
			£50."

Held—the claim was for damages and was not a liquidated demand.

> *Knight* v. *Abbott* (1882) 10 Q.B.D. 11; 52 L.J.Q.B. 131.

Damages for wrongful dismissal are unliquidated. The fact or the chances of the plaintiff having other employment must be taken into consideration.

> *Hartland* v. *General Exchange Bank, Ltd.* (1866) 14 L.T. 863.

A claim for the purchase money of land sold by the plaintiff to the defendant is a claim for unliquidated damages unless the plaintiff avers that the defendant had accepted the title.

> *Leader* v. *Tod-Heatley* [1891] W.N. 38.

Statement of Claim Indorsed on Writ

Formerly the cases where the writ could be " specially indorsed " with a statement of claim were provided for by rule and unless the writ was so indorsed the plaintiff could not apply for summary judgment. The statement of claim can now be indorsed on the writ in all cases. If it is drafted and served separately the action is delayed; moreover, if the plaintiff does not indorse it on the writ when it is reasonable and proper that he should, he may be penalised in respect of any extra costs thereby occasioned.[14] But in some cases—*e.g.*, where the action may well be settled shortly after writ issued, as often happens in collision cases—the drafting of a full statement of claim to be indorsed on the writ instead of a " general " indorsement may be a waste of costs.

A statement of claim so indorsed is the statement of claim in the action [15] and no further statement of claim can be served except by way of amendment. It must be so headed [16] and be signed by

---

[13] See, among many other cases, *Dunlop Pneumatic Tyre Co., Ltd.* v. *New Garage & Motor Co.* [1915] A.C. 79.

[14] See Ord. 62, r. 7. [15] *Anlaby* v. *Praetorius* (1888) 20 Q.B.D. 764.

[16] Ord. 18, r. 6 (1) (*d*).

counsel, if settled by him, otherwise by the plaintiff's solicitor [17] or by the plaintiff himself if acting in person (Order 18, r. 6 (5)). It must comply with all the rules applicable to a pleading (*post*, pp. 84–125) and in particular must give dates and items sufficient to inform the defendant specifically what is the claim made against him, so that he may be able to make up his mind whether he will pay or fight.[18] If he fights, he must (unless other steps are taken) plead to it within fourteen days after the time limited for appearance. It must also state all material facts necessary to constitute a complete cause of action. The more concisely such material facts are stated the better. " But if a man employs the machinery of a specially indorsed writ, he must make his indorsement a full and complete statement of his cause of action." (*Per* Lord Coleridge C.J., in *Fruhauf* v. *Grosvenor & Co.* (1892) 67 L.T. at p. 351.)

Illustrations

The heading " Statement of Claim " and the signature are valuable as distinct indications from which the defendant can learn that he is served, not only with a writ of summons to which he must appear, but also with a statement of claim to which he must plead. In the absence of these judgment in default of defence will not be entered.

   Cassidy & Co. v. *M'Aloon* (1893) 32 L.R.Ir. 368.

   In the absence of sufficient particulars of the claim it may not be clear whether it is truly liquidated and the plaintiff may not be able to enter judgment by default.

   Manchester Advance & Discount Bank, Ltd. v. *Walton* (1893) 62 L.J.Q.B. 158.

Claim for Interest

A claim for interest may be included in an indorsement. Interest may be payable by agreement, express or implied, or by virtue of some statute. In such cases the agreement to pay interest at the rate claimed, or the facts from which such an agreement can be implied, or the facts which bring the case within such statute, must be sufficiently alleged on the writ (not merely in an affidavit),[19] and then interest at the rate agreed or fixed may clearly be claimed up to date of writ. The modern practice is to carry this claim even further—" until payment or judgment "—and this although, as

---

[17] The solicitor's signature by the hand of a duly authorised clerk is sufficient. (*France* v. *Dutton* [1891] 2 Q.B. 208.)

[18] *Smith* v. *Wilson* (1879) 5 C.P.D. 25; *Bickers* v. *Speight* (1888) 22 Q.B.D. 7.

[19] *Gold Ores Reduction Co., Ltd.* v. *Parr* [1892] 2 Q.B. 14; 61 L.J.Q.B. 522.

a general rule, a plaintiff has no right to indorse his writ with any claim that has not at that moment arisen.[20]

In the case of a bill of exchange, promissory note, cheque or any other negotiable instrument to which the Bills of Exchange Act, 1882, applies, interest may be claimed till payment or judgment. And the expenses of noting and protesting the bill may also be claimed on a writ. The Act expressly declares that such claims for interest and expenses are to be " deemed to be liquidated damages." [21]

By the Law Reform (Miscellaneous Provisions) Act, 1934, s. 3 (1), in any proceedings tried in any court of record for the recovery of any debt or damages the court may award interest at such rate and for such period as it thinks fit,[22] but subject to three limitations:

(a) interest on interest is not to be awarded;

(b) this discretionary power does not arise where interest is payable as of right (by agreement or otherwise); and

(c) the damages recoverable for the dishonour of a bill of exchange are not to be affected.

The trial judge [23] may award interest under the Law Reform Act, 1934, although there is no claim for it in the writ or statement of claim [24]; but it is advisable to include it if such interest is sought. It is probably not within the power of the master to award such interest on a summons for judgment under Order 14 except by consent.

By the Administration of Justice Act, 1969, s. 22, the judge must, unless there are special reasons to the contrary, award interest on any award of damages in respect of personal injuries or death

---

[20] Where interest accrues from day to day under the contract and a cause of action for it arises immediately after the debt becomes due, the claim can conveniently be carried down to payment or judgment merely as a matter of calculation. And see Ord. 18, r. 9, and Ord. 13, r. 1. But if, for example, the interest is payable monthly or quarterly and a particular instalment had not become due at the date of the writ, the possibility of objection is more obvious, although the defendant may prefer not to expose himself to the costs of a fresh action by taking the point. " Until payment or judgment " implies whichever first takes place; for after judgment the debt is merged in the judgment and interest is payable upon the amount of the judgment under the Judgments Act, 1838, s. 17, without the necessity for any claim.

[21] Ss. 9 (3), 57; see *London and Universal Bank* v. *Clancarty* [1892] 1 Q.B. 689; *Dando* v. *Boden* [1893] 1 Q.B. 318; and Precedent No. 9.

[22] *Bank of Athens* v. *Royal Exchange Assce.* [1938] 1 K.B. 771; *The Berwickshire* [1950] P. 204.

[23] Or an arbitrator (*Chandris* v. *Isbrandtsen-Moller Co., Inc.* [1951] 1 K.B. 240, 256).

[24] *Riches* v. *Westminster Bank* [1943] 2 All E.R. 725.

exceeding £200. Such interest, however, need not be claimed in the writ or statement of claim; it will normally accrue to the claim for special damages from the date of service of the writ, and to the amount awarded for pain and suffering from the date of the accident, at an appropriate rate.[24a] In such cases, therefore, undue delay in serving the writ may need to be particularly avoided.

Claim for an Account

If a rent-collector, or a commercial traveller, or any other agent or trustee, has received money on behalf of the plaintiff, he is what is called " an accounting party"; that is, he is bound within a reasonable time after demand to render an account of all moneys received by him, showing how much he has paid over to the plaintiff and how much he still has in hand. It is of great importance to the plaintiff to have such an account; he does not know how much money the defendant has in fact received on his behalf; and therefore he does not know what sum to claim on the writ. In such a case he would indorse his writ with a claim to have an account taken.[25] As a rule such an action should be commenced in the Chancery Division (Judicature Act, 1925, s. 56 (1) (*b*)). " Where a writ is indorsed with a claim for an account or a claim which necessarily involves taking an account, the plaintiff may, at any time after the defendant has entered an appearance or after the time limited for appearing, apply for an order under this rule "— *i.e.*, for an account to be taken (Order 43, r. 1 (1)). The application for such order must be made by summons and, if the master so directs, must be supported by affidavit or other evidence (rule 1 (2)) and the order will usually be made unless the defendant satisfies the master that there is some preliminary question to be tried (*e.g.*, to decide whether or not he is an accounting party or has already fully accounted). When making the order the master " may also order that any amount certified on taking the account to be due to either party be paid to him within a time specified in the order " (rule 1 (3)). Moreover, at any stage of the proceedings in any cause or matter the court or a judge may direct any necessary accounts to be taken, notwithstanding that there may be some further relief sought, or some special issue still to be tried (rule 2 (1)).

[24a] See *Jefford* v. *Gee* [1970] 2 Q.B. 130.
[25] See Precedents, Nos. 20, 21 and 22.

.This method of obtaining an account was borrowed from the Court of Chancery; it is of the greatest utility. It is true that an action lay at common law against a bailiff or receiver, or by one merchant against another in respect of their mutual dealings as merchants, for not rendering a reasonable account of profits. And by the Administration of Justice Act, 1705, s. 27 (now repealed) an action of account might be brought by one joint-tenant or tenant in common against the other, as bailiff, for receiving more than his just share or proportion.[26] But in the face of the extensive jurisdiction of the courts of equity in all matters of account these common law actions became practically obsolete. Now, however, in either division of the High Court [27] a plaintiff may indorse his writ with a claim for an account.

If an order be made on such an application, the account may be taken by a master, or a district registrar,[28] or by a special or an official referee.[29] A special referee may be selected by the parties; an official referee (see *post*, p. 264) is an officer of the court to whom matters may be referred by the order of a judge or master. A referee is not bound to take the account in the strict way usually adopted before a master in Chancery Chambers (*post*, p. 347); he may adopt that method if he thinks it convenient, or any other method that in his opinion will best advance the ends of justice.[30] And by Order 43, r. 3, he is empowered to give special directions with regard to the mode in which the account is to be taken or vouched, and in particular may direct that books of account in which the accounts in question have been kept shall be prima facie evidence of the truth of the entries. See also rules 4 and 5 as to procedure. The first step generally is for the defendant to deliver an account. This the plaintiff proceeds to criticise. If he can show that the defendant has taken credit for payments which he never made, he can have the items struck out; that is called " falsifying." To " falsify " is to show that some item is erroneous. If he can show that the defendant has received moneys with which he has not debited himself, in other words, that some items have

---

[26] *Henderson* v. *Eason* (1851) 17 Q.B. 701.
[27] *York* v. *Stowers* [1883] W.N. 174.
[28] *Re Bowen* (1882) 20 Ch.D. 538.
[29] See Ord. 36 and *Rochefoucauld* v. *Boustead* [1897] 1 Ch. 196, 213.
[30] *Re Taylor, Turpin* v. *Pain* (1890) 44 Ch.D. 128. See Seton (7th ed.), Vol. II, pp. 1309–1346, and Precedents, Nos. 23, 24.

been omitted, the plaintiff can have these items added; that is called "surcharging." When this process has been exhausted the referee will have arrived at a correct account, and can then make an order that the defendant shall pay the plaintiff the balance shown by such account to be due to him. (And see *post*, p. 208.)

CHAPTER 4

MATTERS TO BE CONSIDERED AFTER WRIT

SERVICE

WHEN the plaintiff or his solicitor has indorsed the writ, his next step (after obtaining any necessary leave as set out in Chapter 2) is to issue it (as described in Chapter 1).

Next it must be served on the defendant or defendants. If any defendant has a solicitor who will accept service, the writ may be sent to the latter, who indorses it with the words " I accept service hereof on behalf of the defendant A.B.," [1] signs and dates it and returns it to the plaintiff's solicitor. Personal service on that defendant is then unnecessary and the writ is deemed to have been served on him on the date on which the acceptance was indorsed. (Order 10, r. 1 (2).)

Personal service may also be rendered unnecessary by the terms of a contract. The action must be one which the High Court has jurisdiction to hear by virtue of, or independently of, a term of the contract. Then if it specifies a particular manner of service, or a person other than the defendant (*e.g.*, an agent) on whom process may be served, such service will be effective. It may specify a place out of the jurisdiction as a place for service; but in that case leave to serve there must first be obtained as described at pp. 36–39. (Order 10, r. 3.)

A company registered under the present or former Companies Acts may be served with a writ (or any other process) by leaving it at or sending it by post to the registered office of the company.[2] This method of effecting service is frequently adopted even when the company has a solicitor acting for it. A registered trade union may be served in like manner. Other bodies corporate, in respect of which no special statutory provision is made, are served by personally serving the appropriate officer (see Order 65, r. 3). For service on a partnership, see Order 81, r. 3.

---

[1] An undertaking to appear is no longer necessary.
[2] Companies Act, 1948, s. 437; *White* v. *Land, etc., Co.* [1883] W.N. 174.

In other cases personal service is usually necessary (see p. 9); but if this is impracticable the plaintiff may apply to the practice master on affidavit for an order for " substituted service " (Order 65, r. 4). This is particularly useful when the defendant is evading service. The plaintiff must show that he has made genuine but unsuccessful efforts to effect personal service and that the alternative method which he proposes will probably be effective in bringing the writ or other document to be served to the defendant's notice in time.[3] The master may then order service by post, or more rarely by advertisement (which is expensive), or by service upon the defendant's partner or agent or upon a solicitor acting for him but not instructed to accept service. In claims for the possession of land, if no one is in possession of that land, the writ may be allowed to be served (when other means are impracticable) by affixing a copy of it to some conspicuous part of the land (Order 10, r. 4)[3a]; but if the defendant does not enter an appearance, judgment can only be obtained for possession, not for arrears of rent or mesne profits, unless an order for substituted service is obtained.

If the writ has been served personally or by substituted service (but not if service has been accepted by a solicitor or has been waived by the entry of an unconditional appearance) the person serving it must, within three days, make what is called an " indorsement of service " on the original. This must specify the day of the week [3b] and the date and place of service, and the person served. If that person is not the defendant, and is, for example, the manager of a firm but not a partner, it must also specify the capacity in which he is served. Unless this indorsement is made within the three days or any extended time which a master may allow, the plaintiff cannot enter judgment in default of appearance or defence (Order 10, r. 1 (4)).

If the writ is served more than twelve months from the date of issue [3c] it is deemed to have been irregularly served and may be set aside; but the irregularity may be waived if the defendant enters an unconditional appearance (*post*, p. 54). The plaintiff may, before the twelve months is up, apply to the master to renew

---

[3] *Re a Judgment Debtor* [1937] Ch. 137.

[3a] Note the similar provision made by Order 113, r. 4 (2) for service of an originating summons on an unidentifiable trespasser (*ante*, p. 14).

[3b] Service on a Sunday is excluded (except, in case of urgency, with leave). (Order 65, r. 10, *post*, p. 460).

[3c] Including that date (*Trow* v. *Ind Coope, Ltd.* [1967] 2 Q.B. 899.

it. If the master thinks it proper to renew it, either because the defendant cannot be found or for some other reason, he will do so for any period up to twelve months and so on from time to time (Order 6, r. 8). The application to renew can by leave be made after the expiration of the twelve months (or of the extended period), but in that case renewal will not necessarily be granted if there has been delay [3d] or if the effect thereof would be to deprive the defendant of a defence of a statute of limitations which has accrued to him by reason of the plaintiff's delay.[4] For service out of the jurisdiction, see *ante*, pp. 36–40.

APPEARANCE

After the writ has been served upon him a defendant must, if he wishes to defend the action, enter an appearance, unless there has been some irregularity in the issue or service of the writ. He or his solicitor hands or posts to the proper officer at the Central Office in London or at a district registry two copies of a " Memorandum of Appearance "; one copy the officer retains and enters in a book called the " Cause Book "; the other he seals with his official stamp. If someone attends to enter the appearance, the sealed copy is returned to him and he must on the same day send it on to the plaintiff or his solicitor; if the appearance is entered by post, the officer of the court sends the sealed copy to the plaintiff or his solicitor and also sends to the defendant or his solicitor a sealed and dated " Notice of Appearance " showing that the defendant entered an appearance on that date. (Order 12, r. 4.) When the writ is issued out of a district registry and it is stated on the writ that any cause of action arose in the district in which it was issued the defendant *must* enter appearance in the district registry (r. 2 (2)). In the absence of any such statement any defendant who neither resides nor carried on business [5] within the district may appear either in the district registry or at the Central Office at his option (r. 2 (4)).

CONDITIONAL APPEARANCE

The defendant, if not a British subject or a British company, may have valid reasons for objecting to the jurisdiction of our

---

[3d] *Baker* v. *Bowketts Cakes Ltd.* [1966] 1 W.L.R. 861.

[4] *Battersby* v. *Anglo-American Oil Co.* [1945] 1 K.B. 23; *Sheldon* v. *Brown Bayley's Steel Works, Ltd.* [1953] 2 Q.B. 393; *E., Ltd.* v. *C.* [1959] 1 W.L.R. 692; *Heaven* v. *Road and Rail Wagons Ltd.* [1965] 2 Q.B. 355.

[5] Or, in the case of a company, neither has its registered office, nor carries on business (see Ord. 12, r. 2 (3) and *Davies* v. *British Geon, Ltd.* [1957] 1 Q.B. 1).

courts. If he enters unconditional appearance he thereby sets at rest all doubts as to jurisdiction and loses all right to object subsequently, except possibly in the case of a foreign sovereign. Similarly, the entry of unconditional appearance by any defendant usually amounts to a waiver of any irregularity in the issue or service of the writ. If therefore there is any question of jurisdiction or irregularity, the defendant should avail himself of his right under Order 12, r. 7 (1), to enter appearance " under protest," as it were, and thus preserve his rights. If necessary, the court will try the question of jurisdiction as a preliminary point and in a proper case will stay the proceedings. An application to set aside the writ or service of it, or to discharge an order giving leave to serve out of jurisdiction, may be made before entering an appearance of any sort. But there is not always time to do so; and by entering a conditional appearance the defendant's solicitor gets himself upon the record. A conditional appearance will become unconditional unless the defendant makes his application within 14 days, or gets an extension of time, or unless the master orders otherwise. (Order 12, rr.7, 9.)

WRIT ISSUED WITHOUT AUTHORITY

If the defendant has reason to believe that the plaintiff has not really set the law in motion and that the writ purporting to be issued in his name was issued without authority he should apply promptly to set it aside.[5a] He should not wait to deliver his defence. Again, if the plaintiff without authority uses a solicitor's name for the purpose of issuing a writ and indorses it thereon, the proceedings may be stayed.[5b]

INTERIM PAYMENTS

In an action for personal injuries [5c] the plaintiff may, at any time after the writ has been served and the time limited for the defendant to enter an appearance has expired, apply for an order requiring the defendant to make an interim payment. (Order 29 (part II), r. 10.) This rule, made under the Administration of Justice Act, 1969, s. 20, introduced [5d] a swift procedure for the recovery, in appropriate cases, of a sum on account of the damages which ought

5a *Richmond* v. *Branson* [1914] 1 Ch. 968.
5b Ord. 6, r. 5.
5c Defined by Order 29, r. 9, to include an action in which there is a claim for damages in respect of a person's death.
5d On July 20, 1970, see R.S.C. (Amendment No. 2) 1970: S.I. No. 944.

eventually to be awarded to the plaintiff. Application must be made by summons supported by an affidavit verifying the special damages and exhibiting the relevant hospital and medical reports, and these documents must be served on the defendant not less than 10 clear days before the return day (r. 11).

This procedure is appropriate only where the degree of contributory negligence, if any, on the part of the plaintiff is insubstantial and where the defendant can be shown to be liable, or at very serious risk, in damages and able to make some payment. In a proper case the court may order the payment of " such amount as it thinks just, not exceeding a reasonable proportion " of the damages it seems likely the plaintiff will eventually recover (see r. 12 (1) (2)). Payment will normally be made to the plaintiff, but otherwise into court (*post*, pp. 254–258), and may be ordered in one sum or by stated instalments (r. 12 (3) (4)).

The hearing of the application may be treated as a convenient opportunity for the giving of certain directions (*post*, p. 262) depending upon the stage reached in the action when it is made (r. 13) and regardless of the outcome.

A defendant who counterclaims damages for personal injuries may likewise apply for an interim payment from the plaintiff (r. 17) but neither party should ever mention in his pleading the fact that an order has been made, nor should this fact be mentioned to the trial judge until all questions of liability and the amount of the damages have been decided (r. 14). The trial judge must then be so informed in order that his final judgment may be tailored to suit the financial obligations resulting between the parties. Thus, for example, it may be necessary to order the plaintiff to repay to the defendant so much of an interim payment as exceeds the judge's award, or one of several defendants may be found liable to pay to another by way of contribution some part of an interim payment made by one and not the other (r. 16). In the case of a minor or a patient who sues by his next friend or guardian (*ante*, pp. 22–23) money recovered by way of interim payment as well as under a final award will ordinarily be paid into court and dealt with as directed (Order 80, r. 12, and see *post*, p. 256.)

DEFAULT OF APPEARANCE

Brief reference to this topic has been made in Chapter 1. If the defendant does not enter an appearance within the time specified in the writ, the plaintiff is ordinarily entitled to judgment in default of appearance. There are, however, certain exceptions. When the defendant is a minor or a patient, the plaintiff must apply to the master to appoint a guardian *ad litem* for the defendant. When the claim is for special relief not mentioned in Order 13, rr. 1–4 (usually such as before 1873 could only have been given in the Court of Chancery), the procedure is as described *post,* at p. 57. Leave must be obtained: (i) if the plaintiff is a moneylender suing for money lent [6]; (ii) in many hire-purchase claims [6a]; and (iii) in actions in tort between husband and wife.[7] If the plaintiff omits or delays to enter judgment, the defendant may still enter an appearance and defend the action; but he gains no extra time for his defence or for taking any other step through his delay. (Order 12, r. 6 (2).)

The procedure on entering judgment in default of appearance varies according to the nature of the plaintiff's claim. When the writ is indorsed for a liquidated sum [7a] the plaintiff may, on filing an affidavit showing that the writ has been duly served, or on producing the writ indorsed with an acceptance of service by the defendant's solicitor, enter *final* judgment for any sum not exceeding the sum indorsed on the writ, together with interest, if properly claimed (see *ante,* p. 46), at the rate specified (if any), or (if no rate be specified) at the rate of 5 per cent. per annum, to the date of the judgment, and costs. (Order 13, r. 1.) If the defendant after writ issued pays the debt but not the costs and does not appear, the plaintiff may (subject to the County Courts Act, 1959, s. 47, *post,* pp. 406–409) enter judgment for costs only.[8] Moreover, if there are a number of defendants and some appear and some do not, the plaintiff may enter judgment in default of appearance against those who do not appear and issue execution thereon without prejudice to his right to proceed with the action against such of the defendants who have appeared. This rule and Order 19. r. 2, render the decision in *Kendall* v. *Hamilton* ((1879) 4 App.Cas. 504, *ante,* p. 18) inoperative as regards a final judgment in default of appearance or defence for a debt or liquidated demand.[9] And see Order 14, r. 8 (*post,* p. 68). Should, however, this amount be in excess of what is

---

[6] See *post,* pp. 59–60.
[6a] See Ord. 84, and *post,* p. 60. [7] See Ord. 89, r. 2.
[7a] *Ante,* p. 44.
[8] See Ord. 62, Appendix 3, and *Hughes* v. *Justin* [1894] 1 Q.B. 667.
[9] *Parr* v. *Snell* [1923] 1 K.B. 1.

really due to the plaintiff, the judgment is liable to be set aside
(see *post*, pp. 58–59) or its amount reduced.[10] As to actions for an
account, see *ante*, p. 48. If, however, the plaintiff's claim is for
unliquidated damages, he cannot immediately obtain final judgment since the damages have to be assessed. He gets instead what
is called an *interlocutory* judgment which he can afterwards
convert into a final judgment. (Order 13, r. 2.) If the action be
solely in detinue the plaintiff may at his option either enter interlocutory judgment against the defendant for the return of the
goods or their value to be assessed and costs, or enter interlocutory
judgment for their value to be assessed and costs. (Order 13, r. 3.)
If the plaintiff adopts the former course he need not then wait
for an assessment of value, if he suspects that the defendant still
has the goods, but may apply to a master *ex parte* for leave to
issue a writ of delivery (*post*, p. 391). In actions for possession of
land only other than mortgage actions [10a] he may enter final judgment for possession subject to the provisions and requirements of
rule 4. When the writ is indorsed with two or more of the claims so
far mentioned (*i.e.*, for a liquidated demand or unliquidated damages,
or detinue or possession of land) and no other, the plaintiff may
obtain judgment in respect of any such claim as if it were the only
claim indorsed on the writ. (Rule 5.)

But in actions not covered by the preceding rules, including
claims for an injunction or a declaration and other claims which
before the Judicature Acts could only have been brought in the Court
of Chancery, the procedure is different. The plaintiff is not at this
stage allowed to enter any judgment, either final or interlocutory,
upon the claim, even though the defendant has not appeared. After
proving due service of the writ he must, unless the writ is already
fully indorsed, prepare a statement of claim and serve it on the defendant either personally, or by leaving it at his address, or by post,
or in such other manner as the court may direct. (Order 65, r. 5.)
When this has been done the plaintiff may proceed with the action
in the undermentioned way. (Order 13, r. 6 (1).) If the defendant
desires, he may still appear, and, if he does, the action proceeds as if
he had done so at the proper time, and he must serve a defence. But
if he does not appear, he cannot serve a defence, and the plaintiff,

---

[10] *Muir* v. *Jenks* [1913] 2 K.B. 412.
[10a] As to which see Ord. 88.

after waiting fourteen days, can move the court or apply by sum-mons [11] for judgment in default of defence. The statement of claim will stand admitted, and the plaintiff will obtain such judgment as he is entitled to thereon. (Order 19, r. 7 (1).) No evidence is neces-sary or, indeed, admissible.[12] But the court has a discretion as to the order it will make [13]; and also over the costs of the action.[14] If, however, the defendant has satisfied or complied with the claim —*e.g.*, by abating a nuisance complained of—so that it becomes unnecessary for the plaintiff to proceed further with the action, then, if the defendant fails to enter an appearance, the plaintiff may apply by summons for leave to enter judgment against him for costs. (Order 13, r. 6 (2).) If one of several defendants defaults, the plain-tiff may proceed in accordance with Order 19, r. 7 (2). The court can, if need be, give leave to amend the statement of claim; if so, it may in its discretion order re-service and adjourn the application meanwhile.

An interlocutory judgment does not specify what amount is due to the plaintiff, since this has still to be determined. The amount of damages or the value of the chattel must subsequently be assessed by a master, unless reference to an official or special referee, or trial before a judge (with or without a jury), is specially ordered, or unless there are other defendants against whom the action is proceeding to trial. The defendant is given notice of the hearing and the defendant, although he has not appeared, may attend it in person or by solicitor or counsel. He is entitled to cross-examine the witnesses called on behalf of the plaintiff, call evidence himself on the issue of *quantum* and address the court. When the damages (or value of the chattel) have been assessed, then the plaintiff can enter *final* judgment for the amount assessed.[15]

A judgment in default of appearance or defence may be set aside or varied unconditionally or upon terms. (Order 13, r. 9; Order 19, r. 9; and see *Evans* v. *Bartlam* [1937] A.C. at p. 480.) A judgment irregularly obtained used to be set aside as of right. Now, under Order 2, r. 1, the court can make such order (including

---

[11] This alternative was given in 1958. A motion, or, when appropriate, a summons before a judge in chambers, is necessary where relief is claimed which a master has no power to grant, such as an injunction.

[12] *Webster & Co., Ltd.* v. *Vincent* (1897) 77 L.T. 167; *Young* v. *Thomas* [1892] 2 Ch. 134.

[13] *Charles* v. *Shepherd* [1892] 2 Q.B. 622.

[14] *Young* v. *Thomas (supra)*. [15] See Ord. 37, rr. 1–5.

an order as to costs) as it thinks just.[16] The irregularities relied on must be specified in the summons and the application must be made within a reasonable time and before any fresh step is taken after knowledge of the irregularity. (*Ibid.*) But before granting any application to set aside a judgment regularly obtained (*i.e.*, strictly in compliance with the rules), the court will require to be satisfied not only that the defendant had some reasonable excuse, *e.g.*, illness, for failing to enter an appearance, but also as to his " merits," *i.e.*, that in the action itself there is some prospect of his being at least partly successful. An affidavit is usually necessary for this purpose. If a judgment has been set aside on conditions and the defendant does not comply with the conditions, the judgment stands and the plaintiff may proceed upon it unless the master otherwise directs (Order 45, r. 10; see also r. 9), or unless the defendant obtains an extension of time.[17]

A judgment for an amount larger than is due at the time it is entered is bad and will be set aside or reduced.[18] In the case of genuine mistake the plaintiff may get leave *ex parte* to amend, provided he applies before communicating the contents of the judgment to the defendant or taking any steps to enforce it. In other cases where there has been a clerical mistake in the judgment or an error arising from some accidental slip or omission the application must be made on summons under the " slip rule " (Order 20, r. 11, *post*, p. 172).

Moneylenders' Actions

The considerations applying in general to actions by moneylenders for the return of money lent may conveniently be set out here, since in this type of action the defendant through fear of publicity often abstains from appearing or defending the action. Under the Moneylenders Acts, 1900–1927, every person whose business is that of moneylending, or who advertises or holds himself out as carrying on that business, must be licensed. Registration under the Registration of Business Names Act, 1916, may also be required. In the absence of a written acknowledgment and under-taking to pay or other special circumstances, he must bring his action within twelve months from the date when the last payment

---

[16] And see *Anlaby* v. *Praetorius* (1888) 20 Q.B.D. 764; *White* v. *Weston* [1968] 2 Q.B. 647.
[17] *Manley Estates, Ltd.* v. *Benedek* [1941] 1 All E.R. 248, 461; *Reading Trust Ltd.* v. *Spero* [1930] 1 K.B. 492.   [18] *Muir* v. *Jenks* [1913] 2 K.B. 412.

becomes due under the contract. The writ must, *before issue*, be indorsed with a statement that at the material time the lender was licensed as a moneylender (Order 83, r. 2); and the statement of claim, whether indorsed on the writ or not, must contain the details of the transaction prescribed by rule 3. The plaintiff cannot sign judgment in default of appearance or of defence without the leave of a master. If the transaction appears to him to be harsh and unconscionable, he has power upon an application for such leave (but not, except by consent, upon an application for summary judgment under Order 14 [19]) to give relief to the defendant. If the rate of interest exceeds 48 per cent. the transaction is presumed to be harsh and unconscionable unless the contrary is shown.[20] And this may lead to the reopening of earlier connected transactions. The plaintiff may file an affidavit justifying the rate of interest charged, notwithstanding that it exceeds 48 per cent., or he may abandon any claim to interest in excess of 48 per cent., and the master in either case makes such order as he thinks just under the wide powers entrusted to him; these include the power to give directions as though the defendant had appeared (Order 83, r. 4 (4) (*b*)). If a serious issue be raised as to whether the transaction is harsh and unconscionable, the proper course would ordinarily be to order it to be tried; usually, however, the plaintiff prefers the matter to be disposed of summarily by the master and will take his decision as to the fair rate of interest. Upon an application for summary judgment under Order 14, unless a defence is shown to the whole claim under one of the above statutory provisions or otherwise, the master will usually give the plaintiff leave to sign judgment for the balance of principal due and give leave to defend as to the interest if there is a case for relief. Even if the defendant consents to judgment, the master may refuse to give leave for judgment to be entered unless satisfied that the rate of interest is not excessive.[21]

Actions arising out of Hire-Purchase Agreements

The provisions of Order 84 apply to any action for money arising out of a hire-purchase agreement which is brought against a hirer

---

[19] *Wells* v. *Allott* [1904] 2 K.B. 842.
[20] Moneylenders Act, 1927, s. 10; and see *Samuel* v. *Newbold* [1906] A.C. 461; *Reading Trust, Ltd.* v. *Spero* [1930] 1 K.B. 492.
[21] *Mills Conduit Investment, Ltd.* v. *Leslie* [1932] 1 K.B. 233.

or his guarantor unless the money claim is for unliquidated damages or is for no more than the amount due for unpaid instalments. The plaintiff must set out in his statement of claim the circumstances in which his claim arises, and he cannot enter judgment in default without leave. Leave will only be given in respect of such part of the claim as is clearly not a " penalty " (*ante,* pp. 44–45).

CHAPTER 5

PROCEDURE UNDER ORDER 14

ORDER 14 makes provision for a plaintiff to obtain summary judgment upon his claim or part of his claim without the delay and expense of a trial and its preliminaries if he can show to the satisfaction of a master or a judge that there can be no answer to his case. "It is a strong thing to give such a power to a judge, and this court and all the courts have said, therefore, that they would watch strictly the exercise of that power. But they did not mean by that that they would give effect to every pettifogging objection which the ingenuity of a defendant could raise." (*Per* Lord Esher M.R. in *Roberts* v. *Plant* (1895) as reported in 14 R., at pp. 225, 226.) An enormous volume of business is done under the order and the student will do well to make himself thoroughly master of it.

Origin and Present Scope of Order 14

The object of a debtor in a vast number of cases is not necessarily to defeat his creditor altogether but to gain time, which may work grave injustice to the creditor. Before the middle of the nineteenth century a defendant sued in the plainest of plain cases—*e.g.*, for the price of goods sold and delivered or upon a dishonoured cheque—had merely to put upon the record a plea, no matter how devoid of merits or remote from the actual facts, and the case had to go for trial with all the delay and expense necessarily involved. At the trial the defendant very often did not appear. Eventually the bankers and other holders of bills in the City of London complained so vigorously that in 1855 the Summary Procedure on Bills of Exchange Act (commonly called "Keating's Act") was passed. In cases to which that Act applied the defendant had to get leave to appear, which he could only do by paying the money into court or setting out his defence in an affidavit. By the Judicature Act, 1873, and later by the Rules of the Supreme Court, 1883, the procedure was extended to cover cases where the plaintiff sought to recover a debt or liquidated demand in money and actions for the recovery of land. In 1937 the procedure became additionally applicable so far as the Queen's Bench Division only is concerned to all actions except libel, slander, malicious prosecution, false imprisonment, and actions in which fraud is alleged by the plaintiff. Since January 1, 1964, the procedure has been available with the same exceptions in all actions commenced by writ in the Queen's Bench or Chancery Division,[1] and is available not only to a plaintiff but also to a counterclaiming defendant. It was then also extended so as to enable application to be made for judgment on part only of a claim or counterclaim. This was a radical departure from the old rule, which presupposed that if the plaintiff succeeded the expense of a trial would be avoided altogether.

It is only after a defendant has entered an appearance that a plaintiff can ask for summary judgment. And there are many cases in which he should not ask for it. He is not bound to take out a summons for judgment under Order 14; he can do so or not at his pleasure. He should remember that Order 14 is only intended to apply to cases where there is no substantial dispute as to the facts or the law.[1a] If he applies for summary judgment where there is an obvious defence, his summons may be dismissed with costs. (See *post*, p. 71.) And seeing that he is applying for judgment without a trial it behoves him to have his tackle strictly in order in all respects.

Before applying for judgment on part of a claim or on a counterclaim it is wise to consider carefully not only whether the application can technically succeed but also whether, if successful, it will produce any substantially useful result. If there is bound to be a trial of the major issues in dispute, the small advantage of obtaining a preliminary judgment upon some unimportant part of the claim may not be worth the expense of the application. Again, although a defendant may be entitled to summary judgment on a counterclaim, justice may require that execution thereon be stayed until the plaintiff's claim is tried. In some cases the claim of the plaintiff may afford a good defence by way of set-off to the

---

[1] Except actions for specific performance, etc. for which an analogous procedure is provided by Ord. 86.

[1a] See *Dummer* v. *Brown* [1953] 1 Q.B. 710, where in somewhat exceptional circumstances the plaintiff was allowed to sign judgment for damages to be assessed in an action under Lord Campbell's Act.

defendant's counterclaim. Useless applications may be discouraged by the appropriate exercise of the master's discretion as to costs.

The procedure under Order 14 is as follows:

After the defendant, or any particular defendant against whom the application is intended to be made, has entered an appearance and the plaintiff has served a statement of claim upon him, the plaintiff takes out a summons[2] before a master for leave to enter judgment either for the whole claim or for some particular part of the claim. The application should be made promptly; but it may be made even after delivery of a defence, if the plaintiff can satisfactorily explain the delay[3] and show that the defence cannot hold water. A defendant who has served a counterclaim on the plaintiff may make a similar application. The summons in either case must be supported by an affidavit verifying the facts on which the claim (or part) is based and stating that in the deponent's belief there is no defence to it (except as to the amount of damages, if damages are claimed[4]). Formerly the affidavit had to be made by the plaintiff or some other person who could swear positively to the facts. Since 1964 it has become permissible for it to contain statements of information or belief, provided that the sources of the information and the grounds of belief are stated; but it is within the master's discretion to require a further affidavit based on actual knowledge before he will give judgment. A copy of the affidavit and of any exhibits to it must be served with the summons and at least ten clear days[5] must elapse between the day of service and the return day.

If the affidavit is sworn by an officer or servant of a limited company or by some other person on behalf of the plaintiff, it should show how far the facts are within the deponent's own knowledge and that he is authorised to make it.[6] It may verify the claim in general terms: it need not explicitly repeat every allegation made on the writ.[7] But all material facts (for example, an assignment) must be verified, a joint affidavit or more than one affidavit

---

[2] See Precedent No. 90.
[3] *McLardy* v. *Slateum* (1890) 24 Q.B.D. 504.
[4] See *Dummer* v. *Brown* (*ante*).
[5] For the meaning of " clear days " see *post*, p. 74. The time for service of a summons under Ord. 14 is never abridged.
[6] *Chirgwin* v. *Russell* (1910) 27 T.L.R. 21; *Pathé Frères* v. *United Electric Theatres* [1914] 3 K.B. 1253.
[7] *May* v. *Chidley* [1894] 1 Q.B. 451.

being made if necessary.[8] Defects in an affidavit may be cured by the filing of a further affidavit at the hearing [9]; but statements in an affidavit will not cure a defect in the statement of claim.[10]

The defendant may show cause against the application by stating his defence to the claim and showing that there is a real issue which ought to be tried. This is usually done by affidavit, though it is not absolutely essential if the master can be satisfied otherwise. (Order 14, r. 4.) He must state whether the defence alleged goes to the whole or to part only, and (if so) to what part, of the plaintiff's claim. If you appear against a dishonest defendant who puts in a vague affidavit admitting that something is due but seeking to evade a judgment against him by avoiding any actual mention of figures, your proper course is to ask the master to adjourn the matter for the defendant to file a further affidavit specifying in figures how much he admits. The master may, if he thinks fit, order the defendant, or in the case of a body corporate, any officer thereof, to attend and be examined upon oath, or to produce any leases, deeds, books or documents, or copies of or extracts therefrom (Order 14, r. 4 (4)), though such orders are rarely made.

At the hearing the master may give judgment; and he has a wide choice of other orders, the most common of which are often referred to by number,[10a] such as: Order No. 2 (unconditional leave to defend); Order No. 2A (leave to defend as short cause, see *post*, pp. 70, 275); Order No. 3 (leave to defend on bringing a stated sum into court, otherwise judgment for the amount claimed); Order No. 4 (leave to defend whole claim on bringing part into court; in default, judgment for that part; in any event leave to defend as to balance); Order No. 8 (leave to defend and trial before master by consent); Order No. 9 (judgment for plaintiff for damages to be assessed). The master may give leave to defend, either unconditionally, or subject to such terms as to payment into court of the whole or part of the claim, security for costs, time or mode of trial or otherwise as he may think fit. (Order 14, r. 4 (3).) Leave to defend ought to be given whenever there is an issue to be tried, even though the

---

[8] *Les Fils Dreyfus* v. *Clarke* [1958] 1 W.L.R. 300; [1958] 1 All E.R. 459.
[9] *Ibid.*
[10] *Gold Ores Reduction Co., Ltd.* v. *Parr* [1892] 2 Q.B. 14; 61 L.J.Q.B. 522.
[10a] Order No. 1 is now no longer used; it gave leave to enter judgment for the whole claim with costs.

master may think the defendant will fail.[11] In such a case, however, he is not bound to give unconditional leave: he may impose
conditions.[12] Where the conditions merely deal with matters of
procedure, such as time and mode of trial, his discretion may be
freely exercised; but where they deal with other matters, such as
payment into court or giving security, they must not be prohibitive or have the practical effect of debarring the defendant from
raising any triable issue which he may bona fide be entitled to
raise,[13] even though the master may think the circumstances are
suspicious. If, however, there is good ground on the evidence for
believing that the so-called defence is a sham and it is a borderline
case whether the plaintiff should not have judgment forthwith,
it is proper to give leave to defend conditionally upon a payment
into court of the amount claimed,[13a] especially if it is clear that
the defendant's assets will be dissipated and injustice done to the
plaintiff if there is any delay. Such an order if complied with by the
defendant places the plaintiff in the position of a secured creditor.[14]
If the facts alleged by the defendant do not amount to a defence to
the action, either in fact or law, the master will, as a rule, make an
order that judgment be entered for the amount indorsed on the
writ—in a proper case, with interest. And as soon as the judgment
is entered accordingly the plaintiff becomes a judgment creditor.[15]

Defendant Showing Cause

The defendant is not bound to show a good defence on the
merits. He must however satisfy the master that " there is an
issue or question in dispute which ought to be tried or that there
ought for some other reason to be a trial " of the claim (r. 3). " If,
therefore, the defendant shows such a state of facts as leads to the
inference that at the trial of the action he may be able to establish
a defence to the plaintiff's claim, he ought not to be debarred of
all power to defeat the demand made upon him . . . and leave
to defend may be granted either unconditionally or upon such
terms as may be thought just." (*Per* Brett L.J. in *Ray* v. *Barker*

---

[11] *Codd* v. *Delap* (1905) 92 L.T. 510 (H.L.).
[12] *Kodak, Ltd.* v. *Alpha Film Corp.*; *Frederick Huth & Co.* v. *Jackson*, reported
together in [1930] 2 K.B. 340, Scrutton L.J. dissenting.
[13] *Jacobs* v. *Booth's Distillery Co.* (1901) 85 L.T. 262; *Powzechny Bank* v. *Paros*
[1932] 2 K.B. 353; and see *Fieldrank, Ltd.* v. *E. Stein* [1961] 1 W.L.R. 1287.
[13a] See, for example, *Ionian Bank, Ltd.* v. *Couvreur* [1969] 1 W.L.R. 781.
[14] *Re Ford* [1900] 2 Q.B. 211.
[15] See *Re Gurney* [1896] 2 Ch. 863, decided under the former rule.

(1879) 4 Ex.D., at p. 283.) Where a defence of a kind is set up by the defendant, but the master has good reason to doubt its good faith, he may order the defendant to bring money into court (*vide supra*). But whenever a genuine defence, either in fact or law, sufficiently appears, the defendant is entitled to unconditional leave to defend.[16] For the form of some of these various orders, see Precedent No. 89.

The defence must be stated with sufficient particularity to appear to be genuine. A general statement, " I do not owe the money," or a vague suggestion of fraud or other misconduct on the part of the plaintiff, will not suffice. " General allegations, however strong may be the words in which they are stated, are insufficient to amount to an averment of fraud of which any court ought to take notice." [17] A technical defence, such as the Limitation Act, is sufficient. But it must be a defence. An affidavit merely pleading poverty, or showing hardship, or a remedy over against a third person, will not avail, though it may be a ground for a stay of execution (see *post*, p. 396).

The defendant may in answer to the plaintiff's claim rely upon a set-off or a counterclaim.[18] A true set-off is a defence to the action (see *post*, p. 216). Where the defendant relies upon a counterclaim various matters have to be considered. If the counterclaim arises out of the subject-matter of the action or may be treated as an equitable set-off,[19] leave to defend *pro tanto* should be given; and if such a counterclaim overtops or may probably overtop the amount of the plaintiff's claim there will be leave to defend as to the whole, even though part of the plaintiff's claim is admitted. If the counterclaim has no connection with the plaintiff's cause of action, the plaintiff may be given leave to sign judgment on the claim, provided that he is clearly entitled to succeed upon it and would be put to unnecessary expense in having to prove it [20]; but it is within the discretion of the court to stay execution up to the anticipated amount of the counterclaim pending the trial of the counterclaim or further order. This it will ordinarily

---

[16] *Ward* v. *Plumbley* (1890) 6 T.L.R. 198; *Electric Corporation* v. *Thomson-Houston* (1893) 10 T.L.R. 103.

[17] *Wallingford* v. *Mutual Society* (1880) 5 App.Cas., at p. 697; and see pp. 701, 704.

[18] As has been mentioned (*ante*, p. 63), it is also possible for a defendant to apply for summary judgment upon a counterclaim.

[19] *Post*, p. 217; *Morgan & Son, Ltd.* v. *S. Martin Johnson & Co., Ltd.* [1949] 1 K.B. 107; *Hanak* v. *Green* [1958] 2 Q.B. 9.

[20] *Sheppards & Co.* v. *Wilkinson* (1889) 6 T.L.R. 13 (C.A.).

do if the counterclaim appears to be genuine; but it will not necessarily do so, particularly where the plaintiff is suing on a bill of exchange. (*James Lamont & Co., Ltd.* v. *Hyland Ltd.,* [1950] 1 K.B. 585, 588.) Or in appropriate cases a stay may be granted subject to a payment into court by the defendant.

Special provisions apply in the case of actions by money-lenders. (See *ante,* pp. 59–60.)

In answer to technical objections the plaintiff can, if necessary, amend the statement of claim without leave under Order 20, r. 3, or obtain the master's leave to do so under Order 20, r. 5. Provided that the defendant is present or represented or the amendment is a mere matter of form, re-service can be dispensed with. No fresh appearance is necessary.[21] Thus, for example, if the plaintiff has included a claim based on fraud so that Order 14 is inapplicable (*ante,* p. 63), the master will not necessarily dismiss the summons altogether, but may order that claim to be struck out. He has jurisdiction to give summary judgment if there is a good statement of claim before him at the moment when he comes to do so.[22] And if unconditional leave to defend has been given in consequence of any technical defect in the writ, the plaintiff may, after the defect has been cured, make a second application for final judgment.[23]

If it appears that the defence set up by the defendant applies only to a part of the plaintiff's claim, or that any part of his claim is admitted, the plaintiff can have judgment forthwith for such part of his claim as is not covered by the defence or as is admitted, subject to such terms, if any, as to suspending execution or the payment of the amount levied or any part thereof into court by the sheriff, the taxation of costs or otherwise, as the master may think fit (Order 14, r. 3); and the defendant may be allowed to defend as to the residue of the plaintiff's claim. If it appears to the master that any defendant has a good defence to the action, and that any other defendant has no good defence, he may give the former defendant leave to defend and give judgment against the latter. The plaintiff may thereupon issue execution upon such judgment without prejudice to his right to proceed with his action against the former defendant (r. 8). He may thus

---

[21] *Paxton* v. *Baird* [1893] 1 Q.B. 139.
[22] *Roberts* v. *Plant* [1895] 1 Q.B. 597.
[23] *Dombey & Son* v. *Playfair Brothers* [1897] 1 Q.B. 368.

(as in the case of a default judgment) safely take judgment against one of several joint contractors notwithstanding the decision in *Kendall* v. *Hamilton* (1879) 4 App.Cas. 504 (*ante,* pp. 18, 56). But this rule does not apply where the right of action can only be in the alternative against one or other of two defendants. In such a case judgment against one of the defendants is conclusive evidence of an election not to proceed against the other [24]; unless the judgment is drawn up and entered it may not be conclusive.[25]

Judgment may be given under Order 14 against a firm, even though one of the partners be a minor.[26]

Order 14 applies to actions for possession of land in which a tenant has forfeited his lease through non-payment of rent. But rule 10 of that Order expressly provides that such a tenant shall " have the same right to apply for relief after judgment for possession of land on the ground of forfeiture for non-payment of rent has been given under this Order as if the judgment had been given after trial "; that is, he will have the right to apply within six months under section 210 of the Common Law Procedure Act, 1852, to have the judgment set aside on payment of all rent in arrear and costs. Before judgment the tenant may stop the proceedings by tendering or paying into court the rent in arrear and costs (s. 212); and relief may be given by the master in a summary manner pursuant to section 46 of the Judicature Act, 1925.

Further Powers of the Master

In cases involving not more than £750 [27] the master, if he gives leave to defend, will often transfer the action to the appropriate county court, which in such cases he may do even against the will of one of the parties and notwithstanding that the defendant may have a counterclaim exceeding that amount (Order 14, r. 4 (3)). In other cases he may transfer by consent of both parties pursuant to sections 42 and 67 of that Act. (See *post,* p. 265.)

---

[24] *Morel Brothers* v. *Earl of Westmorland* [1904] A.C. 11; *French* v. *Howie* [1906] 2 K.B. 674; *Moore* v. *Flanagan and Wife* [1920] 1 K.B. 919.

[25] See *C. Christopher (Hove), Ltd.* v. *Williams* [1936] 3 All E.R. 68, decided under the old rule.

[26] *Harris* v. *Beauchamp (No. 1)* [1893] 2 Q.B. 534.

[27] See Administration of Justice Act, 1969, s. 2, which came into operation on May 26, 1970, and County Courts Act, 1959, s. 45.

If leave to defend is given and the action is transferred, the costs are ordinarily in the discretion of the county court.[29]

If the claim is unliquidated and the master is satisfied that there is no defence except as to the amount of damages, he may give the plaintiff interlocutory judgment for damages to be assessed. Unless he orders otherwise they will be assessed by a master; but he may refer them to an official or special referee or allow the action to go to trial as to damages only, giving any necessary directions. (Order 37, rr. 1, 4.)

When leave, whether conditional or unconditional, is given to defend or judgment is given with a stay of execution pending the trial of a counterclaim, the master will give directions as to the further conduct of the action as though the application were a summons for directions under Order 25 (see *post*, p. 259), and the provisions of that Order apply with any necessary modifications, save that a counter-notice for directions by the defendant is not required. (Order 14, r. 6 (1).) A fresh summons for directions at a later stage is then unnecessary; but the master will adjourn or give liberty to apply under the summons for further directions if required. The directions may, if all parties consent, provide for trial of the action by a master, which may enable it to be quickly, cheaply and conveniently disposed of. (Order 14, r. 6 (2).) In that case an appeal lies direct to the Court of Appeal. (Order 58, r. 2 (1) (a).)

If the point of the defence is a short one, and particularly if the master has doubts of its honesty, he may direct the case to be tried as a short cause. (See the form of order in Queen's Bench Masters' Practice Forms, App. K., No. 7A.) Such an order is advantageous to a plaintiff since the case may be tried and disposed of quickly and with comparatively little expense. Under Order 14, r. 4 (3), conditions may be imposed as to giving security or time or mode of trial. It may even be ordered under Order 64, r. 4 (2), to be tried in the Long Vacation if there is urgent need of such a speedy trial. If the master thinks that the case is not suitable for the short cause list but that injustice would be caused by delay, he may make an order for speedy trial, directing an application to be

---

[29] County Courts Act, 1959, s. 76. Note that if a special order is made reserving costs to the county court *judge*, this excludes the jurisdiction of the registrar and is often found to be inconvenient in practice.

made to the Clerk of the Lists to fix a day for the hearing.[30] He may order the defendant's affidavit to stand as his defence and dispense with further pleadings. He may not, however, restrict the defences which the defendant may raise [31]; accordingly, leave is usually given to furnish within a limited time—*e.g.*, four days—particulars of any further defence or counterclaim not disclosed in his affidavit. If the master only gives leave to defend as to part and the balance remaining in dispute is small, he may, and commonly does, make an order transferring the case to the appropriate county court for trial as to the disputed part, giving judgment in the High Court for the remainder.

The costs of and incidental to all applications under Order 14 will be dealt with by the master in his discretion on the hearing of the application. In order to discourage plaintiffs from making unnecessary applications for summary judgment, it is provided that if a plaintiff makes an application under rule 1 where the case is not within the Order, or if it appears to the master that the plaintiff knew that the defendant relied on a contention which would entitle him to unconditional leave to defend, the application may be dismissed (rule 7 (1)).[32] In that case the master may either give the defendant his costs " in any event " (see *post*, p. 416) or, provided that the plaintiff is not an assisted person, order them to be paid forthwith.[33] If the plaintiff obtains summary judgment he will ordinarily be awarded the fixed costs provided by Order 62, Appendix 3, or, if the master certifies for counsel, costs to be taxed. If he gives leave to defend, the master usually, though not always, orders " costs in the cause " (see Order 62, r. 3 (2), and *post*, p. 415). Notwithstanding that the " event " of the summons may be said to have been in favour of the defendant, this is likely to be the fair order to make in cases where the plaintiff had good ground to believe that there was no defence and was suddenly faced with the defendant's affidavit raising an issue. It often happens that the contentions of the defendant, though sufficiently specious to entitle him to leave to defend, are really quite unsubstantial.

On an application under Order 14 the master is not concerned to ascertain the truth of the defence put forward in the defendant's

---

[30] L.C.J.'s directions of December 9, 1958 (see *post*, p. 275).
[31] *Langton* v. *Roberts* (1894) 10 T.L.R. 492.
[32] And see *Pocock* v. *A.D.A.C., Ltd.* [1952] 1 T.L.R. 29, 34.
[33] Rule 7 (1); and see Ord. 62, r. 4.

affidavit unless it can be shown conclusively from documentary evidence that it *cannot* be true. A counter-affidavit by the plaintiff may be put in if the master gives leave; but if, as often happens, it serves only to emphasise that there is a dispute to be tried he may disallow the costs of it. If the defendant's affidavit discloses facts which, if true, could reasonably be argued to be a defence to the plaintiff's claim, the master *must* give leave to defend either conditionally or unconditionally although he may have his doubts as to its truth.

A judgment given under Order 14, when the defendant or his solicitor has failed to attend at the hearing of the summons, may be set aside or varied on such terms as the master thinks just (rule 11).

CHAPTER 6

PLEADINGS

A MATTER which normally occupies the attention of the parties in the early stages is pleading. The student must familiarise himself not only with the theory and the art of pleading but also with the rules of procedure governing the exchange of pleadings, and how a party may be relieved of embarrassment caused by the defective or irregular pleading of his opponent.

Time for Pleading

The time for serving, amending or filing any pleading, answer or other document is governed by a fixed timetable laid down by Orders 18 and 20. But such time may be, and often is, enlarged by consent in writing without application to the court. (Order 3, r. 5 (3).) Further, the time fixed for doing any act may be enlarged or abridged by the master, who may enlarge it even though it has already expired (Order 3, r. 5 (1) (2)); but it is unwise to defer the application till so late a date. If an order has been made dismissing the action unless the plaintiff does some act—*e.g.*, serves a statement of claim—within a limited time and the plaintiff defaults,[1] the action is at an end and the time for doing the act cannot thereafter be extended; all that can be done is to ask for an extension of time for appealing against the order dismissing the action.[2] The costs of a summons to extend time will, in default of a special order, fall upon the party applying. (Order 62, r. 3 (4).)

When the time allowed for doing any act is seven days or less, Saturdays, Sundays, Bank holidays, etc., are not counted (Order 3, r. 2 (5)) [2a]; and in any case where an act has to be done at an office of the Supreme Court and time expires on a Sunday, or other

---

[1] As to the meaning of default in this connection, see *Reiss* v. *Woolf* [1952] 2 Q.B. 557.

[2] *Burke* v. *Rooney* (1879) 4 C.P.D. 226.

[2a] No provision is made for the case where a time exceeding seven days for an act not required to be done at an office of the Supreme Court—*e.g.*, the service of particulars—expires on a Sunday, etc. If an act could not reasonably be done on a particular day because, for example, a solicitor's office was not open to receive a document, the court would doubtless deal appropriately with the situation.

day on which the offices of the court are closed (which now includes Saturday), the time is automatically extended to the next day on which the offices are open (rule 4). Where a document (other than a writ or originating summons) is served personally on (or left at the proper address of) the person to be served between 12 noon on a Saturday and midnight on Sunday, or after 4 in the afternoon on any other weekday, it is deemed to have been served on the next day available for court business (Order 65, r. 7.) But no " process " (which includes a writ, petition and originating summons) may be served on a Sunday except, in case of urgency, with leave (rule 10, *post*, p. 460). Except by leave of a master or consent of all parties pleadings may not be served during the Long Vacation (Order 18, r. 5).[2b] If a writ or statement of claim can be amended without leave (see *post*, p. 168) this may be done in the Long Vacation; otherwise no pleading may be amended in the Long Vacation except by leave (Order 20, r. 6). Nor does the Long Vacation count in computing time for serving, filing or amending a pleading unless the master otherwise directs (Order 3, r. 3). In reckoning a period of time for doing an act " after," " from " or " before " a given date, that day is excluded ; if " clear days " are mentioned, the day on which the act is to be done is also excluded (rule 2).

Illustrations

If a writ is served within the jurisdiction, appearance may, under Order 12, r. 5, be entered within " eight days after service of the writ (including the day of service)." Therefore if the writ is served on a Wednesday, a judgment in default of appearance can be entered on, but not before, the following Thursday. But for the words in brackets it would be the Friday. If the writ is served on a Saturday, a judgment in default of appearance cannot be entered until the following Tuesday week (for the defendant could appear on the Monday).

A summons under Order 14 must be served " not less than ten clear days before the return day." As this period is over seven days, Saturdays, Sundays, and the other days mentioned in Order 3, r. 2 (5) must be included in the reckoning. The calculation of the return day may therefore be affected by the day of the week on which the summons is issued.[2c] Hence, if the return day is on Wednesday 14th the summons must be served not later than Saturday 3rd by noon.

Subject to the above rules, if the plaintiff has not served a statement of claim with his writ, he must do so not more than fourteen days after the defendant's appearance (Order 18, r. 1);

[2b] This would not be held to apply to the service of a statement of claim indorsed on the writ.

[2c] See *Practice Direction* [1970] 1 W.L.R. 258.

if he fails to do so, he runs the risk of having his action dismissed for want of prosecution. (Order 19, r. 1.) [3]

Ordinarily a defendant who appears must serve his defence not more than fourteen days after the time limited for appearance or from the service of the statement of claim, whichever is the later. (Order 18, r. 2.) If the plaintiff serves a summons for judgment under Order 14 and the defendant obtains leave to defend, the master usually directs whether or not a defence shall be served and within what time; failing such a direction, the defence must be served within fourteen days after the order giving leave to defend. (Order 18, r. 2 (2).) A defendant who is served with a summons for judgment may and should hold his hand and serve no defence until the summons is disposed of.[4] Under Order 18, r. 2 (2), the time for serving the defence does not run after service of the summons.

If the time expires and no defence is served, the plaintiff may enter judgment by default under Order 19.[5] But, if he delays in doing this, the defendant may put in a defence after time, which will prevent judgment from being entered—though the defendant will probably be ordered to pay any costs incurred through his delay.[6] The plaintiff is not bound to enter judgment in default. In a proper case, *e.g.*, a libel action or where very heavy damages are claimed, he may take out a summons for directions and proceed to trial in the ordinary way.[7]

If the defendant pleads a counterclaim, the plaintiff must within fourteen days (unless the time is extended) reply to it as though he were a defendant serving a defence to a statement of claim; otherwise it is deemed to be admitted. (Order 18, r. 3 (2).) If the defendant by his counterclaim brings in a new party, the latter is subject to a similar rule. (Order 15, r. 3.) If there is no counterclaim, but the plaintiff nevertheless desires to serve a reply, he may do so without leave within fourteen days from the service of the defence (Order 18, r. 3 (4)), or later by leave. If the plaintiff wishes to serve both a reply and a defence to counterclaim, they must be combined in the same document (rule 3 (3)).

---

[3] He may save himself by serving it before the hearing of the summons to dismiss, but not necessarily so. (*Clough* v. *Clough* [1968] 1 W.L.R. 525.)
[4] *Hobson* v. *Monks* [1884] W.N. 8.
[5] Leave is necessary in moneylenders' and certain hire-purchase actions and in actions in tort between husband and wife.
[6] *Graves* v. *Terry* (1882) 9 Q.B.D. 170; *Gill* v. *Woodfin* (1884) 25 Ch.D. 707.
[7] *Nagy* v. *Co-operative Press* [1949] 2 K.B. 188.

Pleadings subsequent to a reply (see *infra*, and p. 234) may occasionally be ordered under Order 18, r. 4. Otherwise the pleadings are deemed to be closed at the expiration of fourteen days after the service of the defence, reply, or defence to counter-claim, as the case may be (rule 20). When the pleadings become closed there is an implied joinder of issue on the pleading last served and every material allegation of fact therein is deemed to be denied (rule 14). At any stage *after* service of the defence or defence to counterclaim, as the case may be, a party may, if necessary, expressly join issue upon the preceding pleading save as to any facts which he may desire to admit (*ibid.*).

The Function of Pleadings

Before judge or jury is ᵗasked to decide any question which is in controversy between litigants, it is in all cases desirable, and in most cases necessary, that the matter to be submitted to them for decision should be clearly ascertained. The defendant is entitled to know what it is that the plaintiff alleges against him; the plaintiff in his turn is entitled to know what defence will be raised in answer to his claim. The defendant may dispute every statement made by the plaintiff, or he may be prepared to prove other facts which put a different complexion on the case. He may rely on a point of law, or raise a cross-claim of his own. In any event, before the trial comes on it is highly desirable that the parties should know exactly what they are fighting about, otherwise they may go to great expense in procuring evidence to prove at the trial facts which their opponents will at once concede. It has been found by long experience that the most satisfactory method of attaining this object is to make each party in turn state his own case and answer that of his opponent before the hearing. Such statements and the answers to them are called the *pleadings*.

The plaintiff naturally begins; if he has not already indorsed his writ with a *Statement of Claim*, he serves one separately. The defendant then puts in his *Defence*, which besides answering the plaintiff's claim, may also set up a *Counterclaim*, after which the plaintiff in turn may serve a *Defence to Counterclaim*, or he may *Reply*, or both. Occasionally the defendant then obtains leave to *Rejoin*. It is very seldom that any further pleadings are ordered, but there may be *Surrejoinders*, *Rebutters*, and *Surrebutters*. Each of these alternate pleadings must in its turn either admit or deny the facts alleged in the last-preceding pleading; it may also allege additional facts, where necessary. The points admitted by either side are thus extracted and distinguished from those in controversy; other matters, though disputed, may prove to be immaterial; and thus the litigation is narrowed down to two or three matters which are the real questions in dispute. The pleadings should always be conducted so as to evolve some clearly defined *issues*, that is, some definite propositions of law or fact, asserted by one party and denied by the other, but which both agree to be the points which they wish to have decided in the action.

When this is properly and fairly done, four advantages ensue:

(i) It is a benefit to the parties themselves to know exactly what are the matters left in dispute. They may discover that they are fighting about nothing at all; *e.g.*, when a plaintiff in an action of libel finds that the defendant does not assert that the words are true, he is often willing to accept an apology and costs, and so put an end to the action.

(ii) It is also a boon to the parties to know precisely what facts they must prove at the trial; otherwise, they may go to great trouble and expense in procuring evidence of facts which their opponent does not dispute. On the other hand, if they assume that their opponent will not raise such and such a point, they may be taken sadly by surprise at the trial.

(iii) Moreover, it is necessary to ascertain the nature of the controversy in order to determine the most appropriate mode of trial. It may turn out to be a pure point of law, which should be decided by a judge; it may involve investigation of complicated accounts, in which case the action should be referred to a referee; or it may be a question proper for a jury.

(iv) It is desirable to place on record the precise questions raised in the action, so that the parties or their successors may not fight the same battle over again.

The function of pleadings then is to ascertain with precision the matters on which the parties differ and the points on which they agree; and thus to arrive at certain clear issues on which both parties desire a judicial decision.[8] In order to attain this object, it is necessary that the pleadings interchanged between the parties should be conducted according to certain fixed rules, which it is our endeavour to state and explain in the following pages. The main purpose of these rules is to compel each party to state clearly and intelligibly the material facts on which he relies, omitting everything immaterial, and then to insist on his opponent frankly admitting or explicitly denying every material matter alleged against him. By this method they must speedily arrive at an issue. Neither party need disclose in his pleading the evidence by which he proposes to establish his case at the trial. But each must give his opponent a sufficient outline of his case.

History of Pleading

This method of arriving at an issue by alternate allegations has been practised in England from earliest times. It is apparently as ancient as any portion of our law of procedure. It certainly existed in substantially the same form in the reign of Henry II. The word " issue " is to be found at the very commencement of the Year Books, *i.e.*, in the first year of Edward II; and the distinction between an *issue en ley* and an *issue en fet* is equally ancient. (See the Year Book, 3 Edw. II, 59.) And even before the reign of Edward II the production of an issue had been not only the constant effect, but the professed aim and object, of pleading.

At first the pleadings were oral. The parties actually appeared in open court and a *viva voce* altercation took place in the presence of the judges. These oral pleadings were conducted either by the party himself or his pleader (called *narrator* or *advocatus*); and it seems that the rule was then already established that none but a professional advocate could be a pleader in any cause not his own. It was the duty of the judge to superintend, or " moderate," the oral contention thus conducted before him. His aim was to arrive at some specific point or matter affirmed on the one side, and denied on the other, which they both agreed was the question requiring decision. When this result was attained, the parties were said to be " at issue "—*ad exitum*— the pleadings were over, and the parties were ready to go before

---

[8] And see Lord Radcliffe's speech in *Esso Petroleum Co., Ltd.* v. *Southport Corporation* [1956] A.C. 218, 241.

a jury, if it were an issue of fact, or before the court, if it were an issue of law. And so strict were the judges in those days, that they allowed only one issue in respect of each cause of action; if a defendant had two defences to the same claim, he had to elect between them; it was only in the reign of Queen Victoria that the parties were allowed to raise more than a single issue, either of law or fact. Hence the question for decision came itself to be called *the issue.*

During the parol altercation one of the officers of the court was busy writing on a parchment roll an official report of the allegations of the parties and of the acts of the court itself during the progress of the pleading. This was called *the Record.*[9] As the suit proceeded, similar entries were made from time to time, each successive entry being called a *continuance,* and, when complete, the roll was preserved " as a perpetual intrinsic and exclusively admissible testimony of all the judicial transactions " which it purported to record.

It is not apparently known when the system of oral pleading fell into disuse; but it gradually became the practice for each pleader in turn to borrow the parchment roll, and enter his statements thereon himself. Later (probably in the reign of Edward IV), the plan was adopted of drawing up the pleadings in the first instance on paper, and interchanging them between the parties in that form; then, after an issue had been arrived at, they were transcribed on to a parchment roll. This was called, " entering the proceedings on the record." But though the practice of oral pleading was abandoned, the ancient method of alternate allegation continued. So that the student may understand the reports of cases which turned on the old system of pleading, note that what we now call a Statement of Claim was before 1875 called a *declaration*; a Defence was called a *plea* or *pleas*; and a Reply was called a *replication.* The names of the further pleadings remain unchanged. A declaration often contained more than one *count,* each of which stated a complete and separate cause of action, and would in fact by itself have been a good and valid declaration. So, too, each plea had to be in itself a complete answer to the count to which it was pleaded. (See Precedents, Nos. 1, 2.) The courts of equity had their own methods of pleading.

[9] See *post,* pp. 82, 252.

The principles on which pleadings were framed, and the rules which regulated them, remained substantially the same till 1852. Their practical utility was, however, seriously impaired by the over-subtlety of the pleaders and by the excessive rigour with which the rules were applied; the merits of the case being constantly subordinated to technical questions of form. A determined effort was made to correct these defects by the provisions of the Common Law Procedure Acts, 1852–1860. In 1873, however, it was found necessary to adopt a more thorough method of reform; and the Judicature Act substituted in the new High Court of Justice the system of pleading which is still in force.

Till the year 1893 in every action commenced by writ there were pleadings as a matter of course, unless both parties agreed to dispense with them. In 1893, by an Order revoked in 1917, power was given to the plaintiff, if he thought fit, to declare on his writ that he intended to proceed to trial without pleadings. If the plaintiff did so declare, there were no pleadings, unless the defendant could persuade a master to order them. In 1897 the rules were amended, and for the first time in the history of our law a plaintiff who wished to deliver a pleading was not allowed to do so without an order from a master. But in 1933 further alterations were made, the effect of which was in substance to revert to the practice prior to 1893. In 1955 the plaintiff was empowered by Order XIVB to include in his writ, if specially indorsed, a notice of his intention to apply for trial without pleadings. And now since 1964 an improved procedure has been made available on application by either party (see *post*, p. 81). As we have seen (*ante*, p. 7) if the real matter for decision is one of the construction of an Act or document, or some other question of law, or if there is not likely to be any substantial dispute of fact, the plaintiff has the option of commencing proceedings by originating summons. (Order 5, r. 4.)

When Pleadings will be Dispensed With

The whole object of pleadings, as we have seen, is to bring the parties to a clear issue, and thus to secure that they both know, before the action comes on for trial, what is the real point to be discussed and decided. But a master has power to order that service of a statement of claim be dispensed with if he is satisfied that pleadings are unnecessary. Again, where the defendant in answer to a summons for judgment has filed an affidavit or has in some other way stated his defence, any further pleading may be unnecessary, and the master may make an order accordingly. (See Order 18, rr. 1 and 21.) So if the questions in dispute have already been argued on an application for an *interim* injunction. Again, if the cause is to be tried by a special jury of the City of London, or if for any other reason it is fit for the commercial list, counsel frequently appear before the judge who takes cases of that class; each states orally what his client's case will be; and then Points of Claim and Points of Defence are usually ordered.

So, too, " the court may order any question or issue arising in a cause or matter, whether of fact or law . . . and whether raised by the pleadings or otherwise, to be tried before, at or after the trial of the cause or matter, and may give directions as to the manner in which the question or issue shall be stated." (Order 33, r. 3.) Then, again, a master may direct the parties to prepare a statement of the issues in dispute (see Order 18, r. 21, *infra*). Such issues take the place of pleadings; they are usually directed to determine whether a particular person was or was not a member of the defendant firm at the time the contract sued on was entered into with that firm, or to determine the liability of a person summoned as a garnishee (see *post*, p. 389), or to decide between rival claimants to property taken in execution by the sheriff or in the hands of a stakeholder (see *post*, pp. 212–213, 387).

Apart from these special instances the master now has a general power under Order 18, r. 21, in actions to which the rule applies, to order trial without pleadings or without further pleadings as the case may be. The procedure is not encumbered with the restrictions and risks involved in the rules of 1955 and may well be found useful. It is available in actions begun by writ with the exception of actions which include a claim by the plaintiff for libel, slander, malicious prosecution, false imprisonment, seduction or breach of promise of marriage or based on an allegation of fraud. Unlike the procedure under Order 14 it may be adopted although it is clear that there is an issue to be tried; and it may be appropriate in many cases where the nature and compass of the dispute have been made clear in correspondence. After appearance by any defendant, the plaintiff or that defendant, whether his opponent consents or not, may take out a summons; and if the master thinks that the issues can be defined, or that the action can properly be tried, without pleadings or further pleadings, he will order accordingly. He may direct the parties to prepare a statement of the issues in dispute and may settle the statement himself if necessary. He will also give appropriate directions as though a summons for directions had been issued, and may do so even though he refuses the application.

The Form of Modern Pleadings

No entries now are made on any parchment roll; the pleadings are written or printed on paper and interchanged between the parties; the solicitor of one party serves his pleading on the solicitor of the other party, or on the party himself, if he does not employ a solicitor. This goes on till the pleadings are " closed." The cause is then set down for trial, for which purpose two bundles, each containing the writ, the pleadings, any particulars (with the order or request therefor), orders made on the summons for directions and any legal aid documents, are lodged with the officer of the court. (Order 34, r. 3 (1).) One bundle is for the use of the judge; the other, which is marked with the stamp denoting the fee paid on entry, is regarded as the record and, unless it is withdrawn as a result of a settlement, will be filed after the trial and show what the issues were on which judgment was given.

Remember that a pleading is a document which passes between the parties and, unless indorsed on the writ, is not in the possession of the court until it is lodged as above on setting the action down for trial. Therefore while it is correct to assume that the trial judge has the pleadings before him, do not waste time on a summons in chambers by asking the master or judge if he has them, but see that they are handed to him forthwith if it is necessary to refer to them. In the Chancery Division they may have been left with the master to peruse before the hearing.

Every pleading should bear at the top the year in which the writ was issued, the letter and number of the action, the title of the action, the Division of the High Court to which, and the name of any judge to whom, the action is assigned (and in a Chancery action any group to which it is assigned), the description of the pleading and, at the foot, the date on which it was served. (Order 18, r. 6.) A statement of claim should also bear the words " Writ issued the . . . . . day of . . . . 19 . . ." in order to show that the cause of action pleaded had accrued before action brought.

It must be indorsed with the name and place of business of the solicitor and agent (if any) who serves it, or the name and address of the party serving it, if he does not act by a solicitor. (*Ibid.*) It may be either written, typewritten or printed on proper sized paper.[10] Every pleading must be divided into paragraphs numbered consecutively. Dates, sums and numbers should be expressed in figures, and not in words. It is not necessary, though it is generally desirable, that a pleading should be drawn or settled by counsel; where it has been, he must sign his name at the end of it; if not settled by counsel, it must be signed by the solicitor or by the party if he sues or defends in person. (*Ibid.*) Below counsel's signature there should appear the words: " Served the . . . . . . day of . . . . 19 . . . by . . . . of (*address*), Solicitor for the [Plaintiff] [Defendant]."

Cardinal Rules in Pleading

The allegations in every pleading must be:

   (i) Material.

   (ii) Certain.

The next two chapters are therefore devoted to Materiality and Certainty.

---

[10] Type lithography or stencil duplicating is permitted in lieu of printing. Facsimile copies of documents for use in court may be made photographically. (Ord. 66, r. 2.)

CHAPTER 7

MATERIAL FACTS

THE fundamental rule of our present system of pleading is this:

"Every pleading must contain, and contain only, a statement in a summary form of the material facts on which the party pleading relies for his claim or defence, as the case may be, but not the evidence by which those facts are to be proved, and the statement must be as brief as the nature of the case admits." (Order 18, r. 7 (1).)

This rule involves and requires four separate things:

(i) Every pleading must state facts and not law.

(ii) It must state material facts and material facts only.

(iii) It must state facts and not the evidence by which they are to be proved.

(iv) It must state such facts concisely in a summary form.

(i) EVERY PLEADING MUST STATE FACTS AND NOT LAW

Conclusions of law, or of mixed law and fact, are no longer to be pleaded. It is for the court to declare the law arising upon the facts proved before it. A plaintiff must not merely aver, " I am entitled to recover £100 from the defendant," or " It was the defendant's duty to do so and so." He must state the facts which in his opinion give him that right, or impose on the defendant that duty; and the judge will decide, when those facts are proved, what are the legal rights and duties of the parties respectively. So, too, a defendant must state clearly the facts which in his opinion afford him a defence to the plaintiff's action. He must not say merely, " I do not owe the money "; he must allege facts which show he does not owe it; e.g., that the goods were never ordered, or were never delivered, or that they were not equal to sample. He may plead that, even assuming every allegation of fact in the statement of claim to be true, the plaintiff has no cause of action against him. This is called

" an objection in point of law." But if he is not prepared to admit them all, he must deal with the facts alleged by his opponent, and deal with each of them clearly and explicitly. If he pleads that he never agreed as alleged, this will be taken to mean that he never in fact made any such contract—not that the contract is bad in law or not binding on him because he is an infant, or because he was induced to enter into it by fraud. All facts tending to show the insufficiency or illegality of any contract must be specially pleaded. To say, " There never was any contract," is a different thing from saying, " There was a contract, but I contend it is invalid." State the facts and prove them, and the judge will then decide the question of validity. He knows the law, and can apply it to the facts of the case without its being stated in the pleadings.

This is one of the greatest improvements introduced by the Judicature Act. Each party was, before 1875, bound to state with reasonable precision the points which he intended to raise; but this he generally did by stating, not the facts which he meant to prove, but the conclusion of law which he sought to draw from them. The other side thus learnt that the party pleading meant to prove *some* set of facts which would sustain a given legal conclusion; but there might be many sets of facts which would sustain that legal conclusion, and which of these would be set up at the trial was not disclosed. For instance, this was a very common form of declaration: " The plaintiff sues the defendant for £——, money payable by the defendant to the plaintiff for money received by the defendant to the use of the plaintiff." [1] That might cover any one of the following cases, and many more besides; and it could not be ascertained from the plaintiff's pleading which would be his case at the trial—

(a) That the defendant was the plaintiff's rent collector, and had received money for him as such.

(b) That the plaintiff was entitled to an office which the defendant also claimed, and under colour of which the defendant had received fees, which the plaintiff sought to recover from him.

---

[1] As to the scope and limits of this form of action, see an excellent speech of Lord Sumner in *Sinclair* v. *Brougham* [1914] A.C., pp. 453–456. And see Precedent No. 1.

(c) That the plaintiff had paid the defendant the price of goods which he was to supply, and the defendant had never supplied them.

(d) That the plaintiff had paid a sum of money to the defendant by mistake, having taken him for another person of similar name or appearance.

Then, again, there were often several alternative legal conclusions which could be drawn from the facts, any one of which would serve the plaintiff's turn; and therefore several " counts " were pleaded in the same declaration, giving various legal aspects of the same transaction, though the evidence given in support of each at the trial would be identical.

So, too, with the defence. In an action for goods sold and delivered, the defendant was allowed to plead " the general issue," as it was called, that he " never was indebted as alleged." This is a conclusion of law, and at the trial it was open to him to give in evidence under this plea any one or more of several totally different defences, of which the following may serve as instances:

(i) That he never ordered the goods.

(ii) That they were never delivered to him.

(iii) That they were not of the quality ordered.

(iv) That they were sold on a credit which had not expired at the time that the action was commenced.

But the defendant might not, under this plea, set up the Statute of Limitations, nor allege payment or a set-off, because each of these defences implies that the defendant *was once* indebted to the plaintiff as alleged. He might deny that any express contract of sale was ever made: he might deny all or any of the matters of fact from which such a contract would by law be implied; but he could not under the plea of " never indebted " insist that the contract, though made in fact, was void in law. Now all such ambiguous formulae are abolished, and the actual facts on which either party relies must be stated as briefly as possible in his pleading.

Illustrations

It is unnecessary to state in a pleading the principles of the common law, or to set forth the contents of a public statute. Thus, law need not be pleaded to show that a plaintiff is entitled to sue upon a dishonoured bill of exchange so long as the necessary facts be alleged; and a defendant may plead simply, " the action is not maintainable without special damage and none is alleged."

But where a particular statute is relied on as the foundation of a claim or defence, the facts necessary to bring the case within the statute should be pleaded and reference should usually be made to the section relied on (see *post*, pp. 98, 109, 145).

Even if this is not done, effect may be given to a statutory defence appearing from the evidence where there has been no surprise.

Singlehurst v. *Tapscott Steamship Co.* [1899] W.N. 133.

" It is said that an implied warranty is not alleged in the pleadings, but all the material facts are alleged, and in these days, so long as those facts are alleged, that is sufficient for the Court to proceed to judgment without putting any particular legal label upon the cause of action."

Per Denning L.J. in *Shaw* v. *Shaw* [1954] 2 Q.B. 429, 441.

It is bad pleading to allege merely that a right or a duty or a liability exists; the facts must be set out which give rise to such right or create such duty or liability. Hence, where the facts stated in the pleading disclose no cause of action, the pleading will be held bad in spite of any allegation to the effect that the act was " unlawful," or " wrongful," or " improper," or " done without any justification therefor or right so to do."

Gautret v. *Egerton* (1867) L.R. 2 C.P. 371.

Day v. *Brownrigg* (1878) 10 Ch.D. 294, 302; 48 L.J.Ch. 173.

It is not sufficient for a plaintiff to say, " under and by virtue of a certain deed I am entitled," etc., for that is an inference of law. The limitations of the deed, and all other facts upon which he proposes to rely as showing that he is so entitled, must be stated.

Riddell v. *Earl of Strathmore* (1887) 3 T.L.R. 329.

A plaintiff may not allege merely that " the defendant has received £—— to the use of the plaintiff "; he must state the facts which make such receipt by the defendant a receipt to the use of the plaintiff.

See Order 18, r. 7.

A statement of claim alleged that the deceased, " two days before his death made a good and valid *donatio mortis causa* to the plaintiff of the whole of his moneys standing on deposit to his account at the Ellesmere Savings Bank," but did not state what the deceased in fact did. It was struck out on the ground that the facts which the plaintiff alleged to amount to a valid *donatio mortis causa* should have been set out in the statement of claim.

Re Parton, Townsend v. *Parton* (1882) 30 W.R. 287.

In an action to recover damages caused to the plaintiff's reversion in a dwelling-house by interference with an easement, it is not sufficient to allege in the statement of claim that the plaintiff is entitled to such easement; the plaintiff must show how he is so entitled, whether by grant, or prescription, or otherwise, and must set out the facts upon which he relies as entitling him to such easement.

Farrell v. *Coogan* (1883) 12 L.R.Ir. 14.

In actions upon bills of exchange, promissory notes or cheques, a defence *in denial* must deny some matter of fact, *e.g.*, the drawing, making, indorsing, accepting, presenting or notice of dishonour of the bill or note.[1a]

See Order 18, r. 13.

In actions for goods bargained and sold or sold and delivered, a defence *in denial* must deny the order or contract, the delivery, or the amount claimed,

---

[1a] This illustration is taken from the wording of Ord. XXI of the R.S.C., 1883, for which the more general language of Ord. 18, r. 13, has been substituted. The principle, however, still holds good.

and in an action for money had and received, a defence *in denial* must deny the receipt of the money, or the existence of those facts which are alleged to make the receipt by the defendant a receipt to the use of the plaintiff.[1a]

See Order 18, r. 13.

In an action of libel or slander, a defendant may not plead merely that " he published the words on a privileged occasion." He must set out the facts and circumstances on which he relies as creating the privilege, and then the judge will decide on the facts proved at the trial whether the occasion was or was not privileged.

Simmonds v. *Dunne* (1871) Ir.R. 5 C.L. 358.

Elkington v. *London Association for the Protection of Trade* (1911) 27 T.L.R. 329.

In an action on an award, if the defendant pleads that the arbitrator never made any such award as alleged, this plea will now be taken to mean that no award was ever made in fact; and it will not be open to the defendant to contend that, though the arbitrator had in fact made an award, it was bad in law because it included matters not within the submission. An award is valid till it is set aside.

See *Bache* v. *Billingham* [1894] 1 Q.B. 107.

When a contract, promise or agreement is alleged in any pleading, a bare denial of the same by the opposite party will be construed only as a denial in fact of the express contract, promise or agreement alleged, or of the matters of fact from which the same may be implied by law, and not as a denial of the legality or sufficiency in law of such contract, promise or agreement whether with reference to the Statute of Frauds or otherwise.

See Order 18, r. 8.

Howatson v. *Webb* [1907] 1 Ch. 537; [1908] 1 Ch. 1.

Whenever the same legal result can be attained in several different ways it is not sufficient to aver merely that that result has been arrived at, but the facts must be stated showing how and by what means it was attained.

Illustrations

Where A claims that an estate formerly held by B is now vested in himself, he must state in his pleading the date and nature of the conveyance or other transfer from B to A, whether it was by deed or by will, etc.

Com.Dig. Pleader (E. 23), (E. 24).

Plaintiff alleged that he had a right of way. It was held that he was bound to say in his statement of claim whether he claimed it by prescription or by grant. But a lost grant may be pleaded without stating its date or parties.

Harris v. *Jenkins* (1882) 22 Ch.D. 481; 52 L.J.Ch. 437.

Palmer v. *Guadagni* [1906] 2 Ch. 494.

A defendant pleading in answer to a claim for trespass upon a road that the road is a highway must set out any specific acts of dedication on which he relies.

Spedding v. *Fitzpatrick* (1888) 38 Ch.D. 410; 58 L.J.Ch. 139.

It is not enough for a plaintiff to reply to a plea of the Limitation Act that the statute " does not apply," or that " the case has been taken out of the statute." There are several modes by which a debt may be taken out of the operation of that statute; and " it is a prejudice to a defendant to be compelled to come prepared to meet three different matters, when perhaps the plaintiff intends to rely on one only."

    Per Parke B. in *Forsyth* v. *Bristowe* (1853) 8 Ex., at p. 350.

It is not sufficient to plead " the said bill of sale is void and of no effect in law." Facts must be stated showing its invalidity, *e.g.*, that it has not been registered, or is not in the form given in the schedule to the Bills of Sale Act, 1882.

It is not sufficient in an action upon a contract for the defendant to plead that " the contract is rescinded." This may mean that the parties met, and in express terms agreed to put an end to the contract; or it may mean that such an intention is to be collected from a long correspondence or a whole series of transactions; or it may mean that the plaintiff himself has broken the contract in such a way as to amount to actual repudiation. The defendant must show in what manner and by what means he contends that it was rescinded.

If a man claims to be a peer, he must state whether he is a peer by writ, or by patent, or by descent, or by prescription. For if he " claims to be a peer by writ, he is not a peer until he has taken his seat. . . . If by patent, the title is complete as soon as the patent is sealed."

    Per Bayley J. in *R.* v. *Cooke* (1824) 2 B. & C., at p. 874.

    And see *St. John Peerage Claim* [1915] A.C., at p. 309.

Where a party claims by inheritance, he must do more than merely state " I am the heir-at-law." He must show how he is heir, *viz.*, as son or otherwise; and if he does not claim by immediate descent he must show the pedigree. For example, if he claims as nephew, he must show how he is nephew, whether brother's son or sister's son, and account for all who would be nearer in blood.

    Dumsday v. *Hughes* (1803) 3 Bos. & Pul. 453.

    And see *Roe* v. *Lord* (1776) 2 Bl.Rep. 1099, and the cases there cited; *Palmer* v. *Palmer* [1892] 1 Q.B. 319; 61 L.J.Q.B. 236.

(ii) EVERY PLEADING MUST STATE MATERIAL FACTS ONLY

What facts are material?

" The word ' material ' means necessary for the purpose of formulating a complete cause of action, and if any one ' material ' fact is omitted, the statement of claim is bad." (*Per* Scott L.J. in *Bruce* v. *Odhams Press, Ltd.*, [1936] 1 K.B. at p. 712.) The same principle applies to defences.

Facts which are not necessary to establish either a cause of action or the defence to it are not, speaking generally, " material " within the meaning of Order 18, r. 7, and should, therefore, be omitted from the pleading unless it is clear that evidence will have to be given of them at the trial.[2] (See *post*, pp. 100–101.) All statements which need not be proved should be omitted.

It is obvious, then, that the question whether a particular fact is or is not material depends mainly on the special circumstances of the particular case. It is a question which it is not

---

[2] *Gaston* v. *United Newspapers, Ltd.* (1915) 32 T.L.R. 143.

always easy to answer, and yet it is a very important one: the result of the case often depends on the ruling of the judge at the trial that it is or is not necessary that a particular fact should be proved. Sometimes it is material to allege and prove that the defendant was aware of a certain fact; at other times it is sufficient to aver that he did some act, without inquiring into the state of his mind. In some cases the defendant's intention is material: in a few cases his motives. The pleader must apply his knowledge of the law, or, better still, his common sense, to the facts stated in his instructions, and decide for himself which he must plead and which he may safely omit. Precedents may afford him some assistance; and so will books like Roscoe's *Evidence in Civil Actions*. But in the end he must rely on his own judgment. No general rule can be laid down.

In early days, when the courts were very strict, they punished either party who pleaded immaterial facts: for if his opponent pleaded to immaterial facts, and issue was joined thereon, they compelled the party who had alleged such facts to prove them literally, although they were immaterial; otherwise he failed in his action. He had himself raised the issue, so he must prove it or take the consequences.[3]

Subsequently, however, the courts adopted a far better method of preventing the parties from raising immaterial issues. They declared that "immaterial allegations were not traversable," *i.e.*, neither party was allowed to plead to any immaterial matter in his opponent's pleading, but must treat it as surplusage and leave it alone. Thus no issue could be raised on it; and the party pleading it was no longer bound to prove it at the trial.[4]

And now the courts never compel either party to prove at the trial more than the substance of his pleading, even though his opponent may have expressly traversed some immaterial averment contained in it lest by the operation of Order 18, r. 3 (1) (*post*, pp. 132, 133), it should be taken to be admitted.

If after consideration you are still in doubt whether a particular fact is or is not material, the safer course is to plead it, if you think you can prove it. For if you omit to plead it, and it

---

[3] See *Wood* v. *Budden* (1617) Hobart 119; *Cudlip* v. *Rundle* (1692) Carthew 202; *Bristow* v. *Wright* (1781) 2 Douglas 665; *Sir Francis Leke's Case* (1580) 3 Dyer 365; 2 Wms.Saund. 206, n. (22).
[4] See *Lane* v. *Alexander* (1608) Yelverton 122; *Osborne* v. *Rogers* (1682) 1 Wms. Saund. 267; *Alsager* v. *Currie* (1843) 11 M. & W. 14.

is held to be material, you cannot strictly give any evidence of that fact at the trial, unless the judge will give leave to amend, and such leave may be upon terms as to payment of costs.[5]

It is sufficient if a pleading states such facts, as would, if proved or admitted, establish the plaintiff's case.

Here is a statement of claim in which a most material allegation has been omitted. What is it? (Look near the top of the next page *after* deciding.)

" The defendant instructed and employed the plaintiff to do certain work (specifying it). The plaintiff's charges for such work amounted to £——, which sum the defendant promised to pay, but has not paid, to the plaintiff."

The consideration for any contract not under seal is always material, and it is advisable to set it out in the statement of claim,[6] except in the case of negotiable instruments, where the consideration is presumed (*post*, p. 96). If the contract be under seal, no consideration need be proved.

In an action against a bailee it is material to know whether he was to be paid for his services, as this affects the degree of diligence which the law expects. But the amount of his remuneration is not material; it is sufficient to aver that he was to carry or warehouse the goods " for reward."

As a rule the precise wording of a document or a conversation is not material, and it is sufficient to state briefly its purport or effect.

Order 18, r. 7 (2).

In an action for the recovery of land, the plaintiff is not bound to set out in his statement of claim the precise words of a will under which he claims, even though a question has arisen as to their true construction. It is enough to state briefly what he alleges to be their effect.

Darbyshire v. *Leigh* [1896] 1 Q.B. 554; 65 L.J.Q.B. 360.

But in an action for libel or slander the precise words complained of are material, and they must be set out *verbatim* in the statement of claim. If the words taken by themselves are not clearly actionable, the plaintiff must also insert in his statement of claim an averment (with particulars in support) of an actionable meaning which he will contend the words conveyed to those to whom they were published. Such an averment is called an innuendo.

Harris v. *Warre* (1879) 4 C.P.D. 125; 48 L.J.C.P. 310.

Collins v. *Jones* [1955] 1 Q.B. 564.

Rubber Improvement Ltd. v. *Daily Telegraph Ltd.* [1963] 2 W.L.R. 1063; and see *post*, pp. 104, 164.

Order 82, r. 3 (1).

Where words of praise are spoken ironically, so as to convey a defamatory meaning, it must be averred that they were so intended and understood; else the statement of claim will disclose no cause of action.

The precise wording of a covenant may be material if it be in an unusual form; for a change of phrase may alter the legal effect of the clause.

Horsefall v. *Testar* (1817) 7 Taunt. 385; 1 Moore 89.

Where either party relies on any custom of the country or of the trade as enlarging or restricting the right given him by the ordinary law of the land or

---

[5] See *Byrd* v. *Nunn* (1877) 5 Ch.D. 781; 7 Ch.D. 284; and *Brook* v. *Brook* (1866) 12 P.D. 19.

[6] See *Cooke* v. *Rickman* [1911] 2 K.B. 1125 at 1129, 1130.

by a written contract, such custom must be specially pleaded with all necessary detail. See the replication in

    Wigglesworth v. *Dallison* (1779) 1 Smith's L.C.

Where the parties expressly agree to limit the liability ordinarily imposed on either of them in contracts of the particular class, such limitation is material and should be alleged by the party who first purports to set out the true contract.

    Sharland v. *Leifchild* (1847) 4 C.B. 529; 16 L.J.C.P. 217.

    Heath v. *Durant* (1844) 12 M. & W. 438; 13 L.J.Ex. 95.

Answer to the first illustration: that the plaintiff did the work

Notice

In an action on a bill of exchange against an indorser, the holder must allege notice of dishonour; in an action against the acceptor he need not.

    Bills of Exchange Act, 1882, s. 48.

But in an action brought against the drawer of a dishonoured cheque, the statement of claim must contain either an allegation that notice of dishonour was given to the drawer, or a statement of the facts excusing the giving of such notice.

    Fruhauf v. *Grosvenor & Co.* (1892) 61 L.J.Q.B. 717.

    May v. *Chidley* [1894] 1 Q.B. 451, 453.

In an action by a creditor against a surety there is no need to allege that the creditor gave the surety notice that the principal debtor had not paid.

    Cutler v. *Southern* (1667) 1 Saund. 116 (and many other cases).

If A's dog bites a human being, the plaintiff must prove that A knew that his dog was of a fierce and savage disposition, either generally or under the special circumstances. The best proof of this will be that A knew that his dog had on some previous occasion bitten or attempted to bite a human being. Mere proof that it had, to A's knowledge, bitten some animal will not suffice.

    Osborne v. *Chocqueel* [1896] 2 Q.B. 109; 65 L.J.Q.B. 534.

    Barnes v. *Lucille Ltd.* (1907) 96 L.T. 680.

But if A's dog bites cattle, horses, mules, asses, sheep, goats, swine or poultry, the owner of the injured animal can recover damages without proof of any such knowledge on the part of A.

    Dogs Act, 1906, s. 1; Dogs (Amendment) Act, 1928, s. 1.

Where the defendant relies on his insanity as a defence to an action of contract, he must not only plead that he was insane at the date of the contract but also that the plaintiff knew that he was then insane.

    Imperial Loan Co. v. *Stone* [1892] 1 Q.B. 599.

Intention and Motive

Whenever an injunction is applied for, it is material to allege that the defendant " threatens and intends " to repeat the illegal act complained of, unless such an intention can be readily inferred from the nature of the case and the facts already pleaded.

    Stannard v. *Vestry of St. Giles* (1882) 20 Ch.D., at p. 195.

In an action brought on a fraudulent prospectus, it is unnecessary for the plaintiff to state the motives which induced the defendants to issue it, or which led to the scheme of which it was a part; it is sufficient to allege that particular statements contained in the prospectus were false to the knowledge of the defendants.

    Herring v. *Bischoffsheim* [1876] W.N. 77.

Yet where collusion is alleged between A and B, the fact that A knew the improper motives which actuated B is material, and for this purpose those improper motives must be stated.

Briton Medical, etc., Life Association v. *Britannia Fire Association* (1888) 59 L.T. 888.

If the plaintiff in a passing-off action proposes to allege at the trial that the defendant purposely made his goods to resemble in appearance the goods of the plaintiff with the intention of misleading the public, this must be explicitly pleaded in the statement of claim.

Claudius Ash & Co. v. *Invicta Co.* (1912) 29 R.P.C. 465.

Where it is alleged that the defendant has obstructed a public right of way, it is immaterial to allege that A B induced the defendant to do so " for his own private interest," etc. The plaintiff should merely plead that the defendant has obstructed the right of way: it does not matter why he did it.

Murray v. *Epsom Local Board* [1897] 1 Ch. 35.

And see *Provincial Bank* v. *Brocklebank* (1890) 26 L.R.Ir. 572.

Each party must state his whole case. He must plead all facts on which he intends to rely, otherwise he cannot strictly give any evidence of them at the trial. " The plaintiff is not entitled to relief except in regard to that which is alleged in the pleadings and proved at the trial." (*Per* Warrington J. in *Re Wrightson* [1908] 1 Ch., at p. 799.) The statement of claim must disclose a good cause of action: the defendant must show a good defence thereto. Omit no averment which is essential to success; do not plead half a defence and leave the rest to be inferred.

Illustrations

By a lease dated March 2, 1889, the plaintiff demised a house to A for the term of twenty-one years at the yearly rental of £120, payable quarterly. A is dead; the defendant is living in the house; three quarters' rent is in arrear, for which the plaintiff has issued a writ. A statement of claim which disclosed those facts and nothing more would be bad; the plaintiff must show that the defendant is assignee of the lease and liable on the covenant to pay the rent thereby reserved; he may be merely a sub-lessee who has regularly paid his rent to A's executors.

Warden of Sir Roger Cholmeley's School v. *Sewell* [1893] 2 Q.B. 254.

A plaintiff seeking to re-enter upon a breach by the defendant of a tenancy agreement alleged in his statement of claim that " it was a term of the said agreement that the said room should be used for office accommodation only " and that the defendant had used it for living accommodation, but omitted to allege a covenant not to use the premises otherwise than for offices and also a proviso for re-entry on breach of such covenant. It was held that the statement of claim disclosed no cause of action.

Whall v. *Bulman* [1953] 2 Q.B. 198.

In an action of slander, if the words are actionable only by reason of their being spoken of the plaintiff in the way of his office, profession or trade, the statement of claim must contain an averment that the plaintiff actually held the office or carried on the profession or trade at the time when the words were spoken. And there should also be an averment that the words were spoken of the plaintiff with reference to such office, profession or trade.

    Gallwey v. *Marshall* (1854) 9 Ex. 300; 23 L.J.Ex. 78.

In an action against a carrier for the loss of a parcel, the defendant cannot set up at the trial that the parcel was above £10 in value, and that no notice of its value was given at the time of its being delivered, as required by the Carriers Act, 1830, unless this defence has been specially pleaded. It is not sufficient merely to deny the contract alleged by the plaintiff.

    Syms v. *Chaplin* (1839) 5 A. & E. 634.

Action of replevin for wrongfully seizing cattle. The defendant avowed taking them in the close in question for rent in arrear. The plaintiff pleaded in bar to this avowry that the cattle were not levant and couchant on the close in question. This was held a bad plea. For it is a general rule of law that all things upon the premises are distrainable for rent in arrear, and the levancy and couchancy of the cattle is immaterial, except under special circumstance such as did not appear by the plea in bar to have existed in this case.

    Jones v. *Powell* (1826) 5 B. & C. 647.

In an action brought by a commoner against a stranger for putting his cattle on the common, *per quod communiam in tam amplo modo habere non potuit*, the defendant pleaded a licence from the lord to put his cattle there, but he did not aver that there was sufficient common left for the commoners; this was held to be no good plea, for the lord had no right to give a stranger such licence unless there was enough common left for commoners. It was urged that it was rather for the plaintiff to reply that there was not enough common left; but the court held that the defendant was bound to plead all such facts as were necessary to make good the defence he had pleaded.

    Smith v. *Feverell* (1686) 2 Mod. 6; 1 Freem. 190.

    Greenhow v. *Ilsley* (1746) Willes 619.

    And see *Ashby* v. *White* (1703) 1 Sm.L.C.

" Regularly whensoever a man doth anything by force of a warrant or authority, he must plead it."

    Co.Litt. 283 a; *ibid.*, 303 b; 1 Wms.Saund. 298, n. (1).

Sometimes the whole point of the action turns on one minute allegation. Thus:

In an action of trespass for assault and battery, the defendant pleaded that a judgment was recovered and execution issued thereupon against a third person, and that the plaintiff, to rescue that person's goods from the execution, assaulted the bailiffs, and that in aid of the bailiffs and by their command the defendant *molliter manus imposuit* upon the plaintiff, to prevent his rescue of the goods. It was held that it was unnecessary to aver any command of the bailiffs, for even without their command the defendant might lawfully interfere to prevent a rescue, which is a breach of the peace.

    Bridgwater v. *Bythway* (1695) 3 Lev. 113.

It is otherwise if not done to prevent a rescue; for in a case where the defendant justifies merely as assistant to, and by command of, a person executing legal process, the command is material and must be alleged, as without it the defendant would be a mere volunteer, meddling in other people's business.

    Britton v. *Cole* (1698) 1 Ld.Raym. 305; 1 Salk. 408.

Do not leap before you come to the Stile

But the pleader should never allege any fact which is not material at the present stage of the action, even though he may reasonably suppose that it may become material hereafter. It is sufficient that each pleading in turn should contain in itself a good prima facie case, without reference to possible objections not yet urged. It is not necessary to anticipate the answer of the adversary; to do so, according to Hale C.J., is " like leaping before one comes to the stile." (*Sir Ralph Bovey's Case* (1684) Vent. 217.)

" It is no part of the statement of claim to anticipate the defence and to state what the plaintiff would have to say in answer to it. That would be a return to the old inconvenient system of pleading in Chancery, which ought certainly not to be encouraged, when the plaintiff used to allege in his bill imaginary defences of the defendant and make charges in reply to them." (*Per* James L.J. in *Hall* v. *Eve* (1876) 4 Ch.D., at p. 345.) So, too, it is quite unnecessary for the defendant to excuse himself from matters of which he is not yet accused, or to plead to causes of action which do not appear in the statement of claim.[7]

Illustrations

It is not normally necessary in a statement of claim for the plaintiff to allege facts which, he hopes, will take the case out of the Limitation Act.
Hollis v. *Palmer* (1836) 2 Bing.N.C. 173 (an action of debt).
Especially if those facts relate to a disability which prevents the running of time.
Dismore v. *Milton* [1938] 3 All E.R. 762.
But in a claim for money due under an agreement which, but for a subsequent acknowledgment, would be statute-barred, it is proper to plead the facts relating to the acknowledgment in the statement of claim rather than in a reply.
Busch v. *Stevens* [1962] 1 All E.R. 412.
In an action of account, it is sufficient for the plaintiff in the first instance to allege facts which show that the defendant is prima facie liable to account to the plaintiff for certain moneys. If the defendant in his defence sets up that all accounts up to a certain date were settled between them (see *post*, p. 208), it will then be for the plaintiff to state in his Reply the facts which may entitle him to have such settled account reopened. Such facts would be immaterial in the original statement of claim.
In pleading a devise of land it is enough to state that A was seised of the land in fee, and devised it by his last will in writing, without alleging that A was

---

[7] *Rassam* v. *Budge* [1893] 1 Q.B. 571.

then of full age. For if he were under twenty-one when he made his will it is for the other party to show this; it need not be denied by anticipation.

Stowell v. *Lord Zouch* (1569) Plowd. 376.

So in claiming a debt due under a bond, it is unnecessary to allege that the defendant was of full age when he executed the bond.

Walsingham's Case (1573) Plowd. 564.

Sir Ralph Bovey's Case (1684) Vent. 217.

It is bad pleading in a statement of claim for trespass and conversion of goods to continue thus: " The defendant committed the alleged trespass and seized and carried away the said goods under colour of a pretended bill of sale alleged to have been given him by the plaintiff, whereby, etc. But the said bill of sale, if any, has never been registered, and is also void in law because it is not in conformity with the form in the schedule to the Bills of Sale Act," etc. This is leaping before you come to the stile. Leave the defendant to set up his bill of sale, if he thinks he can make anything of it; and plead its invalidity in your Reply. He may have some other perfectly good defence, and never plead the bill of sale at all.

In an action for libel, it would be bad pleading for the plaintiff to say in his statement of claim: " The defendant will contend that the said words are part of a fair and accurate report of a judicial proceeding; but such report was neither fair nor accurate." How do you know what the defendant will contend? Do not suggest defences to your opponent. There is no necessity for the plaintiff to mention the judicial proceeding or to state that the words form part of any report.

A charterparty contained a covenant " that no claim should be admitted or allowance made for short tonnage, unless such short tonnage were found and made to appear on the ship's arrival on a survey to be taken by four ship-wrights to be indifferently chosen by both parties." In an action brought on this charterparty to recover for short tonnage, the plaintiff had a verdict; and the defendants moved in arrest of judgment that it had not been averred in the declaration that a survey was taken, and short tonnage made to appear. But the court held that if such survey had not been taken, this was a matter of defence which ought to have been shown by the defendants, and refused to arrest the judgment.

Hotham v. *East India Co.* (1787) 1 T.R. 638; 1 Dougl. 272.

" A party need not plead any fact if it is presumed by law to be true or the burden of disproving it lies on the other party, unless the other party has specifically denied it in his pleading." (Order 18, r. 7 (3).)

Illustrations

A plaintiff need not, in his pleading, set out the consideration for which a bill of exchange was given him, when he sues only on the bill. It will be for the defendant to plead no consideration. It is otherwise when the plaintiff sues on the consideration as a substantive ground of claim; then, of course, he must allege it specifically.

Cf. Bills of Exchange Act, 1882, s. 30.

In an action for goods sold and delivered, it is unnecessary, in addition to the allegation that the plaintiff sold and delivered them to the defendant, to state that they were goods of the plaintiff; for a buyer who has accepted and enjoyed the goods cannot dispute the title of the seller.

Buller, N.P. 139.

In a claim for money lent, it is unnecessary to aver that the money lent was lent by the plaintiff to the defendant *at his request*; for " a loan imports an obligation to pay. If the money is accepted, it is immaterial whether or not it was asked for. The same doctrine will not apply to money paid; because no man can be a debtor for money paid, unless it was paid at his request."
   Victors v. *Davies* (1844) 12 M. & W. 758; 13 L.J.Ex. 241.
   Where the plaintiff is or was in possession of any land or chattel, it is sufficient against a wrongdoer to aver possession only, and the plaintiff need not set out his title. *Omnia praesumuntur contra spoliatorem.*
   Armory v. *Delamirie* (1722) 1 Sm.L.C.

Whenever the rule of law applicable to the case has an exception to it (as it generally has), all facts are material which tend to take the case out of the rule and bring it within the exception. And so are all facts which tend to take the case out of the exception and keep it within the rule.

Whenever there is a conflict between law and equity on any relevant point, all facts are material which tend either to raise or oust the equity.

Whenever the right claimed or the defence raised is the creature of statute, being unknown to the common law, every fact must be alleged necessary to bring the case within the statute.

When the right claimed or the defence raised existed at common law, but the common law applicable to the case has been materially altered in its substance by statute, all facts are material which tend to take the case out of the rule at common law and bring it within the statute. And so are all facts which tend to show that the statute does not apply to the particular case.

But where the right claimed or the defence raised existed at common law, and the subsequent statute has not affected its validity, but merely introduced regulations as to the mode of its existence or performance, the statute does not affect the form of pleading. It is sufficient to allege whatever was sufficient before the statute.[8]

Illustrations

At common law the assignee of a debt could not sue at all; in equity he could sue if he made the assignor a party. But by the Law of Property Act, 1925,

---

[8] See 1 Wms. Saund. 211, n. (2), 276, n. (2); *Birch* v. *Bellamy* (1702) 12 Mod. 540; *Charlie* v. *Belshaw* (1830) 6 Bing. 529; *Prestney* v. *Mayor and Corporation of Colchester* (1882) 21 Ch.D. 111.

s. 136, he can sue alone if the debt be absolutely assigned to him by writing under the hand of the assignor, and express notice in writing of such assignment has been given to the debtor. The statement of claim of such an assignee suing alone must expressly allege—

(a) an absolute assignment
(b) in writing; and
(c) notice of such assignment
(d) given in writing to the debtor before the commencement of the action.

For without these averments the case is not brought within the statute and the plaintiff has no right to bring the action.

Seear v. *Lawson* (1880) 16 Ch.D. 121; 50 L.J.Ch. 139.

By section 146 (1) of the Law of Property Act, 1925, a landlord cannot eject a tenant for breach of covenant to repair without serving on him, a reasonable time before the writ is issued, a notice in writing specifying the repairs that are needed and other matters. Need a landlord suing for recovery of possession allege in his statement of claim that he did give such a notice a reasonable time before action? No: for he has a perfectly good right of entry without it; the statute merely regulates his exercise of that right; in other words, it imposes a fresh condition precedent to his right of action. His due performance of the requirements of the statute will therefore be presumed until the defendant pleads that he never was served with any such notice.

Order 18, r. 7 (4) *post*, p. 99.

Gates v. *W. A. & R. J. Jacobs, Ltd.* [1920] 1 Ch. 567.

At common law no liability attached to a man for using a public highway in an extraordinary manner or to an unusual degree; for he was entitled so to use it. But it was felt that such a person ought to make a special contribution to the funds of the highway authority; and accordingly, by statute, whenever damage has been caused to a highway " by excessive weight passing along the same, or extraordinary traffic thereon," the expense of repairing it can be recovered in an action against the person who caused the damage. In such an action, as there was no liability at common law, the statement of claim must allege all such facts as are necessary to show that the case falls within the statute.

Morpeth Rural District Council v. *Bullocks Hall Colliery Co.* [1913] 2 K.B. 7; 82 L.J.K.B. 547.

[See the pleadings in this action in Bullen & Leake, 11th ed., pp. 492, 1036.]

Colchester Corporation v. *Gepp* [1912] 1 K.B. 477; 81 L.J.K.B. 356.

A plaintiff need not show in his statement of claim that the Statute of Frauds has been complied with. It is for the defendant to plead that it has not; and it will then be for the plaintiff to prove that it has.

Dawkins v. *Lord Penrhyn* (1878) 4 App.Cas. 51, 58; 48 L.J.Ch. 304.

Conditions Precedent

Neither party need allege the performance of any condition precedent. The party who desires to contest the performance or occurrence of any condition precedent must raise the point specifically in his pleading. " A statement that a thing has been done or that an event has occurred, being a thing or event the doing or occurrence of which, as the case may be, constitutes a condition precedent necessary for the case of a party is to be implied in his pleading." (Order 18, r. 7 (4).)

Note the wording of this rule. It does not say such an averment is immaterial; only that it shall be implied. There is a reason for this. Although it is no longer necessary for a plaintiff to plead the due performance of all conditions precedent to his right of action, yet the burden of *proving* due performance is still on him, if the defendant specially plead non-performance. In former days it was essential for a plaintiff to set out in his declaration every condition precedent to his right, and to aver the due performance of it with all particularity. Then came the Common Law Procedure Act, 1852, section 57 of which provided: " It shall be lawful for the plaintiff or defendant in any action to aver performance of conditions precedent generally, and the opposite party shall not deny such averment generally, but shall specify in his pleading the condition or conditions precedent the performance of which he intends to contest." And now a general averment of the due performance of all conditions precedent is implied in every pleading. (A good modern illustration of the technicalities arising under the old system of pleading is to be found in *Bank of New South Wales* v. *Laing* [1954] A.C. 135.)

But what is a condition precedent? And how does it differ from the material facts which must be pleaded?

Where everything has happened which would at common law prima facie entitle a man to a certain sum of money, or vest in him a certain right of action, and yet in this particular case there is something further to be done, or something more must happen before he is entitled to sue, either by reason of the provisions of some statute, or because the parties have expressly so agreed— this something more is called a condition precedent. It is not of the essence of such a cause of action; but it has been made essential. It is an additional formality superimposed on what otherwise would have been valid. Hence the plaintiff can draft a perfectly good statement of claim without any reference to it; and it is for the defendant to raise the point if he thinks the plaintiff has not performed all that is required of him. If neither party refers to the condition, it will probably be because it has been duly complied with; anyhow its due performance will in that event be presumed. (And see pp. 109, 178, *post*.)

Illustrations

A agrees to build a house for B, according to a specification in writing, for £3,000. A has built the house according to the specification. But by the agreement to which such specification is scheduled he agreed that payment should only be made upon the architect's certificate that so much is due. Obtaining and presenting such a certificate is, therefore, a condition precedent to his right to receive the £3,000. But he can draft a statement of claim showing a good prima facie right to the £3,000 without mentioning any certificate. It will be for the defendant to plead that the architect has never certified that the amount is due.

Precedent No. 57.

And see *Hotham* v. *East India Co.* (1787) 1 T.R. 638, *ante*, p. 96.

No solicitor can commence an action for his costs till one month after he has delivered a bill of costs (Solicitors Act, 1957, s. 68). Yet he need not allege in his statement of claim that he duly delivered to the defendant a bill in accordance with the Act. The defendant must plead that no bill was delivered; and then it will be for the plaintiff to prove its delivery.

Lane v. *Glenny* (1837) 7 A. & E. 83.

The giving of the notice required by section 146 (1) of the Law of Property Act, 1925, is a condition precedent to the commencement of the action, but, as we have seen (*ante*, p. 98) it need not be specially pleaded in the statement of claim.

Gates v. *W. A. & R. J. Jacobs, Ltd.* [1920] 1 Ch. 567.

A policy of insurance on an aeroplane contained a condition that the insured should duly observe the statutory regulations for air navigation and further provided that the observance of the conditions of the policy should be a condition precedent to his right to recover. The points of defence in an arbitration purported to put him to proof of the observance of the conditions in four stated respects. Held, that the insurers must prove non-compliance with the conditions.

Bond Air Services, Ltd. v. *Hill* (1955) 2 Q.B. 417.

Matters affecting Damages

A " material fact " has been defined (*ante*, p. 89) as a fact which is essential to the plaintiff's cause of action or to the defendant's defence. But there are many facts which are not material on the main issue whether plaintiff ought to succeed or not, and which will yet be proved and discussed at the trial, because they affect the amount of *damages* which he will be entitled to recover. Such facts are called " matters in aggravation of damages " or " matters in mitigation of damages."

Much learning has in the past been displayed in discussing whether the plaintiff and defendant respectively should state such facts in their pleading. In the light of the rules in their present form and the decision in *Plato Films Ltd.* v. *Speidel* [1961] A.C. 1090, it seems clear that they should. Lord Denning says so expressly at p. 1135 in relation to evidence of the plaintiff's bad character; moreover, Order 18, r. 8 (1) (*b*), requires matter which might take the opposite party by surprise to be specially pleaded. Order 82, r. 7, prohibits a defendant in an action for libel or slander, who does not justify, from giving evidence in chief with a view to mitigation of damages, as to the circumstances under which the libel or slander was published, or as to the character of the plaintiff, without the leave of the judge, unless seven days at least before the trial he furnishes particulars to the plaintiff of the matters as to which he intends to give evidence. This rule was not in force when *Scott* v. *Sampson* ((1882) 8 Q.B.D. 491) decided that facts in mitigation of damages should be pleaded; and the corresponding rule of 1883 was probably made in order to settle certain doubts which had arisen from other decisions. Although particulars furnished under this rule have for many years been referred to among practitioners as " a notice in mitigation of damages," it is to be observed that " particulars " is the word used in the rule— that is to say, particulars under the traverse of damages which is implicit in every defence (Order 18, r. 13 (4)). It is accordingly appropriate that such particulars should appear in the pleading itself. If they do not, they may still be given under the rule.

It is impossible to draw any logical distinction between matters in aggravation and matters in mitigation of damages, and the former also should be pleaded.[9]

In an action of libel or slander the defendant may, by a special plea in mitigation of damages, justify part of the words, provided such part is distinct and severable from the rest.[10] The plea must distinctly identify the portion justified.[11] Without such a plea the defendant can give no evidence that any portion of his words is true, not even though he has given a notice under Order 82, r. 7.

(iii) EVERY PLEADING MUST STATE FACTS, AND NOT THE EVIDENCE BY WHICH THEY ARE TO BE PROVED

Facts should be alleged as facts. It is not necessary to state in the pleadings circumstances which merely tend to prove the truth of the facts already alleged.[11a]

The fact in issue between the parties is the *factum probandum*, the fact to be proved, and therefore the fact to be alleged. It is unnecessary to tell the other side how it is proposed

[9] *Millington* v. *Loring* (1880) 6 Q.B.D. 190.
[10] *Davis* v. *Billing* (1891) 8 T.L.R. 58.
[11] *Vessey* v. *Pike* (1829) 3 C. & P. 512.   [11a] But see *post*, p. 105.

to prove that fact; such matters are merely evidence, *facta probantia*, facts by means of which one proves the fact in issue. Such facts will be *relevant* at the trial, but they are not *material facts* for pleading purposes.[12]

This was always a clear rule of the common law. " Evidence shall never be pleaded, because it tends to prove matter in fact, and therefore the matter in fact shall be pleaded." (*Dowman's Case* (1586) 9 Rep. 9b.)

In the Court of Chancery, however, this rule was never observed: the pleadings there were lengthy narratives which sometimes became intolerably prolix. They stated the evidence on which the party proposed to rely in full detail, with copious extracts from the material documents. They were more like lengthy affidavits than modern pleadings, which still in the Chancery Division are apt to run to length.

This was partly due to the nature of the matters with which equity courts had to deal; for even now an equitable defence or reply is pleaded in the Queen's Bench Division somewhat more in detail than is usual in the case of ordinary legal defences or replies.[13] Moreover, it is not always easy to decide what are the facts to be proved, and what is only evidence of those facts. The question is often one of degree. " There are many cases in which facts and evidence are so mixed up as to be almost indistinguishable." (*Smith* v. *West* [1876] W.N. 55.) But in most cases the line is sharp and clear between the fact in issue and the evidence by which that fact would be proved. " The difference, although not so easy to express, is perfectly easy to understand." (*Per* Brett L.J., in *Philipps* v. *Philipps* (1878) 4 Q.B.D. at p. 133.) " It is an elementary rule in pleading that, when a state of facts is relied on, it is enough to allege it simply without setting out the subordinate facts which are the means of producing it, or the evidence sustaining the allegation." (*Per* Lord Denman C.J., in *Williams* v. *Wilcox* (1838) 8 A. & E. at p. 331.)

Illustrations

Action on a policy of insurance on the life of A. Defence that A committed suicide, in which event the company, by the express terms of the policy, is not

---

[12] See *Re Dependable Upholstery, Ltd.* [1936] 3 All E.R. at p. 743; *Thompson* v. *Thompson* [1957] P. 19; but *cf. Bruce* v. *Odhams Press, Ltd.* [1936] 1 K.B. 697, *post*, p. 158.
[13] See *Heap* v. *Marris* (1877) 2 Q.B.D. 630.

liable. The issue is, Did A kill himself? The facts that he had for weeks been in a moody, miserable state, that he bought a pistol the day before his death, that he was found shot with that pistol in his hand, that on him was found a letter to his wife stating that he intended to kill himself, etc., these are all " evidentiary facts " which go to prove the fact in issue. None of these therefore should be pleaded. The defence should merely state, " The said A died by his own hand," or whatever are the exact words of condition on the back of the policy.

See *Borradaile* v. *Hunter* (1843) 5 Man. & Gr. 639.

It would be still worse pleading to aver in the defence that the coroner had held an inquest on A's body, and that the jury had returned a verdict of *felo de se*. For such a verdict would not be evidence either for or against the company, and such an allegation would be struck out as an attempt to prejudice the fair trial of the action.

See *Smith* v. *The British Insurance Association* [1883] W.N. 232.

In the absence of a special order (see *post*, p. 301) neither the verdict of the coroner's jury nor the depositions of witnesses at the inquest are admissible to prove the cause of death or negligence.

Bird v. *Keep* [1918] 2 K.B. 692; 87 L.J.K.B. 1199.

Barnett v. *Cohen* [1921] 2 K.B. 461; 90 L.J.K.B. 1307.

Where the main question in an action is, Was the defendant partner with his father in a Lime Street business? it would be bad pleading to allege that the defendant shared in the profits and contributed to the losses incurred in the business, or any other facts which tend to show that he was a partner. Plead merely, " The defendant throughout the year 19— carried on business at No. 21 Lime Street, in partnership with his father, under the style or firm name of ' Davis & Son '."

If the only point in dispute be, Had A authority to make a certain contract on behalf of the defendant? the plaintiff may plead either that " the defendant employed A as his agent to make the said contract on his behalf," or that " the defendant held A out as having authority to make the said contract on his behalf." But he may not allege that " when A made the contract he represented that he was the defendant's agent, and that he had authority from him to enter into the said contract on his behalf." And it is ridiculous to plead, as was once done, that A " has all along been regarded by the lessor, the bankers, and the plaintiff himself, as the agent of the defendant."

If the plaintiff's case is that certain damage has happened to him in consequence of some wrongful act of the defendant, it is not necessary to set out the facts which show the connection between the damage and the wrongful act. These are but evidence. It is sufficient to allege the wrongful act, and that the defendant caused it, and then to continue, " The plaintiff has thereby suffered, etc., and been put to a great expense in, etc." (specifying the damages).

" If both the unlawful act and the consequence are stated, it is unnecessary to allege the means by which that act produced that consequence. . . . The means are matter of evidence."

Per Lord Mansfield C.J. and Buller J. in *R.* v. *Eccles* (1783) 3 Dougl. at p. 337.

" Where the facts in a pedigree are facts to be relied upon as facts to establish the right or title, they must be set out; but where the pedigree is the means of proving the facts relied on as facts by which the right or title is to be established, then the pedigree is evidence that need not be set out."

Per Brett L.J. in *Philipps* v. *Philipps* (1878) 4 Q.B.D. at p. 134.

103

So, to a claim for labour and medicines for curing the defendant of a distemper, the defendant pleaded infancy. The plaintiff replied that the action was brought for necessaries. It was objected to this replication, that the plaintiff had not set out how or in what manner the medicines were necessary; but it was adjudged that the replication in this general form was good.

> *Huggins* v. *Wiseman* (1690) Carth. 110.

Where time has not been made of the essence of the contract, it is sufficient to aver that the work was done or the event happened " within a reasonable time." It is unnecessary to explain that the weather was bad, or that the men struck work, or to state any other reason why it took so long: that is the evidence by which you are going to prove your assertion that the time in fact occupied was a reasonable time.

> *Eaton* v. *Southby* (1738) Willes 131.

Where the plaintiff pleaded that he had " been informed by the defendant that," etc., the paragraph was struck out. This was stating the evidence by which he proposed at the trial to prove the fact in issue.

> *Jones* v. *Turner* [1875] W.N. 239.

A statement of claim set out in full a multitude of letters which were said to be material because they contained admissions. But the Court held that if that were so, still admissions were only evidence, and that facts and not evidence should alone be pleaded. The letters were accordingly struck out.

> *Davy* v. *Garrett* (1878) 7 Ch.D. 473; 47 L.J.Ch. 218.

The plaintiff alleged that certain windows of his were ancient lights. The defendant pleaded that in another action the plaintiff had sworn they were not ancient. This allegation was struck out.

> *Lumb* v. *Beaumont* (1884) 49 L.T. 772.

Where M insures his life, assigns the policy to the plaintiff and disappears, and the defendant has reason to believe that the disappearance is fraudulent and collusive, he should plead merely that M is not dead. He should not allege a conspiracy between M and the plaintiff, and set out other frauds which they had jointly committed; for this is, at best, merely evidence that M is not dead, and that is the real question at issue. But if fraud is *material* it must be pleaded (*post*, pp. 123, 145).

> *Provincial Bank* v. *Brocklebank* (1890) 26 L.R.Ir. 572.
> And see *Murray* v. *Epsom Local Board* [1897] 1 Ch. 35.

Every pleading must contain the necessary particulars of any misrepresentation, fraud, breach of trust, wilful default or undue influence on which the party pleading relies.

> Order 18, r. 12 (1) (*a*).

Whenever any condition of mind other than knowledge is alleged (*e.g.*, any disorder or disability, or malice or fraudulent intention) particulars of the facts on which the pleader relies must be given.

> Order 18, r. 12 (1) (*b*). But see Order 82, r. 3 (3) in defamation actions.

Where knowledge or notice is alleged as a fact the court has power if necessary to order particulars of the facts on which the party pleading relies as showing knowledge, or to order particulars of the notice.

> Order 18, r. 12 (4). And see *post*, pp. 157, 163.

In actions for libel or slander particulars of the facts relied on by the plaintiff to show that the words complained of were used in a defamatory sense other than their ordinary meaning must be given.

> Order 82, r. 3 (1). *Ante*, p. 91 and *post*, p. 164.

When a defendant pleads justification he must give particulars of the facts and matters he relies on in support of his allegation that the words are true, and, if he joins a plea of fair comment as to part of the words complained of, he must specify which of them he alleges to be statements of fact.

See Order 82, r. 3 (2), and *post*, p. 164.

If a butcher and a baker each deal at the other's shop, and at the end of the year they settle accounts and strike a balance, showing that the baker owes the butcher £32 18s. 7d., and the baker checks the figures and agrees to the balance, then that is a settled account, on which the butcher can sue, if he likes, as a substantive cause of action. If he sues on the settled account, he must state when and between whom it was settled; but he should not refer to the butcher's meat or to loaves. If, on the other hand, he prefers to sue for the price of the butcher's meat sold and delivered, giving credit for the amount due from him for bread, he can do so; and then his pleading should contain no reference whatever to the account stated, as it is in that action only an admission that so much is due. Or he might sue on the settled account, and add a claim in the alternative for goods sold and delivered.

See *post*, pp. 187, 208, and Precedents, Nos. 10, 61.

The general principle that every pleading must state facts and not the evidence by which they are to be proved is now subject to an important exception. For any party who intends to adduce evidence of a conviction must include in his pleading a statement of his intention to do so, giving particulars of the conviction and its date, naming the court of trial, and specifying the issue in the proceedings to which the conviction is relevant.[13a] Likewise any denial of the conviction, or of its relevance, or an allegation that it was erroneous must be specifically pleaded with due particularity.

(iv) EVERY PLEADING MUST STATE MATERIAL FACTS CONCISELY IN A SUMMARY FORM

In the first place, material facts must be stated clearly and definitely. Be as concise as you can, provided you do not thereby become obscure. Pleadings are useless unless they state facts with precision. The names of persons and places, if material, must be accurately given. Avoid pronouns; it often is not clear whom you mean by " he." Repeat " the plaintiff," or " the said Johnson," whenever " he " would be ambiguous. Use relative pronouns as little as possible; when you do use them see that each has its proper antecedent. Call things by their

---

[13a] Order 18, r. 7A, *post*, p. 433; a new rule which came into force on October 1, 1969, as a necessary adjunct to s. 11 of the Civil Evidence Act, 1968, whereunder the fact of a conviction is made admissible in evidence at the trial if it is relevant to any issue to prove the commission of the criminal offence. A similar provision with regard to findings of adultery and paternity is to be found in s. 12 of the Act to which this rule also applies.

right names, so far as you can, but in any event always allude
to the same thing by the same name. Keep to the same
phraseology throughout the pleading; a change of phrase
suggests a change of meaning. If you are suing on a document,
or relying on an Act of Parliament, do not attempt to improve
on the language of either (however strong the temptation may
be, especially in the latter case).

Illustrations

The plaintiff and defendant should not be mentioned by name in the body of
a pleading. They should always be called " the plaintiff " and " the defendant,"
or, if more than one, " the male plaintiff," " the female plaintiff," " the defendant
Smith," " the defendant Robinson," or, if both defendants bear the same surname, " the defendant Henry," " the defendant John."

The name of any other person, not a party to the suit, should be given in
full, if known, the first time he is mentioned. Afterwards he can be referred to
by his surname only, as " the said Johnson."

It does not matter in the least whether you allude to the cottage claimed by
the plaintiff as " the said cottage," or " the said house," or " the said messuage,"
or " the said premises." But whichever phrase you use the first time should be
used throughout the pleading.

It will lead to confusion if you refer to the same document sometimes as
" the indenture of May 20th, 1867," sometimes as " the said lease," and sometimes as " the agreement between the parties." In fact, it is technically wrong
to call a contract under seal an agreement.

A policy of life insurance by its express terms becomes void " if the assured
shall die by his own hand." Do not plead that " the assured killed himself,"
or that he " committed suicide." Plead in the very words of the policy, " the
assured died by his own hand."

See *Borradaile* v. *Hunter* (1843) 5 Man. & Gr. 639.

A policy of life assurance contains a condition that satisfactory proof of the
title of the claimant, and of the age and death of the assured, must be given
to the directors. The company is now sued on the policy, and relies on the fact
that this condition has not been complied with. Set out the condition, and
then aver that " no satisfactory proof of the title of the plaintiff or of the age
of the deceased has ever been given to the directors of the defendant company."
Do not plead, as was once done, that " no evidence satisfactory to the defendant
company either of the date of the birth of the assured, or the plaintiff's right to
receive the sum assured, has ever been afforded or supplied by the plaintiff,
though he has been often requested by the defendant company so to do."
Such a change of phrase is unnecessary and confusing.

Facts should be alleged as facts. Use terse, short, curt, blunt
sentences, all in the indicative mood. Be positive. Do not beat
about the bush. Go straight to the point. If you mean to allege
a particular fact, state it boldly, plainly, clearly and concisely.
Avoid all " ifs," all introductory averments and all circum-
locution. A pleading is not the place for fine writing, but simply
for hard, downright, business-like assertion.

Avoid, too, the passive voice: always use the most direct and straightforward construction, and that, as a rule, will be the active voice. It is simpler and clearer to say, " He repaid the money on June 24th, 1969," than to say, " The money was repaid by him " on that date.

Above all, avoid participial phrases; never say that the defendant, being so-and-so, did something. Make two sentences of it; say that he was so-and-so, and then that he did something. Avoid all clauses that are introduced by " being " or " having." If a fact is material, it should be stated as a positive fact, and in a separate sentence.

Then, again, it always conduces to clearness to observe the strict order of time. In any case not of the simplest, dates are of the greatest importance. The only way to tell a long or complicated story clearly and intelligently is to keep to strict chronological order.

Illustrations

It is wholly unnecessary to plead:

" The defendant says that he does not admit that the goods referred to in paragraph 3 of the statement of claim, and therein alleged to have been delivered by the plaintiff to the defendant, or any of them, were in fact so delivered, and he puts the plaintiff to the proof of such delivery."

Omit all preamble, and plunge at once *in medias res*. Plead simply—

" The plaintiff never delivered any of the said goods to the defendant."

Again, it is quite unnecessary to preface any plea with saving clauses, such as, " In the alternative," or " The defendant without waiving any other ground of defence says, that, etc." It is quite unnecessary too to apologise for the line of defence which you adopt or to explain why you think fit to adopt it.

Here is a badly drawn statement of claim:

" The defendant is indebted to the plaintiff, as executor of Lavinia Jones, deceased, in the sum of £231 5s. 10d., being the balance still owing of a sum of £700 advanced to the defendant by the said Lavinia Jones in her lifetime, repayable on demand, with interest at 5 per cent. per annum."

It is all one sentence, and the facts are stated in inverse order of date. The pleading should be:

" 1. On May 15, 1954, the late Lavinia Jones lent the defendant £700. He agreed to repay her that sum on demand, with interest at the rate of 5 per cent. per annum, payable quarterly.

" 2. The defendant regularly paid Lavinia Jones, during her lifetime, interest at the said rate. He also repaid her £468 14s. 2d. towards the principal.

" 3. Lavinia Jones died on December 21, 1968. The plaintiff is her executor.

" 4. The plaintiff, as such executor, claims the balance, £231 5s. 10d., with interest thereon at the said rate from September 29, 1968, until payment or judgment."

Here is a badly drafted sentence:

" The plaintiff has suffered damage by breach of contract by bill of lading of goods shipped by the plaintiff, signed by the master of the ship *Mary*, as the defendant's agent, dated the 1st of January, 19—."

In it there are three distinct allegations depending on participles; and it appears to be left to implication that the defendant is the owner of the ship. Surely it would be far better to plead as follows:

" 1. On January 1st, 19—, the plaintiff caused 200 quarters of wheat to be shipped on board the defendant's ship *Mary* at Bilbao.

2. The master of the said ship received the same to be carried to London upon the terms stated in a bill of lading, which he then signed and of which the following clauses are material:

[*Here state the clauses sued on.*]

3. Of the said wheat, 50 quarters were delivered in a damaged condition, and 100 quarters were not delivered at all.

Particulars of damage:

50 quarters at 4s.	..	..	..	£10
100 quarters at 40s.	..	..	..	£200
				£210

The plaintiff claims £210."

This, then, is the *first* essential of good pleading—to be *clear*. The next is to be *brief*. The Rules repeatedly insist on the necessity of brevity.

The fundamental rule cited at the head of this chapter requires that " every pleading must contain, and contain only, a statement in a summary form of the material facts on which the party pleading relies . . . and the statement must be as brief as the nature of the case admits." (Order 18, r. 7 (1).)

If anything is done improperly or unnecessarily—and this includes unnecessary prolixity—the court has power to give appropriate directions to the Taxing Master as to the costs thereby occasioned. (See Order 62, r. 7.) The Taxing Master will in any case only allow such costs as are proper to be allowed under Order 62, r. 28.

Yet, as we have seen (pp. 90–91, 93), each party must state his whole case; he cannot, strictly, prove at the trial any material fact which is not alleged in his pleading. How, then, is the necessary brevity to be attained?

In two ways:

I. By omitting every unnecessary allegation.

II. By omitting all unnecessary detail when alleging material facts.

I. It is bad pleading to insert a single unnecessary allegation.

108

Illustrations

Neither party should set out the provisions of public Acts of Parliament; or of private Acts passed since 1850, unless the Act itself makes it necessary to be cited. Nor should he state in his pleading the propositions of law which he proposes to urge upon the court.

Neither party may plead the evidence by which he proposes to prove the facts on which he relies.

See Order 18, r. 7 (1).

It is " a rule of law that a man shall never traverse that which the plaintiff has not alleged in his declaration."

Per Holt C.J. in *Powers* v. *Cook* (1696) 1 Ld.Raym. 63.

Rassam v. *Budge* [1893] 1 Q.B. 571; 62 L.J.Q.B. 312.

" A party need not plead any fact if it is presumed by law to be true or the burden of disproving it lies on the other party, unless the other party has specifically denied it in his pleading."

Order 18, r. 7 (3), *ante*, p. 96.

Neither party need allege the performance of any condition precedent; such an averment is now implied in every pleading.

Order **18**, r. 7 (4), *ante*, pp. 98–99.

Neither party need set out the whole or any part of any conversation or document, unless its precise words are material. It is sufficient to state its purport or effect as briefly as possible.

Order 18, r. 7 (2).

It is not necessary for any defendant to plead any denial or defence as to damages claimed or their amount; they will be deemed to be traversed in all cases, unless specifically admitted.

Order 18, r. 13 (4).

It is unnecessary for either party to plead any matter, or to plead to any matter, which merely affects costs.

It is unnecessary for either party to plead to his opponent's prayer or claim or to his particulars, or to any matter introduced by a *videlicet*. (See *post*, p. 133.) He need only deal with the allegations contained in the body of the preceding pleading.

Neither party need refer in his pleading to any item for which his opponent has given him credit.

It is unnecessary for either party in his pleading to refer to any interlocutory proceeding in the action, or to recount the history of the case since writ.

It is not necessary for either party to plead any fact which is not yet material to his case, though he may reasonably suppose that it may become material at a later stage. (*Ante*, p. 95.)

Neither party should plead to any matter of law set out in his opponent's pleading. This may be treated as mere surplusage.

Richardson v. *Mayor of Orford* (1793) 2 H.Bl. 182; *post*, p. 132.

II. When pleading material facts, all unnecessary details should be omitted.

A certain amount of detail is essential to ensure clearness and precision. " Although pleadings must now be concise, they must also be precise." (*Per* Kay J. in *Re Parton, Townsend* v. *Parton* (1882) 30 W.R. 287; 45 L.T. 756.) Indeed, Order 18, r. 12,

expressly requires that " every pleading must contain the necessary particulars of any claim, defence or other matter pleaded." [14]
It is sometimes difficult to know what particulars are necessary,
or what degree of particularity is expected of the pleader. Nor does
any other rule give us this information. But here the former
procedure and practice, qualified by the important alterations
made by the Judicature Act, is a guide. Under the old system of
pleading there was much learning on this matter of " certainty,"
as it was called; and so much of it as appears likely to be of use to
beginners in the art of pleading under the present system will be
found in the next chapter.

---

[14] Necessary particulars of any debt, expenses or damages, if they exceed 3 folios
(216 words or figures), must be set out in a separate document referred to in the
pleading, and the pleading must state whether the document has already been
served, and if so when, or is to be served with the pleading (Ord. 18, r. 12 (2))

CHAPTER 8

CERTAINTY

MATERIAL facts must be alleged with certainty. The object of
pleadings is to ascertain definitely what is the question at issue
between the parties; and this object can only be attained when
each party states his case with precision. If vague and general
statements were allowed, nothing would be defined; the issue
would be " enlarged," as it is called; and neither party would
know, when the case came on for trial, what was the real point
to be discussed and decided. On the other hand, a party who
pleads with unnecessary particularity may thereby fetter his
hand at the trial,[1] and lay on himself an increased burden of
proof.[2]

The amount of detail necessary to ensure precision naturally
varies with the nature of each case. The only general rule that
can be laid down is this—that the party pleading must use such
particularity as will make it clear to the court and to his opponent
what is the precise question which he desires to raise. " What
particulars are to be stated must depend on the facts of each case.
But in my opinion it is absolutely essential that the pleading, not
to be embarrassing to the defendants, should state those facts
which will put the defendants on their guard, and tell them what
they will have to meet when the case comes on for trial." (*Per*
Cotton L.J. in *Philipps* v. *Philipps* (1878) 4 Q.B.D., at p. 139.)

The pleader, then, must decide for himself how far it is necessary
for him to set out items and go into figures; how far details of time
and place and other surrounding circumstances are necessary to
make his pleading intelligible and precise. Experience will teach
him this; even common sense without experience will help him
much, for our law is rapidly degenerating into common sense!

Perhaps the best test is this: after you have drafted your pleading, banish your instructions from your mind for a moment, and

---

[1] As in *James* v. *Smith* [1891] 1 Ch. 384.
[2] As in *West* v. *Baxendale* (1850) 9 C.B. 141.

imagine yourself a stranger coming fresh to the matter. Would your draft, read by itself, convey to his mind a clear conception of your client's case? If not, you must make your draft more definite: and this object will often be best attained by omitting half of it. Length does not conduce to perspicuity. Half a dozen neat, short sentences, each clear in itself, will tell your story best.

And note this distinction. If you omit a material fact altogether from your pleading, this slip may lose the case for your client, as in *Collette* v. *Goode* (1878) 7 Ch.D. 842; and *Byrd* v. *Nunn* (1877) 5 Ch.D. 781; 7 Ch.D. 284. If you plead the fact, but with insufficient detail, the worst that can happen is that you have to give particulars —at some small cost to your client.

Where a plaintiff claims a specific sum of money as the total amount due to him on an account containing many items, he must state particulars showing how that figure is arrived at.

Order 18, r. 12 (2), *ante*, p. 110n.

Philipps v. *Philipps* (1878) 4 Q.B.D., at p. 131.

Again, if a plaintiff claims a lump sum for money paid on various occasions, he must give the items and state when and to whom each such payment was made.

Gunn v. *Tucker* (1891) 7 T.L.R. 280.

So if a plaintiff in his statement of claim gives the defendant credit for a certain amount, and claims to recover the balance, he must not merely name a lump sum, but state the dates and items of the amounts credited. For without this information the defendant cannot tell whether it is necessary for him to plead payment or set-off, or to counterclaim for the sums which he has paid the plaintiff.

Godden v. *Corsten* (1879) 5 C.P.D. 17; 49 L.J.C.P. 112.

Similarly, a mortgagee in possession who admits that he has received certain sums on account must give particulars of all sums received.

Kemp v. *Goldberg* (1887) 36 Ch.D. 505.

If, however, a general account is claimed, and the court agrees that such an account must be taken, then no such particulars need be given. But merely asking for an account will not prevent the court from ordering particulars.

Augustinus v. *Nerinckx* (1880) 16 Ch.D. 13.

Blackie v. *Osmaston* (1884) 28 Ch.D. 119; 54 L.J.Ch. 473.

Carr v. *Anderson* (1901) 18 T.L.R. 206.

Where an agreement not under seal is alleged, its date and consideration and the parties to it should be given; it should also be stated whether it was made verbally or in writing. But a party who alleges a verbal agreement will not be ordered to state in whose presence it was made.

Turquand v. *Fearon* (1879) 48 L.J.Q.B. 703.

Cf. Temperton v. *Russell* (1893) 9 T.L.R. 318, 319. (*Post*, p. 158.)

In an action for false and fraudulent misrepresentation the statement of claim should state whether the alleged representations were oral or in writing, and when each of them was made.

Seligmann v. *Young* [1884] W.N. 93.

In an action of slander the plaintiff must state when and to whom each slander was uttered and may be ordered to give sufficient particulars to identify the occasion.

Roselle v. *Buchanan* (1886) 16 Q.B.D. 656; 55 L.J.Q.B. 376.

Roche v. *Meyler* [1896] 2 Ir.R. 35.

As to actions of libel, see *ante*, pp. 43, 91 and *post*, p. 158.

Time

In an action on any negotiable instrument, its date and amount and the parties thereto should be stated.

Walker v. *Hicks* (1877) 3 Q.B.D. 8; 47 L.J.Q.B. 27.

In an action for goods sold and delivered, the date and amount of each consignment should be stated; or identified by reference to some specific account already rendered.

Parpaite Frères v. *Dickinson* (1878) 38 L.T. 178.

Aston v. *Hurwitz* (1879) 41 L.T. 521.

In an action brought by a lessor against a lessee during the continuance of the term for breach of a covenant to repair, the statement of claim must state the time which the term still has to run; for on this depends the value of the lessor's reversion.

Turner v. *Lamb* (1845) 14 M. & W. 412.

Murphy v. *Murphy* [1903] 2 Ir.R. 329.

So a claim for rent must state the dates at which the rent claimed fell due.

Beaufort v. *Ledwith* [1894] 2 Ir.R. 16.

Where the defendant has raised the Limitation Act or any defence of waiver by laches, dates are most material and must therefore be pleaded.

Reeves v. *Butcher* [1891] 2 Q.B. 509; 60 L.J.Q.B. 619.

If in trespass to land the defendant pleads that the *locus in quo* was his freehold, he must allege that it was his freehold " at the time of the alleged trespass "; otherwise the plea is insufficient.

Com.Dig. Pleader (E. 5).

Place

In an action for the recovery of land the property must be described with sufficient certainty to enable the sheriff to put the plaintiff in possession of it, if he succeed in the action.

In an action of trespass the plaintiff should describe the close on which the defendant trespassed so as to identify it.

In an action of replevin the place where the cattle or goods were distrained is material.

Coaker v. *Willcocks* [1911] 2 K.B. 124; 80 L.J.K.B. 1026.

In alleging a right of way the *termini* of the way should be stated.

Harris v. *Jenkins* (1882) 22 Ch.D. 481; 52 L.J.Ch. 437.

Damages

No particulars will ordinarily be required of general damage; for this the law presumes in the plaintiff's favour. But special damage must be alleged with sufficient particularity to inform the defendant of the nature and extent of the loss sustained.

See *post*, pp. 159, 161, 181, 182.

Title

Where either party claims to be the owner of any property, real or personal, or of any right or interest to, in or over it, he must state his title to such property, right or interest, with all due particularity. The pleadings must show title.

But very different degrees of particularity are necessary in different cases. In the first place, our law always respects possession. Possession is a physical fact, and generally an obvious one; it is wholly distinct from ownership, which is often a difficult question of law. The true owner of a field or of a chattel may be in possession of it, or he may not. Again, he may be rightfully out of possession, as where he has let it to a tenant, or lent it to a friend; or he may be wrongfully out of possession, as where he has been evicted from the field by a trespasser, or where the chattel has been stolen.

A man may be said to be in possession of land or of a chattel whenever he has full and uncontrolled physical dominion over it. Thus, he is in possession of a house when he or his servants are living in it; if he or they are absent from it, he would still be held to be in possession, if such absence was only temporary, or if he could return and re-enter at any moment, if he chose, without asking anyone's permission and without any preliminary ceremony. But the moment anyone else enters into and remains in possession of the premises without his consent, the former possessor is ousted; for two persons cannot be in possession of the same property at the same time (unless they be partners or joint occupiers).

I. *Where the person showing title is in possession or was in possession at the date of the wrong complained of*

As against a wrongdoer, it is always sufficient to allege a merely possessory title. (*Armory* v. *Delamirie* (1722) 1 Smith's *Leading Cases.*) Thus, in trover, detinue or trespass to goods it is sufficient to describe them as " the goods and chattels of the plaintiff"; in trespass to land it is sufficient to describe the *locus in quo* as the " close of the plaintiff," or to allege that " the plaintiff was lawfully possessed of a certain close," describing it. So, with respect to incorporeal hereditaments, it is sufficient to allege that the plaintiff was possessed of the corporeal thing in respect of which the incorporeal right is claimed: *e.g.*, " the plaintiff was possessed of a certain messuage " (stating its name and situation), " and by reason thereof was entitled to common of pasture," or to a right of way, etc.

Illustrations

In an action of trespass it is sufficient to allege that the defendant broke and entered certain land of the plaintiff, called —— (describing it).

In an action of trover it is sufficient to say that the defendant converted to his own use the plaintiff's goods (specifying them).

In an action for detinue it is sufficient to allege that the defendant detained from the plaintiff his title deeds of —— (describing the land).

In an action for obstructing a right of way it is sufficient to allege that the plaintiff was possessed of a certain messuage, the occupiers whereof had from time immemorial (*or* for so many years before suit) enjoyed as of right and without interruption a way from the said messuage across a certain close called Blackacre to a public highway, and back again from the said public highway over the said close to the said messuage, for themselves and their servants, on foot and with horses, cattle and carriages, at all times of the year.

See Prescription Act, 1832, and Rights of Way Act, 1932.

As to pleading a prescriptive right at common law to an easement, or to any profit or benefit taken or arising out of land, see 2 Wms.Saund. 401a; *Att.-Gen.* v. *Gauntlett* (1829) 3 Y. & J. 93. As to pleading a period of prescription under the Act, see Prescription Act, 1832, s. 5. And see Bullen & Leake's *Precedents of Pleadings.*

A defendant to an action for the recovery of land must plead specifically every ground of defence on which he relies, and a plea that he is in possession of the land by himself or his tenant is not sufficient. (Order 18, r. 8 (2).) In this respect the law was radically altered by a new rule in force since 1964. Formerly he was only required to plead specifically if he was in possession by virtue of a lease from the plaintiff or his predecessor in title or if he had an equitable defence; all other defences could be raised under the bare plea that he was in possession. Now he must plead them. The defendant in an action for the recovery of land has never been bound to disclose his title or want of title: the plaintiff must recover on the strength of his own title, not on the weakness of his adversary's title. Therefore the defendant may deny the plaintiff's title, or any particular link in it, and put him to the proof of it. If, however, the defendant intends to allege specifically that the plaintiff's ancestor conveyed the property to him, or to trustees who are not parties to the action, he should so plead, especially if it is a matter which might take the plaintiff by surprise. (Order 18, r. 8 (1) and (2).)

A defendant who is in possession of a chattel may also, if he thinks fit, content himself with denying that the goods are the plaintiff's, and so put him to proof of his title.[3] But if the defendant claims any right to the possession of the chattel apart from ownership this should be specially pleaded; otherwise, as soon as the plaintiff proves his title, the right to the possession of his own property (which is always inherent in ownership) will at once attach and displace the prima facie title which the defendant derived from its possession. A plaintiff who has proved his title to the property is not a wrongdoer, and mere possession will not avail against him.

Illustrations

In an action for the recovery of a chattel, the defendant must plead specially that it was hired out to him for a definite period not yet expired, or lent to him for a purpose not yet accomplished, or pawned to him, or that he has a lien on it for warehouse rent, or any other lien. For such defences admit the plaintiff's title to the ownership of the goods, and should therefore be specially pleaded by way of " confession and avoidance " (see *post*, p. 126).

Possession is prima facie seisin against a wrongdoer; and anyone who enters on land which is in the possession of another, against the will of that other, is deemed a wrongdoer till he pleads and establishes his title to the land, or to a right of way over it. If therefore in an action of trespass for assault and battery, the defendant justifies on the ground that the plaintiff wrongfully entered his house, and was making a disturbance there, and that the defendant gently removed him, the plea should be in this form: " the defendant was lawfully possessed of a certain dwelling-house, etc.; and while he was so possessed, the plaintiff was unlawfully in the said dwelling-house," etc. It is not necessary for the defendant to show any title to the house, beyond this of mere possession.

3 Chitt.Pl. (7th ed.), 323.

So in an action of trespass for seizing cattle, if the defendant justifies on the ground that the cattle were damage feasant on his close, it is not necessary for him to show any title to his close, except that of mere possession.

1 Wms.Saund. 221, n. (1), 346; 2 Wms.Saund. 285, n. (3); Bac.Abr. " Trespass " (5th ed.), 613.

Where it is sufficient to allege a mere possessory title, it is a mistake to go into details as to the precise estate of either party.

See *Cudlip* v. *Rundle* (1692) Carthew 202.

Sir Francis Leke's Case (1580) 3 Dyer 365; 2 Wms.Saund. 206, n. (22).

Bristow v. *Wright* (1781) 2 Douglas 665.

II. *Where the party pleading is out of possession and his opponent is in possession*

Here, if the title of the party pleading is material, its *basis*, whether ownership in fee simple or a term of years or an equitable interest, must be pleaded. But how far is it necessary to allege its *origin*?

If he claims possession, he must show possession, either in himself or in someone from whom he claims, prior to the alleged wrongful act or possession of his opponent. As to estates in fee

[3] But note the position where the defendant is a bailee (*post*, p. 121).

simple the old rule was that it was sufficient to state a *seisin* in fee simple without showing the derivation or commencement of the estate; for if that were required the process might be carried back *ad infinitum*. If, however, he was obliged in his pleading to allege seisin in someone other than himself, he was bound to show how the fee passed to him from such other person.[4]

With respect to *particular estates* (which included estates for life, estates tail, terms of years and tenancies at will) the general rule was that he must show the derivation of that title from its commencement, that is to say, from the last seisin in fee simple with all subsequent devolutions, stating the nature and effect of each transfer or conveyance.[5] An exception was, however, permitted in the case of a plea of " *liberum tenementum* " in answer to an action of trespass, where a defendant was (and still is) allowed to allege a general freehold title; the old plea being merely that " the said close was the close, soil and freehold of the defendant," even though he might only have held a particular freehold estate (as was formerly possible).

The Law of Property Act, 1925, and the Settled Land Act, 1925, reduced the number of legal estates and extended the classes of persons entitled to the fee simple, and a tenant for life or in tail has the legal estate in fee simple vested in him. There are now only two legal estates: a fee simple absolute in possession (which does not necessarily mean physical possession),[6] and a term of years absolute. And of equitable estates conferring a right to immediate possession, a tenancy under an agreement for a lease is alone likely to be met with in practice.

There do not appear to be any reported cases as to the pleading of title since 1925, but it would seem that in the main the old rules are still applicable. Thus, provided that the party pleading duly traces title from a fee simple absolute with actual possession, he need go no further. (See Precedents, Nos. 50, 51.) If he has only a term of years, his pleading must show the commencement and derivation of his title. Cases where he has to rely upon an equitable estate will be less frequent, since the owner of the legal estate will usually be the proper party; but if he does, he should show its origin in like manner.

---

[4] See *Stephens on Pleading* (6th ed., 1860), p. 232.
[5] *Ibid.*; and Co.Litt. 303b; *Pinhorn* v. *Souster* (1853) 8 Ex. 138.
[6] Law of Property Act, 1925, s. 205 (xix).

In the case of a term of years the pleading should state fully—

(a) the commencement and derivation of title, if that be material,[7] giving the number of owners, if more than one, at any stage [8];

(b) who granted the lease pleaded and to whom, and any subsequent steps such as assignment; and

(c) the length of the term granted and the period of enjoyment. (Dates are most material in any case of disputed title.)

Illustrations

Where A's fee was conditional on an event which has happened, or is determinable in an event which has not happened, he may allege a present absolute fee without qualification, without showing its commencement.

Seymour's Case (1613) 10 Rep. 98; Doctrina Placitandi, 287.

An action for the breach of a covenant in a lease granted by J. S. to the defendant was brought by the heir of J. S. after his death. The plaintiff, having alleged that J. S. was seised in fee when he granted the lease, must then show how the fee passed to himself, *viz.*, by descent.

Cuthbertson v. *Irving* (1860) 4 H. & N. 742; 6 H. & N. 135.

And see *ante*, p. 89.

In an action for the recovery of land of which the plaintiff has never been in possession, the statement of claim must allege the nature of the deeds and documents upon which he relies in deducing his title from the person under whom he claims. A general statement, that by assurances, wills, documents and Crown grants in the possession of the defendants, without further describing them, the plaintiff is entitled to the land, is embarrassing and liable to be struck out under Order 18, r. 19 (1).

Philipps v. *Philipps* (1878) 4 Q.B.D. 127; 48 L.J.Q.B. 135.

If a lease be granted by J. S. to the defendant, and the plaintiff, claiming as assignee of the reversion, sue the lessee on the covenant therein contained for rent, he must precisely state the conveyances or other transfers of title from J. S. to himself, whereby he became entitled to the reversion. To say generally that the reversion came to him by assignment will not be sufficient without circumstantially alleging all the mesne assignments. The devolution of the estate to the plaintiff must be shown.

Davis v. *James* (1884) 26 Ch.D. 778; 53 L.J.Ch. 523.

Where a plaintiff claims as assignee of a debt originally contracted between the defendant and A, he must show in his pleading how he derives his title; he must allege an absolute assignment in writing, and that notice in writing of such assignment was given to the defendant before action, otherwise he would not be entitled to sue, at all events without joining A as a co-plaintiff. (Law of Property Act, 1925, s. 136; and see *ante*, p. 27.)

Seear v. *Lawson* (1880) 16 Ch.D. 121; 50 L.J.Ch. 139.

---

[7] In an action by a lessor against his lessee title is not usually material (see *post*, p. 119); nor is it material if alleged merely by way of inducement. (*Post*, p. 176.)

[8] An averment of seisin in fee without more means sole seisin (*Gilbert* v. *Parker* (1705) 2 Salk. 629; *Bonner* v. *Walker* (1596) Cro.Eliz. 524).

Title by Estoppel

There is one case in which this particularity is unnecessary. No title need be shown at all where the opposite party is estopped from denying the title. Thus, if a lessor sue the original lessee, or anyone who has attorned tenant to the lessor, *e.g.*, by paying rent, he need allege no title to the premises demised, because in those circumstances a tenant is estopped from denying his landlord's title.[9]

But the tenant is not bound to admit title to any extent greater than would authorise the lease. Hence, if the action be brought not by the lessor himself but by his heir, executor, or other representative or assignee, the title of the lessor must be alleged, in order to show that the reversion is now legally vested in the plaintiff in the character in which he sues.[10] The tenant is not bound to admit that his lessor was seised in fee; and a tenant is not estopped from saying that his landlord's title has determined, or from saying that he paid rent to the plaintiff merely as a collector for his landlord.[11]

Pleading Title in Another

So far we have dealt with the case where the party pleading alleges title in himself. The same rules apply with equal strictness where the party pleading sets up title in some third person, from whom he says he derived the authority to do the act complained of. For instance, where a servant exercises a right of way by his master's order, the right must be pleaded with the same particularity as if the master, whose authority he pleads, had been made a defendant.

Next, we must consider the case where a party alleges title in his adversary with the object of making him liable in respect of the property, real or personal.

In this case it is not necessary to allege title more precisely than is sufficient to show a liability in the party charged, or to defeat his present claim. The reason of this difference is that a party may be presumed to be ignorant of the particulars of his adversary's

---

[9] *Casey* v. *Hellyar* (1886) 17 Q.B.D. 97; *Jones* v. *Stone* [1894] A.C. 122. If the defendant asserts the title to be in himself or a stranger, he thereby incurs a forfeiture; but a mere traverse of the landlord's title, if the title be expressly alleged, does not have this effect. (*Warner* v. *Sampson* [1959] 1 Q.B. 297, overruling a decision in 1935.)

[10] See *Cuthbertson* v. *Irving* (1860) 4 H. & N. 742; 6 H. & N. 135 (in error); *Thriscutt* v. *Martin* (1849) 3 Ex. 454; and the judgment of Willes J. in *Smith* v. *Scott* (1859) 6 C.B.(N.S.) 771.

[11] *Jones* v. *Stone* [1894] A.C. 122.

title, though he is bound to know his own.[12] " It lies more properly in the knowledge of the lessor what estate he himself has in the land, which he demises, than of the lessee who is a stranger to it." [13]

In order to show a liability in the party charged, according to the rule here given, it is in most cases sufficient to allege that your adversary is in possession, and to prove that he has some present interest in chattels, or is in actual possession of land. But this form of pleading is *ex hypothesi* inapplicable if the interest he possesses be by way of reversion or remainder. In that event the party pleading must state his opponent's title in detail. Then, again, there are cases in which to charge a party with mere possession would not be sufficient to show his liability. Thus, if the defendant be sued as assignee of a term of years for arrears of rent due under a covenant in the lease creating that term, it is not sufficient to show that he is in possession of the property demised, but it must be further shown that he is in possession as assignee of the term. But even here the party pleading is not expected to plead all the details of the various assignments of the term, though he must show all the assignments of the reversion; for these are within his knowledge.

Illustrations

In an action of debt, where the defendant is sued for rent as the assignee of the term after several mesne assignments, it is sufficient, after stating the original demise, to allege that " after making the said indenture, and during the term thereby granted, all the estate and interest of the said E F " (the original lessee) " of and in the said demised premises by assignment came to and vested in the defendant," without further showing the nature of the mesne assignments. For the plaintiff is a stranger to the defendant's title, and therefore cannot set it out more particularly.

Cotes v. *Wade* (1678) 1 Lev. 190; 1 Sid. 298.
1 Wms.Saund. 112 (*b*), n. (4).
Derisley v. *Custance* (1790) 4 T.R. 75.

Upon the same principle, if title be laid in an adversary by descent—as, for example, where an action of debt is brought against an heir, on the bond of his ancestor—it is sufficient to charge him as an heir, without showing how he is heir, *viz.*, as son or otherwise; though where a party seeks to entitle himself by inheritance, the mode of descent must be alleged, as we have seen *ante*, p. 89.

Denham v. *Stephenson* (1705) 1 Salk. 355.

Pleading Authority

Whenever the party pleading seeks to justify an act prima facie unlawful, he must show his authority or excuse with precision.

---

[12] See *Rider* v. *Smith* (1790) 3 T.R. 766; *Att.-Gen.* v. *Meller* (1679) Hardr. 459.
[13] *Bradshaw's Case* (1613) 9 Rep. 60b; and see *Cudlip* v. *Rundle* (1692) Carth. 202.

If he seeks to justify it by virtue of any writ, warrant, precept or other authority, he must set it forth particularly in his pleading. If he plead that he did the act by the command of A, he must further show that A had legal right and title so to command. If the plaintiff is in possession of any land or goods, or can otherwise make out a prima facie title to them, it is not enough for the defendant to show a better title in some third person; he must also show that he acted as agent for such third person at the time he did the act complained of.

Illustrations

If you trespass on land of which I am in possession, it is immaterial that the land really belongs to A, unless you claim through or under A, or acted by his authority.

If I deposit goods with a warehouseman and he subsequently refuses to deliver them up to me, it is not enough for him to plead that they belong to B (for he received them from me); he must go further, and plead that he refused to redeliver them, relying upon the title and by the authority of B.

> *Thorne* v. *Tilbury* (1858) 3 H. & N. 534; 27 L.J.Ex. 407.
> *Biddle* v. *Bond* (1865) 6 B. & S. 225; 34 L.J.Q.B. 137.
> *Ex p. Davies* (1881) 19 Ch.D. 86.

The bailee of goods cannot avail himself of the title of a third person to the goods as a defence to an action of detinue by the bailor, except by further showing that he is defending the action on behalf and by the authority of such third person.

> *Rogers & Co.* v. *Lambert* [1891] 1 Q.B. 318; 60 L.J.Q.B. 187.
> *Henderson* v. *Williams* [1895] 1 Q.B. 521; 64 L.J.Q.B. 308.

With respect to acts valid at common law, but regulated as to the mode of performance by statute, it is sufficient to use such certainty of allegation as was sufficient before the statute. See *ante*, p. 100.

But where an act is prima facie illegal, all facts necessary to prove its legality must be alleged and proved with great particularity. *E.g.*, in an action of replevin (*post*, p. 191), if the defendant justifies taking the cattle by alleging that he was bailiff of a landlord who distrained them for rent, he must show by his plea that the land on which such distress was made was demised at a rent certain, specifying it, and that the rent was in arrear; but he need not set out the lessor's estate or title, or any particulars of the demise, except the rent.

> See Precedent No. 76.

> See also *Smith* v. *Feverell* (1686) 2 Mod. 6; 1 Freeman 190 (*ante*, p. 94).

But in an *avowry for distress damage feasant* (as such a defence was formerly called), the defendant is still bound to justify with full particularity; he must show that the cattle were damaging him, else he would have no right to distrain. But need he plead his exact estate or interest in the land on which the cattle were straying, even if he be in possession? (See *ante*, p. 116.) Here we have a conflict between two rules. And it has been decided that it is not enough for the defendant to plead possession merely; that, if a tenant, he must state the details of his tenancy, etc., if a freeholder, he must plead that the land is his freehold; but that he need not go on to state whether he be seised in fee, in tail, or for life. (See Precedent No. 77.)

> *Per* Buller J. in *Dovaston* v. *Payne* (1795) 2 H.Bl. 530. (And see 2 Sm. L.C.)
>
> *Hawkins* v. *Eckles* (1801) 2 Bos. & Pul. 359, 361, n. (a).

Where the act complained of was done in the execution of judicial process, it is not sufficient for the defendant to allege generally that he so acted by virtue of a certain writ or warrant directed to him; he must set it forth particularly in his plea. (1 Wms.Saund. 298, n. (8); Co.Litt. 303 b.) If the party pleading be an officer of the court, he need not also set out the judgment on which such writ or warrant was founded; for it is his duty to execute the process of the court without inquiring into the validity or even the existence of the judgment.[14] But if the party pleading be not an officer of the court, he must set out the judgment as well as the writ.[15] If it be the judgment of a superior court, none of the previous proceedings in that suit need be stated; if it be the judgment of an inferior court, or, it seems, of a foreign court, then so much of the previous proceedings must be pleaded as will show jurisdiction in that court (*e.g.*, that the cause of action arose within its jurisdiction); and if it be a court whose jurisdiction is not defined by any public Act of Parliament of which judicial notice will be taken, the nature and extent of its jurisdiction should also be set forth.[16]

Illustrations

The defendant seized the plaintiff's mare on the wastes of the manor of B. The defendant justified his act under a by-law made by the lord of the manor and the homage at a lawful court, which by-law the plaintiff had broken. This offence was presented at the next court, and thereupon the defendant, being bailiff of the lord of the said manor, did take the mare for the forfeiture incurred by the plaintiff, etc. The court held the plea bad; " for the bailiff cannot take a forfeiture *ex officio*. There must be a precept directed to him for that purpose, which he must show in pleading."

> *Lamb* v. *Mills* (1695) 4 Mod. 377.

A plea, justifying the arrest and detention of a ship under a judgment *in rem* of a competent court having jurisdiction in Admiralty, must state what the charge was, and who were the parties to it, and at whose instance the order was given, and at what time, and for what object, and whether the defendant was a party to the suit or acted as an officer of the court.

> *Collett* v. *Lord Keith* (1802) 2 East 260.

In an action of trover for taking a ship, the defendant set up that the Admiralty of a certain port in the East Indies had given sentence against the said

---

[14] *Andrews* v. *Marris* (1841) 1 Q.B. 3; *Dews* v. *Riley* (1851) 11 C.B. 434.
[15] *Per* Holt C.J. in *Britton* v. *Cole* (1698) 1 Ld.Raym. 305; *Barker* v. *Braham* (1773) 3 Wils. 368.
[16] *Moravia* v. *Sloper* (1737) Willes 30; *Morrell* v. *Martin* (1841) 3 M. & Gr. 581.

ship as a prize. It was held that the plea ought to have shown some special cause for which the ship became a prize; and that the judge who gave sentence should have been named, and the court described with sufficient certainty to identify it.

> *Beak* v. *Tyrrell* (1687) Carth. 31.

Charges of Misconduct and Negligence

Particularity is especially needed where the pleading contains an imputation on the character of your opponent; as then it is only right and fair that he should know definitely before the trial what is the charge which is made against him. Justice requires you to define the accusation you bring against anyone; and this is a very different thing from setting out the evidence by which you intend to establish it. " The court will require of him who makes the charge that he shall state that charge with as much definiteness and particularity as may be done, both as regards time and place." (*Per* Lord Penzance in *Marriner* v. *Bishop of Bath and Wells* [1893] P. at p. 146.) It is no excuse for the omission of such details that the opponent must already be perfectly well aware of the facts.[17] Each party is entitled to know the outline of the case that his adversary is going to make against him, and to bind him down to a definite story. Particulars must always be given of any alleged negligence[18] and as a rule of any contributory negligence.[19]

Illustrations

Every pleading must contain the necessary particulars of any misrepresentation, fraud, breach of trust, wilful default or undue influence on which the party pleading relies.

> Order 18, r. 12 (1) (*a*).

Where a party pleading alleges any condition of the mind of any person, whether any disorder or disability of mind or any malice, fraudulent intention or other condition of mind except knowledge, his pleading must contain particulars of the facts on which he relies.

> Order 18, r. 12 (1) (*b*).

The plaintiff alleged that the defendants had made false entries in certain books; he was ordered to give a list of the entries alleged to be false, and also to state generally the nature of his objections to them.

> *Newport Dry Dock Co.* v. *Paynter* (1886) 34 Ch.D. 88; 56 L.J.Ch. 1021.
> *Harbord* v. *Monk* (1878) 38 L.T. 411.

The plaintiff alleged that the defendant had " in various ways misapplied rent and profits of leaseholds, which he had received on behalf of the plaintiff, and committed breaches of trust." Particulars were ordered.

> *Re Anstice* (1885) 54 L.J.Ch. 1104.

---

[17] *B.* v. *B. and G.* [1937] P. 1, 5.
[18] *Gautret* v. *Egerton* (1867) L.R. 2 C.P. 371; *Fowler* v. *Lanning* [1959] 1 Q.B. 426, 440; *Bills* v. *Roe* [1968] 1 W.L.R. 925 (*post*, p. 159).
[19] *Atkinson* v. *Stewart & Partners, Ltd.* [1954] N.I. 146 (*post*, p. 159).

In an action for the price of work and labour done, if the defendant wishes to prove at the trial that the plaintiff did the work unskilfully, he must plead full particulars of the alleged defects, so as to give the plaintiff notice of the charge that is going to be made against him.

Where the plaintiff alleges that an accident was due to the failure by his employers to provide a safe system of work, the statement of claim ought to set out, so far as is material, what the proper system of work was and in what relevant respects it was not observed.

    Colfar v. *Coggins & Griffith* (*Liverpool*), *Ltd.* [1945] A.C. 197, 203.

" There may be cases in which the plaintiff will not get very far with an allegation of unsafe system of work unless he can show some practicable alternative, but there are also cases . . . in which a plaintiff can fairly say: ' If this is dangerous, then there must be some other way of doing it that can be found by a prudent employer and it is not for me to devise that way or to say what it is '." *Per* Devlin L.J. in *Dixon* v. *Cementation Co.* [1960] 1 W.L.R. 746.

The respondents alleged negligent navigation and management of a vessel in specific respects which were held to be unfounded; but the evidence showed that the stranding was due to an unexplained fracture in the stern frame of the vessel which affected the steering. The pleadings were not amended and did not allege unseaworthiness. *Held,* that the respondents could not afterwards contend that the burden of accounting for the defect was on the appellants and that they had not discharged it.

    Esso Petroleum Co., Ltd. v. *Southport Corporation* [1956] A.C. 218.

In an action of defamation, where the defendant justifies, if the libel or slander consists of one specific charge, it is sufficient to allege generally that the words are true, and ordinarily no further particulars are necessary. But where the defendant justifies a general charge of misconduct, specific instances must be given in the defence, and stated with sufficient particularity to inform the plaintiff precisely what are the facts to be tried, and what is the charge made against him.

    Cumming v. *Green* (1891) 7 T.L.R. 408.

    Arnold & Butler v. *Bottomley* [1908] 2 K.B. 151; 77 L.J.K.B. 584.

    Wootton v. *Sievier* [1913] 3 K.B. 499; 82 L.J.K.B. 1242.

" A defendant should never place a plea of justification on the record unless he has clear and sufficient evidence of the truth of the imputation." *Gatley on Libel and Slander,* 6th ed. (1967), p. 462, para. 1046.

    Associated Leisure Ltd. v. *Associated Newspapers, Ltd.* [1970] 2 Q.B. 450, 456.

And see *post,* p. 207.

When the pleader seeks to avoid the Limitation Act by pleading concealed fraud, he must state his case with the utmost particularity, or the pleading may be struck out.

    Lawrance v. *Lord Norreys* (1890) 15 App.Cas. 210; 59 L.J.Ch. 681.

    Lynn v. *Bamber* [1930] 2 K.B. 72; 99 L.J.K.B. 504.

Uncertainty

We conclude with one practical observation. Counsel often cannot be as precise as they desire, because they cannot obtain definite information. The lay client is abroad, or there is some other reason. Where you cannot be exact, make too broad rather than too narrow an allegation. It is better to claim too much than too little. It is wiser to state your client's right too largely, if you cannot state it exactly; the greater includes the less. Either party will be allowed as a general rule to prove so much of his allegation as is necessary to support his case, although he has alleged more in his pleadings; for, in the language of the old pleaders, " pleadings are construed *distributively*."

Illustrations

If the plaintiff claims £500, he will be allowed to recover £100 or £200; though where the items are divisible and arise out of separate facts, he ought to be made to pay the costs occasioned by his joining the items as to which he has failed.

This was not so in Roman Law; there, if a defendant could show that the plaintiff had claimed too much, he won the action. The plaintiff had to recover the full sum he claimed or nothing at all. This system had some advantages; but such strictness would now be impossible.

In cases of unliquidated damages it is usual to claim damages " at large," but if you wish to insert a definite amount, be sure you claim enough, as the plaintiff cannot recover more than the sum claimed on his writ or statement of claim, unless the judge gives leave to amend.

Modera v. *Modera and Barclay* (1893) 10 T.L.R. 69.

The Dictator [1892] P. 64; 61 L.J.P. 72.

An averment of intention is divisible; so that where a libel is alleged to have been published with intent to defame certain magistrates, and also to bring the administration of justice into contempt, it is sufficient to prove a publication with either of those intentions.

R. v. *Evans* (1821) 3 Stark. 35.

If a defendant pleads that he has paid the plaintiff his whole debt, he will be allowed to prove part payment as a defence *pro tanto*, and the plaintiff will recover judgment only for the balance.

If a defendant in an action for the conversion or detention of goods denies that any of the goods are the plaintiff's, he will be allowed to prove at the trial that some of them are not, though he may have to admit that the rest are, the plaintiff's.

Freshney v. *Wells* (1857) 26 L.J.Ex. 228.

If a defendant chooses on his pleading to deny his liability in respect of every item in the plaintiff's claim, he cannot be compelled to give particulars stating which of them he really intends to dispute at the trial.

James v. *Radnor County Council* (1890) 6 T.L.R. 240.

In a proper case, however, the plaintiff may be allowed to deliver interrogatories to the defendant, who, if his refusal to admit proves unreasonable, may be ordered to pay the costs thereof (see *post*, p. 137).

The plaintiff alleged that his vessel had been injured by the defendant's ship running into it *twice* while it was at anchor, and driving it on the rocks. He failed to prove two separate collisions; but he proved one of sufficient force to drive his vessel ashore. *Held*, that he was entitled to recover.

Tyrer v. *Henry* (1860) 14 Moore 83.

CHAPTER 9

ANSWERING YOUR OPPONENT'S PLEADING

So far we have dealt only with the statement by a party of his own case. But after the first pleading each party must do more than state his own case; he must deal with that presented by his opponent.

Now there are only three ways in which a party who means to fight can deal with his opponent's pleading:

(i) He can deny the whole or some essential part of the averments of fact contained in it. This is called *traversing* an opponent's allegations.

(ii) He can say, " Well, that is true so far as it goes; but it is only half the truth. Here are several other facts which are omitted from your pleading, and which will put a very different complexion on the case." Alleging such facts is called *pleading by way of confession and avoidance*, or, more shortly, *confessing and avoiding*; because the pleader seems to confess that his opponent's statement discloses a good prima facie case—that it is on the face of it good in law and true in fact—and he then goes on to allege new facts by which he hopes to destroy the effect of the allegations admitted.

(iii) He may take a point of law, and say, " Assuming every word contained in this statement to be true, still I say that it is bad in law; it discloses no cause of action " (or " no defence to my action," or " no answer to my plea," as the case may be). This was formerly called *demurring* (from the Latin *demorari*, or French *demorrer*, to " wait " or " stay "); because the party who demurred would not proceed with his pleading, but awaited the judgment of the court whether any case was made out for him to answer. What was formerly a *demurrer* is now called " *an objection in point of law*," which is a short definition rather than a name. (See *post*, p. 147.) However, it exactly expresses what a demurrer was.[1]

Every objection in point of law asserts or implies that the pleading objected to is sufficient on the face of it; hence it admits for the moment that the allegations contained in it are true. Thus, it may be said that a traverse denies, and an objection admits. But they are alike in this, that neither of them introduces any fresh matter; whereas a plea in confession and avoidance neither simply admits nor merely denies; it admits the facts alleged in the opponent's pleading, subject, however, to the new facts by which it seeks to destroy their legal effect.

Formerly, the party pleading had to elect which of these three courses he would adopt; he could not both demur and plead, nor could he traverse any allegation to which he also pleaded by way of confession and avoidance. Now, however, he is not restricted in this way; the same allegation may be traversed in point of fact, objected to as bad in law, and at the same time collateral matter may be pleaded to destroy its effect.[2] Remember, however, that it is foolish to multiply the issues needlessly, as your client may be ordered to pay the costs of those which he fails to prove, even though he succeeds on the main issue.

This may be best explained by one or two instances:

Writ issued November 18, 1970.

Statement of Claim

1. On August 18, 1969, the defendant promised to pay the plaintiff the sum of £800 on November 18, 1969.
2. The defendant did not pay the plaintiff the said sum of £800, or any part thereof, on November 18, 1969, or at all.

And the plaintiff claims the said sum of £800 with interest thereon at the rate of 5 per cent. per annum, from November 18, 1969, till payment or judgment.

To this badly drafted claim the defendant may, if he likes, take three objections in point of law; he is not bound to state them

---

[1] There is, however, this difference between the former demurrer and the present system. Formerly a party who had demurred could always without leave set the demurrer down for argument before the court *in banc*, and thus frequently delay the trial of the action. Nowadays the point of law raised by an objection is disposed of by the judge who tries the cause at or after the trial, unless on a master's order it is argued before the trial (see *Everett* v. *Ribbands* [1952] 2 Q.B. 198, 206).

[2] For example, see Precedent No. 78.

in his pleading but he is entitled to do so (Order 18, r. 11). He will probably also traverse the alleged agreement.

Defence

1. The defendant never promised as alleged. (*Traverse.*)
2. The defendant will object that no consideration is shown for his alleged promise.
3. The defendant will object that the statement of claim discloses no cause of action for interest.
4. The defendant will object that the writ was issued prematurely.

But this is a technical kind of defence. Paragraph 1 is probably untrue, and there was probably also some consideration for the promise, if indeed it was not under seal, and some agreement to pay interest; so that the plaintiff could amend his statement of claim and proceed. Paragraph 4 raises a more serious objection, but this can be got over by the plaintiff's discontinuing this action, paying the costs and issuing a second writ. In the second action the defendant would probably be driven to confess and avoid:

Defence

1. The defendant admits that he promised to pay the plaintiff the said sum of £800 on November 18, 1969; but he promised to do so on condition that the plaintiff had by that date built a stable for the defendant in accordance with a specification, dated May 3, 1969.
2. The plaintiff did not by November 18, 1969, or any other day, build a stable for the defendant in accordance with the said specification, or at all.

We thus learn at last what is the real bone of contention between the parties.

Take another instance:

Statement of Claim
(Indorsed on writ)

1. On April 13, 1963, the defendant agreed that if the plaintiff would supply goods to C D he would see the plaintiff paid therefor.
2. On the faith of this guarantee, the plaintiff supplied C D with the following goods, the price of which is £913 8s. 11d.

(Particulars of the goods supplied, with dates)

3. Neither C D nor the defendant has paid the plaintiff the said price or any part thereof.

And the plaintiff claims £913 8s. 11d.

Defence

1. The defendant never agreed as alleged.
2. There is no memorandum in writing of the alleged agreement sufficient to satisfy the Statute of Frauds.
3. The plaintiff discharged the defendant from all liability by giving time to the principal debtor, the said C D.

128

4. By a deed dated January 18, 1964, made between the plaintiff and the defendant, the plaintiff released the cause of action on which he now sues.

5. Such cause of action, if any, did not accrue within six years, and the defendant will rely on the Limitation Act, 1939.

(*N.B.—Here the first paragraph traverses, the other four
confess and avoid.*)

Reply

1. The plaintiff joins issue with the defendant upon paragraphs 1, 2 and 3 of the Defence.

[*This is a compendious form of traverse which is permitted in a Reply or any subsequent pleading.*]

2. The plaintiff was induced to execute the said release by the fraud of the defendant. Particulars of such fraud are as follows:—(*State them.*)

3. On May 15, 1967, the defendant wrote and signed an acknowledgment that the debt now sued for remained unpaid and due to the plaintiff.

[*Paragraphs 2 and 3 respectively confess and avoid paragraphs 4 and 5 of the Defence. A special Reply is necessary in this case.*]

Besides pleas by way of traverse and pleas by way of confession and avoidance, there were formerly also certain pleas which were called *dilatory pleas*, because they offered a merely formal objection to the proceedings, without presenting any substantial answer to the merits of the action. Such were:

(a) A plea to the jurisdiction, by which the defendant took exception to the jurisdiction of the court to entertain the action. Such an objection is, of course, still possible. It is, however, very seldom met with in practice, owing to the stringent provisions of Order 11, and to the power given to a defendant to apply under Order 12, r. 8, to set aside the service of the writ. Moreover, the defendant waives the objection if, knowing the facts, he enters an unconditional appearance to the writ.

(b) A plea in suspension of the action; a plea which shows some ground for not proceeding in the suit at the present period, and prays that the pleading may be stayed until that ground be removed. The number of these pleas was always small, and none of them was of ordinary occurrence in practice. Their place is now taken by a summons to stay proceedings, on the hearing of which the point is summarily decided.

(c) A plea in abatement; a plea which showed some good reason for abating or quashing the statement of claim on the ground that it was improperly framed, without, at the same time, tending to deny the right of action itself: *e.g.,*

129

the misnomer of a defendant, or the non-joinder of a necessary party. But this plea has long been abolished. The defendant must himself correct the misnomer; and he may, if he thinks fit, take out a summons to have the missing plaintiff or defendant made a party. (See *post*, pp. 193–194.)

In contradistinction to these *dilatory* pleas, traverses and pleas in confession and avoidance were called *peremptory* pleas or *pleas in bar*, because they barred or impugned the right of action altogether.

These three things—traverse, confession and avoidance, and objection in point of law—must be kept clear and distinct. The pleader may adopt any one or two or all three of these methods of pleading, so long as he makes it quite clear which he is adopting. The object of a traverse is merely to compel the opposite party to prove his allegations true in fact; it does not dispute their sufficiency in point of law. If either party desires to object to his opponent's pleading in point of law, he must do so clearly and distinctly by way of objection. A plea, which may be either a traverse or an objection, is embarrassing and will be struck out.[3]

Moreover, an objection in point of law can only be raised where the fault of which you desire to take advantage is apparent on the face of the pleading to which you object. You cannot state new facts in your own pleading or on affidavit, and then contend that the result of the combination is to show that your opponent is wrong in his law. It is the province of a plea in confession and avoidance to state new facts which put your opponent out of court.

Illustrations

If in a statement of claim facts be alleged " by reason whereof the plaintiff became seised, etc." or " the defendant became liable, etc." the defendant must not traverse, denying that " by reason thereof, etc." For if he intends to question the facts from which the seisin or liability is deduced, he should traverse these facts and them only; if he disputes the legal inference drawn from the facts, then the proper course is for him to object; or he may do both, if he keeps the two defences clear and distinct.

Priddle and Napper's Case (1613) 11 Rep. 8, 10.

In an action of covenant, the plaintiff set out a deed which contained a recital that the plaintiff was the inventor of certain looms, and had given the defendants permission to use them in consideration of their paying him certain moneys. The defendants pleaded that the plaintiff was not the true inventor. To this plea the plaintiff should have replied specially, setting up the recital by way of

---

[3] *Stokes* v. *Grant* (1878) 4 C.P.D. 25.

estoppel, as the defendants were estopped from denying the statement made in the deed which they had executed. Instead of doing this, he took issue in fact on the plea. It was held that in that state of the record the defendants were not estopped by the recital of the deed from proving that the plaintiff was not the true inventor. The plaintiff had in fact waived the estoppel by his bad pleading.

> *Bowman* v. *Rostron* (1835) 2 A. & E. 295,n.

So, too, a traverse cannot be made to do the work of a plea in confession and avoidance. Its office is to contradict, not to excuse. Matters justifying an act must not be insinuated into a plea which denies the act. " All matters in confession and avoidance shall be pleaded specially." [4]

As a general rule [5] the burden will lie on your opponent to prove at the trial the facts which you have traversed; but the burden will lie on you to prove the facts which you have alleged by way of confession and avoidance. And you will not be allowed to shift the onus of proof by traversing when you should confess and avoid, even where your opponent has given you the opportunity by introducing an unnecessary averment into the preceding pleading.

Illustrations

A statement of claim in libel or slander always alleges that " the defendant falsely and maliciously wrote [*or* ' spoke '] and published the words." Yet the defendant may not plead " the defendant never wrote [*or* ' spoke '] or published the said words falsely or maliciously or at all." For this, while apparently merely a denial of the fact of publication, is also an insinuation that the words are true, and that the occasion of publication is privileged. It is in fact a traverse and two pleas in confession and avoidance all rolled into one. It is for the plaintiff to prove the publication, and for the defendant to prove truth or privilege.

> *Belt* v. *Lawes* (1882) 51 L.J.Q.B. 359.

And see Precedent No. 80.

So in an action against the master for the dismissal of his servant, the statement of claim will certainly allege that the defendant *wrongfully* dismissed the plaintiff from his employ. But the defendant ought not to traverse this allegation in its entirety. To plead " The defendant never wrongfully dismissed the plaintiff " would be bad pleading; for it is ambiguous. Does it mean " The defendant never in fact dismissed the plaintiff " or " The defendant had a right to dismiss the plaintiff and therefore did so "? The defendant may plead both defences or either, so long as he makes his meaning clear. He may traverse the fact of dismissal, if he wishes. He may go on to justify the dismissal by showing that the plaintiff was guilty of misconduct which entitled the defendant to dismiss him. This would be a plea in confession and avoidance, and it should state the particular acts of misconduct on which the defendant relies as justifying

---

[4] Pleading Rules of Hilary Term, 1853, rr. 12, 17. Now see Ord. 18, r. 8, *post*, pp. 144–145.　　　　[5] But see *post*, pp. 291–292.

the dismissal (*ante*, pp. 123, 124). It is for the plaintiff to prove the dismissal; and for the defendant to show that it was justified.

Lush v. *Russell* (1850) 5 Ex. 203; 19 L.J.Ex. 214.

Horton v. *McMurtry* (1860) 5 H. & N. 667; 29 L.J.Ex. 260.

TRAVERSES

A traverse is the express contradiction of an allegation of fact in an opponent's pleading; it is generally a contradiction in the very terms of the allegation. It is, as a rule, framed in the negative, because the fact which it denies is, as a rule, alleged in the affirmative.

As to traverses, there are two fundamental rules, the object of which is to compel each party in his turn to admit frankly, or deny fully, each allegation of fact in the pleading of his opponent:

I. ANY ALLEGATION OF FACT MADE BY A PARTY IN HIS PLEADING IS DEEMED TO BE ADMITTED BY THE OPPOSITE PARTY UNLESS IT IS TRAVERSED BY THAT PARTY IN HIS PLEADING OR A JOINDER OF ISSUE UNDER RULE 14 OPERATES AS A DENIAL OF IT.[6] (Order 18, r. 13 (1).)

II. EVERY ALLEGATION OF FACT MADE IN A STATEMENT OF CLAIM OR COUNTERCLAIM WHICH THE PARTY ON WHOM IT IS SERVED DOES NOT INTEND TO ADMIT MUST BE SPECIFICALLY TRAVERSED BY HIM IN HIS DEFENCE OR DEFENCE TO COUNTERCLAIM, AS THE CASE MAY BE; AND A GENERAL DENIAL OF SUCH ALLEGATIONS, OR A GENERAL STATEMENT OF NON-ADMISSION OF THEM, IS NOT A SUFFICIENT TRAVERSE OF THEM. (Order 18, r. 13 (3).)

Due observance of these rules will speedily bring the parties to a definite issue.

Note, first, that only allegations of fact should be denied. If your opponent pleads matter of law, you should not traverse it.

Illustrations

In an action of trespass for fishing in the plaintiff's fishery, the defendant pleaded that the *locus in quo* was an arm of the sea, in which every subject of the realm had the liberty and privilege of free fishing; and the plaintiff, in his replication, denied that in the said arm of the sea every subject of the realm had the liberty and privilege of free fishing. This was held to be a traverse of a mere inference of law, and therefore bad.

Richardson v. *Mayor of Orford* (1793) 2 H.Bl. 182.

So where, in an action for improperly removing a wall, the plaintiff alleged that it was the defendant's duty to have taken proper precautions in pulling it down so as not to injure an adjoining vault of the plaintiff; and the defendant pleaded by way of traverse that it was not his duty to have taken any precautions; this was held a bad plea.

Trower v. *Chadwick* (1836) 3 Bing. N.C. 334; 3 Scott 699.

---

[6] An admission is not however to be implied from the pleading of a person under a disability. (Ord. 80, r. 8.)

Formerly, any other matters which were not fit subjects of traverse (see *ante*, p. 109) were not taken to be admitted by the defendant's "pleading over" (*i.e.*, by his omitting all reference to them in his pleading). In particular it was held wrong to plead to matters introduced under a *videlicet* (see *King* v. *Norman* (1847) 4 C.B. 884; 17 L.J.C.P. 23). Now, however, in view of Order 18, r. 13 (1), a defendant may be running a risk if he passes over in silence subsidiary allegations which he deems immaterial, or the "matters of inducement" (*post*, p. 176) which are often set out in the introductory paragraphs of a long pleading. They may, however, conveniently be dealt with by a denial of the matter "as alleged or at all" or of "each of the allegations in paragraph 1 of the statement of claim," or as the case may be; but the vital allegations must be dealt with specifically, pleading to the point of substance (*post*, pp. 140, 195–196). Damages and their amount are always in issue unless expressly admitted [7]; do not therefore plead to them unless you wish to make some admission. Nor should you plead to the prayer or claim for relief at the end of your opponent's pleading. Nor need you plead to particulars (but see *post*, pp. 196–197). Neither party should traverse matter not alleged; he should be content to answer the case that is actually laid against him, not that which he thinks his opponent meant or ought to have raised.

Illustrations

Action against an administratrix founded on a promise made by the intestate. Defence: "The defendant (*i.e.*, the administratrix, not the intestate) never promised as alleged." This was held to be obviously immaterial and bad.
    Anon., 2 Vent. 196.
    Rassam v. *Budge* [1893] 1 Q.B. 571; 62 L.J.Q.B. 312.
    It is quite unnecessary to plead: "The particulars delivered by the plaintiff in pursuance of the order of Master ——, dated July 2, 1970, are insufficient to enable the defendant to check the prices of the items charged for." Plead boldly: "The defendant never agreed to pay the plaintiff the prices which he has charged for the said work, labour and materials. Such prices are unreasonable and exorbitant."
    In an action of debt on a bond conditioned for the payment of £1,550, the defendant pleaded that "part of the sum mentioned in the condition, *to wit*, £1,500, was won by gaming, contrary to the statute in such case made and provided," and that the bond was consequently void. The plaintiff, in his replication, denied that £1,500 was won by gaming as alleged. The court was of opinion that the material part of the plea was that part of the money for which the bond was given was won by gambling; that the words "to wit, £1,500," were only form, of which the replication ought not to have taken notice; and

---

[7] Ord. 18, r. 13 (4). And see *post*, p. 197.

that the replication was ill, because it put the precise sum in issue, and tended to oblige the defendant to prove that the whole £1,500 was won by gaming; whereas the statute avoids the bond if any part of the consideration be on that account." The proper replication would have been: " No part of the sum mentioned in the condition was won by gaming."

Colborne v. *Stockdale* (1722) 1 Stra. 493.

I. *Any allegation of Fact unless traversed is admitted*

The pleader must either admit or deny every material allegation of fact in the pleading of his opponent: and he must make it absolutely clear which facts he admits and which he denies. To ensure this, rule 13 provides that any allegation of fact is deemed to be admitted unless traversed and that a traverse may be made either by a denial or by a statement of non-admission and either expressly or by necessary implication. As a rule, the pleader should deny, when the facts are necessarily within his client's own knowledge: other facts which happen *inter alios*, etc., he may refuse to admit.[8] But he must be just as specific in not admitting as in denying [9]; in either case he must leave no uncertainty as to how much or how little he intends to admit.

What is meant by " necessary implication "? Where the traverse of one allegation necessarily and unmistakably traverses another as well, the latter allegation is denied by necessary implication. Since rule 13 (3) requires that every allegation made in a statement of claim or a counterclaim must be " specifically " traversed, if it is not intended to be admitted, it is safer to deny both expressly if there can possibly be any misconception.

In pleadings subsequent to the defence or defence to counterclaim, as the case may be, instead of dealing specifically with every allegation of fact in the preceding pleading the pleader may say that he " joins issue ": he may do so either generally upon the preceding pleading or with the exception of certain facts which he admits. As we shall see (*post*, p. 234), upon " close of pleadings " there is an implied joinder of issue on the pleading last served. A joinder of issue operates as a denial of every material allegation of fact in the preceding pleading which is not expressly admitted. (Order 18, r. 14.) " There can be no joinder of issue on a statement of claim or counterclaim " (r. 14 (3)) and " a general denial of such allegations, or a general statement of non-admission of them,

---

[8] And see *Warner* v. *Sampson* [1959] 1 Q.B. 297.
[9] *Per* Jessel M.R. in *Thorp* v. *Holdsworth* (1876) 3 Ch.D., at p. 640.

is not a sufficient traverse of them " (r. 13 (3)). Care must therefore be taken to deal specifically with *every* material allegation of fact in a claim or counterclaim.

It is in the power of the party either to admit or to deny each allegation in his opponent's plea, as he thinks fit. If he decides to deny it, he must do so clearly and explicitly. Any equivocal or ambiguous phrase will be construed into an admission of it. There is no third or intermediary stage. If the judge does not find in the pleading a specific denial or a definite refusal to admit, there is an end of the matter; the fact stands admitted.

Illustrations

Claim for specific performance of a contract. Defence: " The defendant puts the plaintiffs to proof of the several allegations in their statement of claim." *Held*, when the defendant did not appear at the trial, that all the plaintiffs' allegations were admitted.

Harris v. *Gamble* (1878) 7 Ch.D. 877; 47 L.J.Ch. 344.

Defence: " The defendants do not admit the correctness of " certain allegations in the statement of claim, " and require proof thereof." *Held*, an insufficient denial. The defendants were ordered to state in what respects they disputed these allegations.

Rutter v. *Tregent* (1879) 12 Ch.D. 758; 48 L.J.Ch. 791.

But the words " The defendants deny the facts alleged in paragraph 3 of the statement of claim " used in pleading to a number of highly material allegations were held by the Court of Appeal under the old rules to be a sufficient traverse of those facts, though such pleading was criticised as being drawn " in a loose and irregular form."

Grocott v. *Lovat* [1916] W.N. 317.

But now see Order 18, r. 13 (3), *ante*, p. 132.

Defence: " The terms of the arrangement were never definitely agreed upon as alleged." *Held*, that such a traverse was an evasive denial and that it admitted that an agreement was in fact made as alleged. Jessel M.R.: " The whole object of pleadings is to bring the parties to an issue, and the meaning of the rules of this Order is to prevent the issue being enlarged, which would prevent either party from knowing, when the cause came on for trial, what the real point to be discussed and decided was. . . . The defendant is bound to deny that any agreement or any terms of arrangement were ever come to, if that is what he means: if he does not mean that, he should say that there were no terms of arrangement come to, except the following terms, and then state what those terms were."

Thorp v. *Holdsworth* (1876) 3 Ch.D. 637; 45 L.J.Ch. 406.

If I deny that the defendant was ever tenant to the plaintiff of certain premises, I deny by necessary implication that the plaintiff ever demised those premises to the defendant. But the converse does not hold. The defendant may now be tenant to the plaintiff, although the plaintiff never demised the premises to him. *E.g.*, the plaintiff's ancestor may have demised the premises to the defendant for a long term which is still unexpired.

As the party pleading has a right either to admit or deny, at his option, there is no need for him to apologize for his denial, or to explain why he does not admit the allegation. For instance, it is quite unnecessary for him to plead: "The defendants do not know when the plaintiffs first published the photographs referred to in the second paragraph of the statement of claim and therein alleged to be photographs representing, etc.; and therefore they do not admit that such photographs were first published and circulated by the plaintiffs in or about the month of October, 1954, as in the said paragraph alleged."

How much ought the party pleading to admit, and how much to deny? Clearly it is wrong to deny plain and acknowledged facts, or any fact which it is not to your client's interest to deny. It was intended by the framers of the Judicature Act that each party in his pleading should frankly admit every statement of fact which he does not intend seriously to dispute at the trial. But this intention has not been carried out. Counsel hesitate to make admissions unless they are expressly instructed to do so—which they very seldom are. Solicitors hesitate to instruct counsel to make admissions, because the facts have not yet been thoroughly sifted; they do not feel sure that they have got to the bottom of the case; and they fear something may turn up hereafter which may make them wish to recall the admission.[10] Either party may at any stage of the case apply for judgment on the admissions which have been made by the other side. (Order 27, r. 3.) You must be careful, therefore, how you admit even introductory paragraphs which may appear immaterial; they were probably inserted for some purpose. Besides, it is sometimes desirable to deny a particular fact so as to compel your opponent to call as *his* witness a person whom you wish to cross-examine, or by whose evidence you hope to prove a particular fact essential to your case; you may thus, perhaps, be able to avoid calling witnesses, and so gain the right to the last word.

On the other hand, in actions for debt or liquidated damages the defendant, by omitting to plead any denial or refusal to admit and pleading affirmatively only, may gain the right to begin. Where, however, the action is brought for unliquidated damages, this consideration does not apply; for in that case the plaintiff has always been entitled to begin, even though the burden of proof lies on the defendant. (See *post*, p. 310.)

But as a rule each party should admit whatever facts can be proved against him without trouble. Moreover, it looks weak to deny everything in your opponent's pleading. It suggests that you have no substantial defence to it. " By rashly traversing statements

---

[10] This, in a proper case, can be done (*Hollis* v. *Burton* [1892] 3 Ch. 226).

which are obviously true, much unnecessary expense may be caused." (*Per* Fletcher Moulton L.J. in *Lever Brothers* v. *Associated Newspapers* [1907] 2 K.B. at p. 628.) There was formerly a useful rule [10a] expressly empowering judges and masters to make a special order as to costs occasioned by unreasonable denials. This has been replaced by the general power under Order 62, rr. 3 and 4, to deal at any stage with any part of the costs incidental to any proceedings. This power should be remembered. Further, by Order 25, r. 4, at the hearing of the Summons for Directions the master must endeavour to secure that the parties make all admissions which ought reasonably to be made. When faced by what seems to be an unreasonable denial it may be prudent to serve a formal notice to admit facts. (See *post*, p. 270.)

There is one case in which it is shameful not to make a proper admission. If your opponent relies on a written document, he will either set out the words of the document in his pleading, or he will state shortly its effect. In the latter case, as your construction of the document will probably differ from his, it is quite legitimate to traverse his version of its effect. But if he sets out the actual words correctly, it is slovenly work to plead, as was sometimes done: " The defendant does not admit that the terms of the said indenture are sufficiently or correctly set forth in paragraph 4 of the statement of claim, and craves leave to refer to the original thereof at the trial for greater certainty as to its terms and effect." Why " crave leave " to do that which you have now an absolute right to do? " Any party to a cause or matter shall be entitled at any time to serve a notice on any other party in whose pleadings or affidavits reference is made to any document requiring him to produce that document for the inspection of the party giving the notice and to permit him to take copies thereof." (Order 24, r. 10.) Obtain a copy of the document under this rule, if you have not one already, and see if its terms are or are not correctly stated by your opponent. If they are, admit that they are, adding such other portions as you yourself rely on. If they are not, then set them out correctly yourself, if you deem them material. One may suspect that the man who " craves leave " is perfectly familiar with the contents of the document all the time.

[10a] R.S.C. 1883, Ord. XXI, r. 9.

II. *Denials must be Specific*

It is not sufficient for a defendant in his defence to deny generally the allegations in the statement of claim, or for a plaintiff in his reply to deny generally the allegations in a counterclaim, but each party must traverse specifically each allegation of fact which he does not intend to admit. The party pleading must make it quite clear how much of his opponent's case he disputes. Sometimes, in order to obey the rule and to deal specifically with every allegation of fact of which he does not admit the truth, it is necessary for him to place on the record two or more distinct traverses to one and the same allegation. Merely to deny the allegation in terms will often be ambiguous.

Illustrations

Claim: " The defendant broke and entered the close of the plaintiff " [*specifying it*]. If the defendant pleads: " The defendant never broke or entered the close of the plaintiff," the more obvious meaning of this allegation is that he never broke or entered the close which the plaintiff claims as his; but it may be that his case is that the close specified does not belong to the plaintiff. The words are capable of that meaning; and if such ambiguity were permitted, pleadings would lose their utility. If the defendant intends at the trial to deny the plaintiff's possession or right to possession of the close in question, he must say so distinctly. A literal traverse of the words of the claim will be taken to deny merely that the defendant, in fact, broke and entered that close. If, then, the defendant desires to raise both defences—to deny both the act complained of and the plaintiff's title to the land—he must put on the record two separate paragraphs, *e.g.*:—

" 1. The defendant never broke or entered the said close."

" 2. The said close is not the plaintiff's close."

Pleading Rules of Hilary Term, 1853, r. 19.

In an action of trover, detinue or trespass to goods, the defendant is similarly required to deny specifically that the goods were the property of the plaintiff. A mere traverse of the conversion, detention or trespass will be taken as denying merely the acts complained of.

Pleading Rules of Hilary Term, 1853, rr. 15, 20.

Again, if the plaintiff alleges that " the said A B executed the said deed on behalf of the defendant, as his agent, acting under a power of attorney duly signed by the defendant," the defendant must not plead " The defendant denies that the said A B executed the said deed on behalf of the defendant, as his agent, under a power of attorney duly signed by the defendant." If he wishes to traverse the whole allegation he must plead:—

" 1. The said A B never executed the said deed.

" 2. The said A B never executed the said deed on behalf of the defendant, or as his agent.

" 3. The defendant never signed any such power of attorney as alleged, nor did A B ever act thereunder."

Otherwise it would not be clear how much of the plaintiff's allegation the defendant really denies.

So, if the defendant says that he never seduced the plaintiff's servant, this will be taken as a denial of the act of seduction. The defence that the girl seduced was not the plaintiff's servant must be specially pleaded.

Torrence v. *Gibbins* (1843) 5 Q.B. 297; 13 L.J.Q.B. 36.

Whenever the cause of action depends on the plaintiff's holding a certain office, or carrying on a profession or trade, the defendant must always specifically deny that the plaintiff had held that office or carried on that profession or trade at date of writ, if such be the fact.

Gallwey v. *Marshall* (1854) 8 Ex. 300; 23 L.J.Ex. 78.

If either party wishes to deny the right of any other party to claim as executor, or as trustee whether in bankruptcy or otherwise, or in any representative or other alleged capacity, or the alleged constitution of any partnership firm, he should deny the same specifically.

Furthermore (as was explicitly stated in the old rules) a traverse must not be evasive, but must answer the point of substance; otherwise it will be liable to be struck out under Order 18, r. 19,[11] as embarrassing. It must be neither too large nor too narrow. The pleader must deny enough and not too much.

Illustrations

If it be alleged that the defendant received a certain sum of money, it will not be sufficient for him to deny that he received that particular amount, but he must deny that he received that sum or any part thereof, or else set out how much he received.

Rules of the Supreme Court, 1883, Order XIX, r. 19.[11a]

The plaintiff alleged that his agent, the defendant, had not handed over to him certain rents which he had received from the plaintiff's tenants. Defence: " The defendant has handed over to the plaintiff all the rent which he has received from the plaintiff's tenants." This is a bad traverse, though it is in the very words of the claim. It is not clear whether the defendant has received all the rent due or part or none of it. He must state whether he has received any, and, if any, how much rent, and what amount he handed over to the plaintiff, and when.

Kennett v. *Mundy*, Judge at Chambers (not reported).

How should a defendant traverse this statement: " The premises were handed over in an unfinished condition "? If he says, " The defendant denies that the premises were handed over in an unfinished condition," this may mean that the premises have never yet been handed over at all. A similar objection will apply if he pleads: " The premises were not handed over in an unfinished condition." The right traverse is: " The premises were finished when handed over."

Dangers of a literal Traverse

Do not traverse too literally in an effort to be specific. It is sufficient to answer the point of substance. A traverse may become evasive, if it follows too closely the precise language of the allegations traversed.

---

[11] See *post*, p. 152.
[11a] See now Order 18, r. 13.

(i) By traversing too literally you may fall into the vice of pleading " a negative pregnant." A negative pregnant is such a form of negative expression as may imply or carry within it an affirmative proposition. It is therefore evasive and ambiguous, and must not be used.

Illustrations

A statement of claim alleged that the defendant offered the plaintiff a bribe of £500. The defendant pleaded " that he had never offered the plaintiff a bribe of £500 "; which would have been true if he had offered £400 or any sum other than £500. Such a denial half admits the main allegation that a bribe of some kind had been offered. It is therefore an unfair and evasive denial. The defendant should have pleaded that he never offered a bribe of £500 or any other sum.

> *Tildesley* v. *Harper* (1878) 7 Ch.D. 403; 47 L.J.Ch. 263; (C.A.) 10 Ch.D. 393; 48 L.J.Ch. 495.
> *Colborne* v. *Stockdale* (1722) 1 Stra. 493, *ante*, pp. 133–134.

In an action of trespass the plaintiff claimed damages for the defendant's entering his house. The defendant pleaded that the plaintiff's daughter gave him licence to do so; and that he entered by that licence. The plaintiff replied that the defendant *did not enter by her licence*. This was considered as a *negative pregnant*; for the pleading left it in doubt whether the plaintiff meant that there never was a licence, or that the defendant did not enter by virtue of it. And it was held that the plaintiff should have traversed the entry by itself, or the licence by itself, and not both together.

> *Myn* v. *Cole* (1606) Cro.Jac. 87.

Action for assault and battery by a sailor against the master of his ship. The defendant justified, saying that he bade the plaintiff do some service in the ship, but the plaintiff refused; wherefore the defendant moderately chastised him. The plaintiff replied that the defendant did not moderately chastise him. And this traverse was held to be a negative pregnant; for it might mean either that the defendant did not chastise the plaintiff at all, or that he chastised him immoderately, and was therefore ambiguous.

> *Auberie* v. *James* (1682) Vent. 70; 1 Sid. 444; 2 Keb. 623.
> And *cf. Pinson* v. *Lloyds, etc., Bank, Ltd.* [1941] 2 K.B. 72, *post*, p. 166.

(ii) Again, there may be many details which were properly introduced into your opponent's pleading, but which it is misleading for you to include in your traverse. By so doing you may raise false issues, and so evade the point of substance. To a denial of the main allegation the addition of the words " as alleged or at all " will often cure this defect.

Illustrations

" If an allegation is made with divers circumstances, it shall not be sufficient to deny it along with those circumstances."

> Rules of the Supreme Court, 1883, Order XIX, r. 19.[11b]

[11b] This rule has been revoked and is now replaced by Order 18, r. 13 (3), (*ante*, p. 132) which is no doubt intended to have precisely the same effect. However, the old, more specific rules still provide many such excellent precepts of good pleading.

The plaintiff pleaded that the Queen, at a manor court held on such a day, by J S, her steward, and by copy of court roll, etc., granted certain land to A. The defendant traversed this allegation *totidem verbis*; he pleaded " that the Queen had not, at a manor court held on such a day, by J S, her steward, and by copy of court roll, granted the said lands to A." The court held that this was a bad traverse. " The Queen never granted the said lands to A " would have been sufficient; for the plaintiff was not bound to prove a grant on any particular day, or by any particular steward.

   Lane v. *Alexander* (1608) Yelv. 122.

If the plaintiff, in an action for wages, alleges that he had served the defendant as a hired servant from March 25, 1968, to June 24, 1969, at Epsom, in the county of Surrey, it would be a bad traverse for the defendant to plead: " The plaintiff did not serve the defendant as a hired servant from March 25, 1968, to June 24, 1969, at Epsom, in the county of Surrey." The defendant must either deny that the plaintiff ever served him at all, or else state for how long he admits the plaintiff did serve him. And he must not traverse the place, unless it is material; but if he does he must say that the plaintiff did not serve him at Epsom " or in any other place."

   Doctrina Placitandi, 360.
   Osborne v. *Rogers* (1682) 1 Wms.Saund. 267.
   Alsager v. *Currie* (1843) 11 M. & W. 14.

To a statement of claim alleging that " the defendant in or about Michaelmas, 1968, called upon several of the plaintiff's tenants at the premises, Nos. 43, 45 and 47 Baynham Street, Camden Town, and spoke and published to them " a slander on the plaintiff's title, it is sufficient to plead, " The defendant never spoke or published the said words," for that answers the point of substance. You may add, if you think it worth while, " nor did he call upon any of the plaintiff's tenants," though this may be considered to be mere matter of inducement denied by implication. To plead that the defendant did not call on several of the plaintiff's tenants, etc., would seem to admit that he called on one or two of them; and to deny that he spoke the words to any of the plaintiff's tenants would be consistent with having spoken them to someone not a tenant of the plaintiff, which might be equally actionable.

(iii) If your opponent's allegation be in the *conjunctive*, you must plead to it in the *disjunctive*; otherwise your traverse may be too large; for it is seldom, if ever, necessary for your opponent to prove at the trial the whole of his allegation precisely as he has pleaded it. In other words, when traversing, remember always to turn " and " into " or," and " all " into " any."

Illustrations

Claim: " The defendants broke and entered the plaintiff's close and depastured the same with sheep and cattle." The proper traverse is: " *Neither* defendant broke *or* entered the plaintiff's close *or* depastured the same with *any* sheep or cattle."

In an action on a policy of insurance, the plaintiff averred " that the ship insured did not arrive in safety; but that the said ship, tackle, apparel, ordnance, munition, artillery, boat and other furniture were sunk and destroyed in the said voyage." The defendant pleaded, denying " that the said ship, tackle, apparel, ordnance, munition, artillery, boat and other furniture were sunk and destroyed in the voyage, in manner and form as alleged." This was held a bad traverse; the defendant ought to have pleaded disjunctively, denying that the ship, *or* tackle, *or* apparel, etc., was sunk or destroyed; because the plaintiff was entitled to recover compensation for anything that was insured and had been lost.

> *Goram* v. *Sweeting* (1682) 2 Wms.Saund. 205.
> *Moore* v. *Boulcott* (1834) 1 Bing.N.C. 323.

See other instances of a traverse being too large—
> *Basan* v. *Arnold* (1840) 6 M. & W. 559.
> *De Medina* v. *Norman* (1842) 9 M. & W. 820.
> *Dawson* v. *Wrench* (1849) 3 Ex. 359; 18 L.J.Ex. 229.
> *Aldis* v. *Mason* (1851) 11 C.B. 132; 20 L.J.C.P. 193.

As to traverses which have been held not too large, see—
> *Palmer* v. *Gooden* (1841) 8 M. & W. 890.
> *Eden* v. *Turtle* (1842) 10 M. & W. 635.

How far should the pleader confine himself to merely traversing? Should he not, after denying his opponent's story, go on to add his own version of the matter?

This is sometimes a difficult question. The pleader must use his own discretion. It is sometimes most desirable to do so, in order to show clearly what is the real point in dispute.[12] If, for instance, a plaintiff in his statement of claim sets out or refers to certain clauses of a written contract on which he relies, the defendant should certainly set out or refer to other clauses, if any, which tell in his favour. Again, if the plaintiff gives his version of the effect of a written document, it will certainly tend to clear the matter up if the defendant, instead of merely denying the plaintiff's version, states also his own construction of the document. And in many cases it may be desirable for a defendant thus to state definitely which his exact contention is. But by so doing he necessarily somewhat limits his case at the trial. He has no longer the same free hand. And there is this further danger, that if the defendant, instead of merely denying, sets up an affirmative case as well, both judge and jury will expect him to prove his affirmative case, and are apt to find against him if he does not. The onus of proof is not really shifted by such a method of pleading.[13] But if, when accused of a tort, the defendant pleads, "It was A who did it, not I," the judge may be inclined to treat this as an admission that either A or the defendant did it, and to conclude that if the defendant cannot prove his assertion that A did it, he must have done it himself.

---

[12] See the judgment of Jessel M.R. in *Thorp* v. *Holdsworth*, part of which is quoted *ante*, p. 135.
[13] *Kilgour* v. *Alexander* (1860) 14 Moore 177.

Illustrations

If the defendant's real case is that he was not guilty of any negligence himself, it may be unwise for him to plead that there was contributory negligence on the part of the plaintiff.

If the defendant's case is that the plaintiff is not seised in fee, he need not state who *is* seised in fee, of the land.

> *Bradshaw's Case* (1613) 9 Rep. 60 b.
> *Argent* v. *Durrant* (1799) 8 T.R. 403, *post*, p. 146.

Where the defendants were sued as sheriffs of London for allowing a debtor, Robinson, to escape, they pleaded that it was their predecessors in office who had allowed Robinson to escape. This was held a bad plea, because it neither traversed nor confessed the allegation that the defendants had allowed Robinson to escape. They should have merely denied the act attributed to themselves, and not have set up affirmatively that others were guilty of it.

> *Mynours* v. *Turke and Yorke* (1550) 1 Dyer 66 b.

Action for breach of copyright under the Copyright Act, 1842 (now repealed). The plaintiff alleged that his song had been duly registered according to the Copyright Act. The defendant pleaded, " The defendant denies that the said song has been duly registered; the date of the first publication thereof is not truly entered." Had he not added the latter clause, he might have won the action; as it was, he failed. For it turned out at the trial that the date of publication was truly entered, but the name of the publisher was not. The Act required both to be truly stated; hence the song had not in fact been duly registered. But Fry J. thought that it was not open to the defendant to raise this point; he held that the manner in which the defendant had pleaded was, in effect, " an admission that, in every respect but that one which was mentioned, the registration was duly effected." And he refused leave to amend.

> *Collette* v. *Goode* (1878) 7 Ch.D. 842; 47 L.J.Ch. 370.

So where a plaintiff alleged that H " agreed by writing under the hand of his agent thereunto lawfully authorised," the defendant pleaded that " H never agreed by writing under the hand of any agent thereunto lawfully authorised," but added that " H was of unsound mind, and therefore could not lawfully authorise any agent." It was held that this addition limited the preceding general words, so that H's unsoundness of mind was the only substantial issue raised; and that if H was of sound mind, the defendant could not go into other matters to show that in fact H never authorised anyone to sign this agreement; because " the denial, being justified by a fact specifically alleged and no other, must be taken to refer to that fact alone."

> *Byrd* v. *Nunn* (1877) 5 Ch.D. 781; (C.A.) 7 Ch.D. 284; 47 L.J.Ch. 1.
> *Cf. Harris* v. *Mantle* (1789) 3 T.R. 307, *post*, p. 180.
> *Angerstein* v. *Handson* (1835) 1 Cr.M. & R. 789, *post*, p. 161.

MATTERS IN CONFESSION AND AVOIDANCE

The party pleading is often willing to admit that the facts alleged by his opponent are so far true, and that they make out a good prima facie case or defence. But he desires to destroy the effect of these allegations either by showing some justification or excuse of the matter charged against him, or some discharge or release from it. A defendant, for instance, may seek to show on the one hand that the plaintiff never had any right of action, because the act charged was under the circumstances justifiable; or on the other that, though the plaintiff once had a right of action, it has been discharged or released by some matter subsequent. In either case, he confesses the truth of the allegation which he proceeds to answer or avoid. Hence such defences are called *pleas in confession and avoidance.*

The effect of such admission, if it stand alone, is extremely strong; for it concludes the party making it, even though the jury should improperly go out of the issue, and find the contrary of what is thus confessed on the record.[14] At the same time, the confession operates only to prevent the fact from being brought into question in the same suit; it is not conclusive as to the truth of that fact in any subsequent action between the same parties. And, even in the same suit, it will not be conclusive, if the party pleading also traverses the facts confessed, as he may do now.

Illustrations

Action of assault. Defence that the defendant did the acts complained of in necessary self-defence. This is a plea in confession and avoidance; for it admits the assault while it justifies it.

Similarly, in an action of libel, a plea that the words are true or that they were published on a privileged occasion, if it stands alone, admits that the defendant published the words of the plaintiff, but justifies or excuses the act.

To plead that the defendant has a lien on certain goods admits that the goods are the plaintiff's, and that the defendant detains them from him.

And generally in any action of tort if the defendant admits the act complained of, but desires to show that it was not wrongful or no breach of duty, he must plead such justification specially by way of confession and avoidance.

Frankum v. *Lord Falmouth* (1835) 2 A. & E. 452; 4 N. & M. 330.
Lush v. *Russell* (1850) 5 Ex. 203; 19 L.J.Ex. 214.

On the other hand, pleas of tender, of payment or set-off, of waiver or accord and satisfaction, or laches or of the Limitation Act, admit that the plaintiff once had a cause of action, but assert that it is now lost, suspended or discharged.

All matter in confession and avoidance must be pleaded specially. The pleader must not attempt to insinuate it under an apparent traverse; he should state it clearly and distinctly and in a separate paragraph. At the same time, he should not confess and avoid where a mere traverse is sufficient. For he will thus introduce collateral matter which his client may have to prove, instead of putting the plaintiff to proof of his allegations.

The rule on this subject (Order 18, r. 8 (1)) is as follows:

---

[14] *Hewitt* v. *Macquire* (1851) 7 Ex. 80.

" A party must in any pleading subsequent to a statement of claim plead specifically any matter, for example, performance, release, any relevant statute of limitation, fraud or any fact showing illegality—

(a) which he alleges makes any claim or defence of the opposite party not maintainable; or

(b) which, if not specifically pleaded, might take the opposite party by surprise; or

(c) which raises issues of fact not arising out of the preceding pleading."

This rule, like the corresponding rule of 1883, " is not confined . . . to a case where a statute is the thing to be pleaded; it applies to all cases of grounds of defence or reply which if not raised would be likely to take the opposite party by surprise or raise issues of fact not arising out of the pleadings. Where the defendant ought to plead things of that sort, the rule does not say that if he does not the court shall adjudicate upon the matter as if a ground valid in law did not exist which does exist. If in the course of the proceedings it was proved that the deed sued upon was a forgery and the defendant does not plead it or did not know it was a forgery, the court would not give judgment upon the deed on the footing that it was a valid deed. The effect of the rule is, I think, for reasons of practice and justice and convenience to require the party to tell his opponent what he is coming to the court to prove. If he does not do that, the court will deal with it in one of two ways. It may say that it is not open to him, that he has not raised it and will not be allowed to rely on it; or it may give him leave to amend by raising it, and protect the other party if necessary by letting the case stand over. The rule is not one that excludes from the consideration of the court the relevant subject-matter for decision simply on the ground that it is not pleaded. It leaves the party in mercy and the court will deal with him as is just." (*Per* Buckley L.J., in *Re Robinson's Settlement, Gant* v. *Hobbs* [1912] 1 Ch., at pp. 727, 728.)

Illustrations

If a defendant merely pleads that " he never agreed as alleged," he cannot insist at the trial that though a contract was made as alleged it is invalid in point of law; for this must form the subject of a special allegation, showing the circumstances out of which the illegality arose.

Order 18, r. 8 (1).

And see *Belt* v. *Lawes* (1882) 51 L.J.Q.B. 359, *ante*, p. 131.

Potts v. *Sparrow* (1835) 1 Bing.N.C. 594.

The plaintiff alleged the negligent provision of an unsafe tool; the defendant traversed the alleged negligence. The plaintiff came to trial prepared to prove the defects in the tool, when it appeared that the real defence was that it had been bought from a reputable supplier and that there was no duty to test or examine it. *Held*, that this was a matter of surprise which should have been specially pleaded. Leave to amend and an adjournment were granted at the defendant's expense.

> *Davie* v. *New Merton Board Mills* [1956] 1 All E.R. 379; [1956] 1 W.L.R. 233.

Under a bare traverse of negligence a defendant may prove facts showing that the accident happened inevitably—*e.g.*, from the shying of a horse without the driver's negligence—where it is obvious from the circumstances that such a defence may arise and there is no surprise.

> *Rumbold* v. *L.C.C.* (1909) 25 T.L.R. 541.

But a particular vice in a horse or latent defect in a machine relied on to support a defence of inevitable accident should be specially pleaded.

If in answer to a charge of cruelty a party intends not merely to deny the commission of acts of cruelty but to suggest that there was consent to what was done, this should be specifically pleaded.

> *Porr* v. *Porr* [1963] 1 W.L.R. 98.

Contributory negligence must be specially pleaded.

> *The Pleiades* v. *Page* [1891] A.C. 259; 60 L.J.P.C. 59.

Fraud, if material, must be specially pleaded. In an action on a bill of exchange the defendant pleaded that the plaintiff was not a bona fide holder for value. It was held that he could not under that plea raise the question of his being privy to a fraud. The only question on such an issue will be, did he give value for the bill?

> *Uther* v. *Rich* (1839) 10 A. & E. 784; 2 P. & D. 579.

But where facts have to be established by the evidence of a party, it may be permissible to challenge his veracity by cross-examination even to the extent of showing his conduct in the transaction in question to have been fraudulent without having pleaded fraud.

> *Wintle* v. *Nye* [1959] 1 W.L.R. 284 at p. 294 (H.L.).

In an action of trespass for breaking and entering the plaintiff's close, the defendant pleaded that the plaintiff demised the close to him for a term of years, by virtue whereof he entered and committed the supposed trespass. This is a good plea in confession and avoidance, for it admits the plaintiff's title, subject to the effect of the demise.

> *Leyfield's Case* (1611) 10 Rep. 91a; 3 Salk. 273.

Action of trespass for breaking and entering plaintiff's close. Defence that J S was seised in fee of the close and demised it to the defendant for a term of years by virtue whereof he entered, which is the alleged trespass. This was held a bad plea. A traverse denying that the close was the plaintiff's was all that was necessary.

> *Argent* v. *Durrant* (1799) 8 T.R. 403.

For illustrations of confession and avoidance in a reply, see pp. 230–231.

In confessing and avoiding, as in traversing, the plea must be neither too wide nor too narrow. It must be as broad and as long as the claim to which it is pleaded and justify or excuse the whole of it; or, if it be intended to apply to part only of such claim, it must be limited accordingly by a prefix " As to so much of the statement of claim as alleges, etc.," or " As to paragraph 4 of the statement of claim." Be careful not to make too wide an averment, whereby you will take on your shoulders an unnecessary burden, or too narrow an averment, which will fetter your hands at the trial.

Illustrations

In an action for slander in these words, " Woor says that M'Pherson is insolvent," it would be insufficient to plead that Woor had in fact said so; the defendant must allege and prove not merely what Woor said but also that what he said was true.

> *M'Pherson* v. *Daniels* (1829) 10 B. & C. 263; 5 M. & R. 251.
> *Duncan* v. *Thwaites* (1824) 3 B. & C. 556; 5 D. & R. 447.

In a plea of privilege it is unwise to allege that the defendant had just and reasonable grounds for believing the charges made against the plaintiff to be true. Such an averment may be intended only as a corollary to a plea of privilege (in which case it would be far better to plead that " the defendant acted bona fide and without any malice toward the plaintiff "); but it runs dangerously near to a justification, and will either be struck out as immaterial (*Cave* v. *Torre* (1886) 54 L.T. 87, 515), or particulars will be ordered of the grounds of such belief.

> *Fitzgerald* v. *Campbell* (1866) 18 Ir.Jur. 153.
> But see *Roberts* v. *Owen* (1890) 6 T.L.R. 172, *post*, p. 166.
> *Alman* v. *Oppert* [1901] 2 K.B. 576; 70 L.J.K.B. 745, *post*, p. 158.

In pleading the Statute of Frauds it is not necessary to plead any particular section; if you do, you may not be allowed to rely upon a different one.

> *James* v. *Smith* [1891] 1 Ch. 384; followed in
> *Hills & Grant, Ltd.* v. *Hodson* [1934] Ch. 53; 103 L.J.Ch. 17.

OBJECTION IN POINT OF LAW

Either party may object to the pleading of the opposite party on the ground that it does not set forth a sufficient ground of action, defence or reply, as the case may be. Such an objection can only be raised where the fault is apparent on the face of the pleading; and the fault must be something more than a mere imperfection, omission or defect in *form*.

Demurrers were abolished in 1883.[15] But it was desirable, and indeed necessary, to preserve some form of objection in point of law, otherwise parties might incur great expense in trying issues of fact which, when decided, would not determine their rights. So it was provided that any party should be entitled to raise by his pleading any point of law (Order 18, r. 11). In some cases this is better left to be disposed of by the judge at the trial. But the master

---

[15] *Special demurrers*, as they were called, *i.e.*, mere objections to the *form* of an opponent's pleading, were entirely abolished by the Common Law Procedure Act, 1852, section 50 of which provided that " on such demurrer the court shall proceed and give judgment according as the very right on the cause and matter in law shall appear unto them, without regarding any imperfection, omission, defect in, or lack of, form."

has a discretion to order that such a point [16] (and also any issue of fact, see *ante*, p. 81) be tried separately (Order 33, rr. 3 and 4 (2)). He may order it to be set down as a preliminary point and may, if he thinks it right, stay other proceedings meanwhile, thus saving the parties the expense of a possibly elaborate contest on the facts and the discovery incidental to it. When the point is decided, if it substantially disposes of the action, judgment may be given accordingly or whatever other order is appropriate may be made (rule 7).

When the matter is one of first impression, or when for any other reason the law on the point is not clear, it may be very desirable to argue an objection and settle the point of law before incurring the expense of a trial with witnesses. But in ordinary cases it is generally wiser to raise the objection on the pleading but not to apply to have it argued before the trial. The usual result of such an argument is that, if the defendant succeeds, the plaintiff obtains leave, on paying the costs of the argument, to amend his statement of claim; and it is better for the defendant that the plaintiff should be driven to such amendment at the trial. Hence, as a rule, it is best not to apply to have any point of law argued before the trial, unless the objection is one which will dispose of the whole action.

You need not be afraid that, by omitting to apply, you are throwing away a chance of success—that the objection, if not taken at once, cannot be taken afterwards. No doubt slight defects, such as slips of the pen, careless omissions, informal pleading, etc., may sometimes be aided by pleading over, and may often be cured by verdict. But it is never worth while in these days to incur the cost of a motion or summons over some purely formal defect. You should always bear in mind the good advice which that great judge, Sir Edward Coke, deduced as a moral from " the first cause that he ever moved in the King's Bench ":

" When the matter in fact will clearly serve for your client although your opinion is that the plaintiff has no cause of action, yet take heed you do not hazard the matter upon a demurrer, in which, upon the pleading and otherwise, more perhaps will arise

---

[16] Particularly when the point, if decided in one way, should be decisive of litigation (*Everett* v. *Ribbands* [1952] 2 Q.B. 198, 206; *Carl Zeiss Stiftung* v. *Herbert Smith & Co.* [1969] 1 Ch. 93).

than you thought of; but first take advantage of the matters of fact, and leave matters in law, which always arise upon the matters in fact, *ad ultimum*, and never at first demur in law, when, after trial of the matters in fact, the matters in law (as in this case it was) will be saved to you." (*The Lord Cromwell's Case* (1581) 4 Rep., at p. 14.) This advice, though more than three hundred years old, is as sound now as it was in the days of Queen Elizabeth I; in fact, owing to the liberal powers of amendment given by the Judicature Acts, its value has increased rather than diminished. Lindley J. laid down the same rule in *Stokes* v. *Grant* (1878) 4 C.P.D., at p. 28: " If the defendant wants to avail himself of his point of law in a summary way, he must demur; but if he does not demur, he does not waive the objection, and may say at the trial that the claim is bad on the face of it." If then the facts are likely to prove in your favour, you should not, as a rule, apply for a preliminary hearing of the point of law. But if at the trial you will be compelled to admit that you have no case on the merits, then by all means take advantage of any point of law you can.

No one is bound to take an objection in point of law; Order 18, r. 11, merely says that a party *may* raise it by his pleading. At the trial he may urge any point of law he likes, whether raised on the pleadings or not.[17] This was decided on June 10, 1886, by a Divisional Court (Day and Wills JJ.) in the case of *MacDougall* v. *Knight* (not reported on this point). And it was also the law under the former system.[18] The provisions of Order 18, r. 8 (1) (*ante*, pp. 144–145), should, however, be borne in mind. Even in cases not within the four corners of that rule the modern tendency in pleading is to avoid taking an opponent by surprise—a course which may cause embarrassment and inconvenience at the trial.

But if either party desires to have any point of law set down for hearing, and disposed of *before* the trial, he should raise it in his pleading by an objection in point of law. Indeed, where the point of law amounts to a plea in bar such as *res judicata*, it would be the correct procedure.[19] And having regard to the words

---

[17] But it is desirable to plead it, especially when the point is a substantial one which may dispose of the whole action. *Independent Automatic Sales, Ltd.* v. *Knowles & Foster* [1962] 1 W.L.R. 974.

[18] *Per* Lindley J. in *Stokes* v. *Grant, supra.*

[19] *Workington Harbour Board* v. *Trade Indemnity Co., Ltd.* (1937) 43 Com.Cas. 235.

of Order 33, r. 7, it is clearly worth while to raise on the pleadings any point of law which will substantially dispose of the whole action or render the trial unnecessary.[20]

Illustrations

It is a common error to suppose that where a man who has made two wills at different times revokes the second, he thereby revives the first will. Suppose a plaintiff in that belief propounds the first will: the defendant would plead it was revoked by the execution of the second will; the plaintiff would reply that the second will was in its turn revoked. If the defendant joins issue on this, the cause would proceed to trial on an issue of fact which is wholly immaterial: for the revocation of the second will would not (without more) re-establish the first; it would merely leave the testator intestate. The defendant should object that the reply affords no answer to the defence.

Where special damage is essential to the plaintiff's cause of action, an objection which may dispose of the whole action can be taken in the following manner: " The defendant will object that the special damage stated is not sufficient in point of law to sustain the action." Similarly, if no special damage be alleged, the defendant may object " that the matters disclosed in the statement of claim are not actionable without proof of special damage, and that none is alleged." See also Precedents, Nos. 69, 78, 79.

When an objection in point of law has been set down for hearing, the party objecting ordinarily has the right to begin.[21] And for the purposes of the argument he is taken to admit all the facts alleged in the pleading to which he objects.[22] The court will, moreover, take the whole record into consideration and give judgment for the party who, on the whole, appears to be entitled to it. Thus, a plaintiff who objects to a defence may find himself called on to defend the sufficiency of his statement of claim; and, if he is unsuccessful, judgment will be given for the defendant.

---

[20] As in *Mayor, etc., of Manchester* v. *Williams* [1891] 1 Q.B. 94.
[21] *Stevens* v. *Chown* [1901] 1 Ch. at p. 900. But this is subject to the judge's discretion (Ord. 35, r. 7 (1)). And see *Seldon* v. *Davidson* [1968] 1 W.L.R. 1083.
[22] *Burrows* v. *Rhodes* [1899] 1 Q.B. at p. 821; *Anderson* v. *Midland Ry.* [1902] 1 Ch. at p. 374.

CHAPTER 10

ATTACKING YOUR OPPONENT'S PLEADING

THESE, then, are the leading rules of our present system of pleading. They are clear, simple and sensible; and, at the same time, they are elastic. Pleadings are no longer cast all in one mould; there is full scope for individuality. " An application to set aside for irregularity any proceedings, any step taken in any proceedings or any document, judgment or order therein shall not be allowed unless it is made within a reasonable time and before the party applying has taken any fresh step [1] after becoming aware of the irregularity." (Order 2, r. 2 (1).) Hence an irregularity [2] may be cured by your opponent's pleading over. And experienced pleaders often break the letter of these rules for the sake of clearness or brevity. Thus, though it is in general unnecessary to allege matter of law, yet it is sometimes convenient to do so, and it may make the statements of fact more intelligible and show their connection with each other. There is no harm in this, if the facts are also stated on which the proposition of law is based.

But what is a pleader to do when he is confronted by some flagrantly bad bit of pleading in flat violation of the rules? Even then, the best thing he can do, as a rule, is to leave it alone. But there are exceptions. As Bowen L.J. said in *Knowles* v. *Roberts* ((1888) 38 Ch.D. at p. 270), " It seems to me that the rule that the court is not to dictate to parties how they should frame their case, is one that ought always to be preserved sacred. But that rule is, of course, subject to this modification and limitation, that the parties must not offend against the rules of pleading which have been laid down by the law; and if a party introduces a pleading which is unnecessary, and it tends to prejudice, embarrass and delay the trial of the action, it then becomes a pleading which is beyond his right." His opponent's

---

[1] See *post*, pp. 192–193.

[2] As contrasted with a defect dealt with under Ord. 18, r. 19 (*post*). A distinction was drawn in such cases as *Craig* v. *Kanssen* [1943] 1 K.B. 256; *Re Pritchard, Decd.* [1963] Ch. 502; *Cooper* v. *Williams* [1963] 2 Q.B. 567 between an irregularity and a nullity. Now by Ord. 2, r. 1, any failure whatsoever to comply with the rules is to be treated as an irregularity and does not nullify the proceedings, which may be set aside, amended or otherwise dealt with as may be just. See *Harkness* v. *Bell's Asbestos & Engineering Co.* [1967] 2 Q.B. 729.

remedy in such a case is to apply to the master at chambers for an order that the whole or any part of a pleading be struck out or amended under Order 18, r. 19 (1), or for an order for particulars under rule 12 (3).

But be careful how you advise any such application. You may materially increase the costs of the action, and yet reap no compensating advantage for your client, even though you succeed. You should also be careful which of these alternatives you adopt. If your opponent has omitted a material allegation, the proper course is to apply under Order 18, r. 19 (1); if, however, he has pleaded a material allegation with insufficient particularity, the appropriate remedy is to apply for particulars.[3]

(1) *Striking out or amending your Opponent's Pleading*

Your attack may be directed at the whole of your opponent's pleading or upon certain objectionable portions of it; the objective may be to expose the entire action or the defence to it as a sham, or one which cannot possibly succeed in law, and to obtain judgment accordingly; or it may be to force your opponent to amend the whole or some part of an embarrassing pleading under pain of having it struck out if he does not.

The provisions of Order 18, r. 19 (1) (set out in full at p. 437, *post*), afford a prompt and summary method of disposing of groundless actions and of excluding immaterial issues. Under this rule a master at chambers has power at any stage to strike out or to order the amendment of the whole or part of any pleading or indorsement which discloses no reasonable cause of action or defence, or which is scandalous, frivolous or vexatious, or which may prejudice, embarrass or delay the fair trial of the action, or which is otherwise an abuse of the process of the court.

The master also has power on these grounds to stay or dismiss any action or to order judgment to be entered accordingly. The various types of application which may be made under this rule must be considered separately.

(i) *Where no reasonable cause of action or defence is disclosed*

On an application based on this ground alone, no evidence is admissible. The application is analogous to a *demurrer* (see *ante*,

---

[3] *Bruce* v. *Odhams Press, Ltd.* [1936] 1 K.B. 697.

pp. 126–127) and the master can look only at the pleadings and particulars, not at any affidavit.[4] The master's power is exercisable at any stage of the proceedings, but he should only strike out a pleading in " plain and obvious cases "[5] and where no reasonable amendment would cure the defect. If the point requires substantial argument and careful consideration, it may be more appropriate to set it down for trial under Order 33; the summary procedure of striking out is only appropriate where it is plainly evident that the statement of claim as it stands is insufficient, even if proved, to entitle the plaintiff to what he asks, or that the defence cannot afford any answer in law to the claim.[6] Hence though you may think that your opponent's pleading discloses no reasonable cause of action or defence to your claim, it by no means follows that you should at once apply to have it struck out or amended. So long as the statement of claim or the particulars served under it[7] disclose *some* cause of action, or raise some question fit to be decided by trial, the mere fact that a case is weak and not likely to succeed is no ground for striking it out.[8] That the plaintiff's action may be barred by the Limitation Act is ordinarily no ground for striking out the statement of claim before pleadings are closed.[9] It is customary at the common law Bar before advising an application to be made under this rule to communicate with your opponent so that he may have an opportunity of amending his pleading.

(ii) *Where action or defence is frivolous, vexatious or an abuse of process*

The court has long exercised an inherent power, which is now set out in the rule, to stay, strike out or dismiss proceedings which are in this category. Here the master is not confined to the pleadings but extrinsic evidence may be put before him on affidavit.[10] If, in

[4] R. 19 (2); *Wenlock* v. *Moloney* [1965] 1 W.L.R. 1238.

[5] *Hubbuck & Sons* v. *Wilkinson* [1899] 1 Q.B. 86, 91.

[6] *Griffiths* v. *London and St. K. Docks Co.* (1884) 13 Q.B.D. at p. 261; *Steeds* v. *Steeds* (1889) 22 Q.B.D. at p. 542. See also *Dyson* v. *Att.-Gen.* [1911] 1 K.B. at p. 414; and the remarks of Selborne L.C. in *Burstall* v. *Beyfus* (1884) 13 Q.B.D. at p. 261; and of the Court of Appeal in *Worthington* v. *Belton* (1902) 18 T.L.R. 438; and *Lea* v. *Thursby* (1904) 90 L.T. 265.

[7] *Davey* v. *Bentinck* [1893] 1 Q.B. 185.

[8] *Boaler* v. *Holder* (1886) 54 L.T. 298; *Moore* v. *Lawson* (1915) 31 T.L.R. 418.

[9] *Dismore* v. *Milton* [1938] W.N. 305.

[10] *Willis* v. *Earl Howe* [1893] 2 Ch. 545, at pp. 551, 554.

all the circumstances of the case, it is obvious that the claim or defence is devoid of all merit or cannot possibly succeed,[11] an order may be made. But it is a jurisdiction which ought to be very sparingly exercised, and only in very exceptional cases. Its exercise would not be justified merely because the story told in the pleadings is highly improbable, and one which it is difficult to believe could be proved.[12]

Illustrations

Where S., for the apparent purpose of delaying the proceedings, denied or refused to admit every allegation in the statement of claim and set up no case of his own, and it was shown that in a previous action he had admitted on oath several of the more material allegations and not denied many of the others. *Held,* that the defence was not honest and bona fide but a sham, put in for the purpose of gaining time, and must be struck out as an abuse of the process.
    Remmington v. *Scoles* [1897] 2 Ch. 1.
    And see *Critchell* v. *L. & S.W. Ry.* [1907] 1 K.B. 860.
    In fresh proceedings R. sought to raise by his defence and rely upon the very same question which had been decided against him as plaintiff in a previous action. This was held to be an abuse of the process and the defence was struck out as being frivolous and vexatious.
    Reichel v. *Magrath* (1889) 14 App.Cas. 665.
    The plaintiff brought a second action upon other defamatory statements in a publication which had already been decided to be a fair and accurate report of a judgment. *Held,* that it was frivolous and vexatious and that a plea of *res judicata* must succeed.
    MacDougall v. *Knight* (1890) 25 Q.B.D. 1.
    And see *Wright* v. *Bennett (No.* 2) [1948] 1 All E.R. 227.

A solicitor who drafts a fictitious indorsement so as to conceal the true nature of the action may be guilty of contempt of court.[13] Moreover, apart from this rule, the court has inherent power, where either party to an action has made repeated frivolous applications to the judge or master, to make an order prohibiting any further applications by him without leave.[14] Such an order is, however, rarely made.

(iii) *Where objectionable matter is included*

    Under the same rule a master may order to be struck out or amended any matter in any pleading which may be scandalous, frivolous or vexatious, or which may tend to prejudice, embarrass

---

[11] *Willis* v. *Earl Beauchamp* (1886) 11 P.D. 59.
[12] *Lawrance* v. *Lord Norreys* (1890) 15 App.Cas. 210, 219.
[13] *R.* v. *Weisz* [1951] 2 K.B. 611.
[14] *Grepe* v. *Loam* (1887) 37 Ch.D. 168; *Kinnaird* v. *Field* [1905] 2 Ch. 306. And see the Judicature Act, 1925 (15 & 16 Geo. 5, c. 49), s. 51; *Re Chaffers* (1897) 13 T.L.R. 363; *Re Jones* (1902) 18 T.L.R. 476; *Re Boaler* [1915] 1 K.B. 21.

or delay the fair trial of the action. In flagrant cases he sometimes awards costs on the common fund basis. But such orders
are not lightly made. One party cannot dictate how the other
shall plead. Any immaterial allegations or irrelevant or unnecessary details which, for example, merely suggest that a party is
dishonest or corrupt, or are designed to degrade him, may be
" scandalous." But remember that " nothing can be scandalous
which is relevant." (*Per* Cotton L.J. in *Fisher* v. *Owen* (1878) 8
Ch.D., at p. 653.) The mere fact that an allegation is unnecessary
is no ground for striking it out; nor is a pleading embarrassing
merely because it contains allegations which are inconsistent or
stated in the alternative.[15] " I take ' embarrassing ' to mean that
the allegations are so irrelevant that to allow them to stand would
involve useless expense, and would also prejudice the trial of the
action by involving the parties in a dispute that is wholly apart
from the issues." (*Per* Pickford L.J. in *Mayor, etc., of London*
v. *Horner* (1914) 111 L.T., at p. 514; and see *Willoughby* v.
Eckstein [1936] 1 All E.R. 650.)

Unless the pleading as it stands is really and seriously
embarrassing, it is often better policy not to attack it; you only
strengthen your opponent's position by compelling him to reform
and thus to improve his pleading. But be careful in drawing a defence
not to aid a defect in the claim in any way; the less said about
that part of the pleading the better. Do not admit it; if need be,
traverse it in so many words; but, after such denial, avoid the
whole topic, if possible, leaving the plaintiff's counsel to explain it
to the judge at the trial, if he can.

Illustrations

" A defendant may claim *ex debito justitiae* to have the plaintiff's case presented
in an intelligible form, so that he may not be embarrassed in meeting it."
      Per James L.J. in *Davy* v. *Garrett* (1878) 7 Ch.D., at p. 486.

In an action to enforce the compromise of a former action, it is unnecessary
and embarrassing for the plaintiff to set out in his new pleading all the facts
on which he relied before; for he will not be allowed to try the former action
over again.
      Knowles v. *Roberts* (1888) 38 Ch.D. 263.

Allegations of dishonesty and outrageous conduct, etc., are not scandalous
if relevant to the issue.
      Christie v. *Christie* (1873) L.R. 8 Ch. 499; 42 L.J.Ch. 544.
      Millington v. *Loring* (1880) 6 Q.B.D. 190; 50 L.J.Q.B. 214.

[15] *Child* v. *Stenning* (1877) 5 Ch.D. 695; *Re Morgan* (1887) 35 Ch.D. 492.

But where a plaintiff in his statement of claim made allegations of dishonest conduct against the defendant, but stated in his reply that he sought no relief on that ground, the allegations were struck out as scandalous and embarrassing. *Brooking* v. *Maudslay* (1886) 55 L.T. 343.

And see *Murray* v. *Epsom Local Board* [1897] 1 Ch. 35.

(2) *Particulars*

The most usual way of attacking your opponent's pleading is by applying for particulars.

" The court may order a party to serve on any other party particulars of any claim, defence or other matter stated in his pleading, or in any affidavit of his ordered to stand as a pleading, or a statement of the nature of the case on which he relies, and the order may be made on such terms as the court thinks just." (Order 18, r. 12 (3).) If either party considers that his opponent's pleading does not give him the information to which he is entitled, he should first apply for further particulars by letter, otherwise he may not get an order (r. 12 (6)); the costs of such a letter are allowable. If the particulars are refused, he should then apply to the master for an order, preferably upon the first hearing of the Summons for Directions (*post*, p. 259). Care should be taken not to make the application prematurely, for under rule 12 (5) particulars will not be ordered before defence unless the master deems them necessary or desirable to enable the defendant to plead or there are other special reasons.

" The object of particulars is to enable the party asking for them to know what case he has to meet at the trial, and so to save unnecessary expense, and avoid allowing parties to be taken by surprise." [16] If your opponent has worded his pleading so vaguely that you cannot be sure what his line of attack or defence will be at the trial, it is worthwhile to apply for particulars, even though you think you can make a shrewd guess at his meaning. It is safer to pin him down to a definite story, otherwise it will be open to him at the trial to give evidence as to any fact which tends to support his vague allegation.[17] It is also most desirable to ascertain whether the plaintiff is relying on parol conversations or written documents as amounting to a misrepresentation or as establishing a contract. Always ask for particulars of losses, expenses and other special damage.

[16] *Spedding* v. *Fitzpatrick* (1888) 38 Ch.D., at p. 413.
[17] *Chester* (*Dean and Chapter of*) v. *Smelting Corporation Ltd.* [1902] W.N. 5; *Hewson* v. *Cleeve* [1904] 2 Ir.R. 536.

Particulars are now ordered much more freely than in former days. Look at such cases as *Gale* v. *Reed* (1806) 8 East 80; *Shum* v. *Farrington* (1797) 1 Bos. & Pul. 640; *Burton* v. *Webb* (1800) 8 T.R. 459; *Cornwallis* v. *Savery* (1759) 2 Burr. 772; and *Forsyth* v. *Bristowe* (1853) 8 Ex., at p. 350. In each of these cases the particulars asked for would now be ordered. " The old system of pleading at common law was to conceal as much as possible what was going to be proved at the trial." (*Per* Cotton L.J. in *Spedding* v. *Fitzpatrick* (1888) 38 Ch.D., at p. 414.) Now we play with the cards on the table.

Under the rules of 1883 it was sufficient to allege knowledge simply as a fact, without giving particulars of the circumstances relied on as showing or raising an inference of knowledge. (See *Burgess* v. *Beethoven Electric Equipment Ltd.* [1943] K.B. 96.) Nor were particulars ordered of an allegation that a party had " notice " of a fact, unless the circumstances were material. Now, however, particulars may in either case be ordered at the master's discretion on such terms as may be just (Order 18, r. 12 (4)). But if a party serves particulars he is bound by them at the trial and there are many cases where knowledge can only be established by cross-examination or after discovery of documents or interrogatories. Accordingly a convenient form of order may often be to the effect that if a party intends to adduce at the trial affirmative evidence showing that the other party knew the thing alleged, he do serve particulars of the facts relied on within so many days after inspection (or not less than so many days before trial, as the case may be). If it is practicable to give the necessary particulars in the pleading the costs of an application will be saved. Again, a plaintiff sometimes pleads " as the defendant ought to have known." In some cases this amounts to no more than an allegation that the defendant had notice of a particular fact, in which case particulars may be ordered at the master's discretion if the circumstances be material.[18] But if the intended effect of the allegation is that the other party was negligent in failing to observe or to infer the existence of a particular thing, particulars of the facts and circumstances relied on as constituting such negligence ought always to be given.[19]

[18] Ord. 18, r. 12 (4); and see *Cresta Holdings, Ltd.* v. *Karlin* [1959] 1 W.L.R. 1055, decided under the former rule.
[19] *Fox* v. *H. Wood (Harrow), Ltd.* [1963] 2 Q.B. 601.

Illustrations

If an agreement is alleged generally (*e.g.*, " it was agreed between the plaintiff and the defendant that," etc.), particulars will be ordered of the alleged agreement, stating its date, and whether the same was verbal or in writing, in the latter case identifying the document.

> *Turquand* v. *Fearon* (1879) 48 L.J.Q.B. 703.

Where it is alleged that " the defendant represented to the plaintiff," etc., an order will be made for similar particulars of the alleged representation.

> *Seligmann* v. *Young* [1884] W.N. 93.

So where the plaintiff alleged that certain directors had instigated the defendant to do something, Kay J. held that the plaintiff ought to state whether such instigation was verbal or in writing, and if verbal by whom it was made, and if in writing the date of such writing.

> *Briton Medical, etc., Association* v. *Britannia Fire Association* (1888) 59 L.T. 888.

In an action for conspiring to induce certain persons by threats to break their contracts with the plaintiffs, the defendant is entitled to particulars, stating the name of each such contractor, the kind of threat used in each case, and when and by which defendant each such threat was made, and whether verbally or in writing; if in writing, identifying the document; but he is not entitled to the names of the workmen in the employ of those contractors whom it is alleged the defendant threatened to " call out."

> *Temperton* v. *Russell* (1893) 9 T.L.R. 318, 319.

Where directors pleaded under the Companies (Consolidation) Act, 1908, s. 84 (now section 43 of the Companies Act, 1948), that they bona fide believed their statements in the prospectus to be true and had reasonable grounds for their belief, they were ordered to deliver particulars of the grounds of their belief.

> *Alman* v. *Oppert* [1901] 2 K.B. 576; 70 L.J.K.B. 745. But see *Stapeley* v. *Annetts* [1970] 1 W.L.R. 22 (malicious prosecution).

If a plaintiff in an action for libel is not identified in the libel by name or description, he must give particulars of the facts from which it is to be inferred that the words refer to him. Such facts are " material facts," and if they are omitted, the defendant is entitled to these particulars as of right.

> *Bruce* v. *Odhams Press, Ltd.* [1936] 1 K.B. 697; 105 L.J.K.B. 318.

So are the actual words of a libel.

> *Collins* v. *Jones* [1955] 1 Q.B. 564.

Particulars in support of an innuendo in an action for libel or slander are now required to be given by rule.

> Order 82, r. 3. And see pp. 91, 104, 164.

Where, however, a material fact is pleaded, particulars will not be ordered of the facts relied on in support of that allegation, if such facts are no more than the evidence by which the allegation is to be proved.

> *Re Dependable Upholstery, Ltd.* [1936] 3 All E.R. 741.

The defendant in an action for seduction applied, before defence, for particulars of the alleged immoral intercourse. But the Divisional Court refused to make any order unless he made an affidavit that he had not seduced the girl.

> *Thomson* v. *Birkley* (1882) 47 L.T. 700; approved in
> *Sachs* v. *Speilman* (1887) 37 Ch.D., at p. 304; 57 L.J.Ch. 658.

In a similar case, a Divisional Court declined to follow this decision, and ordered particulars.

Kelly v. *Briggs* (1888) 85 L.T.J. 78.

But the principle of *Thomson* v. *Birkley* was followed in

Knight v. *Engle* (1889) 61 L.T. 780, and in

Hanna v. *Keers* [1896] 2 Ir.R. 226.

Particulars of the defence of " inevitable accident " were ordered in

Martin v. *M'Taggart* [1906] 2 Ir.R. 120.

But see *ante*, p. 146.

A plaintiff who alleges negligent driving may not be permitted at the hearing to allege that this was due to the insobriety of the defendant unless he has expressly pleaded that this was the cause.

Bills v. *Roe* [1968] 1 W.L.R. 925.

Particulars of contributory negligence will be ordered if reasonably necessary (as they usually are) to enable the plaintiff to know what case he has to meet and to avoid surprise.

Atkinson v. *Stewart & Partners, Ltd.* [1954] N.I. 146.

Where a plaintiff claims a lump sum of money, he must give particulars of the items of which it is composed.

Philipps v. *Philipps* (1878) 4 Q.B.D., at p. 131; 48 L.J.Q.B. 135.

Whenever the plaintiff claims a lump sum for carriage, warehouse rent, work and labour done, and money paid, he will be ordered to give the items composing such lump sum, and to distinguish which sums are charged for carriage, which for warehouse rent, which for work and labour, and which for money paid, and to state when and to whom each such payment was made.

See *Gunn* v. *Tucker* (1891) 7 T.L.R. 280.

A railway company, suing for carriage and other charges, was ordered to deliver particulars showing the price charged for each consignment. It then appeared that various consignments were charged at different rates, some less and some higher than the statutory maximum. Further and better particulars were ordered, distinguishing the charges for conveyance from the terminal and dock charges (if any).

London and North Western Ry. v. *Lee* (1891) 7 T.L.R. 603.

And see *Mansion House Association* v. *G.W. Ry.* [1895] 2 Q.B. 141.

In an action for wrongful dismissal where the contract of service did not state the length of notice required to terminate it, the defendants applied for particulars of (1) the period of time claimed by the plaintiff to be a reasonable notice, and (2) of the special damage alleged, stating whether during the period alleged to constitute a reasonable notice he obtained other employment or employments and if so, when, with whom, date of commencement, salary and whether any such employment is still continuing and if not when it determined.

Held, the defendants were entitled to these particulars and that, as a question of payment into court arose, they were entitled to them before defence.

Monk v. *Redwing Aircraft Co.* [1942] 1 K.B. 182. See also

Phipps v. *Orthodox Unit Trusts, Ltd.* [1958] 1 Q.B. 314. (*Post*, p. 161).

Other decisions as to particulars are set out on pp. 113, 123, *ante*.

In some cases the parties are bound to serve particulars by express enactment. (See in particular Order 18, r. 12; *post*, p. 434.)

Illustrations

In an action under the Fatal Accidents Acts, 1846–1908, the plaintiff must serve with his statement of claim " a full particular of the person or persons for whom and on whose behalf such action shall be brought, and of the nature of the claim in respect of which damages shall be sought to be recovered."

Fatal Accidents Act, 1846, s. 4; see Precedent No. 44.

In an action for infringement of a patent, the plaintiff must serve with his statement of claim particulars of the infringements relied on, specifying which of the claims in the specification are alleged to be infringed and giving at least one instance of each type of infringement alleged.

Order 103, rr. 19 (1) and 20.

If the defendant disputes the validity of the patent, he must serve particulars of his objections (rule 10; and see rule 6); so must any person petitioning or counterclaiming for its revocation (rules 18, 19 (4)). Such particulars must state every ground upon which the validity is disputed, and clearly define every issue intended to be raised (rule 21 (1)); and if one of the objections is want of novelty, they must comply with rule 21 (2).

In defamation actions particulars must be given in accordance with Order 82, rr. 3 and 7 (see *ante*, pp. 101, 158, and *post*, p. 164).

In moneylenders' actions the statement of claim, whether indorsed on the writ or not, must contain the particulars required by Order 83, r. 3. (See Precedent No. 14.)

In certain hire-purchase actions the statement of claim must state the circumstances in which the claim arises.

Order 84, r. 2.

The indorsement of claim on a writ issued against the Crown must contain the particulars required by Order 77, r. 3 (1).

Any party who pleads that at the time when a will, the subject of the action, was alleged to have been executed the testator did not know and approve of its contents must specify the nature of the case on which he intends to rely, and no allegation in support of that plea which would be relevant in support of any of the following other pleas, that is to say—

(a) that the will was not duly executed,

(b) that at the time of the execution of the will the testator was not of sound mind, memory and understanding, and

(c) that the execution of the will was obtained by undue influence or fraud,

shall be made by that party unless that other plea is also pleaded.

Order 76, r. 13 (3).

There is another advantage in obtaining particulars from your opponent. It limits the issue. He is bound by his particulars, and cannot at the trial (without special leave, which will only be granted on terms) go into any matters not fairly included therein.[20] Particulars thus " prevent surprise at the trial, and limit inquiry at the trial to matters set out in particulars. They tend to narrow issues, and ought to be encouraged." (*Per* Watkin Williams J., in *Thomson* v. *Birkley* (1882) 47 L.T. 700.)

[20] *Woolley* v. *Broad* [1892] 2 Q.B. 317.

Particulars

Illustrations

A landlord brought an action of ejectment against his tenant, and gave as particulars of the breaches of covenant on which he relied as a forfeiture: " Selling hay and straw off the premises, removing manure, and non-cultivation." He was not allowed at the trial to give evidence that the defendant had mismanaged the farm by over-cropping, or by deviating from the usual rotation of crops. He was confined to the matters stated in the particulars.

> *Doe dem. Winnall* v. *Broad* (1841) 2 Man. & G. 523.

In an action brought by a landlord against a tenant for not properly cultivating a farm according to the course of good husbandry and the custom of the country where the farm was situate, the declaration alleged that, according to the custom of the country, the defendant ought to have had about one-half only of the arable lands in corn, one-fourth in seeds, and the remaining fourth in turnips or fallow; and alleged as a breach that the defendant had more than one-half in corn, etc., etc. The defendant pleaded, traversing the custom as alleged in the declaration. At the trial the jury found that the custom was not as the plaintiff had alleged, but that the farm had been cultivated contrary to the course of good husbandry in the neighbourhood. *Held*, that the plaintiff had tied himself up to the precise custom as alleged in the declaration, and, having failed to prove it, was not entitled to recover.

> *Angerstein* v. *Handson* (1835) 1 Cr.M. & R. 789; 1 Gale 8.
> And see *Harris* v. *Mantle* (1789) 3 T.R. 307, *post*, p. 180.

Particulars of general damage will very rarely be ordered. But when any special damage is claimed, without sufficient detail, particulars will be ordered of the alleged damage; *e.g.*, if the plaintiff alleges that certain customers have ceased to deal with him, he will be ordered to state their names. This is a very useful order, for if plaintiff cannot give the names, he will be compelled to strike out the allegation of special damage; and the summons should ask that it be struck out if such particulars be not delivered. If he gives the necessary particulars, he will be bound by them; he will not be allowed at the trial to give evidence of any special damage which is not claimed explicitly, either in his pleading or particulars. If ambiguous expressions be used in the statement of claim which may or may not amount to an allegation of special damage, the master will order " particulars of special damage, if any claimed."

> *Watson* v. *North Metropolitan Tramway Co.* (1886) 3 T.L.R. 273.
> *Dimsdale* v. *Goodlake* (1876) 40 J.P. 792.
> *London and Northern Bank, Ltd.* v. *George Newnes, Ltd.* (1900) 16 T.L.R. 433.
> *Hayward* v. *Pullinger & Partners, Ltd.* [1950] 1 All E.R. 581 (*post*, p. 182).

Whenever damage of any kind is an essential portion of the cause of action it is " special damage " within the meaning of this rule. *E.g.*, particulars have been ordered at chambers of a " general loss of business " in a case similar to *Ratcliffe* v. *Evans* [1892] 2 Q.B. 524; 61 L.J.Q.B. 535.

A plaintiff claiming damages for wrongful dismissal may be ordered to give as part of his particulars of special damage in respect of loss of salary an estimate of the amount of tax which he would have had to pay if he had remained in employment and the broad facts relied on in arriving at that estimate.

> *Phipps* v. *Orthodox Unit Trusts, Ltd.* [1958] 1 Q.B. 314.
> *Parsons* v. *B.N.M. Laboratories, Ltd.* [1964] 1 Q.B. 95.
> And see *ante*, p. 159 and *post*, p. 329.

When the plaintiff in an action to restrain the infringement of his trade mark alleged that the defendant had induced " divers persons " to purchase his goods as and for those of the plaintiff, particulars were ordered of the names and addresses of such "divers persons."

Humphries v. *Taylor Drug Co.* (1888) 39 Ch.D. 693.

But see *Duke* v. *Wisden & Co.* (1897) 77 L.T. 67.

It is no objection to an application for particulars that the applicant must know the true facts of the case better than his opponent. He is entitled to know the outline of the case that his adversary will try to make against him, which may be something very different from the true facts of the case. His opponent may know more than he does; in any event it is well to bind him down to a definite story. Particulars will be ordered whenever the master is satisfied that without them the applicant cannot tell *what* is going to be proved against him at the trial. But *how* his opponent will prove it is a matter of evidence of which particulars will not be ordered.

Again, where the party applying is in other respects entitled to the particulars for which he asks, it is not a valid objection to his application that if the order be made it will compel the party giving them to name his witnesses, or otherwise to disclose or give some clue to his evidence. If the only object of the summons be to obtain particulars of the evidence on the other side, it should, of course, be dismissed as an improper application.[21] But where the information asked for is clearly necessary to enable the applicant properly to prepare for trial, or where in other respects the application is a proper one, the information must be given, even though it discloses some portion of the evidence on which the other party proposes to rely at the trial,[22] and even where the plaintiff is privileged from producing documents which would disclose such evidence.[23]

In certain cases, a party who is ordered to give particulars is allowed, before giving them, to interrogate his opponent or to obtain discovery of documents.[24] "It is good practice and good sense that where the defendant knows the facts and the plaintiffs do not, the defendant should give discovery before the plaintiffs deliver particulars." (*Per* Bowen L.J. in *Millar* v. *Harper* (1888)

[21] *Temperton* v. *Russell* (1893) 9 T.L.R. at p. 320.

[22] *Marriott* v. *Chamberlain* (1886) 17 Q.B.D. 154, 161; *Zierenberg* v. *Labouchere* [1893] 2 Q.B. at pp. 187, 188; *Bishop* v. *Bishop* [1901] P. 325.

[23] *Milbank* v. *Milbank* [1900] 1 Ch. 376.

[24] *Whyte* v. *Ahrens* (1884) 26 Ch.D. 717; *Leitch* v. *Abbott* (1886) 31 Ch.D. 374.

38 Ch.D., at p. 112; *Edelston* v. *Russell* (1888) 57 L.T. 927.) But
no hard and fast rule can be laid down to determine when particulars should precede discovery or discovery should precede
particulars. Each case will depend on its own circumstances.[25]

Illustrations

A line can be drawn, though sometimes only with difficulty, between requiring
a plaintiff to make a sufficient statement to prevent the defendant being
taken by surprise at the trial, and requiring him to disclose the evidence on
which he intends to rely. Thus, where the plaintiff alleged that the defendants
" knew or ought to have known, and must be taken to have known, the improper
motives which actuated the directors," the defendants applied for particulars,
stating what were the alleged improper motives, and how and in what manner
they were known to the defendants. Kay J. made an order for particulars of
the alleged improper motives which actuated the directors, but declined to
make the rest of the order asked for. (A wider order might now be made under
Order 18, r. 12 (4). See *ante*, pp. 104, 157.)

> *Briton Medical, etc., Association* v. *Britannia Fire Association* (1888) 50
> L.T. 888.

Where the defendant justified the arrest of the plaintiff on the ground that
he had reasonable and probable cause for suspecting that a felony had been
committed and that the plaintiff had committed it, he was ordered to give
particulars of the alleged felony and of the reasonable and probable cause for
suspicion, but not of the names of those who had given him information against
the plaintiff.

> *Green* v. *Garbutt* (1912) 28 T.L.R. 575.

In any action of slander or slander of title, the defendant is entitled to particulars of the times when, and the persons to whom (and in some cases of the
places where), the alleged slanders were published, if such details are not given
in the statement of claim.

> *Roselle* v. *Buchanan* (1886) 16 Q.B.D. 656; 55 L.J.Q.B. 376.
> *Roche* v. *Meyler* [1896] 2 Ir.R. 35.

Each publication is a separate cause of action, and the defendant is therefore
entitled to this information, although the plaintiff may thus be compelled to
name some of his witnesses.

> *Humphries* v. *Taylor Drug Co.* (1888) 39 Ch.D. 693.

If a libel be contained in a letter or other private document, the name of the
person to whom each publication was made, and the date of such publication,
must be stated in the pleading. This, however, is unnecessary in the case of a
newspaper, prospectus, handbill or other document widely disseminated. A
person libelled in a newspaper cannot be expected to tell the proprietor the
names of all who take his paper. That would be oppressive.

> *British Legal and United Provident Assurance Co.* v. *Sheffield* [1911] 1 Ir.R.
> 69.
> *Davey* v. *Bentinck* [1893] 1 Q.B. 185; 62 L.J.Q.B. 114.

Nor can a plaintiff be compelled to give the names of the persons passing
in the street at the time an alleged slander was uttered.

> *Wingard* v. *Cox* [1876] W.N. 106.
> *Roche* v. *Meyler, supra.*

---

[25] *Waynes Merthyr Co.* v. *Radford* [1896] 1 Ch. 29.

If no facts be stated in a plea of justification, particulars will be ordered of the facts upon which the defendant intends to rely at the trial in support of that plea, unless the charge is specific and precise.

> *Cumming* v. *Green* (1891) 7 T.L.R. 408.
> *Wootton* v. *Sievier* [1913] 3 K.B. 499.

Where a defendant pleads justification, he is not entitled to wait for discovery before giving the necessary particulars.

> *Goldschmidt* v. *Constable & Co.* [1937] 4 All E.R. 293.

Particulars will also be ordered of the facts on which the defendant will rely in support of his plea of fair comment.

> *Digby* v. *Financial News, Ltd.* [1907] 1 K.B. 502; 76 L.J.K.B. 321.

Where a plaintiff alleges that the words or matters complained of were used in a defamatory sense other than their ordinary meaning, he must give particulars of the facts and matters on which he relies in support of such sense.

> Order 82, r. 3 (1). And see *ante*, pp. 91, 104,

Where the defendant pleads that " in so far as the words complained of consist of statements of fact they are true in substance and in fact and in so far as they consist of expressions of opinion they are fair comment on a matter of public interest," [26] or pleads to the like effect, the defendant must give particulars specifying which of the words complained of he alleges are statements of fact and he must also give particulars of the facts and matters he relies on in support of his allegation that the words are true.

> Order 82, r. 3 (2).   And see *post*, p. 207.

Discovery will be limited to the issues as narrowed by the particulars.

> *Yorkshire Provident Co.* v. *Gilbert* [1895] 2 Q.B. 148.
> *Arnold & Butler* v. *Bottomley* [1908] 2 K.B. 151; 77 L.J.K.B. 584.

And the particulars served must go to justify the charges made in the libel or slander, and not some other collateral imputation.

> *Wernher, Beit & Co.* v. *Markham* (1901) 18 T.L.R. 143, 763.

Unless the plaintiff has extended the natural meaning of the words by an innuendo; in which case it will be open to the defendant to plead that the words in that extended sense are true and to give particulars justifying both the words and the innuendo.

> *Maisel* v. *Financial Times, Ltd.* (1915) 84 L.J.K.B. 2145; 112 L.T. 953.

When a plaintiff claims as heir he should in his statement of claim show how he is heir; if he does not, he must give particulars of his descent.

> *Palmer* v. *Palmer* [1892] 1 Q.B. 319; 61 L.J.Q.B. 236 (*ante*, p. 89).

The mere fact that the defendant has already served his defence is no waiver of his right to particulars of the allegations in the statement of claim.[27]   Unless such particulars are necessary in order to enable him to plead, the proper time for his application is upon the first hearing of the Summons for Directions (see *post*, p. 259).   If he makes a separate application earlier or later, as he

---

[26] The rule departs from the wording of the plea, commonly known as " the rolled-up plea," which refers to " fair comment *upon the said facts* " and was held in *Sutherland* v. *Stopes* [1925] A.C. 47 to be a plea of fair comment and not justification. Nevertheless the effect of the rule seems to be that particulars must be given of such a plea.

[27] *Sachs* v. *Speilman* (1887) 37 Ch.D. 295.

may so long as he is not guilty of unreasonable delay, he will probably have to bear the costs, unless there was some very good reason for taking this course.

It is no hardship on a party who has a good case to be ordered to give particulars. It is often a benefit to him, for it compels him to get his case up carefully in good time before the trial. It is also sometimes an advantage to have full particulars of his grievance, loss, expenses, etc., clearly stated in black and white, and laid before the judge with the pleadings.

At the same time, particulars will not be exacted where it would be oppressive or unreasonable to make such an order; as where the information is not in the possession of either party, or could only be obtained with great difficulty, or where the particulars are not applied for till the last moment. An order is often made for " the best particulars the plaintiff can give."

Illustrations

A declaration alleged that the plaintiff was chosen and nominated a knight of the shire by the greater number of the forty-shilling freeholders present. It was objected that the plaintiff does not show the certainty of the number. But it was held that the declaration was " good enough, without showing the number of electors; for the election might be made by voices or hands, or by such other way wherein it is easy to tell who has the majority and yet very difficult to know the certain number of them." And it was laid down that, to put the plaintiff " to declare a certainty where he cannot by any possibility be presumed to know or remember the certainty, is not reasonable nor requisite in our law."

    Buckley v. *Rice Thomas* (1554) Plowd. 118.

Where the defendant on the face of his pleading disputes all the items of the plaintiff's claim, he cannot be made to give particulars stating which of them he really disputes. Where he alleges that all the prices charged by the plaintiff are unreasonable and excessive, he cannot be ordered to state to which items he objects. (But see *ante*, pp. 125, 137, as to costs.)

    James v. *Radnor County Council* (1890) 6 T.L.R. 240.

Particulars of an immaterial allegation will not be ordered; particulars of an allegation which is not necessary may be ordered, if the master in his discretion thinks it right.

    Cave v. *Torre* (1886) 54 L.T. 515.
    Gibbons v. *Norman* (1886) 2 T.L.R. 676.
    Gaston v. *United Newspapers, Ltd.* (1915) 32 T.L.R. 143.

As a rule, particulars will only be ordered of an affirmative allegation—not of a mere traverse or of a joinder of issue.[28] But this simple rule is not quite so easy to apply as might at first appear.

---

[28] *Weinberger* v. *Inglis* [1918] 1 Ch. 133; *La Radiotechnique* v. *Weinbaum* [1928] Ch. 1.

Where a negative allegation is traversed, this implies in some sense an affirmative. The question whether particulars will be ordered seems to depend on whether the traverse imports an affirmative allegation beyond that which is in any event to be implied (*i.e.*, whether the traverse is what is called a pregnant negative, in which case particulars ought to be given [29]), or whether it is a mere traverse. It is not always easy to decide on which side of the line a given case falls. The relevant considerations are discussed at length in *Pinson* v. *Lloyds, etc., Bank, Ltd.* [1941] 2 K.B. 72.

Illustrations

In an action for malicious prosecution the plaintiff alleged that the defendant had prosecuted without any reasonable or probable cause. The defendant admitted that he prosecuted the plaintiff, but denied that he did so without reasonable or probable cause. The plaintiff applied for particulars of the defendant's reasonable and probable cause; but this application was refused. The court did not see its way to order particulars of the traverse without the help of an affidavit showing that they were necessary.

> *Roberts* v. *Owen* (1890) 6 T.L.R. 172.
> And see *Maass* v. *Gas Light and Coke Co.* [1911] 2 K.B. 543, a case on
> interrogatories.

Where the onus of establishing a positive or negative allegation lies on the plaintiff, particulars will not normally be ordered of a mere traverse of that allegation. Even if the defendant's plea is put in an affirmative form they may sometimes be refused if the plea amounts in substance to no more than a traverse of that which the plaintiff has to prove.

> *Weinberger* v. *Inglis* [1918] 1 Ch. 133.

A wife alleged that her husband had withdrawn from cohabitation and had kept and continued away without just cause. The husband denied that he withdrew or remained away without just cause—an undesirable way to plead on any showing (see *ante*, pp. 139–140). *Held*, the plea amounted to an affirmative allegation of which particulars should be given.

> *MacLulich* v. *MacLulich* [1920] P. 439.

The plaintiff alleged that he and his mistress contributed to the purchase of a house in equal shares and that he never intended that any contribution by him should be a gift to her. *Held*, that the negative allegation was of doubtful necessity (there being no matrimonial relationship) but having been pleaded it amounted to a positive averment warranting particulars of the overt acts of the plaintiff (if any) and the facts relied on to show that the contributions were made without such intention.

> *Feeney* v. *Rix* [1968] Ch. 693.

An order for particulars does not automatically stay proceedings until the particulars are given or extend a party's time for pleading. Hence it is wise, and usual, if such further order is required, to ask for it in the summons. An order for particulars made against a plaintiff may contain a term that the action shall be dismissed if

---

[29] *Chapple* v. *Electrical Trades Union* [1961] 1 W.L.R. 1290.   And see *ante*, p. 140.

he fails to comply.[30] A defendant is, on the same principle, often subjected to a condition that any allegations, of which he fails to give particulars, shall be struck out.

It sometimes happens that a party, who in compliance with an order has given all particulars then within his knowledge, subsequently discovers new matter which he desires to add to the particulars already served. In such a case the proper course is to apply for leave to serve further particulars, unless a right to do so has already been reserved to him. For without such leave he has strictly no right to add anything to those already served and by which he is bound.[31] However, service of so-called " voluntary particulars " (without such leave) is becoming increasingly common in practice, by which a party ought to be equally bound. Objection to this course is rarely, if ever, taken though there is no provision for it in the rules.

30 *Davey* v. *Bentinck* [1893] 1 Q.B. 185.
31 *Yorkshire Provident Co.* v. *Gilbert* [1895] 2 Q.B. at p. 152; *Emden* v. *Burns* (1894) 10 T.L.R. 400.

Chapter 11

AMENDMENT

Now look at home. Your opponent may have raised some well-founded objection to your pleading; or new facts may have come to light, independently of your opponent's pleading; or it may even happen (though you should not lightly be moved to alter what you first drafted) that you have regretfully come to the conclusion that your own first thoughts, as expressed in your original pleading, are not the best or only way of framing your client's case. In such event you had best seek to amend before the costs increase. Many amendments can be made without leave. But remember that, if application to the court is necessary, the master can make the order upon the Summons for Directions (*post*, p. 266) and do not make a separate application unless it is essential. Again, further instructions may make it necessary to add another party or another cause of action or some technical defect may come to light, so that you must include the writ as well as the pleadings in the ambit of your review. The relevant rules are mainly to be found in Order 20.

Amending without Leave

After service the writ may be amended once without leave at any time before pleadings are closed. But this facility does not extend to an amendment consisting of the addition, omission or substitution of a party to the action, or an alteration of the capacity in which a party sues or is sued, or the addition or substitution of a new cause of action unless such amendment is made before the writ has been served (rule 1); normally therefore leave to make such an amendment will be necessary. Amendments to a statement of claim indorsed on the writ cannot be made under this rule but are dealt with as amendments to a pleading (see *infra*). Instances of the type of amendment which is permissible under this rule are where there has been a mistake in the spelling of a party's name or other misnomer not amounting to a change of identity [1]; a wrong address

---

[1] A mere misnomer on the writ is often corrected in the statement of claim without formal amendment (see *post*, pp. 174 175).

of the registered office of a limited company; an error in a general indorsement or in the formal parts of the writ; and there are many other possibilities. If the writ has already been served before amendment it must be re-served unless a master dispenses with re-service; the application is made *ex parte*, ordinarily to the Practice Master.[2] The costs of and occasioned by any such amendment fall upon the plaintiff, unless a master on a summons for the purpose orders otherwise (Order 62, r. 3 (3)). To make the amendment the plaintiff or his solicitor takes to the writ room in the Central Office the original writ and a copy marked (usually in red ink) with the amendment which he wishes to make and headed " Amended the — day of — 19— under Order 20, rule 1 " and stamped with the requisite fee; the copy is filed and the original is altered and sealed. If the alterations are so long or elaborate that the altered document would be difficult to read, a fresh document in the amended form must be prepared and reissued (rule 10).

A memorandum of appearance cannot be amended without leave (rule 2).

Any pleading may be amended once without leave at any time before pleadings are closed (rule 3).[3] The amended pleading must be served on the opposite party, and subsequent pleadings, if already served, may if necessary be amended consequentially within the time limited by the rule. The costs of and occasioned by an amendment of the writ or any pleading without leave fall on the amending party unless a master orders otherwise (Order 62, r. 3 (3)). A party served with a writ or pleading amended without leave may within 14 days apply by summons to a master to disallow the amendment, and it may be disallowed or allowed to stand on terms as may be just (Order 20, r. 4).

A writ or statement of claim (but no other pleading) may be amended without leave during the Long Vacation (rule 6).

Amending with Leave

(1) A writ [5] or any pleading may, with leave, be amended at any stage of the proceedings on such terms as may be just (rule 5).

---

[2] See p. 4.

[3] In cases where a writ or statement of claim can be amended without leave, this may be done in the Long Vacation; otherwise leave must be obtained to amend any pleading in that period (r. 6). Before 1964 amendment of pleadings subsequent to the statement of claim could only be made by leave.

[5] And an originating summons, a petition and an originating notice of motion (rule 7).

Certain special rules apply where the amendment involves a change of parties (see *ante,* p. 16); but in general the master, the trial judge and the Court of Appeal have power to allow all such amendments as are necessary to enable justice to be done.[5a]

Either party is ordinarily given leave to make such amendment as is reasonably necessary for the due presentation of his case on payment of the costs of and occasioned by the amendment, provided that there has been no undue delay on his part, and provided also that the amendment will not injure his opponent or affect his vested rights. Where the amendment is necessary to enable justice to be done between the parties, it will be allowed on terms even at a late stage.[6] " However negligent or careless may have been the first omission and however late the proposed amendment, the amendment should be allowed if it can be made without injustice to the other side. There is no injustice if the other side can be compensated by costs; but if the amendment will put them into such a position that they must be injured, it ought not to be made." [7] " Sometimes to correct the error will lead to injustice which cannot be cured, as when a witness who could give evidence cannot be got at, or the solvency of one party is doubtful." [8] If the application be made mala fide, or if the proposed amendment will cause undue delay, or will in any other way unfairly prejudice the other party, or is irrelevant or useless, or would raise merely a technical point, leave to amend will be refused.

Whereas formerly a plaintiff would not be allowed to amend by setting up fresh claims in respect of causes of action which since the issue of the writ had become barred by the Limitation Act,[9] the court should now grant leave to amend under Order 20, r. 5 (1), whenever it is just to do so, and even though it may deprive the defendant of a defence under that Act.[9a] And specific power to do so is granted in three cases if justice so requires. (i) The name of a party may be corrected even if the effect is to substitute a new party, provided that the wrong name was given through a

---

[5a] See *Chatsworth Investments, Ltd.* v. *Cussins (Contractors), Ltd.* [1969] 1 W.L.R. 1; *Sterman* v. *E. W. & W. J. Moore* [1970] 1 Q.B. 596.

[6] *Hunt* v. *Rice & Son, Ltd.* (1937) 53 T.L.R. 931.

[7] *Clarapede & Co.* v. *Commercial Union Association* (1883) 32 W.R. 262, *per* Brett M.R.

[8] *Ibid.,* at p. 263, *per* Bowen L.J.

[9] *Weldon* v. *Neal* (1887) 19 Q.B.D. 394; *Hall* v. *Meyrick* [1957] 2 Q.B. 455; and compare the cases on renewal of a writ (*ante,* p. 53n.).

[9a] See text and cases cited in n. 5a (*supra*).

genuine mistake which was not misleading or such as to cause
any reasonable doubt as to the identity of the intended plaintiff
or defendant.[9b] (As to correcting a mere misnomer not involving
a change of identity, see *ante*, pp. 168–169 and *post*, pp.
174–175.) (ii) The capacity in which a party sues or counterclaims
may be altered to one in which he might have sued at the date of
the writ or counterclaim. (iii) A new cause of action may be added
or substituted if it arises out of the same facts, or substantially the
same facts, as give rise to a cause of action already pleaded. (Order
20, r. 5 (2)–(5).) [9c]

Where the action has been brought on a substantial cause of
action, to which a good defence has been pleaded, the plaintiff will
not be allowed to amend his claim by including in it, for the first
time, a trivial and merely technical cause of action, which such defence may not cover.[10] In some cases the plaintiff may amend
by adding a new defendant.[11] But a defendant cannot, as a rule,
make a third person a defendant without the plaintiff's consent.[12]
No person may be added as a plaintiff without his consent signified
in writing or in such other manner as may be authorised (Order
15, r. 6). In some cases, if not all, the consent of the plaintiff already
on the record will also be required.[13]

(2) Any document in the proceedings (other than a judgment
or order) may be amended under Order 20, rule 8, for the purpose
of determining the real question in controversy between the parties
or of correcting any defect or error in any proceedings. This may
be done on the application of any party or by a master or judge
on his own initiative at any stage of the proceedings. Terms may
be imposed. Under this rule an issue might be ordered to be
amended; answers to interrogatories or other affidavits might be
allowed to be altered and resworn; a notice might be amended;
and there are many other possible examples. Further, under Order 2,
r. 1, irregular proceedings may be set aside or amended or otherwise
dealt with at discretion.

[9b] See for example *Rodriguez* v. *Parker* [1967] 1 Q.B. 116; *Mitchell* v. *Harris
Engineering Co., Ltd.* [1967] 2 Q.B. 703.
[9c] The effect, but not the precise wording of the rule is here given.
[10] *Dillon* v. *Balfour* (1887) 20 L.R.Ir. 600.
[11] *Edward* v. *Lowther* (1876) 45 L.J.C.P. 417.
[12] *McCheane* v. *Gyles* [1902] 1 Ch. 911. But there are exceptions (see *post*, pp.
193–194).
[13] See *Pennington* v. *Caley* (1912) 106 L.T. 591; *Emden* v. *Carte* (1881) 17 Ch.D.
169, 768 (joinder of plaintiff's trustee in bankruptcy).

(3) Clerical mistakes in judgments or orders, or errors arising from any accidental slip or omission, may at any time be corrected on motion or summons without the necessity for an appeal (rule 11). This is known as the " slip rule." It applies to clerical mistakes and accidental slips or omissions both by the officers of the court and by the parties, and has even been held to cover neglect to apply for certain special costs which a party would ordinarily have been given if he had asked for them [14]; but it does not apply where the judgment or order correctly represents what the court in fact, albeit wrongly, intended. Amendments cannot be made under the rule upon an *ex parte* application.

Except where this rule applies, when once a judgment has been entered or an order drawn up, a party who thinks that it is wrong and wishes to have it altered must, in the ordinary way, appeal against it.[15] A judgment or order pronounced or made either in court or chambers may be reviewed or recalled on the application of a party or on the judge's own initiative until it has been entered or drawn up, as the case may be. Meanwhile it is provisionally effective.[16] Even thereafter the court has an inherent power to vary the wording so as to give effect to its original intention if it has been wrongly expressed, but not to correct a mistake of law subsequently discovered.

---

[14] *Re Inchcape (Earl of)* [1942] Ch. 394.
[15] But in *Thynne* v. *Thynne* [1955] P. 272 the court allowed in a decree absolute of divorce an amendment affecting the date and place of the marriage, these not being regarded as essential parts of the decree.
[16] *Re Harrison's Share* [1955] Ch. 260; *Hall* v. *Meyrick* [1957] 2 Q.B. 455.

CHAPTER 12

STATEMENT OF CLAIM

A STATEMENT of claim should state the material facts upon which the plaintiff relies and then claim the relief he desires. As " pleadings now are to be merely concise statements of the facts which the party pleading deems material to his case," it is unnecessary to particularise the form of action in which the relief would in former days have had to be sought. To state what form the plaintiff's right takes is to state a conclusion of law; and it is always unnecessary now for either party to state conclusions of law in his pleading—the court will draw the proper inference from the facts alleged.[1]

" Forms of action " are in fact abolished: it is now no longer necessary to state either on the writ or on the pleadings whether the plaintiff is suing in trespass or on the case, in detinue or in trover. This is a most important alteration. Formerly, everything turned on the form of action in which the plaintiff elected to sue. If he selected the wrong one, he would in the end be non-suited, even though an action would have lain if the declaration had been differently drawn. If he sued on a money count and it turned out that there was a special contract, he was non-suited and had to pay the costs of the first action before he could bring another on the special contract.[2] Again, if he sued in trespass and trespass did not lie, he was non-suited, although trover or detinue would have lain. In all the old reports the form of action is usually stated first in capitals. And the court never decided that *no* action lay on such a set of facts; but only that the action did not lie in that form. Hence in some cases it was only by a costly process of elimination that a plaintiff could ascertain for certain which was his proper legal remedy. In 1875 there were seven different forms of *personal* actions: debt, covenant,

---

[1] *Hanmer* v. *Flight* (1876) 35 L.T. 127; *Shaw* v. *Shaw* [1954] 2 Q.B. 429, 441 (*ante*, p. 87).
[2] See *White* v. *G.W. Ry.* (1857) 2 C.B.(N.S.) 7.

assumpsit, detinue, trespass, trespass on the case, and replevin; there were three *real* actions [3]: dower, writ of right of dower, and *quare impedit*; and one *mixed* action: ejectment (see *post*, p. 186). And each form of action (except that last mentioned [4]) had its appropriate form of declaration; one of these forms, and only one, had to be pleaded.

This strictness had undoubted advantages; it taught barristers to be precise. But it was often disastrous for the suitors and has accordingly been abolished. Each party now states the facts on which he relies; and the court will declare the law arising upon the facts pleaded. If on those facts the plaintiff would have been entitled to recover in any form of action, he will now recover in the action which he has brought.[5]

Parties

Before drafting a statement of claim, counsel must carefully consider whether all necessary parties have been brought before the court, and also whether it was necessary to bring before the court all the parties named on the writ. He has to show in his pleading a right of action in every plaintiff, and a liability on the part of each defendant and he should consider whether an application to amend the writ will be necessary (see *ante*, pp. 169–172). The plaintiff can, at this early stage, discontinue the action against any of the defendants or withdraw any part of his complaint without any summons, merely by giving a notice in writing under Order 21, r. 2 (1). He must, of course, pay the costs occasioned by the matter so withdrawn (see *post*, Chapter 17). The statements of claim served on all defendants who are kept as parties to the action must be identical, although they may show that different relief is claimed against different defendants. If any party sues, or is sued, in a representative character (*e.g.*, as trustee in a bankruptcy or as executor of a will), this fact ought to be stated in the title or heading of the statement of claim, as well as on the writ.[6]

Illustrations

If any party to the action is improperly or imperfectly named on the writ and no change of identity is involved, the misnomer may be corrected in the statement

---

[3] The other real actions had been abolished by the Real Property Limitation Act, 1833.
[4] From 1852 to 1875 there were no pleadings in ejectment; but the plaintiff often had to deliver particulars.
[5] See *Kelly* v. *Metropolitan Ry.* [1895] 1 Q.B., at p. 946.
[6] *Re Tottenham* [1896] 1 Ch. 628.

of claim by inserting the right name with a statement that the party misnamed had sued or had been sued by the name on the writ, *e.g.*, " John William Smythe (sued as ' J. M. Smith ')." The defendant can take no advantage of such an alteration (pleas in abatement of misnomer were abolished as long ago as 1834); but difficulty may arise in executing a judgment unless the plaintiff amends the writ.

Where a defendant has executed a deed by a wrong name, it is right to sue him by the name in which he executed it.

See *Williams* v. *Bryant* (1839) 5 M. & W. 447.
Mayor of Lynne's Case (1613), 10 Rep. 122 b.

Joinder of Causes of Action

The plaintiff may unite in one action several causes of action without leave, provided that such joinder does not contravene the rules of Order 15 (*ante*, pp. 22 *et seq.*). And he ought to join in the one action all causes of action which can conveniently be tried together, and so save costs.

" A statement of claim shall not contain any allegation or claim in respect of a cause of action unless that cause of action is mentioned in the writ or arises from facts which are the same as, or include or form part of, facts giving rise to a cause of action so mentioned; but subject to that, a plaintiff may in his statement of claim alter, modify or extend any claim made by him in the indorsement of the writ without amending the indorsement," *e.g.*, by claiming further relief or stating the same claim in a different way.[7] Otherwise, matters which have arisen at any time, whether before or since the issue of the writ, may be included in any pleading.[8] But this rule does not entitle the plaintiff to add a new and totally different claim. On the other hand, if a plaintiff in his statement of claim omits all mention of a cause of action or a claim for relief which is stated on his writ, he will be deemed to have abandoned it.[9]

The result of Order 18, r. 15 (2), is that a plaintiff may only include in his statement of claim causes of action which existed at the date of the writ. He can nevertheless recover damages accruing since that date from a cause of action vested in him before it or from a continuing cause of action (*ante*, p. 41). But he cannot claim damages in respect of a cause of action against the same defendant, which has vested in him since the date of the writ.

---

[7] Order 18, r. 15 (2); *Large* v. *Large* [1877] W.N. 198; *Graff Brothers Estates Ltd.* v. *Rimrose Brook Joint Sewerage Bd.* [1953] 2 Q.B. 318.

[8] Ord. 18, r. 9.

[9] *Harries* v. *Ashford* [1950] 1 All E.R. 427. And see *Sterman* v. *E. W. & W. J. Moore* [1970] 1 Q.B. 596.

If he wishes to do that, he must issue a second writ,[9a] and then apply to have the two actions consolidated, if they can conveniently be tried together (see *post*, p. 263). Freer use is made of the power to consolidate actions than was formerly possible.[10]

A plaintiff should as a rule avail himself of all his causes of action, and join as many of them as he can in one action. *E.g.*, he should set out every covenant that there is any ground for believing broken, and allege every available breach of such covenant. But the facts upon which each claim is founded should, so far as possible, be stated separately and distinctly.

Illustrations

A repairing lease generally contains three concurrent covenants as to repairs:
(a) A general covenant to repair.
(b) A covenant to repair on three months' notice.
(c) A covenant to paint the outside once in every three years, and the inside once in every seven years.

Each of these is distinct and severable from the others, and every breach of any one of them is a separate cause of action; therefore set out all three and allege that each is broken, as you may win on one, though you fail on the others. See Precedent No. 27.

If the plaintiff sues the defendant for fraud and proves negligence, he cannot recover; hence it may be advisable, in such a case, to plead negligence in the alternative.

    Connecticut Fire Insurance Co. v. *Kavanagh* [1892] A.C. 473; 61 L.J.P.C. 50.

But a plaintiff must sometimes elect between a claim for damages and a claim for an injunction.

    Gent v. *Harrison* (1893) 69 L.T. 307.

It is often desirable to commence a statement of claim with some introductory averments stating who the parties are, what business they carry on, how they are related or connected, and other surrounding circumstances leading up to the dispute. These are called *matters of inducement*, because they explain what follows, though they may not be essential to the cause of action. A good pleader always reduces such prefatory statements to a minimum, and states them as concisely as possible, though the temptation to " tell the story " may be great! Next should come the essential portions of the claim, *i.e.*, the statement of the plaintiff's right which he alleges has been violated; and then the

---

9a Unless it were to be held that, contrary to the settled practice before 1964, the new rules permit an amendment of the writ in such circumstances.

10 See *Horwood* v. *Statesman Publishing Co.* (1929) 98 L.J.K.B. 450; *Bailey* v. *Marchioness Curzon* [1932] 2 K.B. 392.

statement of the breach or wrong complained of. Then comes the allegation of damage, and last the claim for relief. This order should always be followed.

Tort

In an action of tort it is unnecessary to set out the right which has been violated in cases where that right is not peculiar to the plaintiff in any way, but is one possessed by every subject of the Crown. Thus, in actions of libel, slander, false imprisonment or assault, the claim is merely a statement of a wrong. In other cases where the plaintiff claims a special right in himself (*e.g.*, an easement, or copyright), the right must be stated with all due particularity. This is specially so in actions for the recovery of land. (See *ante*, p. 115.) And remember that it is not sufficient to allege in a pleading that a right or a duty or a liability exists; but the facts must be stated which give rise to such right or create such duty or liability (*ante*, p. 87).

Illustrations

Where a plaintiff claims a right of way he must define the course of the path, state its *termini*, and show how the right vested in him, whether by prescription or grant, but he is not bound to give the precise dates of lost grants, or name the parties to them.

    Harris v. *Jenkins* (1882) 22 Ch.D. 481; 52 L.J.Ch. 437.

    Palmer v. *Guadagni* [1906] 2 Ch. 494.

In an action of libel or slander the precise words complained of are material, and they must be set out *verbatim* in the statement of claim.

    Harris v. *Warre* (1879) 4 C.P.D. 125; 48 L.J.C.P. 310.

    Collins v. *Jones* [1955] 1 Q.B. 564.

    And see the remarks of Lord Esher M.R. in *Darbyshire* v. *Leigh* [1896] 1 Q.B. at p. 557.

In an action of slander you should always aver, wherever there is any ground for doing so, that the words were spoken of the plaintiff in the way of his trade. A foundation should be laid for such an averment by alleging in paragraph 1 that " the plaintiff is a ——, carrying on business at ——," etc.

    Foulger v. *Newcomb* (1867) L.R. 2 Ex. 327; 36 L.J.Ex. 169.

Contract

Where the action is brought on a contract, the contract must first be alleged, and then its breach. It should clearly appear whether the contract on which the plaintiff relies is express or implied; in the latter case the facts should be briefly stated from which the plaintiff contends a contract is to be implied. If the contract be by deed, it should be so stated; if it be not by deed, then a consideration should be shown, which must not be a past consideration.

Wherever the contract sued on is contained in a written instrument, the pleader should shortly state what he conceives to be its legal effect; he should not set out the document itself *verbatim* unless the precise words of the document, or some of them, are material. (Order 18, r. 7 (2).) It will be for the defendant, if he disputes the legal effect attributed to it by the plaintiff, to state his own version of the document, or, if he thinks fit, to set it out *verbatim* in the defence, with an allegation that this is the contract referred to in the statement of claim.

The actual contract which was in force between the parties at the date of breach should be the one alleged. There is no need to go into ancient history. If there have at different times been different agreements between the parties, it is unnecessary to set out the original terms which have been dispensed with. It is sufficient to state the contract as it stood when the plaintiff's right of action accrued.[11] And contingencies need not be stated, if the events upon which they were contingent never happened; they do not affect the plaintiff's right or title.

It is no longer necessary for a plaintiff to allege generally the performance of all conditions precedent, as was customary before the Judicature Act. Such an allegation is now implied in his pleading by Order 18, r. 7 (4) (see *ante*, pp. 98–99, 109). Where, however, the plaintiff is conscious that he has not performed a condition precedent, and has a good excuse for such non-performance, he should in his statement of claim state the condition, the non-performance and the facts which afford him his excuse, *e.g.*, that the defendant prevented or discharged him from performing it. At first sight this might appear to constitute an exception to the principle already stated (*ante*, p. 95) " do not leap before you come to the stile." But this is not really so, even though to a certain extent the plaintiff may be anticipating the defence. For had he failed to mention the circumstances of his non-performance, due performance would have been impliedly alleged by virtue of Order 18, r. 7 (4) and a false issue raised. (And see *ante*, p. 98.)

[11] *Boone* v. *Mitchell* (1822) 1 B. & C. 18.

If either the consideration or the promise is in the alternative, this should be stated according to the fact. If the promise or covenant sued on contains an exception or proviso qualifying the defendant's liability, such exception or proviso should be stated; for it would be incorrect to state the contract as an absolute one. But if the promise or covenant sued on is absolute in itself and contains no exception or proviso, and no reference to any exception or proviso, it may be stated as an absolute contract, although there may be in a distinct part of the deed or instrument a proviso defeating or qualifying it in certain events. For such proviso is in the nature of a defeasance, and must be set up by the defendant if the facts permit. If, however, the subsequent clause is referred to by some such words as "save as hereinafter excepted," then strictly the exception or proviso ought to be set out in the statement of claim.

Illustrations

When the action is brought on a written contract, the pleader should describe it as a contract in writing, and give its date, and name the parties to it, so as to identify the document. If he merely states, "It was agreed between the plaintiff and the defendant," the defendant will apply for particulars.

> *Turquand* v. *Fearon* (1879) 48 L.J.Q.B. 703.

It is not necessary for him, however, to state expressly that the written agreement was signed by the defendant, even though the contract sued on be one to which the Statute of Frauds or Lord Tenterden's Act applies.

> *Rist* v. *Hobson* (1824) 1 S. & S. 543.

As to when a plaintiff should base his claim on a special contract, and when on a *quantum meruit* or an implied contract, see Precedent No. 27 and

> *Head* v. *Baldrey* (1837) 6 A. & E. 459.
>
> *White* v. *G. W. Ry.* (1857) 2 C.B.(N.S.) 7; 26 L.J.C.P. 158.

The plaintiff sued the defendant for not repairing the demised premises pursuant to the covenant in his lease, which the plaintiff stated as a covenant to "repair when and as need should require." The plaintiff, at the trial, produced the deed, and it appeared that the covenant was to repair "when and as need should require, *and at farthest within three months after notice.*" *Held*, a fatal variance, as the latter words, which were omitted from the declaration, debarred the plaintiff from suing until three months had elapsed from service of a notice.

> *Horsefall* v. *Testar* (1817) 7 Taunt. 385; 1 Moore 89.

Where there are several covenants in the same deed, some of which are broken and some not, the plaintiff should, of course, omit all allusion to the covenants which he does not allege to have been broken. There is no need for him to set out the whole document. He should first of all set out all the covenants which he alleges have been broken in their order as they occur in the deed, and then allege separately the breach of each covenant in the same order.

See Precedent No. 27.

Breach

The breach of contract, of which the plaintiff complains, must be alleged in the terms of the contract, or in words co-extensive with the effect or meaning of it. If, however, to allege a breach in the very words of the covenant would be too general an averment, particulars of the breaches should be set out in the pleading. But be careful in so doing not to narrow unduly the general averment that the covenant has been broken.

In averring a breach, " and " must always be turned into " or," and " all " into " any." If the contract be to do more things than one, the plaintiff must either state expressly that the defendant has done none of them, or else set out precisely what and how much he has in fact done. And generally the rules as to traversing (*ante*, p. 132) apply to pleading a breach.

Illustrations

Action on a covenant. The breach was thus assigned: " That the defendant has not used the farm in a husbandlike manner, but on the contrary has committed waste." It was held that the plaintiff could not give any evidence of the defendant's using the farm in an unhusbandlike manner, if it did not amount to waste.

Harris v. *Mantle* (1789) 3 T.R. 307.

This case was cited with approval by Pollock B., and acted on, in *Property Investment Company of Scotland* v. *Lucas & Son*, on April 13, 1886. The learned Baron said: " The case of *Harris* v. *Mantle* was decided by one of the greatest lawyers (Buller J.) of the day in my early time, and although it sounds like a technical decision, it is one of the most sensible decisions ever made."

And see *Doe* d. *Winnall* v. *Broad* (1841) 2 Man. & Gr. 523.

Angerstein v. *Handson* (1835) 1 Cr.M. & R. 789; *ante*, p. 161.

Byrd v. *Nunn* (1877) 7 Ch.D. 284; 47 L.J.Ch. 1; *ante*, p. 143.

Collette v. *Goode* (1878) 7 Ch.D. 842; 47 L.J.Ch. 370; *ante*, p. 143.

If the covenant or promise be in the alternative, the pleader must allege that the defendant did neither the one nor the other.

Legh v. *Lillie* (1860) 6 H. & N. 165; 30 L.J.Ex. 25.

If the contract be to pay a sum of money, *e.g.*, £900, the breach alleged must be not merely that the defendant did not pay £900; the plaintiff must add the words " or any part thereof," or else state how much has been paid and give the defendant credit for that amount, claiming only the balance.

So, again, if the promise be to pay on a particular day, the plaintiff must not merely allege that the defendant has not paid the money on that day; he must add the words " or at all."

If the covenant be to deliver up certain boats and masts and nets and tackle on a certain day, the breach must be assigned that " the defendant never delivered up *any* of the said boats *or* masts *or* nets *or* tackle."

The Claim for Damages

As to the allegation of damage, the distinction between special and general damage must be carefully observed. General damage such as the law will presume to be the natural or probable consequence of the defendant's act need not be specifically pleaded. It arises by inference of law, and need not, therefore, be proved by evidence, and may be averred generally. In some cases however, part of the general damages which it is sought to recover may have resulted from the wrong complained of in an unexpected though foreseeable way, in which case particulars should be given so as to avoid surprise at the trial and to enable your opponent to consider making a payment into court.[11a] And in those cases where a claim for exemplary or aggravated damages still lies the facts alleged in support of that claim should be pleaded.[11b]

Special damage, on the other hand, is such a loss as the law will not *presume* to be the consequence of the defendant's act, but which depends in part, at least, on the special circumstances of the case. It must therefore always be explicitly claimed on the pleadings, and at the trial it must be proved by evidence both that the loss was incurred and that it was the direct result of the defendant's conduct. A mere expectation or apprehension of loss is not sufficient. And no damages can be recovered for a loss actually sustained, unless it is either the natural or probable consequence of the defendant's act, or such a consequence as he in fact contemplated or could reasonably have foreseen when he so acted. All other damage is held " remote."[12] Loss of a kind which is foreseeable yet unexpected, and any damage (*e.g.*, loss of profits) which, although the direct result of the wrongful act, may not have been the immediate consequence of it, should be pleaded in enough detail to inform your opponent of the case he will have to meet and, if possible, enable him to make his own calculation of their amount.[11a] In many cases, proof of special damage is essential to the right of action; in these the writ must not be issued till the special damage has accrued, and then it must be alleged with special care.

[11a] *Perestrello e Companhia Limitada* v. *United Paint Co., Ltd.* [1969] 1 W.L.R. 570; *Domsalla* v. *Barr* [1969] 1 W.L.R. 630.

[11b] *Rookes* v. *Barnard* [1964] A.C. 1129.

[12] *The Wagon Mound* [1961] A.C. 388; *Smith* v. *Leech Brain & Co. Ltd.* [1962] 2 Q.B. 405; *Warren* v. *Scruttons Ltd.* [1962] 1 Lloyd's Rep. 497; *Hadley* v. *Baxendale* (1854) 9 Exch. 341.

No general rule can be laid down as to the precise degree of exactness necessary in a claim of special damage. " The character of the acts themselves which produce the damage, and the circumstances under which these acts are done, must regulate the degree of certainty and particularity with which the damage done ought to be stated and proved. As much certainty and particularity must be insisted on, both in pleading and proof of damage, as is reasonable, having regard to the circumstances and to the nature of the acts themselves by which the damage is done. To insist upon less would be to relax old and intelligible principles. To insist upon more would be the vainest pedantry." (*Per* Bowen L.J., in *Ratcliffe* v. *Evans* [1892] 2 Q.B., at pp. 532, 533.) And remember that a plaintiff who succeeds in recovering general damages may yet be ordered to pay the costs occasioned by a claim for special damage which he has failed to substantiate.[13]

Matters in aggravation of damages may be pleaded in the statement of claim, as we have seen already, *ante*, pp. 100–101.

Illustrations

A plaintiff cannot prove that he has lost particular customers, unless he states their names, either in his pleading or particulars. And the persons so named must as a rule be called at the trial to state why they ceased to deal with the plaintiff.

The plaintiff alleged that in consequence of the defendant's slander she had " lost several suitors." This was held too general an allegation ; for the names of the suitors, if there were any, could hardly have escaped the plaintiff's memory.

Barnes v. *Prudlin vel Bruddel* (1680) 1 Sid. 396; Ventr. 4.

Where a plaintiff claimed generally for loss of his lodgers, he was not allowed to prove the loss of a particular lodger.

Westwood v. *Cowne* (1816) 1 Stark. 172.

In an action for an imprisonment, the plaintiff cannot prove as damage that he suffered in health, or was stinted of food in prison, unless he has charged it in the statement of claim.

Pettit v. *Addington* (1791) Peake 62.
Lowden v. *Goodrick* (1791) Peake 46.

In an action for wrongful dismissal, the loss of salary and commission, which the plaintiff would have earned, is special damage which must be specifically pleaded.

Hayward v. *Pullinger & Partners Ltd.* [1950] 1 All E.R. 581.

But in some cases a plaintiff is allowed to allege generally a loss of business or custom, and to prove it, without having recourse to particular instances, *e.g.*, by showing that his receipts have diminished, or that he has

---

[13] *Forster* v. *Farquhar* [1893] 1 Q.B. 564.

done less business, compared with former years, in consequence of the defendant's conduct.

Rose v. *Groves* (1843) 5 M. & Gr. 613; 12 L.J.C.P. 251.

Ratcliffe v. *Evans* [1892] 2 Q.B. 524; 61 L.J.Q.B. 535.

The Claim for Relief

Every statement of claim must state specifically the relief which the plaintiff claims, either simply or in the alternative; but costs need not be specifically claimed (Order 18, r. 15). The same cause of action may entitle the plaintiff to relief of different kinds. In addition to claiming the payment of a debt (with interest, if appropriate, *ante*, p. 46) or damages, he may ask for one or more of the following kinds of relief:

(i) An injunction (either prohibitory or mandatory) (*post*, pp. 184–185).

(ii) Possession of land.

(iii) Delivery up of a chattel.

(iv) A declaration of right or title (*post*, p. 186).

(v) The appointment of a receiver (*post*, p. 184).

(vi) An account (*ante*, pp. 48–50).

(vii) Specific performance of a contract (*post*, p. 185).

But remember that a statement of claim supersedes the writ; hence if some special form of relief be claimed on the writ, and not in the statement of claim, it will be taken that so much of the claim is abandoned.[14]

Damages.—In an action for unliquidated damages, it is not necessary to insert any specific figure as the precise amount of damages claimed.[15] But where the plaintiff's claim is liquidated and can be ascertained exactly, the pleader should, of course, claim only the precise amount. Where he cannot be exact, it is wiser to claim too much rather than too little; for if the jury find a verdict for a larger amount than the plaintiff claimed, that amount cannot be recovered without amending the record. The judge has power to make such an amendment, if he thinks fit. (Order 20, r. 5; *Beckett* v. *Beckett* [1901] P. 85.)

Equitable relief.—But while the common law courts could only compensate an injured plaintiff by awarding him damages

---

[14] *Harries* v. *Ashford* [1950] 1 All E.R. 427.

[15] See *London and Northern Bank, Ltd.* v. *George Newnes, Ltd.* (1900) 16 T.L.R. at p. 434; *cf. Thompson* v. *Goold & Co.* [1910] A.C. 409. But in the county court, where the scales of costs vary with the sum claimed, it is often expedient to do so.

or ordering his goods or land to be restored to him, courts of equity, even where recognising and enforcing exactly the same primary rights and liabilities as the common law courts, applied different remedies to protect and enforce them. And much of the value of the Chancery system depended upon the efficiency of these remedies. Where the common law could only award damages for a wrong when committed, equity could prevent its commission by injunction. Where law could only give damages for a breach of contract, equity could enforce its specific performance. Where law could give damages for fraud or breach of faith, equity could declare the property affected by it to be held in trust for the injured party—in fact, to be his property; or insist on an account being delivered of all moneys received. But now, by virtue of section 37 of the Judicature Act, 1925, every kind of equitable relief can be claimed and given in an action in the Queen's Bench Division. And even where it is not claimed, yet if the right to it appear incidentally in the course of the proceedings, a party may, if necessary, be allowed to amend his claim and the appropriate relief will be granted.

Receiver.—The court has jurisdiction to appoint a receiver in all cases in which it appears to be just or convenient to make such an order, although the defendant may be in possession of the property [16]; and it will give the receiver possession of the property so far as is necessary for the preservation of the plaintiff's rights.[17] A receiver is an officer of the court, not the agent of or trustee for the parties.[18] He must ordinarily give security duly to account for what he shall receive as such receiver and to pay the same as the court shall direct. (Order 30, r. 2 (2).)

Injunction.—An injunction should be claimed whenever there is any reason to apprehend any repetition of the defendant's unlawful act. In such a case it must be averred that the defendant threatens and intends to repeat the unlawful act, unless such an intention is already apparent from the nature of the case or the facts pleaded.[19] Particulars of the alleged threats could always be

---

16 Judicature Act, 1925, s. 45; *Gwatkin* v. *Bird* (1882) 52 L.J.Q.B. 263; *Leney & Sons* v. *Callingham* [1908] 1 K.B. 79.
17 *Charrington & Co., Ltd.* v. *Camp* [1902] 1 Ch. 386.
18 *Boehm* v. *Goodall* [1911] 1 Ch. 155.
19 *Stannard* v. *Vestry of St. Giles* (1882) 20 Ch.D., at p. 195 ; and see *Att.-Gen.* v. *Dorin* [1912] 1 Ch., at p. 378.

ordered; now particulars of any facts relied on as showing intention must also be pleaded (Order 18, r. 12 (1) (b)).

Under the Judicature Act, 1925, s. 45, the court may grant an injunction by interlocutory order in all cases in which it appears to be just or convenient so to do. Application for such an order may, in cases of extreme urgency, be made *ex parte* (Order 29, r. 1 (2)), and even, if necessary, before the writ is issued. If an *ex parte* injunction is granted it will normally be limited to the period necessary for the return to a summons or motion for an interim injunction pending the trial of the action; but the usual course is to apply after notice to the other side, in which case an interlocutory injunction until the trial of the action may be granted, or the defendant may prefer to give an undertaking. The application will normally be made to a judge in chambers in the Queen's Bench Division (in the Chancery Division by motion in open court) unless the terms of the injunction are agreed upon by the parties, in which case a master or district registrar has jurisdiction to grant it.[19a] The evidence is given on affidavit. Notice of motion for an injunction may be served with the writ without leave (Order 8, r. 4) and this rule is in practice deemed to cover a summons for an injunction. If it is desired to serve short notice of motion (less than two clear days) special leave must be applied for (rule 2 (2)). The plaintiff is usually required to give an undertaking to pay all damages caused to the defendant by the granting of an interlocutory injunction if the order ought not to have been made.[20]

Specific Performance.—Formerly the courts of common law could only award damages for a breach of contract. The courts of equity, on the other hand, while they could not award damages, could compel each party to a contract to execute it precisely according to its terms. This was effected by a " decree for specific performance." But now by section 43 of the Judicature Act, 1925, any division of the High Court may give judgment either for damages or for specific performance, or both. Nevertheless actions for specific performance of contracts for the sale of *real estates* and contracts for *leases* are, for the sake of convenience, assigned to the Chancery Division and should properly be commenced therein. (Section 56.) On the other hand, in any action for breach of contract to deliver specific or ascertained

---

[19a] Ord. 32, r. 11 (2).
[20] And see *Wiltshire Bacon Co.* v. *Associated Cinemas* [1938] 1 Ch. 268.

goods, any division of the High Court may direct that the contract shall be performed specifically, without giving the defendant the option of retaining the goods on payment of damages, or upon such other terms and conditions as to the court may seem just (Sale of Goods Act, 1983, s. 52; and *cf.* Order 14, r. 9). But no such order will be made where the plaintiff has been guilty of unreasonable delay in making his application, or has otherwise acted in a harsh or inequitable manner, or where damages would afford the plaintiff adequate compensation for the breach of contract.

Declaration of Right or Title.—In former days, questions of ownership were decided in *real* actions, questions as to possession in *mixed* actions. But real actions fell into disuse owing to the extreme technicality of their procedure, and the mixed action of ejectment was used to determine indirectly questions of title under the guise of a decision merely as to the right to possession of the property. Thus, if both A and B claimed to be seised in fee of Blackacre, and B was in possession of the land, A would not sue in his own name; for, if he did, he would have to bring a *real* action. He pretended that he had demised Blackacre a few days previously to John Doe or Richard Roe; and this fictitious lessee would obligingly lend his name as plaintiff; and as he claimed no title in himself, but only a right to possession derived from the lease, he could sue in ejectment, and the action would be called *Doe dem. A* v. *B.* The plaintiff would plead A's seisin, and the demise to himself: the defendant was not allowed to traverse the fictitious demise, but he would deny A's seisin; and so A's title to the land would become an issue in the action, and be judicially decided. But it was not always possible to resort to this manoeuvre; moreover the Court of Chancery would not make a binding declaration of title, unless a right to " some consequential relief " was shown,[21] and this practice was followed —with some hesitation—in the High Court after the passing of the Judicature Act until 1883.[22] But by the Rules of 1883 and now by Order 15, r. 16, it has been clearly provided that " no action or other proceeding shall be open to objection on the ground that a merely declaratory judgment or order is sought thereby, and the court may make binding declarations of right, whether or not any

---

[21] *Rooke* v. *Lord Kensington* (1856) 2 K. & J. 753.
[22] *Cox* v. *Barker* (1876) 3 Ch.D. at pp. 370–372.

consequential relief is or could be claimed." And this is now the practice. But the power is discretionary and to be used sparingly.[23] The declaration must be of some legal right, not merely in respect of professional ethics.[23a] The High Court may make a declaration, even where it refuses to grant an injunction or to give any other relief, provided there has in fact been a disturbance of the right which the court is asked to declare.[24] (The jurisdiction of the county court in respect of declarations is more limited.) And see Precedents Nos. 52, 53.

The following forms of action call for special notice:

Account Stated

The law as to account stated is discussed in the judgment of Scrutton L.J. in *Joseph Evans & Co.* v. *Heathcote* [1918] 1 K.B. at pp. 434–437, and in the subsequent cases of *Camillo Tank SS. Co.* v. *Alexandria Engineering Works* (1921) 38 T.L.R. 134 and *Siqueira* v. *Noronha* [1934] A.C. 332. From these authorities it appears that there are two kinds of account stated:

(i) Where there are cross-demands, *i.e.*, where A owes B certain moneys and B also owes A money. In such a case, if A and B, either verbally or in writing, state an account with items on both sides, and strike a balance, and agree on it, then if the balance be in favour of B, he can sue for that balance on an account stated. And, prima facie, he can sue for nothing else except that balance: all his other demands are now extinguished, are in fact paid; and the satisfaction of these is the consideration for A's implied promise to pay the balance. An account stated of this kind is usually conclusive, even though it contains items for which B could not have sued; but it may be reopened on the ground of fraud, or if it is shown that there are substantial errors in it, or if any of the items are such as, if actually paid, could have been recovered back. But the fact that some of the earlier items were barred by the Limitation Act is no reason why A should not pay the balance agreed on, for such earlier items are now considered paid. Similar principles apply to the case where

---

[23] *Guaranty Trust Company* v. *Hannay & Co.* [1915] 2 K.B. 536; *Russian Commercial, etc., Bank* v. *British Bank for Foreign Trade* [1921] 2 A.C. 438, 445; *Vine* v. *National Dock Labour Board* [1957] A.C. 488, 500.
[23a] *Cox* v. *Green* [1966] 2 W.L.R. 369.
[24] *Llandudno Urban District Council* v. *Woods* [1899] 2 Ch. 705; *Dysart (Earl)* v. *Hammerton* [1914] 1 Ch. 822; [1916] A.C. 57.

there is an express promise for good consideration to pay a balance arrived at, whether as a result of items on both sides or on one only; but in this case it would seem that the account can only be reopened on the ground of fraud or some other ground which would vitiate the fresh contract, or in the exercise of the court's equitable jurisdiction.

(ii) Where the debt is all on one side, so that there are no cross-items which can be set off one against the other, and no balance to be struck, and there is an acknowledgment of the total amount due, but no fresh consideration to support an express or implied promise to pay it. This kind of account stated is not conclusive, and the debtor, even in the absence of fraud, may go behind it and dispute the validity of the original debt. One might have thought that such an acknowledgment would be, at most, a mere admission by A of the pre-existing causes of action against himself—a useful piece of evidence in any action for the former debt, but not in itself a cause of action. It has been decided, however, that such an acknowledgment or admission of liability is in itself a new cause of action; and, for want of a better name, it also is called " an account stated." [25]

Examination into the original debts may show one of two things:

(a) that they were good and valid debts, in which case they would be a past executed consideration which would support the fresh promise.[26] They will support it even though they could not have been enforced owing to some procedural bar, such as the Statute of Frauds or the Limitation Act—though in this case the account stated would have to be in writing owing to Lord Tenterden's Act,[26a] or

(b) that the original debt was altogether non-existent, or void owing to the operation of a statute such as the Gaming Act—in which case the account stated would not assist the plaintiff—or that the antecedent obligation was executory in its nature, in which case the account stated is merely a piece of evidence like an I.O.U.[27]

[25] *Knowles* v. *Michel* (1811) 13 East 249, 250; *Brown* v. *Tapscott* (1840) 6 M. & W. 123, 124.　　　　　[26] *Lampleigh* v. *Brathwait* (1616) 1 Sm.L.C.
[26a] *Jones* v. *Ryder* (1838) 4 M. & W. 32.
[27] *Lemere* v. *Elliott* (1861) 30 L.J.Ex. 350.

An action on an account stated must be carefully distinguished from a claim for an account (*ante*, p. 48). As to pleading an account stated, see *ante*, p. 105; as to the defence of settled account, *post*, pp. 208–209, and Precedent No. 61.

Action on a Bond

A bond is the acknowledgment of a debt in writing under the hand and seal of the debtor, who is then called the *obligor*. It must be delivered to the creditor, who becomes the *obligee*. Being under seal it requires no consideration to support it, and the previous simple contract debt, if any, merges in the bond. It binds both the real and personal estate of the obligor. (Law of Property Act, 1925, s. 80; and see Precedent No. 25.)

Bonds are of *three* kinds:—

(i) A " single bond," *i.e.*, a bond without any condition. This is now rare and is not further referred to here.

(ii) A " common money bond," *i.e.*, a bond given to secure the payment of a sum of money. In this case the obligor, having borrowed a sum of money, executes a bond whereby he acknowledges to owe the obligee a larger sum (the penalty), and a condition is annexed that if the sum actually borrowed is repaid with interest at the agreed rate on a named day the bond shall be void.

(iii) A bond with a condition, other than a common money bond, *e.g.*, for the discharge of certain duties or the performance of, or abstention from, particular acts agreed to be or not to be done by the obligor or by someone for whom he stands surety.

A change in the procedure in actions on bonds, which had become highly technical, was made in 1957 by Order LIIIG, which provided that, " In an action on a bond, the indorsement of the writ and the statement of claim shall be framed so as to claim the amount which the plaintiff is entitled to recover, regard being had to the rules of equity relating to penalties, and not the penalty provided for by the bond." It was apparently considered unnecessary to reproduce this Order when the rules were revised in 1962, but the practice (which accords with good sense and with the true rights of the plaintiff) seems to continue.

At common law the penalty on a common money bond was recoverable if the condition was not performed to the letter. But equity intervened to prevent the creditor from recovering more than he was entitled to under the condition. Further relief was given by the Administration of Justice Act, 1705, s. 12, where the payment was not in strict accordance with the condition, on payment of the sum borrowed with interest and costs. But if arrears of interest accumulated to such an amount as, together with the principal, to exceed the penalty of the bond, the creditor could claim no more than the penalty, either at law,[28] or in equity,[29] except in special circumstances, as where the obligor had delayed the creditor by vexatious proceedings,[30] and even in that case the excess could only be claimed against the obligor, not against subsequent incumbrancers.[31]

The penalty on a bond with other conditions formerly became due on breach of any part of the condition and judgment might be had and execution issued thereon subject only to the control of a court of equity, if the debtor applied to it for relief. By the Administration of Justice Act, 1696, s. 8 (now repealed), which removed the necessity for proceedings in equity, any plaintiff suing on such a bond was required to state (or *assign*) the breaches which had been committed by the obligor, and although judgment was still signed for the whole penalty, execution was allowed to issue only for the amount of damages actually sustained in consequence of the breaches so assigned, the judgment remaining as a further security for damages sustained by any future breach.[32]

Accordingly the statement of claim in an action on a common money bond should now state the date of the bond and its terms, including the rate of interest reserved and the period for which it is claimed, and should claim the amount actually recoverable and no more. (See Precedent No. 25.) In an action on a bond with other conditions it should set out the terms of the bond and its conditions and state each breach and claim damages as though the bond were an express covenant by the defendant to

---

[28] *Wilde* v. *Clarkson* (1795) 6 T.R. 303; *Hatton* v. *Harris* [1892] A.C. 547.

[29] *Clarke* v. *Seton* (1801) 6 Ves.Jun. 411; *Hughes* v. *Wynne* (1832) 1 Mylne & Keen 20.

[30] *Grant* v. *Grant* (1830) 3 Sim. 340.

[31] *Hatton* v. *Harris, supra.* It has been held in Ireland that where payments had from time to time been made as and for interest on a bond, and had been applied as such, and the amount of the interest due at any one time, together with the principal, had never reached the penalty, the rule which prevents a bond creditor from being paid more than the amount of the penalty did not apply. (*Knipe* v. *Blair* [1900] 1 Ir.R. 372.)

[32] See *Hurst* v. *Jennings* (1826) 5 B. & C. 650.

do the various acts specified in the conditions. The ordinary rules apply in case of default of appearance or defence, and the claim on a common money bond will ordinarily be treated as a liquidated claim and that on the other type as unliquidated.

Replevin

Replevin is the re-delivery to their owner of goods or cattle which have been taken from him, upon his giving security that he will commence and duly pursue an action against the person by whose orders they were taken, and return them should he fail in the action.

The action generally arises where goods have been distrained for arrears of rent, or where cattle have been straying and doing damage.

For a precedent of a statement of claim in replevin, see No. 45; for defences in such an action, see Nos. 76 and 77 in the Appendix of Precedents.

Chapter 13

DEFENCE

The defendant's counsel, before drafting the defence, should carefully consider the statement of claim, and the way in which the action is shaped against his client. Is any cause of action shown at all? Is the action frivolous or vexatious? If so, he may think it right to apply to strike out the statement of claim. (*Ante*, pp. 152–156.) Such an application should be made promptly—as a rule, before any defence is served. Then is the claim properly pleaded? Is any portion of it embarrassing? Or are particulars necessary? Have claims been joined which cannot conveniently be tried together? If so, the defendant should apply to sever them under Order 15, r. 5. Should the defendant interplead? (*Post*, p. 212.) Should the action be transferred to a county court, under section 45 of the County Courts Act, 1959? Or is it from its nature one that ought to be referred, and has the plaintiff ever agreed in writing to submit the dispute to arbitration? If so, the defendant must at once, before serving any pleading or taking any other step in the action, except appearing, apply to a master to stay the proceedings under section 4 of the Arbitration Act, 1950.

Illustrations

A "step in the proceedings" in section 4 of the Arbitration Act, 1950, means some application to the court by summons or motion, and does not include an application by letter or notice from one party to another, or by correspondence between their respective solicitors. Therefore, merely writing to the plaintiff for further time to plead will not preclude the defendant from applying under this section.

Ives and Barker v. *Willans* [1894] 2 Ch. 478; 63 L.J.Ch. 521.
Cf. the remarks of Cave J. in *Rein* v. *Stein* (1892) 66 L.T. at p. 471.

Nor will merely opposing a summons issued, or a motion made, by the plaintiff.

Zalinoff v. *Hammond* [1898] 2 Ch. 92; 67 L.J.Ch. 370.

But if the defendant attends on the hearing of the plaintiff's summons for directions, and any order is made in favour of the defendant, such as an order for discovery, this is a "step."

Richardson v. *Le Maitre* [1903] 2 Ch. 222; 72 L.J.Ch. 779.
Parker, Gaines & Co. v. *Turpin* [1918] 1 K.B. 358.

So if on hearing of such a summons the defendant gives an undertaking to furnish an account to the plaintiff, and then obtains an adjournment of the summons, this is a step, even though no order be actually made.

Ochs v. *Ochs* [1909] 2 Ch. 121; 78 L.J.Ch. 555.

So is appearing before the master on a summons under Order 14 and asking for leave to defend, or even, apparently, filing an affidavit asking for leave to defend, unless a summons to stay is taken out at the same time.

Pitchers, Ltd. v. *Plaza, etc., Ltd.* (1940) 162 L.T. 213.

The entry of an unconditional appearance is a step in the action (save for the purpose of section 4 of the Arbitration Act, 1950), and amounts to a waiver of any irregularity in the writ or service.

Sheldon v. *Brown Bayley's Steel Works Ltd.* [1953] 2 Q.B. 393.

Appealing from an order made against the defendant under Order 14 is a " step."

And so is an application for leave to serve interrogatories.

Chappell v. *North* [1891] 2 Q.B. 252; 60 L.J.Q.B. 554.

So too may perhaps be an application for particulars.

But see *Clarke Brothers* v. *Knowles* [1918] 1 K.B. 128.

Or for security for costs.

Adams v. *Catley* (1892) 66 L.T. 687.

The Assunta [1902] P. 150.

Or taking out a summons for further time to plead.

Ford's Hotel Co. v. *Bartlett* [1896] A.C. 1; 65 L.J.Q.B. 166.

And *a fortiori* the service of a defence.

West London Dairy Society v. *Abbott* (1881) 44 L.T. 376.

But the fact that the arbitrator agreed on by the parties has, since action brought, made an award, is no ground for staying the action.

Doleman & Sons v. *Ossett Corporation* [1912] 3 K.B. 257; 81 L.J. K.B. 1092.

The defendant must also consider whether the proper parties have been placed on the record. He can no longer plead in abatement. If he considers that the proper parties are not before the court, his remedy is to take out a summons under Order 15, rr. 6 and 7, to add or strike out or substitute a plaintiff or a defendant. If, for instance, he is sued alone for a debt due from his firm, he should apply to have his partners joined as co-defendants, if they are still alive and within the jurisdiction, and that the action meantime be stayed.[1] A defendant may accordingly (subject to the rules as to one or more persons representing all the parties, such as Order 15, rr. 12 and 13) apply to the master to add as plaintiff or defendant any person who ought to have been joined (see pp. 15–21) or whose presence is necessary to enable the court effectually and completely to adjudicate upon and settle all the questions involved in the cause or matter. Thus, if he can show a *prima*

---

[1] See *Pilley* v. *Robinson* (1887) 20 Q.B.D. 155.

facie ground for saying that A is jointly liable with him on the contract sued on, the master will make A a co-defendant on the terms that the plaintiff is not to be prejudiced thereby, and that the original defendant shall pay A's costs, if A is held not liable.[3] No such order will be made if the sole purpose of the application is to enable the proposed new defendant to join with the existing defendant in prosecuting a counterclaim.[4] A person whose legal rights will be directly affected by the granting of the relief claimed in the action, and can therefore show that his presence is necessary to enable the court effectually and completely to adjudicate as above stated, may be added as a party upon his own application.[5] The master will make an order to add a defendant more readily than to add a plaintiff.[6] Moreover, a fresh plaintiff can only be added with his consent signified in writing or in such other manner as may be authorised. (Order 15, r. 6, see *ante*, p. 19.) In some cases, if not all, the consent of a plaintiff already on the record will also be required.[7] The defendant should also consider whether third party proceedings should be instituted (see *post*, pp. 210–212).

Has the defendant's counsel all the documents he needs to help him to draft the defence? If any are referred to in the statement of claim, he should at once give notice to the plaintiff to produce them for his inspection under Order 24, r. 10 (1) (*post*, p. 235). Otherwise he must usually wait until the issues are defined. In exceptional cases the master may order discovery of documents before service of defence—or even of the statement of claim; but this power is seldom exercised and never for the purpose of enabling a party to fish out a case (see *post*, p. 238).

As soon as these preliminary questions are disposed of, the defendant's counsel must proceed to draft the defence. The defendant must state in his defence every material fact on which he proposes to rely at the trial. He must deal specifically with every fact alleged in the statement of claim, either admitting or denying

---

3 *Fardell, etc., Co.* v. *Basset* (1899) 15 T.L.R. 204; *Norbury, Natzio & Co.* v. *Griffiths* [1918] 2 K.B. 369.

4 *Atid Navigation Co. Ltd.* v. *Fairplay Towage & Shipping Co. Ltd.* [1955] 1 W.L.R. 336.

5 *Dollfus Mieg* v. *Bank of England* [1951] 1 Ch. 33; *Amon* v. *Raphael Tuck & Sons, Ltd.* [1956] 1 Q.B. 357; *The Result* [1958] P. 174.

6 *Wilson, Sons & Co.* v. *Balcarres Brook Steamship Co., Ltd.* [1893] 1 Q.B. 422; *Roberts* v. *Holland* [1893] 1 Q.B. 665.

7 See *Pennington* v. *Caley* (1912) 106 L.T. 591; *Emden* v. *Carte* (1881) 17 Ch.D. 169, 768 (joinder of plaintiff's trustee in bankruptcy.)

it; he may plead further facts in answer to those he admits; he may object to the whole pleading as insufficient in law; or he may rely on a set-off or counterclaim. (See Chapter 14.) All these separate grounds of defence must be stated, as far as may be, separately and distinctly, especially where they are founded upon separate and distinct facts.

Any number of defences may be pleaded together in the same action, although they are obviously inconsistent. A defendant may " raise by his statement of defence, without leave, as many distinct and separate, and therefore inconsistent, defences as he may think proper, subject only to the provision " contained in Order 18, r. 19, for striking out embarrassing matter. (*Per* Thesiger L.J. in *Berdan* v. *Greenwood* (1878) 3 Ex.D. at p. 255.) And a defence is not embarrassing merely because it contains inconsistent averments,[8] provided such averments are not fictitious.[9]

As to objections in point of law, enough has been said *ante,* p. 147. As to traverses, do not deny everything. It causes useless expense. Admit all you can. But when you traverse, traverse well and boldly.

Denials must be specific

" Any allegation of fact made by a party in his pleading is deemed to be admitted by the opposite party unless it is traversed by that party in his pleading or a joinder of issue under rule 14 operates as a denial of it." (Order 18, r. 13 (1).)

" A traverse may be made either by a denial or by a statement of non-admission and either expressly or by necessary implication." (Order 18, r. 13 (2).)

" Every allegation of fact made in a statement of claim or counterclaim which the party on whom it is served does not intend to admit must be specifically traversed by him in his defence or defence to counterclaim, as the case may be; and a general denial of such allegations, or a general statement of non-admission of them, is not a sufficient traverse of them." (Order 18, r. 13 (3).)

The rules of 1883 dealt with these matters in greater detail and with instances. The effect of the rules is to prevent a defendant pleading the general issue, as it was called (see *ante,* p. 86), and to make him " take matter by matter, and traverse each of them

[8] *Child* v. *Stenning* (1877) 5 Ch.D. 695.
[9] *Re Morgan* (1887) 35 Ch.D., at p. 496.

separately." (*Per* Thesiger L.J. in *Byrd* v. *Nunn* (1877) 7 Ch.D., at p. 287.) Hence a defendant should not plead merely that " he denies specifically every allegation contained in the statement of claim," or he may find that he has broken Order 18, rule 13 (3) and his pleading may be struck out under rule 19 (1). On the other hand he cannot be expected to write out and traverse every sentence in the statement of claim.[10] It is usually considered sufficient, when dealing with matters of inducement or other allegations which do not go to the gist of the action, to plead that " the defendant denies each of the allegations contained in paragraph 3." But when the pleader comes to those allegations which are the gist of the action, he should be more precise and should plead, " The defendant never agreed as alleged," or " never spoke or published any of the said words," or " never made any such representation as is alleged in paragraph 3 of the statement of claim." (See Precedents, Nos. 59, 67, 69, 78.)

There are two important exceptions to the rule that a defendant must specifically traverse every allegation of fact in the statement of claim which he does not admit. Both are legacies from the old procedure and are very sensible and proper provisions.

(i) *Pleading to Particulars*

Before the Judicature Act it was not the practice for the plaintiff to set out in his declaration any details which were not a necessary part of the cause of action; such matters were stated, if at all, in a separate document, subsequently delivered, which was called " Particulars." And it was then a clear rule that the defendant must not plead to anything stated in the " Particulars," but only to the matters alleged in the declaration. The rules of pleading at present in force require a plaintiff to insert all necessary details in his statement of claim, except that particulars of debt, expenses or damages exceeding three folios in length must be served separately [11]; but it still remains the practice that the defendant does not plead specifically to matter alleged under the head of " Particulars," as in answering the body of the pleading he will have dealt with the substantive allegation to which the particulars

---

10 *John Lancaster Radiators Ltd.* v. *General Motor Radiator Co. Ltd.* [1946] 2 All E.R. 685.
11 Order 18, r. 12 (2).

refer and the particulars will ordinarily be covered by implication. Unfortunately, it sometimes happens that a plaintiff inserts in his particulars allegations of fact which go beyond what is alleged in the body of the pleading. This puts the defendant in a difficulty. It would hardly be appropriate to take out a summons attacking the statement of claim as embarrassing, but at the same time it will not be wise for him to allow the action to go for trial without denying the matters in question or pleading the facts which answer them. Hence he usually pleads to them as though they had been stated in their proper place.

(ii) *Do not Plead to Damages*

" Any allegation that a party has suffered damage and any allegation as to the amount of damages is deemed to be traversed unless specifically admitted." (Order 18, r. 13 (4).) This rule applies to damage of all kinds, whether special or general, and whether the alleged damage is part of the cause of action or not.[12]

Illustrations

Action of trespass for chasing sheep, *per quod* the sheep died. It is not necessary to traverse expressly the dying of the sheep.
> *Leech* v. *Widsley* (1681) Vent. 54; 1 Lev. 283.

Action for not properly building a ship, according to covenant, whereby she was obliged to put back and was detained. A plea " to so much of the declaration as relates to the detaining " was held bad.
> *Porter* v. *Izat* (1836) 1 M. & W. 381; 1 Tyr. & G. 639.

" The plea must be an answer to the action ; there is no such thing as a plea to the damages."
> *Per* Tindal C.J., in *Smith* v. *Thomas* (1835) 2 Bing.N.C., at p. 378.

Special Defences

" A party must in any pleading subsequent to a statement of claim plead specifically any matter, for example, performance, release, any relevant statute of limitation, fraud or any fact showing illegality—(a) which he alleges makes any claim or defence of the opposite party not maintainable; or (b) which, if not specifically pleaded, might take the opposite party by surprise; or (c) which raises issues of fact not arising out of the preceding pleading." (Order 18, r. 8 (1).) In all such cases the fresh facts on which the defence is based must be specifically pleaded.

---

[12] See the remarks of Smith L.J. in *Greenwell* v. *Howell* [1900] 1 Q.B. at p. 538.

Defence

Illustrations

The defence that a contract is a wager within the Gaming Acts should be specially pleaded: and the facts which are relied on to bring the transactions within those Acts should be stated.

Colborne v. *Stockdale* (1722) 1 Stra. 493.
Grizewood v. *Blane* (1851) 11 C.B. 526; 21 L.J.C.P. 46.
Willis v. *Lovick* [1901] 2 K.B. 195; 70 L.J.K.B. 656.

So whenever the contract sued on is of a kind prohibited by statute.
Bull v. *Chapman* (1853) 8 Ex. 444; 22 L.J.Ex. 257.

In all cases, however, the court will itself take notice of any illegality of the contract on which the plaintiff is suing, if it appears on the face of the contract or from the evidence brought before it by either party, and even though the defendant has not pleaded the illegality.

Gedge v. *Royal Exchange Assurance* [1900] 2 Q.B. 214.
R. v. *Weisz* [1951] 2 K.B. 611.
Snell v. *Unity Finance Co. Ltd.* [1964] 2 Q.B. 203 and other cases there cited.
Belvoir Finance Co. v. *Harold G. Cole & Co.* [1969] 1 W.L.R. 1877.

Where the contract is not *ex facie* illegal, but the question of illegality depends upon the surrounding circumstances, as a general rule the court will not entertain the question unless it is raised by the pleadings. But it may allow an amendment so as to raise the point and grant an adjournment if justice so requires.

Re Robinson's Settlement [1912] 1 Ch. 717.
North Western Salt Co. v. *Electrolytic Alkali Co.* [1914] A.C. at p. 469.

A plea that the contract sued on was subsequently altered in a material particular by an interlineation is a plea in confession and avoidance and must be specially pleaded.

Hemming v. *Trenery* (1839) 9 A. & E. 926.
Crediton (Bishop) v. *Exeter (Bishop)* [1905] 2 Ch. 455.

A surrender must be specially pleaded, whether it was by deed or by operation of law; in the latter case the facts must be stated which are alleged to constitute such a surrender.

Foquet v. *Moor* (1852) 7 Ex. 870, 875; 22 L.J.Ex. 35.

If a plaintiff sues in a representative capacity, the defence that he is not such executor or administrator must be specially pleaded. If it is not, the objection cannot be raised at the trial. So, if the plaintiff asserts that he is a member of a particular partnership firm, and the defendant intends to dispute this at the trial, he must specifically deny the plaintiff's allegation in his defence.

Hole v. *Bradbury* (1879) 12 Ch.D. 886; 48 L.J.Ch. 673.

In an action brought by a solicitor for his costs, the defence that he was not a duly qualified practitioner at the time the work was done must be specially pleaded.

Hill and Randall v. *Sydney* (1838) 7 A. & E. 956.

And so must the defence that he did not deliver a signed bill of costs in accordance with section 68 of the Solicitors Act, 1957.

Cf. Lane v. *Glenny* (1837) 7 A. & E. 83.

Special Defences

Plea of the Statute of Frauds

" There is no memorandum in writing of the alleged contract sufficient to satisfy the Statute of Frauds." It is not necessary to plead any particular section, and it is wiser not to do so. For if you specify a particular section, you cannot avail yourself of another, unless the judge gives you leave to amend.[13] If the plaintiff sues on a written contract, and then at the trial seeks to rely on a parol agreement, the judge should either exclude all evidence of the parol agreement, or else allow the defendant to amend by pleading the Statute of Frauds if applicable.[14] The operation of the statute was considerably curtailed by the Law Reform (Enforcement of Contracts) Act, 1954.

Plea of the Statute of Limitations

" The plaintiff's cause of action, if any, did not accrue within six[15] years before this suit, and the defendant will rely on the Limitation Act, 1939." The objection that the action is brought too late must be raised by a special plea, even though it appear on the face of the statement of claim.[16] The date at which an action commenced is the date on which the writ was issued and not the date of service.

It is now the same in an action for the recovery of land. The defendant must specially plead the Limitation Act and should do so in this form: " The plaintiff's claim is barred by the Limitation Act, 1939, and his right and title (if any) to the said land were extinguished by virtue of that Act." [17]

Former Proceedings

That the plaintiff brought a previous action and recovered

---

[13] *James* v. *Smith* [1891] 1 Ch. 384; *Hills and Grant, Ltd.* v. *Hodson* [1934] Ch. 53.

[14] *Brunning* v. *Odhams* (1897) 75 L.T. 602.

[15] In the case of actions for damages for personal injuries caused by negligence, nuisance or breach of duty the period is three years (Law Reform (Limitation of Actions, etc.) Act, 1954). In such cases the day on which the accident occurred is excluded from the reckoning, so that the action may validly be commenced on the anniversary of that day (*Marren* v. *Dawson Bentley & Co. Ltd.* [1961] 2 Q.B. 135). Whether the contrary authority of *Gelmini* v. *Moriggia* [1913] 2 K.B. 549 would now be followed in actions of contract seems doubtful. See *Hodgson* v. *Armstrong* [1967] 2 Q.B. 299.

[16] *Hawkings* v. *Billhead* (1636) Cro.Car. 404.

[17] See *Dawkins* v. *Lord Penrhyn* (1878) 6 Ch.D. at p. 323; 4 App.Cas. at pp. 59, 64; and *Tichborne* v. *Weir* (1892) 67 L.T. 735.

damages [18] against the *same* defendant for the same cause of action is a bar to any subsequent action, even though fresh damage has since arisen from the defendant's unlawful act; for the judge or jury in the former action must be taken to have assessed the damages once for all, and the probability or possibility that this subsequent damage would follow should have been submitted to their consideration then. This rule, however, does not apply to cases where special damage is essential to the cause of action; in such cases a second action can be brought if fresh special damage accrues from the same cause of action. [19]

Where more than one person is involved, if there are joint contractors and judgment is signed against one, the other is discharged except where the plaintiff's rights against another defendant in the same action are preserved by Order 13, r. 1, Order 14, r. 8 or Order 19, r. 2. (*Parr* v. *Snell* [1923] 1 K.B. 1, and see *ante*, pp. 56, 68.) Thus, if A and B be in partnership, a previous judgment recovered against A for a breach of contract would be a bar to any action against B for the same cause of action, even though the judgment obtained against A be not satisfied; because both A and B ought to have been sued jointly in the first action. It may also be a bar to a claim for relief which could have been— but was not—made in the first action. (*West* v. *Automatic Salesman Ltd.* [1937] 2 K.B. 398.)

Where the plaintiff sues upon a joint tort, a judgment previously obtained against one joint tortfeasor is now no bar to an action against another; but he cannot execute for more in the aggregate than the amount of his judgment in the first action and he will be at risk as to costs (see Law Reform (Married Women and Tortfeasors) Act, 1935, s. 6 (1)).

If the claim, whether in contract or tort, is founded upon separate causes of action in respect of the same subject-matter, judgment without satisfaction against one defendant does not bar a judgment against another defendant in the same or a subsequent action (*Isaacs & Sons* v. *Salbstein* [1916] 2 K.B. 139; *B. O. Morris Ltd.* v. *Perrott & Bolton* [1945] 1 All E.R. 567).

---

[18] Or accepted money paid into court (*Derrick* v. *Williams* [1939] 2 All E.R. 559).
[19] *Darley Main Colliery Co.* v. *Mitchell* (1886) 11 App.Cas. 127; *Crumbie* v. *Wallsend Local Board* [1891] 1 Q.B. 503; *West Leigh Colliery Co.* v. *Tunnicliffe* [1908] A.C. 27.

Where two persons are liable in the alternative, judgment against one is a bar to an action against the other.[20]

Again, if the former action was unsuccessful, this will also be a bar to a second action against the same defendant; unless, indeed, the plaintiff lost the former action only on some technical ground, and the judge, instead of giving judgment against him, gave him leave to discontinue (see *post*, p. 253). So, if A and B are jointly liable and the plaintiff sues A and fails, the judgment in the action against A will afford B a good defence to a subsequent action against him, provided that A succeeded on a ground which is also open to B.[21]

The defence of *res judicata* cannot be raised, unless it is specially pleaded in the defence.[22] The cause of action must be the same in both actions,[23] and both actions must be brought against the same defendant,[24] or against persons jointly liable on the same cause of action. A long series of cases, many of them difficult to reconcile, has left the law in a rather confused state.

Where, for any reason, the strict defence of *res judicata* is not applicable (*e.g.*, where the actions are not between precisely the same parties or persons suing in the same capacity), still, if the plaintiff is " suing substantially by virtue of the same alleged title," or if the issues raised in the second action are identical with those decided in the first, the court will stay the second action,[25] at all events until the costs of the first action are paid [26]; but not where the former action, though similar in its nature, was brought against a different defendant.[27]

There is machinery for registering in this country judgments of the superior courts of many of the Commonwealth countries, colonies and other territories, and of such foreign countries as give reciprocal facilities, so that execution may be had thereon unless application is made to set the registration aside. Whether registered or not, they are in some circumstances regarded as conclusive

---

[20] *Morel Brothers* v. *Earl of Westmorland* [1904] A.C. 11.
[21] *Phillips* v. *Ward and Others* (1863) 2 H. & C. 717.
[22] *Edevain* v. *Cohen* (1889) 43 Ch.D. 187; *Workington Harbour Board* v. *Trade Indemnity Co., Ltd.* (1937) 43 Com.Cas. 235.
[23] *Serrao* v. *Noel* (1885) 15 Q.B.D. 549; *Ord* v. *Ord* [1923] 2 K.B. 432.
[24] *Isaacs & Sons* v. *Salbstein* [1916] 2 K.B. 139.
[25] *Humphries* v. *Humphries* [1910] 2 K.B. 531; *Cooke* v. *Rickman* [1911] 2 K.B. 1125.
[26] *Martin* v. *Earl Beauchamp* (1883) 25 Ch.D. 12; *MacDougall* v. *Knight* (1890) 25 Q.B.D. 1; *M'Cabe* v. *Bank of Ireland* (1889) 14 App.Cas. 413. Except where the plaintiff is a minor: *Re Payne* (1883) 23 Ch.D. 288.
[27] *Le Mesurier* v. *Ferguson* (1903) 20 T.L.R. 32.

between the parties. (See Administration of Justice Act, 1920; Foreign Judgments (Reciprocal Enforcement) Act, 1933; and Order 71.)

Estoppel

In some cases the law will not allow a litigant to attempt to prove allegations which are directly contrary to that which has already been decided against him, or to that which he has himself deliberately represented to be the fact. He is said to be " estopped " from proving such matters. An estoppel debars a party from raising a particular contention in an action, when to raise it would be inequitable or contrary to the policy of the law. It binds not only the original parties but also all who claim under them. It is not a cause of action but a rule of evidence.

Estoppels are of three kinds:

(i) By record.
(ii) By deed.
(iii) By conduct.

(i) *Estoppel by record, e.g.*, by a judgment of a court of competent jurisdiction.[28] The matter becomes *res judicata* even though judgment is delivered after the commencement of fresh proceedings.[29] So long as that judgment stands, no one who was a party to it can reopen that litigation.[30] The judgment binds the plaintiff, the defendant and the executor, administrator or assign of each of them, and all claiming under them.[31] Where in a first action the defendant does not traverse an allegation which he might have traversed, he will be estopped from traversing a similar allegation in a second action by the same plaintiff.[32] A record will not create an estoppel if the judgment was obtained by fraud or collusion.

(ii) *Estoppel by deed.*—If under his hand and seal a man asserts a thing to be, he cannot set up the contrary in any litigation between him and the other party to that deed. Both parties

---

[28] See *Nokes* v. *Nokes* [1957] P. 213.
[29] *Bell* v. *Holmes* [1956] 1 W.L.R. 1359.
[30] See, for example, *Hill* v. *Hill* [1954] P. 291 and *Wood* v. *Luscombe* [1966] 1 Q.B. 169. But the principle will not operate in matrimonial cases where the court, exercising its statutory duty to inquire into the truth of the petition, decides to reopen the issue. (*Thompson* v. *Thompson* [1957] P. 19.)
[31] *Marchioness of Huntly* v. *Gaskell* [1905] 2 Ch. 656.
[32] *Humphries* v. *Humphries*; *Cooke* v. *Rickman, ante*, p. 201.

are bound by the language of the deed; and so are all claiming under them.[33] But there will be no estoppel if the deed was obtained by fraud or duress, or is tainted with illegality.

(iii) *Estoppel by conduct.*[34]—If A by word or conduct induces B to believe that a certain state of things exists, and B in that belief acts in a way in which he would not have acted unless he so believed and is thereby prejudiced, then A cannot in any subsequent proceeding between himself and B or any one claiming under B be heard to deny that that state of things existed.[35] But A will not be estopped from averring the truth in any other proceeding. The estoppel only arises in favour of some person whom A has induced by word or conduct to do or abstain from doing some particular thing. The words may be written or spoken; the conduct may be any act, omission or neglect, provided it be an omission to do something which A ought to do—the neglect of some legal duty which A owes B; provided also that such omission or neglect misleads B and misleads him to his prejudice.[36] Even silence may be sufficient where there is a duty to speak, and where silence will create an erroneous impression which causes B to alter his position for the worse; as in *Pickard* v. *Sears* (1837) 6 A. & E. 469, where a man stood by and saw his goods sold to a bona fide purchaser.[37]

An estoppel must always be specially pleaded,[38] unless it appears on the face of the adverse pleading, when it is ground for an objection in point of law; or unless there was no opportunity to plead it, as there was not in *Coppinger* v. *Norton* [1902] 2 Ir.R. 241. It cannot be pleaded by a stranger to the estoppel. A plea of estoppel must always be drafted with great care and particularity. It must state in full detail the facts on which the party pleading relies as constituting the estoppel, and should also specify

---

[33] *Bateman* v. *Hunt* [1904] 2 K.B. 530.

[34] The third kind of estoppel was formerly called estoppel *in pais* (*i.e.*, in the country), because it depended on matters outside the four corners of any record or deed. Estoppel by conduct is a clearer phrase.

[35] See *Square* v. *Square* [1935] P. 120; 104 L.J.P. 46.

[36] *Lewis* v. *Lewis* [1904] 2 Ch. 656.

[37] And see *Nana Ofori Atta II* v. *Nana Abu Bonsra II* [1958] A.C. 95.

[38] It has been held that an estoppel by *record* or *deed* must be specially pleaded (*Bowman* v. *Rostron* (1835) 2 A. & E. 295n.) but that an estoppel by conduct might in some cases be given in evidence without being specially pleaded. (*Freeman* v. *Cooke* (1848) 2 Ex. 654; *Phillips* v. *Im-Thurm* (1865) 18 C.B.(N.S.) 400.) Under the present rules the proper course is to plead an estoppel of any kind, if it be practicable to do so (Ord. 18, r. 8 (1)).

the allegations which it is contended the other party is precluded from proving. (See Precedent No. 81.)

Release

This defence must be specially pleaded. (Order 18, r. 8 (1); and see *ante*, pp. 129, 145.) If one of several joint creditors releases the debtor, the other joint creditors are barred, unless the release was obtained fraudulently. So the release of one joint debtor releases all who are jointly liable with him, unless the right to release one without discharging the others was expressly reserved; but where the liability is several, the release of one debtor does not affect the others, except possibly in the case of co-sureties. If the right of one co-surety to contribution be taken away by a release given to another co-surety, both are discharged.[39]

Rescission

This must be specially pleaded. (See Precedent, No. 66).

Lien

This defence must be specially pleaded, for it admits the plaintiff's property in the goods he seeks to recover, but states a good reason why he should, for the time, be deprived of the possession of them. It is thus a plea of confession and avoidance. Where it is pleaded, the master may order the goods to be given up to the plaintiff on his paying into court, to abide the event of the action, the full sum claimed by the defendant as the amount of his lien, together with a further sum for interest and costs. (Order 29, r. 6; and see *Gebruder Naf* v. *Ploton* (1890) 25 Q.B.D. 13.)

Accord and Satisfaction

These are both technical terms, and the plea must allege both. Suppose that B has broken his contract with A; then A and B agree [39a] together that B shall give or do something to or for A, and that A shall accept this in discharge of his cause of action against B. This is an " accord "; and if the matter rests there, there is no defence to an action brought by A on the original contract. But if

[39] *Ward* v. *National Bank of New Zealand* (1883) 8 App.Cas. 755.
[39a] Such agreement must be complete and either under seal or supported by consideration. (*D. & C. Builders Ltd.* v. *Rees* [1966] 2 W.L.R. 288.)

B in pursuance of the " accord " gives to A or does for him what was agreed, this is a " satisfaction," and the two together afford B a good defence to any action on the original contract. *E.g.*, X agrees to sell and deliver to Y a Broadwood piano for £200, but is unable to obtain a Broadwood piano. He asks Y to accept an Erard piano of at least equal value, and Y agrees to do so. This agreement alone affords X no defence to an action by Y, unless and until X delivers the Erard piano to Y. An accord and satisfaction made by a third party on the defendant's behalf, and accepted by the plaintiff in discharge, will be a bar to the action.[40] This defence could not formerly be pleaded to a claim on a bond or other specialty, because there was a maxim that a contract under seal could only be discharged by performance or some other contract under seal. But now an accord and satisfaction is an answer to an action on a specialty debt.[41] (See Precedent No. 55.)

Tender

" The defendant, before action, to wit, on March 23, 1968, tendered to the plaintiff the sum of £——, which the plaintiff claims in this action, but the plaintiff then refused to accept it. And the defendant now brings the said sum of £—— into court ready to be paid to the plaintiff." A plea of tender must show that the tender was made before action brought; and the sum alleged to have been tendered must be brought into court. (Order 18, r. 16.) This plea cannot strictly be pleaded to actions for unliquidated damages, whether sounding in contract or in tort,[42] unless there be some special statutory provision enabling a defendant to tender amends. But there is a difference between a payment into court *simpliciter* and a payment into court with a plea of tender. A tender is a defence proper[43]; hence the plaintiff cannot, without the leave of a master, take out money paid in with a plea of tender (Order 22, r. 4 (1)). If he gets leave and takes the money out in satisfaction, the order of the master must deal with the whole costs of the action or of the cause of action to which

[40] *Jones* v. *Broadhurst* (1850) 9 C.B. 173.
[41] *Steeds* v. *Steeds* (1889) 22 Q.B.D. 537.
[42] *Dearle* v. *Barrett* (1834) 2 A. & E. 82; *Davys* v. *Richardson* (1888) 21 Q.B.D. 202.
[43] But as to the position in Admiralty proceedings see *The Mona* [1894] P. at p. 286.

Defence

the payment relates (*ibid.*); and he would ordinarily award them
to the defendant, since the plaintiff should have accepted the money
tendered and not have sued for it.[44]

As a plea of tender must necessarily disclose the fact that
money has been paid into court, it is one of the exceptions to the
general rule that that fact should not be known to the judge at
the trial (Order 22, r. 7); the issue is simply, was a good tender
made before action brought?

Payment

Payment before action is a matter of defence which must be
pleaded and proved by the defendant. A plea of payment should
state that the payment relied on was made before the issue of the
writ, giving dates and amounts of payments and also any
facts showing an appropriation of such payments to the debt
sued for in the action. But there is no need for the defendant to
plead that he paid any sums for which he is expressly given
credit in the statement of claim. The plaintiff is taken to be
suing for the balance due after crediting payments he admits.

Payment into Court

The fact that money has been paid into court (see *post*, p. 254)
no longer appears, as it used to do, on the face of the defence
except where tender before action or a defence under the Libel
Act, 1843, s. 2, is pleaded (Order 22, r. 7; Order 82, r. 4 (2)).

Fraud

Where fraud is intended to be charged, it must be distinctly
charged, and its details specified. General allegations, however
strong, are insufficient to amount to an averment of fraud of
which any court ought to take notice. (*Wallingford* v. *Mutual
Society* (1880) 5 App.Cas. at p. 697; *Lawrance* v. *Lord Norreys*
(1890) 15 App.Cas. at p. 221.) Counsel must insist on being fully
instructed before placing a plea of fraud on the record. Such a
plea should never be drafted on insufficient material, nor without
warning to the client, if appropriate, that by adopting such an
aggressive line of defence he may double or treble the amount of
damages which he may ultimately have to pay.

[44] *Griffiths* v. *Ystradyfodwg School Board* (1890) 24 Q.B.D. 307.

Justification in Libel and Slander

This also is a most dangerous plea, and should never be placed on the record without careful consideration of the sufficiency of the evidence by which it is to be supported. " Like a charge of fraud, counsel must not put a plea of justification on the record unless he has clear and sufficient evidence to support it." (*Per* Lord Denning M.R. in *Associated Leisure, Ltd.* v. *Associated Newspapers, Ltd.* [1970] 2 Q.B. 450 at p. 456.) Full particulars will almost certainly be ordered (see *ante*, p. 124); and at the trial the strictest proof will be required. (See *Leyman* v. *Latimer* (1877) 3 Ex.D. 15, 352.) And if the plea be not proved, the defendant's persistence in the charge is some evidence of malice, and will always tend to aggravate the damages given against him. The defence cannot be raised without a special plea; and counsel should never draw such a plea without express instructions, and even then should always caution the defendant as to the risk he runs. The plea must justify the precise charge which the defendant has made, and, as a rule, the whole of that charge. In some cases the defendant will be allowed to justify a portion of his words, but only in mitigation of damages. (See *ante*, pp. 100–101.)

Where the defendant did not make a direct charge himself, but only repeated what A said, a general plea that the words are true will be insufficient; he must plead and prove not only that A said so, but in addition that what A said was true.[45] The defendant cannot in any case plead that other words not set out in the statement of claim are true.[46]

Privilege

Formerly, it was unnecessary specially to plead privilege; this defence was available under the plea of Not Guilty, as it still is in criminal cases. But since the Judicature Act privilege must be specially pleaded, and the facts and circumstances on which the defendant will rely as rendering the occasion privileged must be set out either in the plea or in the particulars.[47] Any plea which wears a doubtful aspect, which may be either a plea of

---

[45] *Duncan* v. *Thwaites* (1824) 3 B. & C. 556; *M'Pherson* v. *Daniels* (1829) 10 B. & C. 263.

[46] *Rassam* v. *Budge* [1893] 1 Q.B. 571.

[47] *Simmonds* v. *Dunne* (1871) Ir.R. 5 C.L. 358; *Elkington* v. *London Association for the Protection of Trade* (1911) 27 T.L.R. 329.

privilege, or a mere traverse, or a justification, will be struck out as embarrassing. (See Precedent No. 78.)

Equitable Defences

Equitable defences may now be pleaded in the Queen's Bench Division. And so may equitable counterclaims, *e.g.*, for specific performance or rescission or rectification of an agreement. (See Precedent No. 65.) " If a defendant claims to be entitled to any equitable estate or right, or to relief on any equitable ground against any deed, instrument or contract, or against any right, title or claim asserted by any plaintiff or petitioner in the cause or matter, or alleges any ground of equitable defence to any such claim of the plaintiff or petitioner, the court or judge shall give to every equitable estate, right or ground of relief so claimed, and to every equitable defence so alleged, the same effect by way of defence against the claim of the plaintiff or petitioner, as the Court of Chancery ought formerly to have given, if the like matters had been relied on by way of defence in any suit or proceeding instituted in that court for the like purpose." (Judicature Act, 1925, s. 38.) Equitable defences must be pleaded fully,[48] even in actions for the recovery of land.

Settled Account

A settled account is a statement of the accounts between two parties which is agreed to and accepted by both as correct. It must be final, that is, it must show clearly what balance is due, or that no balance is due. An informal release of all demands may be a settled account. The fact that it is stated with the qualification " errors excepted " will not prevent its being a good settled account. It is not enough for the accounting party merely to deliver his account; there must be some evidence that the other party has accepted it as correct. But such acceptance need not be express; contemporaneous or subsequent conduct may amount to a sufficient acquiescence.[49] The fact that the accounting party delivered up his vouchers to the other party is evidence that both regarded the settlement as final. (See Precedent No. 61.)

The plea of a settled account is a good defence to a claim

---

[48] *Sutcliffe* v. *James* (1879) 40 L.T. 875; *Heap* v. *Marris* (1877) 2 Q.B.D. 630.
[49] *Clark* v. *Glennie* (1820) 3 Stark. 10; *Irvine* v. *Young* (1823) 1 Sim. & St. 333.

for an account; and if coupled with an allegation that the balance shown by such account had before action been paid to the plaintiff, it is also a good defence to an action for money received by the defendant to the use of the plaintiff. In reply to such a plea, however, the plaintiff may allege that the settlement ought to be set aside, because the account contains errors of such a kind, or to such an extent, that it would be inequitable to hold him bound by it. He must, in his reply or other pleading, specify the errors upon which he relies [50]; and if he contends that such errors were made fraudulently, this must also be clearly stated. If he succeeds in proving fraud, the account will be wholly set aside, and the defendant must account *de novo* for every penny which he has received. The same result will follow where there is no fraud, if a considerable number of errors is shown in the account. Indeed, if the parties stand to each other in a fiduciary relation (*e.g.,* as solicitor and client, trustee and *cestui que trust,* guardian and ward), the plaintiff need only prove one " grave or substantial error," and the account will be taken as though there had been no settlement.[51] Where there is no such relation, and no fraud, and the plaintiff cannot prove any large number of errors he will probably only obtain leave to " surcharge and falsify," as it is called. Proof of one " definite and important error " will entitle him to this.[52] It means that the account stands for what it is worth; but that either party may try to amend it, either by adding items in his favour which were wrongly omitted (that is, surcharging), or by striking out items against himself which were wrongly inserted (that is, falsifying). Whether an account shall be opened, or leave only given to surcharge and falsify, is a matter entirely in the discretion of the court; and whenever one party is allowed to surcharge and falsify, the other may do so too.[53] And see *ante,* pp. 49, 188.

Matter arising since Writ

A ground of defence which arose after action brought may nevertheless be pleaded (Order 18, r. 9) or raised subsequently

---

[50] *Parkinson* v. *Hanbury* (1866) L.R. 2 H.L. 1, 19.
[51] *Per* Davey L.J., in *Re Webb* [1894] 1 Ch. at pp. 83–86.
[52] *Parkinson* v. *Hanbury, supra.*
[53] See *Williamson* v. *Barbour* (1877) 9 Ch.D. 529, 532; *Gething* v. *Keighley, ibid.* 547.

by amendment of the defence.[53a]   Faced with this, the plaintiff may consider it useless to continue the action; yet up to this point he may have been fully justified in bringing it.   What is he then to do?   If he cannot effect a settlement, he may apply to a master to stay the proceedings or for leave to discontinue them under Order 21, r. 3 (*post*, p. 253), on such terms as may be just, including the payment of his costs to date.   A difficult question may then arise if the defendant contends that the action would in any event have failed by reason of some other defence which he has.   Since it would be ridiculous to carry the issues to trial merely for the sake of costs, an order which does substantial justice can usually be devised.[54]

In olden times when the pleadings were each entered separately on the record, every entry after the first one was called a *continuance*.   When the matter of defence arose after writ, but before plea or continuance, it was said to be pleaded " to the further maintenance " of the action.   When it arose after plea or continuance, it was called a plea of *puis darrein continuance*— since the last continuance.[55]

Set-off and Counterclaim

Any defendant to an action may now plead a set-off or a counter-claim.   A set-off is a statutory defence to a plaintiff's action: a counterclaim is substantially a cross-action.   In certain cases the defendant may join a third person and make him a party to the counterclaim along with the plaintiff.   These matters are fully dealt with in the next chapter.

Third Parties

Again, there may be someone from whom the defendant, if himself found liable in the action, will be entitled to recover some portion of the amount which he will have to pay the plaintiff— in other words, from whom he is entitled to " contribution." Or there may be someone by whom the defendant, if found liable, will be entitled to be wholly reimbursed—that is, he is

---

[53a] For the converse case where the defendant satisfies the plaintiff's claim and therefore serves no defence, see Ord. 13, r. 6 (2), *ante*, p. 58.

[54] The Rules of 1883 contained somewhat elaborate provisions enabling a defendant to deliver a " further defence " and the plaintiff to deliver a " confession " of such defence. These are now abolished.

[55] See *Howarth* v. *Brown* (1863) 1 H. & C. at p. 697.

entitled to an "indemnity." Thus, the defendant may be sued as a surety, and, if found liable, may be entitled to contribution from a co-surety. He may be sued upon a contract which he made as agent for an undisclosed principal and may be entitled to be indemnified by his principal. Or he may be sued for negligent driving and wish to claim contribution from some other driver whom the plaintiff has not elected to sue. In such cases it is obviously desirable to bring in the third person against whom the defendant claims to have a remedy, so that the decision as to the liability of the defendant and of this third person shall be finally settled in one and the same action. The latter can therefore be served with a third-party notice calling upon him to appear within eight days. Cases of contribution and indemnity were formerly the only ones in which the defendant could do this. Since 1929, however, third-party procedure is also available where the defendant claims that he is entitled to any relief or remedy relating to or connected with the original subject-matter of the action and substantially the same as some relief or remedy claimed by the plaintiff; and also where any question between the defendant and the third party relating to the original subject-matter is substantially the same as some question arising between the plaintiff and the defendant. (Order 16, r. 1; *Re Burford, Burford* v. *Clifford* [1932] 2 Ch. 122; and see Precedent No. 94.)

The notice to the third party can be issued without leave at any time after appearance and before the defence is served, or later with the leave of a master (Order 16, rr. 1 and 2). It must state the nature and grounds of the claim or the nature of the question to be determined, and the relief sought. The third party, on being served, becomes a party to the action *quoad* the defendant as though he had been sued by him; he may appear, defend, and even counterclaim against the defendant.[56] If he appears pursuant to such notice, the master, if satisfied that there is a question proper to be determined as to his liability, may order this question to be tried in such manner as he may direct, or allow him to appear at the trial between the plaintiff and the defendant and take such part in it as may be just. (Order 16, r. 4.) Or, again, he may refuse to make any order, in which case the third-party proceedings fall to the ground. If, on the other hand, the third party does not appear pursuant to the notice, he will be taken to admit

---

[56] *Barclays Bank* v. *Tom* [1923] 1 K.B. 221.

the validity of any judgment which the plaintiff may obtain and his own liability to the defendant to the extent claimed (rule 5). Moreover, a third party may in his turn bring in a fourth party, the fourth a fifth, and so on (rule 9) or he may bring a counter-claim against the defendant.[56a]   A defendant who has entered an appearance may without leave issue a similar notice to a person who is already a party to the action, *e.g.*, a co-defendant (rule 8).   Where the defendant in an action counterclaims, the plaintiff can serve a third party notice on a person from whom he claims contribution, indemnity or similar relief in respect of the counterclaim (rule 11).   The court will endeavour as far as possible to prevent the plaintiff from being embarrassed in his claim against the defendant by the latter's use of third-party procedure.

Severing Defences

If counsel is instructed on behalf of more than one defendant, the question will arise, should he draw one defence for all, or should they put in separate defences?   This depends on what their case will be at the trial.   If for any reason they ought to be separately represented then, they must sever now; if they join in one defence, they cannot appear by different counsel at the hearing. If their interests are practically identical, this does not matter; but if they occupy different positions, hold different offices, or took different shares in the transaction, they had better sever; otherwise a special defence peculiar to one of them may be lost.[57] But a special order as to costs may be made, if defendants improperly sever.[58]

Interpleader

An action is sometimes brought or threatened against a person (such as a banker, warehouseman or stakeholder) in possession of money or goods in which he himself has no interest but which are the subject of rival claims.   It is obviously unjust that he should be put to the expense of defending an action in which he has no interest and he may have no means of knowing who is really entitled; yet if he hands over the property to one claimant he may expose himself to an action by the other.   In such circum-

---

[56a] *The Normar* [1968] P. 362.
[57] *Born* v. *Turner* [1900] 2 Ch. 211.
[58] *Re Isaac* [1897] 1 Ch. 251; *Bagshaw* v. *Pimm* [1900] P. 148.

stances he may bring the claimants before the master and obtain protection by issuing an interpleader summons under Order 17. (This is known as a " stakeholder's interpleader " as distinguished from a " sheriff's interpleader," *post*, p. 387.) He must swear an affidavit showing that he claims no interest in the subject-matter other than for charges or costs; that he does not collude with any claimant; and that he is willing to deal with the subject-matter of the dispute as the master may direct. The master may then, if it seems just, stay proceedings against the applicant and order an issue to be tried between the claimants and give such other directions with regard to the property and generally as may be appropriate.

CHAPTER 14

SET-OFF AND COUNTERCLAIM

EVEN though the plaintiff was the first to commence litigation
it may happen that the defendant has a claim of some kind
against the plaintiff. If so, the question at once arises, must the
defendant issue a separate writ for this, or can he set up his claim
in the plaintiff's action?

If the defendant's claim can be tried without inconvenience
at the same time and by the same tribunal as the plaintiff's, the
defendant will be allowed to plead in the plaintiff's action (a)
in some cases a " set-off," (b) in all cases a " counterclaim."
The distinction between set-off and counterclaim should be
carefully noted, though it must be said that the modern tendency
is rather to slur over the differences and emphasise the similarities.

Speaking generally, a set-off may be described as a shield
which operates only as a defence to the plaintiff's action, and a
counterclaim as a sword with which the plaintiff may be attacked,
but which does not afford the defendant any protection unless
it is of such a nature that it can also be pleaded as a set-off. The
distinction is important; for if A is both a creditor of, and a debtor
to, B in respect of different transactions, and B's solvency is
doubtful, it is obviously to A's advantage to set off one amount
against the other if he can. On the other hand, if the plaintiff's
action is discontinued, it would seem to follow that the defendant's
set-off would fall to the ground; but if he had pleaded a counterclaim, he could obtain judgment upon it.[1]

Both are to a large extent the creatures of statute-law. Under
the old common law a defendant who had any cross-claim against
the plaintiff could not raise it in the plaintiff's action: he had to
bring a cross-action. But two statutes (now repealed) were
passed in the reign of George II, which enabled *mutual debts* to
be set off; the scope of these statutes was, however, somewhat
limited. Courts of equity would also give effect to a set-off,

---

[1] *McGowan* v. *Middleton* (1883) 11 Q.B.D. 464, 470; Order 15, r. 2 (3).

independently of the statute, in cases where it appeared that the defendant ought thus to be protected against the plaintiff's demand.[2] By the Judicature Act, 1873, s. 24 (3) (now section 39 of the Judicature Act, 1925), the court was given power to give a defendant in the plaintiff's action such relief, both in respect of legal and equitable rights, as is properly claimed by his pleading and could have been given in a separate action. Now by Order 18, r. 17, " where a claim by a defendant to a sum of money (whether of an ascertained amount or not) is relied on as a defence to the whole or part of a claim made by the plaintiff, it may be included in the defence and set off against the plaintiff's claim, whether or not it is also added as a counterclaim." And by Order 15, r. 2 (1), a defendant in any action " who alleges that he has any claim or is entitled to any relief or remedy against a plaintiff in the action in respect of any matter (whenever and however arising) may, instead of bringing a separate action, make a counterclaim in respect of that matter; and where he does so he must add the counterclaim to his defence." The court may then pronounce a final judgment in the action, both on the original claim and on the cross-claim. This is subject to the power of the court under Order 15, r. 5, to exclude a counterclaim, if satisfied that the defendant's claim ought not to be disposed of by way of counterclaim but in an independent action.

A counterclaim or set-off in an action by or against the Crown is now permissible, subject to the general law and to the limitations imposed by Order 77, r. 6. No set-off or counterclaim can be raised against the Crown in proceedings for the recovery of taxes, duties or penalties, nor can a claim for repayment of taxes, duties or penalties be pleaded by way of set-off or counterclaim in any proceedings by the Crown. (Rule 6 (1).) Leave must be obtained to raise a counterclaim or set-off in proceedings by or against the Crown in two cases—(a) if the Crown sues or is sued in the name of a government department to which the counterclaim or set-off does not relate; and (b) if the Crown sues or is sued in the name of the Attorney-General (Rule 6 (2)).

Under Order 15, r. 2 (4), where a counterclaim is established against the plaintiff's claim, the court may, if the balance is in favour of one of the parties, give him judgment for such balance without prejudice to the court's discretion as to costs.

[2] *Rawson* v. *Samuel* (1839) 1 Cr. & Ph. 161.

The correct interpretation of the Judicature Act and the rules has been a matter of some doubt. It was at one time thought that their effect was to enlarge the right of set-off, so that any cross-claim by the defendant raised in the plaintiff's action would operate as a defence to the action. This view did not prevail, and it has been held that the alteration has been one of procedure only, and that the rights of the parties are unchanged.[4] The result appears to be that whatever was a good set-off, either at law or in equity, in 1875 is a good set-off still: and nothing else is admissible as a set-off, though it may be an excellent counterclaim. We must therefore approach the subject historically.

Set-off

A set-off is a defence to the whole or to a portion of the plaintiff's claim. Under Order 15, r. 2 (4), the court appears to have no power to give the defendant judgment for the balance of a *set-off* overtopping the plaintiff's claim. And in any case it would not do so unless such balance is " properly claimed by his pleading " (Judicature Act, 1925, s. 39); and the proper way of doing so would seem to be by pleading a counterclaim.[5] At common law a set-off could only be raised by a cross-action, although a defendant sued for the price of goods could give evidence of a breach of warranty in reduction of the price.[6] Under the Insolvent Debtors Relief Act, 1729, s. 13, and the Debtors Relief Amendment Act, 1735, s. 4, mutual debts between plaintiff and defendant (or if either party sued or was sued as executor or administrator, between the deceased and the other party) could be set off. This was so although the debts might be of a different nature (*e.g.*, specialty or simple contract debts); but if either had accrued by reason of a penalty contained in a bond or specialty, judgment would only be entered for the amount justly due (see *ante*, p. 190). It was held under these statutes that there could only be a set-off where both debts were legal debts, such as would support an action of debt, covenant, or assumpsit for the non-payment of money (see *ante*, pp. 173–174); it was not allowed in actions of trespass or upon the case or for general damages; and the demand intended to be set off must have

---

4 *Stooke* v. *Taylor* (1880) 5 Q.B.D. 569; *Stumore* v. *Campbell & Co.* [1892] 1 Q.B. 314.

5 *Stooke* v. *Taylor* and *Stumore* v. *Campbell & Co., supra*; but see *Gathercole* v *Smith* (1881) 7 Q.B.D. 626, 629.

6 See *Street* v. *Blay* (1832) 2 B. & Ad. 456; Sale of Goods Act, 1893, s. 53.

been liquidated and not in the nature of a penalty. The debts must have been due from and to the same parties in the same right [7]; thus, a joint debt could not be set off against a separate one, nor could a defendant, sued as executor, set off a debt due to him personally; a defendant trustee could, however, set off money due to the *cestui que trust*. The debt sought to be set off must have been in existence at the time of the issue of the writ; now, however, a set-off arising after action brought may be relied on by the defendant, if pleaded as such.[8]

Although in the main equity followed the law, the rigidity of these rules was, to a limited extent, mitigated by the Court of Chancery (see *Story on Equity*, Chapter XXXVIII). Even where there was no legal debt, if either of the cross-demands was a matter of equitable jurisdiction and there was some special reason why equity should intervene, an equitable set-off might be allowed. Thus, in the case of the equitable assignment of a debt the debtor could set off another debt due to him from the assignee.[9] Again, a principal indebted jointly with his surety was allowed to set off a separate debt due from the creditor to himself.[10] Matters of complaint connected with the plaintiff's claim may often be set up to reduce or extinguish it; and it may be inequitable for the plaintiff's claims to be insisted on without taking those of the defendant into account, even though they be unliquidated.[11] But nothing which is not a money claim (whether of an ascertained amount or not) can be set off. (Order 18, r. 17.) Since the Judicature Act equitable set-offs are recognised in every division of the High Court. As a result of the fusion of law and equity there may be pleaded by way of set-off (i) mutual debts; (ii) such matters of complaint as are allowable to reduce or extinguish the claim; or (iii) other matters of equity which formerly might have called for injunction or protection.

Illustrations

The defendant owed the plaintiff £45. The defendant was executor of the estate of John Grimes, deceased. The plaintiff owed that estate more than £45. *Held*, that the defendant, when sued for his personal debt of £45, could not set off the debt due from the plaintiff to John Grimes' estate.
Nelson v. *Roberts* (1893) 69 L.T. 352.

---

[7] See *Reeves* v. *Pope* [1914] 2 K.B. 284.
[8] Order 18, r. 9, *ante*, p. 205; *Ellis* v. *Munson* (1876) 35 L.T. 585.
[9] *Cavendish* v. *Geaves* (1857) 24 Beav. 163.
[10] *Ex p. Hanson* (1806) 12 Ves.Jun. 346.
[11] *Hanak* v. *Green* [1958] 2 Q.B. 9 (C.A.) (*post*, pp. 218–219).

A debt which only accrued to the defendant after the death of a testator or intestate cannot be set off against a debt due from the defendant to the testator or intestate in his lifetime.

> *Newell* v. *National Provincial Bank* (1876) 1 C.P.D. 496.
>
> *Hallett* v. *Hallett* (1879) 13 Ch.D. 232; 49 L.J.Ch. 61.

So a debt due from a testator during his lifetime cannot be set off against a sum (*e.g.*, money received from a policy on his life) which never was payable to the testator himself.

> *Re Gregson* (1887) 36 Ch.D. 223; 57 L.J.Ch. 221.

But the costs incurred by an executor in defending an action brought by a legatee for revocation of probate may be set off against the legacy.

> *Re Knapman* (1881) 18 Ch.D. 300; 50 L.J.Ch. 629.
>
> *Re Peruvian Railway Construction Co.* [1915] 2 Ch. 144, 442; 85 L.J.Ch. 129.

And a debt due to an administrator for costs incurred in an action brought by two next-of-kin may be set off by him against the shares of such next-of-kin.

> *Re Jones* [1897] 2 Ch. 190; 66 L.J.Ch. 439.

Where there are mutual debts between A and B, and A becomes bankrupt, B can set off the debt due to him against a claim by A's trustee.

> Bankruptcy Act, 1914, s. 31.

A's solicitor had in hand £15 belonging to A. A became bankrupt. The solicitor then rendered certain professional services to A, the fair remuneration for which was £12 13s. 4d. A's trustee in bankruptcy sued for £15: *Held*, that the solicitor could not set off the £12 13s. 4d. against the trustee's claim; for that was money earned since the bankruptcy.

> *Stumore* v. *Campbell & Co.* [1892] 1 Q.B. 314; 61 L.J.Q.B. 463.

An agent who has received moneys on behalf of a disclosed principal cannot deduct from the amount so received a debt due to himself personally from the same debtor.

> *Richardson* v. *Stormont, Todd & Co., Ltd.* [1900] 1 Q.B. 701.

But a debt due from an agent can be set off against his principal, whenever the principal remains undisclosed and allows the agent to act as principal in the transaction.

> *George* v. *Clagett* (1797) 7 T.R. 359; 2 Sm.L.C. 118.
>
> *Montagu* v. *Forwood* [1893] 2 Q.B. 350.

So a debt due from a *cestui que trust* can be set off against a claim made by a trustee on behalf of that *cestui que trust*.

> *Bankes* v. *Jarvis* [1903] 1 K.B. 549; 72 L.J.K.B. 267.

A debt due from the plaintiff to a third person duly assigned before action by that third person to the defendant may be set off.

> *Bennett* v. *White* [1910] 2 K.B. 643; 79 L.J.K.B. 1133.

The plaintiff can plead in reply to a set-off that it was barred by the Limitation Act, or was for any other reason not an actionable debt at date of writ.

> *Smith* v. *Betty* [1903] 2 K.B. 317; 72 L.J.K.B. 853.

A claim for damages for negligence by a bailee may be set off against an admitted claim for storage charges; but not, it would seem, a totally unconnected claim such as damages for libel.

> *Morgan & Son, Ltd.* v. *S. Martin Johnson & Co., Ltd.* [1949] 1 K.B. 107. And see *Hale* v. *Victoria Plumbing Co. Ltd.* [1966] 3 W.L.R. 47.

Against a claim for damages for failure to complete certain work and for bad workmanship there may be set off claims (i) for extras; (ii) for

loss through failure to admit the defendant's workman; and (iii) for damages for trespass to the defendant's tools.
    Hanak v. *Green* [1958] 2 Q.B. 9.

Counterclaim

As we have seen, the modern counterclaim was entirely the creation of the Judicature Act, 1873. It need not relate to or be in any way connected with the plaintiff's claim, or arise out of the same transaction.[12] It need not be " an action of the same nature as the original action " (*per* Fry J. in *Beddall* v. *Maitland* (1881) 17 Ch.D. at p. 181), or even analogous thereto. If the defendant has any valid cause of action, legal or equitable, against the plaintiff, there is no necessity for him now to bring a cross-action, unless his counterclaim be of such a nature that it cannot conveniently be tried by the same tribunal or at the same time as the plaintiff's claim.

Every cross-claim of whatever kind can now be pleaded as a counterclaim. It does not matter what the amount of it may be. It may be for either liquidated or unliquidated damages. (Order 15, r. 2 (1).) It may exceed in amount the plaintiff's claim [13]; or it may be less than the plaintiff's claim.[14] If the amount which is found due to the plaintiff on his claim exceeds the amount established by the defendant on his counterclaim, the plaintiff will recover the difference; if, on the other hand, the balance is in favour of the defendant, judgment may be given for the defendant for such balance. (Order 15, r. 2 (4).) Or he may be granted such other relief as he may be entitled to on the merits of the case. It is more usual nowadays to give separate judgments upon the claim and counterclaim with the appropriate costs of each instead of one judgment for the balance, but this is entirely a matter of discretion. (See *post*, pp. 225–226.)

In one respect a defendant who is pleading a counterclaim is in a better position than if he were seeking to enforce the same claim as a plaintiff in a separate action. No one can bring an action in our courts against a foreigner resident out of the jurisdiction, except in the cases specified in Order 11 (*ante*, p. 36), unless he can find him temporarily within the jurisdiction and serve

---

[12] Order 15, r. 2 (1). But in "legal aid" cases the authority of the area committee must be obtained to raise an unconnected counterclaim (Legal Aid (General) Regulations, 1962, reg. 15 (3)).
[13] *Winterfield* v. *Bradnum* (1878) 3 Q.B.D. 324.
[14] *Mostyn* v. *West Mostyn, etc., Co.* (1876) 1 C.P.D. 145.

him. But if that foreigner commences an action here, and so brings himself within the jurisdiction of our courts, he is liable to any counterclaim that can conveniently be tried with his claim. And if that counterclaim overtops his claim, judgment may be recovered and enforced against him for the balance, unless he be a foreign sovereign or state (*post*, p. 225).[15]

Illustrations

An equitable counterclaim can be raised in an action at law, and a legal counterclaim in a Chancery suit.

Fleming v. *Loe* [1901] 2 Ch. 594; 70 L.J.Ch. 805.

" A claim founded on tort may be opposed to one founded on contract, or vice versa." *Per* Cockburn C.J. in

Stooke v. *Taylor* (1880) 5 Q.B.D., at p. 576.

In an Admiralty action *in rem* for salvage services the defendant may counterclaim *in personam* for damages for breach of a charterparty.

The Cheapside [1904] P. 339; 73 L.J.P. 117.

If the defendant seeks to bring in some person who is not already a party to the action, and make him defendant to the counterclaim, either that person must be liable to him along with the plaintiff in respect of the subject-matter of the counterclaim, or the relief for which the defendant asks against him must relate to or be connected with the original subject-matter of the action.

Order 15, r. 3 (1); Judicature Act, 1925, s. 39; *post*, p. 222.

Barber v. *Blaiberg* (1882) 19 Ch.D. 473; 51 L.J.Ch. 509.

Smith v. *Buskell* [1919] 2 K.B. 362; 88 L.J.K.B. 985.

In an action of slander, the defendant may counterclaim for damages for a slander uttered some time previously by the plaintiff, though it has nothing to do with the slander on which the plaintiff is suing.

Quin v. *Hession* (1878) 4 L.R.Ir. 35; 40 L.T. 70.

To an action on a solicitor's bill of costs, the defendant may counterclaim for negligence.

Lumley v. *Brooks* (1889) 41 Ch.D. 323; 58 L.J.Ch. 494.

Even a cause of action which has accrued to the defendant since the plaintiff issued his writ can be pleaded as a counterclaim. The words of the rule are " whenever and however arising." (But it should either be stated expressly, or appear clearly from the dates mentioned in the counterclaim, that the defendant's claim arose after action brought, so that the plaintiff may have an opportunity of discontinuing or taking other appropriate action (see *ante*, pp. 209–210).)

Order 15, r. 2 (1); Order 18, r. 9.

A counterclaiming defendant is in no way limited to a claim for damages. The court will give him judgment for such relief as he may be entitled to upon the merits of the case. (Judicature Act, 1925, s. 39 (*ante*, p. 215), and see Precedent No. 65.)

---

[15] *South African Republic* v. *La Compagnie Franco-Belge* [1897] 2 Ch. 487; [1898] 1 Ch. 190.

Illustrations

A defendant may by his counterclaim ask for a declaration of his rights, or for relief against forfeiture, or for a vesting order under section 146 (4) of the Law of Property Act, 1925.

Adams v. *Adams*, 45 Ch.D. 426; [1892] 1 Ch. 369.
Warden, etc., of Cholmeley's School v. *Sewell* [1893] 2 Q.B. 254.

In an action for the infringement of the plaintiff's patent the defendant may counterclaim for the revocation of the plaintiff's patent and, if he does so, must deliver particulars of objection.

Patents Act, 1949, s. 61.

In certain cases, a defendant may, even before serving his counterclaim, apply for an *interim* injunction or for the appointment of a receiver to protect his interests.

Carter v. *Fey* [1894] 2 Ch. 541; 63 L.J.Ch. 723.
Collison v. *Warren* [1901] 1 Ch. 812; 70 L.J.Ch. 382.

A counterclaim is governed by the same rules of pleading as a statement of claim, and the reply to it by the same rules as a defence. All the facts relied on by way of counterclaim must be stated in numbered paragraphs (following on in the same serial from those of the defence, not starting a fresh series) under the heading " Counterclaim," so as to distinguish them from facts alleged by way of defence. If any of the facts on which the counterclaim is founded have been already stated in the defence, they need not be restated in the counterclaim, but may be incorporated by reference, thus: "And by way of counterclaim the defendant repeats the allegations contained in paragraphs 3, 4, 5 and 8 of the defence." It is, however, undesirable thus to repeat paragraphs containing matter which is irrelevant to the counterclaim. A counterclaim may comprise several distinct causes of action; but the facts on which each cause of action is founded must be stated, as far as may be, separately and distinctly, and the relief claimed be stated specifically, either simply or in the alternative. And the several causes of action must be such as could properly be joined in one independent action.[16] The provisions of Order 15 apply to the joinder of various claims in a counterclaim.

Ample provision is made to protect the plaintiff from inconvenient or improper counterclaims. If he can show that the counterclaim is one which cannot conveniently be disposed of in the pending action, or ought not to be allowed, the master may strike it out or exclude it under Order 15, r. 5, leaving the

---

[16] *Compton* v. *Preston* (1882) 21 Ch.D. 138.

defendant to bring a cross-action. If the counterclaim is frivolous or vexatious, or if it discloses no valid cause of action, or if it may prejudice, embarrass or delay the fair trial of the action or is otherwise an abuse of the process of the court, the master may order that it be struck out or amended under Order 18, r. 19 (1). Or objection may be taken to it in point of law under Order 18, r. 11. It must be properly pleaded or further particulars may be demanded under Order 18, r. 12.

A counterclaim must always claim relief against the plaintiff. " A pleading which asks no cross-relief against a plaintiff either alone or with some other person is not a counterclaim." (*Per* Jessel M.R. in *Furness* v. *Booth* (1876) 4 Ch.D. at p. 587.) It has been held that it need not be a claim against the plaintiff in the same capacity as that in which he sues. (*Re Richardson* [1933] W.N. 90, *infra.*)

Illustrations

To a joint claim by two plaintiffs a separate counterclaim against each of them will be allowed.

    Manchester, etc., Ry. v. *Brooks* (1877) 2 Ex.D. 243.

And on a counterclaim against two plaintiffs, the defendant may recover judgment against one.

    Hall v. *Fairweather* (1901) 18 T.L.R. 58.

If one member of a firm sues for a debt due to him personally, the defendant may counterclaim for a debt due to him from the firm and can make the plaintiff's partner a party to the counterclaim or not, as he pleases. If the defendant does not join the partner, the plaintiff can subsequently apply to add him.

    Eyre v. *Moreing* [1884] W.N. 58.

Where a plaintiff sues in his own right, the defendant can counterclaim against him as trustee or executor or administrator, provided that no practical inconvenience will result. It would seem to follow that if the plaintiff sues as trustee or executor or administrator, the defendant could counterclaim against him in his own right.

    Re Richardson [1933] W.N. 90.

The defendant can also plead a counterclaim against the plaintiff along with some other person, not already a party to the action, described as a " defendant to counterclaim " in the title of the action, provided that it either (a) alleges that such other person is liable to the defendant along with the plaintiff in respect of the subject-matter of the counterclaim, or (b) relates to or is connected with the subject-matter of the plaintiff's claim.[17] And

---

[17] Order 15, r. 3 (1); Judicature Act, 1925, s. 39; *Smith* v. *Buskell* [1919] 2 K.B. 362; *Barber* v. *Blaiberg* (1882) 19 Ch.D. 473.

his counterclaim may seek relief jointly, severally, or in the alternative. Or he can plead such a counterclaim against a co-defendant along with the plaintiff. But he cannot counterclaim against any co-defendant or third person alone without the plaintiff, though he can claim contribution, indemnity or other similar relief from such a person as a " third party " under Order 16. (*Ante*, p. 210.)

Whenever such a counterclaim is pleaded, the defendant must place at the head of his defence an additional title, stating the names of all persons whom he has thus made defendants to his counterclaim and serve the counterclaim upon them. (Order 15, r. 3 (2).) Thereafter each defendant to the counterclaim becomes a party in the action " with the same rights in respect of his defence to the counterclaim and otherwise as if he had been duly sued in the ordinary way by the party making the counterclaim " (*ibid*.). Each new defendant must appear to it as though he had been served with a writ and plead to it (rule 3 (5)). Any person thus made defendant to a counterclaim, whether plaintiff, co-defendant or new party, may, before replying, apply to the master to exclude the counterclaim on the ground that it ought to be disposed of in an independent action, and not by way of counterclaim (rule 5). A plaintiff against whom a counterclaim is pleaded can in certain cases counterclaim against the defendant's counterclaim. (See *post*, p. 234.) He may also issue a third-party notice against a person not a party to the action from whom he claims contribution, indemnity or such other relief as is permitted under Order 16.[18] But a new party brought in solely as defendant to a counterclaim cannot counterclaim against either the plaintiff or the defendant.[19]

Where a plaintiff fails to serve a defence to counterclaim, the defendant may sign judgment in default of pleading in any of the ways provided in Order 19, rr. 2 to 7 inclusive (Order 19, r. 8). Further, the procedure under Order 14 is open to a counter-claiming defendant (Order 14, r. 5, *ante*, p. 63).

Illustrations

A counterclaim is admissible against the plaintiff and a new party along with the plaintiff if its matter be connected with that of the plaintiff's claim, even though such new party could not possibly have been made a party in the plaintiff's original action.

Turner v. *Hednesford Gas Co.* (1878) 3 Ex.D. 145.

---

[18] Order 16, r. 11.
[19] *Street* v. *Gover* (1877) 2 Q.B.D. 498; *Alcoy, etc., Ry.* v. *Greenhill* [1896] 1 Ch. 19.

But not if such new party can only be liable in one of two inconsistent alternatives.

> *Evans* v. *Buck* (1877) 4 Ch.D. 432; 46 L.J.Ch. 157.

A defendant cannot join a new party to be a joint plaintiff with himself in a counterclaim against the original plaintiff.

> *Pender* v. *Taddei* [1898] 1 Q.B. 798; 67 L.J.Q.B. 703.

How far a Counterclaim is an Independent Action

For many purposes a counterclaim is substantially a cross-action. " A counterclaim is to be treated, for all purposes for which justice requires it to be so treated, as an independent action." (*Per* Bowen L.J. in *Amon* v. *Bobbett* (1889) 22 Q.B.D. at p. 548.) If, after the defendant has pleaded a counterclaim, the plaintiff's action is for any reason stayed, discontinued or dismissed, the counterclaim may nevertheless be proceeded with. (Order 15, r. 2 (3).) The court may order a counterclaiming defendant to give security for costs [20]; but not where the counterclaim is in substance a defence to the action.[21]

Yet a counterclaim differs in some respects from a cross-action. The issues of fact raised by claim and counterclaim, respectively, must, as a rule, be tried together. But if both parties succeed, there may be two judgments—one for the plaintiff on his claim, with costs, and the other for the defendant on his counterclaim, with costs—though execution will issue only for the balance.[22] A counterclaim, moreover, cannot be transferred to a county court for trial on the ground of lack of means of the party bringing it [23]; though it may be stayed under section 4 of the Arbitration Act, 1950.[24] If foreign plaintiffs bring an action here against a British subject who counterclaims, the court has no jurisdiction to make an order staying proceedings in the action until the foreign plaintiffs give security for damages under the counterclaim.[25]

---

[20] Order 23, r. 1; *Sykes* v. *Sacerdoti* (1885) 15 Q.B.D. 423; *Lake* v. *Haseltine* (1885) 55 L.J.Q.B. 205.

[21] *Neck* v. *Taylor* [1893] 1 Q.B. 560; and see *New Fenix Compagnie* v. *General Accident, etc., Corporation* [1911] 2 K.B. 619.

[22] It is otherwise in the case of a set-off, which is a defence proper. There can be only one judgment—either judgment for the plaintiff for the balance found due; or, if the defendant establishes a set-off equal to or exceeding the amount to which the plaintiff is entitled, judgment for the defendant (see *ante*, p. 216). *Provincial Bill Posting Co.* v. *Low Moor Iron Co.* [1909] 2 K.B. 344; *Sharpe* v. *Haggith* (1912) 106 L.T. 13.

[23] *Delobbel-Flipo* v. *Varty* [1893] 1 Q.B. 663.

[24] *Spartali* v. *Van Hoorn* [1884] W.N. 32; *Chappell* v. *North* [1891] 2 Q.B. 252.

[25] *The James Westoll* [1905] P. 47.

And, although as a rule a counterclaim may be of any amount, overtopping the plaintiff's claim and entitling the defendant to a judgment, still there are two exceptions to this rule, two cases in which a counterclaim, like a set-off, serves only as a defence, and is not a cross-action—or, to employ the time-honoured metaphor, can be used only "as a shield, not as a sword." (*Per* Cockburn C.J. in *Stooke* v. *Taylor* (1880) 5 Q.B.D. at p. 575.)

(i) If a debt be assigned the debtor may in certain cases set off or counterclaim against the assignee a debt due from the assignor to himself; but if the amount of such set-off or counterclaim exceed the amount of the debt assigned, the defendant can recover nothing from the assignee; he must sue the assignor for the balance.[26] In general, any cross-claim arising out of a contract may be set off against an assignee of that contract; but a different rule applies in the case of an assignment of a reversion on a lease.[27]

(ii) A similar rule applies when a sovereign prince or state over whom our courts have no jurisdiction (see *ante*, p. 17) brings an action in this country. The defendant is allowed to plead any set-off or counterclaim against him which is an answer to his demand, but not to recover any judgment against him for the excess, or to raise any counterclaim which is outside and independent of the subject-matter of the claim.[28]

Costs of Set-off and Counterclaim

In the matter of costs, however, a counterclaim which is not a set-off is treated as a cross-action, whereas a set-off remains what it was in the days of George II—a defence to the plaintiff's action. Therefore, a plaintiff, who brings an action and is met by a set-off equal in amount to his claim, must ordinarily pay the defendant his costs of the whole action; for he has failed in the whole action.[29] Whereas, if the defendant can plead only a

---

[26] *Young* v. *Kitchin* (1878) 3 Ex.D. 127; *Government of Newfoundland* v. *Newfoundland Ry.* (1888) 13 App.Cas. 199.
[27] *Reeves* v. *Pope* [1914] 2 K.B. 284.
[28] *Duke of Brunswick* v. *King of Hanover* (1844) 6 Beav. 1, 38; *High Commissioner for India* v. *Ghosh* [1960] 1 Q.B. 134.
[29] *Hanak* v. *Green* [1958] 2 Q.B. 9.

counterclaim and recovers an amount equal to or greater than the plaintiff's claim, the plaintiff will (subject to the court's discretion) recover his costs of the claim, and the defendant only his costs of the counterclaim. The proper principles on which in such a case taxation should be conducted, in the absence of any special order, are laid down in *Atlas Metal Co. v. Miller* [1898] 2 Q.B. 500 and *Medway Oil Co. v. Continental Contractors* [1929] A.C. 88. The costs of the plaintiff's claim should first be taxed as if it were a separate action with no counterclaim. Then the costs occasioned by the counterclaim must be taxed, as though they were part of the costs of a separate action. The taxing master must ascertain what items are really costs of claim and counterclaim, respectively, dealing with the matter as one of substance and not of form; and any items which have been incurred partly on account of each, such as brief fees to counsel, must be divided. But in the absence of a special order, there should be no apportionment of general costs. Then whichever be the smaller amount—the costs of the claim or the costs of the counterclaim—must be deducted from the larger; and the successful party will be entitled to recover the balance. " No costs not incurred by reason of the counterclaim can be costs of the counterclaim." (*Per* Lindley M.R. in *Atlas Metal Co. v. Miller* [1898] 2 Q.B. at p. 505.) Similar principles apply where both claim and counterclaim fail: the proper method is to tax the costs of the defendant except so far as they have been increased by the counterclaim, and to tax the costs of the plaintiff only so far as they have been increased by the counterclaim, with a set-off of the one against the other.[30]

The court, however, has power and is encouraged to make a special order as to costs (*e.g.*, that a proportion only of his total costs shall be paid to the successful party), thus avoiding the complications set out above. (See Order 62, r. 9 (4); *Chell Engineering, Ltd. v. Unit Tool and Engineering Co., Ltd.* [1950] 1 All E.R. 378; *Childs v. Gibson* [1954] 1 W.L.R. 809; which cases illustrate typical points which may arise in practice.)

Where a defendant, who has been sued in the High Court,

---

[30] *James v. Jackson* [1910] 2 Ch. 92; *Medway Oil Co. v. Continental Contractors, supra.*

counterclaims for an amount within the county court jurisdiction, the party succeeding on the counterclaim is entitled to High Court costs; section 47 of the County Courts Act, 1959, does not apply to a counterclaim.[31]

[31] See *Blake* v. *Appleyard* (1878) 3 Ex.D. 195; *Amon* v. *Bobbett* (1889) 22 Q.B.D. 543; and *post*, p. 408.

CHAPTER 15

REPLY, ETC.

IF no defence be served, the plaintiff may enter judgment in default under Order 19.[1] (As to service of defence out of time, see *ante*, p. 75.) The procedure for obtaining final or interlocutory judgment appropriate to the various forms of action described *ante* at pp. 55–61 is followed, but no affidavit of service of the writ is required as the defendant has now entered an appearance.

If the defendant has paid money into court and the plaintiff is content to accept it in satisfaction of his claim, or of those causes of action only in respect of which it was paid in, he may take the money out within fourteen days of the receipt of the notice of payment in (see *post*, p. 255).

If a defence be served containing express or implied admissions of fact, so that it purports to offer an answer to part only of the plaintiff's alleged cause of action, the plaintiff may in most cases, by leave of a master, obtain final or interlocutory judgment for the part admitted, if that part is severable from the rest (Order 27, r. 3).[2] Or the plaintiff may apply for an order that the defendant pay into court any money which he admits is in his hands.[3] He may do this even though he has already served a reply and set the action down for trial[4]; but in that case the defendant should be indemnified against any costs incurred by him through the plaintiff's delay.[5]

Reply

The student should distinguish carefully a "reply" from a "defence to counterclaim" (see *post*, p. 233), although if both are pleaded they must appear in one document (Order 18, r. 3 (3)). A reply, if required, must be served within fourteen days after the

---

[1] Leave is necessary in moneylenders' and certain hire-purchase actions (see *ante*, pp. 59, 60), also in certain claims for possession of land, and in actions in tort between husband and wife.

[2] See *Ellis* v. *Allen* [1914] 1 Ch. 904; *Lancashire Welders, Ltd.* v. *Harland & Wolff, Ltd.* [1950] 2 All E.R. 1096.

[3] *Crompton* v. *Burton* [1895] 2 Ch. 711.

[4] *Brown* v. *Pearson* (1882) 21 Ch.D. 716.

[5] *Tottenham* v. *Foley* [1909] 2 Ir.R. 500.

defence to which it relates has been served, unless the time be extended by consent or by order (r. 3 (4)). A reply is not necessary if its sole object is to deny what the defendant has stated in his defence, for in its absence there is an implied joinder of issue (rule 14 (1) and see *post*, p. 234). Its main function is to raise in answer to the defence any matters which must be pleaded by way of confession and avoidance under rule 8 (*ante*, pp. 144–145), or to make any admissions which you may be disposed to make. And in actions of libel or slander, where the defendant pleads that the words were published on a privileged occasion or as fair comment on a matter of public interest and were so published without malice, the plaintiff, if he intends to set up express malice in answer to such plea of privilege or fair comment, must serve a reply setting out the facts on which he relies. (Order 82, r. 3 (3).) If no reply be served within fourteen days, all material statements of fact in the defence will be deemed to have been denied and put in issue. But where a counterclaim is pleaded, the plaintiff must within fourteen days serve a defence to counterclaim, which is subject to the rules applicable to defences. (Order 18, r. 18 (*b*), and see *post*, p. 233.)

It has hitherto been common practice, when a defence to counterclaim was pleaded, to preface it with a reply stating: " The plaintiff joins issue with the defendant on his defence (save so far as the same consists of admissions)." [6] This is no longer necessary where no special reply is to be pleaded. But it is permissible under rule 14 to say, " The plaintiff admits the facts alleged in paragraph 1 of the defence, but save as aforesaid he joins issue on the defence." There cannot be a mere joinder of issue upon a counterclaim: the plaintiff must plead to it with a " defence to counterclaim " as though he were pleading a defence to a statement of claim (rules 14 (3) and 18). The effect of joining issue is merely to *deny*; it does not confess and avoid. It is simply a comprehensive and compendious *traverse*. " The reply is the proper place for meeting the defence by confession and avoidance." (*Per* James L.J. in *Hall* v. *Eve* (1876) 4 Ch.D. at p. 345.)

The plaintiff must therefore be careful not to join issue merely, where he ought to allege new facts in his reply; for a

---

[6] The words in brackets were always unnecessary, for an admission is not an allegation of fact to which it is necessary to plead.

joinder of issue only contradicts the facts alleged by the defendant.

Illustrations

Action of trespass. Defence, that it was defendant's own freehold. Replication, a mere joinder of issue. At the trial, the plaintiff was not allowed on these pleadings to give evidence of a lease from defendant's ancestor to himself, as that was a new fact consistent with the plea traversed, and should therefore have been specially pleaded in the replication by way of confession and avoidance.

> Y.B. 5 Hen. 7, 10a, pl. 2.

To a plea of the Limitation Act, plaintiff must specially reply any fact upon which he relies to take the case out of the statute; *e.g.*, that the plaintiff himself was and still is an infant.

> *Chandler* v. *Vilett* (1680) 2 Wms.Saund. 120; ed. 1871, p. 391.

Or any acknowledgment in writing; see *ante*, p. 129.

> *Forsyth* v. *Bristowe* (1853) 8 Ex. 347; 22 L.J.Ex. 70.
> *Skeet* v. *Lindsay* (1877) 2 Ex.D. 314; 46 L.J.Ex. 249.

To a declaration for non-payment of money due under a covenant, the defendant pleaded that the cause of action did not accrue within twenty years. Replication that it did accrue within twenty years. *Held*, that under the Civil Procedure Act, 1833, ss. 3 and 5, the plaintiff could not, in support of this issue, give evidence of an acknowledgment by letter within the twenty years.

> *Kempe* v. *Gibbon* (1846) 9 Q.B. 609; 16 L.J.Q.B. 120.

Action for money had and received to the use of the plaintiff. Plea of the Statute of Limitations. Reply, that the defendant had received the money to the use of the plaintiff within six years. It was proved at the trial that the defendant had fraudulently received the money more than six years ago. *Held*, that the plaintiff could not on this issue give any evidence to show that the defendant had, till within six years before action, fraudulently concealed the fact that he had received the money.

> *Clark* v. *Hougham* (1823) 2 B. & C. 149; 3 D. & R. 322.

Such a ground of reply must be specially pleaded, and with great particularity.

> *Gibbs* v. *Guild* (1882) 8 Q.B.D. 296; 9 Q.B.D. 59.
> *Lawrance* v. *Lord Norreys* (1890) 15 App.Cas. 210; 59 L.J.Ch. 681.
> *Betjemann* v. *Betjemann* [1895] 2 Ch. 474; 64 L.J.Ch. 641.

And the fraud alleged must be the fraud of the person setting up the statute or of someone through whom he claims.

> *Re McCallum* [1901] 1 Ch. 143; 70 L.J.Ch. 206.

If the defendant obtained from the plaintiff a release of his cause of action either fraudulently or by duress, the fraud or duress must be specially pleaded in reply to the plea of release.

To a plea of infancy, the plaintiff must reply specially that the goods sold and delivered " were necessaries suitable to the then degree, estate and condition of the defendant."

> *Peters* v. *Fleming* (1840) 6 M. & W. 42.

To a justification setting out a conviction, or to a plea of a previous action, the plaintiff must reply specially that there is no such record, if it be the fact; or, if the conviction be erroneously stated in the defence (as in *Alexander* v. *N.E. Ry.* (1865) 6 B. & S. 340; 34 L.J.Q.B. 152), the plaintiff may set it out correctly in his reply. Or to such a justification the plaintiff may reply a pardon (*Cuddington* v. *Wilkins* (1616) Hob. 67, 81; 2 Hawk.P.C., c. 37, s. 48; *Rawley's Case* (1619) Hutton 21), or that he had undergone his sentence, which may have the same effect.

Leyman v. *Latimer* (1877) 3 Ex.D. 15, 352; 47 L.J.Ex. 470.

To a plea of a settled account, the plaintiff must specially reply the facts on which he relies to reopen the account; *e.g.*, he must specify the errors in the account on which he relies. (*Ante*, p. 209.)

Parkinson v. *Hanbury* (1866) L.R. 2 H.L. 1; 36 L.J.Ch. 292.

To a plea of the Statute of Frauds, the plaintiff may plead specially a part performance, where such a reply is applicable.

Ungley v. *Ungley* (1877) 5 Ch.D. 887; 46 L.J.Ch. 854.

Maddison v. *Alderson* (1883) 8 App.Cas. 467; 52 L.J.Q.B. 737.

But a plaintiff cannot plead the Statute of Frauds to a contract pleaded by the defendant, unless the defendant claims a set-off, or counterclaims, under that contract.

Miles v. *New Zealand Alford Estate Co.* (1886) 32 Ch.D. at pp. 278, 279.

In answer to a set-off or counterclaim, he can and must plead it, if he wishes to rely upon it.

Chapple v. *Durston* (1830) 1 Cr. & J. 1.

Action for specific performance of an agreement to grant a lease. Defence, breaches of contract, which entitled the defendant to put an end to the agreement, and to refuse to grant any lease. The plaintiff, in his reply denied all such breaches, but pleaded also that if any were committed, they were waived, and this reply was held good. A plaintiff may confess and avoid by his reply; for it is no part of the statement of claim to anticipate the defence, and the old rule of pleading still holds, " that you should not leap before you come to the stile." (See *ante*, pp. 95–98.)

Hall v. *Eve* (1876) 4 Ch.D. 341, 347; 46 L.J.Ch. 145.

A reply must not refer to an independent document, such as plaintiff's answer to interrogatories, as containing facts on which the plaintiff relies, without setting out the material part of such document itself as part of the reply. A reply must not set up new claims. A reply must not plead mere evidence or argument, or state conclusions of law to be drawn or inferred from the facts pleaded.

Williamson v. *L. & N.W. Ry.* (1879) 12 Ch.D. 787; 48 L.J.Ch. 559.

Departure

It is at the stage of reply that the rule against what is called " a departure in pleading " applies for the first time. " A party shall not in any pleading make any allegation of fact, or raise any new ground of claim, inconsistent with a previous pleading of his." (Order 18, r. 10.)

A departure takes place when in any pleading the party deserts the ground that he took up in his preceding pleading, and resorts to another and a different ground; or, to give Sir Edward Coke's definition, " A departure in pleading is said to be when the second plea containeth matter not pursuant to his former, and which fortifieth not the same; and therefore it is called *decessus,* because he departeth from his former plea." (Co.Litt. 304a.) This is clearly embarrassing; a reply is not the proper place in which to raise new claims; to permit this would tend to spin out the pleadings to an intolerable length. The plaintiff must amend his statement of claim by adding the new matter as a further or alternative allegation.

Illustrations

If the statement of claim alleges merely a negligent breach of trust, the reply must not assert that such breach of trust was fraudulent. The statement of claim must be amended.

> *Kingston* v. *Corker* (1892) 29 L.R.Ir. 364.

In an action of debt brought on a bond conditioned to perform an award so that the same were delivered to the defendant by a certain time, the defendant pleaded that the arbitrators did not make any award. The plaintiff replied that the arbitrators did make an award to such an effect, and that the same was tendered by the proper time. The defendant rejoined that the award was not so tendered. On demurrer, it was held that the rejoinder was a departure from the plea: " for in the plea the defendant says that the arbitrators made no award, and now, in his rejoinder, he has implicitly confessed that the arbitrators have made an award, but says that it was not tendered according to the condition, which is a plain departure; for it is one thing not to make an award, and another thing not to tender it when made."

> *Roberts* v. *Mariett* (1682) 2 Wms.Saund. 188.

Claim for one-half of £500, which the defendant had received as trustee for himself and the plaintiff in equal shares.

Defence: I only received £311, for half of which I admit liability.

Reply: You ought to have received the full £500, but you wrongfully compromised with the debtor; so I still claim one-half of £500.

Held, that this reply violated the rule, as it was really setting up a new case, which should have been set out in the plaintiff's statement of claim.

> *Earp* v. *Henderson* (1876) 3 Ch.D. 254; 45 L.J.Ch. 738.

(If and in so far as this case purports to show that a plaintiff cannot in his reply traverse and, in the alternative, confess and avoid, it is to that extent overruled by *Hall* v. *Eve* (1876) 4 Ch. 341, *ante*, p. 229.)

Action for the recovery of land, with a claim for mesne profits. Defence: " The following letters passed between the defendant and the plaintiff's late father, who was seised in fee of the lands, which amount to a binding agreement for a lease." The plaintiff cannot turn round and say in his reply: " Very well; then pay me the rent mentioned in those letters." For by his statement of claim he treats the defendant as a trespasser; he must abandon that position before he can claim rent from him as his tenant.

For the same reason, if a plaintiff claims rent on his writ, he cannot claim the same sum in his reply as damages for unlawfully " holding over."

> *Duckworth* v. *McClelland* (1878) 2 L.R.Ir. 527.

In an action on a bond conditioned to keep the plaintiffs harmless and indemnified from all suits, etc., of one Thomas Cook, the defendants pleaded that they had kept the plaintiffs harmless, etc. The plaintiffs replied that Cook sued them, and so the defendants had not kept them harmless, etc. The defendants rejoined that they had not any notice of the damnification. And the court held first, that the matter of the rejoinder was bad, as the plaintiffs were not bound to give notice; and secondly, that the rejoinder was a departure from the plea; for, in the plea, the defendants plead that "they have saved harmless the plaintiffs, and in the rejoinder confess that they have not saved harmless, but allege that they had not notice of the damnification; which is a plain departure."

Cutler v. *Southern* (1679) 1 Wms.Saund. 116.

So in an action of debt on a bond conditioned to perform covenants, one of which was, that the defendant should account for all sums of money that he should receive, the defendant pleaded performance. The plaintiff replied, that the defendant had received £26, for which he had not accounted. The defendant rejoined that he had accounted for that £26 *modo sequente, viz.*, that certain malefactors broke into his counting-house and stole it, wherewith he acquainted the plaintiff. And it was objected that the rejoinder was a departure; for the rejoinder did not show an accounting, but an excuse for not accounting. But the court held that showing he was robbed of a sum of money was giving an account of it, and that therefore there was no departure.

Vere v. *Smith* (1683) 2 Lev. 5; Ventr. 121.

Yet a plaintiff might always "new assign" in his reply; in other words, though he might not set up a new claim, he might explain and define his original claim, a thing which it was often necessary to do in the days when declarations were worded in very general terms.

Illustration

In an action for repeated trespasses to a close of land, if the defendant pleaded that he had a right of way across that close, the plaintiff might reply that his action was brought, not in respect of the defendant's exercise of the right of way but because he constantly wandered out of the line of way on to other parts of the close. Such a reply would not be a departure; for it merely points out the exact nature and extent of the plaintiff's original claim.

Pratt v. *Groome* (1812) 15 East 235.

Oakley v. *Davis* (1812) 16 East 82.

And see *Breslauer* v. *Barwick* (1876) 24 W.R. 901; 36 L.T. 52.

Collett v. *Dickinson* (1878) 26 W.R. 403.

Defence to Counterclaim

"There can be no joinder of issue, implied or express, on a statement of claim or counterclaim." (Order 18, r. 14 (3).) Thus the plaintiff *must* plead to a counterclaim if only for the purpose of denying specifically those allegations of fact in it which he does not admit. The correct pleading for this purpose is a defence to counterclaim and not a reply (rule 3 (2)). If he does not serve a defence to counterclaim, the allegations of fact in the counterclaim are deemed to be admitted (rule 13). As we have seen, the plaintiff may go further and serve a reply if it is needed for compliance with rule 8 (see *ante*, p. 229). If so, it must be included in the same document (rule 3 (3)). He may pay money into court in satisfaction of a counterclaim in accordance with the rules applicable to a defendant paying in, with the necessary modifications. (Order 22, r. 6.) He may even in rare cases counterclaim to it.[7]

Rejoinder, etc.

The defendant's answer, if any, to a reply, is called a Rejoinder; but it is now very seldom pleaded, except where there has been a counterclaim and the defendant desires to confess and avoid some allegation in the defence to counterclaim. The rejoinder is then, in effect, a reply to the defence to counterclaim. (See Precedent No. 85.) Further pleadings are possible; there can be a Surrejoinder, a Rebutter, and a Surrebutter; but they are very seldom met with.

None of these pleadings can be served without leave (Order 18, r. 4) and the time for serving them will be stated in the master's order. He must be satisfied that such a pleading is necessary. If to any such pleading no answer is delivered, every material statement in it will be deemed to be denied, not admitted (rule 14). The principle of rule 8 of Order 18 applies to all these subsequent pleadings. Hence, if the defendant desires to give evidence at the trial of any fresh facts by way of confession and avoidance in answer to the plaintiff's reply, he must allege them specially in his rejoinder, and not merely join issue.

Unless a pleading subsequent to a reply is ordered the pleadings are deemed to be closed at the expiration of fourteen days after service of the reply or defence to counterclaim; or, if there is no reply or defence to counterclaim, fourteen days after service of the defence (rule 20). There is then (except in the case of a counterclaim to which no defence has been pleaded) an implied joinder of issue and every material allegation of fact in the pleading last served is deemed to have been denied (rule 14). The issues are now clear and the parties can take stock of the position and proceed to discovery.

---

[7] *e.g.,* if any cross-claim has accrued to him either before or after the issue of the writ, which arose at the same time and out of the same transaction as the counterclaim and is not strictly pleadable as a set-off, provided that the plaintiff desires to use such cross-claim merely as a shield against the defendant's counterclaim; otherwise he must amend his statement of claim or issue a fresh writ. See *Toke* v. *Andrews* (1882) 8 Q.B.D. 428; *Renton Gibbs & Co., Ltd.* v. *Neville & Co.* [1900] 2 Q.B. 181.

CHAPTER 16

DISCOVERY OF DOCUMENTS

THE issues in the action being now clearly stated in the pleadings, each party naturally proceeds to consider how he shall prove his case. What evidence is available? Some letters have, as a rule, passed between the parties before the action was commenced, and these may contain important admissions, or be evidence of some material fact; but the plaintiff has the defendant's letters, and the defendant has the plaintiff's; and, in the absence of copies, neither set is properly intelligible without the other. It is most desirable that anyone who intends to give evidence should, if possible, read over his own letters before he enters the witness-box. For his recollection of an interview which took place many months ago is probably somewhat hazy now, and far less reliable than his account of it, given in a letter written at the time, which remains in black and white as clear and intelligible now as it ever was. Moreover, there is no better material for cross-examining an opponent than his letters written before the dispute arose. Hence it is generally desirable for each party to see all material documents in the possession of his opponent, and to take copies of the more important ones. Such disclosure is obtained by the process—formerly only available in equity, but now freely used in all divisions of the High Court—called "Discovery of Documents." Two stages are involved: the disclosure of what documents exist (coupled with any claim that any of them are privileged from production) and the inspection of such of those documents as the opposite party is entitled to see.

Disclosure of What Documents Exist

It may be that one party has, in his pleading or particulars, or in an affidavit, whether filed or not, referred to some document; and he cannot say that it is not material as he relies on it himself. His opponent is entitled at once (or later) to give notice under Order 24, r. 10, that he desires to see that document and take a copy of it, if he deems it sufficiently material. The party who has referred to the document must then name a time within seven days when, and a place where, the document can be inspected, and state any grounds he has for objecting to the production of it. The power of the court to order production can then, if necessary, be invoked (*post*, p. 247). Or it may be that one party knows or suspects that the other has certain material documents, or a class of documents, in his possession though they are not referred to in any pleading or affidavit. In such a case he may be able to obtain an order for specific discovery of them (*post*, pp. 237–238). But in most cases neither party has any clear idea as to the documents in his opponent's possession. He may be able to guess at some of them; but he would like a detailed list of all that are material—and this he can generally obtain.

Under the former rules discovery of documents took place as the result of an application which was usually made at the first or at an adjourned hearing of the " summons for directions " (see next chapter). Now, the plaintiff and defendant in an action begun by writ will normally exchange lists of documents between themselves in accordance with Order 24, rr. 1 and 2, without the necessity of attending before a master. Unless dispensed with by order or by agreement this must be done within fourteen days of the close of pleadings. To allow time for this and for the inspection of the documents disclosed, the summons for directions need not be issued until one month from the close of pleadings.

The list of each party must set out all the documents " which are or have been in his possession, custody or power relating to any matter in question between them in the action." (Order 24, r. 2 (1).) How far the addition of the word " custody " to the rule extends the former scope of discovery is referred to at p. 244, and must await the decision of the court. Either party is at liberty to serve a notice on the other requiring him to verify his list by affidavit, and this may be done at any time before the summons for directions is taken out (r. 2 (7)). If, however, the parties agree that discovery is not necessary at all, or that only limited discovery is necessary, they may dispense with or limit it accordingly, without the intervention of the court. If one party is willing to dispense with or limit it, but the other will not agree, or if either party thinks that it should be postponed, he may apply by summons to a master under rule 2 (5); and if the master thinks that immediate and full discovery is not necessary either for disposing fairly of the action or for saving costs he will make an appropriate order.

In " collision cases " (*i.e.*, all cases arising out of an accident on land due to a collision or apprehended collision involving a vehicle) discovery should not be made *by a defendant* unless the master so orders.[1] And in actions for the recovery of any penalty under a statute the defendant need not make discovery.[2]

There are many cases in which the foregoing provision for " automatic " discovery does not apply—*e.g.*, in actions begun by originating summons and in civil proceedings to which the Crown is a party.[3] Or your opponent may fail to give the discovery which he is required to give. Accordingly, rule 3 gives power to the master to order a party to furnish a list of all the relevant documents which are or have been in his possession, custody or power, and if necessary to verify it by affidavit. This is sometimes referred to as an order for " general discovery." The order may be limited to certain classes of documents or to certain issues in the action; or its operation may be postponed until certain issues have been tried. And discovery is sometimes ordered as to special damage only (including documents relating to the plaintiff's industrial injury, industrial disablement or sickness benefit rights); or discovery on the issue of damage may be postponed until the questions of liability have been tried. The power is subject to this overriding limitation, that discovery will not be ordered except where it is necessary either for disposing fairly of the action or for saving costs (rule 8). The party seeking discovery should see that the master's order is drawn up and should, if necessary, serve it on his opponent.

Subject to the same limitation the master has power under rule 7 to order discovery of particular documents or classes of documents. This he may do at any stage of the action. He may be asked to do so before general discovery takes place because a party has reason to believe that the other has relevant documents in his possession which it is necessary in the interests of justice

---

[1] Rule 2 (2). The master might do so, for example, where improper maintenance of the brakes or lights of the defendant's vehicle is alleged.
[2] Rule 2 (3). And see *post*, p. 243.
[3] Order 77, r. 12 (1).

that the applicant should see at once. Discovery, whether general or specific, is seldom ordered before close of pleadings and never for the mere purpose of enabling a party to fish out some case [4]; but there are rare occasions when it may properly be ordered at this stage. Or, again, you may have grounds for believing that material documents have been omitted from the list which your opponent has furnished under rule 2 or in pursuance of an order under rule 3. In such cases you may take out a summons, or apply under the summons for directions, specifying the document or class of document of which discovery is sought and asking for an order requiring your opponent to state whether he has or ever has had it in his possession, custody or power, and, if he has parted with it, what has become of it (rule 7).[5] The application must be supported by an affidavit stating that the deponent believes, with the grounds of his belief, that the other party has, or has had, the document or class of document and that it is relevant. If the other party has already made an affidavit verifying his list of documents so as to show that he has not, and has not had, any relevant documents other than those which he has disclosed, his oath must in some way be displaced. In an application under rule 7 this can be done by an affidavit disclosing prima facie grounds for supposing that specific documents or classes of documents are relevant and that they exist. If the existence of further documents is then disclosed, but they are sworn not to be material, the matter can be tested upon an application for production; but such further oath is usually regarded as conclusive.[6] The master may, however, inspect the document in order to arrive at a decision (rule 13 (2)).

Apart from rule 7, further discovery can only be obtained in special circumstances. A list which, for example, omits all reference to the documents which the deponent once had but has not now in his possession will be deemed an insufficient compliance with the rules and a proper list may be ordered under rule 3. But if a list of documents be drawn up in proper form and verified by affidavit, it is as a rule conclusive. No counter-affidavit will be

---

[4] See, for example, *Gale* v. *Denman Picture Houses, Ltd.* [1930] 1 K.B. 588; *Disney* v. *Longbourne* (1876) 2 Ch.D. 704 (a case on interrogatories).

[5] And see *White* v. *Spafford* [1901] 2 K.B. 241; *Astra-National Productions, Ltd.* v. *Neo-Art Productions, Ltd.* [1928] W.N. 218.

[6] *Chowood, Ltd.* v. *Lyall* [1929] 2 Ch. 406.

permitted except on an application under rule 7.[7] But if it can be shown from the list itself, or from the documents disclosed in it, or from any admission made by the party, or from correspondence or other documents, that he has in his possession other material documents which he has not disclosed, a further and better list may be ordered under rule 3 [8]; so also where it is clear that a party has compiled his list under a misconception of the real issues and that he almost certainly must have documents which ought to have been disclosed and which he would have disclosed if he had rightly conceived his case.[9]

The List of Documents

The documents contained in the list must be described with particularity sufficient to identify them, should the court think fit to order any of them to be produced.[10] If objection is to be made to their production, the grounds must be set out.[11] All material documents must be specified—immaterial documents should be altogether omitted. Any document set out is admitted to be material.

There is thus placed on the practitioner the somewhat invidious burden of deciding whether a document is material or not. If he decides it is not, the correct course is to omit all mention of it; thus the correctness of his decision on materiality is not capable of challenge in the same way as it would be on, say, a doubtful claim to privilege (see p. 248). If his opponent has good ground for supposing that a document exists and that it is material, his only remedy is to apply for further discovery in the manner already described.

But if a document is material, the fact that a party intends to object to its production or does not propose himself to put the document in evidence is no ground for not disclosing it; still less if it may assist his opponent. If it throws light on any part of the case, it is material. If parts only are relevant and he does not wish to disclose the whole, he should specify the relevant parts; it is

---

[7] *Edmiston* v. *British Transport Commission* [1956] 1 Q.B. 191.
[8] *Compagnie Financière du Pacifique* v. *Peruvian Guano Co.* (1882) 11 Q.B.D. 55; *Kent Coal Concessions, Ltd.* v. *Duguid* [1910] 1 K.B. 904; [1910] A.C. 452.
[9] *British Assn. of Glass Bottle Mfrs., Ltd.* v. *Nettlefold* [1912] 1 K.B. 369; [1912] A.C. 709; *Chowood, Ltd.* v. *Lyall* [1929] 2 Ch. 406.
[10] r. 5 (1); *Taylor* v. *Batten* (1878) 4 Q.B.D. 85.
[11] r. 5 (2); see *post*, p. 240.

in his possession and he must take the responsibility.[12] Both
discovery and inspection are strictly limited to the " matters in
question " in the action.

Documents are material which not only would be evidence upon any issue
but which it is reasonable to suppose contain information which may either
directly or indirectly enable the party seeking discovery either to advance his
own case or to damage the case of his adversary, or which may fairly lead
him to a train of inquiry which may have either of those consequences.
>   *Compagnie Financière du Pacifique* v. *Peruvian Guano Co.* (1882) 11
>   Q.B.D. 55.
>   *Astra-National Productions, Ltd.* v. *Neo-Art Productions, Ltd.* [1928]
>   W.N. 218.
If either party has served particulars, he will be entitled to discovery of such
documents only as are relevant to the issues as limited by such particulars.
>   *Arnold & Butler* v. *Bottomley* [1908] 2 K.B. 151; 77 L.J.K.B. 584.
>   The proprietor of a newspaper sued for a libel which has appeared in his
columns need not, as a rule, give inspection of the manuscript.
>   *Hope* v. *Brash* [1897] 2 Q.B. 188; 66 L.J.Q.B. 653.
>   *Kelly* v. *Colhoun* [1899] 2 Ir.R. 199.
>   Where the only issue in an action was the value of a lightship at the
time of its destruction by a collision, the plaintiffs were ordered to produce
for the inspection of the defendant certain books and documents in their
possession which showed the original cost of the lightship and details of its
subsequent depreciation.
>   *The Pacuare* [1912] P. 179; 81 L.J.P. 143.

The list of documents and the affidavit by which it is verified
must be in Forms Nos. 26 and 27 in Appendix A of R.S.C. (rule
5; see Precedents, Nos. 95, 96). The list itself has two schedules,
and the first schedule has two parts. In Schedule 1, Part 1, the
plaintiff or defendant sets out the documents relating to the matters
in question in the action which he has in his possession, custody
or power, and is willing to produce; in Part 2, he sets out all
documents which, although relevant, he objects to produce on
the ground of privilege. The claim of privilege with " a sufficient
statement of the grounds " must be set out in paragraph 2 of the
body of the list. In Schedule 2 he sets out documents which he once
had in his possession, custody or power, but which, at the date of
service of his list, he no longer has. He must state in paragraph 4
of the body of the list what has become of them and in whose
possession they now are. In each schedule he must " enumerate
the documents in a convenient order and as shortly as possible "

[12] *Yorkshire Provident Co.* v. *Gilbert* [1895] 2 Q.B. 148, 153.

but describe each of them, or, in the case of bundles of documents of the same nature, each bundle, sufficiently to enable it to be identified (rule 5 (1)).

At the end of the list is appended a " notice to inspect " which sets out the place at which and the date and time when the documents which a party is willing to produce may be inspected by his opponent.

Claim of Privilege

In all cases where privilege is claimed for a document the court may itself inspect the document for the purpose of deciding whether the claim is valid (Order 24, rr. 12 and 13 (2)).

The fact that a document was written on a privileged occasion, in the special sense in which that term is used in actions of defamation, is no reason for refusing to produce it; it is not on that ground privileged from inspection.[13] Certain former privileges from production were abolished by the Civil Evidence Act, 1968, s. 16. But production for inspection by your opponent may be lawfully refused on the following grounds:

1. *Documents of title.*—No party need produce any document which he can truthfully say relates solely to his own title to any real property, corporeal or incorporeal, and to contain nothing which tends to establish the title of his opponent.[14] If, however, the documents are material to his opponent's title, a party must disclose them, even though he be a purchaser for value without notice.[15] So, where the defendant claims title through the plaintiff, or one of the plaintiff's predecessors in title, the plaintiff is entitled to see the deeds under which such title is alleged to have passed to the defendant.[16]

2. *Communications between solicitor and client.*—Any document which a man at any time prepared in order that his solicitor might advise him on the facts stated therein, or that it might be submitted to counsel for his advice, is privileged from production although it was prepared before the present or any litigation was contemplated.[18] So are all documents which were prepared

[13] *Webb* v. *East* (1880) 5 Ex.D. 23, 108; *Schneider* v. *Leigh* [1955] 2 Q.B. 195 (*post*, p. 243).
[14] *Morris* v. *Edwards* (1890) 15 App.Cas. 309: *Chowood, Ltd.* v. *Lyall* [1929] 2 Ch. 406.
[15] *Ind Coope & Co.* v. *Emmerson* (1887) 12 App.Cas. 300.
[16] *Att.-Gen.* v. *Storey* (1912) 107 L.T. 430.
[18] *Minet* v. *Morgan* (1873) L.R. 8 Ch. 361.

by a solicitor with a view to some previous litigation.[19] So are all opinions of counsel.[20] But when in an action it is specifically alleged with some show of reason that the defendant has been guilty of a crime, or of some definite fraud not amounting to a crime, communications between him and his solicitor relating to the alleged crime or fraud or to its subject-matter are not privileged from production merely because they passed between solicitor and client, even though it be not alleged that the solicitor was a party to the alleged crime or fraud.[21] The privilege does not extend beyond the legal profession,[22] *e.g.*, to a chartered accountant, although in appropriate cases the party seeking discovery may be required to give an undertaking not to divulge the contents of the documents to any person otherwise than for the purposes of the litigation and not to use the information thereby obtained for any collateral purpose.

3. *Documents prepared with a view to litigation.*—All documents, including copies of documents,[23] which are called into existence for the purpose—but not necessarily for the sole or primary purpose—of assisting a party or his legal advisers in any actual or anticipated litigation are privileged from production.[24] Thus, all proofs, briefs,[25] draft pleadings, etc., are privileged; but not counsel's indorsement on the outside of his brief,[26] nor any deposition or notes of evidence given publicly in open court.[27] So are all papers prepared by any agent of the party bona fide for the use of his solicitor for the purposes of the action, whether in fact so used or not.[28] But this privilege from production is the privilege of the litigant and his successors in title and does not

19 *Calcraft* v. *Guest* [1898] 1 Q.B. 759; *Curtis* v. *Beaney* [1911] P. 181.
20 *R.* v. *Godstone R.D.C.* [1911] 2 K.B. 465.
21 *Postlethwaite* v. *Rickman* (1887) 35 Ch.D. 722; *Williams* v. *Quebrada* [1895] 2 Ch. 751; *O'Rourke* v. *Darbishire* [1920] A.C. 581.
22 *Slade* v. *Tucker* (1880) 14 Ch.D. 824; *Chantrey Martin* v. *Martin* [1953] 2 Q.B. 286.
23 *Watson* v. *Cammell Laird & Co.* (*Shipbuilders and Engineers*), *Ltd.* [1959] 1 W.L.R. 702.
24 *Seabrook* v. *British Transport Commission* [1959] 1 W.L.R. 509, where the long line of authorities is reviewed. But it must be an appreciable purpose, not an improbable contingency (*Longthorn* v. *B. T. C., ibid.*, 530). As to the meaning of " anticipated," see *Jarman* v. *Lambert & Cooke Contractors, Ltd.* [1951] 2 K.B. 937. See also *Re Duncan, decd., Garfield* v. *Fay* [1968] P. 306.
25 See *Hobbs* v. *Hobbs and Cousens* [1960] P. 112.
26 *Walsham* v. *Stainton* (1863) 2 H. & M. 1; *Nicholl* v. *Jones* (1865) 2 H. & M. 588.
27 *Goldstone* v. *Williams Deacon & Co.* [1889] 1 Ch. at p. 52; *Lambert* v. *Home* [1914] 3 K.B. 86.
28 *Southwark and Vauxhall Water Co.* v. *Quick* (1878) 3 Q.B.D. 315.

operate in favour of the author of a libellous medical report prepared for use in some other litigation, although the occasion of publication may have been privileged.[29] Privileged also are documents passing between an assured and the insurance company indemnifying him where a claim by a third party is anticipated.[30] Reports by a company's servant, if made in the ordinary course of routine, are not privileged, even though it is desirable that the solicitor should have them and they are subsequently sent to him; but if the solicitor has requested that such documents shall always be prepared for his use and this was one of the reasons why they were prepared, they are privileged.[31] But the privilege does not extend to letters passing between co-defendants unless privileged on other grounds[32]; nor generally to communications made to third parties who have to decide whether or not legal proceedings shall be taken.[33]

4. " *Without prejudice* " *documents.*—If documents come into being under an express or a tacit agreement that they should not be used to the prejudice of either party, an order for production in an action between them on the same dispute will not be made.[34]

5. *Incriminating documents.*—It is also a ground of privilege that the documents, if produced, would tend to expose the party producing them, or his spouse, to proceedings for a criminal offence or for the recovery of a penalty. But a party cannot refuse to make a list of documents on the ground that he might thereby criminate himself. He must take the objection in the list [35] and in terms clear and express. He alone can raise the objection, and he must verify it on oath if required to do so. It is not sufficient for him to state merely : " the production will, to the best of my information and belief, tend to criminate me." [36] The extent of the former privilege from production of incriminating documents has been both limited and extended by section 14 (1) of the Civil Evidence Act, 1968.

6. *Documents which are the property of a third person.*— Before revised rules came into force on January 1, 1964, the

---

[29] *Schneider* v. *Leigh* [1955] 2 Q.B. 195.
[30] *Westminster Airways, Ltd.* v. *Kuwait Oil Co., Ltd.* [1951] 1 K.B. 134.
[31] *Ankin* v. *L. & N.E. Ry.* [1930] 1 K.B. 527.
[32] *Hamilton* v. *Nott* (1873) L.R. 16 Eq. 112.
[33] *Jones* v. *Great Central Ry.* [1910] A.C. 4; but see note 30, *supra.*
[34] *Rabin* v. *Mendoza & Co.* [1954] 1 W.L.R. 271; and see *post*, p. 321.
[35] *Spokes* v. *Grosvenor Hotel Co.* [1897] 2 Q.B. 124, 130; *Nat. Assn. of Plasterers* v. *Smithies* [1906] A.C. 434.
[36] *Roe* v. *New York Press* (1883) 75 L.T.J. 31.

law was as stated later in this section. Now, however, instead of referring to documents in the " possession or power " of a party the rules say " possession, *custody* or power." The list of documents must include all such documents as are relevant; but if the party who has custody of them has no right or power to deal with them and is therefore in a difficulty about producing them, he must take the objection in his list. Whether the court will now compel him merely for the purpose of discovery to produce documents which belong to someone who is not a party to the action and who objects to their production remains to be decided. In this connection reference should be made to the decisions under Order 38, rule 13 (*post*, p. 249n.).

The law formerly was (and may still be) as follows :

A man will not be compelled to produce documents which he holds merely as agent or trustee for another, who is not a party to the action and who objects to their production. " ' Possession or power ' for the purposes of an order for production . . . as distinct from inclusion in an affidavit of documents . . . does not mean actual corporeal possession irrespective of legal ownership, but sole legal possesion, conferring on the party against whom production is sought a right and power to deal with the documents in question." [37] Thus, if an action be brought against the secretary of a company, he will not be ordered to produce any document which is the property of the company, if the directors forbid it. So, too, a solicitor who is a party to an action may refuse to produce documents of which he is in possession solely as a solicitor for a client. [38] Again, a party will not as a rule, be ordered to produce documents which are in the joint possession of himself and another person not a party to the action, unless that person consents. [39] A clerk or servant cannot be compelled to make and exhibit copies of documents which are the property of his employer in answer to interrogatories as to their contents. [40] But no privilege can be claimed for private letters written to the deponent by

---

[37] *Chantrey Martin* v. *Martin* [1953] 2 Q.B. 286, where it was held that working accounts brought into existence by chartered accountants in the course of an audit were their own property and not that of the client.

[38] *Procter* v. *Smiles* (1886) 2 T.L.R. 474; *Ward* v. *Marshall* (1887) 3 T.L.R. 578.

[39] *Hadley* v. *McDougall* (1872) L.R. 7 Ch. 312; *Kearsley* v. *Philips* (1882) 10 Q.B.D. 36, 40; 465 (C.A.); but see *Rattenberry* v. *Monro* (1910) 103 L.T. 560 (*post*, p. 284). As to a solicitor's lien see *post*, p. 248.

[40] *Balfour* v. *Tillett* [1913] W.N. 70.

a stranger to the suit, even though they are expressed to be written in confidence, and the writer forbids their production.[41]

7. *State documents.*—Sometimes, also, production may be refused on the ground of public policy, *e.g.*, where one party to the suit is officially in possession of State documents of importance. But the protection of documents from discovery on this ground is not limited to public official documents of a political or administrative character. "The principle to be applied in every case is that documents otherwise relevant and liable to production must not be produced if the public interest requires that they should be withheld. This test may be found to be satisfied either (a) by having regard to the contents of the particular document, or (b) by the fact that the document belongs to a class which, on grounds of public interest, must as a class be withheld from production." [42] But the class to which they belong and the reason must be specified,[43] for the court undoubtedly has an overriding power to order discovery, if necessary, after an examination of the document itself.[44] If the court is of the opinion that the refusal is not bona fide, or that no reasonable ground of public interest exists,[44a] it will order discovery. If, on the other hand, the document belongs to a class which it is contended ought to be withheld for reasons which the court is not competent to weigh, its production will not be ordered if disclosure of documents of that class would do harm to the functioning of the public service.[44b] "Cases would be very rare in which it could be proper to question the view of the responsible minister that it would be contrary to the public interest to make public the contents of a particular document." [44c] The claim of privilege based on (b) *ante* has in the past given rise to real difficulty and sometimes injustice, however, due mainly to the inherent reluctance of courts to gainsay the representations of a responsible minister. Thus the court must now not only give due weight to such representations and the reasons for them, but can, if it thinks

---

[41] *Hopkinson* v. *Lord Burghley* (1867) L.R. 2 Ch. 447; and see *M'Corquodale* v. *Bell* (1876) 1 C.P.D. 471.

[42] *Duncan* v. *Cammell Laird & Co.* [1942] A.C. 624, 636.

[43] *Re Grosvenor Hotel, London* [1964] Ch. 464; *Merricks* v. *Nott-Bower* [1965] 1 Q.B. 57.

[44] *Conway* v. *Rimmer* [1968] A.C. 910.

[44a] *Re Grosvenor Hotel, London (No. 2)* [1965] Ch. 1210; *Wednesbury Corporation* v. *Ministry of Housing and Local Government* [1965] 1 W.L.R. 262; *Conway* v. *Rimmer (supra)*.

[44b] *Conway* v. *Rimmer* [1968] A.C. 910.

[44c] *Ibid.*, per Lord Reid, at p. 945.

it is necessary or desirable, call for and inspect the document(s) concerned before deciding, on balance, whether the administrative considerations of the executive or the requirements of the fair and proper administration of justice are to prevail.[44d]

If the disclosure of a document would be injurious to the public interest and the law consequently authorises or requires it to be withheld, the provisions of Order 24 are subject to the rule of law and an order for discovery or inspection will not be made (Order 24, r. 15). And then not only will the document be withheld from production but oral evidence based upon it at the trial will also be excluded.[45] If the defendant be a subordinate officer of a public department sued in his official capacity, he cannot on his own authority claim privilege on the ground of public policy; production can only be refused on that ground by the head of the department.[46] But it may not always be necessary that the head of the department should himself attend or make an affidavit, so long as it is made clear to the court that the mind of the responsible person has been brought to bear upon the document in question.[47]

In an action in which the Crown is a party even the existence of a relevant document may be suppressed if in the opinion of any minister of the Crown it would be injurious to the public interest to disclose its existence.[48] In this connection " one facet of the public interest is that justice should always be done and should be seen to be done." [49]

There are a number of statutes which prohibit the disclosure for any other purpose of information obtained for the purposes of and under powers conferred by the Act. Where these apply, objection might well be taken to the making of an order for production of documents; and the validity of the objection would depend upon the provisions of the statute and the nature and origin of the documents.

Production and Inspection

A party who has served a list of documents on any other party, whether he has done so as part of the process of " automatic "

[44d] *Ibid., per* Lord Pearce, at p. 988.   [45] *Gain* v. *Gain* [1962] 1 All E.R. 63.
[46] *Beatson* v. *Skene* (1860) 5 H. & N. 838.
[47] See *Re Grosvenor Hotel, London (No.* 2) [1965] Ch. 1210 and other cases there cited; and see *Practice Note* [1933] W.N. 272.
[48] Crown Proceedings Act, 1947. s. 28; Ord. 77, r. 12 (2).
[49] *Per* Morris L.J. in *Ellis* v. *Home Office, ante.*

discovery under rule 2 or because he has been ordered to do so under rule 3, must allow the other party to inspect and take copies of all the documents other than those which he objects to produce. To this end he must, together with the list, serve a notice stating a time within seven days when and a place where the documents may be inspected (rule 9). Again, as we have seen (*ante*, pp. 235–236), a party may be bound to produce a document because he has referred to it in his pleading, particulars or an affidavit and therefore have been required to serve a similar notice under rule 10. Failure in either case to serve the requisite notice offering inspection, or an offer of inspection at an unreasonable time or place, entitles the other side to apply to a master for an order to produce the documents for inspection (rule 11). And a flagrant defiance of these rules may be dealt with under the wide, and if necessary penal, provisions of rule 16 (see *post*, p. 249). Also under rule 11 an application may be made for the production of documents which a party objects to produce and the master will rule on the grounds of objection; furthermore the master has a discretionary power to order inspection to be given to a party who would not otherwise be entitled to ask for it—*e.g.*, to a plaintiff by a third party and vice versa—provided that the application be supported by an affidavit specifying or describing the documents which the applicant wishes to inspect and stating his belief that the other party has them and that they are relevant. If a party has disclosed the existence of a document as a result of an order for specific discovery under rule 7, he becomes liable to produce it under rule 10 as a document referred to in an affidavit. Moreover, at any stage of the proceedings the master may order any party to produce any relevant document to him, and may deal with it when produced as he thinks right (rule 12). If objection is taken to the production of a document, either to another party or to the master, on the ground of privilege, irrelevance or any other ground, the master may look at the document, before formally ordering its " production," for the purpose of deciding whether the objection is valid (rule 13 (2)). All the before-mentioned powers of the master are subject to two overriding limitations: he must only exercise them in so far as he is of opinion that his order is necessary either for disposing fairly of the cause or matter or for saving costs (rule 13 (1)); and he must not order production of, or even look at, a document if a rule of law authorises or requires it to be withheld on the ground that its disclosure would be injurious to the public interest (rule 15).[50]

The party producing any book or document may seal or cover up any part which he can truthfully say is not material to any issue in the action.[51] No order will be made for inspection of a document which is not relevant to any question in the action, even though it has been disclosed in the list.[52] It is not an answer to an application for production of documents that they are in the hands of a party's former solicitors, who claim a lien over them for costs, and that he disputes the bill; but the order for production will contain liberty to apply in case he really cannot obtain the documents.[53]

The inspecting party is entitled to make a copy of any document produced to him.[54] In a proper case (*e.g.*, where one party denies that he wrote an important document which purports to be in his handwriting), the master will order the party in possession of the document to permit his opponent to take photographic or facsimile copies of it on such terms as may be just.[55]

It is on an application under rule 11 that the validity of any claim of privilege from inspection will be generally tested. The master may in every case inspect the document himself, if he thinks fit.[56] Otherwise the only question is whether the party has in his list said enough about the document to entitle him to refuse production on the ground of privilege—unless the master is satisfied that the party has misrepresented or misconceived its effect.[57]

Any party to the action may be ordered to attend at any stage of the proceedings for the purpose of producing—subject to a

---

[50] Nor may the court hear evidence based on it—*Gain* v. *Gain* [1962] 1 All E.R. 63, *ante*, p. 246.
[51] *Blanc* v. *Burrows* (1896) 12 T.L.R. 521; *Pardy's Mozambique Syndicate, Ltd.* v. *Alexander* [1903] 1 Ch. 191.
[52] *Hope* v. *Brash* [1897] 2 Q.B. 188; *Angell* v. *John Bull, Ltd.* (1915) 31 T.L.R. 175.
[53] *Lewis* v. *Powell* [1897] 1 Ch. 678.
[54] *Ormerod, Grierson & Co.* v. *St. George's Ironworks* [1905] 1 Ch. 505. Usually copies are supplied by the solicitor for the disclosing party on payment of the prescribed charges. (See Ord. 62, Appendix 2, item 83.) If the document has been prepared for use in the Supreme Court, the party who prepared it is usually bound to supply a copy of it, if it is written or typewritten, and up to ten copies if printed, on payment of the charges (see Ord. 66, r. 3).
[55] *Lewis* v. *Earl of Londesborough* [1893] 2 Q.B. 191.
[56] Rule 13 (2); *Ehrmann* v. *Ehrmann* [1896] 2 Ch. 826.
[57] *Roberts* v. *Oppenheim* (1884) 26 Ch.D. 724.

claim of privilege—any document named in the order.[58] A person not a party to the action may also be ordered to attend and produce specified documents for the purpose of a proceeding,[59] and such an order has the effect of a *subpoena duces tecum* (*post*, pp. 298, 323); but the rule does not confer a right of discovery against persons not parties to the action.[60]

Where there are several defendants each one is entitled, after he has pleaded, to have free, on request, a copy of the list of documents, and any affidavit in support of it, served on the plaintiff by each of the others.[61] A similar rule applies in favour of a plaintiff against whom, together with others, a counterclaim is made.

A party who serves a list of documents is himself deemed to have been served with a notice to produce at the trial all the documents in his list which he states are in his possession, custody or power.[62] And a party upon whom a list is served is, unless he gives notice or has already pleaded to the contrary, deemed to admit the authenticity of all the documents set out in the list.[63] As a result of this new rule it will less often be necessary for notices to admit and produce to be served (see *post*, pp. 296, 297) and in a great many cases the necessity will not arise at all.

Copies of business books properly verified by affidavit may be ordered to be produced for inspection if production of the originals is, in the opinion of the master, unnecessary.[64]

Default in making Discovery

If any party fails to discover or produce or allow inspection of documents as provided by any of the foregoing rules, or as ordered, the court has power under rule 16 (1) to make any order it thinks just. This includes, in particular, the power to order that an action be dismissed, or that a defence be struck out with judgment to be entered accordingly.[65] Normally, however, the court is reluctant to exercise such power and will only do so when a party

---

[58] Ord. 38, r. 13; *Straker* v. *Reynolds* (1889) 22 Q.B.D. 262; *Elder* v. *Carter* (1890) 25 Q.B.D. 194.
[59] Ord. 38, r. 13.
[60] See cases in note 58, *supra*.
[61] Rule 6 (1), (2).
[62] Ord. 27, r. 4 (3).
[63] *Ibid.* r. 4 (1), (2).
[64] Ord. 24, r. 14.
[65] And see *Salomon* v. *Hole* (1905) 53 W.R. 588.

has at least once disobeyed a peremptory order insisting, for example, that he make discovery within a time specified in the order. A party who fails to comply with an order for discovery or production is also liable to committal (rule 16 (2)). These are highly penal provisions and will only be enforced in the last resort, where it seems clear that the party in default really intends not to comply with an order of the court.

CHAPTER 17

SETTLING OR WITHDRAWING AN ACTION

THE possibility of settling the action is probably in the minds of the parties at all stages of the proceedings, but assumes special prominence after discovery, when each party has a clearer picture of the strength or weakness of his case. An action is often settled by agreement before or at the trial (see *post*, p. 326), or is allowed to go to sleep without any definite settlement being arranged. If the plaintiff does not proceed, the defendant can apply for it to be dismissed with costs for want of prosecution; but this is not always wise. If an action lies dormant and no proceeding is taken for a whole year, any party desiring to proceed must give a month's notice of his intention. (Order 3, r. 6.)

If no order of the court is required and all parties have given their written consent, an action may be withdrawn before trial without any leave by producing the consents to the appropriate officer of the court (Order 21, r. 2 (4)). If an order staying proceedings on terms agreed is required, it may be made by a master. The applicant issues a summons setting out the order required, and the signed consent of the solicitors for the other parties is indorsed upon it, unless for any special reason they wish to see the master. The applicant may then take the summons so indorsed to the Practice Master [1] to make the order. It is unnecessary to put the summons in the list or to obtain a special appointment from the master to whom the action is assigned unless it is one in which the approval of the court or an order for investment of funds is required, as where a minor or patient is a party, or where damages have been recovered for a widow under the Fatal Accidents Acts.[2] In such cases an appointment is obtained and both sides usually attend. And if a claim by a minor or a patient is settled before proceedings are begun, Order 80, r. 11, makes it

---

[1] See *ante*, p. 4.
[2] See Ord. 80, rr. 10–15. Apart from these rules, which deal with money claims on behalf of such persons, a minor or a patient may repudiate a contract if it is not for his benefit; therefore it is wise to obtain the court's approval of a settlement in all cases where they are parties.

possible to apply for the approval of the court and any necessary directions by originating summons.

It is wise to ask that the stay of proceedings should take effect after the terms have been complied with, or " except for the purpose of carrying out this order," and for liberty to apply; otherwise, in case of default, the party aggrieved may have no remedy except to commence fresh proceedings to enforce the terms.[3] If the action has been set down for trial, the solicitors *must* inform the Clerk of the Lists or, in assize cases, the district registrar or the associate [4] that it has been settled and the summons should ask " that the record be withdrawn." This means that the copies of pleadings which are required to be lodged with the court when the action is set down (see *ante*, p. 82) are returned to the solicitors and the action is withdrawn from the list. It does not mean that all records of the proceedings which the court is required to keep—*e.g.*, the cause book,[5] or the filed copy of the writ [5a] or other documents—are erased; although, no doubt, if any scandalous matter which constituted an abuse of the process of the court appeared therein, the court might order it to be struck out or expunged, as is occasionally done in the case of an affidavit.[5b] If your client is an assisted person under the Legal Aid and Advice Act, 1949, do not omit to ask in the summons (apart from any order as to costs to be paid to him by the opposite party) that his own costs be taxed in accordance with the Third Schedule to the Act.

A defendant may acknowledge that the claim against him is well founded, though he may think that the damages claimed are excessive; he may therefore desire to insure himself, as it were, against the plaintiff's probable success; this he can do by making a payment of money into court (see *post*, p. 254). Or it may be that the plaintiff is now satisfied that he cannot succeed. If so, he may at any time consent to judgment against himself; and from that two results will follow: (a) he must pay the defendant his costs; (b) he can never take any subsequent proceeding upon the same cause of action against the defendant (see *ante*, p. 201). But there is a less drastic course open to him, namely, discontinuance.

---

[3] See *Green* v. *Rozen* [1955] 1 W.L.R. 741; in special circumstances such a stay may be removed: *Cooper* v. *Williams* [1963] 2 Q.B. 567.
[4] See *post*, p. 306, note 2.
[5] See Ord. 1, r. 4.
[5a] See Ord. 6, r. 7 (5).
[5b] Ord. 41, r. 6.

Discontinuance

A plaintiff, who is compelled through lack of some necessary piece of evidence or for some other adequate reason to abandon his present proceedings, may yet desire to preserve his right to bring a fresh action under more favourable circumstances. At common law, before the Judicature Act, he was allowed to discontinue his action at any time before judgment, or to withdraw the record before the jury were sworn, or to elect to be non-suited,[6] and was yet at liberty to re-enter the cause, or bring a second action. But now this liberty has been greatly curtailed; there is no longer such a thing as a non-suit in the High Court.[7] The plaintiff may now discontinue the action, or withdraw any part of it, by giving notice in writing to the defendant. If he does so before the defence is served, or within fourteen days after its service, he may discontinue without leave (Order 21, r. 2) and may yet bring a second action. He must, however, pay the other party's costs (Order 62, r. 10 (1)) and any further action may be stayed until he does so.[8] At any later stage of the action he can only discontinue by leave, and the master or the trial judge can make it a condition of giving such leave that no subsequent action shall be brought. (Order 21, r. 3.) The fact that the defendant is anxious to interrogate the plaintiff is no ground for refusing the plaintiff leave to discontinue.[9]

A defendant who wishes to discontinue his counterclaim, or withdraw any part of it, is subject to similar rules.

Withdrawal of Defence

In some cases it may be better and cheaper for a defendant who has no real answer on liability to put in no defence and let judgment go by default (*e.g.*, in an action for breach of promise of marriage). Damages are then assessed by a master, unless he orders some other mode of assessment (see *ante*, p. 58). A defendant who has put in a defence, but is minded to withdraw it, or any part of it, may do so at any time without leave by giving notice to the plaintiff in writing (Order 21, r. 2 (2) (*a*)). If the whole

---

[6] *Clack* v. *Arthur's Engineering Ltd.* [1959] 2 Q.B. 211.
[7] *Fox* v. *The Star Newspaper Co., Ltd.* [1898] 1 Q.B. 636; [1900] A.C. 19; *aliter* at present in the county court (see *Clack* v. *Arthur's Engineering Ltd., supra*).
[8] Ord. 21, r. 5.
[9] *Hess* v. *Labouchere* (1898) 14 T.L.R. 350.

defence is withdrawn, the plaintiff can enter judgment in default with costs under Order 19. If only part is withdrawn it may be possible for the plaintiff to enter judgment for any part of his claim which stands admitted. But where only one of several defences to the same claim is withdrawn—*e.g.* a plea of justification in a libel action, while a plea of privilege remains—he will have to make a special application for any costs to which he has been put by the matter withdrawn.

Payment into Court

A defendant who has no defence should pay money into court. This he can do at any stage of the action after appearance, and before the judgment or summing-up begins, but the earlier the better. Similarly, if he admits part of the claim, he should at once pay in what he admits. The defendant may pay into court whether the claim is liquidated or unliquidated and he may pay in without specifying whether he admits or denies liability. The right is a valuable one for the protection of defendants and practically ensures that a plaintiff cannot continue litigation oppressively against a defendant who submits and is willing to give the plaintiff his rights. For the court in its discretion over costs may, and ordinarily will, order that a plaintiff, who insists on continuing his action and does not recover more than the amount paid in, shall pay the costs of both sides incurred after payment in (see *post*, p. 256).

Not only is a defendant thus protected when faced with a claim for a liquidated amount which he admits to be due. He also has a powerful weapon to curb the zeal of a plaintiff where the claim is unliquidated, *e.g.*, in an accident case. The plaintiff, faced with a substantial payment in, where damages are at large, will hesitate long before incurring the risk of going on and perhaps having to pay the costs of both sides.

Payment into court is thus not strictly a defence; it is rather an attempt to force a compromise.[10] No such plea was known to the common law; it is entirely the creature of statute. In 1834 payment into court was permitted in actions of contract; in 1843 in actions of newspaper libel; in 1852 in some actions of tort. But in 1875 payment into court was for the first time permitted

[10] But see the observations of Lord Greene M.R. in *Monk* v. *Redwing Aircraft Co.* [1942] 1 K.B. 182.

in all actions for debt or damages. In such cases a defendant is now allowed [11]—after appearance—to pay money into court whether he admits or denies liability.

If the statement of claim contains two or more independent causes of action, the defendant has two courses open to him: he may make separate payments of specified amounts in respect of each or of any two or more of the causes of action, identifying them; or he may make a single payment stated to cover either all the causes of action or any one or more of them. Leave is not required to make a " general " payment in covering more than one cause of action without allocating a sum to each; but if the result is to embarrass the plaintiff, the defendant may be ordered to make such an allocation (Order 22, r. 1 (5)). He may also pay in a sum of money which takes into account both the plaintiff's claim and the whole or part of any counterclaim of his own, expressing his intention to satisfy at one and the same time all such causes of action (rule 2). Where a defendant, after complying with an order to make an interim payment (*ante*, pp. 54–55), pays money into court he must state in his notice of payment (*infra*) that he has taken the award into account (Order 29, r. 15).

The payment in is made at the Pay Office of the Central Office or a District Registry [12] and a notice [13] is sent to the plaintiff and to the co-defendants (if any). The plaintiff must acknowledge its receipt within three days. If the payment in is made *before* the hearing, the plaintiff may, within fourteen days from receipt of the notice (but in any event before the trial begins), accept the money in satisfaction of his claim, or of the causes of action in respect of which it was paid in, by giving a notice of acceptance [14] to all defendants. But where the payment in is made, or increased, *after* the hearing has begun, the plaintiff must make up his mind before the judge begins his judgment (or summing-up to a jury), and in any case within two days, whether or not to accept the money. Only if the plaintiff decides to accept may he or his counsel mention the payment to the judge.[15]

On the plaintiff accepting money paid into court, further

---

[11] If he resides abroad, the leave of the Treasury may be required under the Exchange Control Act, 1947.

[12] But see Order 22, r. 1 (7) relating to actions triable at assizes which have been transferred.

[13] See Precedent No. 92.

[14] See Precedent No. 93.

[15] See rule 7.

proceedings in the action, or upon a particular cause of action, are stayed both against the defendant making the payment and any other defendant sued jointly with or in the alternative to him (Order 22, r. 3 (4)) except (a) where the plaintiff is a minor or a patient, in which case the approval of the court is required (Order 80, r. 12); and (b) in defamation actions, as to which see *post*, p. 257. No fresh action can be brought upon the same cause of action; but exceptionally (*e.g.*, in a case of fraud) a plaintiff might be allowed to resile from his acceptance and have the stay removed.

If notice of acceptance is given, the plaintiff can usually get the money out of court without leave, tax his costs to the time of receipt of the notice of payment in and sign judgment for them if not paid (see *post*, p. 412). But in some cases an order of the court is required and this must further deal with the costs (Order 22, r. 4). This is so (a) in the case of a minor or a patient; (b) where the money was paid in by some only of defendants sued jointly or in the alternative, unless the plaintiff discontinues against the others and they consent in writing to the payment out; (c) where the money was paid in with a defence of tender before action; (d) where the money was paid in in satisfaction of causes of action arising both under the Fatal Accidents Acts and the Law Reform (Miscellaneous Provisions) Act, 1934; or under the Fatal Accidents Acts only, where more than one person is entitled to the money; and (e) in cases where the Exchange Control Act, 1947, applies (see rule 9).

After fourteen days the plaintiff needs leave to take the money out of court, and this will not necessarily be granted.[17] Or he may continue the action in the hope that he will obtain a larger amount, but in that case he cannot take the money out of court—he can only do this in satisfaction of his claim. If he goes on with the action, claiming more, the money must remain in court (r. 5), and the plaintiff may have to pay the defendant a substantial sum for costs, if he is not awarded more than the sum paid into court.[18]

Hence, if the defendant pays money into court at all, he will be wise to pay in a good round sum. The court will give judgment without reference to the amount paid in; indeed, neither the fact that money has been paid into court, nor the amount paid in,

---

[17] Rule 5; *Cumper* v. *Pothecary* [1941] 2 K.B. 58; *Practice Note (Millar* v. *Building Contractors (Luton) Ltd.)* [1953] 1 W.L.R. 780; [1953] 2 All E.R. 339.

[18] See *J. R. Munday, Ltd.* v. *London County Council* [1916] 2 K.B. 331.

may ordinarily be mentioned to the judge or jury until all questions as to liability and the amount of debt or damages to be awarded have been decided (r. 7.) If it is, the judge must in his discretion decide whether the case should continue or be retried elsewhere.[19]

A third party, or a co-defendant against whom a claim for contribution is made as a joint tortfeasor pursuant to the Law Reform (Married Women and Tortfeasors) Act, 1935, may make a written offer to contribute to a specified extent to such debt or damages as may be recovered by the plaintiff and obtain advantages similar to those accruing from a payment into court.[20] And a plaintiff or other defendant to a counterclaim may pay in (see Order 22, r. 6).

In libel and slander there are two peculiarities. Formerly in a defamation action a defendant could only pay in if he admitted liability. Now that it is no longer necessary to state, when paying in, whether liability is admitted or denied, a plaintiff who thinks the sum paid in is sufficient but wishes to clear his name may, on accepting the payment, apply to a judge in chambers for leave to make in open court a statement in terms approved by the judge. (Order 82, r. 5 (1).) If such an action is settled without such a payment having been made into court, it can nevertheless be ordered to be set down in the list so that an approved statement may be made (see r. 5 (2)). Secondly, if one of two or more defendants sued jointly in a defamation action pays money into court in satisfaction of the cause of action against him, and the plaintiff accepts it, the action is not stayed against the others; but the plaintiff, if he gets judgment against them, can only execute for any excess which may be awarded to him against any defendant over and above the sum paid into court; and he will get no costs against a defendant after the date of payment in, unless either he is awarded some excess against him or the judge considers that he had reasonable ground for proceeding with the action against him (rule 4).

A defendant may at any time without leave increase the amount which he has paid into court, in which case the time for acceptance

---

[19] *Millensted* v. *Grosvenor House, Ltd.* [1937] 1 K.B. 717.
[20] See Ord. 16, r. 10; Ord. 62, r. 5; *Bragg* v. *Crossville Motor Services Ltd.* [1959] 1 W L.R. 324.

257

runs from the receipt of the last notice of increase. But if he wishes to withdraw or amend the notice, he must obtain leave (Order 22, r. 1 (3)). Thus in special circumstances a defendant who has paid money into court may apply to take some or all of it out again, and the master or trial judge may grant or refuse leave at his discretion.[21]

---

[21] *Cumper* v. *Pothecary* [1941] 2 K.B. 58.

CHAPTER 18

SUMMONS FOR DIRECTIONS

As we have seen, under Order 18, r. 20, unless a subsequent pleading has been ordered, the pleadings are deemed to be closed at the expiration of fourteen days after service of the defence, or of the reply or defence to counterclaim (if any). It then becomes the duty of the plaintiff within one month to take out a " summons for directions " returnable in not less than fourteen days. (Order 25, r. 1 (1).)[1] These periods are designed to enable discovery to take place before the summons is heard and to give all parties an opportunity to consider what directions they should ask for. If the plaintiff fails to issue the summons, any defendant may do so or may apply for an order to dismiss the action, whereupon the master may either dismiss the action on such terms as may be just, or deal with the application as though it were a summons for directions (rule 1 (4) and (5)).

This rule applies to all actions begun by writ with the exceptions listed in rule 1 (2). (See Appendix, p. 448, where the whole Order should be carefully studied.) The exceptions most commonly met with (apart from patent actions) are actions where directions have been given upon an application for summary judgment or for trial without pleadings, actions which have been referred for trial to a referee and actions in which an application for transfer to the commercial list is pending or such transfer has been ordered. In such cases the referee or the judge, as the case may be, will give the directions.

The object of the summons for directions is to provide an occasion for the consideration by the master of the preparations for the trial of the action, so that—

---

[1] This does not mean that he cannot in any circumstances take out a summons for directions unless and until the pleadings are closed (see *Nagy* v. *Co-operative Press* [1949] 2 K.B. 188). If a party has to make any interlocutory application at an earlier stage, he may include therein all matters upon which he then desires the master's directions; but it is not ordinarily convenient to give extensive directions before the issues have been defined, and a summons under Order 25 would still be necessary at the appropriate time.

(a) all matters which must or can be dealt with on interlocutory applications and have not already been dealt
with may so far as possible be dealt with; and

(b) such directions may be given as to the future course of
the action as appear best adapted to secure the just,
expeditious and economical disposal thereof. (Order
25, r. 1 (1).)

This tends to cheapen the cost of litigation in two ways: first,
by reducing the number of interlocutory applications; and, secondly,
by providing a stock-taking process before the action comes to
trial, so that the parties shall not incur unnecessary expense at the
trial, *e.g.*, by calling witnesses to prove facts which could be proved
by production of a document or which, although formally in issue
upon the pleadings, are not seriously contested and might, with a
little encouragement, be admitted. It is not always possible when the
summons first comes to be heard to give all the directions which
may eventually be found necessary; but rule 2 requires the master to
deal forthwith with all the matters which it is possible then to deal
with; if he thinks it expedient to adjourn the summons for
consideration of any matters at a later stage, he will do so.

The summons must be issued in the form provided (see
Precedent No. 90) and served on all parties to the action who
may be affected by it. It is returnable in not less than fourteen
days. Each party served must, seven days before the hearing,
give to the plaintiff and to any other parties written notice of any
further or other directions which he may wish the master to make,
including so far as possible all matters capable of being dealt with
on interlocutory application (rule 7). If the summons is adjourned,
any party desiring directions not already asked for must give
written notice not less than seven days before the resumed hearing.
The master has power to give such directions as he thinks proper,
whether the parties have asked for them or not; indeed, as we shall
see, there are certain matters which he is specifically required by
rules 3 and 4 to consider of his own motion if necessary; and it
is his duty under rule 2 (3) to endeavour to secure that all outstanding matters which must or can be dealt with by interlocutory
application are dealt with either upon the first or any resumed
hearing of the summons for directions.

Any interlocutory application after the hearing of the summons for directions has been completed should be made by issuing a notice for further directions under the summons; two clear days' notice to the other parties is necessary stating the grounds of the application. On issuing a notice for further directions, as contrasted with an adjournment of the summons, a fee of one pound is payable as on the issue of a summons. If the order asked for is one which could have been granted at the hearing of the original summons, the applicant may have to bear the cost unless the master thinks that there was sufficient reason for the separate application (Order 62, r. 7).

In these ways the object of reducing the number of interlocutory applications is in many cases achieved.

Since discovery now takes place before the summons is heard, an adjournment will less often be necessary. Nevertheless there may be cases where it will be preferable for the plaintiff to ask the master to postpone certain questions until an adjourned hearing, either to save expense or because they are not yet ripe for decision. For example, you may need to ask for leave to make an amendment to the writ or pleadings which will give a completely new turn to the action, or to ask for an order for further discovery. Again, considerable expense may be caused to your client by drafting elaborate interrogatories which, when the summons comes before the master, are found unnecessary because your opponent is willing to make admissions or to give particulars. Again, it may seem likely that an important witness will be unable to attend the trial; but this may be ascertainable with greater certainty at a later date, so that it would be premature to ask for him to be examined now or for his statement to be admitted under the provisions of the Civil Evidence Act, 1968. On the other hand, in simple actions for personal injuries full directions can usually be given forthwith. If the summons is expected to be simple and straightforward, it will be issued in the ordinary morning list; if, however, it is expected to be long, the master should be asked to fix a special appointment for it.

To secure that the pre-trial stocktaking shall in fact take place in all cases to which Order 25 applies it is provided by rule 2 (4) that, unless all parties agree, no order as to the place or mode of trial shall be made until all the matters required by the Order to be considered have been dealt with. This does not apply where the master orders the action to be transferred to a county court or to an official referee; in the latter case an application for directions must be made to the referee.

Some of the problems likely to arise upon the stocktaking are dealt with in Chapter 20 on Advice on Evidence; and thought should have been given to them on those lines before the parties come before the master. It is the duty of the parties and their advisers under rule 6 to give (subject to any claim to privilege) all such information and produce all such documents to the master as he may reasonably require in order to deal properly with the summons. If they are not ready with it upon the hearing or refuse to give it they are likely at the least to be penalised in costs and in flagrant cases may have their pleadings struck out.

No affidavit is to be used on the hearing of the summons without the leave or direction of the master except where it is specifically required by some other rule—*e.g.*, in support of an application to take evidence before an examiner, or an application for discovery of specific documents.

Power to Give Directions

It follows from rule 1 (1) that the master may give all such directions as he may think proper with a view to the just, expeditious and economical disposal of the action. Further, the court has inherent jurisdiction to give directions for the conduct of an action [2]; but how far this power will be exercised in any particular case in the absence of a specific rule is doubtful. [3] In many cases the parties are before the master upon an earlier application in the action and he is empowered by rule to give directions at that stage as to all matters capable of being dealt with on interlocutory application. Thus if leave to defend is given on an application for summary judgment, all appropriate directions will be given then (Order 14, r. 6). There are many other instances. [4] In actions

---

[2] *Henly* v. *Evening Standard* (unreported), 1942, H. No. 340 (July 1942) Lewis J.; *Nagy* v. *Co-operative Press* [1949] 2 K.B. 188 (C.A.); and see Judicature Act, 1925, s. 103.

[3] See *Sigley* v. *Hale* [1938] 2 K.B. 630.

[4] See, for example, Ord. 18, r. 21 (trial without pleadings); Ord. 24, r. 4 (preliminary issue); Ord. 29, rr. 7, 13 (preservation orders, interim payments, etc.); Ord. 83, r. 4 (moneylenders); Ord. 86, r. 6 (specific performance).

transferred to the Commercial List or to a referee, the judge or referee will give the necessary directions.

Matters Dealt With on the Summons

The wide scope of the summons can be seen from the form provided (Precedent No. 90). This form is of considerable length and refers to numerous orders which might be made, not all of which are applicable in any particular action. This is done partly in order to help in the speedy disposal of the summons by saving the master from much writing and partly to ensure that nothing of importance which ought to be dealt with on the hearing shall be overlooked; but the list is not exhaustive. It will be convenient to notice the various topics in the order in which they appear on the form.

Consolidation of actions.—The master has power to consolidate actions pending in the same Division of the High Court (Order 4, r. 10). It is exercisable where some common question of law or fact arises in all the actions to be consolidated; or where the rights to relief arise out of the same transaction or series of transactions; and generally where in the master's discretion it seems desirable (*ibid.*). Thus actions brought by the same persons against different defendants in respect of the same libel [5] or other connected cause of action [6] can be consolidated; so can actions for negligence by different plaintiffs against the same defendant arising out of the same accident [7]; and generally when the plaintiffs could have joined in one action under the provisions of Order 15, r. 4, consolidation may often appropriately be ordered. The master may in his discretion order consolidation, subject to any special directions which he may think fit to give,[8] or refuse it. If consolidated, the several actions concerned proceed thenceforth in chambers and at the trial as a single action.

A simpler method which has many of the advantages of consolidation is to apply by summons before a master for an order that the two actions come into the list before the same judge on the same day, reserving to the judge all questions as to procedure and costs.[9]

---

[5] *Stone* v. *Press Association* [1897] 2 Q.B. 159.

[6] *Bailey* v. *Marchioness Curzon; Same* v. *Duggan* [1932] 2 K.B. 392.

[7] *Brady* v. *McDonald* [1931] N.I. 345.

[8] See *Healey* v. *A. Waddington & Sons, Ltd.* [1954] 1 W.L.R. 688.

[9] But see *John Fairfax & Sons* v. *de Witt* [1958] 1 Q.B. 323, *post*, p. 402.

Sometimes when the same point arises for decision in several actions proceeding simultaneously, all parties agree that one shall be tried first as a test action and to be bound by that decision. Any such agreement may be recorded in the orders for directions and the other proceedings may be stayed temporarily or ordered to be set down later.

Transfer to an official referee.—Official referees (of whom there may be up to four) are officers of the court with almost the full powers of a judge. Each has a court in the Royal Courts of Justice, but they may (and sometimes do) hold sittings anywhere in the country. Business may be referred to them for inquiry and report or for trial,[10] or for arbitration.[11] Reference for trial may be made upon application by any party interested if the nature of the case makes it desirable, whether on grounds of expedition, economy, convenience or otherwise; any question or issue of fact arising in a cause or matter may be referred for inquiry and report whether any party applies or not. Both these powers are subject to any right to trial by jury (*post*, pp. 273–274). Disputes on building contracts and schedules of dilapidations are often so referred. Cases involving a charge of fraud, or of negligence against a professional man, may now properly be referred for trial by an official referee [12] especially if one of the above-mentioned reasons makes this desirable.

Reference to a special referee or a master.—In addition to the power to refer an action by consent for trial by a master under Order 14, r. 6 (2) (*ante*, p. 70), there is power under Order 36, rr. 8 and 9, with consent of both parties, to order the trial of the action or any issue or question of fact arising therein before a master or special referee; and under the same rules such matters may without consent be referred to a master or special referee for inquiry and report. A master will, if practicable, arrange to sit continuously from day to day to hear a long case, if suitable to be referred to him.

Transfer to a county court.—This may be done in the following cases—

---

[10] Administration of Justice Act, 1956, s. 15; Order 36, rr. 1, 2; see also *Practice Direction* [1968] 1 W.L.R. 1425.

[11] Arbitration Act, 1950, s. 11.

[12] *Scarborough R.D.C.* v. *Moore* (1968) 112 S.J. 986.

(1) By consent in any Queen's Bench action of whatever nature to any county court and whatever the amount involved. (County Courts Act, 1959, s. 67.)[13] There must be a memorandum of consent signed by the parties or their solicitors conferring jurisdiction in that action on the particular court. This may conveniently be done by indorsing on the summons the words " We agree that the —— County Court shall have jurisdiction in this action " and signing it.

(2) Upon the application of any party (whether the other side consent or not) in an action in any Division where the plaintiff's claim is founded on contract or on tort, and the amount claimed or remaining in dispute on the claim does not exceed £750 (whether there is a counterclaim exceeding that amount or not), or where the only matter remaining to be tried is a counterclaim not exceeding £750 founded on contract or on tort (*ibid.*, s. 45).[14-15] Under this section the action may be transferred to any county court in which it might have been commenced if the subject-matter and amount had been within the jurisdiction of that court, or to any county court which the master may deem most convenient to the parties.

(3) Transfer may similarly be ordered in certain actions for the recovery of land by a landlord, where the net annual value for rating is under £400 per annum (*ibid.*, s. 50). The section applies, for example, to a claim against a tenant or his assignee who is holding over or has incurred a forfeiture for non-payment of rent, but not for breaches of other covenants.

(4) Transfer of certain Chancery, Admiralty and Probate proceedings may be ordered in appropriate cases (*ibid.*, ss. 54, 59, 63).

(5) Interpleader proceedings (see pp. 212, 387), where the subject-matter of the dispute does not exceed £750 in

---

[13] See also ss. 42 and 53; and *Williams* v. *Settle* [1960] 1 W.L.R. 1072.

[14-15] Increased from £500 since May 26, 1970, by s. 2 of the Administration of Justice Act, 1969 (Commencement No. 2) Order, 1970, (S.I. No. 672); and see, as to costs, *post*, p. 407.

amount or value, may be transferred to the appropriate county court (*ibid.*, s. 68).

Amendments of the writ or pleadings.—See Chapter 11, pp. 168–172. Now is the time when you can make any necessary application to amend without incurring the costs of a special summons, although you may have to bear the costs of actually making the amendment and any costs thrown away as a result of it; and now is the time when such application should be made unless it was desirable to apply earlier. Before the summons look carefully through the proceedings to see whether any amendment is necessary or desirable and draft it; for although this is one of the matters which by Order 25, r. 3, the master is specifically required to consider on the hearing of the summons, if necessary of his own motion, the initiative should come from the parties and not from the master, who may be seeing the case for the first time and will be reluctant to interfere with counsel's pleadings unless application is made. Consider also whether any further pleading (*ante*, p. 233) is necessary, and save the costs of a separate application by asking on this summons for leave to serve it.

Particulars.—See Chapter 10, pp. 156–167. The first hearing of the summons for directions is the time when an application to the court for an order for particulars can and should be made, unless an earlier application was essential. In the first instance you should normally apply by letter, otherwise an order—or at least the costs of the application—may be refused (Order 18, r. 12 (6)). Much time and trouble may be saved if your opponent gives all or some of the particulars beforehand.

Security for costs.—The defendant may in certain cases ask for an order to compel the plaintiff to give security for the costs of the action (Order 23, r. 1), *e.g.*, where the plaintiff is ordinarily resident abroad, and has no substantial property, real or personal, in England [16]; or is a merely nominal and impecunious plaintiff suing for the benefit of some other person; or is an insolvent company [17]; or has deliberately omitted or misstated his address in the writ; or has changed his address with a view to evading the consequences of litigation. But the mere fact that an

---

[16] See *Kevorkian* v. *Burney* (*No.* 2) [1937] 4 All E.R. 468.
[17] See Companies Act, 1948, s. 447.

individual is insolvent, or is a Scotsman resident in Scotland,[18] is not sufficient ground for such an order.

Discovery and inspection of documents.—See Chapter 16. In so far as an order for discovery or further discovery or for inspection may be required it will usually be appropriate to be dealt with when the summons for directions first comes to be heard.

Interrogatories.—See Chapter 19. Whether it is advisable to ask for leave to serve interrogatories upon the first hearing of the summons may often be a matter of considerable doubt. Interrogatories are usually drafted by counsel and are often lengthy and expensive. Such expense may be obviated if it appears on the hearing of the summons that admissions can be made or particulars given which will render interrogatories unnecessary. This, therefore, is one of the matters which, unless the proposed interrogatories are of the simplest kind, it will often be wise to ask the master to deal with on an adjourned hearing of the summons; but on the first hearing the possible need for interrogatories should be mentioned to him so that alternative methods of achieving the object in view may first be explored.

Inspection or preservation of real or personal property.— The master may under Order 29, r. 2, provide for the preservation or inspection of any property or thing to which the action relates. This rule, however, applies only to physical things and not, for instance, to a process of manufacture.[19] Inspection should first be requested in writing. If it is not given and the master makes an order, he may take the refusal into consideration when dealing with the costs of the application. Rule 3 empowers him to order samples to be taken or experiments to be made. Under rule 4 he may order the sale of perishable property, but it is at an earlier stage of the action that occasion for this would be likely to arise.

Evidence.—Subject to the Rules of the Supreme Court, to the Civil Evidence Act, 1968, and to any other enactment relating to evidence, any fact required to be proved by the evidence of witnesses at the trial of any action begun by writ is to be proved by the examination of the witnesses orally and in open court.

---

[18] *Findlay* v. *Wickham* [1920] W.N. 317.
[19] *Tudor Accumulator Co.* v. *China Navigation Co.* [1930] W.N. 200; though, exceptionally, such an inspection may be ordered in a patent action.

(Order 38, r. 1.) The expense of calling witnesses bulks largely in a bill of costs, but it may be significantly reduced if thought is given to the numerous provisions by which other methods of proof may be substituted. Before the summons for directions or the adjourned hearing, as the case may be, each party should carefully consider what are the facts which it will be incumbent on him to prove and how he can most satisfactorily prove them, with due regard to the expense involved; and the observations in Chapter 20 on " Advice on Evidence " should be borne in mind. Upon the hearing of the summons the master should be asked to make all such orders as it is then possible to make with regard to method of proof so as to achieve the maximum saving of costs. (See *post*, p. 271.) This is a matter which he is required to consider, if necessary of his own motion; but it is more difficult for the master to achieve the object in view if the parties do not exercise forethought and initiative.

A very brief summary of the effect of the Civil Evidence Act, 1968, is set out, *post*, p. 301. This is supplemented by the following provisions.

An order may be made that *all or any of the evidence* shall be given by affidavit. (Order 38, r. 2.) Unless the order, or some subsequent order, otherwise directs, the deponent will not be subject to cross-examination and need not attend the trial. As to affidavit evidence generally, see Order 41. If an affidavit contains statements of information or belief—as it may on interlocutory proceedings or, if the master or judge so orders, when used as evidence at the trial—the sources and grounds of the belief must be stated. An affidavit in the form " I am informed and verily believe that . . . " will not be accepted unless the deponent states by whom he was informed.

Under Order 38, r. 3, the master may order that evidence of any particular *fact* shall be given at the trial in such manner as may be specified by the order.[21] In particular, he may order it to be given by statement on oath of information and belief; by the production of documents or entries in books; by copies of documents or entries in books; or, in the case of a fact which is or

---

[21] Under s. 99 (1) (i) and the proviso to s. 101 of the Judicature Act, 1925, rules of court may be made *regulating* the means by which *particular facts* may be proved. Whether a rule which provides that evidence of *any* particular fact may be given in whatever way the court chooses to order is within the power conferred by the Act may be open to question.

was a matter of common knowledge either generally or in a particular district, by the production of a specified newspaper which contains a statement of that fact.

Now, therefore, is the time when the master should be asked to order, for example, that a statement or measurements in a police report should be admissible without calling the constable; or that the date when the Derby was run and the winner—for the court does not take judicial notice of this—should be proved by production of a newspaper; or that the price at which shares were dealt with on a particular day on the Stock Exchange, or goods upon the market, should be proved by an official or trade publication, and so forth.

As to admissions, see *post*, p. 270.

It may also be necessary to have the evidence of some person abroad taken under letters of request or before a British consul or a special examiner (see *post*, p. 295), or to have a witness who is dangerously ill or about to go abroad examined here before the trial (see *post*, p. 295); or to obtain a copy of an entry in a banker's book under the Bankers' Books Evidence Act, 1879 (*post*, p. 300); or of entries in other business books under Order 24, r. 14.

The master may order that the number of medical or expert witnesses who may be called at the trial shall be limited. (Order 38, r. 4.) In actions for personal injuries he will frequently order that unless a medical report be agreed [22] the medical evidence be limited to two doctors on each side. The order is not made as of course, because in some cases—*e.g.*, where the substantial question in the action depends on medical opinion or where a doctor is charged with negligence—it may be necessary that the judge should hear the witnesses examined and cross-examined.[23] The parties cannot be forced to exchange medical reports with a view to agreement, though it is often desirable that they should do so.[24] In collision cases the oral evidence of a motor engineer is not receivable at the trial except by leave of the judge or special order unless a copy of his report has been disclosed to the other parties before the hearing of the summons and the master authorises the admission of the evidence. (Order 38, r. 6.)

---

[22] See *Harrison* v. *Liverpool Corpn.* [1943] 2 All E.R. 449.
[23] *Proctor* v. *Peebles (Papermakers) Ltd.* (1941) 57 T.L.R. 375.
[24] *Worrall* v. *Reich* [1955] 1 Q.B. 296.

The use of plans, photographs and models at the trial is restricted by Order 38, r. 5. Unless for special reasons the master or the judge gives leave, no plan, photograph or model is receivable in evidence in any case unless at least ten days before the trial the other parties have been given an opportunity of inspecting it and agreeing to its admission without further proof. In collision cases the costs of a scale plan will not be allowed on taxation unless an order authorising it was obtained before the trial or the taxing master is satisfied that it was reasonable to prepare it.[24a]

Admissions.—The parties should make all admissions and all agreements as to the conduct of the proceedings which ought reasonably to be made, and the master is to do his best to secure that they do so (Order 25, r. 4). Here again forethought by the parties will lighten the master's task and speed the hearing of the summons. If they do not co-operate, the master may specially note the refusal to admit or to agree, so that the trial judge may deal appropriately with the costs thereby occasioned; or if the refusal to admit were clearly unreasonable, the master himself might make an appropriate order as to the costs of proving the relevant facts, subject to the discretion of the trial judge (see *ante*, p. 137). A stronger weapon, of which far too little use has hitherto been made, is the service of a notice to admit facts under Order 27, r. 2 (1); for under Order 62, r. 3 (5), unless the facts in the notice are admitted within seven days or any extended time, the cost of proving them falls automatically upon the other side, whatever the result of the action, unless an order to the contrary is obtained. The process should not be abused by calling on the other side to admit matters which, from the nature of the action, must obviously be seriously in issue. The admissions are for the purposes of the action only and may by leave be amended or withdrawn on terms. The notice must be given not later than twenty-one days after the action has been set down for trial. It may be done much earlier, even at the time when the statement of claim is delivered. The expense of interrogatories may sometimes be avoided by judicious use of this procedure; or, if interrogatories have subsequently to be resorted to, your opponent may have to pay the costs of them. (As to admissions of documents, see *post*, pp. 296–297.)

[24a] See Ord. 62, App. 2, pt. X, para. 4 (1).

Right of appeal.—Costs can be saved if the parties agree, as they may, that there shall be no appeal from the decision of the trial judge, or that any appeal shall be limited to the Court of Appeal or to questions of law only. It is not for the court to try to force the parties into an agreement of this kind, but the order for directions may record any such agreement which, it seems, would not be enforceable unless embodied in an order.[25] (Order 25, r. 5.)

Other matters.—All matters capable of being dealt with by interlocutory application ought, so far as possible, to be dealt with on the summons for directions. It is impossible to enumerate them all, but the following should also be mentioned—

Accounts.—On this summons the master may order the delivery of an account under Order 43 (see *ante*, p. 48), or the usual partnership accounts.

Attendance of witnesses.—In the event of a dispute as to whether the author of a statement can or should be called as a witness, the master may be asked to determine the matter on a summons under Order 38, r. 27 issued by either party and this may be dealt with at the summons for directions.

Hearsay statements.—Many other matters of evidence arising under rules 28, 30 or 33 may conveniently be dealt with at this stage by the giving of directions. (And see *post*, p. 302.)

Court expert.—In non-jury cases involving any question for an expert witness either party may apply under Order 40 for the appointment of an independent expert, called the court expert, to inquire and report upon any question of fact or of opinion not involving questions of law or construction. Leave may be obtained to cross-examine the court expert upon his report and provision is made for the calling of one (or in exceptional cases more than one) expert witness by each party.[25a] Unexpected difficulties are sometimes encountered in the practical application of this procedure, though it has been found of use particularly in Probate actions. Reference to a skilled arbitrator or special referee is

---

[25] *Re Hull and County Bank* (1879) 13 Ch.D. 261. *Aliter* in the county court (County Courts Act, 1959, s. 111).

[25a] But the costs will not be allowed on taxation unless the judge certifies that the calling of the witness was reasonable (Ord. 62, App. 2, pt. X, para. 4 (2)).

often preferred by the parties, notwithstanding that they may then be at the expense of calling their own expert witnesses.

Stay of proceedings.—Again, on a summons for directions the master has power to stay all proceedings by consent, or if the action be frivolous and vexatious (see *ante*, pp. 153–154), or should have been brought elsewhere,[26] or be premature,[27] or if the plaintiff's mode of conducting the action be oppressive and vexatious,[28] or if he is in contempt of court through a failure to pay costs which he has been ordered to pay.[29] But the mere fact that a plaintiff has not paid costs which he was ordered to pay upon an interlocutory application in the present action, is not a ground for staying proceedings, if the plaintiff really is unable to pay them.[30] The master has power to stay an action between husband and wife if it appears to him that the parties will not gain any substantial benefit from the proceedings if they are continued, or if he thinks that the case is one which could more conveniently be dealt with under the Married Women's Property Act, 1882, s. 17, in which case he may give appropriate directions.[31]

Place of trial.—The place of trial is fixed by the master on the summons for directions (Order 33, r. 4); but except where the action is transferred to a county court or to an official referee no order as to the place or mode of trial is to be made (unless by consent) until all matters required to be dealt with on the summons have been dealt with.[32] The place of trial will be determined, as a rule, by considerations of economy and convenience; the master will fix it in the place which he deems least expensive and most convenient for both parties and the majority of the witnesses on both sides, and will have regard to the date when the trial can take place according to the state of the lists and the facilities for trial at any particular assize. Neither party has any prima facie right of preference, except that the Crown can insist on trial

[26] *Logan* v. *Bank of Scotland* [1906] 1 K.B. 141.
[27] *Smith and wife* v. *Selwyn* [1914] 3 K.B. 98 (action stayed pending the taking of criminal proceedings in case of felony). See also *Jack Clark* (*Rainham*), *Ltd.* v. *Clark* [1946] 2 All E.R. 683.
[28] *Norton* v. *Norton* [1908] 1 Ch. 471.   [29] *Leavis* v. *Leavis* [1921] P. 299.
[30] *Graham* v. *Sutton, Carden & Co.* (*No.* 2) [1897] 2 Ch. 367.
[31] Law Reform (Husband and Wife) Act, 1962, s. 1; the exercise of this power should be considered upon the hearing of the *first* summons in the action which comes before the master (Ord. 89). Note that when s. 1 of the Administration of Justice Act is brought into force all s. 17 applications will be assigned to the Family Division and the Masters will then, instead of giving directions, transfer the matter to the Family Division.
[32] Ord. 25, r. 2 (4); and see *Southey-Roberts Estates, Ltd.* v. *Roe* [1956] 1 W.L.R. 946.

in London.[33] Where the cause of action arose has but little to do with the question. But if for any reason it appears that a fair trial could not be had at the place which would otherwise be most convenient, the master will fix it elsewhere. He will, however, have regard to the burden imposed on jurors, if any.

The decision of the master as to the place or mode of trial may be varied without appeal by a subsequent order made at or before the trial (Order 33, r. 4; and see *post*, p. 304).

Mode of trial.—The master must also direct the mode of trial. Shall it be with or without a jury, by a judge or by an official or special referee? The order must ordinarily contain an estimate of the length of the trial and in London cases must specify the list into which it is to be put.[34] (Order 34, r. 2 (3).) If it is to be tried without a jury, it will usually be entered in the Short Cause List or the Non-jury List, according to the master's estimate of the length of the trial, those up to about two hours being appropriate for the Short Cause List in the Queen's Bench Division.[35]

The rights of the parties to a jury in a civil case were limited by the Administration of Justice (Miscellaneous Provisions) Act, 1933. It is a matter of discretion in most actions in the Queen's Bench Division, whether there shall be trial by jury.[36] Matters to be taken into consideration include whether there is likely to be an acute conflict of evidence, and whether the issues either as to liability or damage are such as can better be decided by a consensus of ordinary lay opinion than by a single judge. But in a personal injury case trial by jury will now be ordered only in exceptional circumstances.[36a] A party may, however, claim a jury as of right if a charge of fraud against him is in issue; so can either party where a claim [37] in respect of libel, slander, malicious prose-

---

[33] Order 77, r. 13 (1).
[34] The following lists exist for the trial of Queen's Bench actions in Middlesex: the Jury List; the Non-jury List (sub-divided into the General and Fixture Lists, *post*, p. 307); the Short Cause List; the Commercial List (*post*, p. 275); the Revenue List (not to be confused with the Revenue Paper in the Ch.D.); the Motions for Judgment List; and the Special Paper List (for the trial of miscellaneous matters such as issues of fact without pleadings (*ante*, p. 80) or points of law (*ante*, p. 147)). (L.C.J.'s Directions of December 9, 1958.)
[35] As to Ch.D. see *post*, p. 344.
[36] And see *Hope* v. *G.W. Ry.* [1937] 2 K.B. 130.
[36a] See *Ward* v. *James* [1966] 1 Q.B. 273; *Hodges* v. *Harland & Wolff Ltd.* [1965] 1 W.L.R. 523.
[37] See *Shordiche-Churchward* v *Cordle* [1959] 1 W.L.R. 351.

cution or false imprisonment is in issue; provided always that the trial will not require prolonged examination of documents or accounts or any scientific or local investigation which cannot conveniently be made with a jury.[38]   In such a case, even though the master has ordered trial by jury, the judge in charge of the list may order the case to be transferred to the Non-jury List, whether the parties consent or not.[39]   The right to claim a jury by virtue of the Act of 1933 must be exercised before the master first fixes the place and mode of trial.[40] Afterwards, although there is always a discretion to vary the former order,[41] a party can no longer insist on it.

A trial will not be held with a jury in the Chancery Division; but if the issues are such that one of the parties would be entitled to a jury if the action were in the Queen's Bench Division, he may apply that the action be transferred to that Division.

Formerly when a jury was ordered, either party could demand a special jury. Special jurors were drawn from a panel with a somewhat higher property qualification than common jurors. But this ancient distinction was abolished in 1949 and all juries are alike, with the sole exception of the City of London Special Jury, which is sometimes ordered in commercial cases (*post*, p. 276).

If the trial is without a jury, it may be either before a judge alone, or a judge sitting with assessors,[42] or before an official or special referee or a master (see *ante*, p. 264), or a commissioner.[43]   Assessors are professional or scientific persons who assist the judge with their special knowledge; they are most frequently seen in the Admiralty Court in cases of collision between two vessels; but they may also sit in the Queen's Bench Division if any issue requires scientific investigation,[44] or if questions of seamanship and navigation arise.[45]

The master has power to order that different issues be tried by different modes of trial, if more convenient, or that some issue or issues be tried before others. (Order 33, r. 4 (2).) The power is exercised sparingly and only for rather special reasons.

---

[38] Administration of Justice (Miscellaneous Provisions) Act, 1933, s. 6.
[39] *Mayhead* v. *Hydraulic Hoist Co.* [1931] 2 K.B. 424.
[40] Order 33, r. 5.
[41] Order 33, r. 4 (1).
[42] Judicature Act, 1925, s. 98; Order 33, rr. 2 and 6.
[43] Judicature Act, 1925, s. 70.
[44] *Swyny* v. *N.E. Ry.* (1896) 74 L.T. 88.
[45] *Esso Petroleum Co. Ltd.* v. *Southport Corporation* [1956] A.C. at pp. 222, 238.

In a personal injury action, for example, if the issues of liability and damages are sufficiently separate and distinct an early determination of the former and a postponement of the court's decision on the latter may sometimes be of undoubted advantage.

Time of trial.—On the summons for directions the master must fix a period within which the plaintiff is to set the action down for trial—*e.g.*, within so many days after the date of the order or after inspection of documents (Order 34, r. 2). If it appears that a London action ought to have an early trial, he may direct an application to be made to the Clerk of the Lists to fix a date for the hearing.[46] This is commonly called an " order for a speedy trial." The application must be made within a week and the earliest practicable date for the trial will be arranged, subject to the right to apply to the judge in charge of the list. A judge has power also upon an application for an interlocutory injunction to make an order for an early trial (Order 29, r. 5). If a Queen's Bench action [47] is not expected to take more than about two hours to try it may be put in the Short Cause List, where it will be likely to be heard without much delay. In appropriate cases an action may be ordered to come on for trial together with or immediately after another named action.

Commercial cases.—These are causes arising out of the ordinary transactions of merchants and traders—amongst others, those relating to the construction of mercantile documents, export or import of merchandise, affreightment, insurance, banking and mercantile agency and usages. (Judges' Regulations, 1895; see The Supreme Court Practice, Part 4G.) A separate list in charge of a Queen's Bench judge is kept for the trial of such causes.[47a] The reasons for the existence of this list are discussed in *Butcher, Wetherly & Co.* v. *Norman* [1934] 1 K.B. 475.[48] The judge sitting in the Commercial Court has no wider jurisdiction than any other judge of the Queen's Bench Division, except by consent of the parties. In practice, however, consent is given as a matter of course to various departures from the usual procedure with a view to expediting business. Thus, points of claim and defence are frequently ordered instead of

---

[46] L.C.J.'s Directions of December 9, 1958, para. 3.
[47] As to Ch.D. see *post*, p. 344.
[47a] And see generally Practice Statement [1967] 1 W.L.R. 1545.
[48] The New Procedure List with which this case also deals has been abolished.

pleadings, and lists of documents instead of affidavits. (See Precedents, Nos. 36, 68 and 91.) By consent, matters may be decided mainly or even exclusively on documentary evidence or by evidence which would not ordinarily be admissible. (See the observations of Roche J. reported in [1931] W.N. 132.) When a jury is required, the action is tried by a special jury of the City of London. (Order 72, r. 9.)

Application for transfer to the commercial list is made on the summons for directions, which may be issued even before the defendant appears, and is heard by the judge in charge of that list. If on a summons for directions before a master it appears that the action may be suitable for trial in the commercial list, he may adjourn the summons to be heard by the judge and treated as an application to transfer. The judge will give directions in the action, if transferred. Either party may appeal against an order transferring an action to the commercial list on the ground that it is not a commercial cause at all.[49]

Costs

The master has power under Order 62, r. 4, to deal at the summons for directions not only with the costs of the summons itself, but of any incidental proceedings in the action. Orders for further discovery of books, accounts and other documents often cause great expense and so may orders for interrogatories. Although such orders may appear necessary in the interests of justice at the time when they are made, only too often the practical result which is produced turns out to be negligible. Yet for lack of a special application the costs are allowed to be " costs in the cause " (see *post*, pp. 415–416) and the general cost of the litigation is thereby unduly swollen. You should, therefore, when appropriate, ask the master to reserve the costs *occasioned by* such an order, even though the costs *of* the application may properly be costs in the cause.

---

[49] *Sea Insurance Co.* v. *Carr* [1901] 1 K.B. 7; *Hagen* v. *National Provincial Bank* [1938] 1 K.B. 169.

CHAPTER 19

INTERROGATORIES

BESIDES discovery of documents the parties may also require discovery of facts. Indeed, they will especially require this in those cases where there are no material documents to be disclosed. For it is in those very cases that there is almost sure to be a conflict of evidence; and that makes it all the more desirable for the parties to ascertain before the hearing what are the exact points on which there will be this conflict. Take, for instance, an action for personal injuries caused by a collision on a railway. Such documents as exist may not throw much light on the matter. Yet it is most important for the plaintiff to know before he comes into court whether at the trial the defendant will seriously contend that no such collision ever took place, or that the plaintiff was not a passenger in either train on the day of the collision, or that he was not injured thereby. Hence in a proper case the court allows one party to administer a series of questions to the other, and compels that other to answer them on oath before the trial; and the admissions obtained by means of these " Interrogatories " often save trouble and expense in preparing for the trial. Sometimes, however, both discovery of documents and interrogatories are necessary; and discovery of documents will generally come first; inspection of the documents disclosed may render the proposed interrogatories or some of them unnecessary.

At one time it was possible for one party to administer interrogatories to the other without leave and subject only to the power of the court to disallow such as were improper. Nowadays this can only be done with leave and for the purpose of fairly disposing of the issues or for saving costs. Throughout this chapter therefore, where it is stated on authority that a party is " entitled " to interrogate, it must be understood that this is subject to the master's overriding discretion. The cases are a guide to how the discretion will normally be exercised. The appropriate time to apply is upon the first or an adjourned hearing of the summons for directions.

So far as possible all matters capable of being dealt with on interlocutory application are to be dealt with when that summons first comes to be heard; but drafting and answering interrogatories is apt to be an expensive procedure, and if the action is of a type where an adjournment of the summons is likely to be necessary an application on the first hearing may add unnecessarily to the costs. The better course will usually be to serve on your opponent with the summons a notice to admit facts (*ante*, p. 270); then if he does not admit them you may proceed to interrogate him and gain some advantage in the matter of costs. The master should at any rate be informed at the first hearing that you may wish to interrogate and he may encourage your opponent to make admissions if he thinks it reasonable. Save in exceptional circumstances interrogatories will not be in order before defence, as the defence may contain admissions which will render them unnecessary.

Either party may at the trial read in evidence any one or more of the answers, or any part of an answer, which he has obtained to the interrogatories served upon his opponent. He need not put in the rest of them unless the judge directs him so to do (Order 26, r. 7). In some cases the master when ordering interrogatories may impose a condition as to the admissibility of the answers; see for instance, *Leeke* v. *Portsmouth Corporation* (1912) 106 L.T. 627.

As a general rule, interrogatories may be allowed whenever the answers to them will serve either to maintain the case of the party administering them or to destroy the case of his adversary (*per* Esher M.R., in *Hennessy* v. *Wright* (*No.* 2) (1888) 24 Q.B.D., at p. 447n.; and *per* Stirling L.J. in *Plymouth Mutual, etc., Society* v. *Traders' Publishing Association* [1906] 1 K.B., at p. 416; and see *Lyle-Samuel* v. *Odhams, Ltd.* [1920] 1 K.B. 135). But " ever since they were first invented, it has been recognised that they constitute a process which might become oppressive, and be used for improper purposes; and therefore that the allowance or disallowance of interrogatories is a matter for discretion, and they should be allowed or disallowed on the merits of the particular case." (*Per* Vaughan Williams L.J. in *Heaton* v. *Goldney* [1910] 1 K.B., at p. 758.) Either party may apply by summons to the master for an order giving him leave to serve interrogatories on any other party and requiring him to answer them on oath within such period as may be allowed. (Order 26, r. 1.) The interrogatories must have a note at the foot stating which of them are to be answered by each of the other parties. The particular interrogatories sought to be served must be submitted to the master, who will allow such of them only as he considers necessary either for disposing fairly of the matter or for saving costs. (Order 26, r. 1.) He will " take into account any offer made by the party to be interrogated to give particulars or to make admissions or to produce documents relating to any matter in question." (*Ibid.*)

The object of interrogating is twofold: first, to obtain admissions to facilitate the proof of your own case; secondly, to ascertain, so far as you may, the case of your opponent. There is therefore some art required in drawing interrogatories. Think rather of the answer the defendant will probably give you than of the answer which you are instructed he ought to give. The defendant's version of the matter must differ from the plaintiff's version, and your object is to discover precisely where and to what extent they differ. Your questions then should be framed so as to elicit, if possible, the admission you desire; and at the same time, failing that admission, to get at all events some definite statement sworn to, from which the party interrogated cannot afterwards diverge. Leave him no loophole of escape. If he will not answer the question your way, still at least find out how far he is prepared to go in the opposite direction. To secure this, it is well to ask a series of short questions rather than one long question. Each additional detail should be put in a question by itself.

Illustrations

If you are instructed that the plaintiff gave evidence in the Bankruptcy Court on May 15, 1963, that a certain cheque was in the handwriting of the defendant, it will be of little use to ask merely: " Did you not state on oath, in the Bankruptcy Court, on May 15, 1963, that the cheque sued on was in the defendant's handwriting? " as the plaintiff may simply answer " No." The only way to discover precisely what it is the plaintiff denies is to split the question up into several—" Were you not examined as a witness in the Bankruptcy Court on May 15, 1963, or on some other and what day? Was not a cheque then and there produced to you? Was not the said cheque the one mentioned in paragraph 2 of the statement of claim, or some other and what cheque? Did you not identity the handwriting of the said cheque? Did you not state the handwriting to be that of the defendant or some other and what person?

Here is a bad interrogatory: "Do you deny that the delay occasioned in the signing of the contract for the sale of the said brewery to the said purchasers arose wholly or in part from the fact that the 'tied houses' alleged to be connected with said brewery were not in your possession or connected with the said brewery?" This should be split up into eight or nine separate questions. As it stands, it assumes the existence of numerous facts, each of which may be in dispute. Possibly only one of them may be really in dispute, but an interrogatory in this shape will not help you to ascertain which one that is.

And see Precedents, Nos. 97–100.

What Interrogatories are Admissible

There are certain rules which determine what interrogatories may be administered and what not:

1. Interrogatories must be relevant to the matters in issue. If particulars have been delivered which restrict the issue, the interrogatories must be confined to the matters stated in such particulars.[1] Not every question which could be asked of a witness in the box may be put as an interrogatory. Thus, questions which are only put to test the credibility of the witness (questions "to credit," as they are called) will not be allowed, although of course they may be asked in cross-examination. (See Order 26, r. 1 (*a*).) "We have never allowed interrogatories merely as to the credibility of a party as a witness." (*Per* Cockburn C.J. in *Labouchere* v. *Shaw* (1877) 41 J.P. 788.) "Scandalous" interrogatories will not be allowed. A scandalous interrogatory may be described as an insulting or degrading question which is irrelevant or impertinent to the matters in issue. "Certainly nothing can be scandalous which is relevant." (*Per* Cotton L.J. in *Fisher* v. *Owen* (1878) 8 Ch.D. 653; and see *Kemble* v. *Hope* (1894) 10 T.L.R. 254.)

Again, no question need be answered which is not put bona fide for the purposes of the present action, but with a view to future litigation.[2] Interrogatories will not be allowed if they are oppressive, that is, if they put an undue burden on the party interrogated[3]; nor if their object be only to establish certain facts which, if proved, would be no defence in law to the action.[4]

---

[1] *Yorkshire Provident Co.* v. *Gilbert* [1895] 2 Q.B. 148; *Arnold & Butler* v. *Bottomley* [1908] 2 K.B. 151.

[2] *Edmondson* v. *Birch & Co., Ltd.* [1905] 2 K.B. 523; *Chapman* v. *Leach* [1920] 1 K.B. 336.

[3] *Heaton* v. *Goldney* [1910] 1 K.B. 754.

[4] *Rogers & Co.* v. *Lambert & Co.* (1890) 24 Q.B.D. 573.

Admissibility

A defendant cannot be asked: " If you did not print the libel, did M'C. & Co., or some other and what firm print it? "

Pankhurst v. *Wighton & Co.* (1886) 2 T.L.R. 745.

" If A's carriage is damaged by a collision in the street, and B is sued for damages as having caused the collision . . . A must establish that the vehicle which ran into his carriage was B's vehicle, and he ought not to be allowed to interrogate B to say if it was not B's vehicle, whose vehicle it was."

Per Cozens-Hardy M.R. in *Hooton* v. *Dalby* [1907] 2 K.B., at p. 20.

If the proprietor of a newspaper accepts liability for a libel which has appeared in his paper, he cannot be interrogated as to the name of the writer of the libel, or of the person who sent it to him for publication, unless the identity of such person is a fact material to some issue raised in the present action.

Hennessy v. *Wright (No.* 2) (1888) 24 Q.B.D. 445n.

Hope v. *Brash* [1897] 2 Q.B. 188; 66 L.J.Q.B. 653.

The plaintiff has, however, a statutory right to obtain discovery by interrogatories of the name of the printer, publisher or proprietor of a newspaper.

See *Hillman's Airways, Ltd.* v. *Soc. Anon. D'Editions Aéronautiques,* [1934] 2 K.B. 356; 103 L.J.K.B. 670.

In an action for a declaration that a certain piece of land was purchased by the defendant and C as partners, interrogatories as to other prior and subsequent purchases by them in order to prove partnership in those transactions were held irrelevant and oppressive and were disallowed.

Kennedy v. *Dodson* [1895] 1 Ch. 334; 64 L.J.Ch. 257.

And see *Ramsey* v. *Ramsey* [1956] 1 W.L.R. 542.

Interrogatories asking the plaintiff whether similar charges had not been made against him previously in a newspaper, and whether he had contradicted them or taken any notice of them on that occasion, are clearly irrelevant.

Pankhurst v. *Hamilton* (1886) 2 T.L.R. 682.

But interrogatories are not, like pleadings, confined to the material facts on which the parties intend to rely; they should be, and generally are, directed to the evidence by which the party interrogating desires to establish such facts at the trial.[5] " Discovery is not limited to giving the plaintiff a knowledge of that which he does not already know, but includes the getting of an admission of anything which he has to prove on any issue which is raised between him and the defendant." [6] Either party may be allowed to interrogate as to any link in the chain of evidence necessary to substantiate his own case; the question is relevant as leading up to a matter in issue in the action.

[5] *Attorney-General* v. *Gaskill* (1882) 20 Ch.D. 519.
[6] *Ibid.,* at p. 528.

Illustrations

If the defendant denies that he wrote a material document, he may be asked whether other documents produced to him are not in his handwriting, though such other documents have nothing to do with the action, and will only be used for comparison of handwriting.

> *Jones* v. *Richards* (1885) 15 Q.B.D. 439.

When a defendant has pleaded that his words are true, he may interrogate as to any fact material to his case on that issue.

> *Marriott* v. *Chamberlain* (1886) 17 Q.B.D. 154; 55 L.J.Q.B. 448.
> *Peter Walker & Son, Ltd.* v. *Hodgson* [1909] 1 K.B. 239; 78 L.J. K.B. 193.

In an action for libel or slander where the defendant pleads that the words or matters complained of are fair comment on a matter of public interest or were published on a privileged occasion, no interrogatories as to the defendant's sources of information or grounds of belief shall be allowed.

> Order 82, r. 6.

Similar interrogatories were disallowed in an action for malicious prosecution.

> *Maass* v. *Gas Light and Coke Co.* [1911] 2 K.B. 543.

In some cases also interrogatories are admissible as to matters which are only relevant in aggravation or mitigation of damages; but as a rule such interrogatories are not encouraged.[7]

Illustrations

Where the defendant has served a notice in mitigation of damages under Order 82, r. 7, he may be allowed to administer interrogatories to the plaintiff, as to the matters referred to in such notice. Presumably the plaintiff may also be allowed to interrogate the defendant on such matters, *e.g.*, as to the circumstances under which the libel was published.

> *Scaife* v. *Kemp & Co.* [1892] 2 Q.B. 319; 61 L.J.Q.B. 515.

A plaintiff is entitled to obtain an approximate statement in round numbers of the circulation of any obscure newspaper, in which a libel has appeared. But in the case of any well-known London or provincial newspaper such an interrogatory would be held unnecessary and vexatious.

> *Whittaker* v. " *Scarborough Post* " [1896] 2 Q.B. 148; 65 L.J.Q.B. 564.
> *James* v. *Carr* (1890) 7 T.L.R. 4.

2. The party interrogating may put his whole case to his opponent if he thinks fit, though it is not always wise to do so; he may also interrogate in full detail as to matters common to the case of both parties; but he is not entitled to obtain more than an outline of his opponent's case. He can compel his adversary to disclose the facts on which he intends to rely, but not the evidence by which he proposes to prove those facts.[8] He cannot claim to " see his opponent's brief," or ask him to

---

[7] *Heaton* v. *Goldney* [1910] 1 K.B. 754.
[8] *Lever Brothers* v. *Associated Newspapers* [1907] 2 K.B. 626, 629.

name the witnesses whom he means to call at the trial.[9]   The
party interrogating may ask anything to support his own case
or answer his opponent's case; he is entitled to know precisely
what is the charge made against him, and what is the case which
he will have to meet.   But he is not entitled to discover in what
way his opponent intends to prove his case.[10]

Illustrations

In an action for the recovery of land, the defendant is entitled to know the
facts showing the nature of the plaintiff's title, and he may, therefore,
administer to the plaintiff interrogatories as to the links through which he
traces his pedigree, etc.; but he is not allowed to inquire into the evidence
by which the plaintiff seeks to prove his title.

   Flitcroft v. *Fletcher* (1856) 11 Ex. 543; 25 L.J.Ex. 94.
   Stoate v. *Rew* (1863) 14 C.B.(N.S.) 209; 32 L.J.C.P. 160.

The plaintiff in such an action is entitled to interrogate the defendant
on all matters relevant to his own case; and he will not be deprived of that
right merely because such discovery may have the effect of disclosing the
defendant's case.   But he cannot compel the defendant to disclose any
matter which relates exclusively to his own title.

   Lyell v. *Kennedy* (1883) 8 App.Cas. 217; 52 L.J.Ch. 385.
   Pye v. *Butterfield* (1864) 5 B. & S. 829; 34 L.J.Q.B. 17.

In an action for seduction in which the defendant denied that he was
father of the child, the plaintiff sought to interrogate the defendant as to
whether he alleged carnal intercourse with the plaintiff's daughter by other
persons, and, if so, by whom.   The interrogatory was not allowed.

   Hooton v. *Dalby* [1907] 2 K.B. 18; 76 L.J.K.B. 652.

On an issue whether the plaintiff is or is not a moneylender, the defendant
is entitled to interrogate the plaintiff as to what other loans (if any) he had
transacted during a reasonable period before and after the loan in question, and
on what security and at what rate of interest, and generally as to the circumstances
and terms of such loans; but not to require the plaintiff to disclose the names
of the borrowers.

   Nash v. *Layton* [1911] 2 Ch. 71.
   Marshall v. *Goulston Discount (Northern), Ltd.* [1967] Ch. 72.

So, interrogatories as to the sources from which articles alleged to
infringe the plaintiff's patent had been obtained were allowed in

   Osram, etc. v. *Gabriel Lamp Co.* [1914] 2 Ch. 129; 83 L.J.Ch. 624.

A party cannot be asked to give the names of those who were present
when any material act was done.   This would be asking him to name his
witnesses.[10a]

   Eade v. *Jacobs* (1877) 3 Ex.D. 335; 47 L.J.Ex. 74.

But if the party interrogating is in other respects entitled to certain
information, he will not be debarred from it merely because supplying it
will necessarily disclose the names of persons whom the party interrogated
may hereafter wish to call as his witnesses, or otherwise give some clue to
his evidence.

---

[9] *Knapp* v. *Harvey* [1911] 2 K.B. 725.
[10] *Ridgway* v. *Smith & Son* (1890) 6 T.L.R. 275.
[10a] Divorce practice differs: *Bishop* v. *Bishop* [1901] P. 325.

Marriott v. *Chamberlain* (1886) 17 Q.B.D. 154; 55 L.J.Q.B. 448.
Birch v. *Mather* (1883) 22 Ch.D. 629; 52 L.J.Ch. 292.
Ashworth v. *Roberts* (1890) 45 Ch.D. 623; 60 L.J.Ch. 27.
Thus, a plaintiff is entitled to interrogate the defendant as to whether he did not speak the words complained of in the presence of persons named in the plaintiff's particulars or any and which of them.
Dalgleish v. *Lowther* [1899] 2 Q.B. 590; 68 L.J.Q.B. 956.
And see cases cited as to particulars, *ante*, pp. 163–164.

3. But even in interrogating as to your own case, the questions asked must not be "fishing," that is, they must refer to some definite and existing state of circumstances, and not be put merely in the hope of discovering something which may help the party interrogating to make out *some* case. They must be confined to matters which there is ground for believing have actually occurred. Thus, if in an action of defamation the plaintiff relies in his statement of claim on publications only to A, B and C, he cannot, as a rule, interrogate the defendant as to whether he did not also publish the words to X, Y or Z.[11] In *Rofe* v. *Kevorkian* [1936] 2 All E.R. 1334 at pp. 1337–1338 Greer L.J. described as "fishing" an interrogatory "by a man who is trying to make a case and has not already the evidence which would justify him in making the case."

Illustrations

Where the plaintiff was charged with having used certain blasphemous phrases, interrogatories were disallowed as "fishing," the object of which was to show that if plaintiff had not said what he was charged with saying, still he had on other occasions said something very much like it.
Pankhurst v. *Hamilton* (1886) 2 T.L.R. 682.
But the defendant in an action of slander may be asked whether he did not speak "the words set out in paragraph 3 of the statement of claim, or some and which of them, or some other and what words *to the same effect.*"
Dalgleish v. *Lowther* [1899] 2 Q.B. 590; 68 L.J.Q.B. 956.
Saunderson v. *Baron Von Radeck* (1905) 119 L.T.Jo. 33 (H.L.).

4. Interrogatories are not ordinarily allowed as to the contents of written documents, unless there is evidence that such documents have been lost or destroyed. But leave may be given in special circumstances, as where production of the original has been refused on the ground that someone not a party has joint possession of it.[13] But you may ask what has become of a particular document. Nor will interrogatories be allowed, the object of which is to contradict a written document.[14] A party may be

---

[11] See *Barham* v. *Lord Huntingfield* [1913] 2 K.B. 193; *Russell* v. *Stubbs,* *ibid.,* p. 200n. (H.L.).
[13] *Rattenberry* v. *Monro* (1910) 103 L.T. 560.
[14] *Moor* v. *Roberts* (1857) 2 C.B.(N.S.) 671.

asked whether he wrote a certain letter, but, if the letter or a copy of it is not in his possession he may demand to see it before he answers.[15]

If the party from whom discovery is sought has not made a list of documents, he may be interrogated as to any document which there is good reason for believing was once, at all events, in his possession; *e.g.*, he may be asked whether that particular document was ever in his possession or control; whether he did not receive it from a certain person on a given day; whether it is not now in his possession or control; if nay, when did he part with it, and to whom? Once the party sought to be interrogated has made a list of documents verified by affidavit there is great difficulty in going behind it, and it is very doubtful whether any such interrogatories can be administered after discovery of documents.[16] In such a case the safer course is to apply under Order 24, r. 7 (1). (*Ante*, pp. 237–238.)

5. Questions which tend to criminate may be asked if they are relevant, though the party interrogated is not bound to answer them.[17] Such questions are not scandalous, unless they are either irrelevant or " fishing," and will not, therefore, be disallowed; the party interrogated must take the objection on oath in his answer. That the interrogatories will tend to criminate others (except the spouse of the party interrogated) is no objection, if they be put bona fide for the purposes of the present action.[18] That to answer them would expose the party interrogated, or third persons, to civil actions was never an objection.[19]

6. Interrogatories may now be administered to the defendant in an action for the recovery of land even if the answers might subject him to a forfeiture.[20] Thus, a tenant may be interrogated as to whether he has not assigned or underlet the premises contrary to a covenant in his lease. And he may be interrogated as to whether his term or other interest has not expired or been duly determined by a notice to quit.[21] Again, leave will not be given to administer interrogatories in any action brought to recover

---

[15] See *Dalrymple* v. *Leslie* (1881) 8 Q.B.D. 5.
[16] See *Hall* v. *Truman* (1885) 29 Ch.D. 307; *Morris* v. *Edwards* (1890) 15 App.Cas. 309.
[17] *Alabaster* v. *Harness* (1894) 70 L.T. 375; and see *post*, pp. 288–289.
[18] *McCorquodale* v. *Bell* [1876] W.N. 39; Civil Evidence Act, 1968, s. 14 (1).
[19] *Tetley* v. *Easton* (1856) 18 C.B. 643.
[20] Civil Evidence Act, 1968, s. 16 (1) (a).
[21] *Wigram on Discovery*, 81.

penalties under a statute.[22]   And a person may refuse to answer on the ground of privilege any interrogatory if to do so would tend to expose him or his spouse to proceedings for the recovery of a penalty provided for by criminal law.[22a]

7. Moreover, the court has a wide discretion as to interrogatories; and only such interrogatories will be allowed as the master " considers necessary either for disposing fairly of the cause or matter or for saving costs." [23]   But there is no general rule of practice that interrogatories are not to be allowed in accident cases.[24]

Answers to Interrogatories

The interrogatories allowed by the master must be answered in full detail and on oath within the time prescribed by him, unless some valid objection can be raised to any of them.[25]   If a person objects to answering an interrogatory on the ground of privilege, he may take the objection in his affidavit in answer (Order 26, r. 4).[26]   Privilege for this purpose includes an objection that the answer may tend to criminate.[27]

The answers must be carefully drawn.   The party interrogated may answer guardedly, and make qualified admissions only, so long as both the admission and the qualification are clear and definite.   He may answer " Yes " or " No " simply, so long as it is clear how much is thus admitted or denied.   The following answer was held sufficient in *Dalrymple* v. *Leslie* (1881) 8 Q.B.D. 5: " I kept no copy and have no copy of the said letter, and I am unable to recollect with exactness what the statements contained therein were."   It is quite admissible to say " I do not know " where the matter is clearly not within the deponent's own knowledge.   He is not bound to procure information from others for the

---

[22]   *Martin* v. *Treacher* (1886) 16 Q.B.D. 507; *Saunders* v. *Weil* [1892] 2 Q.B. 321; *Derby Corporation* v. *Derbyshire C.C.* [1897] A.C. 550.

[22a] Civil Evidence Act, 1968, s. 14 (1).

[23] Ord. 26, r. 1 (3); and see *Cochrane* v. *Smith* (1895) 12 T.L.R. 78; *Ramsey* v. *Ramsey* [1956] 1 W.L.R. 542.

[24] *Griebart* v. *Morris* [1920] 1 K.B. 659.

[25] The affidavit must be filed and the party interrogating can obtain an " office copy," which will be admissible at the trial as evidence of the answers: see *post*, p. 299.

[26] The rules formerly permitted objection to be taken in the answer on the ground that the interrogatory was scandalous or irrelevant or on other grounds, notwithstanding that the interrogatory had previously been allowed by the master. This is no longer permissible.

[27] *Lamb* v. *Munster* (1882) 10 Q.B.D. 110; *Ex p. Reynolds* (1882) 20 Ch.D. 294, 299.

purpose of answering.[28]   If, however, he "is interrogated about acts which are done in the presence of persons employed by him, their knowledge is his knowledge, and he is bound to answer in respect of that." (*Per* North J. in *Rasbotham* v. *Shropshire Union Ry. and Canal Co.* (1883) 24 Ch.D., at p. 113.)   A party to a cause is not excused from answering relevant interrogatories if such matters are within the knowledge of his agents or servants, and such knowledge was acquired by them in the ordinary course of their employment.   A banker or solicitor may be such an agent.[29] In such a case the party interrogated is bound to obtain the information from his agents or servants, unless he can satisfy the master that it would be unreasonable to require him to do so. The officer of a company, answering interrogatories on its behalf, is only bound to answer as to his knowledge acquired in the course of his employment by the company; he is not bound to disclose information which has come to him accidentally or in some other capacity.[30]

Illustrations

Action by the owners of a cargo against the owners of a ship for a loss alleged to have arisen from negligence in the navigation which caused the ship to run ashore and be stranded.   Interrogatories as to what was done by those on board with regard to such navigation at the time of the accident.   The defendants answered that they were not on board at the time, and had no knowledge or information respecting the matters inquired into, except as appeared by the protest, of which the plaintiffs had had inspection.   This answer was held insufficient, as it did not appear that there was any difficulty in the defendants obtaining the required information from those who were in charge of the ship at the time of the accident.

   Bolckow, Vaughan & Co. v. *Fisher and others* (1882) 10 Q.B.D. 161; 52 L.J.Q.B. 12.

   Action by owners of water-mills against a canal company for wrongfully diminishing the quantity of water in the river to the injury of the plaintiffs. The defendants interrogated the plaintiffs, and asked them to give a list of the days between the specified dates on which they alleged that the working of their mills was interfered with by the negligence of the defendants.   The plaintiffs answered that they were unable to specify the particular days:— *Held*, that there was nothing to show that this answer was not genuine, and that the plaintiffs were not bound to state whether they had made inquiries of their agents, servants and workmen.

   Rasbotham v. *Shropshire Union Ry. and Canal Co.* (1883) 24 Ch.D. 110; 53 L.J.Ch. 327.

   Action for the value of certain missing casks, of which full particulars were given.   Interrogatories by the plaintiffs asking whether the defendant

---

[28] *Per* Brett J. in *Phillips* v. *Routh* (1872) L.R. 7 C.P. 287; and see *Rofe* v. *Kevorkian* [1936] 2 All E.R. 1334.
[29] *Alliott* v. *Smith* [1895] 2 Ch. 111.
[30] *Welsbach, etc. Co.* v. *New Sunlight Co.* [1900] 2 Ch. 1.

company had not received the casks, whether they had lost them, or what had become of them. The information asked for was admittedly contained in the books of the defendant company, or of their agents, Messrs. Pickford & Co. and Chaplin and Horne. The defendant company refused the information, on the ground that it would be a great trouble to search through all these books for many years back, and that such an inquiry would be attended with great expense:—*Held*, by Lord Coleridge C.J. and Denman J. (Grove J. *dissentiente*) that the defendant company must answer the interrogatories.

  Hall v. *L.N.W. Ry.* (1877) 35 L.T. 848.

  But it is not reasonable to require a party to make admissions as to matters which are not within his own knowledge, and as to which he can only obtain information by writing to his rivals in the trade, or by asking his own servants for information which they have acquired accidentally and not in the course of their employment by him.

  Ehrmann v. *Ehrmann* [1896] 2 Ch. 611; 65 L.J.Ch. 745.

  Welsbach, etc., Co. v. *New Sunlight Co.* [1900] 2 Ch. 1.

An objection to answering any one or more of several interrogatories should be taken in the affidavit in answer. It is usually in the following or some similar form:

1. " I object to answer on the ground that the question constitutes an inquiry as to communications passing between me and my solicitor confidentially and in his professional capacity." (See *Conlon* v. *Conlons, Ltd.* [1952] 2 All E.R. 462, where it was held that the privilege did not extend to communications which the client had instructed the solicitor to repeat to the other party.) On this ground a client may, for example, refuse to disclose information which he only obtained from his solicitor since action, and which was the result of inquiries instituted by the solicitor for the purposes of the litigation.[31] If the person interrogated be a solicitor, it is a sufficient answer to state, " I have no real personal knowledge of the matter referred to in this interrogatory, and the only information and belief that I have received or have respecting any of such matters has been derived from and is founded on information of a confidential character procured by me as solicitor of the said C, and not otherwise, for the purpose of litigation between the plaintiff and the said C, either pending or threatened by the plaintiff. I claim to be privileged from answering this interrogatory further." (*Procter* v. *Smiles* (1886) 55 L.J.Q.B. 467, 527.)

2. " In answer to the fifth interrogatory, I say that to answer the said interrogatory would tend to criminate me, and I therefore

---

[31] *Procter* v. *Raikes* (1886) 3 T.L.R. 229.

submit that I am not bound to make any further or other answer to the same." This objection must be stated in clear and unequivocal language. In *Lamb* v. *Munster* (1882) 10 Q.B.D. 110, it was held sufficient for the defendant to state on oath, " I decline to answer all the interrogatories upon the ground that my answer to them might tend to criminate me." [32]

Further Answers

If any of the answers are insufficient the court may make an order requiring the party interrogated to make a further answer either by affidavit or on oral examination. (Order 26, r. 5). But an order for such examination is seldom made. The application is made by a notice under the summons for directions or by a notice for further directions, as the case may be. (See *ante*, p. 261.) The notice should specify the interrogatories or parts of interrogatories to which a better answer is required [33]; it should be given within a reasonable time after the answers are delivered.[34]

Default in Answering Interrogatories

Any party failing to answer interrogatories is liable to the same penalties by way of committal and having his action dismissed or defence struck out, as in the case of failure to give discovery of documents (*ante*, pp. 249–250); and the power of the court so to order is exercised upon the like principles (see Order 26, r. 6).

---

[32] And see *Jones* v. *Richards* (1885) 15 Q.B.D. 439.
[33] *Anstey* v. *N. & S. Woolwich Subway Co.* (1879) 11 Ch.D. 439.
[34] *Lloyd* v. *Morley* (1879) 5 L.R.Ir. 74.

Chapter 20

ADVICE ON EVIDENCE

WHEN discovery is completed, and preferably before the summons for directions is issued, the papers should be laid before counsel for his advice on evidence. This should be done by both sides, even in cases apparently simple; otherwise the action may be lost for want of some certificate or other formal piece of proof, as in *Collins* v. *Carnegie* (1834) 1 A. & E. 695. Every document in the case should be sent to counsel; especially, if there has been discovery, the lists of documents, the answers to interrogatories, and the draft notices (if any) to admit and to produce documents. Also the statements of all witnesses who have been interviewed during the preparation of the case.

If counsel has been instructed before the summons for directions or any adjourned hearing thereof, he should first consider whether any interlocutory application of whatever nature ought to be made at the hearing and advise accordingly; he should also cast his mind forward to the trial on the lines set out later in this chapter, so that the master may be asked to make all such orders as to the mode of proof of his case as may be calculated to save expense at the trial. Even if the hearing of the summons for directions has already been concluded, further directions may always be asked for by notice thereunder (*ante*, p. 261).

Before writing his advice on evidence counsel should, therefore, consider whether everything is in proper order for the trial. Answers to interrogatories or documents disclosed by the other party may throw a new light on the matters in dispute. Is any amendment of the pleadings or particulars necessary to enable his client's case to be properly presented at the trial? If so, he must promptly apply for leave to add such new matter. Are his opponent's answers to interrogatories sufficient? Should not more documents be disclosed or produced? Is it desirable for some surveyor or other agent to inspect the *locus in quo*, or take samples of the goods in dispute? If so, an order can be applied for under Order 29, r. 3. (See *ante*, p. 267.) Should an application be made under the Banker's Books Evidence Act, 1879? (See *post*, p. 300.) Should any notice, or further notice, be given under Order 38, r. 21? (See *post*, pp. 301–302.) Then, when counsel is satisfied that all preliminaries are in order, and that all material questions are properly raised on the pleadings, he can proceed to write his opinion.

Advising on evidence is, perhaps, the most important piece of work which a junior barrister has to do; success at the trial so much depends on the care with which the case is got up beforehand; and the solicitor, who may have had but little experience in litigious work, will look to counsel for advice on every necessary detail. The best and clearest method of advising on evidence is first to set out briefly what are the issues in the action, and on whom the burden of proving each issue lies, and then to state seriatim how each is to be proved or rebutted. See Precedents, Nos. 101–103.

Burden of Proof

What the issues are appears, or ought to appear, clearly from the pleadings. From the pleadings also it can at once be ascertained on which party lies the initial burden of proof on each issue. The " burden of proof " is the duty which lies on a party to establish his case. It will lie on A, whenever A must either call some evidence or have judgment given against him. As a rule (but not invariably) it lies upon the party who has in his pleading maintained the *affirmative* of the issue; for a *negative* is in general incapable of proof. *Ei incumbit probatio qui dicit, non qui negat.* The affirmative is generally, but not necessarily, maintained by the party who first raises the issue. Thus, the onus lies, as a rule, on the plaintiff to establish every fact which he has asserted in the statement of claim, and on the defendant to prove all facts which he has pleaded by way of confession and avoidance, such as fraud, performance, release, rescission, etc. It is important to distinguish between the legal burden which rests on a party by law to satisfy the court upon the whole of the evidence that he has proved his case and a provisional burden which is raised by the state of the evidence.[1] As the case proceeds,

---

[1] See *Huyton-with-Roby U.D.C.* v. *Hunter* [1955] 1 W.L.R. 603, 609; *Brown* v. *Rolls Royce, Ltd.* [1960] 1 W.L.R. 210.

the latter burden frequently shifts from the person on whom it rested at first to his opponent. This occurs whenever a prima facie case has been established on any issue of fact or whenever a rebuttable presumption of law has arisen.

Illustrations

In an action on a bill of exchange, the holder is prima facie deemed to be a holder in due course (see sections 29 and 30 of the Bills of Exchange Act, 1882); the onus, therefore, lies on the defendant to prove that the acceptance of the bill was obtained by fraud. But as soon as this is established, then it is for the plaintiff to prove that he took the bill in good faith, and for value, and without notice of the fraud.

Tatam v. *Haslar* (1889) 23 Q.B.D. 345; 58 L.J.Q.B. 432.

Talbot v. *Von Boris* [1911] 1 K.B. 854.

In some cases the onus lies on one party, although the issue was first raised by his opponent. Thus, if a defendant pleads the Limitation Act, the onus lies on the plaintiff to prove that his cause of action arose within the prescribed period; it does not lie on the defendant to prove the negative.

Wilby v. *Henman* (1834) 2 Cr. & M. 658; 4 Tyr. 957.

As a general rule, he who makes an assertion must prove it true; otherwise the jury will deem it untrue. If no affirmative evidence be given, the opposite proposition, the negative of the issue, will be taken as established.

Catherwood v. *Chabaud* (1823) 1 B. & C. 150; 2 D. & R. 271.

The precise form into which the pleading is cast does not matter; the judge will look at the substance of the allegation. Thus, in a plea of privilege, it is immaterial whether the defendant pleads that he published the words bona fide, or that he published them " without malice "; in either case the plaintiff must prove malice, if the occasion be held one of qualified privilege.

There are, however, exceptions to this rule that the burden of proof lies on the party who affirms. Thus, in an action for malicious prosecution, it is for the plaintiff to establish that there was no reasonable and probable cause for the prosecution.

Abrath v. *N.E. Ry.* (1886) 11 App.Cas. 247; 55 L.J.Q.B. 457.

Brown v. *Hawkes* [1891] 2 Q.B. 718; 61 L.J.Q.B. 151.

And where, for example, the defendant admits a conviction alleged in the statement of claim, but denies that he committed the offence or alleges that for some other reason it was erroneous, the plaintiff should still, it seems, put in the statements of the witnesses to prove the facts supporting the conviction as part of his case notwithstanding section 11 (2) of the Civil Evidence Act, 1968.

If the defendant in an action of libel has pleaded a plea under section 2 of Lord Campbell's Libel Act, the onus lies on him to prove that the libel was inserted without gross negligence.

Peters v. *Edwards* (1887) 3 T.L.R. 423.

So where the defendant has sold a book or newspaper which, unknown to him, contains a libel, the onus lies on him to prove that it was not through any negligence on his part that he was unaware of the existence of the libel.

Emmens v. *Pottle* (1885) 16 Q.B.D. 354; 55 L.J.Q.B. 51.

Vizetelly v. *Mudie's Select Library, Ltd.* [1900] 2 Q.B. 170.

So on an issue whether A be still alive or not, the party asserting the negative, *viz.*, that A is not living, must prove his death; the presumption is in favour of the continuance of life, until the contrary be shown, or until seven years have elapsed since he was last heard of.

  Chard v. *Chard* [1956] P. 259.

  Thompson v. *Thompson* [1956] P. 414.

  As to survivorship in cases of air-raids, etc., see *Hickman* v. *Peacey* [1945] A.C. 304.

  Upon an issue whether A and B were married it was held sufficient for the plaintiff to prove for the purpose of establishing his entitlement to property under a will that they had lived together as man and wife; for, unless it were clearly proved to the contrary, the law presumed that they were validly married.

  Re Taylor (decd.) [1961] 1 W.L.R. 9.

Having determined what facts your client has to prove at the trial, you may proceed to state how they are to be proved, what witnesses must be called, and what documents must be put in on each issue. Each party must be prepared with evidence not only to prove the issues which lie upon him, but also to rebut his adversary's case. But remember:—

1. There are some matters which need not be proved at all, *e.g.*, the law of England, public statutes, private statutes passed since 1850, official seals and certain facts so well known that the court takes judicial notice of them without proof.[3] But foreign law (including the law of Scotland, Ireland or the Channel Islands), or the custom of any particular county, or of a city such as London or Bristol, the practice of an inferior or foreign court, resolutions of the House of Commons,[4] or the existence of a war between foreign countries, or the internal constitution or economy of a foreign state,[5] must be proved as facts. All these may be proper subjects for a special order under the summons for directions as to mode of proof.

2. Again neither party need prove that which the law already presumes in his favour, *e.g.*, the plaintiff in an action of libel need not prove that the words are false; the holder of a bill of exchange need not prove that he gave value for it.

3. But even where there is no presumption of law in your favour, it is often only necessary for you to give prima facie evidence. You need not prove any fact up to the hilt. The circumstances, though unexplained, may in themselves be sufficient to establish a prima facie case; or some letter may contain

---

[3] See, for instance, *George* v. *Davies* [1911] 2 K.B. 445, and Civil Evidence Act, 1968, s. 9.

[4] *Stockdale* v. *Hansard* (1837) 7 C. & P. 731, 736.

[5] *Rendal* v. *Arcos, Ltd.* [1936] 1 All E.R. 623.

an admission which will shift the onus of proof on to your opponent.

Illustrations

Strict proof of the plaintiff's special character is not, as a rule, required. In order to prove that a man holds a public office, it is not, as a rule, necessary to produce his written or sealed appointment; it is sufficient to show that he acted in that office, and then it will be presumed that he acted legally.

> *Berryman* v. *Wise* (1791) 4 T.R. 366.
> *Cannell* v. *Curtis* (1835) 2 Bing.N.C. 228; 2 Scott 379.

If a letter be properly addressed to A, and posted, with the postage prepaid, and has not been returned through the Dead Letter Office, it will be presumed that A received it. But this presumption is rebuttable.

> *Walthamstow* v. *Henwood* [1897] 1 Ch. 41.

Witnesses

Counsel must decide what witnesses his client should subpoena to attend the court to give evidence. It is as well to name them in the advice on evidence. If it be necessary to bring up a prisoner to give evidence, an order may be obtained from the Home Office under the Criminal Justice Act, 1961, s. 29; alternatively an application may be made *ex parte* to the judge at chambers for an order under the Criminal Procedure Act, 1853, s. 9. For the latter purpose an affidavit must be sworn, stating where the prisoner is confined, and for what crime, and when and where his attendance will be required. In the case of a person confined upon civil process, the latter statute does not apply, but a writ of *habeas corpus ad testificandum* may be obtained upon application on affidavit to a judge at chambers. A patient may be brought up from a mental hospital under such a writ, if he is fit for examination.[6] A witness residing in Scotland or Northern Ireland can be compelled to attend by a *subpoena ad testificandum* issued under the Judicature Act, 1925, s. 49, by the special leave of a master.

It is sometimes erroneously assumed that a witness who has given a statement to or has been subpoenaed by one party may not be approached by the solicitor on the other side with a view to giving a statement. There is no property in a witness and so long as there is no question of tampering with him or seeking to persuade him to change his story it is permissible to interview him and to take a statement from him. Great discretion should be exercised in order to avoid even the suspicion of irregularity

---

[6] *Fennell* v. *Tait* (1834) 1 Cr.M. & R. 584.

in the approach. Any attempt to intimidate or influence a witness would amount to contempt of court.[7] It is contrary to professional etiquette to interview the *client* of another solicitor, particularly in pending proceedings, without that solicitor's consent.

It may be necessary to apply to postpone the trial, *e.g.*, to secure the attendance of witnesses who are ill or absent abroad. Or it may be necessary to apply for the examination before trial of a witness who is abroad or about to leave the country or who is dangerously ill. (Order 39, r. 1.) The old procedure of obtaining evidence out of the jurisdiction by writ of commission is obsolete. The appropriate procedure is different for different countries and will be found in the notes to Order 39 in *The Supreme Court Practice*. In some cases the evidence may be ordered to be taken before a special examiner or before a British consul. But several foreign governments object to commissions being issued and to examiners administering oaths to witnesses within their dominions. Consequently the Foreign and Commonwealth Office, at the request of the Senior Master, often sends through diplomatic channels a " letter of request " addressed to the tribunal of such other country asking the judges of that tribunal to order the required evidence to be taken and remitted to the English court. The English High Court returns the compliment, and will on request take evidence for a foreign tribunal under Order 70.

A defendant will obtain an order for the examination of witnesses more readily than a plaintiff who has chosen his own *forum*.[8] The affidavit filed in support of such an application must state the name of at least one witness whom it is desired to examine,[9] and the general nature of the evidence which he is expected to give.[10] If such evidence is not directly material to some issue in the cause, but only incidentally useful in corroboration of other evidence, the application will almost certainly not be granted.[11] The plaintiff himself will not be allowed to give his evidence before an examiner save on very exceptional grounds [12]; it should be given before the court. But a defendant, if resident

---

[7] See *Welby* v. *Still* (1872) 8 T.L.R. 202.
[8] *Ross* v. *Woodford* [1894] 1 Ch. 38.
[9] *Howard* v. *Dulau & Co.* (1895) 11 T.L.R. 451.
[10] *Barry* v. *Barclay* (1864) 15 C.B.(N.S.) 849.
[11] See *Ehrmann* v. *Ehrmann* [1896] 2 Ch. 611.
[12] See *Donn* v. *Feinstein* [1956] 1 W.L.R. 478.

abroad, will be allowed this indulgence.[13] The application is not usually made till the pleadings are closed; but it may be made earlier, if there be special reasons for such urgency. The application will fail if it can be shown that the witnesses could be brought to England without much greater expense, or that witnesses now in England could give the same evidence. Sometimes the mere delay, which will thus necessarily be caused, is a sufficient reason for refusing the application. The costs of the examination must be borne by the party who applied for it, unless the judge at the trial makes some other order in respect of them. It is in every way a misfortune not to have the evidence of an important witness given orally in court. The deposition, when read aloud at the trial, produces but a faint effect; if there is a jury, they like to see the man and hear him examined and cross-examined. Moreover, your opponent learns beforehand exactly what your case is, and has plenty of time to prepare his answer to it.

Documentary Evidence

Counsel must next consider what documents will be required to prove his client's case, whether leave should be asked to prove particular facts by documentary rather than by oral evidence, and also what documents will be needed for the cross-examination of the witnesses called by the other side. On this several questions arise: Are such documents still in existence? In whose handwriting are they? Are they within the jurisdiction? If the originals cannot be produced, is any secondary evidence of their contents procurable? If so, is it admissible?

Much needless expense would be incurred at the trial if it were necessary formally to prove all the documents intended to be read. Hence the opposing party may be called upon beforehand to admit their authenticity. Furthermore a copy cannot strictly be put in evidence unless a notice (or the equivalent) has been given to the other side to produce the original at the trial and the original is not produced. Thus an important step in preparing for trial was always to give proper notices to admit and to produce documents under Order 27, r. 5. However, Order 27, rule 4 (see *ante*, p. 249) has in some cases made such notices unnecessary and in nearly all cases has reduced their scope, since a party who serves a list of documents under Order 24 is put in much the same position as if he

---

[13] *New* v. *Burns* (1894) 64 L.J.Q.B. 104.

had served his opponent with a notice to admit and had himself been served with a notice to produce the documents in his list. Nevertheless there will still be many cases where such notices must be served.

Unless your opponent within a limited time—usually twenty-one days after inspection—serves you with a notice stating that he does not admit the authenticity of any particular documents in your list and requires them to be proved at the trial, he is deemed to admit them all (in the sense indicated below). This is subject to any special order of the master or to any extension of time which he may grant. The admission deemed to be made is that any document described in the list as an original is an original and was printed, written, signed or executed as it purports to have been, and that any document described as a copy is a true copy; but it does not prejudice his right to object to the admissibility of the document in evidence at the trial (Order 27, r. 4 (1) and (2)). Since a party can hardly be expected to admit the authenticity of documents which he has not seen, it may often be prudent to serve a notice of non-admission of the documents for which privilege has been claimed.

If you have not had to serve a list of documents upon any particular party and yet wish to put some documents in evidence at the trial, or if you wish to put in any documents not included in your list (*e.g.* because they are in someone else's possession), you can within twenty-one days after the action is set down for trial serve a notice to admit their authenticity, and if a notice of non-admission is not served within twenty-one days thereafter, they are deemed to be admitted (r. 5 (1)–(3)).

If you refuse to admit a document you should ask the master or the trial judge to certify that your refusal was reasonable, otherwise you will have to pay your opponent's costs of proving it, whatever the result of the trial. (Order 62, r. 3 (6).)

Again, if you have served a list of documents on any party, you are ipso facto deemed to have been served by him with a notice to produce them at the trial and vice versa. (Order 27, r. 4 (3).) In cases not covered by that sub-rule a written notice to produce particular documents may be served (r. 5 (4)). The effect of giving a notice to produce, whether express or implied, is to enable a party to give secondary evidence of the contents of any document referred to in the notice if it is not produced at the trial.

It does not of itself oblige your opponent to produce the document, even though he has it; when it is called for in court, his counsel may say that he does not produce it, in which case it is open to you to put in a copy or give oral evidence of its contents if you can.

When advising on evidence you should therefore carefully consider in the light of the above rules whether it is necessary to serve any notice or counter-notice, or to ask for any extension of time or other order of a master.

If the correspondence is voluminous it will be necessary to have an agreed bundle for the use of the judge, the paging of which should be identical with that of the bundles for counsel on both sides. In default of a special agreement, only such letters in the bundle as are actually read at the trial will be taken to be in evidence, and agreeing a bundle does not constitute an admission that all the letters contained in it are admissible in evidence.

Subject to certain statutory exceptions (*post*, pp. 300–301), the rule is that the originals of documents must be available to be produced in court, if they still exist and can be found within the jurisdiction. If they are in the possession of the other side, notice to produce them should, if necessary, be given a reasonable time before the trial; if in the possession of a third person within the jurisdiction, he should be served with a *subpoena duces tecum* [14]; if in the possession of a third person out of jurisdiction, all that you can do is to impress upon him the importance of his attending the trial or sending the document and offer him such inducements as may be necessary. If the original document be produced, it may be necessary to call witnesses to handwriting: as to this, see *post*, p. 320. If it be not produced, there may be considerable difficulty in proving a copy; see *post*, pp. 322–323.

In addition to the provisions of the common law as to the admissibility in certain cases of secondary evidence, several statutes have been passed which make copies of registers and other public and official documents admissible in evidence, if duly authenticated, although the originals are still in existence, so as to save the necessity for conveying ancient records up and down the country. Such copies are of three kinds:—

---

[14] The court can always set aside a subpoena, if it has not been obtained bona fide for the purpose of the trial: *R*. v. *Baines* [1909] 1 K.B. 258.

(i) An examined copy; *i.e.*, a copy which someone, who is called as a witness, swears he has compared with the original, and found to be correct and complete.

(ii) A certified copy, *i.e.*, a copy which some public officer, officially in charge of the original, certifies to be a true copy; he need not be called as a witness, if he has properly sealed or stamped or otherwise authenticated the copy.

(iii) An office copy, *i.e.*, a copy made in the office of the High Court of Justice by an officer having custody of the original; this, in the same court, is accepted as equivalent to the original.

Counsel must be careful to advise the solicitor to obtain the proper kind of copy which is made admissible by the particular Act.

Illustrations

" Office copies of writs, records, pleadings and documents filed in the High Court shall be admissible in evidence in any cause or matter and between all parties to the same extent as the original would be admissible."

Order 38, r. 10 (1).

As to foreign judgments, public registers, etc., see Evidence (Foreign, Dominion and Colonial Documents) Act, 1933, at present of limited application.

An affidavit verifying a list of documents or an answer to interrogatories made in the cause can be proved either by an office copy, or by producing the copy of the affidavit received from the deponent's solicitor, whose act in forwarding it to his opponent amounts to an admission that it is a correct copy.

See *Slatterie* v. *Pooley* (1840) 6 M. & W. 664.

Order 41, r. 10.

A certified copy of an entry in the " Register of Newspaper Proprietors " kept at Somerset House is " sufficient prima facie evidence of all matters and things thereby appearing, unless and until the contrary thereof be shown."

Newspaper Libel and Registration Act, 1881, s. 15.

The by-law of a local authority is proved by the production of a printed copy certified by the clerk to the authority.

Local Government Act, 1933, s. 252.

The " Law List " is admissi le as prima facie evidence that every one whose name appears therein as a solicitor is qualified to practise.

Solicitors Act, 1957, s. 17.

Similarly, the " Medical Register " is prima facie evidence that the persons specified therein are duly registered medical practitioners.

Medical Act, 1956, s. 46.

Otherwise than under the provisions of the Civil Evidence Act, 1968, s. 11, a conviction can be proved: (1) by a certified copy of the record (Evidence Act, 1851, s. 13); (2) a conviction on indictment by a certificate in shorter form signed by the clerk of the court or his deputy (Prevention of Crimes Act, 1871, s. 18); (3) a summary conviction by a copy of the conviction signed by a Justice of the Peace or the clerk (*ibid.*, s. 18), or by a certified extract from the register (Magistrates' Courts Rules, 1952, r. 56); (4) a conviction of a witness by a certificate as in (2), *supra* (Criminal Procedure Act, 1865, s. 6). Evidence of identity is also necessary.

Four instances in which the strict rules of evidence have been relaxed deserve special attention.

(i) By the Bankers' Books Evidence Act, 1879, as extended by the Revenue, Friendly Societies and National Debt Act, 1882, s. 11, a copy of an entry in the book of any banker or any company carrying on the business of bankers is in all legal proceedings made prima facie evidence of such entry, and of the matters, transactions and accounts therein recorded, provided that (1) the book was at the time of the making of the entry one of the ordinary books of the bank, and (2) the entry was made in the usual and ordinary course of business,[15] and (3) the book is in the custody or control of the bank. The copy must be verified by the affidavit of a partner or officer of the bank, who must state that the copy has been examined with the original entry, and is correct. On the application of any party to an action, an order may be made that he shall be at liberty to inspect and take copies of entries in the books of any bank for the purposes of the litigation (Bankers' Books Evidence Act, 1879, s. 7), provided the case be one in which the applicant could, before the Act, have compelled the banker to attend at the hearing and produce his books.[16] Such an order will be made, although the bank be in Scotland or Northern Ireland.[17] It can be made although the account to which the entries relate is kept in the name of a stranger, provided the entries would be evidence in the action [18]; but in this case the jurisdiction will be exercised with the greatest caution.[19] No banker or officer of a bank can in any proceedings to which the bank is not a party be compelled to produce books, or to give evidence of the contents

---

[15] It is sufficient if the book be kept for reference, though it may not be in daily use: *Asylum for Idiots* v. *Handysides* (1906) 22 T.L.R. 573.

[16] *Arnott* v. *Hayes* (1887) 36 Ch.D. 731.

[17] See *Kissam* v. *Link* [1896] 1 Q.B. 574.

[18] *South Stafford Tramway Co.* v. *Ebbsmith* [1895] 2 Q.B. 669.

[19] *Pollock* v. *Garle* [1898] 1 Ch. 1.

of books, which may be proved by copies under the Act, unless by the order of a judge for special cause (s. 6).

(ii) Where production of any business books for inspection is applied for, the master may, instead of ordering production of the original books, order a copy of any entries therein to be supplied and verified by the affidavit of some person who has examined the copy with the original books; such affidavit must state whether or not there are in the original book any and what erasures, interlineations or alterations. (Order 24, r. 14.) And such copies will be evidence against the party supplying them.[20] But the master may always order the book from which the copy was made to be produced for inspection. If there are numerous alterations, photographic copies are likely to be most convenient.

(iii) By Order 38, rr. 2 and 3, the master on the hearing of the summons for directions or otherwise, or the judge at the trial, may order evidence to be given by affidavit, or facts to be proved in some special manner, *e.g.*, by production of documents or copies thereof. (See *ante*, pp. 268–269.)

(iv) By the Civil Evidence Act, 1968,[21] certain out-of-court statements tending to establish relevant facts are admissible in evidence in civil proceedings either by agreement of the parties or subject to certain conditions. The Act defines a statement to include any representation of fact whether made in words or otherwise, and deals specifically with statements made out-of-court by any person (s. 2), previous statements made by a person called as a witness (s. 3), statements contained in a document being, or forming part of, a record (s. 4), and statements contained in a document produced by a computer (s. 5). Documents are defined to include not only a document in writing but (*inter alia*) any map, plan, photograph, disc or tape (s. 10). Thus counsel must consider a variety of matters when advising on evidence having the provisions of the Act and the rules made thereunder in mind. Note that under s. 6 the court can allow in many cases the production of a copy whether or not the original document is still in existence.

Order 38, rr. 21 to 31 inclusive provide the procedures to be adopted where it is intended to adduce " hearsay evidence " under the Act by any one of the several methods authorised. The rules themselves are of some complexity whereas the actual procedure to

---

[20] *Slatterie* v. *Pooley* (1840) 6 M. & W. 664, 669; *Stowe* v. *Querner* (1870) L.R. 5 Ex. 155, 159.
[21] See principally ss. 2 to 5 inclusive.

be followed in any given situation appears to be relatively simple. The party wishing to take advantage of the procedure by adducing hearsay or secondary evidence at the trial must accept the disadvantage of disclosing that evidence to the other side in advance. He must give notice of his intention (r. 21) and state his reasons (if any) (r. 25), and he must give all the necessary particulars of the evidence he is seeking to adduce (see rr. 22, 23 and 24). Unless objection is taken he will be allowed to adduce that evidence at the trial provided it is relevant and otherwise admissible. If objection is taken he should in due course receive a counter-notice (r. 26) giving the reason (if any) why the witness should attend to give oral evidence. Any dispute whether a witness is available to testify or can be expected to recollect the facts must be determined, if possible, before the trial by a master (see p. 271 *ante*, and r. 27 *post*, p. 456) whose decision is subject to review on fresh evidence but will normally be final (r. 27 (3)). If it is found to have been unreasonable to require the attendance of a witness named in the counter-notice the party seeking to secure his attendance may be penalised in costs (r. 32; and see Order 62, r. 7 (1)). Where it is desired to give in evidence a statement made in previous legal proceedings (r. 28) notice under r. 21 must still be given, but, instead of serving a counter-notice your opponent must, if he objects to its admissibility, apply to the court for directions (r. 26 (3)).

Under rule 29 the court has an overriding discretion to allow a statement to be given in evidence at the trial by a party applying to do so notwithstanding his non-compliance with the rules. On the other hand if that party has complied with the rules and no counter-notice has been served (or he can show that his witness cannot attend) he must ordinarily be allowed to put the statement in evidence (see section 8 (3) (*a*) of the Act).

Remember that sometimes your opponent may have in his possession material with which to attack the credibility of your witness, or another and inconsistent statement made by him, in which case (subject to the conditions mentioned in rr. 30 and 31 respectively) he may be allowed to adduce this evidence. You will normally, but not necessarily, be forewarned that such attack is to be made, though your opponent ought at least to have served a counter-notice requiring the attendance of the witness; but even if he has not done so he may get leave from the judge at the trial to adduce the evidence he desires.

Subject to the above qualifications,[22] an order providing for the proof of particular facts by means of a document without producing the original or calling the maker of the statement may be made by the master or the trial judge. The weight which the court will attach to any such statement [22a] depends upon the circumstances in which and the time at which it was made, and a statement by an interested person [23] *post litem motam* will almost certainly be excluded.

Evidence in Aggravation or Mitigation of Damages

The plaintiff may also bring evidence in aggravation, the defendant in mitigation, of damages. (See *ante*, pp. 100–101.) In all actions for libel or slander in which the defendant does not by his defence assert the truth of the statement complained of his counsel must consider the advisability of giving a notice under Order 82, r. 7. For by that rule " the defendant shall not be entitled on the trial to give evidence in chief, with a view to mitigation of damages, as to the circumstances under which the libel or slander was published, or as to the character of the plaintiff, without the leave of the judge, unless seven days at least before the trial he furnishes particulars to the plaintiff of the matters as to which he intends to give evidence." This rule in no way affects the right of cross-examination; and it in no way alters the substantive rules of evidence, but only the procedure relative thereto. It makes nothing admissible in evidence which was not admissible before. Thus, evidence that the plaintiff is of general bad character is admissible in reduction of damages, but not evidence of particular facts and circumstances tending to show misconduct on his part, still less evidence of rumours prejudicial to his character.[24] The pleading, however, may be the proper place for allegations which go to reduce the damages although they are not strictly " material facts." (See *ante*, pp. 100–101.) And it is only fair to the plaintiff that he should have some notice before the trial that this peculiarly offensive line will be taken by the defendant. Hence the rules require particulars of such evidence as is otherwise

---

[22] Whether and to what extent the powers of the court have been enlarged by Order 38, r. 3, may be a matter for judicial decision.

[22a] And any statement admitted under the Act (s. 6).

[23] See, for example, *Kelleher* v. *T. Wall & Sons, Ltd.* [1958] 2 Q.B. 346; *Constantinou* v. *Frederick Hotels Ltd.* [1966] 1 W.L.R. 75.

[24] *Plato Films, Ltd. & Others* v. *Speidel* [1961] A.C. 1090.

admissible in mitigation of damages, if not stated (as it should be) in the defence, to be stated in the particulars so served. (See Precedent No. 75.)

Varying Mode or Place of Trial

The master will have dealt with these matters when giving directions; but his decision then is not final; it may be varied without appeal by a subsequent order made at or before the trial. (Order 33, r. 4.) Circumstances may have changed since then; matters may have arisen which alter the complexion of the case. Counsel should therefore now consider whether it would be better for his client to apply [25] that the action should be tried at a different assize, or by an official referee, or by a judge alone, or by judge and jury (see *ante*, pp. 272–275). An application under section 6 of the Administration of Justice (Miscellaneous Provisions) Act, 1933, for a jury as of right cannot, however, be made after the mode and place of trial have been fixed (r. 5). If the trial is to be by judge and jury, counsel should consider whether it is necessary for the jury to have a preliminary " view " of the *locus in quo*. The master will alter the place of trial if he is satisfied that there is no probability of a fair trial in the place originally fixed, *e.g.*, if a local newspaper of extensive circulation has recently published unfair attacks on either party with reference to the subject-matter of the action.[26] Such extraneous facts must be proved by affidavit.

Legal Aid Cases

Where either party is an assisted person the question of his liability for costs has to be specially considered by the judge at the trial. In this connection the means of a non-assisted party, whose opponent is assisted, are also relevant; since, if he wins, the hardship caused to him by relieving his assisted opponent from liability to pay his costs has to be considered. He will therefore be well advised in a proper case to file an affidavit setting

---

[25] If doubt arises whether a belated application of this kind should be made to the judge in charge of the list or to a master (as to which see *post*, p. 307), the Clerk of the Lists (Room 419, R.C.J.) or the Practice Master should be consulted.

[26] *Thorogood* v. *Newman* (1906) 23 T.L.R. 97.

out his financial position under the Legal Aid (General) Regulations, 1962, reg. 16 (7). Counsel should also consider whether the leave of the Area Committee is necessary under Regulation 15 for any particular step which he may advise, such as obtaining experts' reports or evidence.

CHAPTER 21

TRIAL

BEFORE dealing with the proceedings at the trial let us see how the action comes into a list for trial so that the parties know when to attend.

Setting Down, Fixtures and Postponements

As we have seen (*ante*, p. 275) the master will have given directions for the action to be set down for trial. If the plaintiff fails to do so, the defendant may set it down himself or may apply to the master to dismiss it for want of prosecution. (Order 34, r. 2.) It sometimes happens that because of negotiations for settlement or for other reasons the action is not set down in time. The head clerk of the Crown Office is at present authorised by the masters to allow a London action to be set down out of time on production of up-to-date consents, provided that the delay is not more than a year; otherwise the leave of the practice master must be obtained. Failing that, a summons to extend the time is necessary. The plaintiff must take or send to the " proper officer " [1] a request to set the action down at the place directed, together with two bundles of the pleadings and other necessary documents (see *ante*, p. 82); and within 24 hours after doing so he must notify the other parties (r. 8). This requirement supersedes the old " notice of trial."

In assize cases the district registrar [2] keeps a list in the

---

[1] In Q.B. actions for trial in London, the head clerk of the Crown Office and Associates' Department; in actions for trial at Birmingham, Leeds, Liverpool and Manchester, the appropriate district registrar; in actions for trial at Aylesbury, Chelmsford, Hertford or Kingston-upon-Thames (referred to as " home counties towns ") where there are no district registrars, the associate of the circuit (see note 2, *infra*); in actions for trial elsewhere, the district registrar; in Chancery actions for trial in London, the cause clerk of the Chancery registrars' office; in actions in the Family Division for trial in London, the chief clerk of the contentious department of the principal registry of that division. (Order 34, r. 3).

[2] Or at the " home counties towns " (*supra*, note 1) the associate. The associates are officers of the Supreme Court, who, in the Queen's Bench Division, superintend the entry of actions, and are present at the hearing, sitting below the judge, to record the orders of the court, swear the witnesses, list the exhibits and perform other requisite duties both in London and at assizes.

order in which the actions were set down, and subject to any special application they will come on in that order. At Birmingham, Leeds, Liverpool and Manchester actions may be set down even during the currency of the assize; the district registrar fixes a date before which the action is not to be tried; a list is published of the actions likely to be tried in the first week; the district registrar may entertain applications for postponement made before the commencement of the assize, after which they must be made to the circuit judge; any other application affecting the order of the list can only be granted by a judge in person. At other assize towns the action (if it is to be tried at the next assize) must be set down not less than fourteen days before commission day and the district registrar can only entertain applications for postponement made before that date; all other applications must be made to a judge in person (ordinarily the judge going the circuit), who may give leave for late setting-down in exceptional cases (rr. 6, 7).

Actions set down for trial in the Queen's Bench Division [3] in London in the Non-Jury List are in the first instance set down in a Non-Jury General List. Thence, if a fixed date of trial is desired, they may be transferred to a " Fixture List " on application in proper time and manner to the Clerk of the Lists.[4] He will either fix a date or, if it is objected that the date proposed is too far ahead, he may leave the action in the General List, if necessary marking it not to come on before a certain date so as to give the parties time to prepare for trial. A party who is dissatisfied may within seven days apply to the judge in charge of the Non-Jury List; otherwise no alteration of a fixed date (except to allot an earlier vacated date) will be permitted without the judge's leave. A postponement will only be allowed for good cause and the action may be sent back to the General List.

For each week of each sittings a " Pending List " of non-jury actions is published on the Monday containing (a) the " Week's List " comprising actions both in the Fixture and General Lists expected to be tried that week; (b) other actions in the General List except those which have by order or by

---

[3] As to Chancery actions, see *post*, p. 344.
[4] The practice here set out is mainly governed by the L.C.J.'s Directions of December 9, 1958. Inquiries on any matter of doubt should be made to Room 419, Royal Courts of Justice, or to the practice master.

consent been stood out; and (c) other actions in the Fixture List fixed for trial during the current sittings. Each day there is published a " Daily Cause List " showing the actions to be tried that day; and this also contains the " Warned List," comprising actions likely to be taken on the following day.

As the trial draws near, one or other of the parties often desires to postpone the hearing of the case owing, perhaps, to the illness of himself or of an important witness, or because a late amendment of the pleadings or further discovery has become necessary. If the other side agree and the case is *not* in the Fixture or the Warned List, a consent for a postponement, signed by all parties may on proper grounds be lodged with the Clerk of the Lists to be approved by the judge and the case may then be taken out of the list and restored when the parties are ready. If the action is in the Fixture or the Warned List, an application to the judge in charge of the list showing good cause will probably be necessary. But your opponent may object strongly to any postponement, or to any application which will have that result. A contested application involving an adjournment of a case in the General List but not yet in the Warned List may be brought before a master on summons. But whenever an application regarding the date of any trial has to be made or is referred to the judge in charge of any list, it must be made at the sitting of the court (unless he directs otherwise) and counsel must be instructed and at least one clear day's notice given to the other side, specifying the nature and grounds of the application. If he is applying for the case to stand out of the list until a certain date, counsel should ask that it may keep its place, or it will go to the bottom of the week's list for whatever date it is restored. He must show some good ground for any postponement; " counsel's convenience " is not sufficient, unless he is in another case before the House of Lords or Privy Council or there are other exceptional circumstances. The judge will have regard to the wishes and interests of the parties, the state of the lists and all the circumstances of the case. If he dismisses the application with costs, an appeal lies to the Court of Appeal; but the latter are reluctant to interfere.[5]

It is the duty of all parties at once to inform the officer who keeps the list, whether in London or at assizes, if their case is or

---

[5] *Maxwell* v. *Keun* [1928] 1 K.B. 645.

is likely to be settled or of a different length from that estimated. This is the joint responsibility of counsel, their clerks and solicitors.[6]

Procedure at the Trial

If neither party appears when the case is called on for trial, the action may be struck out of the list; then if the plaintiff wishes to proceed, he must obtain a judge's direction that it be restored. If the plaintiff appears and the defendant does not, the plaintiff may be allowed to prove his claim and obtain judgment in the defendant's absence; if the defendant has a counterclaim the plaintiff will ordinarily ask to have it dismissed with costs.[7] If the defendant appears, and not the plaintiff, the defendant may be given judgment at once, dismissing the plaintiff's claim in the action [7a]; if he has a counterclaim, he may prove it. (Order 35, rr. 1, 2.) But any verdict or judgment obtained in the absence of one party may be set aside upon terms, if application be made within seven days after the trial.[8]

The trial will take place in open court,[9] unless for some solid and special reason the judge orders trial *in camera, e.g.,* on grounds of national security [10] or where a hearing in public would defeat the ends of justice.[11] An official shorthand note or recording of the oral evidence and of the judge's summing-up and judgment will normally be taken (Order 68).

If both parties appear, the jury (if any) is sworn. Formerly junior counsel for the plaintiff had to " open the pleadings " to a jury, briefly stating their effect. This ceremony has now been abolished (*Practice Direction* [1960] 1 W.L.R. 658). If the action is brought for unliquidated damages, counsel must not state the amount claimed.[12] And on no account must he mention the

---

[6] Order 34, r. 8 (2); *Practice Direction* [1959] 1 W.L.R. 258.
[7] *Lumley* v. *Brooks* (1889) 41 Ch.D. 323.
[7a] See *Armour* v. *Bate* [1891] 2 Q.B. 233.
[8] Order 35, r. 2; and see *Schafer* v. *Blyth* [1920] 3 K.B. 140; *Grimshaw* v. *Dunbar* [1953] 1 Q.B. 408. In *Re Barraclough, decd.* [1965] 3 W.L.R. 1023 such an application was refused where the defendant was purposely absent and there was no element of mistake or lack of opportunity.
[9] See *McPherson* v. *McPherson* [1936] A.C. 177; *Hawksley* v. *Fewtrell* [1954] 1 Q.B. 228; *Stevens* v. *Stevens* [1954] 1 W.L.R. 900.
[10] *Baker* v. *Borough of Bethnal Green* [1945] 1 All E.R. 135, 143.
[11] See *Badische, etc.,* v. *Levinstein* (1883) 24 Ch.D. 156; but see *B. (orse.P.)* v. *Attorney-General* [1967] P. 119.
[12] *Per* Lord Halsbury in *Watt* v *.Watt* [1905] A.C. at p. 118.

fact that money has been paid into court in satisfaction save in the excepted cases.[12a]

First may arise the question as to which side begins. Normally the plaintiff will begin by " opening his case " (Order 35, r. 7 (2)), but this depends to a large extent on the pleadings, for where the burden of proof of *all* the issues in the action lies on the defendant he will invariably begin (r. 7 (6)). If the burden of proving but one issue be on the plaintiff, it does not matter that there are others which lie on the defendant, the plaintiff will begin unless the judge otherwise directs. Thus, whenever damages (particularly unliquidated damages) are in issue, the plaintiff should begin, unless a precise sum is claimed which the defendant admits that the plaintiff is prima facie entitled to recover.[13] If the damages claimed be liquidated, still, if the defendant has traversed any material allegation which is essential to the plaintiff's case, the plaintiff should begin. But the defendant may have made admissions in his defence with a view to gaining the advantage of the first word. Moreover, unless no evidence is called on the opposite side, the first word means the last word too; and to have the last word is always important. The defendant may not, when the case is called on, make admissions which are not on the pleadings, so as to gain this advantage [14]—unless, indeed, he can persuade the judge to amend the pleadings then and there. If both parties claim the right to begin, the judge will most probably decide between them according to the pleadings as they stand. The test hitherto has always been, how would judgment be entered on these pleadings if no evidence at all were given on either side? The party against whom judgment would in that event be given was then entitled to begin. But now, in every case, the trial judge may give directions as to the party to begin and the order of speeches (r. 7 (1)).

The leading counsel for the plaintiff (if the plaintiff is to begin) will now " open his case "; that is, he states in chronological order the facts on which the plaintiff relies. Sometimes he deals with the defences pleaded, discounting them in anticipation; sometimes he prefers to leave them unnoticed. He must not open any fact which he is not prepared with evidence to prove. As a rule, the opening speech is purposely pitched in a

---

[12a] See Order 22, r. 7 and *ante*, p. 206.
[13] *Carter* v. *Jones* (1833) 6 C. & P. 64; *Mercer* v. *Whall* (1845) 5 Q.B. 447, **462, 463.**
[14] *Price* v. *Seaward* (1841) Car. & M. 23.

less combative and less confident tone than the final reply; for witnesses often disappoint counsel who has opened his case strongly. Counsel for the plaintiff then calls the first witness, who is generally the plaintiff himself, and examines him " in chief," as it is called. The witness is cross-examined by the defendant's counsel, and re-examined by counsel for the plaintiff. The next witness is then called and examined by one or other of the plaintiff's counsel, and so the case proceeds. When two counsel for a party are briefed they can take the witnesses alternately or as may be convenient.[14a] When all the plaintiff's witnesses have been examined, and all documents material to his case—including such of the defendant's answers to interrogatories as the plaintiff desires to use—have been put in and read, the plaintiff's case is closed.

The defendant's counsel must now make up his mind whether to call evidence or whether to submit that the plaintiff has made out no case to answer in law. He will not ordinarily be allowed to submit no case unless he tells the judge that he intends to rely on the submission alone and call no evidence. If counsel for the defendant adopts this course, counsel for the plaintiff will be entitled to reply to his submission that there is no case for the defendant to answer in law. If the judge overrules the submission, judgment will then be entered for the plaintiff. Another course which the defendant's counsel may adopt at the close of the plaintiff's case is to state, if such be the fact, that he does not intend to call any witnesses; and in that event the plaintiff's counsel at once addresses the court (Order 35, r. 7 (3)),[15] summing up his own evidence, and commenting on the defence, so far as it has been foreshadowed by the cross-examination, and also, no doubt, on the fact that the defendant does not venture to go into the box. The defendant's counsel then addresses the court, criticising the evidence for the plaintiff. But if the defendant's counsel intends to call witnesses, he is entitled to address the court at the end of the plaintiff's case, opening the defence. He then calls his witnesses, each of whom may be examined, cross-examined and re-examined, and he usually makes a second speech for the defendant, at the conclusion of which the

[14a] The leader in his discretion sometimes entrusts the examination of the client to his junior, who has probably acquired some knowledge of the client's idiosyncrasies from conferences in the interlocutory stages.

[15] Formerly, if the defendant's counsel put in a document in the course of the plaintiff's case he lost the last word.

leading counsel for the plaintiff replies on the whole case. This disadvantage necessarily attends calling witnesses for the defendant; it gives the plaintiff the last word; and in a doubtful case the reply of an able advocate can determine the result of the action in his client's favour, especially in a jury case. But, on the other hand, the judge and jury like to see the defendant in the box, and to learn from his own lips his reasons for his conduct. If there are two defendants who appear separately or are separately represented, the order of speeches is governed by rule 7 (5).

When counsel having the last word raises in his speech any fresh point of law or cites any authority not previously mentioned during the course of the trial, his opponent may reply to the point of law or deal with the authority cited (r. 7 (7)).

In citing reported cases it is helpful to the court first to summarise the proposition of law in support of which the case is cited, then to give distinctly and accurately the name of the case and its reference in the law reports, giving the judge time to make a note of it, and then to read such passages as bear upon the point at issue. Counsel owe a duty to the court to bring to its notice all relevant authorities of which they are aware even though they may tell against their case. The *ratio decidendi*, or principle of law on which a case is decided, alone has binding force, as opposed to *obiter dicta* of the judges as to matters not necessary to their decision or not argued before them. Decisions of the House of Lords on questions of law bind all inferior courts, and normally the House itself; [15a] those of the Privy Council, though not technically binding, have almost equal authority. Decisions of the Court of Appeal must be followed by courts of first instance; they also bind the court itself unless (1) there is some conflicting decision of its own; (2) the decision is inconsistent with a decision of the House of Lords, or (3) the decision was given *per incuriam*.[16] Decisions of Divisional Courts bind courts of first instance and are usually followed by other Divisional Courts. A judge of the High Court, while he will allow great weight to the decision of another judge of that court, is not bound by it or relieved from considering the point for himself.[17]

When speeches by counsel are finished, the judge sums up the whole case to the jury, and then follow verdict and judgment;

[15a] See Practice Statement of July 26, 1966 (1 W.L.R. 1234).
[16] See *Young* v. *Bristol Aeroplane Co., Ltd.* [1944] 1 K.B. 718.
[17] *Green* v. *Berliner* [1936] 2 K.B. 477, 493.

if there is no jury, the judge delivers (or reserves) judgment (see *post*, p. 330).

It is improper for counsel in a civil case to invite the jury to stop the case before the judge has summed up,[18] though the judge himself may do so subject to the right of the plaintiff's counsel to address them.

Examination in Chief

The witnesses are always examined *viva voce* and in open court, unless a master or the trial judge has ordered that an affidavit or written statement shall be admissible [19] (see *ante*, pp. 268–269). Any witness who has been subpoenaed to attend the trial may refuse to give any evidence, unless he is first paid his proper expenses for attending. This is so even though the witness has been sworn.[20]

The success of a case depends largely on how the witnesses are handled. The timid witness must be encouraged; the talkative witness repressed; the witness who is too strong a partisan must be kept in check; and yet such management must not be obvious. Counsel has a discretion to call such witnesses as he thinks proper and in whatever order he considers most appropriate.[20a] It is a great art to cross-examine well. It requires even greater skill to examine in chief with uniform success, the chief aim being to bring out clearly and in proper chronological order just so much as is wanted and no more. Nothing will induce some witnesses to swear up to their proofs; from forgetfulness or some other reason they omit the most material circumstance, and supply in its place a host of immaterial details. And yet counsel must not seem to suggest anything to the witness.

Objections are frequently taken either to questions put by counsel or to something which the witness is endeavouring to say. An objection to the admissibility of any evidence must be taken as soon as it is tendered; no objection can be raised after the

---

[18] *Alexander* v. *H. Burgoine & Sons, Ltd.* [1940] W.N. 8; *Beevis* v. *Dawson* [1957] 1 Q.B. 195.
[19] At one time affidavit evidence could be admitted by written agreement of the parties. Order 38, r. 2, does not so provide; but if the parties are agreed, there should be no difficulty in obtaining the necessary order. A statement is also admissible by agreement of the parties under s. 1, Civil Evidence Act, 1968.
[20] *Re Working Men's Mutual Society* (1882) 21 Ch.D. 831.
[20a] *Briscoe* v. *Briscoe* [1966] 2 W.L.R. 205.

evidence has once been received. Such an objection is often stated in the compendious form, " That is not evidence." This may mean one or other of two very different things: either (a) that the fact sought to be proved is irrelevant to every issue in the action, or (b) that the proposed method is not the proper method of proving a relevant fact. Anything that goes to prove a material fact is relevant; everything else will be rigorously excluded. And relevant facts must be proved in a legitimate way; a fact may be most material, but that is no reason why you should be allowed to prove it by inadmissible evidence. Counsel examining in chief must keep rigidly to what is relevant, and must properly prove all relevant facts by admissible evidence.

And he may not ask leading questions. A " leading question " is one which suggests to the witness the answer which it is desired he should give to it. Counsel may not, therefore, put such a question to his own witness, unless it is merely introductory, or relates to matters as to which there is no dispute. In most cases, however, it is necessary to prove a certain number of uncontested facts, in order that judge and jury may understand the position of the parties and the circumstances surrounding the case. As to these matters, leading questions are often put with the permission of counsel on the other side. Leading questions may also be proper to contradict evidence already given by a witness on the other side; *e.g.*, if the plaintiff has sworn that the defendant said: " The goods need not all be equal to sample," the defendant can, and should, be asked in chief: " Did you ever say to the plaintiff that the goods need not all be equal to sample, or any words to that effect? "

In no circumstances may a party attack the character of a witness whom he has called himself, or call evidence to discredit him; but he may call evidence to contradict him upon a fact which is material and not merely collateral,[21] or where—as in the case of an attesting witness to a will—he is compelled by law to call him.[22] If a party voluntarily places a witness before the court to give evidence, he represents that he is worthy of belief. Sometimes, however, the judge will allow a witness, who has given evidence adverse to the party who called him, to be treated as hostile, and then he may be cross-examined and

[21] *Friedlander* v. *London Assurance Co.* (1832) 2 L.J.K.B. 16.
[22] *Coles* v. *Coles and Brown* (1886) L.R. 1 P. & D. 70.

contradicted. He may be asked leading questions. He can also be asked about any previous statement made by him orally or in writing, such as a signed proof of his evidence; and if he denies that he made the statement, proof that he did so may by leave of the judge be given, and the statement, if in writing, may be put in evidence to contradict him. (Criminal Procedure Act, 1865, s. 3.) That statement then becomes admissible as evidence of any fact stated therein by virtue of section 3 of the Civil Evidence Act, 1968. Counsel may not treat a witness as hostile merely because the evidence he is giving is unfavourable to the party who called him. Permission will only be given where the witness shows a decided bias against that party, and a reluctance to state anything that tells in his favour.[24]

A witness should always state what happened according to his own personal recollection, and not according to what he has since been told. But he is allowed to refresh his memory, when in the box, by looking at any entry or memorandum which he himself wrote or dictated very shortly after the event which it records, or even at an entry made by someone else, which he saw, read and approved as correct very shortly after the event. It does not matter that the document is not evidence for either party, or even that it should be and is not stamped.[25] The witness should not read it aloud to the jury, unless the other side consent: he should merely refer to it to refresh his memory. And he must have in court the original entry, and not a fair copy of it.[26] Counsel on the other side is entitled to look at any document by which the witness has refreshed his memory and to cross-examine him on it; and he may, if he thinks fit, put it in evidence.

Cross-examination

Counsel, when cross-examining, has a much freer hand than when examining in chief. He may and often should ask leading questions, although answers which a witness is thus induced to give are not always so convincing. And he need not confine his questions to the fact in issue; he may branch out into many collateral matters; he may attack the character and impugn the credit of the witness

[24] *Greenough* v. *Eccles* (1859) 5 C.B.(N.S.) 786.
[25] *Maugham* v. *Hubbard* (1828) 8 B. & C. 14; *Birchall* v. *Bullough* [1896] 1 Q.B. 325.
[26] *Burton* v. *Plummer* (1834) 2 A. & E. 341.

to any extent which his instructions justify. But he should use this liberty guardedly. Moreover, the judge may disallow vexatious and irrelevant questions.

This much counsel is bound to do, when cross-examining: he must put to each of his opponent's witnesses so much of his own case, in substance, as concerns that particular witness or in which that witness had any share. Thus, if the plaintiff has deposed to a conversation with the defendant, it is the duty of the counsel for the defendant to indicate by his cross-examination how much of the plaintiff's version of the conversation he accepts, and how much he disputes, and to suggest what the defendant's version will be. If he asks no question about it, he will be taken to accept the plaintiff's account in its entirety.

But in all other matters it is often safer to ask too little than too much. It is quite unnecessary to take the witness through the whole of the story which he has already given in chief: the usual result of doing so is that the witness merely repeats his former evidence with greater emphasis and clearness and brings out many minor incidents and considerations which elaborate his tale and serve to make it sound all the more convincing.

Moreover, reckless cross-examination often lets in awkward pieces of evidence which hitherto were not admissible. Thus, if you ask a witness called by the other side whether he did not meet Mr. X at Ilminster Fair last September, and whether Mr. X did not then tell him so and so, your opponent, in reply, will be able to ask the witness what Mr. X really did say to him on that occasion, although this was not admissible in chief, because your client was not present at the conversation. Again, if one entry in a book is tendered in evidence or is used by a witness to refresh his memory, and you take the book and cross-examine as to other entries which you find there, you may make such other entries evidence and part of your case.[27]

Witnesses may be cross-examined not only as to the facts of the case but also " to credit," that is, as to matters not material to the issue, with the view of impugning their credit and thus shaking their whole testimony. But, in order to prevent the case from thus branching out into all manner of irrelevant issues, it is wisely provided that on such matters the answer of the witness must ordinarily be treated as final, no evidence

[27] *Gregory* v. *Tavernor* (1833) 6 C. & P. at p. 281.

being admissible to contradict it. There are important exceptions to this rule. Thus, a witness can always be asked whether he has been convicted of a crime, and if he either denies the fact, or refuses to answer, the opposite party may prove such conviction, however irrelevant to the issue the fact of such conviction may be. (Criminal Procedure Act, 1865, s. 6; and see *ante*, p. 300.) (See further the Civil Evidence Act, 1968, s. 11, as to the admissibility and effect of evidence that a person has been convicted of an offence which should have been properly pleaded in compliance with Order 18, r. 7a (*ante*, p. 105).)

If the witness has previously made a statement material to the issue which is inconsistent with his present testimony, the previous statement may be proved. If it was oral, the circumstances under which it was made must first be put to him, and he must be asked if he admits having made it. If it was in writing, he may be cross-examined upon it without it being shown to him; but if it is intended to put it in evidence, the material parts must be shown to him so that he may have an opportunity of explaining the inconsistency. In any case the judge may insist on seeing the document and may put it in evidence if he thinks it right to do so. (Criminal Procedure Act, 1865, ss. 4 and 5.) The contents of the document then become admissible as provided by Civil Evidence Act, 1968, s. 3.

There are some questions, moreover, which a witness will not be compelled to answer, either in cross-examination or in chief:

(i) He may refuse to answer any question which tends, directly or indirectly, to show that he or his spouse has committed a crime, and there is reasonable ground for apprehending that criminal proceedings may be taken against him; or which tends to expose him or his spouse to proceedings for the recovery of a penalty.[28]

(ii) No barrister or solicitor may, unless his client consents, disclose any fact which his client communicated to him in his professional capacity, or the professional advice he gave his client—nor can the client be compelled to make any such disclosure—so long as such communication

---

[28] Evidence Act, 1851, s. 3; *Macleod* v. *J. J. Lane, Ltd.* (*The Times*, October 25, 1938); Civil Evidence Act, 1968, s. 14 (1).

was not made, nor such advice given, in furtherance of any criminal or fraudulent purpose.[33]

(iii) No juror is allowed to give evidence as to the discussions in the jury box or in the jury room.[34] No judge should be called to give evidence as to facts which can equally well be proved by someone else.[35] Apart from this, a judge of a superior court appears to be privileged from testifying as to proceedings before him, though he may give evidence as to extraneous matters—*e.g.*, a riot in court.[36] No member of the Privy Council may disclose what occurred in the Council.[37] The same rule would probably apply to members of the Cabinet. The Speaker or a Member of Parliament may be called upon to state whether a particular member spoke on a debate, but not what he said or how he voted unless by leave of the House.[38] It has been held that a person in the service of the Crown cannot be compelled to disclose any official communication made to him by any other state official, whether superior or inferior, unless the head of his department permits him so to do.[39] But the court has refused to uphold a claim by the Crown to set aside a subpoena upon a person not in its service, when it was alleged that it was not in the public interest that that person's evidence should be given orally.[40]

Re-examination

The object of re-examination is merely to give the witness an opportunity of explaining any seeming inconsistency in his answers, and of stating the whole truth as to any matter which was touched on, but not fully dealt with, in cross-examination. Counsel, when re-examining, can ask no question that does not

---

[33] *Williams* v. *Quebrada* [1895] 2 Ch. 751; *Minter* v. *Priest* [1930] A.C. 558.

[34] *Ellis* v. *Deheer* [1922] 2 K.B. 113; see also *R.* v. *Thomas* [1933] 2 K.B. 489; and *Ras Behari Lal* v. *The King-Emperor* [1933] W.N. 207.

[35] *Florence* v. *Lawson* (1851) 17 L.T.(o.s.) 260; *R.* v. *Gazard* (1838) 8 C. & P. 595.

[36] *R.* v. *Harvey* (1858) 8 Cox C.C. 99; *Duke of Buccleuch* v. *Metropolitan Board of Works* (1872) L.R. 5 H.L. 418, 433; *R.* v. *Earl of Thanet* (1799) 27 How.St. Tr. 845.

[37] See *Layer's Case* (1722) 16 How.St.Tr. 94, 224.

[38] *Plunkett* v. *Cobbett* (1804) 5 Esp. 136; *Chubb* v. *Salomons* (1851) 3 Car. & Kir. 75.

[39] *Chatterton* v. *Secretary of State for India* [1895] 2 Q.B. 189; and see Official Secrets Act, 1911.

[40] *Broome* v. *Broome* [1955] P. 190.

arise out of the cross-examination, except by consent; he has no more right to ask his own witness leading questions at this stage than at any other; and it is a mere waste of time to ask over again questions already put in chief.

When counsel have finished with the witness, the judge often asks him a few questions. Neither counsel has any right to re-examine the witness on the answers which he has given to the judge; but he may ask the judge to put another question to the witness to make those answers clear. After a witness has once left the box, he cannot be recalled, except by the leave of the judge; and counsel, when asking leave, is expected to indicate the matters on which he desires him to give further evidence. If the judge consents, and the witness is recalled, the counsel recalling him will be confined to the matters so indicated; but his opponent may, apparently, cross-examine him generally with a view to shaking his testimony. The judge has power to call and examine a witness who has not been called by either party, but only if neither party objects.[41] If he does so, neither party has a right to cross-examine that witness without leave; this, however, will always be granted if the evidence is adverse to either party.[42]

Documents

Subject to certain statutory exceptions (*ante*, pp. 300–301) the original document itself must be produced at the trial, if it be possible to obtain it. And if the plaintiff puts it in, the defendant is entitled to have the whole of it read as part of the plaintiff's case. If the original be not produced, it should be satisfactorily accounted for, and its loss or destruction proved. But where a large number of copies are printed from the same type, or lithographed at the same time by the same process, none of them are copies in the legal sense of the word, for they are all counterpart originals, and each is primary evidence of the contents of the rest.

If a person is only called to produce a document and is not sworn or asked any question in chief, the other side has no right to cross-examine him; sometimes he is called on to produce a document while some other witness is in the box, and is himself

---

[41] *Re Enoch and Zaretzky, Bock & Co.'s Arbitration* [1910] 1 K.B. 327; but see *R.* v. *Dora Harris* [1927] 2 K.B. 587, and *R.* v. *McMahon* (1933) 24 Crim.App.R. 95, as to the rule in criminal cases.
[42] *Coulson* v. *Disborough* [1894] 2 Q.B. 316.

called as a witness at a later period of the case. A party who is under notice to produce is not bound to comply with it; when the other side calls for a document, his counsel may say, " I do not produce it." Counsel must not say more; for he is not entitled to give evidence; his witnesses may subsequently explain why it is not produced, *e.g.*, that it has been lost or destroyed.

If the original be produced, a dispute may arise as to who wrote it; and it may be necessary to call witnesses to prove the handwriting. Anyone who has ever seen A write (even though only once) can be called to prove his handwriting. So can anyone who has corresponded with A, or seen letters which have arrived in answer to letters addressed to A. Thus, a clerk in a merchant's office, who has corresponded with A on his master's behalf, may be called to prove his handwriting, though he has never seen A write.[43] The usual course is for the counsel who tenders the document merely to ask the witness, " Do you know Mr. A's handwriting? " leaving it to his opponent to cross-examine as to the extent of the witness's acquaintance. Such cross-examination will only weaken the force of his evidence, not destroy its admissibility. Moreover, section 8 of the Criminal Procedure Act, 1865, provides that " Comparison of a disputed writing with any writing proved to the satisfaction of the judge to be genuine shall be permitted to be made by witnesses; and such writings, and the evidence of witnesses respecting the same, may be submitted to the court and jury as evidence of the genuineness or otherwise of the writing in dispute." It may be necessary to call some expert in handwriting. But the jury generally receive the evidence of experts with caution; so it is well to back it up with evidence of witnesses who have seen the person write. If the suggestion is that the document was written by either party to the suit and he is present in court, he may be then and there required to write something which the court and jury may compare with the document in dispute.[44]

Every material document is prima facie admissible in evidence against the writer. It is, however, manifestly desirable that the parties to a dispute should be free to enter into negotiations with a view to compromise without running the risk of having their letters given in evidence against them if the negotiations fail and

43 *Cf. R.* v. *Turner* [1910] 1 K.B. at pp. 357, 358.
44 *Doe* d. *Devine* v. *Wilson* (1855) 10 Moo.P.C. at p. 530.

an action ensues. They are therefore allowed after a dispute has arisen, whether proceedings have been commenced or not, to mark any documents which form part of such negotiation with the words " Without prejudice," and documents so marked cannot be read at the trial of an action between them on the same dispute, even on a question of costs, without the consent of the writer.[45] The expression " without prejudice " means that the document is not to be used to the prejudice of either party in the dispute, if the negotiations fail.

Sometimes, too, when a document is tendered in evidence, the officer of the court takes the objection that it ought to be, and is not, stamped. It is considered unprofessional (except in revenue cases) for counsel to object to a document on the ground that it is not sufficiently stamped, unless such defect goes to the validity of the document as opposed to its admissibility. Some documents, such as most bills of exchange and promissory notes, cannot be stamped after they are issued; and in such cases the objection is fatal; no copy can be put in, even by consent, after it is known to the court that the original is unstamped. If, however, the document is one which can by law be stamped after its issue or execution, the objection can be met by paying the proper officer the amount of the stamp duty and a penalty; or, if the document be insufficiently stamped, the amount of the deficiency and a penalty. If there is any question as to the necessity for a stamp, or as to its proper amount, the judge decides it then and there; if he admits the document, his decision is final, and a new trial will not be granted nor will an appeal lie if he is subsequently proved to have been wrong. (Order 59, r. 11 (5).) If the judge holds that the stamp is insufficient, the party tendering the document must either dispense with it or pay the penalty.

Sometimes, also, grave difficulty is experienced in putting in evidence some official document, *e.g.*, a letter or memorial sent to a Secretary of State or to some government department. An objection is often taken that the production of such documents is against public policy. If this objection is duly raised in proper form by the proper officer, whether he be a party to the action or not, the document cannot be read, nor can any other evidence be given of its contents. If the original is privileged from production

---

[45] *Stretton* v. *Stubbs, Ltd.* (*The Times,* February 28, 1905); *Rabin* v. *Mendoza & Co.* [1954] 1 W.L.R. 271.

O.P.—11

on the ground of public policy, the same public policy requires that no secondary evidence of it shall be given.[46] But proof *aliunde* of some fact stated in a privileged document is not rendered inadmissible merely because it is contained therein.[47] The objection must ordinarily be taken by the head of the public department of state, who is able to assess whether the production of the document will or will not be injurious to the public service. It is, however, ultimately a decision for the judge at the trial, if necessary, after he has been shown the document.[48] As a rule the judge does not trouble the head of the department to attend court in person, provided a suitable representative from the office attends on his behalf and satisfies the judge that the mind of the responsible head of the department has been brought to bear on the document in question. (See *ante*, p. 246.) Privilege from production may sometimes be claimed under the provisions of a statute.[49]

All documents put in evidence at the trial are marked and listed as exhibits by the associate (Order 35, r. 11). At the conclusion of the trial each party by his solicitor applies for the return of the exhibits which he puts in; and he must carefully preserve them in case there should be an appeal (r. 12).

Secondary Evidence of Documents

If the original document has been lost or destroyed, secondary evidence may be given of its contents. But—subject to the provisions of the Civil Evidence Act, 1968, and of Order 38, r. 3 (*ante*, p. 301)—its loss or destruction must first be proved. It is not necessarily enough for a witness to say it is lost; he must show that he has made a real search for it, before he will be allowed to produce a copy or state his recollection of its contents. If counsel seeks to put in a copy, he must usually, in the absence of agreement or special leave, prove that it is a correct copy by calling the man who made it or otherwise. But copies of correspondence are generally agreed and allowed to be read when it is common ground that such letters were in fact written and received. Where words are written, or a paper placarded, on a wall, so that the writing

---

[46] *Home* v. *Lord Bentinck* (1820) 2 Brod. & B. 130; *Dawkins* v. *Lord Rokeby* (1873) L.R. 8 Q.B. 255; *Asiatic Petroleum Co.* v. *Anglo-Persian Oil Co.* [1916] 1 K.B. 822; *Ankin* v. *L. & N.E. Ry.* [1930] 1 K.B. 527; and see Practice Note [1933] W.N. 272.
[47] *Broome* v. *Broome* [1955] P. 190.
[48] *Conway* v. *Rimmer* [1968] A.C. 910; and see *ante*, p. 245.
[49] *Rowell* v. *Pratt* [1938] A.C. 101; 106 L.J.K.B. 790.

cannot conveniently be brought into court, secondary evidence of it may be given.[50]

Where, however, the document is still in existence and capable of being brought into court, the party desiring to give secondary evidence of its contents must ordinarily prove that he has done all in his power to obtain the original document. Thus, the plaintiff is entitled to give secondary evidence if the original is in the defendant's possession and is not produced when called for, provided it is among the documents set out in his list for discovery or due notice to produce it was served on the defendant's solicitor a reasonable time before the trial; and also if the document is in the possession of someone beyond the jurisdiction of the court, who refuses to produce it on request, although informed of the purpose for which it is required. If it be in the possession of a third person within the jurisdiction, but a stranger to the cause, who refuses to produce it, although duly served with a *subpoena duces tecum* for the purpose, then the right to give secondary evidence of its contents appears to depend on whether such refusal be rightful or wrongful. If it be a *wrongful* refusal, the remedy of the party is against the witness only.[51] If it be a *rightful* refusal, then secondary evidence is, as a rule, admitted, as the party has done all in his power to produce primary proof. Even here, however, the privilege arising from considerations of public policy may prevent *any* evidence being given of the contents of the document. But where the privilege is only of a private character, secondary evidence may be given of the contents of documents privileged from production, *e.g.*, of a document entrusted to a solicitor by his client.[52]

Rebutting Evidence

In some cases, at the close of the defendant's case, the plaintiff may be allowed to call further evidence to answer an affirmative case raised by the defendant.[53] Thus, if the defendant has pleaded an excuse or justification for his conduct, the plaintiff may, if he chooses, deal with this defence and call evidence to rebut the justification in the first instance; or he may, at the judge's discretion, be allowed to confine his original case to prov-

---

[50] *Per* Lord Abinger in *Mortimer* v. *M'Callan* (1840) 6 M. & W. at p. 68; *Bruce* v. *Nicolopulo* (1855) 11 Ex. at p. 133; 24 L.J.Ex. at p. 324.
[51] *R.* v. *Inhabitants of Llanfaethly* (1853) 2 E. & B. 940; *Rowell* v. *Pratt* [1938] A.C. at p. 116.   [52] *Calcraft* v. *Guest* [1898] 1 Q.B. 759.
[53] *Beevis* v. *Dawson* [1957] 1 Q.B. 195.

ing what the defendant did, and, when a prima facie defence has been established, to deal with it in his reply. But the plaintiff cannot, in the absence of special circumstances, call some evidence to rebut the justification in the first instance, and more afterwards in reply, thus dividing his proof.[54]

" *Nonsuit* "

Strictly, there is no longer such a thing as a nonsuit in the High Court (see *ante*, p. 253), the procedure of " discontinuance," which can be allowed by leave and on terms even at the trial, having taken its place. But the word is sometimes loosely used to denote the act of the judge when he withdraws the case from the jury and directs judgment to be entered for the defendant without (or in spite of) their verdict, or in non-jury cases when he enters judgment for the defendant without calling upon him to prove his defence.[54a] At the close of the plaintiff's case, the defendant's counsel sometimes contends that there is " no case to answer " (see *ante*, p. 311), or that there is no evidence fit to be laid before a jury of the facts which the plaintiff must establish in order to succeed in the action. This contention may raise important questions both of law and of fact. Do the facts which the plaintiff has proved give him any and what right of action? If not, may the judge and jury infer from the facts which he has established other facts which are necessary to complete the plaintiff's case? In other words, has the plaintiff proved enough to throw the burden of proof upon his opponent? (See *ante*, pp. 291–292.) Every point of law on which either party intends to rely must, as a rule, be raised before verdict; if it is not raised when it ought to have been raised, the party will be deemed to have waived it.[55] The judge at the trial has full power to allow the plaintiff to alter or amend[56] his writ or any party to amend his pleading on such terms as may be just (Order 20, r. 5),[57] and to add, or strike out, or substitute, a party under Order 15, r. 6.

---

[54] *Browne* v. *Murray* (1825) Ry. & Moo. 254.

[54a] *Westgate* v. *Crowe* [1908] 1 K.B. 24.

[55] *Graham* v. *Mayor, etc., of Huddersfield* (1895) 12 T.L.R. 36; and see *post*, p. 379.

[56] The amendment should actually be made in writing. See (*inter alia*) J. *Leavey & Co. Ltd.* v. *G. H. Hirst & Co., Ltd.* [1944] 1 K.B. 24; and *Hall* v. *Meyrick* [1957] 2 Q.B. 455, 481.

[57] And see *Hunt* v. *Rice & Son Ltd.* (1937) 53 T.L.R. 931; *G. L. Baker Ltd.* v. *Medway Building & Supplies Ltd.* [1958] 1 W.L.R. 1216.

A plaintiff should not be nonsuited on his counsel's opening except by the consent of his counsel.[58] The proper time for the defendant's counsel to submit to the judge that there is no case for him to answer is at the close of the plaintiff's case; or in a jury case he may submit at the conclusion of the whole of the evidence that there is no evidence to go before the jury.[59] If he makes a submission at the close of the plaintiff's case he will probably be required to elect to call no evidence.[60] The matter is one of discretion for the judge, whether sitting alone or with a jury,[61] and the rule does not apply, for example, to defamation cases where the defendant submits that there is no evidence of malice, or that the words are not actionable without proof of special damage. But when the judge is sitting alone it is so highly inconvenient that he should be asked to express an opinion on the evidence until he has heard it all [62] that the Court of Appeal have said that he ought to refuse to rule on the submission unless counsel for the defendant says that he intends to call no evidence, and that that is the practice which ought to be followed in most cases and, in particular, in actions of negligence.[63] If through oversight or misapprehension the judge does not put counsel to his election, and counsel does not either expressly or impliedly in fact elect, counsel may call evidence as though the submission had not been made.[64] It is generally best to discuss the law of the case after all the evidence has been given.

It is not always easy to determine whether the plaintiff has or has not made out a prima facie case.

Illustrations

Where the plaintiff was injured by a barrel of flour falling upon him from a window above the defendant's shop, this was held to be prima facie evidence of negligence on the part of the defendant. *Res ipsa loquitur.*

> *Byrne* v. *Boadle* (1863) 2 H. & C. 722; 33 L.J.Ex. 13.
> *Kearney* v. *L.B. & S.C. Ry.* (1871) L.R. 6 Q.B. 759.
> *Walsh* v. *Holst & Co. Ltd.* [1958] 1 W.L.R. 800.

---

[58] *Fletcher* v. *L. & N.W. Ry.* [1892] 1 Q.B. 122.
[59] *Grinsted* v. *Haddrill* [1953] 1 W.L.R. 696.
[60] See *ante*, p. 311, and *Payne* v. *Harrison & Another* [1961] 2 Q.B. 403.
[61] *Muller* v. *Ebbw Vale Steel Co.* (1936) 52 T.L.R. 655; *Young* v. *Rank* [1950] 2 K.B. 510, where most of the earlier cases are reviewed.
[62] *Alexander* v. *Rayson* [1936] 1 K.B. 169 at p. 178.
[63] *Parry* v. *Aluminium Corpn.* [1940] W.N. 44; *Laurie* v. *Raglan Building Co.* [1942] 1 K.B. 152. It will ordinarily be followed in divorce cases also (*Wilson* v. *Wilson* [1958] 1 W.L.R. 1090).
[64] *Yuill* v. *Yuill* [1945] P. 15.

So if a passenger is injured by a collision between two trains belonging to the same company, this is prima facie evidence of negligence and it lies upon the defendant company to rebut it if possible.

Carpue v. *L. & B. Ry.* (1844) 5 Q.B. 747, 751.

On the other hand, the unexplained happening of an accident when the facts are equally consistent with negligence on the part of either party is no ground for inferring negligence on the part of the defendant.

Wakelin v. *L. & S.W. Ry.* (1886) 12 App.Cas. 41; 56 L.J.Q.B. 229.

Pomfret v. *Lancashire and Yorkshire Ry.* [1903] 2 K.B. 718; 72 L.J.K.B. 729.

Where the plaintiff is injured as the result of an accident between two motor vehicles, and from the evidence it appears probable that one or both of the defendants was negligent, the judge ought not to dismiss either defendant from the action, but should hear the whole case before coming to a decision.

Hummerstone v. *Leary* [1921] 2 K.B. 664; 90 L.J.K.B. 1148.

A collision between two motor vehicles in the centre of a straight road or at cross-roads of equal status may in itself be evidence of negligence on the part of each driver.

Baker v. *Market Harborough Industrial Co-operative Society, Ltd.* [1953] 1 W.L.R. 1472.

France v. *Parkinson* [1954] 1 W.L.R. 581.

See also *Bray* v. *Palmer* [1953] 1 W.L.R. 1455.

Settlement

Actions are frequently settled during the trial.[65] In jury cases a juror is often withdrawn, sometimes at the suggestion of the judge. This means that neither party cares for the case to proceed. If no special terms are agreed on, the effect of withdrawing a juror is that the action is at an end, that no fresh action can be brought for the same cause of action, and that each party pays his own costs.[66] Sometimes a defendant will submit to judgment by consent for an agreed sum, or a plaintiff, whose case has gone badly, may consent to submit to judgment with some concession about the amount of costs he shall pay the defendant. In non-jury cases where for any reason one side or the other wishes to avoid having a judgment recorded against it, the procedural machinery by which a compromise is effected is less stereotyped.[67] A common form is to adjourn *sine die* by consent. In all cases it should be appreciated that a compromise at the trial involves two elements: (i) it is a contract whereby

---

[65] As to settlement at an earlier stage see Chapter 17. Many of the observations there made apply also to a settlement at the trial.

[66] See *Strauss* v. *Francis* (1866) 4 F. & F. 939, 1107; *Moscati* v. *Lawson* (1835) 7 C. & P. 35n.; *Norburn* v. *Hilliam* (1870) L.R. 5 C.P. 129.

[67] The effects of various methods which may be adopted were reviewed in *Green* v. *Rozen* [1955] 1 W.L.R. 741.

new rights or immunities are created between the parties in substitution for, and in consideration of the abandonment of, the former claims or contentions of either or both of them; (ii) it will ordinarily be necessary for the court to take some action agreed upon by the parties, *e.g.*, to give judgment, make an order of discontinuance or stay, or adjourn the matter either indefinitely or for a stated time and perhaps to make an order for the taxation of costs, particularly where either party is an assisted person under the Legal Aid and Advice Act, 1949. If the aid of the court is or may be desired to enforce the terms in any case where judgment is not taken, the terms agreed should include the words " Judge's order if necessary "; and in all cases of any doubt or difficulty it is well to reserve " Liberty to apply." [67a] The utmost care is needed in drawing up a settlement and it is commonly said with some truth that it is more trouble to settle an action than to fight it. In all cases it is important to ensure that no fresh action can be started on the same facts.

Any terms agreed on should be indorsed on counsel's briefs, and each indorsement signed by the leading counsel on both sides. Counsel has full authority to make such a compromise, unless expressly forbidden to do so by his client at the time,[68] provided the compromise does not include or affect matters outside the scope of the action.[69]

As to the settlement of any action in which a minor or a patient is concerned, see *ante*, p. 251.

Verdict

If the progress of the trial is not arrested by either a " nonsuit " or a compromise, then, in jury cases, as soon as all the evidence has been heard and the counsel on both sides have addressed the jury, the judge sums up the evidence. He may either leave the jury to return a general verdict for the plaintiff or for the defendant, or ask them to answer certain questions; in the latter case it will be for the judge to determine subsequently what is the legal result of their findings. If either party desires

---

[67a] This enables a party to ask the court to deal with matters affecting the working out of its judgment; but not to vary it—see *Cristel* v. *Cristel* [1951] 2 K.B. 725.

[68] *Strauss* v. *Francis* (1866) L.R. 1 Q.B. 379; *Neale* v. *Gordon Lennox* [1902] A.C. 465; *Shepherd* v. *Robinson* [1919] 1 K.B. 474.

[69] *Swinfen* v. *Swinfen* (1857) 1 C.B.(N.S.) 364; *Kempshall* v. *Holland* (1895) 14 R. 336.

that any question be left to the jury other than those which the judge is proposing to leave, he should ask the judge to put that question also to the jury before the verdict is given.[70] Once the jury has given a general verdict, the judge is not entitled to ask them any further question.[71]

The jury now consider their verdict.[72] They must determine all issues of fact, and, if they are in favour of the plaintiff, they must also assess the damages. Where there are two or more distinct causes of action, they should assess the damages on each of them separately.[73] In arriving at the amount, the jury must not have regard to any questions of costs; that is a matter for the judge. And they must not be informed that any money has been paid into court. In some cases the amount to which the plaintiff is entitled can be ascertained by mere arithmetic, or calculated according to a scale of charges or some other accepted rate or percentage. The damages are then said to be *liquidated* or " made clear." When, however, the amount to be recovered depends on all the circumstances of the case, and on the conduct of the parties, or is fixed by opinion or by an estimate, the damages are said to be *unliquidated.* Thus, in an action on a bill of exchange or a promissory note, the amount of the verdict, if it be for the plaintiff at all, can be reckoned beforehand: so much for principal, so much for interest, so much for notarial expenses. But in an action of libel, for instance, it is open to the jury to award the plaintiff a penny, or two pounds, or a hundred pounds; and no one can say beforehand what the precise figure will be. Where the damages are unliquidated, the sum which the jury awards to a successful plaintiff may be:

    (i) Contemptuous;
    (ii) Nominal;
    (iii) Substantial; or
    (iv) Exemplary.

(i) Contemptuous damages are awarded when the jury consider that the action should never have been brought. The

---

[70] *Weiser* v. *Segar* [1904] W.N. 93.
[71] *Arnold* v. *Jeffreys* [1914] 1 K.B. 512.
[72] As to taking a verdict in the judge's absence, see *Hawksley* v. *Fewtrell* [1954] 1 Q.B. 228.
[73] *Weber* v. *Birkett* [1925] 2 K.B. 152; but see *Barber* v. *Pigden* [1937] 1 K.B. 664.

defendant may have just overstepped the line, but the plaintiff may also be to blame or have rushed into litigation unnecessarily; so he only recovers a penny.

(ii) Nominal damages are awarded where the action was a proper one to bring, but the plaintiff has not suffered any special damage, and does not desire to put money into his pocket; he has established his right or cleared his character, and is content to accept two pounds and his costs.

(iii) Substantial damages are awarded where the jury seriously endeavour to arrive at a figure which will fairly compensate the plaintiff for his actual loss or injury in all the circumstances of the case. His liability to tax, estimated on broad lines, is a relevant consideration.[74]

(iv) Exemplary damages are awarded where the jury desire to mark their disapproval of the defendant's conduct towards the plaintiff; they therefore punish him by awarding the plaintiff damages beyond the amount which would be adequate compensation for his actual loss or injury. They are only allowed to give such damages in actions where there has been oppressive, arbitrary or unconstitutional conduct by a government official, or where the defendant has sought to achieve some financial or material gain for himself unless such damages are expressly authorised by statute.[74a] Everything which aggravates or mitigates the conduct of the defendant may be taken into consideration, including the means of the parties.[74b]

Where the cause of action is continuing (as in cases of nuisance, non-repair, or continuing trespass), the jury must assess the damages down to the time of assessment; and the plaintiff can bring a second action for any subsequent damage if it continues. But where the cause of action consists of one isolated act or omission (*e.g.*, one assault, one libel, or one piece of negligence), the jury must assess the damages once for all. No fresh action can, as a rule, be brought for any subsequent damage; hence, the jury must now take into their consideration every loss which will naturally result in the future from the

---

[74] *British Transport Commission* v. *Gourley* [1956] A.C. 185; *Beach* v. *Reed Corrugated Cases, Ltd.* [1956] 1 W.L.R. 807. And see *Parsons* v. *B.N.M. Laboratories Ltd.* [1964] 1 Q.B. 95.

[74a] See, for example, the Reserve and Auxiliary Forces (Protection of Civil Interests) Act, 1953, s. 13 (2) and the Copyright Act, 1956, s. 17 (3).

[74b] For the rules of common law relating to exemplary damages, see *Rookes* v. *Barnard & Others* [1964] A.C. 1129, *per* Lord Devlin at p. 1221 *et seq.*

defendant's conduct, though they must not speculate on mere contingencies.[75]

Judgment

As soon as the verdict, be it general or special, has been returned, counsel for the successful party formally asks for judgment. No motion for judgment is necessary; the judge will direct that judgment be entered as he thinks right. In non-jury cases he gives judgment at the conclusion of counsel's speeches, stating his reasons.[75a] Sometimes, if difficult questions are raised, the judge does not give judgment at once, but takes time to consider it.[76] As a rule, however, he gives judgment then and there, according to the findings of the jury if there is one. When distinct issues are separately left to the jury, the judge may accept their verdict on those issues on which they agree, and discharge them on others on which they cannot agree.[77] A judgment debt carries interest. (Judgments Act, 1838, s. 17.) The rate of interest, originally 4 per cent. under that Act, is now variable (see Administration of Justice Act, 1970, s. 44).

In the Chancery Division, where issues are apt to be more complicated and parties more numerous (see *post*, p. 354), it is usual for the judge to give an oral judgment indicating the general sense in which he decides the action but not to direct the entry of judgment there and then. Before this is done junior counsel on each side must agree " minutes of judgment " and

---

[75] There is one exception to this rule. In cases where special damage is essential to the cause of action, it has been held that a second action can be brought, if fresh special damage arises from the same cause of action after the writ in the first action was issued: see *ante*, pp. 41, 200. Hence, in such actions, the jury should confine their attention to the special damage which has actually happened and is alleged and proved before them, and leave the future for some other jury to deal with.

[75a] The word " judgment " is used in two senses. Strictly it means the formal judgment (see Precedent No. 104) which is sealed and issued to the successful party and entered in the books of the court. But it is also commonly used to mean the reasoned judgment which is delivered by a judge sitting without a jury or by a Lord Justice in the Court of Appeal. In the House of Lords " speech " rather than " judgment " is the correct word when it is used in this sense.

[76] This is indicated in law reports by the abbreviation c.a.v. (*curia advisari vult*). For the procedure upon " further consideration " in the Chancery Division, see *post*, p. 348. In the Q.B.D. there may be argument upon the jury's findings, which is similar to a motion for judgment (*ante*, pp. 57–58, and *post*, p. 344), and this must be heard, if possible, by the judge who tried the case (Judicature Act, 1925, s. 60).

[77] *Marsh* v. *Isaacs* (1876) 45 L.J.C.P. 505; and see *Nevill* v. *Fine Arts Insurance Co.* [1895] 2 Q.B. at p. 158.

these are handed in to the registrar and form the basis of the formal judgment which is then drawn up. (See *post*, p. 345.)

But the duties of counsel are not yet over. Now is the time to ask for any special costs, such as the costs of taking evidence abroad, of photographic copies of any document, of transcripts of recorded evidence or shorthand notes,[78] the costs of proving particular documents or facts,[79] and any costs reserved to be disposed of at the trial,[80] or specifically mentioned in the order for directions. The party who has incurred these costs will have to bear them, unless, before judgment is entered, he obtains an order for their allowance on taxation. No fresh order can be made for such costs after the judgment has been drawn up; they must then be borne by the party who has incurred them,[81] unless the judge can be persuaded to amend his order under the " slip rule "[82] on the ground that there has been an accidental omission. The application for such amendment may well involve the client in additional expense and reflects no credit on the counsel responsible for the omission. Counsel for the successful party must also ask for the general costs of the action, which are in the discretion of the trial judge. (Order 62, r. 3.) This discretion must, of course, be exercised judicially. If any money has been paid into court and is still in court, the judge should be asked to make some order with regard to it. (Order 22, rr. 5 and 8.) He may only be informed of a payment into court in satisfaction after all questions of liability and amount of debt or damages have been decided (rule 7). If the defendant is entitled to any costs, his counsel may ask the judge to direct that such money remain in court until after taxation with liberty to apply.[83] If the plaintiff's damages are assessed at a figure less than the amount paid into court, the judge will take that fact into consideration when exercising his discretion as to costs. If either party is an assisted person under the Legal Aid and Advice Act, 1949, his counsel should ask for a direction that his costs be taxed in accordance with the third schedule to that Act, so that the proper amount payable out of

---

[78] See Order 68.

[79] See Order 62, r. 3 (5), (6).

[80] *British Provident Association* v. *Bywater* [1897] 2 Ch. 531; *How* v. *Winterton* (1904) 91 L.T. 763.

[81] *Ashworth* v. *Outram* (1878) 9 Ch.D. 483.

[82] Order 20, r. 11 (*ante*, p. 172); see *Re Inchcape (Earl of)* [1942] 1 Ch. 394.

[83] Under Order 22, r. 5, an order may be made *after trial* to pay money out otherwise than in satisfaction of the causes of action in respect of which it was paid in.

the legal aid fund may be ascertained; otherwise extra expense may be caused by the necessity for a subsequent application.

The counsel for the unsuccessful party, if he desires a stay of execution because he thinks of appealing or on other grounds (see *post*, p. 396), should now apply for it, although an application may be made later (Order 47, r. 1). To obtain a stay of execution from the court below is not to take a benefit under the judgment so as to preclude the appellant from seeking to set it aside.[84] As a rule a stay pending appeal will only be granted on terms. A usual condition is that the unsuccessful party shall bring a sum of money into court and give notice of appeal within so many days; and the costs of the trial may be ordered to be taxed and paid, subject to an undertaking by the respondent's solicitor to refund them if the appeal is successful. Interest will be allowed for the period during which execution has been delayed by the appeal, unless an express order to the contrary is made (Order 59, r. 13). The lodging of a notice of appeal does not itself operate as a stay of execution, but the Court of Appeal can order a stay (*ibid.*). The application should, however, be made in the first instance to the court below (rule 14 (4)).

A judgment finally disposes of all controversy as to any of the matters in issue in the action. The rights of the parties as to any such matter depend in future wholly on the judgment. As long as that judgment stands, none of the issues raised in the action can be re-tried.[85] The original cause of action is gone—*transit in rem judicatam*—it is merged in the judgment. This result is peculiar to a judgment: a mere stay of proceedings, or the acceptance of money paid into court, has not the same effect.[86] Clerical mistakes in a judgment or order, or errors arising from any accidental slip or omission, may be corrected on motion or summons (Order 20, r. 11, *ante*, p. 172); but a judge has no power under this rule to alter the substance of his judgment, once it has been formally drawn up.

---

[84] *Evans* v. *Bartlam* [1937] A.C. at p. 479.
[85] *Ralli* v. *Moor Line* (1925) 22 Ll.L.R. 530.
[86] *Coote* v. *Ford* [1899] 2 Ch. 93.

CHAPTER 22

ACTIONS BY WRIT IN THE CHANCERY DIVISION

BEFORE considering the course of a typical action commenced by writ in the Chancery Division, which in many ways closely resembles the course of a similar action in the Queen's Bench Division and in many ways is strikingly dissimilar, it is necessary to consider what matters are exclusively within the jurisdiction of the Chancery Division and why. The answer is partly historical, for the present Chancery Division is the historic successor of the old Equity Courts, and has by virtue of that very fact inherited a large part of their jurisdiction. But the main answer, which mirrors the historical, lies in the different organisation of the two Divisions. From the very beginnings of Equity, the Courts of Chancery have had a large staff of officials to whom complicated accounts and inquiries can be referred. The result was that litigious business requiring such accounts or inquiries tended to find its home there. And the fundamental distinction between the Chancery and Queen's Bench Divisions as they exist today lies simply in the fact that where a matter of account arises (other than an extremely simple one [1]), or an inquiry, or a judgment which needs careful working out, is required, the action is one which should be brought in the Chancery Division.[1a] And whilst, as we shall see in a moment, certain particular matters are by statute assigned to that Division, it also has complete jurisdiction in any action not expressly assigned to another Division,[2] though such matters will readily be transferred back to their more usual habitat unless the circumstances warrant their retention.

The Chancery Division of the High Court normally sits only in London; but writs in actions assigned to this Division can issue out of the appropriate district registry,[3] and accounts and

---

[1] *York* v. *Stowers* [1883] W.N. 174.

[1a] See, *e.g.*, the Administration of Justice Act, 1970, ss. 37 and 38, which while extending the jurisdiction of the county court in actions for possession by mortgagees, exclude actions for foreclosure (in which accounts have to be taken) or sale (by the court: which requires experienced chambers staff).

[2] A trustee in bankruptcy must commence many purely common law actions in this Division: Bankruptcy Rules, 1952, r. 121.

[3] Order 6, r. 7 (2).

inquiries can, if necessary, be referred to the district registrar.[4] It is because of the close nexus between the types of action brought in this Division and the chamber organisation noted above that, although such actions may theoretically be ordered to be tried at Assize,[5] such orders are very seldom made. Experience has shown that difficulties invariably arise upon the working out of the judgment in such cases. Suitable causes or matters may be transferred to the Lancaster Palatine Court,[6] where no such difficulty arises.

To the Chancery Division are assigned all causes and matters of which exclusive jurisdiction was under any Act given to the Court of Chancery, or to any judge thereof, and all causes and matters for any of the following purposes:

The administration of the estates of deceased persons;

The dissolution of partnerships or the taking of partnership or other accounts;

The redemption or foreclosure of mortgages, and claims for payment or possession thereunder[7];

The raising of portions or other charges on land;

The sale and distribution of the proceeds of property subject to any lien or charge;

The execution of trusts, charitable or private;

The rectification or setting aside or cancellation of deeds or other written instruments;

The specific performance of contracts between vendors and purchasers of real estate, including contracts for leases;

The partition or sale of real estate;

The wardship of infants [7a] and the care of infants' estates:

and generally all causes and matters, which under any enactment or by direction of the Lord Chancellor are assigned to the Division.[8] These include:

Proceedings in Bankruptcy[9];

---

4 *Re Smith* (1877) 6 Ch.D. 692.   5 Order 33, rr. 1, 4 (3).
6 Court of Chancery of Lancaster Act, 1952.
7 Order 88, r. 2. See Administration of Justice Act, 1970, ss. 37 and 38 as to the exclusive county court jurisdiction in actions where possession is claimed.
7a Order 91. But see Administration of Justice Act, 1970, s. 1 and Sch. 1 whereunder proceedings in relation to the wardship of minors will be transferred to the new Family Division of the High Court when constituted, and Sch. 2 which will amend this clause to read " The appointment of a guardian of a minor's estate alone." Contested probate actions will also be transferred to the Chancery Division; *ibid.*
8 Judicature Act, 1925, ss. 56 (1), 57 (1).
9 See [1921] W.N. Part II, pp. 362 and 369.

Proceedings under the Companies Acts [10];

Proceedings under the Patents and Registered Designs Acts [11];

The Revenue Paper [12];

Applications under the Landlord and Tenant Acts, 1927 and 1954 [13];

Proceedings under Part I of the Restrictive Trade Practices Act, 1956 [14]; and

Appeals under the Finance Act, 1894 and Administration of Justice (Miscellaneous Provisions) Act, 1933. [15]

The jurisdiction in relation to persons unable through mental infirmity to manage their own affairs—then known as the jurisdiction in Lunacy—was in 1956 transferred from the Lords Justices to the judges of the Chancery Division [16] and they are now the nominated judges under the Mental Health Act, 1959, s. 100, for the management of the property and affairs of patients. In that capacity they will exercise powers in addition to and also on appeal from the Court of Protection.

Commencement of an Action

The chamber organisation of the Chancery Division makes itself felt immediately upon the issue of the writ. Exactly the same procedure as for the issue of a writ in the Queen's Bench Division is followed but all writs in the Chancery Division are assigned to one of two groups of judges, Group A or Group B. The Group is determined in the usual case by ballot when the writ is issued,[17] but may be determined in some cases by the nature of the action [18] or the existence of previous proceedings. [19] This assignment, taken together with the reference letter, determines the master before whom all subsequent proceedings in the matter will come. However, in order to distribute such cases more equitably amongst the masters, actions concerning mortgages, where the plaintiff is a bank or a building society, are dealt with by the master to whom the matter would be assigned if it bore the distinguishing letter of the first or only defendant.[20]

[10] Order 102, r. 6 (1).　　　　　　　　　　　[11] Order 103, r. 2.
[12] Redistribution of Business (Revenue Paper) Order, 1962.
[13] Order 97, r. 2.　　　　　　　　　　　　　[14] Order 105, r. 2.
[15] Order 90.　　　　　　　　　　[16] See [1956] 2 All E.R. 248.
[17] Order 4, r. 1 (1).
[18] Order 4, r. 1 (4) and (5).
[19] See p. 336, *post*.　　　　　　[20] Practice Direction [1950] W.N. 513.

Formerly the assignment was to a judge, not a group of judges, and as Chancery actions have a habit of lasting for a very long time, it frequently happens that it becomes necessary to know to what group and master an action started long ago is now assigned, for the purpose of taking some further proceedings in an action such, for example, as a summons for payment of money out of court. Elaborate tables are accordingly kept which allow the descent of an action to be traced from judge to judge until finally the right group is ascertained. Where any cause or action in the Chancery Division is closely connected with a previous cause or action, the later action must be assigned, if practicable, to the same group of judges which tried the earlier action. A note indorsed on the originating process by a master of the group which tried the earlier action, or the registrar of the district in which it was begun, will be sufficient authority for the assignment of the later action.[21]

Apart from the above, the issue [22] and service [23] of the writ, entry of appearance,[22] and procedure on default of appearance [23] (which is, however, almost invariably to move a motion for judgment) follow the same general rules as in the Queen's Bench Division.

Summary Judgment

Whilst the procedure of applying for summary judgment under Order 14 in actions commenced by writ [24] is perfectly applicable to the Chancery Division, in practice, from the very nature of the actions dealt with, it is but rarely resorted to. There is, however, a corresponding procedure under Order 86,[25] only applicable to the Chancery Division, under which summary judgment may be obtained in any action commenced by a writ indorsed with a claim for specific performance of an agreement, whether or not in writing, for the sale, purchase or exchange of any real or personal [26] property, or for the grant or assignment of a lease of any property, or for rescission of such an agreement, or for the forfeiture or return of any deposit made under such an agreement.[27]

---

[21] Order 4, r. 1 (6).
[22] See Chapter 1, *ante.*
[23] See Chapter 4, *ante.*
[24] See Chapter 5, *ante.*
[25] Note that Order 14 does not apply to any action to which Order 86 applies: Order 14, r. 1 (3).
[26] *Woodlands* v. *Hinds* [1955] 1 W.L.R. 688.   [27] Order 86, r. 1.

It was formerly necessary (a) for the contract to have been in writing, (b) for the defendant to have appeared, and (c) for the relief actually sought to be that of specific performance. It was also confined to contracts for sale or purchase. None of these limitations now apply.[28]

Where there is no real defence to the action, the plaintiff may in such cases, on affidavit made by any person who can swear positively to the facts verifying the cause of action and stating that in his belief there is no defence, apply by summons for an order for the appropriate judgment. The summons must be accompanied by full minutes of the order to which the plaintiff considers himself to be entitled: we shall have something to say later about the minutes of Chancery Orders in general (*post*, p. 345): a copy of the affidavit in support and any exhibits must be served upon the defendant together with the summons, which is returnable not less than four clear days after service.[29]

Thereupon, unless the defendant by affidavit, by his own *viva voce* evidence, or otherwise, can satisfy the master (or judge, if either party or the master wishes the matter to be referred to him [29a]) that he has a good defence to the action on the merits, or discloses such facts as obviously entitle him to a hearing, judgment will be given for the plaintiff.[30] Leave to defend may be given unconditionally or subject to such terms as to giving security or time or mode of trial or otherwise as the master or judge may think fit, and where such leave is given, further directions must be given as to the further conduct of the action, as if the application for judgment was a summons for directions.[31]

Such procedure must not, of course, be resorted to where the plaintiff knows that there is in fact a substantial issue to be tried: if he does resort to it in such a case, his summons will be dismissed and in all probability with costs, which may be ordered

---

[28] *Woodlands* v. *Hinds* [1955] 1 W.L.R. 688 and Order 86, r. 1.

[29] Order 86, r. 2

[29a] See as to the general procedure before the master in the Chancery Division pp. 339, 340 *post*.

[30] Order 86, r. 4. Masters will not normally make summary orders for specific performance except (i) by consent or (ii) if the agreement sued on is a formal written contract and the defendant is in default of appearance or does not appear at the hearing or there is clearly no defence. In all other cases the matter will be adjourned to the judge. See Practice Direction [1970] 1 W.L.R. 762; [1970] 1 All E.R. 1183.

[31] Order 86, rr. 5, 6.

to be paid forthwith.[32]   Such procedure is, in any event, not available against the Crown.[33]

Pleadings

All the rules of pleading which we have already elaborated [34] apply just as much to the statement of claim and subsequent pleadings in a Chancery action as they do to one in the Queen's Bench Division.   On the whole, however, pleadings in the Chancery Division tend to be longer and more detailed.   The reason is not far to seek; for in general one or other of the parties will be seeking some equitable relief, or relying upon some equitable defence, which involves the exercise of the court's discretion. Such exercise always necessitates the consideration of the whole of the surrounding circumstances, many of which would not be material in an action at law.   Thus specific performance may be refused upon the ground of unilateral mistake [35]; or an injunction upon the ground of hardship [36]; or any remedy because the plaintiff does not come to the court " with clean hands." [37]   Both the plaintiff and the defendant must therefore plead very much more of the surrounding circumstances than is either necessary or desirable in a common law action.

The biggest difference lies, however, in the nature of the relief claimed, which is normally much more complicated than that sought at common law,[37a] and almost invariably involves, for the reasons we have already given, an account or an inquiry of some sort.   As equitable relief can always be moulded to suit the facts disclosed in any particular case, it often happens that precisely the right relief is not sought in the first instance; thus, to serve as a reminder to counsel, the heads of relief claimed invariably end up with the two heads of " Further or other relief " and " Costs."

---

[32] Order 86, r. 7.

[33] Order 77, r. 7 (1).   [34] See Chapters 6 to 9, *ante.*

[35] *Weston* v. *Bird* (1853) 2 W.R. 145.

[36] *Behrens* v. *Richards* [1905] 2 Ch. 614.   And consider the facts a careful pleader would have needed to plead in *Redland Bricks, Ltd.* v. *Morris* [1970] A.C. 652 to have obtained the relief which the House of Lords said might properly have been granted in that case (limited mandatory injunction).

[37] *Davis* v. *Symonds* (1787) 1 Cox Eq.Cas. 402.

[37a] See *e.g., Redland Bricks, Ltd.* v. *Morris, supra.*

Interlocutory Proceedings

The summons for directions,[38] discovery [39] (which originated in Courts of Equity), applications for particulars,[40] service of interrogatories,[41] and other cognate interlocutory matters follow the same course as in an action in the Queen's Bench Division, and any necessary applications to the court (other than those made by notice under the summons for directions) will be by summons. The master, whose powers are governed by different provisions from those governing a Queen's Bench Master's,[42] will deal with any such application in the first instance.[43] Indeed, subject to the right of any party to have an adjournment to the judge in person without any fresh summons for that purpose, the master has power to transact all such business and exercise all such authority and jurisdiction as may be transacted and exercised by a judge in chambers.[44] If an aggrieved party requests an adjournment to the judge in person,[45] the hearing before the judge is not in any sense an appeal,[46] but merely a continuation of the hearing of the summons in chambers. Such applications for the matter to be sent to the judge must, however, be made promptly: preferably then and there, or, after a short adjournment to consider the matter of proceeding further. In any event, if not made before the order has been drawn up, the right to go thus summarily to the judge will be lost,[47] and the party dissatisfied with the master's order will have to move a motion in open court within fourteen days to discharge the order.[48] Once again, however, this is really in the nature of a re-hearing, not an appeal, so that, for example, there is no shift of any *onus*.

Assuming that the application to adjourn to the judge has been made in time, the master will adjourn the summons either

---

[38] See Chapter 18.   [39] See Chapter 16.
[40] See Chapter 10.   [41] See Chapter 19.
[42] A Chancery Master's powers are in general regulated by Order 32 r. 14 (1) and the directions of the Chancery judges given thereunder (as to which see Practice Direction [1970] 1 W.L.R. 762; [1970] 1 All E.R. 1183); a Queen's Bench Master's by Order 32, r. 11.
[43] See Order 32, r. 14 (1).
[44] Order 32, r. 14 (1). The master's powers are subject to any limitations imposed by the direction of the Chancery judges, and the present practice is governed by directions summarised at [1970] 1 W.L.R. 762; [1970] 1 All E.R. 1183.
[45] *Re Agriculturist Cattle Insurance Co.* (1861) 3 De G.F. & J. 194.
[46] *Re Watts* (1883) 22 Ch.D. 5; and see also Practice Direction [1965] 1 W.L.R. 1259; [1965] 3 All E.R. 306.
[47] Practice Direction 1965, *supra*, See *London Permanent Benefit Building Society* v. *De Baer* [1968] 1 Ch. 321.
[48] *Holloway* v. *Cheston* (1881) 19 Ch.D. 516.

to come on as a Monday Morning Chamber Summons, if by reason of the lack of difficulty or shortness of the point it is capable of being disposed of summarily, or else, if not, into open court as a Procedure Summons.

Interlocutory Relief

It is principally in the matter of obtaining interlocutory relief that the form of a Chancery action before judgment differs from that in the Queen's Bench Division. Most interlocutory relief is obtained by means of a motion, made to the judge in open court, upon two days' notice.[49] This affords an extremely speedy way of obtaining urgent relief with a minimum of delay, and accordingly is universally followed in contentious matters.[49a] But where the parties are agreed upon the desirability of some form of interlocutory relief—for example, the appointment of a receiver—the application can as well be made by summons.

Motions normally should be, and usually are, made upon notice to the party against whom the order is sought, but where delay would be fatal (" I never wait till the axe is laid to the root of the tree," said Lord Eldon), motions may be made *ex parte*,[50] and, in extreme cases, before the issue of the writ.[51]

Normally, however, even in a case of extreme urgency there is still time to issue a writ, and the notice of motion can be served together with the writ.[52] The difficulty in the way of bringing a motion on notice is that it must be a two clear days' notice.[53] Accordingly, an application will be made to the appropriate judge of the group to which the action is assigned at the afternoon resumption of the sitting of the court *ex parte* for leave to serve short notice of motion.[53] This enables service to be effected in any case for the next motion day (at present Tuesdays and Fridays). The court is also often asked to grant an interim injunction over that day in order to preserve the *status quo* in the meantime. If granted, such an interim injunction is upon such terms as to costs, and subject to such undertaking, if any, as the court may think fit to impose. The party restrained is theoretically at liberty to move the court to

---

[49] Order 8, r. 2 (2).
[49a] Any relief obtainable by summons in the Chancery Division can equally well be obtained by motion: *Heywood* v. *B.D.C. Properties, Ltd.* [1964] 1 W.L.R. 971 *per* Harman L.J. at p. 974.
[50] Order 8 r. 2 (1).
[51] *Carr* v. *Morice* (1873) 16 Eq. 125.
[52] Order 8, r. 4.
[53] Order 8, r. 2 (2).

discharge any order so made,[54] but, from the nature of the situation, it is not often a right of which he can take advantage in time.

The notice of motion itself must be in writing,[55] addressed to the parties against whom the order is sought, and must state on its face on whose behalf it will be made. If leave to serve short notice of the motion has been obtained from the judge, this must be stated on its face,[55a] and a defendant is at liberty to disregard a short notice of motion which does not show that such leave has been obtained.[56] One notice of motion may include claims for several different species of relief and the separation of claims will be actively discouraged in costs.[57] It is impossible to list all the types of relief which can be obtained; the two commonest are injunctions and the appointment of receivers; but the validity of the writ can also be attacked in this way, the defendant may be made to bring money into court, an order of committal (usually for disobedience to an Order of the Court) may be obtained,[57a] and so on.

The notice of motion should be settled by counsel—the cost of this will always be allowed upon taxation[58]—and should specify the relief sought, whatever it is, in precise terms. Evidence upon the motion will in the first instance be given by affidavit,[59] usually drafted by counsel at the same time as the notice of motion; and, since the relief sought is interlocutory, evidence upon information and belief may be received, provided the sources and grounds thereof are given[60]—a qualification often forgotten. The court may, and in a proper case will, make an order for the attendance of the deponents for cross-examination.[59]

The notice of motion is served in the same way as any other document requiring service during the course of an action, unless its object is to commit the person to whom it is addressed, in which case personal service should be made if at all possible.[61] In such cases and in certain others also, copies of the affidavit evidence must be served together with the notice.[62] In general, as a matter of courtesy between solicitors, copies of any affidavit

---

[54] Order 8, r. 2 (1).   [55] Order 8, r. 3 (1).
[55a] Order 8, r. 3 (1).   [56] *Moggridge* v. *Thomas* (1847) 2 Coop.temp.Cott. 166.
[57] *Hawke* v. *Kemp* (1840) 3 Beav. 288.   [57a] Order 52, r. 4 (1).
[58] Practice Note [1929] W.N. 105.
[59] Order 38, r. 2 (3).   [60] Order 41, r. 5 (2).
[61] *D.* v. *A. & Co.* [1900] 1 Ch. 484; *Re a Solicitor* [1892] W.N. 22.
[62] Order 52, r. 4 (2).

proposed to be used on a motion will be automatically sent to the other side, though it is theoretically the duty of the solicitors to search the file for all affidavits filed up to the date named in the notice of motion for the original hearing. Express notice should be given of any affidavits filed thereafter.[63] In practice, it frequently happens, owing to the time factor, that affidavits have to be used before they are filed: and in such circumstances counsel has to give an undertaking on behalf of his client that this will be duly attended to.

Motions are heard in open court on the fixed motion days. They are not listed, but, subject to the absolute priority of a motion for the discharge of a prisoner, as touching the liberty of the subject,[64] are moved by counsel in order of seniority, each counsel having the right to move two opposed motions before the next senior is called upon to move.[65] Frequently, however, with the consent of the senior counsel making an opposed motion, unopposed motions are disposed of first. Here again, it frequently happens that a defendant appears by counsel before having entered an appearance. In such cases it is the duty of counsel to inform the court of this fact, and undertake on his behalf that appearance will be entered forthwith, and to see that his instructing solicitors understand that this must be done.[66]

Frequently it is necessary to adjourn the motion from time to time in order to enable the opposition to file evidence in answer, or for the party moving to file evidence in reply. Justice is usually served in such cases by putting the party moved against upon terms when adjourning, in order to preserve the *status quo*.[67] Usually all that is required is a suitable undertaking on his behalf; it rarely proves necessary actually to obtain an injunction, but if the party moved against is not willing to assist in preserving the position, whilst at the same time he desires time to answer the evidence (to which he is, of course, clearly entitled), the party moving may move *ex parte*, immediately after the motion has been stood over, for the same relief.

Often the hearing of the motion is, in simple cases, by consent treated as the trial of the action, and an immediate order in the

---

[63] *Clement* v. *Griffith* (1837) Coop.Pr.Cas. 470.
[64] *Ashton* v. *Shorrock* (1880) 29 W.R. 117.
[65] *Soltau* v. *De Held* (1851) 15 Jur. 1151.
[66] Practice Note [1934] W.N. 228.
[67] Order 8, r. 5.

usual form taken. Thus in, say, a partnership dispute, where one partner moves for a receiver and manager, the other partner may clearly realise that the partnership must be dissolved. Accordingly, in such a case by consent of both parties an immediate order for the dissolution of the partnership would be made, and the usual accounts and inquiries directed, thus saving any further pleadings; and so also in many others.

Often, again, the action is compromised on the hearing of the motion: and here, as at any other stage of the action, the proper form of Order (colloquially known as a " Tomlin Order," see Practice Note [1927] W.N. 290) is to stay all further proceedings upon the terms scheduled to the order except for the purpose of carrying such terms into effect, with liberty to apply for that purpose.

If, for any reason, the applicant does not desire to move his motion, he may save it, either by agreement or by mentioning it to the court. But, if it is not so moved or saved to be heard at the trial, it is treated as abandoned, and the costs thereof will be the respondent's in any event.[68]

Where, before the coming into force of the Rules of the Supreme Court (No. 3), 1959 [69] (The Supreme Court Costs Rules, 1959, now Order 62), the order finally made upon the motion was silent as to the incidence of costs, the well settled rules [70] were as follows:

(a) The party making a successful motion was entitled to his costs as costs in the cause; but the party opposing it was not entitled to his costs as costs in the cause.

(b) The party making a motion which failed was not entitled to his costs as costs in the cause; but the party opposing it was entitled to his costs as costs in the cause.

(c) If a motion was made by one party and not opposed by the other, the costs of both parties were costs in the cause.

It is thought that the same principles will continue to be followed but the costs will now have to be dealt with explicitly at some stage.[71]

---

[68] *Harrison* v. *Leutner* (1881) 16 Ch.D. 559.
[69] S.I. 1959 No. 1958 (L. 13).
[70] *Per* Leach V.-C. (1823) 1 Sim. & St. 357.
[71] Order 62, rr. 3 (1); 4 (1).

Motions for Judgment

So far we have been speaking of motions for interlocutory relief in the course of an action. In a large number of cases the mode of obtaining judgment is by motion for judgment; and the types of action in which this procedure is necessary [72] are in general precisely the types which find their natural forum in the Chancery Division. In addition, in this Division this is the correct procedure where judgment is sought upon admissions of fact.[73]

In contradistinction to interlocutory motions, such motions are set down in the cause book and are listed. If it is considered that they will not take more than ten minutes, then upon production of a certificate of counsel to this effect they will be marked as a short cause and come into the list on the next short cause day.[74] If this certificate cannot be given, they will come into the lists in their proper turn.

In all such cases the notice of motion for judgment must state the judge before whom the motion will be heard,[75] and must either set out the exact order sought in the body thereof,[76] or, more usually, be accompanied by, minutes of order. This is so even when all that is asked for is a " common form " order. It must also state that it has been marked short if this is the case.

The defendant must be given two clear days' notice of the motion.[77] If it is moved in default of his appearance, there is no necessity for the production of a certificate of non-appearance at the hearing, but one must be produced to the registrar before the order is drawn up.[78]

Trial and Judgment

Chancery actions are set down for trial at the office of the Chancery registrars.[79] At present there is only one witness list for both groups. As we have already seen, the place of trial will in all cases normally be in London, though in a proper case an order may be made for trial at assizes.[80]

---

[72] See *ante*, pp. 57–58.
[73] *Cook* v. *Heynes* [1884] W.N. 75.
[74] *Green* v. *Moore* (1891) 39 W.R. 421. At present this is Wednesday.
[75] *Jackson* v. *Webster* [1920] W.N. 295.
[76] *De Jongh* v. *Newman* (1887) 56 L.T. 180.
[77] Order 8, r. 2 (2).
[78] *Re Thomas* [1940] W.N. 319.
[79] Order 34, r. 3 (5).   [80] Order 33, rr. 1, 4 (3).

In all Chancery actions (other than those estimated to last not more than two days, for which a special procedure exists [80a]) a date is fixed for hearing quite automatically in accordance with the following procedure. Within ten days of setting an action down for trial the solicitors for each party must lodge with the cause clerk a certificate signed by the counsel who settled the pleadings stating the length of time which the trial is expected to occupy. Where practicable, there should be a single certificate signed by all the counsel concerned. Thereafter the action appears in what is known as Part I of the witness list twenty-three days after being set down, with a notification of the date fixed for the trial. This date is not earlier than three weeks from the date of the first appearance of the case in the lists. Thereafter the date so fixed will only be changed in exceptional circumstances, such as the illness or absence abroad of a party or an essential witness.[81]

The actual course of the trial will follow the course of a normal trial without a jury in the Queen's Bench Division. We have already noted the proper form of order if the action is compromised.[82] When the judge has given his judgment, either at the conclusion of the hearing or after *curia advisari vult* (commonly abbreviated to c.a.v. and meaning that the court takes time to consider its decision), the question often arises as to the precise form in which the result of that judgment should be embodied in an order. In such cases, junior counsel are often directed by the judge to settle and sign a minute, or settle and circulate a minute, in order that proper consideration can be given to the exact terms in which it should be framed. If, as not infrequently happens, junior counsel cannot agree, the action must be mentioned again to the judge on the form of the minutes, and he will then settle any items in dispute.

For, of course, the forms of Chancery judgments, following the form of the relief sought, differ greatly from the form of the normal Queen's Bench judgment. Indeed, whilst in the latter division the whole of the litigation is normally finished as soon as judgment is pronounced, in the usual Chancery action it has

---

[80a] Practice Notes [1966] 1 W.L.R. 1125; [1966] 2 All E.R. 720 and [1969] 1 W.L.R. 322; [1969] 1 All E.R. 787. Such cases go into what is known as Part II of the witness list.

[81] Practice Direction [1954] 1 W.L.R. 693; [1954] 1 All E.R. 946 and [1966] 1 W.L.R. 1125; [1966] 2 All E.R. 720.

[82] *Ante,* p. 343.

barely begun: the terms of the judgment have yet to be worked out.

The great storehouse of this branch of the law is the three volumes of *Seton on Judgments and Orders*,[82a] where precedents appropriate to many actions may be found. There is, however, a very great art in drawing such judgments and orders with precision, and the ultimate arbiters are the Chancery registrars,[83] who are finally responsible for the form of orders in all cases, though if the judge has directed the signature of a minute by counsel [84] their task is rendered comparatively simple. In other cases the procedure can be very complicated,[85] though the details are too specialised to mention here.

Working Out of the Judgment

It is impossible in the space at our disposal to follow up all the different possible types of action which can be brought, and consider all the various types of judgments and the working out which they necessitate. But the typical Chancery judgment directs an account, or an inquiry, or involves the settlement of some document, or the sale of some property. In all such cases the matter is referred back to chambers for the master to take the account, hold the inquiry, or do whatever else is necessary in order to make the judgment effective. The further consideration of the action by the judge is postponed until after the result of the proceedings before the master is known.

Let us assume that the order has directed some form of accounts and inquiries: the reader may usefully compare the course which the procedure would follow in the Queen's Bench Division (*ante*, pp. 48–50). In such a case, unless the judge has for some reason given the carriage of the order to some other party,[86] the plaintiff must within ten days of the same being passed and entered, bring it into chambers, and thereupon a

---

[82a] 7th ed., 1912. Atkin's *Court Forms*, 2nd ed., *current*, contains the more modern forms.

[83] The Chancery registrars perform the same duties as the associates in the Queen's Bench Division so far as proceedings in court are concerned, but their principal functions are to act as watchdogs in all matters of practice and to draw up all judgments and orders. A committee has recently reported upon the arrangement of business in Chancery chambers and the Chancery Registrars' office; no major reorganisation has been proposed.

[84] See Practice Direction (Minutes of Order) [1960] 1 W.L.R. 1168.

[85] See Practice Direction (Orders drawn by Chancery Registrars) [1961] 1 W.L.R. 47.

[86] Order 15, r. 17.

summons to proceed under the order will be issued. If the person having the carriage of the order does not bring it in within this time, any other party may.[87]

The summons to proceed must be served on all parties to the action. On the return of the summons, the master will decide whether all the persons interested in the result of the action are before the court or bound by the action. If not— for example, though *one* beneficiary under a trust may have an order against the trustees for the carrying of the trusts into execution, clearly *all* beneficiaries will be interested parties— he may give directions for the service of notice of the judgment or order on the interested parties. After such notice, they will be bound by the judgment as if they had originally been parties, and equally will be at liberty to move upon notice to set the judgment aside or apply by summons to vary or add to it.[88]

As soon as the master is satisfied that all the interested parties are accounted for, he will give directions as to the way in which each account or inquiry is to proceed, the evidence which he will require upon each, who is to attend the proceedings under each, and fix any necessary time limits for carrying out such directions. [89] Thus in an action for the administration of an estate, advertisements for creditors and beneficiaries will normally be directed,[90] and if the next-of-kin of the deceased are unknown, one of the parties may be directed to bring in a pedigree of the deceased; in an action for specific performance various accounts are normally directed and the accounting party will be directed to bring in a properly vouched account.

The course of the proceedings in front of the master follows as near as may be that of a motion in open court, except that in general it will be conducted by the parties' solicitors, and counsel will only be brought in on points of difficulty or perhaps of principle. Thus the evidence is all given by affidavit in the first instance. If during the course of taking the account or inquiry any point of principle arises upon which any party desires to challenge the master's ruling, he must take out a summons raising the point in question, and have that summons adjourned into court, normally as a Procedure Summons. If any point or matter other than on a question of principle arises,

[87] Order 44, r. 2.
[88] Order 44, r. 3.
[89] Order 44, r. 4.
[90] Order 44, r. 10.

any party may have the matter adjourned to the judge for his decision, normally as a Monday Morning Chamber Summons, without taking out a summons for this purpose.[91]   As before, such adjournment is in neither case an appeal, merely a re-hearing.

When the accounts and inquiries have finally been answered, the master makes his report of the result to the judge in the form of a certificate which is filed in the central office.[92]   At any time within eight clear days after filing any party who wishes may take out a summons to vary the certificate, or, if necessary, discharge it altogether.   If no summons is taken out within this time, the certificate will become binding on all parties,[93] though, even thereafter, it is possible to obtain its variation or discharge by the judge in person in a proper case.   The application may in such cases be made by summons or motion.[94]

Further Consideration

Apart from the further consideration of (i) debenture holders' actions, or for the distribution of an insolvent estate, or the estate of an intestate, (ii) an order made in chambers and (iii) when the order directs the further consideration to take place in chambers, all of which take place in chambers,[95] all further consideration of the action is heard in open court.   The action must be set down for further consideration in the cause book, and six days' notice given to all parties affected thereby.[96]   At the time of setting the action down certain papers must be left for the judge, including a copy of the writ, a copy of the pleadings (if any), a copy of the order reserving the further consideration, a copy of the master's certificate, and two copies of the minutes of the proposed order.[96a]   As the order will be based upon the master's certificate, there is no need to read the evidence upon which that certificate is founded, unless of course there is a summons to vary the certificate which for convenience has been adjourned to come on with such further consideration.   Exceptionally, however, it may be desired to read such evidence, or even to read fresh evidence, and in these cases notice must be given to the other parties of such intention.

[91] Order 44, r. 20.
[93] Order 44, r. 23.
[95] Order 44, r. 24.
[96a] Order 44, r. 25 (1).

[92] Order 44, rr. 21, 22.
[94] Order 44, r. 23 (3).
[96] Order 44, r. 25.

The order on further consideration will be drawn up by the registrar in the normal way.   If it, in its turn, as sometimes happens, directs further accounts and inquiries, or the settlement of documents, the further consideration of the action will again be adjourned and the procedure in chambers which we have already outlined will recommence in connection with such further inquiries.

Costs

The costs of and incidental to all proceedings in the Supreme Court, including the administration of estates and trusts, are in the discretion of the court or judge [96b] (see Chapter 26 for general principles on costs).   But it is expressly provided that where a person is or has been a party to any proceedings in the capacity of trustee, personal representative or mortgagee, he is to be entitled to his costs (so far as they are not recovered from or paid by any other person) out of the trust fund, estate, or the mortgaged property, as the case may be.   And the court can only deprive him of these costs on the ground that the person concerned has acted unreasonably, or, in the case of a trustee, or personal representative, has in substance acted for his own benefit rather than for the benefit of the fund.[97]   Moreover, on any taxation of costs of a trustee or personal representative which are payable out of the trust fund or estate, only those costs may be disallowed which should not have been incurred if the trustee or personal representative had properly discharged his duty to the trust estate.[98]   (And see *post*, pp. 404–405.)

Again, in a large number of cases, which in the space at our disposal it is impossible to particularise, a plaintiff or defendant may be entitled to his costs " on the common fund basis " (see *post*, p. 403).   The upshot is that in a Chancery action the question of costs nearly always merits separate consideration, and we have already seen that the result is that it is customary to claim " costs " expressly in the writ and statement of claim.

[96b] Order 62, r. 3 (2).
[97] Order 62, r. 6 (2).
[98] Order 62, r. 31 (2).

Execution and Appeals

The method of enforcement of an order, whether interlocutory or final, or a judgment, in the Chancery Division is the same as that of enforcing a judgment in the Queen's Bench Division [99]; and, except that many of the possible grounds of appeal will not apply, the procedure on appeal to the Court of Appeal and the House of Lords is also the same.[1]

---

[99] See Chapter 25.
[1] See Chapter 24.

CHAPTER 23

OTHER CAUSES AND MATTERS IN THE CHANCERY DIVISION

BEFORE discussing the other possible forms of proceedings in the Chancery Division, it will be as well to notice the way in which business is normally organised in the Division.[1] The system of the two groups has already been noted: at the moment there are four judges in each group. The senior judge of the division is called the " Vice-Chancellor." [1a] There are also two Patent judges whose functions are self-explanatory. In general, so many of the judges in each group as are from time to time required will sit during term time for the disposal of both parts [1b] of the witness list. One of the judges of each group will sit on Mondays to deal with Chamber Summonses; on Tuesdays to deal with Further Considerations, Motions, Petitions and Adjourned Summonses; on Wednesdays to deal with Short Causes and Adjourned Summonses; on Thursday to deal with Adjourned Summonses; and on Fridays to deal with Motions and Adjourned Summonses. As Adjourned Summonses (which are in the main Originating Summonses) are normally heard without witnesses, this judge is commonly said to be taking the non-witness list. A judge of Group A will sit on Mondays to deal with Companies Business; and a judge of Group B will sit at the same time to deal with Bankruptcy Business. These two will then deal with the witness or non-witness list as the pressure of business demands. There are also certain special matters dealt with in the Chancery Division which are assigned to a particular Group (*e.g.,* company business, which is assigned to Group A) or to a particular judge (*e.g.,* proceedings under the War Damage Act, 1943).

Of all these various matters, we have dealt with the witness list and incidental applications. We shall accordingly now deal with Originating Summonses, Originating Notices of Motion and

---

[1] Generally as to the distribution of business in the Division see the Chancery Division (Arrangement of Business) Order 1961 as amended by Practice Direction, May 21, 1962.

[1a] Administration of Justice Act, 1970, s. 5.

[1b] See p. 345, *ante.*

Petitions, prefacing such consideration with the observation that in many cases there is a choice of the method of approach to the court, although that most frequently encountered is the choice between an approach by Writ and Originating Summons. Provided the applicant is able to approach the court in the manner he has selected, the jurisdiction of the court is the same in all cases. The choice to be made therefore depends upon which is the less expensive mode of application; and a litigant who adopts a more expensive method may find himself deprived of part or the whole of his costs on this account.[2]

Illustration

Thus in *Re Johnson* (1885) 53 L.T. 136 a plaintiff who successfully challenged certain items in a trustee's account was deprived of the whole of his costs, since he could and should have proceeded by summons under what is now Order 85, r. 2, instead of by writ.

Originating Summonses

This is one of the four originating procedures.[3] Where an application is to be made to the High Court, or a judge, under any Act, then this is the appropriate originating procedure, unless under the Rules or the Act the application is expressly required or authorised to be commenced in some other fashion.[4] Except in the case of proceedings which must be commenced by writ,[5] either as a result of the provisions of the Rules or any Act, proceedings may be begun either by writ or originating summons as the plaintiff thinks fit.[6]

Where the main point at issue is one of construction of a document or statute, or is one of pure law, then this is the appropriate procedure. It is not, however, appropriate where there is likely to be any substantial dispute of fact. It is also inappropriate if the plaintiff thinks that the action is one in which summary judgment can be obtained.[7] (See *ante*, pp. 6–7.)

Before the recent revisions of the Rules of the Supreme Court there was no general right to proceed by originating summons; but its simplicity and speed had led to a great and growing number of rules and statutes prescribing this procedure. It is

---

[2] *Re Arnold* [1887] W.N. 122; *Re Johnson* (1885) 53 L.T. 136; *Curwen* v. *Milburn* (1889) 42 Ch.D. 424.
[3] Order 5, r. 1.
[4] Order 5, r. 3.
[5] See *ante*, p. 6.
[6] Order 5, r. 4 (1).   [7] Order 5, r. 4 (2).

352

now, as we have seen above, available generally. Its merits lie in the fact that there are no pleadings or (in general) witnesses, the question for decision being raised directly by the summons itself, and the evidence being given by affidavit, and that in general there is no necessity to resort to any interlocutory proceedings such as discovery.

There are no less than three different types of originating summons: the general form, to which an appearance must be entered; a special form in cases where an appearance need not be entered; and an *ex parte* form.[8] Where the application is made, as it usually is, under the provisions of an Act of Parliament, it must always be headed in the matter in which the question arises, and in the matter of that Act.[9]

Illustration

An application for the appointment of new trustees of the statutory trusts affecting the estate of an intestate would be headed:
" In the matter of the Statutory Trusts arising upon the intestacy of John Doe, deceased, by virtue of the Intestates' Estates Act, 1952,
and
In the matter of the Trustee Act, 1925."

The general form of summons will be used in all cases unless it is taken out under the provisions of an Act or order which provides that no appearance must be entered thereto,[9a] when it will be in the special form; and the *ex parte* form will be used only upon applications where there are no opponents (*e.g.*, an application by all the beneficiaries under a trust for the appointment of a new trustee upon the death of a sole trustee). The Rules, and if necessary the appropriate Act, must be consulted to see if there are any special rules as to parties. If not, the normal rules as to parties apply, including the usual rules as to parties under disability.[10] Where, however, as frequently happens, the rights *inter se* of beneficiaries under a trust or will are in question, as under the common " construction summons " under Order 85, r. 2, there can obviously be no following of the general rule that the trustees or executors

---

[8] See R.S.C. Appx. A, Forms Nos. 8, 9 (District Registry), 10 and 11.
[9] *Re Law* (1842) 4 Beav. 509.
[9a] See Order 57 (Divisional Court Proceedings): Order 89 (proceedings under Married Women's Property Act, 1882, s. 17): Order 94 (5) (proceedings under the Representation of the People Acts): and Order 106 (proceedings under the Solicitors Act, 1957).
[10] See Order 15 generally.

sufficiently represent the estate and the beneficial interests, and all the beneficiaries interested in the questions in debate must be made parties to the application, either as plaintiffs or defendants. This may result in very large numbers of parties, in which case they should all be lettered or numbered in order to assist the court.[11] If, however, the persons who have exactly the same interest are very numerous, or difficult or expensive to discover, a representation order appointing one of the class to represent the whole may sometimes be obtained.[12]

An originating summons is prepared in the same way as a writ, and must bear an indorsement of address. It must in the body thereof raise the exact questions which it is desired to have determined, ideally in such a form that the court will be able merely to pronounce for one of the alternatives propounded. The court will in general only determine the exact points raised, and will not determine anything not specifically raised unless the plaintiff or applicant agrees,[13] but in a suitable case it is now possible for a defendant to make a counterclaim.[13a]

The summons will be issued and sealed at the Central Office,[14] and at the same time it will be assigned to one or other of the two groups of judges.[15] If it is closely connected with a cause or matter already assigned to one group of judges, it must also, if practicable, be assigned to that group, and a note indorsed upon the summons by a master of that group or the registrar in whose district the earlier cause was begun will be sufficient authority for the assignment of the earlier group.[16]

Service of an originating summons must be personal service, to be effected in the same way as service of a writ,[17] including the time-limit for service.[18] Orders for substituted service,[19] or service out of the jurisdiction,[20] may be obtained in proper cases. Appearance, if required, should be entered in the normal way within eight days after service, for although appearance may be entered at any time prior to the hearing, no extra time will be allowed at any stage on account of such delay.[21]

---

[11] Practice Note [1948] W.N. 73.   [12] Order 15, r. 13.
[13] *Re Carter* (1893) 41 W.R. 140.
[13a] Order 28, r. 7.
[14] Order 7, r. 5 (2). In certain cases it can be issued out of a district registry (*ibid.*).
[15] Order 4, r. 1 (1).
[16] Order 4, r. 1 (6).   [17] Order 10, r. 5.
[18] Order 6, r. 8; Order 7, r. 6.   [19] Order 65, r. 4.
[20] Order 11, r. 9.   [21] Order 12, r. 6 (2).

As soon as all appearances have been entered—or sufficient time has elapsed to enable this to be done [22]—an appointment will be taken before the master to whom the matter has been assigned, and notice of this appointment, in the prescribed form, must be served upon the defendants or respondents, at the address given for service in the memorandum of appearance, at least four clear days before the return day. In the case of summonses to which no appearance is required to be entered, the return day is fixed on the issue of the summons and is stated in the body thereof: in the case of *ex parte* summonses it is fixed in chambers on the production of the original summons and is indorsed in the margin.[23]

Hearing of Summons

When the summons first comes before him the master will give all necessary directions as to the further conduct of the proceedings as he thinks best adapted to secure the just, expeditious [23a] and economical disposal thereof.[24] Normally, the initial directions will be as to the filing of evidence. Such evidence is invariably given by affidavit in the first instance, and an affidavit on behalf of the plaintiff or applicant supporting the summons is normally sworn and filed shortly after issue. Very often no further evidence will be required, but all the other parties will require to take advice on the point, and the master will accordingly adjourn the appointment from time to time until the evidence is completed. The master does not merely act as a ring-keeper, but may and frequently does require of his own motion the filing of further evidence which he thinks he will require (if the summons is one which he has power, and proposes, to deal with himself) [25] or which he thinks may be of assistance to the judge, and the joinder of additional parties. Or, indeed, he may at any time give any directions which could have been given if the proceedings had been commenced by writ and a summons for directions therein were before him.[26]

[22] Order 28, r. 2: Order 28 constitutes a complete code of the procedure upon originating summons.
[23] Order 28, r. 2 (2).
[23a] Special directions have been given as to the conduct of business in chambers with a view to avoiding delay: Practice Direction (Ch.D.). (Interlocutory Proceedings: Avoidance of Delay) [1970] 1 W.L.R. 95; [1970] 1 All E.R. 11.
[24] Order 28, r. 4 (2).
[25] For the practice, see [1970] 1 W.L.R. 762; [1970] 1 All E.R. 1183.
[26] Order 28, r. 4 (3); see Chapter 18.

Indeed, with the introduction of a choice, in many cases, of a writ or summons as the originating process, it may well turn out that a wrong choice was made: accordingly, the master can, if it appears that the proceedings ought properly to continue as if commenced by writ, so order.[26a] He may at the same time order that any affidavits shall stand as pleadings, and give (or refrain from giving) liberty to any of the parties to add thereto or apply for particulars thereof.[26a] This procedure applies even where the proceedings could not have been commenced by writ in the first place.[26b] Thereafter, of course, the action will continue along the lines noted in the preceding chapter.

Where no such order has been made, then when the evidence is complete, the master may himself deal with the matter if he has, under the rules and the direction of the judges from time to time,[27] power so to do. Some matters must be dealt with by the judge in person, for example, questions as to the construction of documents or questions of law [27a]; others can be dealt with by the master, for example, an order for general administration in a creditor's administration action where the estate appears to be insolvent. Even, however, when the master has the power, he may refuse to exercise it himself and send the matter to the judge. If, however, he can and does deal with it himself, any party has the same right to require him to send it to the judge in person as in the case of interlocutory proceedings in an action (*ante*, p. 340) and under the same conditions.

In a typical case, however, the master will adjourn the summons to the judge without first expressing any opinion upon the matter, and may either adjourn it into open court, when it will take its turn in the non-witness list (if it is to be heard without cross-examination of witnesses, or if it is adjourned " into court with witnesses, to go into the non-witness list," as happens when the proposed cross-examination will be short) Part I or Part II [27b] of the witness-list (if either party wishes to cross-examine the deponents at length) or into chambers.[27c] It is entirely in the discretion of the judge whether he hears any matter in court or chambers, although he will normally adhere to the well settled

---

[26a] Order 28, r. 8.
[26b] Order 28, r. 8 (3).
[27] Order 32, r. 14; see note 30, p. 337, *ante*.
[27a] Order 32, r. 14 (2).
[27b] See p. 345, *ante*.
[27c] See Practice Direction [1969] 1 W.L.R. 1257; [1969] 2 All E.R. 1132.

practice of the court as to the matters suitable for hearing in chambers, basically those which raise questions of pure administration. Matters can be adjourned if necessary, from court to chambers and vice versa.[28] If the summons is adjourned into chambers, and there are no unusual or difficult features in the case, and there is unlikely to be any strenuous opposition, the master will place it in the Monday morning list of Chamber Summonses. But if the matter is lengthy, or difficult, or there will be serious opposition, though it still ought to be considered in chambers (for example, an application by trustees under section 57 of the Trustee Act, 1925, for permission to carry out a beneficial transaction not authorised by the terms of their trust), the matter cannot be disposed of on a Monday morning, but the parties must apply to the appropriate judge at any afternoon sitting of the court to fix a special time for the hearing of the matter.

It will be apparent from this sketch of the procedure that it is primarily designed to deal with questions of law or discretion arising upon facts substantially not in dispute, and, indeed, where there is any choice in the matter, it is wrong to bring proceedings by originating summons if it is known that the facts are disputed.[29] But, as we have already noticed, sometimes the procedure is obligatory even in cases where there may be very substantial disputes of fact; for example, in a case under the Inheritance (Family Provision) Act, 1938,[30] the question whether the testator has made reasonable provision for his dependants may be bitterly fought by those who inherit under his will. The evidence in chief is still given in such cases by affidavit; but upon the request of any opposite party the deponents will be ordered to attend for cross-examination, and the master will adjourn the summons into court to be heard with witnesses, and in this case (unless the oral evidence would not seriously add to the length of the hearing) it will take its place in the appropriate part of the Witness List. [31]

Whilst it also follows from what we have above stated that interlocutory applications are not normal in proceedings commenced by originating summons, yet, if necessary, applications can

---

[28] Order 32, r. 18.
[29] *Re Powers* (1885) 30 Ch.D. 291; Order 5, r. 4 (2).
[30] Order 99.
[31] Practice Direction of October 22, 1951; 101 L.Jo. 696.

be made for the appointment of receivers,[32] and for discovery,[33] or for any other interlocutory relief which could be granted in an action commenced by writ.

Further, the summons may be amended like a writ, but not so as to include a claim to a right which was not in existence at the date when it was issued.[34]

There are special Chancery rules as to the costs. In general, the costs of the proceedings are, like the costs of any other proceedings, in the discretion of the court or judge.[35] But where the summons is not hostile in spirit (*e.g.*, a summons to determine the true construction of an obscure will or trust instrument) and there is a common fund (residuary estate, trust fund, etc.), the general rule is that the costs, on the common fund or trustee basis, as the case may be, of all proper parties,[36] whether successful or unsuccessful in the issue, will come out of such common fund in a due course of administration.[36a] But all parties having a common interest should arrange for their joint representation, as unless the circumstances justify separate representation only one set of costs of the hearing may be allowed.[37] In cases where the litigation is hostile in spirit, however, costs, as between party and party, normally follow the event.[38]

Appeals

If the matter has been disposed of in chambers, the judge's reasons for his decision are not fully available for consideration by the Court of Appeal, which is a disadvantage if it desired to take the matter further. Accordingly, there is no direct right of appeal to the Court of Appeal (save in a few special cases) from a decision in chambers without leave of the judge or of the Court of Appeal itself. If such leave cannot be obtained, then an application may be made by motion in open court within fourteen days of the Order for its discharge. If the application is refused, it may be appealed without leave.[39]

---

[32] *Re Francke* (1888) 57 L.J.Ch. 437.
[33] See Order 24, r. 3.
[34] *Coutts & Co.* v. *Duntroon Investment Corpn. Ltd.* [1958] 1 W.L.R. 116.
[35] Order 62, r. 3 (2).
[36] But see *Re Preston, Raby* v. *Port of Hull Society's Sailors' Orphans' Home* [1951] 2 All E.R. 421.
[36a] See Order 62, r. 28 (5).
[37] Order 85, r. 3; *Re Amory* [1951] 2 All E.R. 947n.
[38] *Re Buckton* [1907] 2 Ch. 406.
[39] Order 58, r. 7. See *Holloway* v. *Cheston* (1881) 19 Ch.D. 516.

Originating Notices of Motion

Proceedings may be commenced by Originating Notice of Motion if, but only if, this procedure is permitted by the Rules or a statute.[40] It is in fact prescribed by the Rules [41] for many applications under the Companies Act, 1948, *e.g.*, an application under section 165 of that Act for an order that the affairs of the company ought to be investigated. Such a motion may or may not be *ex parte*. It will be intituled, like an originating summons, in the matter in which the question arises, and in the matter of the Act under which the application is made.[42] It must be prepared in the normal way as for an ordinary motion,[43] and must ask for the appropriate relief.[44]

When prepared, it must be taken to the Writ department, where assignment to the appropriate group of judges will be made, and where it will be issued.[45] Once issued, it must be indorsed and served in the same way as a writ of summons. Substituted service or service out of the jurisdiction may be ordered in a proper case.[46] The rule or statute must be consulted as to the length of notice required: in default of any such provision it is two clear days.[47] No appearance is required to be entered by the respondent to an originating notice of motion.

The motion will be heard in open court on the day named in the notice, which must be one of the usual motion days. It will then be moved by counsel as in the case of any other motion, in the appropriate order of seniority.[48] Evidence will normally be given by affidavit, and the respondents will be entitled to have the motion adjourned in the first instance in order to enable them to put in evidence in reply. The court can if necessary order the attendance of the deponents for cross-examination.

[40] Order 5, r. 5.
[41] See also *e.g.*, Order 53, r. 3.
[42] See note 9, *ante*, p. 353.
[43] See Chapter 22.
[44] Order 8, r. 3 (2).
[45] Order 4, r. 1.
[46] Order 65, r. 4; Order 11, r. 9; Order 73, r. 7.
[47] Order 8, r. 2 (2).
[48] See Chapter 22.

Petitions

A petition is a written application, in the nature of a pleading, setting out a party's case in detail and made in open court. Formerly it might or might not have been an originating process; now it is originating only.[49] It is only available where the Rules or a statute expressly prescribe this method of procedure.[50]

There are no prescribed forms which a petition should follow, but the form is in fact well settled by long usage.[51] The title follows that of an originating summons or notice of motion. It is addressed to Her Majesty's High Court of Justice, and states by whom it is presented, and his address. It then sets out the facts upon which the petitioner relies in consecutively numbered paragraphs in the manner of a statement of claim. Where, as was formerly the case, petitions were presented for the payment of moneys out of court, the precise terms of the document under which the money was claimed had to be set out *verbatim* in inverted commas so that the attention of the court was specifically directed thereto.[52] The principle still applies.

The petition then concludes with a prayer asking for the relief to which the petitioner considers himself entitled, if necessary in the alternative, and also asking for such other order as the court thinks fit to make. It concludes with the words " And your petitioner will ever pray, etc.," the abbreviation being found thus in even the oldest books of Chancery precedents.

The persons who are to be the respondents to the petition and upon whom it will be necessary to serve it, are set out in a footnote. If it is not intended to serve it on anybody—as, for example, in the case of the presentation by a company of a petition to wind itself up—this must also be stated.[53] All the normal rules as to parties apply, and the petitioner must make respondents to his petition all the persons who will be affected by the order he wishes to have made.

Subject to any special provisions under the rules or any Act, a petition must be presented by leaving it at the Chancery Registrars' office,[54] or in the district registries of Liverpool or

---

[49] Order 9, r. 5.
[50] Order 5, r. 5.
[51] See Precedent No. 86.
[52] Note " Petitions " [1896] W.N. 203, 211.
[53] Order 9, r. 2 (2).
[54] Order 9, r. 3 (2).

Manchester, but not elsewhere.[55] The usual assignment to a group will then take place, and it will also then be given a reference number.[56]

All petitions require answering. This is a purely formal matter, and consists in the chief registrar endorsing upon the petition an order fixing a day for the hearing of the petition.[57]

Except with special leave, service must be effected at least seven clear days before the day fixed for the hearing.[58] It must be served as near as possible in the same way as a writ, substituted service [59] and service out of the jurisdiction [60] being permitted in proper cases.

A respondent to a petition does not need to enter an appearance. He may simply appear on the hearing, which is normally on a Tuesday, or, in the case of a petition under the provisions of the Companies Act, 1948, on a Monday morning. Petitions are listed and taken in rotation, unopposed petitions normally being taken first, although (apart from the Companies Courts) there are now very few petitions presented. It must be borne in mind that a petition is as much a litigious procedure as any other, and that accordingly the petitioner can properly be considered a plaintiff for the purposes of interrogatories, and discovery can be had if requisite.[61] Applications will in such cases be made by summons before the appropriate master.

The evidence follows what we have already seen to be the normal Chancery procedure on originating applications, and is usually given by affidavit, though attendance for cross-examination can be had if desired.

The hearing of a petition may be adjourned from time to time either to complete the evidence, or to allow the respondent to put in his evidence.[62] If, on any adjournment, the petitioner is not represented, the respondents present are entitled to have the petition dismissed with costs against the petitioner. Apart from this, the costs normally follow the event in a hostile petition.

[55] Order 9, r. 3 (1).
[56] Order 9, r. 1; Order 4.
[57] Order 9, r. 4.
[58] Order 9, r. 4 (2).
[59] Order 6, r. 4.
[60] Order 11, r. 9 (3).
[61] *Re Credit Co.* (1879) 11 Ch.D. 256.
[62] Order 8, r. 5.

Where the order in the petition is an interlocutory order the time for appealing is fourteen days; in the case of orders for the winding up of a company or in bankruptcy, twenty-one days; and in all other cases six weeks.[63] An appeal from an order winding up a company (which is always made on petition) in view of the commercial urgency of the matter will be put into the interlocutory list of appeals,[64] although there is hardly anything so final as an order winding up a limited liability company.

---

[63] Order 59, r. 4.
[64] *Re Reliance Properties, Ltd.* [1951] 2 All E.R. 327n.

CHAPTER 24

APPEALS

UNDER English law a litigant has no inherent right to appeal
against the decision of any tribunal which has found against him;
such a right must always be sought in the provisions of some
statute.[1]

Jurisdiction

In ordinary litigation a right to appeal to the Court of Appeal
against the whole or any part of any judgment or order [2] of the
High Court is, subject as otherwise provided, conferred by the
Judicature Act, 1925, s. 27. The Court of Appeal also has jurisdiction to hear motions for a new trial after trial by jury (s. 30).

An appeal lies direct to the House of Lords from the High
Court [2a] on a point of law of general public importance. The right
to do so is founded in the Appellate Jurisdiction Act, 1876, s. 4,
as extended by section 14 of the Administration of Justice Act,
1969, and is subject to certain conditions (see *post*, p. 367).

Appeals from county courts lie on points of law,[3] provided
that they were taken below,[4] and in some cases, where a substantial amount is at stake, on questions of fact,[5] and are heard
by the Court of Appeal.[6] So are appeals from other inferior
courts of record, where there is a special provision to that effect
(see Judicature Act, 1925, ss. 28, 208). All appeals from the
Mayor's and City of London Court lie to the Court of Appeal;
they are treated as county court appeals except in true

---

[1] *Att.-Gen.* v. *Sillem* (1864) 10 H.L.C. 704. As to the old procedure by writ
of error or bill of exceptions from inferior courts, see *Darlow* v. *Shuttleworth*
[1902] 1 K.B. 721.

[2] See *Lake* v. *Lake* [1955] P. 336.

[2a] By what is sometimes called the "leap-frog" procedure, introduced for the
first time on January 1, 1970 (Administration of Justice Act, 1969 (Commencement No. 1) Order, 1969, S.I. No. 1607).

[3] County Courts Act, 1959, s. 108. The adequacy of damages awarded is a
question of fact unless it can be shown that the county court judge misdirected himself as to the factors to be taken into consideration (*Shave* v.
J. W. Lees (Brewers), Ltd. [1954] 1 W.L.R. 1300).

[4] *United Dominions Trust, Ltd.* v. *Bycroft* [1954] 1 W.L.R. 1345.

[5] See County Courts Act, 1959, s. 109, and *Leslie* v. *Liverpool Corpn.* [1960]
1 W.L.R. 1.

[6] Administration of Justice (Appeals) Act, 1934, s. 2.

" Mayor's Court " cases where the High Court procedure has been adopted (Administration of Justice (Miscellaneous Provisions) Act, 1938, s. 15. See also County Courts Act, 1959, s. 197, and City of London (Courts) Act, 1964, ss. 10, 19, 20).

There is a statutory right to require a case to be stated by the Lands Tribunal and certain other tribunals for determination by the Court of Appeal and these appeals are governed by Order 61.[7] Appeals lie on law from the Restrictive Practices Court to the Court of Appeal under the Restrictive Trade Practices Act, 1956, and are governed by Order 60. Appeals may also be brought to the High Court (not the Court of Appeal) by way of case stated from certain decisions of Ministers of the Crown, government departments and tribunals, under various enactments, and from quarter sessions and justices: all these are dealt with by a Divisional Court (*post*, pp. 381–382) under Order 56.

In all cases of contempt of court a defendant may appeal against any punitive order made, and so also may any person applying for committal. Such appeals are heard by a Divisional Court or the Court of Appeal, broadly speaking according to the general rule governing appeals from the court in question, or by the House of Lords (see Administration of Justice Act, 1960, s. 13). The procedure on such an appeal is governed by Order 59, r. 20.

An appeal lies to the Court of Appeal from the decision of an official referee (a) on a point of law; (b) on a question of fact relevant to a charge of fraud or breach of professional duty; (c) in certain cases where he has ordered or refused to order committal; and in no other circumstances.[8] But where a matter has been referred to him for inquiry and report, the High Court may vary his report or remit it for further consideration.[9]

While most appeals from Queen's Bench masters go to a judge in chambers [10] some lie direct to the Court of Appeal. This is so when he has given a final, not interlocutory, judgment, order or decision on the trial of an action, issue or reference, including on, for instance: an assessment of damages under Order 37 or otherwise; or on the hearing or determination of any interpleader or garnishee matter or issue [10] or of an application under Order 84, r. 3, in a hire-

---

[7] And see Practice Direction [1956] 1 W.L.R. 1112.
[8] Administration of Justice Act, 1956, s. 15 (2); Ord. 58, r. 5.
[9] Ord. 36, r. 3.   [10] See *post*, pp. 366–367.

purchase case.[10a] To the Court of Appeal go also appeals in matters tried under Order 36 by a Chancery master or a special referee.[10b]

Subject to the following limitations and except where the Divisional Court has jurisdiction (*post*, pp. 381–382), an appeal lies to the Court of Appeal from any decision of a judge in chambers in the Queen's Bench Division.[12] Every appeal from a judge in matters of practice and procedure [13] goes to the Court of Appeal (Judicature Act, 1925, s. 31 (3)).

IN SOME CASES NO APPEAL TO THE COURT OF APPEAL LIES AT ALL—

(a) from any judgment of the High Court in any criminal cause or matter [14] (Judicature Act, 1925, s. 31 (1) (*a*));

(b) from a judgment of the High Court in civil proceedings after leave to appeal direct to the House of Lords has been granted by the House (Administration of Justice Act, 1969, s. 13 (2) (*a*));

(c) from an order extending time for appeal (Judicature Act, 1925, s. 31 (1) (*b*));

(d) from an order of a judge *giving* unconditional leave to defend an action (*ibid.* s. 31 (1) (*c*)) [15];

(e) where any statute provides that there shall be no appeal, except with the leave of some specified person, and he refuses to give leave [16];

(f) from any decision of the High Court or a judge thereof declared by statute to be final (*ibid.* s. 31 (1) (*d*)) [17];

(g) from the decision of an official referee, except as stated *ante*, p. 364 (Order 58, r. 5);

10a Ord. 58, r. 2. 10b Ord. 58, rr. 3, 6.

12 Ord. 58, r. 7. As to the Chancery Division, see *ante*, p. 358.

13 That is to say, decisions of an " adjective " as opposed to a " substantive " nature in connection with a cause or matter in the High Court. See in particular *Lever Brothers, Ltd.* v. *Kneale* [1937] 2 K.B. 87; *Re Shoesmith* [1938] 2 K.B. 637.

14 These words have been construed very comprehensively. No appeal is allowed on " any question raised in or with regard to proceedings, the subject-matter of which is criminal, at whatever stage of the proceedings the question arises." (*Per* Lord Esher M.R. in *Ex p. Woodhall* (1888) 20 Q.B.D. at p. 836.) And the subject-matter is deemed to be criminal whenever the proceedings *may* end in the imprisonment of the defendant (*Seaman* v. *Burley* [1896] 2 Q.B. 344), unless a statute has expressly declared the money sought to be recovered by such proceedings to be " a civil debt." (*Southwark and Vauxhall Water Co.* v. *Hampton U.D.C.* [1899] 1 Q.B. 273.) An appeal lies to the Criminal Division of the Court of Appeal against a conviction on indictment.

15 See *Commissioners of Customs and Excise* v. *Anco Plant & Machinery Co., Ltd.* [1956] 1 W.L.R. 1048.

16 *Lane* v. *Esdaile* [1891] A.C. 210; *Ex p. Stevenson* [1892] 1 Q.B. 394, 609.

17 And see *Re Northwood and L.C.C.* [1927] W.N. 144.

(h) where the parties have by agreement excluded their right of appeal, and such agreement is embodied in an order (see Order 25, r. 5; *Re Hull and County Bank*, 13 Ch.D. 261). In county court actions the parties may validly exclude their right of appeal by a written agreement without any order (County Courts Act, 1959, s. 111);

(i) where a party takes the benefit of a judgment, he cannot afterwards be heard to appeal against it.[18]

IN SOME CASES AN APPEAL TO THE COURT OF APPEAL LIES ONLY IF LEAVE IS GIVEN. Where such leave may be given either by the court below or by the Court of Appeal, application should be made in the first instance to the court below (Order 59, r. 14 (4)). If leave is there refused, an application to the Court of Appeal for leave should be made *ex parte* in the first instance (unless the time for appeal has expired). (Rule 14 (2)). The appeals referred to are:

(a) from the determination by a Divisional Court of any appeal to the High Court (Judicature Act, 1925, s. 31 (1) (*f*)). Leave may be given by the Divisional Court or by the Court of Appeal;

(b) from an order of the High Court or a judge thereof (i) made with the consent of the parties, or (ii) as to costs only which by law are left to the discretion of the court (*ibid.* s. 31 (1) (*h*)). Leave of the court or judge making the order is necessary;

(c) in the Chancery and Probate, Divorce and Admiralty Divisions from any decision of a judge in chambers unless an application to set it aside has been unsuccessfully made to the judge sitting in court (Order 58, r. 7). Leave of the judge or of the Court of Appeal is necessary;

(d) from an interlocutory [19] order or judgment of a judge,

---

[18] *Harris* v. *Minister of Munitions* (1921) 124 L.T. 489; *Evans* v. *Monmouthshire, etc., Indemnity Society* (1937) 30 B.W.C.C. 196; but see *Evans* v. *Bartlam* [1937] A.C. 473.

[19] The decisions as to whether any given order is interlocutory or final are numerous and conflicting. The test sometimes applied is whether the application is of such a nature that whatever order is made thereon it must finally dispose of the matter in dispute; another test is whether the order as made finally disposes of the rights of the parties (see *Egerton* v. *Shirley* [1945] 1 K.B. 107). On the latter principle an order giving leave to enter judgment under Order 14 has been held to be final (*ibid.*). But an order dismissing an action under Order 18, r. 19 (1) (*a*), or for want of prosecution, is treated as interlocutory (*Hunt* v. *Allied Bakeries, Ltd.* [1956] 1 W.L.R. 1326), possibly because a fresh action might be brought.

with certain exceptions (see *post*, p. 368) (*ibid.* s. 31 (1) (*i*)). Leave may be given by the judge or by the Court of Appeal;

(e) from the summary decision of a judge against a claimant in an interpleader matter (Order 58, r. 8 (1)). Leave may be given by the judge or by the Court of Appeal;

(f) from the decision of a county court judge in most actions —other than actions for the recovery of land or where an injunction is claimed—where the claim is under £20 (County Courts Act, 1959, s. 108). Leave of the county court judge is necessary.

IN ONE CASE AN APPEAL LIES ONLY IF A CERTIFICATE *and* LEAVE IS GIVEN. If certain conditions are satisfied a High Court judge may grant a certificate (with the consent of all parties) at the conclusion of the trial giving, as it were, leave to apply for leave to appeal direct to the House of Lords (Administration of Justice Act, 1969, s. 12). Armed with such certificate any party may then apply [19a] to the House of Lords for leave to appeal (*ibid.* s. 13 (1)). The judgment to be appealed *must* involve a point of law of general public importance *either* relating to the construction of a statute or statutory instrument *or* being one which the High Court felt itself bound by precedent to follow (*ibid.* s. 13 (3)) *and* the trial judge must be satisfied that a sufficient case for a direct appeal has been made out so as to justify the grant of his certificate. In this way an appeal lies not only from the decision of a High Court judge but also from a decision of the Divisional Court in any case where there would otherwise be a right to go to the Court of Appeal first. There is no appeal against the grant or refusal of a certificate (*ibid.* s. 12 (5)) but in the event of refusal the disappointed party may still go to the Court of Appeal in the customary way.

Interlocutory Appeals

From any order made by a master or district registrar (except in the cases mentioned *ante*, at p. 364) an appeal lies as of right to the judge in chambers (Order 58, r. 1). The appeal is brought by notice in writing given within five days [20] to attend before the judge without a fresh summons (*ibid.*). The master's order need not be drawn up. The judge is in no way fettered by

[19a] Applications are determined without a hearing (s. 13 (3)) and may be dealt with by a committee of the House consisting of three or more Lords of Appeal (s.13 (4)). For the detailed procedure see Practice Note [1970] 1 W.L.R. 97.
[20] Seven days on appeal from a district registrar (Order 58, r. 4).

any exercise of discretion on the part of the master.[21]   As we have seen, an appeal lies from the judge to the Court of Appeal —but as a rule only by leave of the judge or the Court of Appeal. In the following cases, among others, leave is unnecessary:

(a) where the liberty of the subject or the custody of minors is concerned (Judicature Act, 1925, s. 31 (1) (*i*));

(b) where an injunction or the appointment of a receiver is granted or refused (*ibid.*);

(c) where unconditional leave to defend an action has been *refused (ibid.* s. 31 (2)).[21a]

A solicitor acting for an assisted person under the Legal Aid and Advice Act, 1949, before applying for leave to appeal in an interlocutory matter, must, unless the legal aid certificate already provides for it, obtain the authority of the area committee (Reg. 15 (3)).

An appeal from an interlocutory judgment or order [22] may be heard by two judges. (Judicature Act, 1925, s. 68 (1).) It must be brought within the prescribed time (see *post*, p. 370).

Procedure

Every appeal to the Court of Appeal [23] from a final judgment or order [24] must be heard, except by consent of all parties, by not less than three judges of the Court of Appeal (Judicature Act, 1925, s. 68). The procedure is mainly governed by Order 59,[25] and, except in the case of an application for a new trial or merely to set aside a verdict, finding or judgment, is by way of rehearing (rr. 2, 3). [25a]

Notice of appeal.—The appeal is brought by notice of motion,[25b] hereafter referred to as a " notice of appeal," which may be given in respect of the whole or any specified part of the judgment appealed from. It must specify the grounds of the appeal and the

---

[21] *Evans* v. *Bartlam* [1937] A.C. at p. 478.
[21a] Nor under this subsection is leave required by either party to appeal against an order granting leave to defend on conditions. (*Gordon* v. *Cradock* [1964] 1 Q.B. 503.)
[22] See *ante*, p. 366n.
[23] As to Divisional Courts, see *post*, pp. 381–382.
[24] See *ante*, p. 366n.
[25] Special rules apply to appeals in matrimonial causes, patent actions, from county courts and from the Lands Tribunal and certain other tribunals, as to which, except where specially noted hereafter, see Order 59, rr. 16–20 and Order 61.   [25a] And see *Curwen* v. *James* [1963] 1 W.L.R. 748.
[25b] To which Order 8 applies (Order 59, r. 14 (1)).

precise form of the order [26] which the appellant proposes to ask the Court of Appeal to make; and except with the leave of the Court of Appeal the appellant will not be entitled to rely (though the court itself may act [27]) upon any grounds or to apply for any relief not specified in the notice (r. 3 (3)). It may, however, be amended without leave by supplementary notice [28] served within a week after the day on which the appeal is first listed as one of those " next to be heard," or with leave at any time (r. 7). One of the objects is " to eliminate points not intended to be put in issue and so to save expense in copying documents and preparing the case. The grounds of appeal are intended to be shortly and simply stated, but not to be set out in detail or at great length. The broad issues to be raised should be stated and not the detailed reasons in support of them." [29] (See Precedent No. 105.) But it is not enough for the appellant merely to say, for example, that he complains of " misdirection "; the notice must state how the jury were misdirected.[30] The notice must further specify the list of appeals in which the appellant proposes to apply to set down the appeal (*e.g.*, Queen's Bench Division Final and New Trial List; Chancery Division Interlocutory List; County Courts Final and New Trial List *or* Interlocutory List; etc.) (r. 3 (4)). A notice may be struck out if it is plain that there is no right of appeal in the circumstances.[30a]

The title of the notice in the Court of Appeal (unlike the House of Lords) remains the same as in the court of trial. The parties continue to be called in the notice " Plaintiff " and " Defendant," although the usual practice at the hearing is to call the party appealing the "Appellant " and his opponent the " Respondent."

Cross-appeal.—If a respondent desires to contend on the hearing of the appeal that the decision of the court below should be varied, either in any event or in the event of the appeal being allowed in whole or in part, he need not enter a separate substantive motion of his own but must, within twenty-one days (or in an interlocutory appeal within seven days) after being

---

[26] Including any amendment of the pleadings (*G. L. Baker Ltd.* v. *Medway Building & Supplies Ltd.* [1958] 1 W.L.R. 1216, 1242).

[27] Rule 10 (4).

[28] Which may be in the form of a letter (*Sansom* v. *Sansom* [1956] 1 W.L.R. 945).

[29] *Ibid.*

[30] *Murfett* v. *Smith* (1887) 12 P.D. 116; *Taylor* v. *John Summers & Sons Ltd.* [1957] 1 W.L.R. 1182.

[30a] *Aviagents, Ltd.* v. *Balstravest Investments Ltd.* [1966] 1 W.L.R. 150.

served with notice of appeal serve on the appellant and any other parties directly affected a notice called a " respondent's notice " (r. 6). This he must also do if he contends that the decision should be affirmed on grounds other than those relied on by the court below. The notice must specify the grounds of his contention and, if he asks for a variation, the precise form of the order for which he proposes to ask. In default of notice he will not be entitled to raise any such contentions without leave.[30b] The notice may be amended in like manner as a notice of appeal. Two copies must be furnished to the appropriate registrar within two days after service.

Service of notice.—A notice of appeal must be served on all parties to the proceedings in the court below who are directly affected by the appeal (r. 3 (5)). The Court of Appeal may, however, direct that it be served on any other person, whether a party or not (r. 8). In that event the appeal may, if necessary, be adjourned and an order may be made as though the person served had originally been a party. In the case of a county court appeal, the notice must also be served on the county court registrar (r. 19).

Any party served with notice of appeal is prima facie entitled to attend the hearing, and, if the appeal fails, to be paid his costs (subject to the discretion of the court under Order 62, r. 4 (2)), but not where his attendance is obviously unnecessary or useless.[31]

Time for appeal.—Except where otherwise stated the following times run from the date on which the judgment or order of the court below was signed, entered or otherwise perfected (Order 59, r. 4). Notice of appeal must be served in the case of an appeal:

(a) from an interlocutory order (except in winding-up or bankruptcy matters), from a judgment or order under Orders 14 and 86, and in an interpleader or garnishee matter or issue, within fourteen days;

(b) in a winding-up or bankruptcy matter, within twenty-one days;

[30b] See, for example, *Thomas* v. *Marconi's Wireless Telegraph Co. Ltd.* [1965] 1 W.L.R. 850.

[31] *Ex p. Webster* (1882) 22 Ch.D. 136; *Re New Callao* (1882) *ibid.* 484.

(c) from a county court, within six weeks [31a] from the date of the judgment or order of the county court (r. 19 (3));

(d) against a decree nisi of divorce or nullity, within six weeks from the date on which the decree was pronounced;

(e) from the Appeal Tribunal under section 85 of the Patents Act, 1949, six weeks from the date of the decision or such further time as the tribunal may allow;

(f) from a decision in respect of which a certificate has been granted under section 12 of the Administration of Justice Act, 1969, from the end of the time during which (in accordance with section 13 (5) of that Act) no appeal lies to the Court of Appeal; and

(g) in any other case, within six weeks.

(As to appeals to a Divisional Court, see *post*, pp. 381–382.)

(As to appeals to the House of Lords, see *post*, p. 383.)

Where an *ex parte* application has been refused by the court below, it may be renewed to the Court of Appeal within seven days (r. 14 (3)).

In proper cases [32] the time may be extended by the Court of Appeal at any time under Order 3, r. 5. Except in case (d) it may be extended by the court below if application is made before the time expires (Order 59, r. 15), and this is the course which should normally be adopted (r. 14 (4)).

Setting down.—Within seven days after service of the notice of appeal, or such further time as may be allowed by the registrar, the appellant must apply to set down the appeal (r. 5). In ordinary cases this is done in the office of the chief registrar of the Chancery Division, but other officers are appointed for particular appeals (see r. 5 (5)). The judgment or order appealed from, or an office copy, must be produced and a copy of it must be left there together with two copies of the notice of appeal, one of which must bear the appropriate stamp (ordinarily £5, but £2 in interlocutory and certain other appeals), and the other must be indorsed with the date on which the notice was served. The appeal will then be set down in its proper list and will come on to be heard in strict turn unless otherwise ordered. The appellant must within two days give notice of setting-down, specifying

---

[31a] Fourteen days in the case of an interlocutory order and twenty-one days in winding-up or bankruptcy matters dealt with in a county court.

[32] *Kevorkian* v. *Burney* (*No.* 1) [1937] 4 All E.R. 97. See also *Practice Direction* [1958] 2 All E.R. 493.

the list, to all parties on whom the notice of appeal was served. Two copies of any supplementary notice of appeal must be sent to the registrar within two days of service.

Documents for use on appeal.—The appellant's solicitor must lodge the further papers necessary for the hearing with the Lords Justices' clerks (R.C.J. Room 135A) at least a week before the appeal is likely to come on (r. 9). Three numbered and indexed sets are ordinarily required, and should include:

The notice of appeal (and any respondent's or supplementary notice).

The judgment or order of the court below.

The pleadings and particulars.

The transcript of the official shorthand note or recording of the judgment, or, failing that, the judge's own note, if any, of his reasons.

All *relevant* affidavits and exhibits, or parts thereof, including correspondence.

The transcript of the official shorthand note or recording, or, where the judge has intimated that his note will be sufficient, the judge's note of *relevant* parts of the evidence.

An official shorthand writer still attends the trial of many witness actions in the High Court and takes a note of the evidence, summing-up and judgment (Order 68) though provision exists under this Order for a record of the proceedings to be made by mechanical means and this is quite frequently done. The costs of transcribing or copying unnecessary parts of the evidence or correspondence will be disallowed.[33] Provision is made for the supply of transcripts in certain cases at the public expense where a party is in poor financial circumstances. But in " legal aid " cases the authority of the area committee is necessary unless the Law Society has generally authorised it (Reg. 15 (4) and (5)).

Powers of the Court of Appeal

The Court of Appeal has all the powers, authority and jurisdiction of the High Court over any action or matter brought before it on appeal (Judicature Act, 1925, s. 27) and all the powers and duties as to amendment and otherwise of the High Court (Order 59, r. 10 (1)). It has full discretionary power to receive further

---

[33] *Lyus* v. *Stepney B.C.* [1941] 1 K.B. 134, 153; *Dixon* v. *City Veneering Mill Ltd.* [1953] 1 W.L.R. 1369.

evidence upon questions of fact, either orally or by affidavit or deposition; but where there has been a hearing below upon the merits, no further evidence except as to matters which occurred since the hearing will be admitted save on special grounds (r. 10 (2)).[33a] It may draw inferences of fact and give any judgment and make any order which ought to have been given or made or such further or other order as the case may require (r. 10 (3)). But it would seem that where there has been a trial by jury such inferences must not be inconsistent with the jury's findings unless the latter are such as no reasonable men could have arrived at.[34] It may direct issues to be tried, accounts to be taken and inquiries to be held (r. 10 (1)). It has complete discretion as to the costs of an appeal and in the court below (Order 62, r. 4 (2)) [35] and may, in special circumstances,[36] order security to be given (Order 59, r. 10 (5)). It may stay execution; but an appeal does not of itself operate as a stay or invalidate any intermediate act or proceeding (r. 13). Interest for such time as execution has been delayed by an appeal is allowed unless otherwise ordered (*ibid.*).

New Trial

On the hearing of any appeal the Court of Appeal may make any such order as could be made in pursuance of an application for a new trial or to set aside a verdict, finding or judgment of the court below (r. 11 (1)). Motions for a new trial are regulated by Order 8. (Order 59, r. 10 (1).)

Where a judgment has been obtained by fraud, the appropriate procedure is to bring an action to set it aside, giving full particulars of the fraud alleged [37]; but a motion in the Court of Appeal for a new trial may be made in special cases.[38] Leave to bring such an action is not required.[39] Such an action will also lie in cases where, since judgment, fresh material evidence has

---

[33a] See *Ladd* v. *Marshall* [1954] 1 W.L.R. 1489; *Curwen* v. *James* [1963] 1 W.L.R. 748; *Jenkins* v. *Richard Thomas & Baldwins Ltd.* [1966] 1 W.L.R. 476; *Roe* v. *Robert McGregor & Sons, Ltd.* [1968] 1 W.L.R. 925.

[34] *Mechanical Inventions Co. Ltd.* v. *Austin* [1935] A.C. 346.

[35] But see Order 62, r. 4 (3), as to assessment or taxation of the costs below.

[36] See *Weldon* v. *Maples, Teesdale & Co.* (1887) 20 Q.B.D. 331; *Hills* v. *L.P.T.B.* [1937] W.N. 339.

[37] *Jonesco* v. *Beard* [1930] A.C. 298.

[38] *Hip Foong Hong* v. *H. Neotia & Co.* [1918] A.C. 888 ; *Byatt* v. *Byatt* [1958] 1 W.L.R. 1.

[39] *Isherwood, Foster & Stacey, Ltd.* v. *Miglio* [1938] W.N. 189.

been obtained, which could not previously have been procured [40]; alternatively, an application may be made to the Court of Appeal for a new trial (*post*, pp. 375–376).

A new trial may be ordered on any question without interfering with the decision on any other question; and if some miscarriage of justice affects part only of the matter in controversy or some only of the parties, an appropriate order can be made.[41]

The main grounds [42] on which an application for a new trial may be founded are:

    (i) That the judge misdirected the jury.

    (ii) That the judge wrongly received or wrongly rejected evidence.

    (iii) That there was no evidence to go to the jury.

    (iv) That the verdict was against the weight of evidence.

    (v) That fresh evidence has been newly discovered.

    (vi) Surprise.

    (vii) Misbehaviour.

    (viii) That the damages are excessive or inadequate.

(i) and (ii) Misdirection for this purpose includes nondirection and the wrongful withdrawal from the jury of matters which ought to have been left to them. The Court of Appeal is not bound to order a new trial on the ground of misdirection, or improper admission or rejection of evidence, or because the verdict of the jury was not taken upon a question which the judge was not asked to leave to them, unless in the opinion of the court some substantial wrong or miscarriage has been thereby occasioned.[43] But where, through misdirection, the jury have failed to address their minds to the question of damages at all, that amounts to a miscarriage of justice, and the Court of Appeal will not speculate as to what amount the jury, if properly directed, would have awarded.[44]

Neither the wrongful withholding of a document by a third party who has been subpoenaed to produce it, nor his failure to attend on his subpoena is by itself sufficient ground for granting

---

[40] *Charles Bright & Co.* v. *Sellar* [1904] 1 K.B. 6; *Ladd* v. *Marshall* [1954] 1 W.L.R. 1489; *Crook* v. *Derbyshire* [1961] 1 W.L.R. 1360.

[41] Order 59, r. 11 (3); *Marsh* v. *Isaacs* (1876) 45 L.J.C.P. 505.

[42] There must be some solid grounds for the exercise of the discretion (see *Automatic Woodturning Co., Ltd.* v. *Stringer* [1957] A.C. 544).

[43] Order 59, r. 11 (2); *Bray* v. *Ford* [1896] A.C. 44; *Tait* v. *Beggs* [1905] 2 Ir.R. 525; *Lionel Barber & Co.* v. *Deutsche Bank* [1919] A.C. 304.

[44] *Farmer* v. *Hyde* [1937] 1 K.B. 728, 740.

a new trial.[45]　Nor is the wrong ruling of the judge admitting a document after a stamp objection.[46]　The court will not grant a new trial if it is satisfied that the jury, if rightly directed, would still have returned the same verdict.[47]

(iii) and (iv) That there was no evidence to go to the jury on a particular issue is an objection in point of law; it means that there was no evidence worthy of being considered by the jury— in the technical language of the courts, there must be more than a mere *scintilla* of evidence.　On the other hand the objection that the verdict was against the weight of the evidence raises a question of fact.　The judge and jury below who saw the witnesses and heard them cross-examined are the best judges of the weight of their evidence.　It does not matter how many witnesses swore one way, and how few the other.　Where there is any evidence on both sides proper to be submitted to a jury, their verdict once found must stand.[48]　If it is obvious that on all the available evidence no verdict for the plaintiff could be supported and a new trial would therefore be a waste of time, the Court of Appeal may order judgment to be entered for the defendant.[49]　In the absence of any misdirection, the court will not interfere to set aside a verdict or grant a new trial on the ground that the verdict was against the weight of evidence, unless the verdict was one which no reasonable men could have found.[50]　" If reasonable men might find the verdict which has been found, I think no court has jurisdiction to disturb a decision of fact which the law has confided to juries, not to judges." [51]

(v) A new trial may be granted upon the ground that fresh evidence has been discovered, but only when it could not with reasonable diligence have been discovered before the trial, and further, when it is so conclusive as to make it practically certain that the verdict would have been different, if it had been

---

[45] *Rowell* v. *Pratt* [1938] A.C. 101, 116; 106 L.J.K.B. 790.

[46] Order 59, r. 11 (5); and see *ante*, p. 321.

[47] *Per* Lord Esher M.R., in *Merivale* v. *Carson* (1887) 20 Q.B.D. at p. 281.

[48] *Commissioner for Railways* v. *Brown* (1887) 13 App.Cas. 133.

[49] *Mechanical Inventions Co., Ltd.* v. *Austin* [1935] A.C. 346.

[50] *Winterbotham, Gurney & Co.* v. *Sibthorp & Cox* [1918] 1 K.B. 625; *Mechanical Inventions Co., Ltd.* v. *Austin, ante.*

[51] *Per* Lord Halsbury in *Metropolitan Ry.* v. *Wright* (1886) 11 App.Cas. at p. 156, But see the judgments of Lopes L.J., in *Spencer* v. *Jones* (1897) 13 T.L.R. 174. and the speeches of the Lords in *Jones* v. *Spencer* (1897) 77 L.T. 536.

adduced.[52]   (As to the power of the Court of Appeal to receive fresh evidence, see *ante*, pp. 372–373.)

(vi) " Surprise " is the term used to cover cases in which either party has been prevented from having a fair trial through no fault of his own; *e.g.*, if the case be unexpectedly called on when he was reasonably absent; if his opponent misled him as to time or place of trial; if the case took a wholly unexpected turn which could not reasonably have been anticipated; or if a material witness was kept away by his opponent.[53]   Whenever a new trial is moved for on the ground of surprise, there must be an affidavit setting out the facts.   " Surprise is a matter extrinsic to the record and the judge's notes, and consequently can only be made to appear by affidavit." [54]

(vii) The " misconduct " of the jury, or of an officer of the court or other person,[55] or of counsel,[56] or even of the judge,[57] is ground for a new trial, if it really prevented either party having a fair trial.   A new trial will not be granted merely on the ground that the jury expressed an opinion during the judge's summing-up inconsistent with their subsequent verdict,[58] or on the ground that either judge or jury prematurely expressed a strong opinion as to the case either way [59]; or that the jury separated after the summing-up and before giving their verdict.[60] It would be otherwise if a juror before being sworn had expressed a determination to give his verdict a certain way [61]; or if the jury arrived at their verdict by drawing lots, or in any other way made an improper compromise without really trying the issues submitted to them [62]; or if handbills abusing the plaintiff were distributed in court, and shown to the jury on the day of the trial.[63]

[52] *Phosphate Sewage Co.* v. *Molleson* (1879) 4 App.Cas. 801; *Turnbull & Co.* v. *Duval* [1902] A.C. 429; *cf. Robinson* v. *Smith* [1915] 1 K.B. 711; *Meek* v. *Fleming* [1961] 2 Q.B. 366; *Ellis* v. *Scott* (*No. 2*) [1965] 1 W.L.R. 276.
[53] See *Isaacs* v. *Hobhouse* [1919] 1 K.B. 398.
[54] *Per* Maule J. in *Hoare* v. *Silverlock* (*No. 2*) (1850) 9 C.B. 22.
[55] *Goby* v. *Wetherill* [1915] 2 K.B. 674.
[56] *Beevis* v. *Dawson* [1957] 1 Q.B. 195.
[57] *Jones* v. *National Coal Board* [1957] 2 Q.B. 55.
[58] *Napier* v. *Daniel* (1836) 3 Bing.N.C. 77.
[59] *Lloyd* v. *Jones* (1866) 7 B. & S. 475; *De Freville* v. *Dill* [1927] W.N. 133; *Hobbs* v. *Tinling* [1929] 2 K.B. 1.
[60] *Fanshaw* v. *Knowles* [1916] 2 K.B. 538.
[61] *Ramadge* v. *Ryan* (1832) 9 Bing. 333; *Allum* v. *Boultbee* (1854) 9 Ex. 738; 23 L.J.Ex. 208.
[62] *Falvey* v. *Stanford* (1874) L.R. 10 Q.B. 54.
[63] *Coster* v. *Merest* (1822) 3 B. & B. 272.

(viii) Where the damages claimed are unliquidated, the court seldom grants a new trial on the ground that the amount awarded by the jury is either too small or too great. " The assessment of damages is peculiarly the province of the jury" (*Davis* v. *Shepstone* (1886) 11 App.Cas. at p. 191) and the court will not interfere unless the verdict is out of all proportion to the facts.[64] That the award of a jury does not conform to a level which judges have thought appropriate does not prove that the jury is wrong. " The views of juries may form a valuable corrective to the views of judges " (*Scott* v. *Musial* [1959] 2 Q.B. 429, *per* Morris L.J. at p. 438). The court will not grant a new trial on the ground of excessive damages, unless it thinks that, having regard to all the circumstances of the case, the damages are so large that no jury could reasonably have given them.[65] But a new trial will be granted if the court comes to the conclusion that the jury applied a wrong measure of damages or must have taken into consideration matters which they ought not to have considered.[66] The Court of Appeal on an application for a new trial has no power, without consent, to alter the amount of damages awarded by the jury; but it may do so with the appropriate consent [67]; or if the appeal is by way of rehearing after trial by a judge alone it may re-assess or assess them, as the case may be, without such consent.[68]

Still rarer are the cases in which a new trial has been granted on the ground that the amount of the verdict is too small. The rule is that where there has been no misconduct on the part of the jury, no error in the calculation of figures and no mistake in law on the part of the judge, a new trial will not be granted.[69] But a new trial will be granted if it can be shown that the jury wholly omitted to consider some substantial element of damage, which they ought to have taken into their consideration.[70]

---

[64] *Bocock* v. *Enfield Rolling Mills Ltd.* [1954] 1 W.L.R. 1303.
[65] *Praed* v. *Graham* (1889) 24 Q.B.D. 53.
[66] *Johnston* v. *G.W. Ry.* [1904] 2 K.B. 250; *Cavanagh* v. *Ulster Weaving Co. Ltd.* [1960] A.C. 145; *Lewis* v. *Daily Telegraph Ltd.* [1963] 1 Q.B. 340.
[67] See Order 59, r. 11 (4), embodying *Watt* v. *Watt* [1905] A.C. 115, and *Lionel Barber & Co.* v. *Deutsche Bank* [1919] A.C. 304.
[68] *Reaney* v. *Co-operative Wholesale Soc.* [1932] W.N. 78; *Roach* v. *Yates* [1938] 1 K.B. 256.
[69] *Rendall* v. *Hayward* (1839) 5 Bing.N.C. 424; *Forsdike* v. *Stone* (1868) L.R. 3 C.P. 607.
[70] *Phillips* v. *L. & S.W. Ry.* (1879) 5 Q.B.D. 78; *Johnston* v. *G.W. Ry.* [1904] 2 K.B. 250.

Where the appeal is from the decision of a judge alone, the Court of Appeal will not interfere, although they might themselves have awarded a different amount, unless satisfied that he acted upon a wrong principle of law or misapprehended the facts or that the amount awarded was so extremely high or low as to make it an entirely erroneous estimate.[71]

Questions of Law and of Fact

An appeal on a matter of law has, as a rule, a greater chance of success than an appeal on any question of fact. If matters of fact only are involved, the judges of the Court of Appeal are naturally very reluctant to disturb the finding of the judge or jury below, who saw and heard the witnesses and had the opportunity of judging their demeanour in the box.[72] If the action was tried by a judge without a jury, the Court of Appeal must decide whether, not having those advantages, they are in a position to say that the judge was plainly wrong.[73] If the appellant convinces them of that, the decision will be reversed [74]— even though the judge has clearly relied on the demeanour of the witnesses in deciding the facts [75]; if the matter is left in doubt, the Court of Appeal will not alter it.[76] In particular, when a party has been acquitted of fraud the decision should not be displaced on appeal except on the clearest grounds.[77] And when the action was tried by a judge with a jury, it is still more difficult to disturb an adverse finding of fact. (See *ante*, p. 375.)

The great growth in recent years of the practice of trying cases with a judge alone has led to a great increase in appeals (many of them successful) on points of fact. As was pointed out by Lord Sumner in *S.S. " Hontestroom "* v. *S.S. " Sagaporack "* ([1927] A.C. 37, at p. 47), where the trial judge's estimate of the witness as a man and his assessment of his credit enter substantially into the process of arriving at his finding of fact, the

[71] *Owen* v. *Sykes* [1936] 1 K.B. 192; *Davies* v. *Powell Duffryn Assd. Collieries Ltd.* [1942] A.C. 601, 617
[72] *Clarke* v. *Edinburgh, etc., Tramways Co.*, 1919 S.C.(H.L.) 35.
[73] *Powell* v. *Streatham Manor Nursing Home* [1935] A.C. 243; *Watt* v. *Thomas* [1947] A.C. 484.
[74] *Hicks* v. *British Transport Commission* [1958] 2 All E.R. 39, 50.
[75] *Yuill* v. *Yuill* [1945] P. 15.
[76] *Colonial Securities Trust Co.* v. *Massey* [1896] 1 Q.B. 38; *Coghlan* v. *Cumberland* [1898] 1 Ch. 704.
[77] *Akerhielm* v. *de Mare* [1959] A.C. 789.

appellate court ought not as a rule to disturb such a finding. But once findings of fact pass beyond simple direct testimony and become inferential in character, then the Court of Appeal is at no particular disadvantage compared with the trial judge and may reverse his conclusions, though it will give due weight to his views. In short, a distinction must be drawn between " the perception and evaluation of facts " (*per* Viscount Simonds in *Benmax* v. *Austin Motor Co., Ltd.* [1955] A.C. 370).[78] The reasons given by a judge alone for arriving at conclusions which would be matters for the jury, if there were a jury, are not to be treated as citable propositions of law.[79]

Appeals may be brought on points of law or mixed law and fact, either alone or in conjunction with appeals on fact. A common ground of appeal, which in strictness is one of law, is that there was no evidence entitling the judge to decide as he did. Where a point of law is relied on it must be one which was raised at the trial below, unless the appellant was taken by surprise or there are other special circumstances which excuse the omission.[80] If either party at the trial deliberately elects to fight one question only, on which he is beaten, he cannot afterwards on appeal raise another question, although that question was at the trial open to him on the pleadings and on the evidence.[81] The respondent, however, may as a rule support the finding of the court below on any ground, whether raised at the trial or not, provided he has given due notice (*ante*, pp. 369–370). It is the duty of every court to prevent any abuse of its process; hence it may at any stage of the proceeding raise of its own motion the question of the illegality of the contract sued on, although the point had not been pleaded nor raised in the argument before it.[82] Also it is the duty of counsel to prevent any court from enforcing an illegal transaction; it seems that he ought, therefore, to inform the court of such illegality even though it has not been pleaded.[82a]

---

[78] And see the observations of Denning L.J. on primary facts and the conclusions to be drawn from them in *British Launderers' Research Assn.* v. *Hendon Rating Authority* [1949] 1 K.B. at pp. 471–472.

[79] *Qualcast (Wolverhampton) Ltd.* v. *Haynes* [1959] A.C. 743, 744.

[80] *Clouston & Co. Ltd.* v. *Corry* [1906] A.C. 122; *Wilson* v. *United Counties Bank Ltd.* [1920] A.C. 102, 106. In appeals from county courts the rule is inflexible (*United Dominions Trust, Ltd.* v. *Bycroft* [1954] 1 W.L.R. 1345).

[81] *Martin* v. *G.N. Ry.* (1855) 16 C.B. 179; *Gloucester Union* v. *Gloucester Industrial Society* (1907) 96 L.T. 168; 5 L.G.R. 493.

[82] *Snell* v. *Unity Finance Co. Ltd.* [1964] 2 Q.B. 203, and earlier cases there cited.

[82a] See *Mercantile Credit Co. Ltd.* v. *Hamblin* [1964] 1 W.L.R. 423.

Where a discretionary jurisdiction is given to the trial judge, the Court of Appeal will not ordinarily interfere with his decision except on a point of law, unless it is shown that on other grounds (for example, that he has not given adequate weight to considerations which ought to have weighed with him) injustice will result.[83]

As to an appeal on the question of damages, see *ante*, pp. 377–378.

Appeal as to Costs

By section 31 (1) (*h*) of the Judicature Act, 1925, no order made by the High Court of Justice or any judge thereof by the consent of parties, or as to costs only,[84] when such costs are by law left to the discretion of the court or that judge, shall be subject to any appeal, except by leave of the court or judge making such order.[84a]

The effect of this section and the many cases decided under it was exhaustively considered by the House of Lords in *Donald Campbell & Co., Ltd.* v. *Pollak* [1927] A.C. 732, from which the following propositions emerge:

(1) If on appeal the merits of the case are raised bona fide, however small their pecuniary value may be in comparison with the costs, an appeal will lie. (*Per* Lord Dunedin, at p. 756.) So if a decision, which in form affects costs only, is really a decision on the merits or implies that one of the parties has been guilty of some misconduct, an appeal is allowed: *e.g.*, where a trustee,[85] or an executor,[86] or a mortgagee,[87] or an official liquidator[88] is refused costs. So where a solicitor is ordered to pay costs personally.[89]

---

83 *Evans* v. *Bartlam* [1937] A.C. 473, 481; *Phillips* v. *A. Lloyd & Sons* [1938] 2 K.B. 282, 288; see also *Maxwell* v. *Keun* [1928] 1 K.B. 645.

84 The rule that no appeal is allowed as to costs only does not apply to an appeal from a master to a judge at chambers in the Queen's Bench Division. (*Foster* v. *Edwards* (1879) 48 L.J.Q.B. 767.)

84a But in the case of an appeal involving other matters besides costs, the Court of Appeal has jurisdiction to deal with the question of costs even though the appeal fails with regards to the other matters and no prior leave was obtained. (*Wheeler* v. *Somerfield & Others* [1966] 2 Q.B. 94.

85 *Cotterell* v. *Stratton* (1872) L.R. 8 Ch. 295; *Re Isaac* [1897] 1 Ch. 251.

86 *Farrow* v. *Austin* (1881) 18 Ch.D. 58.

87 *Re Beddoe* [1893] 1 Ch. at p. 555.

88 *Re Silver Valley Mines* (1882) 21 Ch.D. 381.

89 *Re Bradford* (1883) 15 Q.B.D. 635; and see *Stevens* v. *Metropolitan District Ry.* (1885) 29 Ch.D. at p. 73.

(2) Where a discretion as to costs has been exercised on material that is illegitimate, or non-existent,[90] or in violation of some principle of substantive right, an appeal will be entertained. (*Per* Lord Haldane, at p. 752.) The words of Lord Halsbury in *Civil Service Co-operative Society* v. *General Steam Navigation Co.* [1903] 2 K.B. 756, were cited with approval: " No doubt, where a judge has exercised his discretion upon certain materials which are before him, it may not be, and I think is not, within the power of the Court of Appeal to overrule that exercise of discretion. But the necessary hypothesis of the existence of materials upon which the discretion can be exercised must be satisfied." Thus where the trial judge awards costs without jurisdiction, an appeal lies.[91] Again, in the words of Viscount Cave in *Donald Campbell & Co., Ltd.* v. *Pollak*, at p. 812: " If a judge were to refuse to give a party his costs on the ground of some misconduct wholly unconnected with the cause of action, or of some prejudice due to his race or religion, or (to quote a familiar illustration) to the colour of his hair, then the Court of Appeal might well feel itself compelled to intervene. But when a judge, deliberately intending to exercise his discretionary powers, has acted on facts connected with or leading up to the litigation, which have been proved before him or which he himself has observed during the progress of the case, then it seems to me that a Court of Appeal, although it may deem his reasons insufficient and may disagree with his conclusions, is prohibited by the statute from entertaining an appeal from it."

But it must be borne in mind that in this case the Lords were dealing with a judge's discretion as to costs, precisely defined by statutes and statutory rules, and the propositions laid down do not necessarily apply to other instances of discretionary powers.[92]

Appeal to a Divisional Court

Divisional Courts may be held in any Division under the Judicature Act, 1925, s. 63, for the transaction of any business assigned

---

[90] See *Wagman* v. *Vare Motors Ltd.* [1959] 1 W.L.R. 853.
[91] *Re Mills' Estate* (1886) 34 Ch.D. 24.
[92] See *Evans* v. *Bartlam* [1937] A.C. at p. 486.

to them by the Rules. They have jurisdiction in numerous matters other than appeals, including applications for orders of mandamus, prohibition and certiorari and writs of *habeas corpus ad subjiciendum* and proceedings for contempt of court [92a]; and extensive appellate jurisdiction, *e.g.*, from certain tribunals, by case stated from quarter sessions or justices, and in some cases of contempt of court.[92b] Their appellate jurisdiction over references and issues tried by masters, assessments of damages, and interpleader and garnishee matters, was transferred to the Court of Appeal in 1957 (*ante*, p. 364).

They retain jurisdiction to hear appeals from certain inferior courts of civil jurisdiction, but since county court appeals were transferred to the Court of Appeal in 1934 few occasions now arise for its exercise. In such cases notice of motion must be served and the appeal entered within twenty-eight days. (See Order 55, r. 4.)

Appeals from orders made by county courts in bankruptcy matters lie to a divisional court of the Chancery Division (Order 55, r. 1 (3)) and the same procedure is followed as on an appeal to the Court of Appeal from a county court.

An appeal lies to a divisional court of the Queen's Bench Division under the Tribunals and Inquiries Act, 1958, s. 9, on points of law from the decisions of certain tribunals, including Rent Tribunals and National Health Service Tribunals and from the Minister of Transport and Civil Aviation on appeal from the Traffic Commissioners; and by case stated from those tribunals and from Agricultural Land Tribunals. It lies also from certain decisions of the Minister of Housing and Local Government under the Town and Country Planning Acts.[93] The procedure, including the persons to be served and the time for appeal, is regulated by Orders 55, 56 and 94.

From a decision of a divisional court an appeal ordinarily lies to the Court of Appeal (Judicature Act, 1925, s. 27), but in some cases only with leave (*ante*, p. 366). In certain cases, however, an appeal may be made direct to the House of Lords (see *ante*, p. 367).

[92a] As to which see Order 52.
[92b] Administration of Justice Act, 1960, s. 13.
[93] See Town and Country Planning Act, 1959, ss. 31, 32.

Appeal to the House of Lords

From the Court of Appeal there is an appeal to the House of Lords—but only with the leave of the Court of Appeal or of the House of Lords. (Administration of Justice (Appeals) Act, 1934, s. 1.) The practice on such an appeal is regulated by the Appellate Jurisdiction Acts, 1876 and 1887, and by certain standing orders and directions which will be found in the *Supreme Court Practice*, 1970, Vol. II, paras. 2531-2612. Accurate information may be obtained from a document supplied free of charge by the House of Lords, entitled " Form of Appeal, Method of Procedure and Standing Orders."

The practice on appeals from the High Court direct to the House of Lords under Part II of the Administration of Justice Act, 1969, has already been dealt with (see *ante*, pp. 363, 365, 367). The application for a certificate should be made immediately after judgment, though in a proper case the judge has power to entertain an application made within fourteen days thereafter (*ibid.* s. 12 (4)). If the certificate is granted, the application for leave to appeal should be made to the House of Lords within one month, though again, an extension of time may be granted (*ibid.* s. 13 (1)).

Appeals are heard in the presence of not less than three (usually five) Lords of Appeal—a body consisting of the Lord Chancellor, the seven Lords of Appeal in Ordinary and such peers as hold or have held high judicial office. Lay peers do not in practice vote on judicial questions. Unless leave has been granted by the Court of Appeal, the appeal must be certified by two counsel as reasonable; and it must in any event be lodged within three months of the last order appealed from. A petition for leave to appeal must be lodged within one month. The documents and contentions of each party are set out in a case signed by one or more counsel and printed or duplicated in a form approved by the Clerk of the Parliaments. Copies of any recognised law reports of the decisions below may be lodged instead of reprinting the judgments in an appendix. The appellant is ordinarily required to give security for costs by recognisance to the amount of £500 and a bond for £200 with two sureties. Legal aid under the Legal Aid and Advice Act, 1949, is available for appeals to the House of Lords.

CHAPTER 25

EXECUTION AND ENFORCEMENT OF JUDGMENTS

WE now come to the process by which a judgment of the court is enforced.[1] And it behoves a successful plaintiff to act promptly, lest he lose the fruits of his victory. Unlike the county court the High Court has no officers of its own for the purpose of executing its judgments or orders.[2] They are enforced either by one of the various writs of execution directed to the sheriff of a county[3] commanding him to take the appropriate steps; or by charging the debtor's property, appointing a receiver, or attaching debts due to him; or, when the law permits, by committing him to prison. Another potent weapon in the hands of a judgment creditor is the threat or issue of a bankruptcy notice. A money judgment of the High Court may be enforced in a county court as if it were a county court judgment (County Courts Act, 1959, ss. 139, 120); but if for any reason this is not appropriate, the judgment creditor may obtain from a master an order under Order 48 that the debtor be examined as to his means, which may lead to the issue of whatever form of execution may be appropriate; or he may by leave issue a judgment summons before a judge of the Chancery Division in Bankruptcy, which may lead to a committal order. Each of these remedies will be explained in turn.

Enforcement of Money Judgments

Until 1966 the form of a money judgment was " that the plaintiff recover against the defendant £——," and execution against the debtor's goods would issue upon it if it was not satisfied forthwith. If the defendant was ordered to pay money into court or to do any other act, the court could order that it be done within a limited

---

[1] The whole system has been considered by a committee presided over by Mr. Justice Payne. Its recommendations will cause many changes. See the *Report* (Cmnd. 3909) of November 21, 1968; the Administration of Justice Act, 1970, Part II; and see Preface.

[2] Except the tipstaff, who conducts to prison anyone committed under an order of committal for contempt committed in the face of the court (and whose authority may now extend to other types of contempt).

[3] Or sometimes to other persons such as sequestrators (*post*, p. 393), or, in the case of ecclesiastical property, to the bishop of the diocese.

time, and disobedience could be visited by proceedings against the person or by sequestration. But a judgment for the recovery of money did not specify any time and it was held that it could not be supplemented by an order fixing a time for payment.

The essential words of a money judgment under the existing [3a] rules are " that the defendant do pay the plaintiff £———."[4] The judgment need not, though it may, specify a time for payment,[5] and a time may be added or altered by a subsequent order made on a summons which must be served on the person ordered to pay.[6]

A judgment or order for the payment of money may ordinarily be enforced in various ways,[7] each of which will be explained in this chapter. The judgment creditor may issue a writ of *fieri facias* (commonly abbreviated to *fi. fa.*) against the debtor's goods under Order 45, r. 1, or apply for a charging order against his land or his securities under Order 50; or, in some cases, he can apply under Orders 51 and 30 for equitable execution by means of a receiver. If he knows of anyone who owes money to the judgment debtor, he can attach the debt by what are known as garnishee proceedings under Order 49. If the judgment specifies a time for payment and the defendant disobeys, it may, with the leave of the court, also be enforced by a writ of sequestration against his property and (subject to the provisions of the Debtors Acts 1869 and 1878) by committal.

Fi. fa.—The most ordinary form of execution is by writ of "*fieri facias*." [8] This writ commands the sheriff to *cause to be made* out of the goods and chattels of the judgment debtor the sum recovered by the judgment, together with interest at the rate of £4 per cent. and costs of execution, and immediately after the execution of the writ to pay the money and interest to be paid to the judgment creditor. The writ may not be indorsed to levy the costs of execution where the judgment is for less than £100 [8a] and

---

[3a] September 1970.

[4] In its full form it is accompanied by such recitals and ancillary provisions as circumstances demand. (See Order 42, r. 1, and Precedent No. 104.) Judgments entered before October 1, 1966, in the old form may be enforced by the methods applicable to the new form other than committal or sequestration (Order 45, r. 13).

[5] Order 42, r. 2 (2). [6] Order 45, r. 6.

[7] See Order 45, r. 1.

[8] See Form No. 53 in Appendix A to the R.S.C. There are also special writs which go, under Order 47, r. 5, against the incumbent of a benefice who has no goods in the county except ecclesiastical property. They are executed by the diocesan officers of the bishop. (See R.S.C., Appendix A, Forms Nos. 58 and 59.)

[8a] See R.S.C. (Amendment) 1970 (S.I. No. 671).

385

does not carry costs (Order 47, r. 4). Immediately after execution the sheriff must make an indorsement on the writ showing how it has been executed and send a copy to the plaintiff. By the authority thus given him the sheriff may enter the house of the execution debtor and seize what goods can be found there belonging to the debtor; he must not seize goods which are the property of someone else. He may also enter the house of a third person, if the goods of the debtor be actually therein; but in this case there is always the risk that the house may contain nothing belonging to the debtor, and then the sheriff would be liable to an action of trespass.

Under a *fi. fa.* the sheriff may seize and sell all the personal goods and chattels belonging to the execution debtor which he can find and which can be sold, with the exception of the wearing apparel and bedding of the judgment debtor or his family, and the tools and implements of his trade; provided the value of such excepted articles does not exceed in the whole £50,[9] or such larger amount as the Lord Chancellor may prescribe.[10] The sheriff can sell under a *fi. fa.* a lease or term of years belonging to the debtor, and execute an assignment of it under his seal of office to the purchaser. But he cannot sell an estate in fee, or for life, or an equitable interest such as an equity of redemption, or things which are fixed to the freehold and which at common law would have passed on death to the heir, and not to the executor, of the owner. Growing corn and other crops which are raised by the industry of man may be taken in execution; but fruits of the earth which yield no annual profit, or which are produced without the labour of man, cannot be seized by the sheriff. The seizure and sale of straw, chaff, turnips, manure, hay, grasses, roots, vegetables and growing crops on land let to farm are regulated by the express provisions of the Sale of Farming Stock Act, 1816, and the Landlord and Tenant Act, 1851, s. 2. The sheriff cannot take goods which are already in the custody of the law, *e.g.,* by distress; but since the passing of the Judgments Act, 1838, s. 12, he may seize *choses in action*, such as bank-notes, cheques, bills of exchange, bonds and other securities for money[11]; and the goods so seized he may safely proceed to sell unless he receives notice that a third

---

[9] S.I. 1297 of 1963 (L. 12).
[10] Small Debts Act, 1845, s. 8; Administration of Justice Act, 1956, s. 37. (Under the County Courts Act, 1959, s. 124, a bailiff has the like powers.)
[11] See *Johnson* v. *Pickering* [1908] 1 K.B. 1.

person claims them as his property (see Bankruptcy and Deeds of Arrangement Act, 1913, s. 15).

It often happens, however, that when a sheriff seizes goods under an execution some third person intervenes and claims that the goods are his, or that he has a charge on them under a bill of sale or otherwise. In such cases the sheriff applies to a master for protection by means of an interpleader summons (see *ante*, p. 212), which he serves on both the claimant and the execution creditor. All three parties then appear before the master, who generally by consent disposes of the case summarily, if the amount in dispute is not large and no difficult question of law or fact arises. In other cases, he may direct an issue between the claimant and the execution creditor, which is tried like an ordinary action. If the claimant will pay into court a reasonable amount to abide the event of the issue, the sheriff will be ordered to withdraw from possession of the goods; if not, the master may order so many of the goods to be sold as will realise the amount of the judgment. If the value of the goods does not exceed £500 he may transfer the proceedings to a county court. The procedure on a sheriff's interpleader is regulated by Order 17.

Charge on land.—If the debtor has land, the creditor under a judgment or order for the payment of money may apply under Order 50, r. 1, for a charging order pursuant to section 35 of the Administration of Justice Act, 1956, which Act abolished the old writ of *elegit.* Application for an order *nisi* is made *ex parte* to a master with an affidavit identifying the judgment to be enforced, giving the name of the judgment debtor, stating the amount unpaid under the judgment, specifying the land on which, or on an interest in which, it is sought to impose a charge, and the deponent's belief (with the sources and grounds) that it belongs to the judgment debtor. The order *nisi* imposes a charge until the return day, when on proof of service it will be made absolute with or without modifications unless sufficient cause is shown to the contrary. The order has the like effect for securing the payment of any moneys due or to become due under the judgment or order as an equitable charge created by the debtor in writing under his hand [12] and it may be made subject to conditions as to the time when the charge is to become enforce-

---

[12] It seems that the creditor cannot sell or appoint a receiver without further application to the court.

able and generally. The creditor will be wise to register the order at the Land Charges Registry even before it is made absolute.

Charge on stock.—An order charging stock or shares belonging to the judgment debtor or money in court in which he has a beneficial interest may be applied for under Order 50. The procedure is similar to that applicable to a charge on land. An order *nisi* prevents the transfer or disposition of the debtor's shares or interest until it is made absolute. Thereafter it has the same effect as though it were a charge executed by the debtor himself, but proceedings to enforce it may not be taken until six months after the order *nisi.*

Equitable execution.—In some cases in which execution could not be had at law, equitable relief could be obtained by the appointment of a receiver. Though called equitable execution, " it is not execution, but a substitute for execution." (*Per* Bowen L.J. in *Re Shephard* (1889) 43 Ch.D. at p. 137.) Thus, a receiver will be appointed to receive a fund in court, or a legacy not yet payable, or a share of the proceeds of the sale of land not yet sold. The appointment of such a receiver operates as an injunction to restrain the judgment debtor from himself receiving the moneys and prevents his dealing with them to the prejudice of the execution creditor.[13] In this way, too, an execution creditor can sometimes secure payment of his debt out of an equity of redemption or any other interest in land which could not be reached by the ordinary process of execution at law.

The appointment of a receiver is one of the three ways in which a judgment or order for the payment of money into court may be enforced, the others being committal and sequestration (see *post,* pp. 392–393). (Order 45, r. 1 (2).)

The Judicature Act, 1925, s. 45, provides that a receiver may be appointed by interlocutory order in all cases in which it appears to the court to be just or convenient so to do. But this section does not confer any wider jurisdiction than existed before 1873.[14] It will not be exercised if there is no hindrance, by reason of the nature of the property, to obtaining execution at law or merely because it would be a more convenient mode of obtaining satisfaction than the usual modes of execution.[15] The Administration of

[13] *Re The Marquis of Anglesey* [1903] 2 Ch. 727.
[14] *Morgan* v. *Hart* [1914] 2 K.B. 183.
[15] *Ibid.*, and *Harris* v. *Beauchamp* (*No.* 2) [1894] 1 Q.B.D. 801.

Justice Act, 1956, s. 36, has, however, extended the power so as to operate in relation to all estates and interests in land and it may be so exercised whether or not a charge has been imposed under section 35 (*ante,* p. 387). In determining whether such appointment would be just or convenient regard is to be had to the amount of the judgment debt, the amount which will probably be obtained by the receiver and the probable costs of his appointment (Order 51, r. 1). The receiver may be required to give security and must render periodical accounts; the machinery is provided by Order 30, rr. 2–6.

The judgment creditor of a man who is a partner in a firm can, under section 23 of the Partnership Act, 1890, obtain an order charging that partner's interest in the partnership property and profits with payment of the amount of the judgment debt and interest thereon, and by the same or a subsequent order a receiver may be appointed of that partner's share of profits (whether already declared or accruing) and of any other money which may be coming to him in respect of the partnership. (And see Order 81, r. 10.)

Attachment of debts.[15a]—Any debt owing to the judgment debtor from any other person within the jurisdiction of the court can be recovered by the judgment creditor towards the satisfaction of his judgment, by a process known as "attachment of debts." In order to ascertain what debts are owing to the debtor, it is often necessary to obtain an order for his examination. (See Order 48, r. 1.) If the judgment debtor disobeys the order, he is liable to be committed to prison. Either before or after any oral examination of the judgment debtor, the judgment creditor may apply *ex parte* to a master for an order, which is technically known as a "Garnishee Order *nisi.*" He must present an affidavit showing that judgment has been recovered, and is still unsatisfied, and to what amount, and that a person named and within the jurisdiction owes the judgment debtor money. The master thereupon may make an order attaching the debt "due or accruing due "[16] to the judgment debtor from such person (who is henceforth called "the garnishee"), and ordering the garnishee to appear and show cause why he should not pay

---

[15a] See *ante,* p. 384, n. 1.
[16] See *Dunlop & Ranken Ltd.* v. *Hendall Steel Structures Ltd.* [1957] 1 W.L.R. 1102. The words of the former rule were " owing or accruing."

such debt to the judgment creditor, or so much of it as may suffice to satisfy his claim. (Order 49, rr. 1–3.) This order must be served personally upon the garnishee; and, as soon as it is served on him, it binds the debt in his hands [17]; he must not, therefore, after service pay any money to the judgment debtor. The garnishee must appear as the order directs, if he wishes to dispute the debt or his liability to be thus garnished. If the garnishee does not appear in obedience to the order *nisi*, or does not dispute his liability, the master may make the order absolute, so that unless the garnishee pays over the amount due from him, or so much thereof as may be sufficient to satisfy the judgment debt, execution can issue against him forthwith (r. 4). If the garnishee appears and disputes his liability, the master, instead of ordering that execution shall issue, may direct that any issue or question necessary for determining his liability be tried (r. 5). Payment by, or execution levied on, the garnishee under any such order is a valid discharge to him of his debt to the judgment debtor, to the amount paid or levied, even though such an order be subsequently set aside, or the judgment reversed (r. 8).

Committal.—See *post*, pp. 393–394.

Sequestration.—See *post*, pp. 392–393.

Bankruptcy Notice.—It is beyond the scope of this work to describe in detail this method of enforcing judgments but, broadly speaking, the procedure is to serve on the judgment debtor a notice which requires him to pay the judgment debt within a specified time and if he does not do so he commits an act of bankruptcy, on which a petition may be presented and he may be adjudicated bankrupt.

Enforcement of other Judgments

The commonest judgments other than for the payment of money are for possession of land and for delivery of goods. The form of judgments for possession is prescribed by R.S.C. Appendix A, Nos. 42 and 42A. (See Order 42, r. 1). The plaintiff either gets a judgment, following nearly the form of order common in the Chancery Division in mortgage cases, " that the defendant do give the plaintiff possession " of the land,[18] or, in summary proceedings under Order 113,

---

[17] Rule 3; *Edmunds* v. *Edmunds* [1904] P. 362. By this method the debtor's bank balance (if any) may be attached, which is how the process is most often used.
[18] See form in R.S.C., Appendix A, No. 42; (Order 42, r. 1).

a judgment " that the plaintiff do recover possession " of the land. In actions of detinue the plaintiff ordinarily gets a judgment that the defendant do deliver to the plaintiff the goods described or pay their value to be assessed and, if claimed, damages for their detention to be assessed.[19]   As in the case of a money judgment, these judgments may contain or be supplemented by a time for performance (Order 42, r. 2, *ante*, p. 385).   There may be other judgments or orders requiring the defendant to do an act, and in those cases the time for performance must be specified (*ibid.*).

Judgments for possession of land and delivery of goods are enforceable, respectively, by writ of possession and writ of delivery. If a time of performance is fixed they may also, by leave, be enforced by sequestration and in some circumstances by committal.

Writ of possession.—This writ commands the sheriff to enter the land and cause the plaintiff to have possession of it.[20] It may be combined with a writ of *fi. fa.* It will not issue without leave except in mortgage actions and after a final order for possession made in summary proceedings under Order 113.[21] To obtain leave the plaintiff should first give notice of the judgment to the defendant and all persons in actual occupation (other than members of the defendant's family living with him), so that they may have an opportunity of applying for relief if so advised.   The application is then made *ex parte* to the practice master on an affidavit showing that notice has been given to all such persons and that there is no obstacle to execution—*e.g.*, that the defendant has some statutory protection.[22] The costs of a writ of possession are usually allowed as fixed costs.[23] If the defendant gets in again after the sheriff has notionally restored possession to the plaintiff, a writ of restitution may issue; but leave is necessary for the issue of any supplementary writ in aid of execution.[24]

Writ of delivery.—If a plaintiff has obtained judgment for the delivery of goods, his precise remedy depends upon the form of

---

[19] *Ibid.* Form No. 41. But except in the case of judgment by default the judgment need not necessarily provide the alternative of paying the assessed value (see Order 45, r. 4 (1)).

[20] See R.S.C., Appendix A, Forms Nos. 66 and 66A.

[21] Order 45, r. 3; Order 113, r. 7.

[22] Order 46, r. 4. See *Peachey Property Corpn. Ltd.* v. *Robinson* [1966] 2 W.L.R. 1386.

[23] Order 62, Appendix 3, Part IV, para. 12.

[24] Order 46, r. 3. And see R.S.C., Appendix A, Form No. 68.

his judgment.[25] If it makes no alternative provision for the payment of assessed value he may enforce it without leave by a writ of specific delivery,[26] or, if it specifies a time, he may get leave to enforce it by committal or sequestration. (Order 45, r. 4 (1).) If it does make such alternative provision, leave must be obtained before a writ of specific delivery will issue, and sequestration may be allowed if a time is specified (r. 4 (2)). A supplementary order may also be obtained requiring the delivery of the goods within a limited time, and if this is disobeyed, an application for committal may follow (r. 5 (3)). The only remedy open *without leave* to a plaintiff where the judgment gives the alternative is to issue an ordinary writ of delivery[27] to recover the goods or their assessed value. (r. 5 (3)). Either form of writ may be combined with a *fi. fa.* for any sum of money payable under the judgment in respect of damages or otherwise.

Writ of sequestration.—If a time for performance is specified in or has been added to a judgment or order, whether it orders payment of money, giving possession of land, delivery of goods or any other act (such as the abatement of a nuisance or the delivery of an account), and the defendant refuses or neglects to obey within the time limited, a writ of sequestration may by leave be issued against his property (or against the property of any director or officer of a corporate defendant). (Order 45, r. 5.) So also if a person disobeys a judgment or order requiring him to abstain from doing an act (*ibid.*). Leave may only be obtained by motion to a judge (Order 46, r. 5).

Before sequestration can issue, a copy of the judgment or order indorsed with a penal notice to the effect that if the party neglects to obey or disobeys he is liable to process of execution, must be served personally on him before any time for compliance expires [28];

---

[25] See *ante*, note 19.

[26] R.S.C., Appendix A, Form No. 64 (Order 45, r. 12.)

[27] *Ibid.* Form No. 65. This form commands the sheriff to cause the goods to be delivered to the plaintiff and, *if possession cannot be obtained*, to levy the assessed value. If strictly enforceable this would seem not to give the defendant the alternative contemplated by the judgment. The extent of the sheriff's powers must therefore be regarded as open to question if the defendant has the goods and will not hand them over. (The old form commanded the sheriff to distrain all the defendant's goods until those the subject of the judgment were found.) The plaintiff's remedy in such a case is to apply for leave to issue a writ of specific delivery, and leave may, if necessary, be given to supplement this by a writ of assistance (Form No. 69; Order 46, r. 1).

[28] Order 45, r. 7; but note sub-rule (6).

but such service may be dispensed with if the court thinks it just, *e.g.* when he has already had notice of the judgment or order and is evading formal service.[29]

Such a writ [30] is directed to commissioners, not less than four in number, called sequestrators, giving them authority to enter on the lands of the person in contempt and sequester and receive into their hands the rents and profits of all his real and personal estate, and to detain them until the contempt be cleared. All moneys that come into the hands of the sequestrators may be applied by them to meet the demand of the party prosecuting the writ. But they must apply for leave before they sell any of the goods and chattels sequestered, and the proceeds of such a sale will be dealt with as the court may direct.

Committal.[31]—The court has a general power to punish contempt by committing the offender to prison.[32] In this chapter we are concerned in particular with disobedience to a judgment or order. In the case of a money judgment there is an independent power under the Debtors Acts, 1869 and 1878, to commit a person who wilfully refuses to pay when he has or has had the means to do so (see " Debtors Acts and Judgment Summons " *post,* p. 395, and Order 45, r. 1 (3)). Apart from this, committal may be ordered under the Rules of the Supreme Court, Order 45, rr. 1 (1) (2) and 5, but in the case of a money judgment this power is subject to the provisions of the Debtors Acts (r. 5 (1) (iii)). These Acts, as we shall see, prevent imprisonment for default in payment of money save in the excepted cases. Committal, like sequestration, may be ordered for refusal or neglect to obey a judgment or order when a time for performance is specified, or for disobedience to a prohibitive order (see *ante,* p. 392).

The procedure is governed by Order 52, rr. 4 and 6–8. The application is made by motion to a judge, supported by an affidavit. A copy of the judgment or order indorsed with a penal

---

[29] *Ibid.,* and see *Kistler* v. *Tettmar* [1905] 1 K.B. 39.

[30] See R.S.C., Appendix A, Form No. 67.

[31] The analogous process of " attachment " has been abolished. *Note* that when Part II of the Administration of Justice Act, 1970, comes into force on a day to be appointed, and in particular s. 11, the power to commit for default in payment of judgment debts will be strictly limited. Furthermore, an elaborate machinery for attaching earnings will also be brought into force, largely to operate in the county court, but also to operate in the High Court to secure payments under a High Court Maintenance Order. (See ss. 13–30 of the Administration of Justice Act, 1970.)

[32] It also has power to fine him (see Order 52, r. 9).

notice must first have been served as already described under " sequestration." [33] The notice of motion, stating the grounds of the application, and a copy of the supporting affidavit must also be served personally unless the court dispenses with such service. [34] A committal order may be suspended for such period or on such terms as the judge may specify [35]; and after committal the court may, on the application of the person committed, discharge him, [36] although it is unlikely while he continues in disobedience.

General Rules

If judgment has been recovered against a firm, execution can ordinarily issue without leave against all property of the firm within the jurisdiction, and also against the goods of any person who has entered an appearance in the action as a partner, or who was served with the writ as a partner and failed to appear, or has admitted on the pleadings that he is, or who has been adjudged to be a partner. But the plaintiff cannot without leave issue execution against any other person. Thus, for example, if the writ was served not on a partner but on the person in control, and judgment was entered in default of appearance, leave must be obtained before execution can be levied on the private goods of the partners. If such person dispute his liability, an issue will probably be directed to determine whether he was a partner or held himself out as a partner at the date of the contract. (Order 81, r. 5.) [37]

A writ of execution, if unexecuted, remains in force for a year from its issue and may be renewed from year to year thereafter. (Order 46, r. 8). Execution may not be effected on a Sunday except, in case of urgency, with leave. (Order 65, r. 10.) Leave to issue execution is also required under Order 46, r. 2 in the following cases:

    (a) where six years or more have elapsed since the judgment or order;

    (b) where any change has taken place, whether by death or otherwise, in the parties entitled or liable to execution;

    (c) where judgment is against the assets of a deceased;

    (d) where under the judgment any person is entitled to relief

---

[33] Order 45, r. 7. In the case of an order for discovery or production of documents or to answer interrogatories, service upon his solicitor is sufficient to cast on a party the burden of showing that he had no notice or knowledge of the order (Order 24, r. 16 (3); Order 26, r. 6 (3)).

[34] Order 52, r. 4.   [35] *Ibid.*, r. 7.   [36] *Ibid.*, r. 8.

[37] *Davis* v. *Hyman & Co.* [1903] 1 K.B. 854.

subject to the fulfilment of any condition which it is alleged
has been fulfilled; and

(e) where any of the goods sought to be seized are in the hands
of a receiver appointed by the court or a sequestrator.

Leave is also necessary pursuant to the Reserve and Auxiliary
Forces (Protection of Civil Interests) Act, 1951, if the defendant
is performing a service described in the First Schedule.

Debtors Acts and Judgment Summons

Before the Debtors Act, 1869, a judgment debtor who failed to
pay even through poverty was liable to indefinite imprisonment.
Section 4 of that Act provided that with certain exceptions no person
should be arrested or imprisoned for making default in payment
of a sum of money. Within the exceptions are penalties other
than under a contract, sums recoverable summarily before justices,
sums ordered to be paid by defaulting trustees, costs payable personally by a solicitor for misconduct and money which he has been
ordered to pay as an officer of the court, salary or income which
a bankrupt has been ordered to pay for the benefit of his creditors,
and sums which the court orders a debtor to pay under section 5
(*post*). Sums payable in respect of death duties and purchase tax
are also excepted, although the debtor has the protection of section
4 in respect of other debts due to the Crown.[38] Furthermore, that
section provides that even in the excepted cases imprisonment
shall not exceed one year. It was at one time held that in the case
of defaulting trustees and solicitors the court was bound to order
imprisonment if it was asked for. Since the Debtors Act, 1878,
such an order is discretionary. Under the Debtors Act, 1869, s. 5,
a person who defaults in payment after an order or an instalment
order has been made for payment of a debt may be ordered to be
imprisoned for a term not exceeding six weeks (subject to earlier
release if he pays) if it is proved that he has, or since the date of the
order, has had, the means to pay.[39] This is established by the
procedure of a judgment summons.

A judgment summons may be and usually is issued in the county
court, which has jurisdiction even though a High Court judgment

---

[38] Crown Proceedings Act, 1947, s. 26 (2).
[39] Debtors Act, 1869, s. 5, proviso (2); *Buckley* v. *Crawford* [1893] 1 Q.B. 105. Such
imprisonment does not extinguish the debt (s. 5, proviso (2)).

is involved.[40] In the High Court it comes before a judge of the Chancery Division in Bankruptcy[41]; the applicant must obtain leave to issue it and must show by affidavit why it should issue in the High Court.[42] The debtor is then examined as to his means and may be committed if he does not attend. If the judge comes to the conclusion that he has not paid as much as he could have done, he may commit him to prison then and there; but he usually orders him to pay by stated instalments, making an order that he be committed on failure to do so.

Enforcement of Foreign and Dominion Judgments

The Administration of Justice Act, 1920, provides for the enforcement in many of the Dominions and Colonies of judgments of our courts and vice versa. The Foreign Judgments (Reciprocal Enforcement) Act, 1933, contains similar provisions with regard to such foreign countries as give corresponding facilities. The procedure in each case is governed by the provisions of Order 71.

Staying Execution

Although the court will not without good reason delay a successful plaintiff in obtaining the fruits of his judgment, it has power to stay execution if justice requires that the defendant should have this protection. Ancient arguments as to the extent of this power have now become academic.[43] Apart from a general power to stay proceedings under the Judicature Act, 1925, s. 41,[44] and the power to make instalment orders under the Debtors Act, 1869 (*ante*, p. 395), the court has wide powers under the Rules of the Supreme Court.[45]

Under Order 47, r. 1, if a judgment is given or an order made for the payment of money the debtor may apply then or later for a stay. The judge or master, if satisfied that there are special circumstances which render it inexpedient to enforce the judgment or that the judgment debtor is unable from any cause to pay

---

[40] County Courts Act, 1959, ss. 139, 120; County Court Rules, 1936, Order 25, r. 33.

[41] Bankruptcy Act, 1914, s. 107.

[42] *Practice Direction* [1956] 2 All E.R. 928. Ordinarily not less than £50 must be due.

[43] A number of cases were referred to in the eighteenth edition of this work, to which reference could be made if necessary.

[44] The extent of which in relation to execution is not clearly defined, but is presumably exercisable in accordance with rules of court.

[45] Under the Execution Act, 1844, s. 62, a judge also has discretionary power to suspend or stay any judgment, order or execution if he is satisfied by evidence that a debtor is unable to pay due to sickness or unavoidable accident.

the money, may stay execution by *fi. fa.* either absolutely or for such period and subject to such conditions as he thinks fit. The order may subsequently be varied or revoked. If the application is not made when judgment is given, it may be made later by summons, even though the defendant may not have entered an appearance. The summons must be supported by an affidavit showing the grounds and relevant facts; in case of inability to pay, the applicant's income, property and liabilities must be disclosed.

Again, in the case of any judgment or order to do an act, whether it be to pay money or not, the court has an indirect power to postpone its operation by fixing a time for performance or extending a time already fixed.[46] For if a time be fixed, the party is not in default until the time has expired. Or if matters have occurred since judgment which would make it just to stay execution, the court may do so under Order 45, r. 11. A master who gives summary judgment against a defendant under Order 14 is expressly empowered to stay execution pending a counterclaim.[47]

The Court of Appeal or the court below may stay execution pending an appeal, but the mere service of a notice of appeal does not operate as a stay (Order 59, r. 13 (1)).

[46] Order 42, r. 2; Order 45, r. 6.
[47] Order 14, r. 3 (2).

CHAPTER 26

COSTS

LAST comes the important question of " Costs." The word is sometimes used to denote the remuneration which a party pays to his own solicitor. But it also means that sum of money which the court or a judge orders one litigant to pay to another to compensate the latter for the expense which he has incurred in the litigation. The amount so awarded seldom, if ever, repays the whole outlay which the successful litigant has been compelled to make; unless agreed the costs have to be taxed, and the taxing master very rarely allows the full amount which the successful party has to pay to his own solicitor. The amount allowed on taxation is called " taxed costs," and this, as a rule, is all that the unsuccessful party has to pay to his opponent. The difference between " taxed costs " and the amount which the successful party is liable to pay to his own solicitor is known as " extra costs," and this the successful party must pay out of his own pocket. There are different bases on which costs may be taxed which are explained hereafter (pp. 402–406).

Power to Order Costs

The Court of Chancery assumed from its commencement the power to deal with all questions of costs without the aid of the legislature. But in the courts of common law the right to costs was the creature of statute and was, by the earlier statutes at all events, made to depend entirely on the result of the litigation (or, in legal language, the costs followed the event). Whichever party had judgment recorded in his favour recovered costs; and the judge had no discretion in the matter until the seventeenth century, and then only of a very limited kind. Now, however, in every division the court has complete discretion over the costs of the proceedings, subject to the express provisions of the rules or of any statute (see *post*, pp. 406–410). " Subject to the provisions of this Act and to rules of court and to the express provisions of any other Act, the costs of and incidental to all proceedings in the Supreme Court, including the administration of estates and trusts, shall be in the discretion of the court or judge, and the court or judge shall have full power to determine by whom and to what extent the costs are to be paid." (Judicature Act, 1925, s. 50.) And by Order 62, r. 2 (4), the powers and discretion of the court under that section are to be exercised subject to and in accordance with that Order.

Except as otherwise provided in the rules one party can only recover costs from another under an order of the court (r. 3 (1)). Exceptions are made in a number of cases, *e.g.*, where judgment is signed in default and the table of fixed costs applies (r. 32 (4) and Appendix 3); where the plaintiff amends without leave (r. 3 (3)), or applies for an extension of time (r. 3 (4)) or discontinues without leave (r. 10 (1)), or accepts before trial money paid into court (r. 10 (2)–(4)). And there are some other exceptions. Costs may be dealt with by the court at any stage of or after the proceedings and may, unless the paying party is an assisted person, be ordered to be paid forthwith (r. 4 (1)). The costs usually allowable in any case are taxed costs (r. 9 (1)); but the court may instead direct the payment of a gross sum,[1] thus saving the parties the expense of taxation, or may order a specified proportion [2] of the taxed costs, or taxed costs from or up to a particular stage, to be paid (r. 9 (4)). The judge generally deals expressly with the costs in his judgment; if he does not, the successful party should ask for them, not forgetting to ask also for any special costs which might not otherwise be allowed (see *ante*, p. 331).

Exercise of Discretion

The judge in his discretion may say expressly that he makes " no order as to costs." In that case each party must pay his own.[3] If he does make an order as to costs the general rule is that he

---

[1] Taking care to see that this does not exceed what the party would have to pay if the costs were taxed (*Wilmott* v. *Barber* (1881) 17 Ch.D. 772, 774).

[2] See *Bourne* v. *Swan & Edgar Ltd.* [1903] 1 Ch. 211, and *post*, p. 411.

[3] If so intended this may be equivalent to an order that a trustee shall not be entitled to retain his costs out of the estate (*Re Hodgkinson* [1895] 2 Ch. 190). But the judge cannot make such an order in the case of a trustee, personal representative or mortgagee, except on special grounds (see *post*, pp. 404–405).

shall order the costs to follow the event,[4] except when it appears to him that in the circumstances of the case some other order should be made as to the whole or any part [5] of the costs (r. 3 (2)). But he must not apply this or any other general rule in such a way as to exclude the exercise of the discretion entrusted to him [6]; and materials must exist upon which the discretion can be exercised.[7] " This discretion, like any other discretion, must, of course, be exercised judicially, and the judge ought not to exercise it against the successful party, except for some reason connected with the case " (*per* Viscount Cave in *Donald Campbell & Co., Ltd.* v. *Pollak* [1927] A.C. 732, at pp. 811, 812). It is not a judicial exercise of the judge's discretion to order a party, who has been completely successful and against whom no misconduct is even alleged, to pay costs.[8]

A successful party may sometimes be deprived of his costs. A successful plaintiff may moreover be ordered to pay the costs of the defendant,[9] but a defendant who is absolutely successful will not be made to pay the whole costs of the action.[10]

" The judge should look, in the first place, at the result of the action itself, namely, the verdict of the jury, and he should look also at the conduct of the parties to see whether either of them had in any way involved the other unnecessarily in the expense of litigation, and beyond that he should consider all the facts of the case so far as no particular fact was concluded by the finding of the jury." (*Per* Bowen L.J. in *Jones* v. *Curling* (1884) 13 Q.B.D., at p. 272.) " Should the jury, in an action for an assault or libel, award the plaintiff an ignominious compensation, it would not follow that the judge ought as of course to deprive him of his costs, although he might treat it as an indication of the opinion of the jury, in which he coincided, that the character of the plaintiff was worthless, and that the action never ought to have been brought, and was therefore oppressive." (*Per*

---

[4] As to the meaning of " the event " see *Reid, Hewitt & Co.* v. *Joseph* [1918] A.C. 717. The term may have to be construed distributively as between separate issues.

[5] As to the costs of separate issues see *post*, pp. 410–412.

[6] *Bew* v. *Bew* [1899] 2 Ch. 467.

[7] *Civil Service Co-op. Soc.* v. *Gen. Steam Navigation Co.* [1903] 2 K.B. 756.

[8] *Kierson* v. *Joseph L. Thompson & Sons* [1913] 1 K.B. 587.

[9] *London Welsh Estates, Ltd.* v. *Phillip* (1931) 100 L.J.K.B. 449.

[10] *Dicks* v. *Yates* (1881) 18 Ch.D. 76, 85; *Re Foster and G.W. Ry.* (1882) 8 Q.B.D. at pp. 521, 522; but see the *dicta* in *Gray* v. *Lord Ashburton* [1917] A.C. 26; and see *Ottway* v. *Jones* [1955] 1 W.L.R. 706 (*post*, p. 402).

Hawkins J. in *Roberts* v. *Jones* and *Willey* v. *G. N. Ry.*
[1891] 2 Q.B., at p. 198.) " The judge is not confined to the
consideration of the defendant's conduct in the actual litigation
itself, but may also take into consideration matters which led
up to and were the occasion of that litigation." (*Per* A. L.
Smith L.J. in *Bostock* v. *Ramsey U.D.C.* [1900] 2 Q.B., at
p. 622.)

Illustrations

If the action is unfairly or oppressively brought or persisted in, there will
be ground for depriving the plaintiff of the ordinary costs. *Per* Lord Esher
M.R., in
> *Barnes* v. *Maltby* (1889) 5 T.L.R. 207.

But bringing an action to recover money which is in fact due to the
plaintiff cannot be said to be oppressive. *Per* Lord Esher M.R., in
> *Wilts. etc., Dairy Association* v. *Hammond* (1889) 5 T.L.R. 196.

That the defendant won the action by relying on a merely technical
defence is no ground for depriving him of costs.
> *Granville & Co.* v. *Firth* (1903) 72 L.J.K.B. 152.

Nor is the mere fact that a plaintiff in an action for unliquidated
damages claimed £600 and only recovered £50. *Per* Lord Esher M.R., in
> *Pearman* v. *Baroness Burdett-Coutts* (1887) 3 T.L.R., at p. 720.

But where a plaintiff preferred an extravagant and extortionate claim,
supported it by fraudulent statements and dishonest acts, and endeavoured
to substantiate it before the jury by evidence which they very properly
disbelieved, the judge at the trial, the Court of Appeal, and the House of
Lords all agreed that there was good ground for depriving him of his
costs, although he had recovered £50 damages.
> *Huxley* v. *West London Extension Ry.* (1889) 17 Q.B.D. 373; 14
> App.Cas. 26

And where a plaintiff claimed two sums of £85 and 6s., was nonsuited
in his original action without any order as to costs being made, and
recovered only 6s. in a second action, he was ordered to pay the defendant's
costs of both actions, which the court regarded as vexatious.
> *Harris* v. *Petherick* (1879) 4 Q.B.D. 611.
> See also *Perry* v. *Stopher* [1959] 1 W.L.R. 415.

Whenever a defendant by his misstatements, made under circumstances
which impose an obligation upon him to be truthful, brings litigation on
himself and renders an action against him reasonable, he may properly be
deprived of costs although successful.
> *Sutcliffe* v. *Smith* (1866) 2 T.L.R. 881.
> *East* v. *Berkshire C.C.* (1911) 106 L.T. 65.

And so may a plaintiff if the action be brought for political motives and
not from a bona fide desire to obtain redress for a grievance.
> *O'Connor* v. *The Star Newspaper Co. Ltd.* (1893) 68 L.T. 146.

The fact that the plaintiff's witnesses gave exaggerated evidence as to
the damages is not, by itself, a sufficient reason for depriving the plaintiff
of his costs.
> *Lipman* v. *Pulman* [1904] W.N. 139.

The judge may order a successful plaintiff to pay the costs occasioned
by a claim for special damage which he has failed to substantiate.
> *Forster* v. *Farquhar* [1893] 1 Q.B. 564; 62 L.J.Q.B. 296.

Or any costs unnecessarily inflicted on the defendant by the successful plaintiff's conduct of the action.

> *Roberts* v. *Jones* [1891] 2 Q.B. 194; 60 L.J.Q.B. 441.
> *Hill* v. *Morris* (1891) 8 T.L.R. 55.

So, too, the judge " has power to order a successful defendant to pay such part of the plaintiff's costs as has been caused by the defendant's misconduct in the action." *Per* Channell J. in

> *Andrew* v. *Grove* [1902] 1 K.B., at p. 628.

E.g., where the costs have been increased by the defendants improperly severing in their defences.

> *Re Isaac* [1897] 1 Ch. 251; 66 L.J.Ch. 160.
> *Bagshaw* v. *Pimm* [1900] P. 148; 69 L.J.P. 45.

Where the plaintiff establishes facts sufficient to give the court jurisdiction to grant some discretionary relief—*e.g.*, an order for possession of premises within the Rent Restrictions Acts—but the relief is refused, the defendant may, in exceptional cases, be ordered to pay the plaintiff's costs.

> *Ottway* v. *Jones* [1955] 1 W.L.R. 706.

An unsuccessful plaintiff in one of two actions, listed and tried together but not consolidated, cannot be ordered to pay costs incurred in the other action to which he was not a party.

> *John Fairfax & Sons* v. *de Witt & Co.* [1958] 1 Q.B. 323.

If either party desires to appeal from the judge's decision as to costs and from that only, his counsel must ask for leave to appeal; otherwise the Court of Appeal will not entertain an appeal as to costs only, nor will it as a rule hear an appeal against the refusal of the trial judge to give the necessary leave.[11] But, as we have seen (*ante*, p. 380n.), if the appeal involves other matters besides costs, the Court of Appeal can deal with the question of costs, even though the appeal as to the other matters fails and no leave has been obtained from the trial judge.[11a]

There are some instances in which the judge's discretion over costs is affected by statute and these are dealt with at pp. 406–410.

Bases of Taxation

There are now four different bases on which costs may be taxed, the principles having been greatly simplified by rules made in 1959 and now contained in Order 62. These bases are:

   (i) Party and party;
   (ii) common fund;
   (iii) trustees';
   (iv) solicitor and own client.

The court may in its discretion order that the costs payable by

---

[11] *Ex p. Stevenson* [1892] 1 Q.B. 609, 611.
[11a] *Wheeler* v. *Somerfield & Others* [1966] 2 Q.B. 94.

the unsuccessful party shall be taxed on either of the first two bases and sometimes on the third; but no power is conferred by the rules to order a party without consent (which is sometimes given, for example, when an action is settled) to pay costs to be taxed as between solicitor and own client.[12]   The first two bases are applicable to costs which under the rules or an order or direction of the court are to be paid to a party to any proceedings either by another party to those proceedings or out of any fund (other than a fund which the party to whom the costs are to be paid holds as trustee or personal representative) (r. 28 (1))—*e.g.*, where a legatee is given costs out of the estate.

(i) *Party and party.*—This, unless some special order is made, is the ordinary basis for the taxation of the costs which an unsuccessful litigant has to pay to his opponent. On this basis " there shall be allowed all such costs as were necessary or proper for the attainment of justice or for enforcing or defending the rights of the party whose costs are being taxed " (r. 28 (2)).

" Any charges merely for conducting litigation more conveniently may be called luxuries, and must be paid by the party incurring them " (*per* Malins V.-C. in *Smith* v. *Buller* (1875) L.R. 19 Eq. at p. 475).   Thus costs incurred through over-caution, negligence or mistake, special fees to counsel and other unusual expenses will usually be disallowed, as they may be on a taxation on the common fund basis also.   The taxing master will be guided by the scale set out in Order 62, Appendix 2, many of the items in which are discretionary as to amount, and by the notes thereto and the general provisions in Part X of that appendix, which are important.   Except in special cases he cannot, when taxing on the party and party or common fund basis, allow for items not mentioned in the scale or any higher amount than is there prescribed (r. 32).

(ii) *Common fund.*—Sometimes the court orders that the costs payable shall be taxed not " as between party and party " but " on the common fund basis " and then a more generous allowance may, if the circumstances warrant it, be made.

Before 1959 this result was achieved by ordering costs to be taxed " as between solicitor and client " and there were various

---

[12] Even before the new rules it was doubted whether this power existed. (See *Morgan* v. *Carmarthen Corpn.* [1957] Ch. 455, 456.)

kinds of solicitor and client taxation according to the circumstances. There was also some obscurity as to the extent of the court's jurisdiction to make such an order except in matters of equitable jurisdiction. These niceties have now been swept away and it is provided by rule 28 (3) that the court, in awarding costs to which the rule applies, may order them to be taxed on the common fund basis in any case in which it thinks fit to do so. The discretion must, of course, be exercised judicially as it used to be in ordering costs to be taxed as between solicitor and client —*e.g.*, where a portion of a pleading is struck out as scandalous. The term " as between solicitor and client " has now disappeared as a category of costs in the High Court; but there remains " as between solicitor and own client."

In a taxation on the common fund basis there will be allowed a reasonable amount in respect of all costs reasonably incurred; but the taxing master must ordinarily observe Order 62, Appendix 2 (r. 32, *ante*, p. 403), and should apply the rules formerly applicable on a taxation as between solicitor and client where the costs were to be paid out of a common fund in which the client and others were interested (r. 28 (4)),[13] whether or not the costs are in fact so to be paid.

This is also the basis on which the costs of an assisted person are to be taxed under the Legal Aid and Advice Act, 1949, 3rd Schedule [14]; but no question is to be raised as to the propriety of any act for which prior approval of the Area Committee was obtained (see paragraph 4 of that schedule). When a party is an assisted person under the Act a direction for taxation of his own costs in accordance with the schedule should be applied for at the conclusion of the proceedings, whether he be successful or unsuccessful. This is usually necessary in order that the machinery by which his legal advisers obtain their remuneration from public funds may be set in motion. (Legal Aid (General) Regulations, 1962, reg. 19.)

(iii) *Trustees' costs.*—" Where a person is or has been a party to any proceedings in the capacity of trustee, personal representative or mortgagee, he shall, unless the court otherwise orders, be entitled to the costs of those proceedings, in so far as they

---

[13] As illustrated by *Reed* v. *Gray* [1952] Ch. 337 and *Gibbs* v. *Gibbs* [1952] P. 332.
[14] As to which, see *Lyon* v. *Lyon* [1952] 2 All E.R. 831; *W. & F. Marshall, Ltd.* v. *Barnes & Fitzpatrick* [1953] 1 W.L.R. 639.

are not recovered from or paid by any other person, out of the fund held by the trustee or personal representative or the mortgaged property, as the case may be; and the court may otherwise order only on the ground that the trustee, personal representative or mortgagee has acted unreasonably or, in the case of a trustee or personal representative, has in substance acted for his own benefit rather than for the benefit of the fund " (r. 6 (2)). That rule deals with the right of a trustee, personal representative or mortgagee to recoup himself out of the fund which he holds and is automatic in the absence of any order to the contrary. But it is further provided that when awarding costs which are to be paid by one party to another, if the recipient of the costs is or was a party to the proceedings in the capacity of a trustee or personal representative, the court has a discretion to order the costs which he recovers from the other party to be taxed on the trustees' basis; so also, if costs are to be paid out of any fund, the court may order them to be so taxed although the fund is one which the recipient does not hold as trustee or personal representative (r. 28 (5)).

In a taxation on the trustees' basis " no costs shall be disallowed except in so far as those costs or any part of their amount should not, in accordance with the duty of the trustee or personal representative as such, have been incurred or paid, or should for that or any other reason be borne by him personally " (r. 31 (2); and see *Re Grimthorpe* [1958] Ch. 615).

(iv) *Solicitor and own client.*—It must not be supposed that even if the successful party is awarded costs on the common fund basis he may not be called upon to pay some portion of his solicitor's bill. For on a taxation of a solicitor's bill to his own client for contentious business (other than a taxation under the Legal Aid and Advice Act, 1949) " all costs are to be allowed except in so far as they are of an unreasonable amount or have been unreasonably incurred " (r. 29). All costs incurred with the express or implied approval of the client are conclusively presumed to have been reasonably incurred and, where the amount has been so approved, to have been reasonable in amount; save that costs of an unusual nature which would not be allowed on a party and party basis are presumed, until the contrary is shown, to have been unreasonably incurred unless the solicitor expressly informed the client before they were incurred that they might not be so allowed (*ibid.*). Items altogether outside the solicitor's retainer and not approved by the client and items in excess of what the solicitor is by law permitted to charge would be disallowed.

Review of Taxation

Any party who is dissatisfied with a taxing master's decision as to any items may (ordinarily within fourteen days) deliver written objections to his opponent and to the master, at the same time calling upon the latter to review the taxation as to those items. Answers to these objections may then be delivered by the party interested to dispute them, if he so desires, and a review of the decision will be made accordingly. Thereafter any party may apply to a judge in chambers by summons for an order for a further review, whereupon the judge may make such order as the circumstances require, *e.g.*, for the taxing master's certificate to be amended or for any item in dispute (except as to amount) to be remitted to the same or another taxing master for taxation (rr. 33–35).

Statutes Affecting Discretion

By section 1 of the Slander of Women Act, 1891, in any action for words spoken and made actionable by that Act, " a plaintiff shall not recover more costs than damages, unless the judge shall certify that there was reasonable ground for bringing the action." Hence, in this case the plaintiff's counsel must ask at the conclusion of the trial[14a] for a certificate, unless the verdict is so large that it clearly exceeds the amount at which the costs of the action will be taxed. Section 17 (2) of the Rent and Mortgage Interest (Restrictions) Act, 1920, provides that if a person takes proceedings under that Act in the High Court which he could have taken in the county court, he shall not be entitled to recover any costs. There are other statutes which contain special provisions as to costs; but these do not always deprive the judge of his power in a proper case to make a discretionary order as to costs.

But by far the most important instance is section 47 of the County Courts Act, 1959. This section only applies to such actions as could have been commenced in the county court.[15]

[14a] Although a later application can be made to the trial judge if necessary. (*Russo* v. *Cole* [1966] 1 W.L.R. 248.)

[15] See *Solomon* v. *Mulliner* [1901] 1 K.B. 76.

It is therefore necessary to remember that the county court has no jurisdiction except by consent to try actions for libel, slander, seduction, or actions for recovery of land or involving the title to any hereditament, the land or hereditament being of a net annual value for rating exceeding £400, or the title to any toll, fair, market or franchise (ss. 39, 48 and 51). Apart from such actions, the county court can try any action founded on contract or tort where the amount claimed does not exceed £750.[16] It can also try actions for the recovery of land, and actions in which the title to any hereditament comes in question or in which an easement or licence over a hereditament is claimed, where the net annual value of the land or hereditament for rating does not exceed £400 (ss. 48, 51). Subject to these fundamental limitations, section 47 (1) provides that, if the plaintiff commences in the High Court an action founded on contract or tort and " recovers " [17] less than £100, he will be entitled to no costs whatever; if he recovers £100 or upwards, but less than £500,[17a] he will be entitled to county court costs only, unless in either event the case falls within one of the following exceptions:

(a) if it appears to the High Court or a judge thereof (or where the matter is tried before a referee or officer of the Supreme Court to that referee or officer) that there was reasonable ground for supposing the amount recoverable in respect of the plaintiff's claim to be in excess of the amount recoverable in an action commenced in the county court, the question of costs is not affected by the section;

(b) if the same authority [18] is satisfied either that there was sufficient reason for bringing the action in the High Court or that the defendant or one of the defendants objected to the transfer of the action to a county court, he may make an order allowing the costs or any part of the costs on the High Court scale or on any one of the county court scales.

---

[16] Section 39. Increased from £500 since May 26, 1970, by the Administration of Justice Act, 1969 (Commencement No. 2) Order, 1970 (S.I. No. 672).

[17] See *post*, p. 408. Money paid into court and accepted is " recovered." (*Parr* v. *Lillicrap* (1862) 1 H. & C. 615; *Parkes* v. *Knowles* [1957] 1 W.L.R. 1040; *Colton* v. *McCaughey* [1970] 1 W.L.R. 63.

[17a] Increased from £400 (see footnote 16).

[18] Or, in the case of a remitted action, the county court judge (County Courts Act, 1959, s. 76).

A plaintiff is to be treated for this purpose as recovering the full amount recoverable in respect of his claim without regard to any deduction made in respect of contributory negligence on his part or otherwise in respect of matters not falling to be taken into account in determining whether the action could have been commenced in the county court.

In both cases, therefore, it is the duty of the plaintiff's counsel to apply to the judge for such a certificate or special order.

In actions brought to enforce a right to recover possession of goods, whether or not a claim for payment of any debt or damages is included, the amount " recovered " is the aggregate amount recovered by the plaintiff, including the value of any goods in respect of which he obtains an order for delivery or for payment of their value (section 47 (1A)).[18a]

The section applies whenever the plaintiff's claim is reduced below the limit by an admitted set-off, as distinct from a counterclaim [19]; but not where it is so reduced by a set-off which he does not admit, or by a counterclaim,[20] or even by a payment made to the plaintiff out of court after action brought.[21] It does not apply to any counterclaim; the defendant is always entitled to the costs of his counterclaim, if he recovers under it any amount, however small, because he is not responsible for the action being commenced in the High Court.[22] Nor does the section apply as between the defendant and a third party whom he has brought in.[23] Moreover, if the plaintiff, in addition to recovering nominal damages, obtains an injunction or other relief claimed as a matter of substance, he will be entitled to his costs in spite of the section.[24]

The section applies if the action is founded either on contract or tort, and the distinction is for this purpose immaterial. It is however material for some purposes. Very often a cause of action may be framed and treated either as a breach of contract or as a tort. But when the court is compelled to draw a hard

[18a] This sub-section is added by the Administration of Justice Act, 1969, s. 4, and affects actions commenced on or after May 26, 1970.
[19] *Lovejoy* v. *Cole* [1894] 2 Q.B. 861.
[20] *Stooke* v. *Taylor* (1880) 5 Q.B.D. 569; *Goldhill* v. *Clarke* (1892) 68 L.T. 414.
[21] *Pearce* v. *Bolton* [1902] 2 K.B. 111; *Lamb Brothers* v. *Keeping* (1914) 111 L.T. 527. But see *Colton* v. *McCaughey* [1970] 1 W.L.R. 63.
[22] *Blake* v. *Appleyard* (1878) 3 Ex.D. 195; *Amon* v. *Bobbett* (1889) 22 Q.B.D. 543.
[23] *Per* Field J. in *Bates* v. *Burchell* [1884] W.N. 108.
[24] *Keates* v. *Woodward* [1902] 1 K.B. 532.

and fast line the distinction depends on the facts of the case, not on the form of the pleadings. When a tort is committed by a party in contractual relationship with another, the test is, can the plaintiff maintain an action without setting up and relying on a contract? If so, it is an action of tort. " Where the breach of duty alleged arises out of a liability independently of the personal obligation undertaken by contract, it is tort, and it may be tort even though there may happen to be a contract between the parties, if the duty in fact arises independently of that contract. Breach of contract occurs where that which is complained of is a breach of duty arising out of the obligations undertaken by the contract." (*Per* Greer L.J. in *Jarvis* v. *Moy, Davies & Co.* [1936] 1 K.B., at p. 405.) [24a]

Illustrations

An action founded on the common law liability of a bailee for negligence is an action of tort within the meaning of the section, although the bailment was a contract.

> *Turner* v. *Stallibrass* [1898] 1 Q.B. 56; 67 L.J.Q.B. 52. See also *Chesworth* v. *Farrar* [1966] 2 W.L.R. 1073 and cases there cited.

The defendant demised certain premises to the plaintiff, and then wrongfully removed the fixtures. *Held*, that the action was founded on tort.

> *Sachs* v. *Henderson* [1902] 1 K.B. 612; 71 L.J.K.B. 392.

An action by a passenger against a railway company for personal injuries caused by negligence is an action founded on tort, although he took a ticket.

> *Taylor* v. *Manchester, etc., Ry.* [1895] 1 Q.B. 134; 64 L.J.Q.B. 6.
> *Kelly* v. *Metropolitan Ry.* [1895] 1 Q.B. 944; 64 L.J.Q.B. 568.

But a claim for damages by a workman against his employers for breach of duty in failing to provide a safe system of work may be framed in contract so as to enable an order for service out of the jurisdiction to be made. (See *ante*, p. 37.)

> *Matthews* v. *Kuwait Bechtel Corporation* [1959] 2 Q.B. 57.

An action of detinue is, for the purpose at any rate of costs, one of tort.

> *Bryant* v. *Herbert* (1878) 3 C.P.D. 389; 47 L.J.C.P. 670.
> *Cohen* v. *Foster* (1892) 61 L.J.Q.B. 643.

But the plaintiff will be entitled to costs if the goods detained be recovered *in specie*.

> *Keates* v. *Woodward* [1902] 1 K.B. 532.
> *Du Pasquier* v. *Cadbury Jones & Co.* [1903] 1 K.B. 104; 72 L.J.K.B. 78.
> *Deverell* v. *Milne* [1920] 2 Ch. 52; 89 L.J.Ch. 305.

[24a] Applied in *Bagot* v. *Stevens Scanlan & Co. Ltd.* [1966] 1 Q.B. 197 (at pp. 203–204); where it was held that under a building contract the duty of an architect to exercise reasonable skill and care arose under the contract alone and not in tort.

An assisted person under the Legal Aid and Advice Acts, 1949 and 1960, is placed on a special footing as regards liability for his opponent's costs. He is to be ordered to pay such amount as is reasonable having regard to all the circumstances including the means of both parties and their conduct in connection with the dispute (Legal Aid and Advice Act, 1949, s. 2 (2) (*e*)). The amount of any damages awarded to him may at this stage be taken into consideration.[25] As to the determination of the amount of his liability for costs see the Legal Aid (General) Regulations, 1962, regulation 18.

An unassisted person may sometimes be justified in making an application for an order under the Legal Aid Act, 1964, s. 1, for his own party and party costs to be paid out of the legal aid fund if he is successful in an action against an assisted party. His own means are relevant, for no such order can be made unless the court is satisfied that he will otherwise suffer severe financial hardship.[25a] In that case, provided the proceedings in the court of first instance were instituted by his opponent, the court may award the whole or any part of his costs if (and only if) it is satisfied that it is just and equitable in all the circumstances. As to the procedure for making and hearing applications, see the Legal Aid (Costs of Successful Unassisted Parties) Regulations, 1964.

Costs of Separate Issues

Although the judge may award one party the general costs of the action, he may yet order him to pay the costs of any separate issues on which he has failed. " An isolated question of fact is not an ' issue.' An ' issue ' is that which results in a determination or adjudication in favour of one party or the other." [26] There was formerly a rule which provided that the costs of separate issues should follow their own event, but this was revoked in 1929. While these cases have therefore lost much of their former importance, they are still useful as a guide for the exercise of judicial discretion in deciding whether or not a special order should be made. Thus a party against whom judgment is

---

[25] *Nolan* v. *C. & C. Marshall, Ltd.* [1954] 2 Q.B. 42.

[25a] See *Nowotnik* v. *Nowotnik* [1965] P. 83; and *In re Spurling's Will Trusts* [1966] 1 W.L.R. 920; *Hanning* v. *Maitland (No.* 2) [1970] 2 W.L.R. 151.

[26] *Per* Buckley L.J. in *Howell* v. *Dering* [1915] 1 K.B. at p. 63; see also *Reid, Hewitt & Co.* v. *Joseph* [1918] A.C. 717; *Williams* v. *Stanley Jones & Co.* [1926] 2 K.B. 37.

entered may yet fairly expect to be awarded the costs of any separate issues upon which he has succeeded, or that some equivalent order will be made. The general costs of the action will be found as a rule to exceed the costs of any number of issues, but the taxing master will divide any items of costs which are attributable to more than one issue. A judge sometimes makes a special order giving one party the costs of the action, except in so far as they have been increased by some particular issue having been raised.[27] Or he will in some cases direct that the whole of the successful party's costs of the action be taxed, and that he shall receive only a certain proportion of the amount at which they are taxed—a course strongly recommended by Kekewich J. in *Re Pollard* [1902] W.N. 49, and held in *Cinema Press, Ltd.* v. *Pictures and Pleasures, Ltd.* [1945] 1 K.B. 356, to be the simplest method—or he may award any party a lump sum in lieu of taxed costs. (Order 62, r. 9 (4); and see *ante*, p. 399.)

But when the plaintiff sues on two distinct *causes of action*, fails on one and wins on the other, the defendant is entitled, subject to the judge's discretion, to all his costs referable solely to the first cause of action, the plaintiff to all his costs referable solely to the second cause of action, the costs common to both causes of action being apportioned between them.[28]

As to the costs of a counterclaim, see *ante*, pp. 225–227.

Illustrations

In an action for libel the defendant pleaded justification and privilege. The judge ruled that the occasion was privileged; the jury negatived malice, but found that the words were not true. *Held*, that the defendant was entitled to the general costs of the action, the plaintiff to the costs of those witnesses only whose evidence related exclusively to the issue whether the words were true or false.

> *Harrison* v. *Bush* (1855) 5 E. & B. 344; 25 L.J.Q.B. 99.
> *Brown* v. *Houston* [1901] 2 K.B. 855; 70 L.J.K.B. 902.

In an action for damages for the obstruction of a right of way, claimed alternatively as a public and as a private right of way, the jury found that there was a public, but not a private, right of way. *Held*, that the plaintiff was entitled to the general costs of the action, and the defendant only to the costs of the issue on which he had succeeded, namely, as to the private right of way.

> *Smyth* v. *Wilson* [1904] 2 Ir.R. 40.

The Registrar of Trade Marks granted W. C. & Co. leave to register a trade mark. The R. B. P. Co. appealed against the order, and on the

---

[27] *The Adams* (1919) 88 L.J.P. 129.
[28] *Todd* v. *N.E. Ry.* (1903) 88 L.T. 112.

appeal raised several issues as to the user and non-user of the trade mark before 1875 and its subsequent abandonment. On these issues the R. B. P. Co. failed, but the appeal was allowed and the order of the registrar reversed. Byrne J. ordered W. C. & Co. to pay to the R. B. P. Co. all the costs of the appeal, except so far as such costs had been increased by the issues of fact found against them.

Re Wright, Crossley & Co. [1900] 2 Ch. 218, 229.

Payment into Court

If the defendant pays a sum of money into court, and the plaintiff accepts it in satisfaction of the cause of action, or all the causes of action, in respect of which he claims, the plaintiff is entitled to his costs up to the time of receipt of the notice of payment in, even though the sum paid in be only sixpence [29]—unless (a) the master otherwise orders,[30] which he may do for good cause in exceptional circumstances, *e.g.*, if the whole action is useless or malicious [31]; or (b) the case is covered by the County Courts Act, 1959, s. 47.[32] If the plaintiff does not accept the sum paid into court, but continues his action in the hope of recovering more, the judge must take the payment and its amount into consideration to such extent, if any, as may be appropriate in the circumstances (Order 62, r. 5). The plaintiff will ordinarily be entitled to the whole of his costs of the action if the amount of the ultimate judgment be larger than the sum paid into court. But if he recovers an amount not greater than the sum in court, the plaintiff is, subject to the judge's discretion, entitled to have his costs of the action up to the time when the money was paid into court, and the defendant to have his costs incurred after that time, less any severable costs subsequent to the payment into court in respect of any issue on which the plaintiff has succeeded.[33] Or the judge may give the plaintiff his costs up to payment in, give each party the costs since payment in of the issue on which he has succeeded, and order the general costs to be apportioned.[34]

[29] Order 62, r. 10; *M'Sheffrey* v. *Lanagan* (1887) 20 L.R.Ir. 528.
[30] Order 62, r. 10.
[31] *Broadhurst* v. *Willey* [1876] W.N. 21.
[32] See *ante*, pp. 406–409, and *Parr* v. *Lillicrap* (1862) 1 H. & C. 615; *Parkes* v. *Knowles* [1957] 1 W.L.R. 1040.
[33] *Powell* v. *Vickers, Sons & Maxim, Ltd.* [1907] 1 K.B. 71; *Fitzgerald* v. *Thomas Tilling, Ltd.* (1907) 96 L.T. 718; *The Blanche* [1908] P. 259.
[34] *Willcox* v. *Kettell* [1937] 1 All E.R. 222.

Illustrations

Payment into court is a necessary part of a plea under section 2 of Lord Campbell's Libel Act. Hence, if the jury find a verdict for the plaintiff for an amount less than the sum paid into court, but also find that the defendant was guilty of malice or gross negligence, the plaintiff will be entitled to the general costs of the action, because the defendant has failed to prove the whole of his plea.

> *Oxley* v. *Wilkes* [1898] 2 Q.B. 56; 67 L.J.Q.B. 678.

In all other cases, where a plaintiff recovers an amount not greater than the sum which the defendant has paid into court, the defendant is prima facie entitled to the general costs of the action, but may be ordered to pay the costs of any issue on which he has failed, even though that issue was not one going to the whole cause of the action.

> *Hubback* v. *British North Borneo Co.* [1904] 2 K.B. 473.
> *Ridout* v. *Green* (1902) 87 L.T. 679.

Whether a plaintiff is entitled to the costs of an issue is a matter for the discretion of the trial judge.

> *Hultquist* v. *Universal Pattern and Precision Engineering Co. Ltd.* [1960] 2 Q.B. 467, 481, 482.

The plaintiff claimed damages for personal injuries caused by the defendants' negligence. The defendants denied the negligence, but paid £450 into court. The jury found that the defendants were guilty of the negligence, and assessed the damages at £200. *Held,* that under these circumstances the proper course was for the judge to direct that the plaintiff should have the general costs of the action up to the time of the payment into court, and that the defendants should have the general costs subsequent to that date other than the costs attributable to the issue, negligence or no negligence.

> *Davies* v. *Edinburgh Life Assurance Co.* [1916] 2 K.B. 852; 85 L.J.K.B. 1662.

The plaintiffs claimed an injunction and damages. On a motion for an interlocutory injunction the defendants gave an undertaking, and the costs of the motion were reserved. Later the defendants paid into court a sum of money, at the same time denying the plaintiffs' right to an injunction. The plaintiffs accepted in satisfaction the sum paid in, and abandoned their claim for an injunction. It was held that they were nevertheless entitled to the costs of the motion.

> *Wiltshire Bacon Co.* v. *Associated Cinemas* [1938] 1 Ch. 268; 107 L.J.Ch. 49.

Married Women

A married woman may be ordered to pay costs as if she were a *feme sole* (Law Reform (Married Women and Tortfeasors) Act, 1935, s. 1). Since the Married Women (Restraint upon Anticipation) Act, 1949, has abolished any such restriction, the whole of a married woman's property is now liable for costs.

Several Parties

When several persons join in one action as plaintiffs and some succeed and others fail, the defendant should ask for an order for any special costs occasioned by the joinder of those who failed (see *ante*, p. 30). Before 1959 he was entitled to them automatically unless the judge otherwise ordered.

Where a plaintiff sues two defendants who defend jointly by the same solicitor, and judgment is given in favour of one defendant and against the other, the successful defendant is, in the absence of any agreement between him and his co-defendant as to how their costs are to be borne *inter se*, entitled to recover from the plaintiff half the costs of the defence.[35] In an action claiming relief against two defendants in the alternative, if the judge is satisfied that it was a reasonable and proper course for the plaintiff to join both defendants, he may order the plaintiff to pay the costs of the successful defendant and then to add those costs to the costs which the unsuccessful defendant is ordered to pay to the plaintiff. This is commonly called a " Bullock order " after the case of *Bullock* v. *London General Omnibus Co.* [1907] 1 K.B. 264. He may do so whether one defendant has blamed the other or not[36]; it is a matter of discretion.[37] In some cases the unsuccessful defendant is ordered to pay the successful defendant's costs to him directly.[38] When one of several co-defendants who are ordered to pay the plaintiff's taxed costs pays the whole of such costs, he is entitled to obtain contribution from the others without an independent proceeding.[39]

The court has a complete discretion in regard to the costs of third or subsequent parties.[39a]

Illustrations

The plaintiff was injured by a collision between an omnibus and a cart. He brought an action against the owners of both vehicles charging them both jointly and severally with negligence. The jury found negligence on the part of the driver of the omnibus, and negatived negligence on the part of the driver of the cart. The judge entered judgment for the plaintiff against the first-named defendant, and judgment for the successful defendant, with costs in each case.

---

[35] *Beaumont* v. *Senior and Bull* [1903] 1 K.B. 282; *Ellingsen* v. *Det Skandinaviske Co.* [1919] 2 K.B. 567.

[36] *Besterman* v. *British Motor Cab Co. Ltd.* [1914] 3 K.B. 181.

[37] *Hong* v. *A. & R. Brown Ltd.* [1948] 1 K.B. 515.

[38] *Sanderson* v. *Blyth Theatre Co.* [1903] 2 K.B. 533; *The Esrom* [1914] W.N. 81; *Parkes* v. *Knowles* [1957] 1 W.L.R. 1040; and see *Mayer* v. *Harte & Others* [1960] 1 W.L.R. 770, *per* Harman L.J. at p. 776, where it was said that in a case not tried with a jury, prima facie the *Sanderson* form of order should be followed.

[39] *Newry Salt Works Co.* v. *Macdonnell* [1903] 2 Ir.R. 454.

[39a] *Edginton* v. *Clark* [1964] 1 Q.B. 367.

The judge further ordered that the costs so payable by the plaintiff should be included in the costs recoverable from the first-named defendant.

> *Bullock* v. *L.G.O. Co.* [1907] 1 K.B. 264; 76 L.J.K.B. 127; approved in *Compania Sansinena, etc.* v. *Houlder Brothers* [1910] 2 K.B. 354; 79 L.J.K.B. 1094.

In a similar case, the Court of Appeal held that the judge had a discretion to make such an order, although before the issue of the writ the motor cab company had not intimated to the plaintiff their intention to throw the responsibility for the accident on the other defendant.

> *Besterman* v. *British Motor Cab Co., Ltd.* [1914] 3 K.B. 181; 83 L.J.K.B. 1014.

But note that in 1870, where the plaintiff bought land from F, who asserted that he had authority to sell it on behalf of himself and his co-owners, and they proved that he had no such authority, it was held that the plaintiff could recover from F the costs of the action only up to the date when the plaintiff had received and considered certain answers to interrogatories in which the co-owners had sworn that F had no such authority.

> *Godwin* v. *Francis* (1870) L.R. 5 C.P. 295; 39 L.J.C.P. 121.

Costs of Proceedings in Chambers

" Costs may be dealt with by the court at any stage of the proceedings " (Order 62, r. 4). " The court " in these rules includes masters and district registrars (r. 1). The provision in rule 3 that costs will be ordered to follow the event except when it appears to the court that in the circumstances of the case some other order should be made as to the whole or any part of the costs, is applicable to proceedings in chambers no less than at the trial. It is, however, not quite clear whether in relation to interlocutory proceedings " the event " is intended to mean the event of the particular application or the event of the whole action, in which latter case the master should, subject to his discretion to order otherwise, order " costs in the cause." (This means that whoever has to pay the general costs of the action will also have to pay both parties' costs of the application.) An interlocutory application—*e.g.*, a summons for directions—may not have an " event " of its own at all. But whichever interpretation be adopted, it is clear that the master must in each case exercise his discretion; and in interlocutory applications the circumstances of the case may often in fairness require some special order to be made. If the application is a proper one, " costs in the cause " frequently gives a just result.

The master sometimes orders " plaintiff's [*or* defendant's] costs in the cause "; this means that the costs of the party so named follow the general costs of the action; if he wins he gets them from the other party, but the other party has to pay his own whatever happens. If the master orders " plaintiff's [*or* defendant's] costs in any event " it means that the opposite party will have to pay the costs of the application on both sides, whatever the result of the action; but not at once—they will be taken into account in the ultimate taxation. If the person against whom the order is made is not an assisted person, the master may order " costs to be paid forthwith " (Order 62, r. 4). If an application is dismissed " with costs " it means costs to be taxed as between party and party and paid forthwith. The general power under r. 28 (3), to order costs to be taxed on the common fund basis, may be exercised in appropriate cases by the master.

No costs are allowed in respect of counsel attending before a master in chambers unless the master certifies that the attendance was proper in the circumstances. Before a judge in chambers one counsel is allowed without certificate, but for more than one the judge must be asked to certify. (Order 62, App. 2, Pt. X, para. 2 (3).) This is usually done by junior counsel.

An appeal lies from the master's decision to the judge in chambers, even where it only affects costs.[40] But if the order be not appealed from at the time, the judge at the trial has no power to vary it.[41]

Costs in the Court of Appeal

In the Court of Appeal costs ordinarily follow the event; and if nothing is said by the court as to costs, the order will be so drawn up. Thus if the appeal is dismissed, the respondent retains his order for costs in the court of trial and gets his costs of resisting the appeal. But if the court is allowing the appeal and reversing the decision of the trial judge, including his award of costs to the unsuccessful respondent, the normal order in the Court of Appeal will be " Appeal allowed with costs here and below." The court, however, has full discretion over the costs

---

[40] *Foster* v. *Edwards* (1879) 48 L.J.Q.B. 767.
[41] *Koosen* v. *Rose* (1897) 76 L.T. 145.

of an appeal, and in the court below, and can make such order as to the whole or any part of them as may be just.[42] Hence it may, in a proper case, refuse costs to the successful party; thus an appellant has been deprived of his costs where he succeeded on a point not raised in the court below,[43] or on fresh evidence,[44] or on a mere point of law, after having failed to prove allegations of fraud.[45] So where the appellants were innocent persons, who had used due diligence, but had been made the victims of a forgery, their appeal was dismissed without costs.[46] But the mere omission by the respondent to inform his opponent that he has a preliminary objection which proves fatal to the appeal is not a sufficient reason for depriving him of costs.[47]

The costs of an appeal may include the cost of the transcript of the judgment of the court below whether taken down and transcribed by an official shorthand writer or transcribed from a mechanical recording. Formerly the cost of a transcript of the evidence was only allowed in special circumstances.[48] Nowadays where such a transcript is a document required for use on appeal (see *ante*, p. 372) the cost of relevant portions would normally be allowable.

If the Court of Appeal reverses the judgment of the court below, it should be asked to award the successful party the costs of the trial in addition to the costs of appeal.

If the Court of Appeal orders a new trial, the costs of the first trial abide the event of the second, unless any special order be made when the new trial is granted, or at the second trial.[49] And by " the event " of the second trial is meant the result of that trial as to costs.[50]

The costs of a successful application for a new trial will, as a rule, be given to the applicant.[51]

---

[42] Order 62, r. 4 (2); *North London, etc., Co.* v. *Moy* [1918] 2 K.B. 439. But see Order 62, r. 4 (3) as to assessment or taxation of the costs below.
[43] *Hussey* v. *Horne-Payne* (1878) 8 Ch.D. 670; *Dye* v. *Dye* (1884) 13 Q.B.D. 147.
[44] *Arnot's Case* (1887) 36 Ch.D. 710; *Chard* v. *Jervis* (1882) 9 Q.B.D. 178.
[45] *Ex p. Cooper* (1878) 10 Ch.D. 313.
[46] *Cooper* v. *Vesey* (1881) 20 Ch.D. 611.
[47] *Ex p. Shead* (1885) 15 Q.B.D. 338.
[48] *Pilling* v. *Joint Stock Institute* (1896) 73 L.T. 570; *Castner Kellner* v. *Commercial, etc., Corp.* [1899] 1 Ch. 803.
[49] *Creen* v. *Wright* (1877) 2 C.P.D. 354; *Field* v. *G.N. Ry.* (1878) 3 Ex.D. 261.
[50] *Brotherton* v. *Metropolitan District Ry. Joint Committee* [1894] 1 Q.B. 666; but see *Dunn* v. *S.E. & C. Ry.* [1903] 1 K.B. 358.
[51] *Hamilton* v. *Seal* [1904] 2 K.B. 262.

The powers of the Court of Appeal to deal with applications under the Legal Aid Act, 1964, s. 1, by successful unassisted litigants are the same as those of other courts. It may either dismiss such an application forthwith, or adjourn it, and may refer it to a taxing master or district registrar for his decision or for an inquiry and report.[52]

---

[52] Legal Aid (Costs of Successful Unassisted Parties) Regulations, 1964, reg. 11; and see *ante*, p. 410.

RULES OF PARTICULAR USE TO STUDENTS

ORDER 5

MODE OF BEGINNING CIVIL PROCEEDINGS IN HIGH COURT

Mode of beginning civil proceedings

1. Subject to the provisions of any Act and of these rules, civil proceedings in the High Court may be begun by writ, originating summons, originating motion or petition.

Proceedings which must be begun by writ

2. Subject to any provision of an Act, or of these rules, by virtue of which any proceedings are expressly required to be begun otherwise than by writ, the following proceedings must, notwithstanding anything in rule 4, be begun by writ, that is to say, proceedings—

(*a*) in which a claim is made by the plaintiff for any relief or remedy for any tort, other than trespass to land;

(*b*) in which a claim made by the plaintiff is based on an allegation of fraud;

(*c*) in which a claim is made by the plaintiff for damages for breach of duty (whether the duty exists by virtue of a contract or of a provision made by or under an Act or independently of any contract or any such provision), where the damages claimed consist of or include damages in respect of the death of any person or in respect of personal injuries to any person or in respect of damage to any property;

(*d*) . . . .

(*e*) in which a claim is made by the plaintiff in respect of the infringement of a patent.

In this rule " personal injuries " includes any disease and any impairment of a person's physical or mental condition.

Proceedings which must be begun by originating summons

3. Proceedings by which an application is to be made to the High Court or a judge thereof under any Act must be begun by originating summons except where by these rules or by or under any Act the application in question is expressly required or authorised to be made by some other means.

This rule does not apply to an application made in pending proceedings.

Proceedings which may be begun by writ or originating summons

4.—(1) Except in the case of proceedings which by these rules or by or under any Act are required to be begun by writ or originating summons or are required or authorised to be begun by originating motion or petition, proceedings may be begun either by writ or by originating summons as the plaintiff considers appropriate.

(2) Proceedings—

(*a*) in which the sole or principal question at issue is, or is likely to be, one of the construction of an Act or of any instrument made under an Act, or of any deed, will, contract or other document, or some other question of law, or

(*b*) in which there is unlikely to be any substantial dispute of fact,

are appropriate to be begun by originating summons unless the plaintiff intends in those proceedings to apply for judgment under Order 14 or Order 86 or for any other reason considers the proceedings more appropriate to be begun by writ.

ORDER 6

GENERAL PROVISIONS WITH RESPECT TO WRITS OF SUMMONS

Indorsement of claim

2.—(1) Before a writ is issued it must be indorsed—

(*a*) with a statement of claim or, if the statement of claim is not indorsed on the writ, with a concise statement of the nature of the claim made or the relief or remedy required in the action begun thereby;

(*b*) where the claim made by the plaintiff is for a debt or liquidated demand only, with a statement of the amount claimed in respect of the debt or demand and for costs and also with a statement that further proceedings will be stayed if, within the time limited for appearing, the defendant . . . pays the amount so claimed . . .

Indorsement as to capacity

3.—(1) Before a writ is issued it must be indorsed—

(*a*) where the plaintiff sues in a representative capacity, with a statement of the capacity in which he sues;

(*b*) where a defendant is sued in a representative capacity, with a statement of the capacity in which he is sued.

(2) Before a writ is issued in an action brought by a plaintiff who in bringing it is acting by order or on behalf of a person resident outside the scheduled territories, it must be indorsed with a statement of that fact and with the address of the person so resident.

ORDER 7

GENERAL PROVISIONS WITH RESPECT TO ORIGINATING SUMMONSES

Contents of summons

3.—(1) Every originating summons must include a statement of the questions on which the plaintiff seeks the determination or direction of the High Court or, as the case may be, a concise statement of the relief or remedy claimed in the proceedings begun by the originating summons with sufficient particulars to identify the cause or causes of action in respect of which the plaintiff claims that relief or remedy.

ORDER 13

DEFAULT OF APPEARANCE TO WRIT

Claim for liquidated demand

1.—(1) Where a writ is indorsed with a claim against a defendant for a liquidated demand only, then, if that defendant fails to enter an appearance, the plaintiff may, after the time limited for appearing, enter final judgment against that defendant for a sum not exceeding that claimed by the writ in respect of the demand and for costs, and proceed with the action against the other defendants, if any.

(2) A claim shall not be prevented from being treated for the purposes of this rule as a claim for a liquidated demand by reason only that part of the claim is for interest accruing after the date of the writ at an unspecified rate, but any such interest shall be computed from the date of the writ to the date of entering judgment at the rate of 5 per cent.

Claim for unliquidated damages

2. Where a writ is indorsed with a claim against a defendant for unliquidated damages only, then, if that defendant fails to enter an appearance, the plaintiff may, after the time limited for appearing, enter interlocutory judgment against that defendant for damages to be assessed and costs, and proceed with the action against the other defendants, if any.

Claim in detinue

3. Where a writ is indorsed with a claim against a defendant relating to the detention of goods only, then, if that defendant fails to enter an appearance, the plaintiff may, after the time limited for appearing, at his option enter either—

(*a*) interlocutory judgment against that defendant for the return of the goods or their value to be assessed and costs; or

(*b*) interlocutory judgment for the value of the goods to be assessed and costs;

and proceed with the action against the other defendants, if any.

Claim for possession of land

4.—(1) Where a writ is indorsed with a claim against a defendant for possession of land only, then, subject to paragraph (2), if that defendant fails to enter an appearance the plaintiff may, after the time limited for appearing, and on producing a certificate by his solicitor, or (if he sues in person) an affidavit, stating that he is not claiming any relief in the action of the nature specified in Order 88, r. 1, enter judgment for possession of the land as against that defendant and costs, and proceed with the action against the other defendants, if any.

(2) Notwithstanding anything in paragraph (1), the plaintiff shall not be entitled, except with the leave of the court, to enter judgment under that paragraph unless he produces a certificate by his solicitor, or (if he sues in person) an affidavit, stating either that the claim does not relate to a dwelling-house or that the claim relates to a dwelling-house of which the rateable value exceeds, in Greater London £400, and elsewhere £200.

(3) An application for leave to enter judgment under paragraph (2) shall be by summons stating the grounds of the application, and the summons must, unless the court otherwise orders and notwithstanding anything in Order 65, rule 9, be served on the defendant against whom it is sought to enter judgment.

(4) If the court refuses leave to enter judgment, it may make or give any such order or directions as it might have made or given had the application been an application for judgment under Order 14, rule 1.

(5) Where there is more than one defendant, judgment entered under this rule shall not be enforced against any defendant unless and until judgment for possession of the land has been entered against all the defendants.

Mixed claims

5. Where a writ issued against any defendant is indorsed with two or more of the claims mentioned in the foregoing rules, and no other claim, then, if that defendant fails to enter an appearance, the plaintiff may, after the time limited for appearing, enter against that defendant such judgment in respect of any such claim as he would be entitled to enter under those rules if that were the only claim indorsed on the writ, and proceed with the action against the other defendants, if any.

Other claims

6.—(1) Where a writ is indorsed with a claim of a description not mentioned in rules 1 to 4, then, if any defendant fails to enter an appearance, the plaintiff may, after the time limited for appearing and upon filing an affidavit proving due service of the writ on that defendant and, where the statement of claim was not indorsed on or served with the writ, upon serving a statement of claim on him, proceed with the action as if that defendant had entered an appearance.

(2) Where a writ issued against a defendant is indorsed as aforesaid, but by reason of the defendant's satisfying the claim or complying with the demands thereof or any other like reason it has become unnecessary for the plaintiff to proceed with the action, then, if the defendant fails to enter an appearance, the plaintiff may, after the time limited for appearing, enter judgment with the leave of the court against that defendant for costs.

(3) An application for leave to enter judgment under paragraph (2) shall be by summons which must, unless the court otherwise orders, and notwithstanding anything in Order 65, rule 9, be served on the defendant against whom it is sought to enter judgment.

ORDER 14

SUMMARY JUDGMENT

Application by plaintiff for summary judgment

1.—(1) Where in an action to which this rule applies a statement of claim has been served on a defendant and that defendant has entered an appearance in the action, the plaintiff may, on the ground that that defendant has no defence to a claim included in the writ, or to a particular part of such a claim, or has no defence to such a claim or part except as to the amount of any damages claimed, apply to the court for judgment against that defendant.

(2) Subject to paragraph (3), this rule applies to every action in the Queen's Bench Division or Chancery Division begun by writ other than one which includes—

    (*a*) a claim by the plaintiff for libel, slander, malicious prosecution, false imprisonment. . . . or

    (*b*) a claim by the plaintiff based on an allegation of fraud.

(3) This Order shall not apply to an action to which Order 86 applies.[1]

Manner in which application under rule 1 must be made

2.—(1) An application under rule 1 must be made by summons supported by an affidavit verifying the facts on which the claim, or the part of a claim, to which the application relates is based and stating that in the deponent's belief there is no defence to that claim or part, as the case may be, or no defence except as to the amount of any damages claimed.

---

[1] *i.e.* Any action in the Chancery Division in which (*inter alia*) specific performance is claimed.

(2) Unless the court otherwise directs, an affidavit for the purposes of this rule may contain statements of information or belief with the sources and grounds thereof.

(3) The summons, a copy of the affidavit in support and of any exhibits referred to therein must be served on the defendant not less than 10 clear days before the return day.

Judgment for plaintiff

3.—(1) Unless on the hearing of an application under rule 1 either the court dismisses the application or the defendant satisfies the court with respect to the claim, or the part of a claim, to which the application relates that there is an issue or question in dispute which ought to be tried or that there ought for some other reason to be a trial of that claim or part, the court may give such judgment for the plaintiff against that defendant on that claim or part as may be just having regard to the nature of the remedy or relief claimed.

(2) The court may by order, and subject to such conditions, if any, as may be just, stay execution of any judgment given against a defendant under this rule until after the trial of any counterclaim made or raised by the defendant in the action.

Leave to defend

4.—(1) A defendant may show cause against an application under rule 1 by affidavit or otherwise to the satisfaction of the court.

(2) Rule 2 (2) applies for the purposes of this rule as it applies for the purposes of that rule.

(3) The court may give a defendant against whom such an application is made leave to defend the action with respect to the claim, or the part of a claim, to which the application relates either unconditionally or on such terms as to giving security or time or mode of trial or otherwise as it thinks fit.

(4) On the hearing of such an application the court may order a defendant showing cause or, where that defendant is a body corporate, any director, manager, secretary or other similar officer thereof, or any person purporting to act in any such capacity—

(*a*) to produce any document;

(*b*) if it appears to the court that there are special circumstances which make it desirable that he should do so, to attend and be examined on oath.

Application for summary judgment on counterclaim

5.—(1) Where a defendant to an action in the Queen's Bench Division or Chancery Division begun by writ has served a counterclaim on the plaintiff, then, subject to paragraph (3), the defendant may, on the ground that the plaintiff has no defence to a claim made in the counterclaim, or to a particular part of such a claim, apply to the court for judgment against the plaintiff on that claim or part.

(2) Rules 2, 3 and 4 shall apply in relation to an application under this rule as they apply in relation to an application under rule 1 but with the following modifications, that is to say—

(*a*) references to the plaintiff and defendant shall be construed as references to the defendant and plaintiff respectively;

(*b*) the words in rule 3 (2) " any counterclaim made or raised by the defendant in " shall be omitted; and

(*c*) the reference in rule 4 (3) to the action shall be construed as a reference to the counterclaim to which the application under this rule relates.

(3) This rule shall not apply to a counterclaim which includes any such claim as is referred to in rule 1 (2).

Directions

6.—(1) Where the court—

(*a*) orders that a defendant or a plaintiff have leave (whether conditional or unconditional) to defend an action or counterclaim, as the case may be, with respect to a claim or a part of a claim, or

(*b*) gives judgment for a plaintiff or a defendant on a claim or part of a claim but also orders that execution of the judgment be stayed pending the trial of a counterclaim or of the action, as the case may be,

the court shall give directions as to the further conduct of the action, and Order 25, rules 2 to 7, shall, with the omission of so much of rule 7 (1) as requires parties to serve a notice specifying the orders and directions which they require and with any other necessary modifications, apply as if the application under rule 1 of this Order or rule 5 thereof, as the case may be, on which the order was made were a summons for directions.

(2) In particular, and if the parties consent, the court may direct that the claim in question and any other claim in the action be tried by a master under the provisions of these rules relating to the trial of causes or matters or questions or issues by masters.

Costs

7.—(1) If the plaintiff makes an application under rule 1 where the case is not within this Order or if it appears to the court that

426

the plaintiff knew that the defendant relied on a contention which would entitle him to unconditional leave to defend, then, without prejudice to Order 62, and, in particular, to rule 4 (1) thereof, the court may dismiss the application with costs and may, if the plaintiff is not an assisted person, require the costs to be paid by him forthwith.

(2) The court shall have the same power to dismiss an application under rule 5 as it has under paragraph (1) to dismiss an application under rule 1, and that paragraph shall apply accordingly with the necessary modifications.

Right to proceed with residue of action or counterclaim

8.—(1) Where on an application under rule 1 the plaintiff obtains judgment on a claim or a part of a claim against any defendant, he may proceed with the action as respects any other claim or as respects the remainder of the claim or against any other defendant.

(2) Where on an application under rule 5 a defendant obtains judgment on a claim or part of a claim made in a counterclaim against the plaintiff, he may proceed with the counterclaim as respects any other claim or as respects the remainder of the claim or against any other defendant to the counterclaim.

Judgment for delivery up of chattel

9. Where the claim to which an application under rule 1 or rule 5 relates is for the delivery up of a specific chattel and the court gives judgment under this Order for the applicant, it shall have the same power to order the party against whom judgment is given to deliver up the chattel without giving him an option to retain it on paying the assessed value thereof as if the judgment had been given after trial.

Relief against forfeiture

10. A tenant shall have the same right to apply for relief after judgment for possession of land on the ground of forfeiture for non-payment of rent has been given under this Order as if the judgment had been given after trial.

Setting aside judgment

11. Any judgment given against a party who does not appear at the hearing of an application under rule 1 or rule 5 may be set aside or varied by the court on such terms as it thinks just.

ORDER 15

CAUSES OF ACTION, COUNTERCLAIMS AND PARTIES

Joinder of causes of action

1.—(1) Subject to rule 5 (1), a plaintiff may in one action claim relief against the same defendant in respect of more than one cause of action—

    (*a*) if the plaintiff claims, and the defendant is alleged to be liable, in the same capacity in respect of all the causes of action, or

    (*b*) if the plaintiff claims or the defendant is alleged to be liable in the capacity of executor or administrator of an estate in respect of one or more of the causes of action and in his personal capacity but with reference to the same estate in respect of all the others, or

    (*c*) with the leave of the court.

(2) An application for leave under this rule must be made ex parte by affidavit before the issue of the writ or originating summons, as the case may be, and the affidavit must state the grounds of the application.

Joinder of parties

4.—(1) Subject to rule 5 (1), two or more persons may be joined together in one action as plaintiffs or as defendants with the leave of the court or where—

    (*a*) if separate actions were brought by or against each of them, as the case may be, some common question of law or fact would arise in all the actions, and

    (*b*) all rights to relief claimed in the action (whether they are joint, several or alternative) are in respect of or arise out of the same transaction or series of transactions.

(2) Where the plaintiff in any action claims any relief to which any other person is entitled jointly with him, all persons so entitled must, subject to the provisions of any Act and unless the court gives leave to the contrary, be parties to the action and any of them who does not consent to being joined as a plaintiff must, subject to any order made by the court on an application for leave under this paragraph, be made a defendant.

This paragraph shall not apply to a probate action.

(3) Where relief is claimed in an action against a defendant who is jointly liable with some other person and also severally liable, that other person need not be made a defendant to the action; but where persons are jointly, but not severally, liable under

a contract and relief is claimed against some but not all of those persons in an action in respect of that contract, the court may, on the application of any defendant to the action, by order stay proceedings in the action until the other persons so liable are added as defendants.

Court may order separate trials, etc.

5.—(1) If claims in respect of two or more causes of action are included by a plaintiff in the same action or by a defendant in a counterclaim, or if two or more plaintiffs or defendants are parties to the same action, and it appears to the court that the joinder of causes of action or of parties, as the case may be, may embarrass or delay the trial or is otherwise inconvenient, the court may order separate trials or make such other order as may be expedient.

(2) If it appears on the application of any party against whom a counterclaim is made that the subject-matter of the counterclaim ought for any reason to be disposed of by a separate action, the court may order the counterclaim to be struck out or may order it to be tried separately or make such other order as may be expedient.

Misjoinder and nonjoinder of parties

6.—(1) No cause or matter shall be defeated by reason of the misjoinder or nonjoinder of any party; and the court may in any cause or matter determine the issues or questions in dispute so far as they affect the rights and interests of the persons who are parties to the cause or matter.

(2) At any stage of the proceedings in any cause or matter the court may on such terms as it thinks just and either of its own motion or on application—

(*a*) order any person who has been improperly or unnecessarily made a party or who has for any reason ceased to be a proper or necessary party, to cease to be a party;

(*b*) order any person who ought to have been joined as a party or whose presence before the court is necessary to ensure that all matters in dispute in the cause or matter may be effectually and completely determined and adjudicated upon be added as a party;

but no person shall be added as a plaintiff without his consent signified in writing or in such other manner as may be authorised.

(3) An application by any person for an order under paragraph (2) adding him as a defendant must, except with the leave of the court, be supported by an affidavit showing his interest in the matters in dispute in the cause or matter.

Representative proceedings

12.—(1) Where numerous persons have the same interest in any proceedings, not being such proceedings as are mentioned in rule 13, the proceedings may be begun, and, unless the court otherwise orders, continued, by or against any one or more of them as representing all or as representing all except one or more of them.

(2) At any stage of proceedings under this rule the court may, on the application of the plaintiff, and on such terms, if any, as it thinks fit, appoint any one or more of the defendants or other persons as representing whom the defendants are sued to represent all, or all except one or more, of those persons in the proceedings; and where, in exercise of the power conferred by this paragraph, the court appoints a person not named as a defendant, it shall make an order under rule 6 adding that person as a defendant.

(3) A judgment or order given in proceedings under this rule shall be binding on all the persons as representing whom the plaintiffs sue or, as the case may be, the defendants are sued, but shall not be enforced against any person not a party to the proceedings except with the leave of the court.

(4) An application for the grant of leave under paragraph (3) must be made by summons which must be served personally on the person against whom it is sought to enforce the judgment or order.

(5) Notwithstanding that a judgment or order to which any such application relates is binding on the person against whom the application is made, that person may dispute liability to have the judgment or order enforced against him on the ground that by reason of facts and matters particular to his case he is entitled to be exempted from such liability.

(6) The court hearing an application for the grant of leave under paragraph (3) may order the question whether the judgment or order is enforceable against the person against whom the application is made to be tried and determined in any manner in which any issue or question in an action may be tried and determined.

ORDER 18

PLEADINGS

Service of statement of claim

1. Unless the court gives leave to the contrary or a statement of claim is indorsed on the writ, the plaintiff must serve a statement of claim on the defendant or, if there are two or more

defendants, on each defendant, and must do so either when the writ, or notice of the writ, is served on that defendant or at any time after service of the writ or notice but before the expiration of 14 days after that defendant enters an appearance.

Service of defence

2.—(1) Subject to paragraph (2), a defendant who enters an appearance in, and intends to defend, an action must, unless the court gives leave to the contrary, serve a defence on the plaintiff before the expiration of 14 days after the time limited for appearing or after the statement of claim is served on him, whichever is the later.

(2) If a summons under Order 14, rule 1, is served on a defendant before he serves his defence, paragraph (1) shall not have effect in relation to him unless by the order made on the summons he is given leave to defend the action and, in that case, shall have effect as if it required him to serve his defence within 14 days after the making of the order or within such other period as may be specified therein.

Service of reply and defence to counterclaim

3.—(1) A plaintiff on whom a defendant serves a defence must serve a reply on that defendant if it is needed for compliance with rule 8; and if no reply is served, rule 14 (1) will apply.

(2) A plaintiff on whom a defendant serves a counterclaim must, if he intends to defend it, serve on that defendant a defence to counterclaim.

(3) Where a plaintiff serves both a reply and a defence to counterclaim on any defendant, he must include them in the same document.

(4) A reply to any defence must be served by the plaintiff before the expiration of 14 days after the service on him of that defence, and a defence to counterclaim must be served by the plaintiff before the expiration of 14 days after the service on him of the counterclaim to which it relates.

Pleadings subsequent to reply

4. No pleading subsequent to a reply or a defence to counterclaim shall be served except with the leave of the court.

Service of pleadings in Long Vacation

5. Pleadings shall not be served during the Long Vacation except with the leave of the court or with the consent of all the parties to the action.

Pleadings: formal requirements

6.—(1) Every pleading in an action must bear on its face—

(*a*) the year in which the writ in the action was issued and the letter and number of the action,

(*b*) the title of the action,

(*c*) the division of the High Court to which the action is assigned and the name of the judge (if any) to whom it is assigned or, if it is assigned to the Chancery Division, the group of judges (if any) to which it is assigned,

(*d*) the description of the pleading, and

(*e*) the date on which it was served.

(2) Every pleading must, if necessary, be divided into paragraphs numbered consecutively, each allegation being so far as convenient contained in a separate paragraph.

(3) Dates, sums and other numbers must be expressed in a pleading in figures and not in words.

(3A) Where a pleading contains a claim for a sum of money which includes an amount expressed in shillings and pence, the equivalent of that sum must also be stated in the pleading.

(4) Every pleading of a party must be indorsed—

(*a*) where the party sues or defends in person, with his name and address;

(*b*) in any other case, with the name or firm and business address of the solicitor by whom it was served and also (if the solicitor is the agent of another) the name or firm and business address of his principal.

(5) Every pleading of a party must be signed by counsel, if settled by him, and, if not, by the party's solicitor or by the party if he sues or defends in person.

Facts, not evidence, to be pleaded

7.—(1) Subject to the provisions of this rule and rules 7A, 10, 11 and 12, every pleading must contain, and contain only, a statement in a summary form of the material facts on which the party pleading relies for his claim or defence, as the case may be, but not the evidence by which those facts are to be proved, and the statement must be as brief as the nature of the case admits.

(2) Without prejudice to paragraph (1), the effect of any document or the purport of any conversation referred to in the pleading must, if material, be briefly stated, and the precise words of the document or conversation must not be stated, except in so far as those words are themselves material.

(3) A party need not plead any fact if it is presumed by law to be true or the burden of disproving it lies on the other party, unless the other party has specifically denied it in his pleading.

(4) A statement that a thing has been done or that an event has occurred, being a thing or event the doing or occurrence of which, as the case may be, constitutes a condition precedent necessary for the case of a party is to be implied in his pleading.

Conviction to be adduced in evidence: matters to be pleaded

7A.—(1) If in any action which is to be tried with pleadings any party intends, in reliance on section 11 of the Civil Evidence Act, 1968 (convictions as evidence in civil proceedings) to adduce evidence that a person was convicted of an offence by or before a court in the United Kingdom or by a court-martial there or elsewhere, he must include in his pleading a statement of his intention with particulars of—

(*a*) the conviction and the date thereof,

(*b*) the court or court-martial which made the conviction, and

(*c*) the issue in the proceedings to which the conviction is relevant.

(2) If in any action which is to be tried with pleadings any party intends, in reliance on section 12 of the said Act of 1968 (findings of adultery and paternity as evidence in civil proceedings) to adduce evidence that a person was found guilty of adultery in matrimonial proceedings or was adjudged to be the father of a child in affiliation proceedings before a court in the United Kingdom, he must include in his pleading a statement of his intention with particulars of—

(*a*) the finding or adjudication and the date thereof,

(*b*) the court which made the finding or adjudication and the proceedings in which it was made, and

(*c*) the issue in the proceedings to which the finding or adjudication is relevant.

(3) Where a party's pleading includes such a statement as is mentioned in paragraph (1) or (2), then if the opposite party—

(*a*) denies the conviction, finding of adultery or adjudication of paternity to which the statement relates, or

(*b*) alleges that the conviction, finding or adjudication was erroneous, or

(*c*) denies that the conviction, finding or adjudication is relevant to any issue in the proceedings,

he must make the denial or allegation in his pleading.

Matters which must be specifically pleaded

8.—(1) A party must in any pleading subsequent to a statement of claim plead specifically any matter, for example, performance, release, any relevant statute of limitation, fraud or any fact showing illegality—

(*a*) which he alleges makes any claim or defence of the opposite party not maintainable; or

(*b*) which, if not specifically pleaded, might take the opposite party by surprise; or

(*c*) which raises issues of fact not arising out of the preceding pleading.

(2) Without prejudice to paragraph (1), a defendant to an action for possession of land must plead specifically every ground of defence on which he relies, and a plea that he is in possession of the land by himself or his tenant is not sufficient.

Matter may be pleaded whenever arising

9. Subject to rules 7 (1), 10 and 15 (2), a party may in any pleading plead any matter which has arisen at any time, whether before or since the issue of the writ.

Departure

10.—(1) A party must not in any pleading make any allegation of fact, or raise any new ground of claim, inconsistent with a previous pleading of his.

(2) Paragraph (1) shall not be taken as prejudicing the right of a party to amend, or apply for leave to amend, his previous pleading so as to plead the allegations or claims in the alternative.

Points of law may be pleaded

11. A party may by his pleading raise any point of law.

Particulars of pleading

12.—(1) Subject to paragraph (2), every pleading must contain the necessary particulars of any claim, defence or other matter pleaded including, without prejudice to the generality of the foregoing words—

(*a*) particulars of any misrepresentation, fraud, breach of trust, wilful default or undue influence on which the party pleading relies; and

(*b*) where a party pleading alleges any condition of the mind of any person, whether any disorder or disability of mind or any malice, fraudulent intention or other condition of mind except knowledge, particulars of the facts on which the party relies.

(2) Where it is necessary to give particulars of debt, expenses or damages and those particulars exceed 3 folios, they must be set out in a separate document referred to in the pleading and the pleading must state whether the document has already been served, and if so, when, or is to be served with the pleading.

(3) The court may order a party to serve on any other party particulars of any claim, defence or other matter stated in his pleading, or in any affidavit of his ordered to stand as a pleading, or a statement of the nature of the case on which he relies, and the order may be made on such terms as the court thinks just.

(4) Where a party alleges as a fact that a person had knowledge or notice of some fact, matter or thing, then, without prejudice to the generality of paragraph (3), the court may, on such terms as it thinks just, order that party to serve on any other party—

(*a*) where he alleges knowledge, particulars of the facts on which he relies, and

(*b*) where he alleges notice, particulars of the notice.

(5) An order under this rule shall not be made before service of the defence unless, in the opinion of the court, the order is necessary or desirable to enable the defendant to plead or for some other special reason.

(6) Where the applicant for an order under this rule did not apply by letter for the particulars he requires, the court may refuse to make the order unless of opinion that there were sufficient reasons for an application by letter not having been made.

Admissions and denials

13.—(1) Subject to paragraph (4), any allegation of fact made by a party in his pleading is deemed to be admitted by the opposite party unless it is traversed by that party in his pleading or a joinder of issue under rule 14 operates as a denial of it.

(2) A traverse may be made either by a denial or by a statement of non-admission and either expressly or by necessary implication.

(3) Subject to paragraph (4), every allegation of fact made in a statement of claim or counterclaim which the party on whom it is served does not intend to admit must be specifically traversed by him in his defence or defence to counterclaim, as the case may be; and a general denial of such allegations, or a general statement of non-admission of them, is not a sufficient traverse of them.

(4) Any allegation that a party has suffered damage and any allegation as to the amount of damages is deemed to be traversed unless specifically admitted.

Denial by joinder of issue

14.—(1) If there is no reply to a defence, there is an implied joinder of issue on that defence.

(2) Subject to paragraph (3)—

(a) there is at the close of pleadings an implied joinder of issue on the pleading last served, and

(b) a party may in his pleading expressly join issue on the next preceding pleading.

(3) There can be no joinder of issue, implied or express, on a statement of claim or counterclaim.

(4) A joinder of issue operates as a denial of every material allegation of fact made in the pleading on which there is an implied or express joinder of issue unless, in the case of an express joinder of issue, any such allegation is excepted from the joinder and is stated to be admitted, in which case the express joinder of issue operates as a denial of every other such allegation.

Statement of claim

15.—(1) A statement of claim must state specifically the relief or remedy which the plaintiff claims; but costs need not be specifically claimed.

(2) A statement of claim must not contain any allegation or claim in respect of a cause of action unless that cause of action is mentioned in the writ or arises from facts which are the same as, or include or form part of, facts giving rise to a cause of action so mentioned; but subject to that, a plaintiff may in his statement of claim alter, modify or extend any claim made by him in the indorsement of the writ without amending the indorsement.

(3) Every statement of claim must bear on its face a statement of the date on which the writ in the action was issued.

Counterclaim and defence to counterclaim

18. Without prejudice to the general application of this Order to a counterclaim and a defence to counterclaim, or to any provision thereof which applies to either of those pleadings specifically,—

(a) rule 15 (1) shall apply to a counterclaim as if the counterclaim were a statement of claim and the defendant making it a plaintiff;

436

(*b*) rules 8 (2), 16 and 17 shall, with the necessary modifications, apply to a defence to counterclaim as they apply to a defence.

Striking out pleadings and indorsements

19.—(1) The court may at any stage of the proceedings order to be struck out or amended any pleading or the indorsement of any writ in the action, or anything in any pleading or in the indorsement, on the ground that—

(*a*) it discloses no reasonable cause of action or defence, as the case may be; or

(*b*) it is scandalous, frivolous or vexatious; or

(*c*) it may prejudice, embarrass or delay the fair trial of the action; or

(*d*) it is otherwise an abuse of the process of the court;

and may order the action to be stayed or dismissed or judgment to be entered accordingly, as the case may be.

(2) No evidence shall be admissible on an application under paragraph (1) (*a*).

(3) This rule shall, so far as applicable, apply to an originating summons and a petition as if the summons or petition, as the case may be, were a pleading.

Close of pleadings

20.—(1) The pleadings in an action are deemed to be closed—

(*a*) at the expiration of 14 days after service of the reply or, if there is no reply but only a defence to counterclaim, after service of the defence to counterclaim, or

(*b*) if neither a reply nor a defence to counterclaim is served, at the expiration of 14 days after service of the defence.

(2) The pleadings in an action are deemed to be closed at the time provided by paragraph (1) notwithstanding that any request or order for particulars has been made but has not been complied with at that time.

Trial without pleadings

21.—(1) Where in an action to which this rule applies any defendant has entered an appearance in the action, the plaintiff or that defendant may apply to the court by summons for an order that the action shall be tried without pleadings or further pleadings, as the case may be.

(2) If, on the hearing of an application under this rule, the court is satisfied that the issues in dispute between the parties can

be defined without pleadings or further pleadings, or that for any
other reason the action can properly be tried without pleadings
or further pleadings, as the case may be, the court shall order
the action to be so tried, and may direct the parties to prepare
a statement of the issues in dispute or, if the parties are unable to
agree such a statement, may settle the statement itself.

(3) Where the court makes an order under paragraph (2), it
shall, and where it dismisses an application for such an order, it
may, give such directions as to the further conduct of the action
as may be appropriate, and Order 25, rules 2 to 7, shall, with the
omission of so much of rule 7 (1) as requires parties to serve a
notice specifying the orders and directions which they desire and
with any other necessary modifications, apply as if the application
under this rule were a summons for directions.

(4) This rule applies to every action begun by writ other than
one which includes—

(*a*) a claim by the plaintiff for libel, slander, malicious prosecution, false imprisonment. . . .; or

(*b*) a claim by the plaintiff based on an allegation of fraud.

ORDER 22

PAYMENT INTO AND OUT OF COURT

Payment into court

1.—(1) In any action for a debt or damages any defendant may
at any time after he has entered an appearance in the action pay
into court a sum of money in satisfaction of the cause of action
in respect of which the plaintiff claims or, where two or more
causes of action are joined in the action, a sum or sums of money
in satisfaction of any or all of those causes of action.

(2) On making any payment into court under this rule, and on
increasing any such payment already made, the defendant must
give notice thereof in Form No. 23 in Appendix A to the plaintiff
and every other defendant (if any); and within 3 days after
receiving the notice the plaintiff must send the defendant a written
acknowledgment of its receipt.

(3) A defendant may, without leave, give notice of an
increase in a payment made under this rule but, subject to that and
without prejudice to paragraph (5), a notice of payment may not
be withdrawn or amended without the leave of the court which may
be granted on such terms as may be just.

(4) Where two or more causes of action are joined in the

action and money is paid into court under this rule in respect of all, or some only of, those causes of action, the notice of payment—

(*a*) must state that the money is paid in respect of all those causes of action or, as the case may be, must specify the cause or causes of action in respect of which the payment is made, and

(*b*) where the defendant makes separate payments in respect of each, or any two or more, of those causes of action, must specify the sum paid in respect of that cause or, as the case may be, those causes of action.

(5) Where a single sum of money is paid into court under this rule in respect of two or more causes of action, then, if it appears to the court that the plaintiff is embarrassed by the payment, the court may, subject to paragraph (6), order the defendant to amend the notice of payment so as to specify the sum paid in respect of each cause of action.

(6) Where a cause of action under the Fatal Accidents Acts 1846 to 1959 and a cause of action under the Law Reform (Miscellaneous Provisions) Act 1934 are joined in an action, with or without any other cause of action, the causes of action under the said Acts shall, for the purpose of paragraph (5), be treated as one cause of action.

(7) Where—

(*a*) an action proceeding in a district registry is being tried at an assize town within the district of another district registry or at the Royal Courts of Justice, or

(*b*) an action proceeding in the Royal Courts of Justice is being tried at an assize town within the district of a district registry,

any payment into court under this rule made after the trial or hearing has begun may, if the defendant so desires, be made at the district registry within the district of which the assize town is situated or, if the action is being tried at the Royal Courts of Justice, in the same manner as if the action were being tried there.

Payment in by defendant who has counterclaimed

2. Where a defendant, who makes by counterclaim a claim against the plaintiff for a debt or damages, pays a sum or sums of money into court under rule 1, the notice of payment must state, if it be the case, that in making the payment the defendant has taken into account and intends to satisfy—

(*a*) the cause of action in respect of which he claims, or

(*b*) where two or more causes of action are joined in the counter-claim, all those causes of action or, if not all, which of them.

439

Acceptance of money paid into court

3.—(1) Where money is paid into court under rule 1, then, subject to paragraph (2), within 14 days after receipt of the notice of payment or, where more than one payment has been made or the notice has been amended, within 14 days after receipt of the notice of the last payment or the amended notice but, in any case, before the trial or hearing of the action begins, the plaintiff may—

    (*a*) where the money was paid in respect of the cause of action or all the causes of action in respect of which he claims, accept the money in satisfaction of that cause of action or those causes of action, as the case may be, or

    (*b*) where the money was paid in respect of some only of the causes of action in respect of which he claims, accept in satisfaction of any such cause or causes of action the sum specified in respect of that cause or those causes of action in the notice of payment,

by giving notice in Form No. 24 in Appendix A to every defendant to the action.

(2) Where after the trial or hearing of an action has begun—

    (*a*) money is paid into court under rule 1, or

    (*b*) money in court is increased by a further payment into court under that rule,

the plaintiff may accept the money in accordance with paragraph (1) within two days after receipt of the notice of payment or notice of the further payment, as the case may be, but, in any case, before the judge begins to deliver judgment or, if the trial is with a jury, before the judge begins his summing up.

(3) Rule 1 (5) shall not apply in relation to money paid into court in an action after the trial or hearing of the action has begun.

(4) On the plaintiff accepting any money paid into court all further proceedings in the action or in respect of the specified cause or causes of action, as the case may be, to which the acceptance relates, both against the defendant making the payment and against any other defendant sued jointly with or in the alternative to him, shall be stayed.

(5) Where money is paid into court by a defendant who made a counterclaim and the notice of payment stated, in relation to any sum so paid, that in making the payment the defendant had taken into account and satisfied the cause or causes of action, or the specified cause or causes of action in respect of which he claimed, then, on the plaintiff accepting that sum, all further proceedings on the counterclaim or in respect of the specified cause or causes of action, as the case may be, against the plaintiff shall be stayed.

(6) A plaintiff who has accepted any sum paid into court shall subject to rules 4 and 10 and Order 80, rule 12, be entitled to receive payment of that sum in satisfaction of the cause or causes of action to which the acceptance relates.

Order for payment out of money accepted required in certain cases

4.—(1) Where a plaintiff accepts any sum paid into court and that sum was paid into court—

(a) by some but not all of the defendants sued jointly or in the alternative by him, or

(b) with a defence of tender before action, or

(c) in an action to which Order 80, rule 13, applies,[2] or

(d) in satisfaction either of causes of action arising under the Fatal Accidents Acts 1846 to 1959 and the Law Reform (Miscellaneous Provisions) Act 1934, or of a cause of action arising under the first mentioned Acts where more than one person is entitled to the money,

the money in court shall not be paid out except under paragraph (2) or in pursuance of an order of the court, and the order shall deal with the whole costs of the action or of the cause of action to which the payment relates, as the case may be.

(2) Where an order of the court is required under paragraph (1) by reason only of paragraph (1) (a), then if, either before or after accepting the money paid into court by some only of the defendants sued jointly or in the alternative by him, the plaintiff discontinues the action against all the other defendants and those defendants consent in writing to the payment out of that sum, it may be paid out without an order of the court.

(3) Where after the trial or hearing of an action has begun a plaintiff accepts any money paid into court and all further proceedings in the action or in respect of the specified cause or causes of action, as the case may be, to which the acceptance relates are stayed by virtue of rule 3 (4), then, notwithstanding anything in paragraph (2), the money shall not be paid out except in pursuance of an order of the court, and the order shall deal with the whole costs of the action.

Money remaining in court

5. If any money paid into court in an action is not accepted in accordance with rule 3, the money remaining in court shall not be paid out except in pursuance of an order of the court which may be made at any time before, at or after the trial or hearing

---

[2] *i.e.*, an action involving a person under disability.

of the action; and where such an order is made before the trial or hearing the money shall not be paid out except in satisfaction of the cause or causes of action in respect of which it was paid in.

Counterclaim

6. A plaintiff against whom a counterclaim is made and any other defendant to the counterclaim may pay money into court in accordance with rule 1, and that rule and rules 3 (except paragraph (5)), 4 and 5 shall apply accordingly with the necessary modifications.

Non-disclosure of payment into court

7. Except in an action to which a defence of tender before action is pleaded, and except in an action all further proceedings in which are stayed by virtue of rule 3 (4) after the trial or hearing has begun, the fact that money has been paid into court under the foregoing provisions of this Order shall not be pleaded and no communication of that fact shall be made to the court at the trial or hearing of the action or counterclaim or of any question or issue as to the debt or damages until all questions of liability and of the amount of debt or damages have been decided.

Money paid into court under order

8.—(1) Subject to paragraph (2), money paid into court under an order of the court or a certificate of a master or associate shall not be paid out except in pursuance of an order of the court.

(2) Unless the court otherwise orders, a party who has paid money into court in pursuance of an order made under Order 14—

    (a) may by notice to the other party appropriate the whole or any part of the money and any additional payment, if necessary, to any particular claim made in the writ or counterclaim, as the case may be, and specified in the notice, or

    (b) if he pleads a tender, may by his pleading appropriate the whole or any part of the money as payment into court of the money alleged to have been tendered;

and money appropriated in accordance with this rule shall be deemed to be money paid into court in accordance with rule 1 or money paid into court with a plea of tender, as the case may be, and this Order shall apply accordingly.

ORDER 24

DISCOVERY AND INSPECTION OF DOCUMENTS

Mutual discovery of documents

1.—(1) After the close of pleadings in an action begun by writ there shall, subject to and in accordance with the provisions of this Order, be discovery by the parties to the action of the documents which are or have been in their possession, custody or power relating to matters in question in the action.

(2) Nothing in this Order shall be taken as preventing the parties to an action agreeing to dispense with or limit the discovery of documents which they would otherwise be required to make to each other.

Discovery by parties without order

2.—(1) Subject to the provisions of this rule and of rule 4, the parties to an action between whom pleadings are closed must make discovery by exchanging lists of documents and, accordingly, each party must, within 14 days after the pleadings in the action are deemed to be closed as between him and any other party, make and serve on that other party a list of the documents which are or have been in his possession, custody or power relating to any matter in question between them in the action.

Without prejudice to any directions given by the court under Order 16, rule 4, this paragraph shall not apply in third party proceedings, including proceedings under that Order involving fourth or subsequent parties.

(2) Unless the court otherwise orders, a defendant to an action arising out of an accident on land due to a collision or apprehended collision involving a vehicle shall not make discovery of any documents to the plaintiff under paragraph (1).

(3) Paragraph (1) shall not be taken as requiring a defendant to an action for the recovery of any penalty recoverable by virtue of any enactment to make discovery of any documents.

(4) Paragraphs (2) and (3) shall apply in relation to a counterclaim as they apply in relation to an action but with the substitution, for the reference in paragraph (2) to the plaintiff, of a reference to the party making the counterclaim.

(5) On the application of any party required by this rule to make discovery of documents, the court may—

(*a*) order that the parties to the action or any of them shall make discovery under paragraph (1) of such documents or classes of documents only, or as to such only of the matters in question, as may be specified in the order, or

(*b*) if satisfied that discovery by all or any of the parties is not necessary, or not necessary at that stage of the action, order that there shall be no discovery of documents by any or all of the parties either at all or at that stage;

and the court shall make such an order if and so far as it is of opinion that discovery is not necessary either for disposing fairly of the action or for saving costs.

(6) An application for an order under paragraph (5) must be by summons, and the summons must be taken out before the expiration of the period within which by virtue of this rule discovery of documents in the action is required to be made.

(7) Any party to whom discovery of documents is required to be made under this rule may, at any time before the summons for directions in the action is taken out, serve on the party required to make such discovery a notice requiring him to make an affidavit verifying the list he is required to make under paragraph (1), and the party on whom such a notice is served must, within 14 days after service of the notice, make and file an affidavit in compliance with the notice and serve a copy of the affidavit on the party by whom the notice was served.

Order for discovery

3.—(1) Subject to the provisions of this rule and of rules 4 and 8, the court may order any party to a cause or matter (whether begun by writ, originating summons or otherwise) to make and serve on any other party a list of the documents which are or have been in his possession, custody or power relating to any matter in question in the cause or matter, and may at the same time or subsequently also order him to make and file an affidavit verifying such a list and to serve a copy thereof on the other party.

(2) Where a party who is required by rule 2 to make discovery of documents fails to comply with any provision of that rule, the court, on the application of any party to whom the discovery was required to be made, may make an order against the first-mentioned party under paragraph (1) of this rule or, as the case may be, may order him to make and file an affidavit verifying the list of documents he is required to make under rule 2 and to serve a copy thereof on the applicant.

(3) An order under this rule may be limited to such documents or classes of document only, or to such only of the matters in question in the cause or matter, as may be specified in the order.

Discovery and Inspection of Documents

Form of list and affidavit

5.—(1) A list of documents made in compliance with rule 2 or with an order under rule 3 must be in Form No. 26 in Appendix A, and must enumerate the documents in a convenient order and as shortly as possible but describing each of them or, in the case of bundles of documents of the same nature, each bundle, sufficiently to enable it to be identified.

(2) If it is desired to claim that any documents are privileged from production, the claim must be made in the list of documents with a sufficient statement of the grounds of the privilege.

(3) An affidavit made as aforesaid verifying a list of documents must be in Form No. 27 in Appendix A.

Order for discovery of particular documents

7.—(1) Subject to rule 8, the court may at any time, on the application of any party to a cause or matter, make an order requiring any other party to make an affidavit stating whether any document specified or described in the application or any class of document so specified or described is, or has at any time been, in his possession, custody or power, and if not then in his possession, custody or power when he parted with it and what has become of it.

(2) An order may be made against a party under this rule notwithstanding that he may already have made or been required to make a list of documents or affidavit under rule 2 or rule 3.

(3) An application for an order under this rule must be supported by an affidavit stating the belief of the deponent that the party from whom discovery is sought under this rule has, or at some time had, in his possession, custody or power the document, or class of document, specified or described in the application and that it relates to one or more of the matters in question in the cause or matter.

Discovery to be ordered only if necessary

8. On the hearing of an application for an order under rule 3 or rule 7 the court, if satisfied that discovery is not necessary, or not necessary at that stage of the cause or matter, may dismiss or, as the case may be, adjourn the application and shall in any case refuse to make such an order if and so far as it is of opinion that discovery is not necessary either for disposing fairly of the cause or matter or for saving costs.

Inspection of documents referred to in list

9. A party who has served a list of documents on any other party, whether in compliance with rule 2 or with an order under rule

3, must allow the other party to inspect the documents referred to in the list (other than any which he objects to produce) and to take copies thereof and, accordingly, he must when he serves the list on the other party also serve on him a notice stating a time within 7 days after the service thereof at which the said documents may be inspected at a place specified in the notice.

Inspection of documents referred to in pleadings and affidavits

10.—(1) Any party to a cause or matter shall be entitled at any time to serve a notice on any other party in whose pleadings or affidavits reference is made to any document requiring him to produce that document for the inspection of the party giving the notice and to permit him to take copies thereof.

(2) The party on whom a notice is served under paragraph (1) must, within 4 days after service of the notice, serve on the party giving the notice a notice stating a time within 7 days after the service thereof at which the documents, or such of them as he does not object to produce, may be inspected at a place specified in the notice, and stating which (if any) of the documents he objects to produce and on what grounds.

Order for production for inspection

11.—(1) If a party who is required by rule 9 to serve such a notice as is therein mentioned or who is served with a notice under rule 10 (1)—

    (*a*)   fails to serve a notice under rule 9, or as the case may be, rule 10 (2), or

    (*b*)   objects to produce any document for inspection, or

    (*c*)   offers inspection at a time or place such that, in the opinion of the court, it is unreasonable to offer inspection then or, as the case may be, there,

then, subject to rule 13 (1), the court may, on the application of the party entitled to inspection, make an order for production of the documents in question for inspection at such time and place, and in such manner, as it thinks fit.

(2) Without prejudice to paragraph (1), but subject to rule 13 (1), the court may, on the application of any party to a cause or matter, order any other party to permit the party applying to inspect any documents in the possession, custody or power of that other party relating to any matter in question in the cause or matter.

(3) An application for an order under paragraph (2) must be supported by an affidavit specifying or describing the documents of which inspection is sought and stating the belief of the deponent

that they are in the possession, custody or power of the other party and that they relate to a matter in question in the cause or matter.

Order for production to court

12. At any stage of the proceedings in any cause or matter the court may, subject to rule 13 (1), order any party to produce to the court any document in his possession, custody or power relating to any matter in question in the cause or matter and the court may deal with the document when produced in such manner as it thinks fit.

Production to be ordered only if necessary, etc.

13.—(1) No order for the production of any documents for inspection or to the court shall be made under any of the foregoing rules unless the court is of opinion that the order is necessary either for disposing fairly of the cause or matter or for saving costs.

(2) Where on an application under this Order for production of any document for inspection or to the court privilege from such production is claimed or objection is made to such production on any other ground, the court may inspect the document for the purpose of deciding whether the claim or objection is valid.

Production of business books

14.—(1) Where production of any business books for inspection is applied for under any of the foregoing rules, the court may, instead of ordering production of the original books for inspection, order a copy of any entries therein to be supplied and verified by an affidavit of some person who has examined the copy with the original books.

(2) Any such affidavit shall state whether or not there are in the original books any and what erasures, interlineations or alterations.

(3) Notwithstanding that a copy of any entries in any book has been supplied under this rule, the court may order production of the book from which the copy was made.

Document disclosure of which would be injurious to public interest: saving

15. The foregoing provision of this Order shall be without prejudice to any rule of law which authorises or requires the withholding of any document on the ground that the disclosure of it would be injurious to the public interest.

Failure to comply with requirement for discovery, etc.

16.—(1) If any party who is required by any of the foregoing rules, or by any order made thereunder, to make discovery of documents or to produce any documents for the purpose of inspection or any other purpose fails to comply with any provision of that rule or with that order, as the case may be, then, without prejudice, in the case of a failure to comply with any such provision, to rules 3 (2) and 11 (1), the court may make such order as it thinks just including, in particular, an order that the action be dismissed or, as the case may be, an order that the defence be struck out and judgment be entered accordingly.

(2) If any party against whom an order for discovery or production of documents is made fails to comply with it, then, without prejudice to paragraph (1), he shall be liable to committal.

(3) Service on a party's solicitor of an order for discovery or production of documents made against that party shall be sufficient service to found an application for committal of the party disobeying the order, but the party may show in answer to the application that he had no notice or knowledge of the order.

(4) A solicitor on whom such an order made against his client is served and who fails without reasonable excuse to give notice thereof to his client shall be liable to committal.

Revocation and variation of orders

17. Any order made under this Order (including an order made on appeal) may, on sufficient cause being shown, be revoked or varied by a subsequent order or direction of the court made or given at or before the trial of the cause or matter in connection with which the original order was made.

ORDER 25

SUMMONS FOR DIRECTIONS

1.—(1) With a view to providing, in every action to which this rule applies, an occasion for the consideration by the court of the preparations for the trial of the action, so that—

    (*a*) all matters which must or can be dealt with on interlocutory applications and have not already been dealt with may so far as possible be dealt with, and

    (*b*) such directions may be given as to the future course of the action as appear best adapted to secure the just, expeditious and economical disposal thereof, the plaintiff must, within one month after the pleadings in the action are deemed to be closed, take out a summons (in these rules referred to as a summons for directions) returnable in not less than 14 days.

(2) This rule applies to all actions begun by writ except—

(*a*) actions in which the plaintiff or defendant has applied for judgment under Order 14, or in which the plaintiff has applied for judgment under Order 86, and directions have been given under the relevant Order;

(*b*) actions in which the plaintiff or defendant has applied under Order 18, rule 21, for trial without pleadings or further pleadings and directions have been given under that rule;

(*c*) actions in which an order has been made under Order 2 or rule 4, for the trial of an issue or question before discovery;

(*d*) actions in which directions have been given under Order 29 rule 7;

(*e*) actions in which an order for the taking of an account has been made under Order 43, rule 1;

(*f*) actions in which an application for transfer to the commercial list is pending;

(*g*) actions which have been referred for trial to an official referee;

(*h*) actions for the infringement of a patent; and

(*i*) actions ordered to be tried as Admiralty short causes.

(3) Where, in the case of any action in which discovery of documents is required to be made by any party under Order 24, rule 2, the period of 14 days referred to in paragraph (1) of that rule is extended, whether by consent or by order of the Court or both by consent and by order, paragraph (1) of this rule shall have effect in relation to that action as if for the reference therein to one month after the pleadings in the action are deemed to be closed there were substituted a reference to 14 days after the expiration of the period referred to in paragraph (1) of the said rule 2 as so extended.

(4) If the plaintiff does not take out a summons for directions in accordance with the foregoing provisions of this rule, the defendant or any defendant may do so or apply for an order to dismiss the action.

(5) On an application by a defendant to dismiss the action under paragraph (4) the court may either dismiss the action on such terms as may be just or deal with the application as if it were a summons for directions.

(6) In the case of an action which is proceeding only as respects a counterclaim, references in this rule to the plaintiff and defendant

449

shall be construed respectively as references to the party making the counterclaim and the defendant to counterclaim.

Duty to consider all matters

2.—(1) When the summons for directions first comes to be heard, the court shall consider whether—

    (*a*) it is possible to deal then with all the matters which, by the subsequent rules of this Order, are required to be considered on the hearing of the summons for directions, or

    (*b*) it is expedient to adjourn the consideration of all or any of those matters until a later stage.

(2) If when the summons for directions first comes to be heard the court considers that it is possible to deal then with all the said matters, it shall deal with them forthwith and shall endeavour to secure that all other matters which must or can be dealt with on interlocutory applications and have not already been dealt with are also then dealt with.

(3) If, when the summons for directions first comes to be heard, the court considers that it is expedient to adjourn the consideration of all or any of the matters which, by the subsequent rules of this Order, are required to be considered on the hearing of the summons, the court shall deal forthwith with such of those matters as it considers can conveniently be dealt with forthwith and adjourn the consideration of the remaining matters and shall endeavour to secure that all other matters which must or can be dealt with on interlocutory applications and have not already been dealt with are dealt with either then or at a resumed hearing of the summons for directions.

(4) Subject to paragraphs (5) and (6), and except where the parties agree to the making of an order under Order 33 as to the place or mode of trial before all the matters which, by the subsequent rules of this Order, are required to be considered on the hearing of the summons for directions have been dealt with, no such order shall be made until all those matters have been dealt with.

(5) If, on the summons for directions, an action is ordered to be transferred to the county court or some other court, paragraph (4) shall not apply and nothing in this Order shall be construed as requiring the court to make any further order on the summons.

(6) If, on the summons for directions, the action or any question or issue therein is ordered to be tried before an official referee, paragraph (4) shall not apply and the court may, without giving any further directions, adjourn the summons so that it can be

heard by the referee, and the party required by Order 36, r. 6, to apply to the referee for directions may do so by notice without taking out a fresh summons.

(7) If the hearing of the summons for directions is adjourned without a day being fixed for the resumed hearing thereof, any party may restore it to the list on 2 days' notice to the other parties.

Particular matters for consideration

3. On the hearing of the summons for directions the court shall in particular consider, if necessary of its own motion, whether, any order should be made or direction given in the exercise of the powers conferred by any of the following provisions, that is to say—

    (*a*) any provision of Part I of the Civil Evidence Act, 1968 (hearsay evidence) or of Part III of Order 38;

    (*b*) Order 20, rule 5, Order 38, rules 2 to 7, and Order 75, rule 25 (4).

Admissions and agreements to be made

4. At the hearing of the summons for directions, the court shall endeavour to secure that the parties make all admissions and all agreements as to the conduct of the proceedings which ought reasonably to be made by them and may cause the order on the summons to record any admissions or agreements so made, and (with a view to such special order, if any, as to costs as may be just being made at the trial) any refusal to make any admission or agreement.

Limitation of right of appeal

5.   Nothing in rule 4 shall be construed as requiring the court to endeavour to secure that the parties shall agree to exclude or limit any right of appeal, but the order made on the summons for directions may record any such agreement.

Duty to give all information at hearing

6.—(1) Subject to paragraph (2), no affidavit shall be used on the hearing of the summons for directions except by the leave or direction of the court, but, subject to paragraph (4), it shall be the duty of the parties to the action and their advisers to give all such information and produce all such documents on any hearing of

451

the summons as the court may reasonably require for the purpose of enabling it properly to deal with the summons.

The court may, if it appears proper so to do in the circumstances, authorise any such information or documents to be given or produced to the court without being disclosed to the other parties but, in the absence of such authority, any information or document given or produced under this paragraph shall be given or produced to all the parties present or represented on the hearing of the summons as well as to the court.

(2) No leave shall be required by virtue of paragraph (1) for the use of an affidavit by any party on the hearing of the summons for directions in connection with any application thereat for any order if, under any of these rules, an application for such an order is required to be supported by an affidavit.

(3) If the court on any hearing of the summons for directions requires a party to the action or his solicitor or counsel to give any information or produce any document and that information or document is not given or produced, then, subject to paragraph (4), the court may—

(*a*) cause the facts to be recorded in the order with a view to such special order, if any, as to costs as may be just being made at the trial, or

(*b*) if it appears to the court to be just so to do, order the whole or any part of the pleadings of the party concerned to be struck out, or, if the party is plaintiff or the claimant under a counterclaim, order the action or counterclaim to be dismissed on such terms as may be just.

(4) Notwithstanding anything in the foregoing provisions of this rule, no information or documents which are privileged from disclosure shall be required to be given or produced under this rule by or by the advisers of any party otherwise than with the consent of that party.

Duty to make all interlocutory applications on summons for directions

7.—(1) Any party to whom the summons for directions is addressed must so far as practicable apply at the hearing of the summons for any order or directions which he may desire as to any matter capable of being dealt with on an interlocutory application in the action and must, not less than 7 days before the hearing of the summons, serve on the other parties a notice specifying those orders and directions in so far as they differ from the orders and directions asked for by the summons.

(2) If the hearing of the summons for directions is adjourned and any party to the proceedings desires to apply at the resumed

hearing for any order or directions not asked for by the summons or in any notice given under paragraph (1), he must, not less than 7 days before the resumed hearing of the summons, serve on the other parties a notice specifying those orders and directions in so far as they differ from the orders and directions asked for by the summons or in any such notice as aforesaid.

(3) Any application subsequent to the summons for directions and before judgment as to any matter capable of being dealt with on an interlocutory application in the action must be made under the summons by 2 clear days' notice to the other party stating the grounds of the application.

ORDER 38

EVIDENCE

I. *General Rules*

General rule: witnesses to be examined orally

1. Subject to the provisions of these rules and of the Civil Evidence Act, 1968, and any other enactment relating to evidence, any fact required to be proved at the trial of any action begun by writ by the evidence of witnesses shall be proved by the examination of the witnesses orally and in open court.

Evidence by affidavit

2.—(1) The court may, at or before the trial of an action begun by writ, order that the affidavit of any witness may be read at the trial if in the circumstances of the case it thinks it reasonable so to order.

(2) An order under paragraph (1) may be made on such terms as to the filing and giving of copies of the affidavits and as to the production of the deponents for cross-examination as the court thinks fit but, subject to any such terms and to any subsequent order of the court, the deponents shall not be subject to cross-examination and need not attend the trial for the purpose.

(3) In any cause or matter begun by originating summons, originating motion or petition, and on any application made by summons or motion, evidence may be given by affidavit unless in the case of any such cause, matter or application any provision of these rules otherwise provides or the court otherwise directs, but

the court may, on the application of any party, order the attendance for cross-examination of the person making any such affidavit, and where, after such an order has been made, the person in question does not attend, his affidavit shall not be used as evidence without the leave of the court.

Evidence of particular facts

3.—(1) Without prejudice to rule 2, the court may, at or before the trial of any action, order that evidence of any particular fact shall be given at the trial in such manner as may be specified by the order.

(2) The power conferred by paragraph (1) extends in particular to ordering that evidence of any particular fact may be given at the trial—

(a) by statement on oath of information or belief, or
(b) by the production of documents or entries in books, or
(c) by copies of documents or entries in books, or
(d) in the case of a fact which is or was a matter of common knowledge either generally or in a particular district, by the production of a specified newspaper which contains a statement of that fact.

Limitation of expert evidence

4. The court may, at or before the trial of any action, order that the number of medical or other expert witnesses who may be called at the trial shall be limited as specified by the order.

Limitation of plans, etc., in evidence

5. Unless, at or before the trial, the court for special reasons otherwise orders, no plan, photograph or model shall be receivable in evidence at the trial of an action unless at least 10 days before the commencement of the trial the parties, other than the party producing it, have been given an opportunity to inspect it and to agree to the admission thereof without further proof.

Expert evidence in action arising out of accident

6.—(1) In an action arising out of an accident on land due to a collision or apprehended collision, unless at or before the trial the court otherwise orders, the oral expert evidence of an engineer sought to be called on account of his skill and knowledge as respects motor-vehicles shall not be receivable unless a copy of a report from him containing the substance of his evidence has been made available to all parties for inspection before the hearing of the summons for directions and an order made on the summons for directions or an application thereunder authorises the admission of the evidence.

(2) The references in this rule to the summons for directions include references to any summons or application to which, under any of these rules, Order 25, rules 2 to 7, are to apply, whether with or without modifications.

III. Hearsay Evidence

20.—(*Interpretation and application*)

Notice of intention to give certain statements in evidence

21.—(1) Subject to the provisions of this rule, a party to a cause or matter who desires to give in evidence at the trial or hearing of the cause or matter any statement which is admissible in evidence by virtue of section 2, 4 or 5 of the Act must—

(*a*) in the case of a cause or matter which is required to be set down for trial or hearing or adjourned into court, within 21 days after it is set down or so adjourned, or within such other period as the Court may specify, and

(*b*) in the case of any other cause or matter, within 21 days after the date on which an appointment for the first hearing of the cause or matter is obtained, or within such other period as the Court may specify

serve on every other party to the cause or matter notice of his desire to do so, and the notice must comply with the provisions of rule 22, 23 or 24, as the circumstances of the case require.

(2) Paragraph (1) shall not apply in relation to any statement which is admissible as evidence of any fact stated therein by virtue not only of the said section 2, 4 or 5 but by virtue also of any other statutory provision within the meaning of section 1 of the Act.

(3) Paragraph (1) shall not apply in relation to any statement which any party to a probate action desires to give in evidence at the trial of that action and which is alleged to have been made by the deceased person whose estate is the subject of the action.

(4) Where by virtue of any provision of these rules or of any order or direction of the Court the evidence in any proceedings is to be given by affidavit then, without prejudice to paragraph (2), paragraph (1) shall not apply in relation to any statement which any party to the proceedings desires to have included in any affidavit to

be used on his behalf in the proceedings, but nothing in this paragraph shall affect the operation of Order 41, rule 5, or the powers of the Court under Order 38, rule 3.

(5) Order 65, rule 9, shall not apply to a notice under this rule but the Court may direct that the notice need not be served on any party who at the time when service is to be effected is in default as to entry of appearance or who has no address for service.

Determination of question whether person can or should be called as a witness

27.—(1) Where in any cause or matter a question arises whether any of the reasons specified in rule 25 applies in relation to a person particulars of whom are contained in a notice under rule 21, the Court may, on the application of any party to the cause or matter, determine that question before the trial or hearing of the cause or matter or give directions for it to be determined before the trial or hearing and for the manner in which it is to be so determined.

(2) Unless the Court otherwise directs, the summons by which an application under paragraph (1) is made must be served by the party making the application on every other party to the cause or matter.

(3) Where any such question as is referred to in paragraph (1) has been determined under or by virtue of that paragraph, no application to have it determined afresh at the trial or hearing of the cause or matter may be made unless the evidence which it is sought to adduce in support of the application could not with reasonable diligence have been adduced at the hearing which resulted in the determination.

Directions with respect to statement made in previous proceedings

28. Where a party to a cause or matter has given notice in accordance with rule 21 that he desires to give in evidence at the trial or hearing of the cause or matter—

(*a*) a statement falling within section 2 (1) of the Act which was made by a person, whether orally or in a document, in the course of giving evidence in some other legal proceedings (whether civil or criminal), **or**

(*b*) a statement falling within section 4 (1) of the Act which is contained in a record of direct oral evidence given in some other legal proceedings (whether civil or criminal),

any party to the cause or matter may apply to the Court for directions under this rule, and the Court hearing such an application may give directions as to whether, and if so on what conditions, the party desiring to give the statement in evidence will be permitted to do so and (where applicable) as to the manner in which that statement and any other evidence given in those other proceedings is to be proved.

Costs

ORDER 62

COSTS

When costs follow the event

3.—(1) Subject to the following provisions of this Order, no party shall be entitled to recover any costs of or incidental to any proceedings from any other party to the proceedings except under an order of the court.

(2) If the court in the exercise of its discretion sees fit to make any order as to the costs of or incidental to any proceedings, the court shall, subject to this Order, order the costs to follow the event, except when it appears to the court that in the circumstances of the case some other order should be made as to the whole or any part of the costs.

(3) The costs of and occasioned by any amendment made without leave in the writ of summons or any pleading shall be borne by the party making the amendment, unless the court otherwise orders.

(4) The costs of and occasioned by any application to extend the time fixed by these rules, or any direction or order thereunder, for serving or filing any document or doing any other act (including the costs of any order made on the application) shall be borne by the party making the application, unless the court otherwise orders.

Stage of proceedings at which costs to be dealt with

4.—(1) Costs may be dealt with by the court at any stage of the proceedings or after the conclusion of the proceedings; and any order of the court for the payment of any costs may, if the court thinks fit, and the person against whom the order is made is not an assisted person, require the costs to be paid forthwith notwithstanding that the proceedings have not been concluded.

Costs arising from misconduct or neglect

7.—(1) Where in any cause or matter any thing is done or omission is made improperly or unnecessarily by or on behalf of a party, the court may direct that any costs to that party in respect of it shall not be allowed to him and that any costs occasioned by it to other parties shall be paid by him to them.

(2) Without prejudice to the generality of paragraph (1), the court shall for the purpose of that paragraph have regard in particular to the following matters, that is to say—

(a) the omission to do any thing the doing of which would have been calculated to save costs;

(b) the doing of any thing calculated to occasion, or in a manner or at a time calculated to occasion, unnecessary costs;

(c) any unnecessary delay in the proceedings.

(3) The court may, instead of giving a direction under paragraph (1) in relation to any thing done or omission made, direct the taxing officer to inquire into it and, if it appears to him that such a direction as aforesaid should have been given in relation to it, to act as if the appropriate direction had been given.

Order 65

SERVICE OF DOCUMENTS

Personal service: how effected

2. Personal service of a document is effected by leaving a copy of the document with the person to be served and, if so requested by him at the time when it is left, showing him—

(a) in the case where the document is a writ or other originating process, the original, and

(b) in any other case, the original or an office copy.

Personal service on a body corporate

3. Personal service of a document on a body corporate may, in cases for which provision is not otherwise made by any enactment, be effected by serving it in accordance with rule 2 on the mayor, chairman or president of the body; or the town clerk, clerk, secretary, treasurer or other similar officer thereof.

Substituted service

4.—(1) If, in the case of any document which by virtue of any provision of these rules is required to be served personally on any person, it appears to the court that it is impracticable for any reason to serve that document personally on that person, the court may make an order for substituted service of that document.

(2) An application for an order for substituted service may be made by an affidavit stating the facts on which the application is founded.

(3) Substituted service of a document, in relation to which an order is made under this rule, is effected by taking such steps as

458

the court may direct to bring the document to the notice of the person to be served.

Ordinary service: how effected

5.—(1) Service of any document, not being a document which by virtue of any provision of these rules is required to be served personally, may be effected—

(*a*) by leaving the document at the proper address of the person to be served, or

(*b*) by post, or

(*c*) in such other manner as the court may direct.

(2) For the purposes of this rule, and of section 26 of the Interpretation Act 1889, in its application to this rule, the proper address of any person on whom a document is to be served in accordance with this rule shall be the address for service of that person, but if at the time when service is effected that person has no address for service his proper address for the purposes aforesaid shall be—

(*a*) in any case, the business address of the solicitor (if any) who is acting for him in the proceedings in connection with which service of the document in question is to be effected, or

(*b*) in the case of an individual, his usual or last known address, or

(*c*) in the case of individuals who are suing or being sued in the name of a firm, the principal or last known place of business of the firm within the jurisdiction, or

(*d*) in the case of a body corporate, the registered or principal office of the body.

(3) Nothing in this rule shall be taken as prohibiting the personal service of any document or as affecting any enactment which provides for the manner in which documents may be served on bodies corporate.

Effect of service after certain hours

7.—Any document (other than a writ of summons or other originating process) service of which is effected under rule 2 or under rule 5 (1) (*a*) between 12 noon on a Saturday and midnight on the following day or after 4 in the afternoon on any other weekday shall, for the purpose of computing any period of time after service of that document, be deemed to have been served on the Monday following that Saturday or on the day following that other weekday, as the case may be.

Rules of particular use to Students

Service of process on Sunday

10.—(1) No process shall be served or executed within the jurisdiction on a Sunday except, in case of urgency, with the leave of the court.

(2) For the purposes of this rule " process " includes a writ, judgment, notice, order, petition, originating or other summons or warrant.

APPENDIX 2

PRECEDENTS

I.—PLEADINGS BEFORE THE JUDICATURE ACT

II.—INDORSEMENTS ON WRIT

INDORSEMENTS FOR AN ACCOUNT

III.—STATEMENTS OF CLAIM

IN ACTIONS FOR BREACH OF CONTRACT

Precedents

Precedents

463

I.—PLEADINGS BEFORE THE JUDICATURE ACT

No. 1

A Declaration

In the Queen's Bench.

The 1st day of February, A.D. 1869

Middlesex, to wit.

A B, by C D, his attorney, sues E F, for money payable by the defendant to the plaintiff for goods sold and delivered by the plaintiff to the defendant, and for goods bargained and sold by the plaintiff to the defendant, and for work done and materials provided by the plaintiff for the defendant at his request, and for money lent by the plaintiff to the defendant, and for money paid by the plaintiff for the defendant at his request, and for money received by the defendant for the use of the plaintiff, and for interest upon money due from the defendant to the plaintiff and forborne at interest by the plaintiff to the defendant at his request, and for money found to be due from the defendant to the plaintiff on accounts stated between them.[1]

And the plaintiff claims £——.

No. 2

Pleas

In the Queen's Bench.

F. ⎧   The 3rd day of March, A.D. 1869.
ats.⎨   1. The defendant by G H, his attorney, says that he
B. ⎩ never was indebted as alleged.

2. And for a second plea the defendant says that before action he satisfied and discharged the plaintiff's claim by payment.

---

[1] This was called the common indebitatus count. See *ante*, pp. 79, 86.

II.—INDORSEMENTS ON WRIT

No. 3

SPECIMEN FORM OF WRIT

1970.   J.—No. 210.

In the High Court of Justice,
  Queen's Bench Division.

Between Davy Jones	. . . .	Plaintiff
and		
Richard Robinson	. . .	Defendant.

(as executor of John Corbould deceased and in his personal capacity).

ELIZABETH THE SECOND, by the grace of God of the United Kingdom of Great Britain and Northern Ireland and of Our Other Realms and Territories Queen, Head of the Commonwealth, Defender of the Faith:

To Richard Robinson, of 50 Fleet Street, in the City of London.

We command you, that within eight days after the service of this writ on you, inclusive of the day of such service, you do cause an appearance to be entered for you in an action at the suit of Davy Jones; and take notice that in default of your so doing the plaintiff may proceed therein and judgment may be given in your absence.

Witness, QUINTIN MCGAREL, BARON HAILSHAM OF ST. MARYLEBONE, Lord High Chancellor of Great Britain, the sixth day of May, 1970.

Note:—This writ may not be served later than 12 calendar months beginning with the above date unless renewed by order of the court.

DIRECTIONS FOR ENTERING APPEARANCE

The defendant may enter an appearance in person or by a solicitor either (1) by handing in the appropriate forms, duly completed, at the Central Office, Royal Courts of Justice, Strand, London, W.C.2, or (2) by sending them to that office by post. The appropriate forms may be obtained by sending a postal order for 1s. (5p.) with an addressed envelope, foolscap size, to the Controller of Stamps, Royal Courts of Justice, Strand, London, W.C.2.

The defendant is sued as executor of the late John Corbould, and also in his personal capacity.

The plaintiff's claim [1a] is for £——, balance of money received by the said John Corbould during his lifetime, and by the defendant since his death, to the use of the plaintiff.

And for an account.

And for a receiver.

This writ was issued by F. W. Williams of 19 Ludgate Hill, London, E.C., solicitor for the said plaintiff, whose address is 145 Belsize Park Gardens, Hampstead, N.W.

This writ was served by me at 50 Fleet Street, London, E.C., on the defendant Richard Robinson on Monday, the 13th day of May, 1970.

Indorsed the 13th day of May, 1970.

(Signed)   W. Forsyth,

(Address)   19 Ludgate Hill, London, E.C.

(*Ante*, p. 42)

No. 4

FRAUD

The plaintiff's claim is for damages for fraudulent misstatements contained in an advertisement issued by the defendant for the sale of a confectionery business at ——.

No. 5

LIBEL

The plaintiff's claim is for damages for a libel contained in the —— *Independent* for Tuesday, November 5, 1969, being an article headed " A New Trick " in the first column of page 5 of that issue.

[*See Order* 82, *r*. 2.]

No. 6

MONEY LENT

The plaintiff's claim is as assignee of ——, for £—— money lent by the said ——, being then a licensed moneylender, to the defendant, and interest.

[*See Order* 83, *r*. 2.]

No 7

TRESPASS: INJUNCTION

The plaintiff's claim is for £—— damages for the wrongful entry by the defendants on to the plaintiff's land, known as Red Meadow, Whitchurch, Hampshire; and for an injunction restraining the defendants, their servants, workmen and agents, from entering

---

[1a] If the plaintiff's claim is for a debt or liquidated demand only it must be followed by an additional indorsement claiming " 8 day costs " which is not set out here (see R.S.C., Appendix A, Form No. 1).

on the plaintiff's said meadow, or from destroying or otherwise injuring the hedge or fence on the east side thereof, or from erecting or causing to be erected a wooden or other fence on the east side thereof, or from in any way interfering with the plaintiff's use and enjoyment of the said meadow.

No. 8

POSSESSION OF LAND AND ARREARS OF RENT

The plaintiff's claim is, as against all the defendants, for possession of No. 34 High Street, Camden Town, N.W., now in the occupation of the defendants A, B and C, as sub-tenants of the defendant K; and also, as against the defendant K, for £—— arrears of rent due from him under the lease of the said premises granted him by the plaintiff on the —— day of ——, for damages for breach of the covenants therein, for mesne profits, and for a receiver.[2]

No. 9

BILL OF EXCHANGE

The plaintiff's claim is for £820 11s. 6d. (£820·57½), for principal, interest and notarial expenses, payable by the defendant to the plaintiff on a bill of exchange for £800, dated January 1, 1969, drawn by A B on the defendant, and accepted by him, payable three months after date to the order of E F, and indorsed by E F to the plaintiff.

Particulars

1969	£	s.	d.	
April 4—Principal due	800	0	0	(£800·00)
Interest	20	10	0	(£20·50)
Noting	0	1	6	(7½p.)
Total	£820	11	6	(£820·57½)

The plaintiff also claims interest on £800 of the above sum at £5 per cent. from date hereof until payment.

Signed ——

No. 10

GOODS SOLD AND DELIVERED—ACCOUNT STATED

The plaintiff's claim is for £162 15s. 2d. (£162·76), balance of the price of goods sold and delivered by the plaintiff to the defendant.

---

[2] If the property is sublet, it is as well to ask for the appointment of a receiver. See *Gwatkin* v. *Bird* (1882) 52 L.J.Q.B. 263.

Particulars

	£	s.	d.	
1968—December 31—Butcher's meat supplied to this date	155	12	8	(£155·63½)
1969—January 1 to March 31—Butcher's meat supplied between these dates	15	13	0	(£15·65)
Cr.	171	5	8	(£171·28½)
1969—March 31—By cash	8	10	6	(£8·52½)
Balance due £162	15	2		(£162·76)

The plaintiff will also seek to recover the same amount as money payable by the defendant to the plaintiff on an account stated between them.

Particulars

	£	s.	d.	
1969—May 15—Balance found to be due on an account stated in writing by the plaintiff and verbally agreed by the defendant to be correct this day	162	15	2	(£162·76)

Signed ——

[*If the particulars are lengthy, they must be set out in a separate document; and then the indorsement on the writ should conclude* as *follows*: " Full particulars which exceed three folios in length are served herewith," *or*, " Full particulars which exceed three folios in length were served upon the defendant on 24th June, 1969."]

No. 11

GUARANTEE

[For a precedent of an indorsement in an action on a guarantee, see *ante*, p. 128.]

No. 12

WORK AND LABOUR DONE

The plaintiffs' claim is for £313 3s. 11d. (£313·19½,) balance of an account for services rendered and work done by the plaintiffs as advertising agents and contractors for advertisements, in printing, posting, and advertising for the defendants, and also for moneys paid by the plaintiffs for the defendants at their request.

Particulars

				£ s. d.
1969—April 18 to September 30—To account rendered				408 19 11
				(£408.99½)
Cr.			£ s. d.	
1969—May 5—By cheque on account			4 5 0	
July 3—Goods shipped to plain-	£ s. d.		(£4.25)	
tiffs' order at Ostend	116 0 0			
	£ s. d.	(£116.00)		
Less 10% discount	11 12 0			
	(£11.60)			
Freight and duty 12 17 0	24 9 0	91 11 0	95 16 0	
(£12.85)	(£24.45)	(£91.55)	(£95.80)	

£313 3 11
(£313.19½)

Signed ――

No. 13

ON A TRUST

1. By his will A B, deceased, bequeathed to the defendants the sum of £5,000 upon trust to invest the same and to pay the interest arising therefrom to the plaintiff during her life by half-yearly instalments.

2. The defendants invested the said sum in 3½ per cent. War Stock and duly paid the said instalments up to the end of June, 1965, but they have failed to pay the instalment due in December, 1965.

And the plaintiff claims:—

£ s. d.
Six months' interest on £5,000 3½ per cent. War Stock 87 10 0 (£87.50)

Signed ――

No. 14

[*Under Order* 83, *r.* 3]

CLAIM BY A MONEYLENDER

The plaintiff's claim is for principal and interest owing by the defendant under his promissory note dated September 1, 1969, in favour of the plaintiff whereunder, in consideration of the principal sum of £40 lent to him by the plaintiff the defendant promised to pay to the plaintiff the sum of £60 by twelve consecutive monthly instalments of £5 commencing on October 1, 1969. The sum of £60 represents £40 principal and £20 interest equivalent to interest at the rate of 92·3 per cent. per annum calculated in accordance with the First Schedule to the Money-lenders Act, 1927. The said note provided that in default of payment of any instalment the whole balance of principal then unpaid should become due and payable forthwith together with interest at the rate aforesaid on any overdue amount until payment and default has been made.

The plaintiff was at the time when the loan was made and is a licensed moneylender.

Particulars

1969	£	s.	d.
1st Sept.—To Principal	40	0	0 (£40·00)
17th Oct.—Repayment £5			
⌈ Sum allocated to principal	3	6	8 (£3·33½)
⎮	36	13	4 (£36·66½)
⎮ Allocated to interest £1 13s. 4d.			
⌊ Leaving interest unsatisfied [3]	3	1	9 (£3·09)
Interest on the sum of £36 13s. 4d. at 92·3 per cent. per annum from 17th Oct. 1969, to date of writ	7	4	8 (£7·23½)
Amount claimed	£46	19	9 (£46·99)

The plaintiff further claims interest on the sum of £36 13s. 4d. (£36·66½) from the date of writ until payment or judgment at the rate of 92·3 per cent. per annum as provided by the said note.

Particulars pursuant to Order 83, *rule* 3 *of the Rules of the Supreme Court*

(a) The loan was made on 1st September, 1969.

(b) The amount actually lent to the borrower was £40.

(c) The rate per cent. per annum of interest charged was 92·3.

(d) The date when the contract for repayment was made was 1st September, 1969.

(e) A memorandum of the contract was made and was signed by the borrower.

(f) A copy of the memorandum was delivered to the borrower on 1st September, 1969.

(g) The amount repaid is £5.

(h) The amount due but unpaid at the date hereof is £36 13s. 4d. (£36·66½) principal and £10 6s. 5d. (£10·32) interest.

(i) The principal sum accrued due on 1st October, 1969, and interest accrued due then and from day to day thereafter.

(j) The amount of interest accrued due is £3 1s. 9d. (£3·09) for the period 1st—17th October, 1969, and £7 4s. 8d. (£7·23½) thereafter.

Signed ——

----

[3] See Moneylenders Act, 1927, s. 7.

No. 15

Possession of Land where the Term has Expired

The plaintiff's claim is for possession of two plots of land at Waxham, in the parish and manor of Horsey, in the county of Norfolk, numbered 491 and 492 in the Ordnance Survey, which were demised by the plaintiff to the defendant by an agreement in writing bearing date September 17, 1955, for a term which expired on September 29, 1970.

The plaintiff also claims mesne profits from September 29, 1970, till possession of the said plots is delivered up to him.[4]

Signed ——

No. 16

Possession of Land where the Tenancy had been Determined

(a) Tenancy at Will

1. The plaintiff's claim is for possession of certain premises situate in the parish of M, in the manor of N, in the county of S, and known as Hepthorp House, and for mesne profits from December 23, 1965.

2. The defendant was tenant at will to the plaintiff of the said premises; but the plaintiff on December 23, 1969, duly determined such tenancy and demanded possession of the said premises; yet the defendant refuses to deliver up possession thereof to the plaintiff.

Signed ——

[See Precedents, Nos. 80 and 84.]

No. 17

(b) Oral Tenancy

1. By oral agreement made on or about January 1, 1969, the plaintiff let to the defendant certain premises known as Laurel Cottage, St. Anne's Churchyard, in the borough of Petersfield, in the County of Hampshire, upon a monthly tenancy at a rent of £3 a month; the said tenancy was determinable by one calendar month's notice in writing on either side.

2. The plaintiff duly determined the said tenancy by serving on the defendant on October 29, 1969, a notice to quit the said

---

[4] The plaintiff is entitled to have the mesne profits calculated up to the date of his obtaining possession of the land. (*Southport Tramways Co.* v. *Gandy* [1897] 2 Q.B. 66; 66 L.J.Q.B. 532.)

premises on December 1, 1969; yet the defendant refuses to deliver up possession thereof to the plaintiff.

3. The plaintiff also claims the mesne profits of the said premises from December 1, 1969, till possession be delivered up.

Signed ——

[See another precedent in *Daubuz* v. *Lavington* (1884) 13 Q.B.D. 347; 53 L.J.Q.B. 283.]

For the form of statement of claim to be indorsed on the writ where a tenant has incurred a forfeiture through not paying his rent, see Precedent No. 49.

No. 18

DETENTION OF A CHATTEL

1. By a written agreement made between the plaintiffs and the defendant on January 1, 1969, the defendant agreed to hire from the plaintiffs an Austin motor-car No. ABC 123F, the property of the plaintiffs, for the sum of £60 per month, payable as to the first payment on February 1, 1969, and thereafter on the first day of each month until the said agreement should be determined in the manner therein provided.

2. The defendant paid sums of £60 on February 1, March 1 and April 20, 1969, since when he has paid nothing.

3. The plaintiffs by a letter to the defendant, dated July 2, 1969, duly determined the said agreement and demanded the return of the said motor-car. Yet the defendant by letter, dated July 10, 1969, refused to return the said motor-car and still detains the same.

And the plaintiffs claim:—

(1) The return of the said motor-car or its value.

(2) Money due for the hire thereof:—

	£	s.	d.
May 1, 1969	60	0	0
June 1, 1969	60	0	0
July 1, 1969	60	0	0
	£180	0	0

(3) Damages for the detention of the said motor-car.

Signed ——

No. 19

POSSESSION UNDER A MORTGAGE[5]

1. The plaintiff is entitled to the possession of a house and land known as The Manor, at Harpenden, in the county of Hertford.

2. By a deed made between the plaintiff and the defendant on June 23, 1946, the defendant demised the said house and land to the plaintiff for a term of 1,000 years by way of mortgage to secure the sum of £2,500 and interest thereon, and the said mortgage is still subsisting.

3. By the said deed the defendant covenanted to pay interest on the said sum at the rate of 5 per cent. per annum by half-yearly instalments on January 1 and July 1, in every year.

4. The defendant has failed to pay the instalment of interest due on July 1, 1969.

5. The defendant has never given up possession of the said house and land to the plaintiff, but remains wrongfully in possession thereof.

The plaintiff claims:—

    (i) possession of the said house and land; and

    (ii) the sum of £62 10s. (£62·50).

Signed ——

INDORSEMENTS FOR AN ACCOUNT

(*Ante*, pp. 48–50)

No. 20

CLAIM BY AN EXECUTOR

The plaintiff's claim is, as executor of A B, deceased, for an account of all moneys received and paid by the defendant as the agent of A B.

Particulars

1. On December 1, 1965, A B employed the defendant to collect the rents of his property, known as Beaconsfield Terrace, Walthamstow.

---

[5] Unless assigned for some special reason to the Family Division, all such actions for relief by a mortgagee are assigned to the Chancery Division (Order 88, r. 2); they should normally be commenced by originating summons (Order 88, r. 1).

2. The defendant collected the said rents from December 1, 1965, till April 19, 1969; he paid over to A B certain moneys as and for the rents of the said property up to December 31, 1967. He has made no payment since either to A B or to the plaintiff.

3. A B died on June 13, 1968, having by his last will, dated March 5, 1968, appointed the plaintiff his executor. Yet the defendant has refused to make any payment or render any account to the plaintiff.

No. 21

CLAIM AGAINST AN AGENT

The plaintiffs' claim is for £932, moneys had and received by the defendant as the plaintiffs' agent on their behalf and for their use; and also for an account of all moneys had and received by the defendant as such agent, and for payment of the amount found due on taking such account.

No. 22

MUTUAL DEALINGS

The plaintiffs' claim is, as trustee in bankruptcy of one James Smith, for £640 1s. 10d. (£640·9), money payable by the defendant to the plaintiff for goods sold and delivered by the said J. S. to the defendant, and for money received by the defendant to the use of the said J. S., and for an account of all mutual dealings between the defendant and the said J. S. from May 3, 1969, up to the present time, and of all moneys received by the defendant from the said J. S. between these dates; and that the defendant may be ordered to pay to the plaintiff the amount found due to him on taking such account.

[And see Precedent No. 23.]

III.—STATEMENTS OF CLAIM

IN ACTIONS FOR BREACH OF CONTRACT

No. 23

AGENT LIABLE TO ACCOUNT

In the High Court of Justice
Queen's Bench Division   1969. J.—No. 345
     Writ issued the 10th day of May 1969.

Between
> Davy Jones . . . . . . Plaintiff
> and
> Robert Robinson . . . . . Defendant.

[Amended] Statement of Claim

1. The plaintiff is a merchant in England, having business transactions on the west coast of Africa.

2. On September 2, 1966, the plaintiff appointed the defendant his agent for the collection of certain debts due to him on the west coast of Africa, and, for the purpose of such collection, delivered certain securities to the defendant.

3. The defendant did not collect all the said debts; he has not accounted for any of the said debts; and he disposed of certain of the securities without collecting the said debts.

[Particulars]

And the plaintiff claims an account.

> (signed) John Doe.

Served on the 24th day of May, 1969, by Snodgrass & Co. of 510 Bedford Row, London, W.C., the Plaintiff's solicitors [and re-served as amended pursuant to Order 20, rule 3, on the 9th day of June, 1969].

No. 24

AGENT LIABLE TO ACCOUNT—DETINUE

1. From April 1, 1968, until August 7, 1969, the plaintiff employed the defendant as his solicitor and confidential agent in the management of building estates and otherwise.

2. The defendant, as such solicitor and agent, received large sums of money for the plaintiff, for which he refuses to account.

3. The defendant wrongfully detained, and still detains, from the plaintiff the plaintiff's deeds, books, account-books, papers and writings.

The plaintiff claims ——

> (1) An account of all sums received and paid by the defendant as solicitor and agent of the plaintiff.
>
> (2) Payment of the amount found due to the plaintiff on taking such account.
>
> (3) A return of the said deeds, books, account-books. papers and writings.
>
> (4) Damages for their detention.

Precedents

No. 25

Action on a Common Money Bond against the Executor
and Devisee of the Obligor

1. William Smith, by his bond dated April 16, 1963, bound himself and his heirs to pay the plaintiff the penal sum of £1,000, subject to the condition that if he or they paid the plaintiff the sum of £500 on April 16, 1968, with interest thereon at the rate of 5 per centum per annum, the said bond should be void.

2. On April 16, 1968, William Smith paid the plaintiff £25, being interest on £500 at the agreed rate for one year; he paid the plaintiff the like sum on April 16, 1969. He made no other payment to the plaintiff.

3. On February 21, 1970, William Smith died.

4. The defendant, George, is the eldest son and executor of William Smith. The defendant, Mary, is his widow, to whom, by his last will, dated February 9, 1970, he devised all his real estate. The defendant, George, has assented to this devise.

And the plaintiff claims from each of the defendants

	£	s.	d.	
Principal.......................................	500	0	0	(£500·00)
Interest from April 16, 1969, to date of writ	79	3	4	(£79·16½)
Amount due	£579	3	4	(£579·16½)

The plaintiff further claims interest at the said rate from the date of writ until payment or judgment.

See *ante*, pp. 47, 190.

No. 26

Commission

1. The plaintiffs are auctioneers and estate agents, carrying on business at ——; the defendant was at all times hereinafter mentioned the owner of the brewery known as —— Brewery, Burton-on-Trent.

2. The defendant was, in the months of September and October, 1968, desirous of selling his said brewery; he employed the plaintiffs as his agents to find him a purchaser; and he undertook in the event of the plaintiffs introducing a buyer for the said brewery, to pay them a commission of 1½ per cent. on the purchase-money, payable on the purchase being completed and the money paid.

3. The defendant represented to the plaintiffs that the said brewery was making a net profit of £7,000, on a turnover of

£25,000 a year; that there were sixty-five public-houses in Birmingham and elsewhere " tied " to the said brewery; and that the trade he was then doing was 200 barrels a week, at a profit of 15s. a barrel.

4. The plaintiffs did introduce to the defendant a buyer who agreed with the defendant to purchase the brewery and the defendant's interest in the said public-houses for £68,000.

5. The said buyer was always ready and willing to complete the said purchase and pay the defendant the said price, until he discovered that the representations made by the defendant as to the profit made and the trade done by the said brewery, and as to the number of tied houses attached thereto, were untrue. He then declined to complete the said purchase or to pay the said price.

6. The plaintiffs were thus prevented through the defendant's default from earning their commission on the said purchase-money, which at the rate of 1½ per cent. amounts to £1,020.

7. The plaintiffs also seek to recover the said sum of £1,020 as money payable by the defendant to the plaintiffs for services rendered by the plaintiffs to the defendant, and for work and labour done by them for the defendant at his request.

And the plaintiffs claim £1,020

    (i) as commission earned;

    (ii) as damages under paragraphs 5 and 6;

    (iii) on a *quantum meruit.*

No. 27

COVENANTS IN A LEASE

1. By a lease, dated December 11, 1960, the plaintiff demised to the defendant a public-house, known as The King's Arms, High Street, in the City of Manchester, for a term of twenty-one years from September 29, 1960, at a yearly rental of £900.

2. By the said lease the defendant covenanted (*inter alia*):

    (i) To pay the said rent to the plaintiff by equal quarterly payments on the usual quarter days.

    (ii) During the said term to keep the inside of the said premises, together with the fittings, fixtures, etc., in as good and tenantable repair and decorative condition as they were in on December 11, 1960.

    (iii) Within three calendar months after notice in writing of any defects of repair should have been given to the defendant, or left upon the said premises, to repair, decorate and amend the same accordingly.

(iv) That no act should be done or committed, or omitted, or any offence or offences committed, whereby the licence for the time being for the vending of beer and other malt liquors on the said premises might become forfeited, or the renewal thereof refused.

(v) To keep open the said public-house for the sale of beer and other malt liquors at all times allowed by law.

(vi) That the said business of a beer retailer should at all times be managed and conducted on the said premises in a lawful and orderly and proper manner.

3. The defendant has broken all the said covenants:—

(i) He has not paid the rent which accrued due on June 24, September 29, and December 25, 1968, respectively, or any part thereof.

(ii) He has not repaired the premises in accordance with the covenant in that behalf.

(iii) Notice in writing of all defects of repairs was given to the defendant on July 21, 1968, and also left upon the said premises on August 17, 1968, yet the defendant did not, within three calendar months from the delivery thereof, or within a reasonable time thereafter, repair, decorate or amend the said premises.

(iv), (v), (vi) The retail business at the said public-house was not conducted in a lawful or orderly or proper manner, whereby the justices, on September 23, 1968, refused to renew the licence of the said public-house. And since the date of such refusal the said public-house has not been kept open for the sale of any malt liquors; but the said premises have ever since remained closed and unlicensed.

4. By reason of the said breaches of covenants, and of the wrongful acts complained of, the plaintiff has suffered damage, and has been greatly injured in his reversion.

And the plaintiff claims:—

(i) £675 for rent in arrear.

(ii) Damages for the said breaches of covenants.

No. 28

GOODS SOLD AND DELIVERED—NON-ACCEPTANCE

1. On October 20, 1969, the defendants by their agent A B agreed to buy from the plaintiff, and the plaintiff bargained and sold to the defendants certain barley, then lying on the plaintiff's premises, *viz.*, 306 sacks, at the price of £3 per sack.

2. All the said barley has been delivered by the plaintiff to the defendants; but the defendants have refused and still refuse to pay for the same.

3. Alternatively, the plaintiff says that the defendants have accepted part of the said barley, *viz.*, 44 sacks; but have refused and still refuse to accept the remainder of the said barley, or to pay for the said 44 sacks.

The plaintiff claims—
    (a) under paragraphs 1 and 2—£912; or
    (b) under paragraph 3
        (i) £132.
        (ii) Damages.
        [See Precedents, Nos. 62, 82.]

No. 29

GOODS OF INFERIOR QUALITY

1. On January 3, 1969, the defendant agreed to sell and deliver to the plaintiff 200 sacks of flour of the kind known as " seconds " at forty-five shillings a sack.

2. The defendant duly delivered to the plaintiff 200 sacks in alleged compliance with his agreement. But the flour in them was not " seconds," but an inferior quality worth only thirty-three shillings a sack.

And the plaintiff claims damages.

No. 30

NON-DELIVERY OF GOODS

1. The plaintiff is an iron merchant carrying on business at ——. The defendant is the owner of the —— Mine at Cleveland, in the County of York.

2. By letters passing between the plaintiff and the defendant and dated respectively January 31, February 2 and February 5, 1969, the defendant agreed to sell to the plaintiff, and the plaintiff agreed to buy from the defendant, 200 tons of scrap iron at the price of £4 a ton, and the defendant agreed to deliver the same to the plaintiff free on rail at Hull on or before April 1, 1969.

3. The defendant has only delivered eighty tons of the said iron, and he did not deliver that quantity till June 13, 1969.

Particulars of damage:—

	£	s.	d.
Loss of profit on 120 tons at £2 per ton	240	0	0
Loss by delay on 80 tons at 22s. 6d. (£1·12½) per ton	90	0	0
	£330	0	0

And the plaintiff claims £330 damages.

No. 31

LOST LUGGAGE

1. The plaintiff, on July 24, 1969, was received by the defendants as a passenger for the purpose of being carried with her suitcase by train on the defendants' railway from Liverpool to London, for reward to the defendants.

2. The defendants thereupon received and took charge of the said suitcase, which contained the plaintiff's wearing apparel, and placed it in their luggage van at Liverpool in the train in which the plaintiff was about to travel, for the purpose of its being carried to London.

3. The defendants did not carry the said suitcase to London, nor did they deliver it to the plaintiff on her arrival by the said train there, or within a reasonable time thereafter, or at all.

4. The defendants have either lost or retained the said suitcase, whereby the plaintiff has been and still is deprived of the said suitcase and its contents, and has suffered great inconvenience, and has incurred expense in endeavouring to recover possession thereof.

And the plaintiff claims damages.

No. 32

MONEY OVERPAID

1. By an indenture, dated November 16, 1964, J. S. guaranteed to the defendants the payment of any sum which might thereafter become payable to them by his son, Charles S.

2. On April 18, 1968, Charles S. was adjudicated bankrupt. On that day he owed the defendants £1,081 16s. (£1,081·80), and no more. No further sums have become payable by him to the defendants.

3. Since that date J.S. paid the defendants £325 (£325·00) on account of his indebtedness to them under the said guarantee.

4. J. S. died on August 8, 1968. By his last will he appointed his widow, the plaintiff, his executrix.

5.   Since the death of J. S. the plaintiff, in ignorance of the facts alleged in paragraphs 3 and 6, has paid the defendants various sums, amounting in all to £812 (£812·00).

6.   The defendants have received from the estate of Charles S. dividends on £1,081 16s. 0d., (£1,081·80), amounting in all to £326 16s. 0d. (£326·80). But they have not paid the same over to the plaintiff or given her credit therefor.

7.   The plaintiff has thus overpaid the defendants the amount of £382 (£382·00) which, as executrix of J. S., she claims from the defendants as money received by them to her use.

No. 33
Money Paid

1.   By an indenture of lease, dated April 24, 1896, the plaintiff demised to the defendant a house, No. 3 Albion Terrace, Hackney, at the yearly rent of £——, payable quarterly; and the defendant covenanted with the plaintiff that he would at all times during the term " pay the land-tax, sewers rate, and all other taxes, rates, duties, assessments and impositions, parliamentary, parochial or otherwise, which now are or shall at any time during the demise be assessed or imposed on or in respect of the said demised premises or of the rent hereby reserved (landlord's property tax only excepted)."

2.   In the month of May, 1896, the drains of the said house were defective and injurious to the health of the neighbourhood.

3.   Thereupon the Hackney Vestry, on June 5, 1896, served a notice upon the plaintiff under the Public Health (London) Act, 1891, ordering and requiring him to abate the nuisance arising from the state of the drains of the said house, and for that purpose to take up the existing drains and lay down new and proper drains throughout the premises.

4.   The plaintiff did the work required by the said vestry, and thereby incurred an expense of £148. He has demanded payment of this sum from the defendant, who refuses to pay the same.

And the plaintiff claims £148.

[See *Brett* v. *Rogers* [1897] 1 Q.B. 525; 66 L.J.Q.B. 287.]

No. 34
Warranty on the Sale of a Car [7]

1.   The plaintiff is a minor who sues by his brother, C D, as his next friend. The defendant is a car dealer carrying on business

---

[7] Contrast this claim in contract with claims in tort for fraudulent misrepresentation, such as Precedents Nos. 37 and 38.

at Goodsales Garage, Downlands Road, Reading, in the County of Berks.

2. On January 3, 1968, the defendant offered the plaintiff a Ford motor car, index no. PGR 505E, for sale at the price of £775, and to induce the plaintiff to purchase it at that price the defendant warranted that it was " in spanking good condition and thoroughly roadworthy."

3. The said warranty was oral and given at the premises aforesaid, and it induced the plaintiff to purchase the said car. Relying on the defendant's said warranty the plaintiff paid the sum of £775.

4. During the next two days the plaintiff observed the following defects in the said car:—

Particulars

Near side rear brake shoes missing;
Brake fluid reservoir leaking;
3 pistons cracked;
Off side rear leaf spring fractured;
Steering column bent;
Radiator blocked and rusted;
Crankshaft badly worn at all main bearings.

5. In the premises the said car was not in good condition nor was it in a roadworthy state.

6. By reason of the breach of warranty aforesaid the car was of no use to the plaintiff who, at a cost of £235 for replacement parts, repaired the same himself.

[*Particulars of special damage*]
And the plaintiff claims £235.

No. 35

Wrongful Dismissal

1. Prior to April 16, 1969, the defendant had entered into a contract with the S—— Local Board for the construction of a reservoir, etc., on Heaton Moor, in the County of York.

2. On April 14, 1969, the defendant verbally engaged the plaintiff as manager for the completion of the said contract and of all works connected therewith at a weekly salary of £30 from that date until the final settlement of accounts in respect of the same between the defendant and the said Board.

3. The plaintiff entered into the employ of the defendant and served him as such manager until he was wrongfully dismissed, as hereinafter mentioned. He always was and now is ready and willing to continue to serve the defendant as such manager until such final settlement of accounts is effected.

4. Yet the defendant, on October 9, 1970, gave the plaintiff one week's notice to quit his employment, and wrongfully dismissed the plaintiff from his post of manager, and refused to retain the plaintiff in his service after October 16, 1970, although the final settlement of accounts has not yet been effected between the defendant and the said Board.

5. The plaintiff has thereby lost the salary which he would have derived from continuing in the defendant's service, and has been unable to obtain another situation, and has remained unemployed from that date until now.

6. While the plaintiff was in the defendant's service the defendant did not pay him the agreed weekly salary of £30 regularly or at all, and the sum of £2,190 was, on October 15, 1970, and is now, due and payable to the plaintiff by the defendant for arrears of salary.

And the plaintiff claims—

    (i) Damages.

    (ii) £2,190 for arrears of salary to October 15, 1970.

No. 36

POINTS OF CLAIM IN A COMMERCIAL CASE

1. The defendant chartered the plaintiff's ship by charter dated May 1, 1969.

2. Lay days began at the port of loading on June 1, 1969, when the ship entered the Avonmouth dock; and expired on June 10, 1969. But the ship was not loaded till June 20.

The plaintiff claims £400, being ten days' demurrage at £40 a day.

IN ACTIONS OF TORT

No. 37

FRAUDULENT MISREPRESENTATION ON THE SALE OF A BUSINESS— WARRANTY—RETURN OF DEPOSIT

1. In the months of March and April, 1969, the defendant was desirous of selling, and offered to sell to the plaintiff, a baker's shop, situate at 99 Queen Street, Chelsea, and the goodwill of the business carried on thereat. And the plaintiff entered into negotiations with the defendant with a view to purchasing the same.

2. In the course of such negotiations, on April 10, 1969, the defendant warranted and represented to the plaintiff that

483

the said business had made a profit of £1300 during the preceding six months.

3. The plaintiff was thereby induced to purchase the said shop and goodwill from the defendant, and then and there paid him the sum of £650 as a deposit in part payment of the purchase-money, relying on the truth of what the defendant had stated.

4. The defendant's statement was not true. The said business had not during the preceding six months made a profit of £1300, or any other sum. On the contrary, it had made a loss during that period.

5. The defendant was well aware of the facts stated in the preceding paragraph when he made the said statement, and he made the same fraudulently with the intention of inducing the plaintiff to purchase the said shop and goodwill, and to pay the said deposit on the faith thereof.

6. The plaintiff, on discovering that the defendant's said statement was false, repudiated the said purchase, and refused to complete the same; and the consideration for his said deposit of £650 has, therefore, wholly failed.

And the plaintiff claims—

(1) The return of the said deposit of £650 with interest thereon at the rate of 5 per cent. per annum from April 10, 1969, till payment or judgment.

(2) Damages for the said misrepresentation and breach of warranty.

No. 38

FRAUDULENT MISREPRESENTATION AS TO DRAINS

1. In the month of April, 1969, the defendant was desirous of selling to the plaintiff a house known as No. 37 —— Street, London, S.W., as a residence for the plaintiff, his wife, children and servants.

2. In order to induce the plaintiff to purchase the said house, the defendant represented to the plaintiff that the drains of the said house had been properly constructed and were then in perfect order, and in particular that the main drain of the said house was properly trapped at the end of the yard.

3. The plaintiff was thereby induced to purchase the said house and did purchase it, relying on the truth of the defendant's statements, and paid the defendant £—— for the said house, and went to reside therein with his wife, children and servants, in the month of May, 1969.

4. The said drains had not been properly constructed and were not then in perfect order, and the said main drain of the said house was not in any way trapped at the end of the yard or at all.

5. The defendant made the said statements well knowing them to be untrue, or with a reckless disregard as to whether they were true or false.

6. In consequence of the defects of the said drainage, foul and noxious gases escaped from the drains into the said house, and injured the health of the plaintiff, his wife, children and servants; and in the months of July and August, 1969, the plaintiff, his wife, and two sons, and a servant became very seriously ill and suffered pain, and were prevented from attending to their work and business, and the plaintiff has incurred expense in nursing and curing himself and them, and for medical attendance, and in and about the inspection and repair and reconstruction of the said drains.

[Particulars]

And the plaintiff claims damages.

No. 39

INFRINGEMENT OF COPYRIGHT

1. The plaintiff is the author of a book entitled " Hints to Poultry Fanciers " and the owner of the copyright therein.

2. The defendant has infringed the plaintiff's copyright in the said book:—

[Here give full particulars of the alleged infringements.]

3. The defendant has in his possession a large number of copies of the plaintiff's said book which the defendant caused to be printed without the plaintiff's consent. The plaintiff before action demanded these copies from the defendant, but he refused and still refuses to deliver them to the plaintiff.

[Add particulars of special damage, if any.]

4. The defendant threatens and intends to continue his infringements of the plaintiff's copyright.

And the plaintiff claims:—

(1) Damages.

(2) Delivery up to the plaintiff of all copies of his said book now in the defendant's possession.

(3) An injunction to restrain the defendant from any further infringement of the plaintiff's copyright.

No. 40

Liability of a Lighterman

1. The defendants are wharfingers and lightermen, carrying on business at the —— Wharf, Wapping.

2. On January 7, 1969, the defendants, as such wharfingers and lightermen, agreed with the plaintiffs for reward safely to tranship and carry from the ship *Rosalba*, then moored in the Millwall Docks, to the said —— Wharf and there to land and warehouse, 197 bags of gum arabic, the property of the plaintiffs.

3. The defendants began to tranship and carry off the said goods, in pursuance of their said agreement, and, in doing so, they loaded the said goods upon a lighter called *The Thomas*, which sank on January 8, 1969, and the said goods were thereby greatly damaged.[9]

4. The said lighter was, on January 8, 1969, in the custody and control of the defendants, their servants or agents, who so negligently and carelessly navigated, moored and kept the said lighter that by reason thereof she sank, and the said goods were greatly damaged as aforesaid.

5. The defendants warranted that the said lighter was a tight, staunch, strong lighter, in every way suitable and reasonably fit for loading and carrying the said goods without damage.

6. The said lighter was not tight, staunch or strong, and was not at all suitable or fit for loading or carrying the said goods, but leaked, let in water and sank, whereby the said goods were greatly damaged as aforesaid.

Particulars of damage	£	s.	d.
Value of 197 bags of (double) gum arabic, weighing, when sound, 380 cwt., at 45s. per cwt. (51 kilos)	672	0	0 (£672·00)
Less price realised on sale of the same 197 bags as damaged......................................	176	1	8 (£176·08½)
	£495	18	4 (£495·91½)

---

[9] The statement of claim might end here. It is not necessary for the plaintiff to aver negligence on the part of the defendant, as in exercising the employment specified he had incurred the liability of a common carrier. (*Liver Alkali Co.* v. *Johnson* (1874) L.R. 9 Ex. 338; *Hill* v. *Scott* [1895] 2 Q.B. 713.)

The plaintiffs claim £495 18s. 4d. (£495·91½).
[See Precedent No. 71.]

No. 41

MALICIOUS PROSECUTION

1. The plaintiff is a plumber, carrying on business at ——.
2. On January 18, 1970, the plaintiff did some work for the defendant at his residence at ——.
3. On the following day the defendant, maliciously and without reasonable or probable cause, accused the plaintiff of having stolen a gold ring when at work in the defendant's house, and preferred a charge of larceny against the plaintiff before a justice of the peace.
4. The said justice, after hearing the evidence of both the defendant and the plaintiff, dismissed the charge.
5. The plaintiff has thereby been injured in his reputation, and has suffered the following special damage:—
   [*Particulars of special damage, if any.*]
And the plaintiff claims damages.

No. 42

NEGLIGENCE OF A SOLICITOR

1. The plaintiff is a married woman, the wife of A B, of ——.
2. The defendant is a solicitor of the Supreme Court, and was employed by the plaintiff in the year 1968 to advise her as to the investment of certain moneys, and in other business.
3. The defendant as such solicitor, in the month of October, 1968, advised the plaintiff to invest the sum of £5000 on a second mortgage of six leasehold houses situate in St. Mark's Road, Dulwich. The defendant recommended the said mortgage to the plaintiff as an excellent security for that amount.
4. The plaintiff, relying on the advice and skill of the defendant, invested the said sum of £5000 on the said mortgage, and the defendant acted as solicitor for the plaintiff in effecting this investment.
5. No solicitor exercising ordinary care and skill would have advised a client to lend money on a security of such a nature as that on which the defendant advised the plaintiff to lend this money.
6. The defendant was further guilty of negligence in not obtaining a report of a surveyor as to the condition and value

of the said property before he advised the plaintiff to advance money thereon.

7. The defendant was also guilty of negligence as a solicitor in not ascertaining the condition, state of repair and rental value of the said premises, and in representing to the plaintiff that the property was let at a net rental of £1500 a year; whereas three of the six houses were then void, the other three were let to unsubstantial and unsatisfactory tenants at £200 a year each, and all six houses were very much out of repair.

8. The plaintiff paid to the defendant the sum of £8 15s. 6d. as his charges in respect of the said investment.

9. The first mortgagees have now taken possession of the property which has proved insufficient to satisfy their claim, and the plaintiff has lost the whole of the said sum of £5000 and the interest thereon from December 25, 1968.

The plaintiff claims:—

(1) £5000, and interest thereon at the rate of 5 per cent. per annum from December 25, 1968, till judgment.

(2) £8 15s. 6d. (£8·77½) referred to in paragraph 8.

No. 43

Personal Injuries in a Collision

1. The plaintiff is a clerk in the employ of Messrs. X & Co.

2. On July 21, 1969, the first defendants accepted the plaintiff as a passenger, to be by them safely carried in their motor-coach from London to Brighton for reward.

3. The first defendants did not safely carry the plaintiff, but so negligently managed their coach in which the plaintiff was then being carried that it came into collision in London Road, Purley, with a motor-car owned and driven by the second defendant. Alternatively the said collision was caused by the negligence of the second defendant or of both defendants.

[Particulars of Negligence of first defendants.]

[Particulars of Negligence of second defendant.]

4. By reason of the premises the plaintiff suffered personal injury and pain and has been put to loss and expense.

[Particulars of Injuries.]

Statements of Claim

PARTICULARS OF SPECIAL DAMAGE

	£	s.	d.	
Suit damaged beyond repair	25	0	0	(£25·00)
Medical attendance by Dr. A.	16	5	0	(£16·25)
Extra food and nourishment	10	0	0	(£10·00)

Loss of salary (10 weeks at
£12 per week) .... £120 0 0 (£120·00)
Less half the value of sickness
benefit received (£21 10 0) [10] £10 15 0 (£10·75)   109 5 0 (£109·25)

£160 10 0 (£160·50)

And the plaintiff claims damages.

No. 44

CLAIM ARISING FROM DEATH BY ACCIDENT

1. The plaintiff brings this action as administratrix of A B, deceased, who died intestate on August 10, 1968. Letters of administration were granted to the plaintiff on October 21, 1968.

2. On or about August 1, 1968, the deceased was lawfully riding a bicycle upon the highway known as Castle Hill, Winchester, in the County of Hants, when the defendant so negligently drove his motor-car that a collision occurred between the said bicycle and motor-car, whereby the deceased suffered personal injuries and pain and was put to expense and his expectation of life was shortened. The deceased died as a result of the said injuries, and the plaintiff has incurred funeral expenses.

[Particulars of Negligence.]
[Particulars of Injuries.]
[Particulars of Special Damage.]

3. This action is brought for the benefit of the deceased's estate under the Law Reform (Miscellaneous Provisions) Act, 1934, and also under the Fatal Accidents Acts, 1846–1959, on behalf of the following persons who have suffered damage by the death of the deceased:—

The plaintiff, C B, aged ——, the widow of the deceased;
D E B, aged ——, his son;
F G B, aged ——, his daughter.

The deceased was a gardener in the employ of Y Z, earning £16 10s. (£16·50) a week and was the sole support of his said wife and children.

And the plaintiff claims damages.

---

[10] See Law Reform (Personal Injuries) Act, 1948, s. 2; *Flowers* v. *George Wimpey & Co., Ltd.* [1956] 1 Q.B. 73; *Hultquist* v. *Universal Pattern and Precision Engineering Co., Ltd.* [1960] 2 Q.B. 467.

No. 45

REPLEVIN [11]

On March 31, 1969, the defendant wrongfully seized the goods of the plaintiff [*enumerate them*] in his house at —— [*or* wrongfully seized six cows, the property of the plaintiff], and took the same away and deprived the plaintiff of the use thereof, and unjustly detained the same from him whereby the plaintiff has suffered damage.

And the plaintiff claims damages.

No. 46

SLANDER

1. The plaintiff is a road contractor, carrying on business at W., in the county of N.

2. In the months of March, April and May, 1969, the plaintiff was employed by the W. Urban District Council under a contract in writing dated March 4, 1967, to make up certain roads within the district, the names of which are set out in the schedule to the said contract.

3. On July 12, 1969, the defendant falsely and maliciously spoke and published of the plaintiff and of him in the way of his said business the words:—

" The work is scandalously badly done. Wilkins has broken his contract in many important particulars; and he ought not to be paid a penny more of the ratepayers' money until his work is thoroughly examined."

4. The said words were spoken to A B, C D, E F, and others whose names are at present unknown to the plaintiff.

5. The defendant meant and was understood to mean thereby that the plaintiff was a dishonest and fraudulent person who claimed money from the said District Council to which he was not entitled, and that the plaintiff was incompetent and not fit to be trusted or employed to carry out any public work.

[*Particulars of facts and matters relied on in support of the innuendo.*]

6. In consequence of the said words the plaintiff was injured in his credit and reputation and in his said business, and the H. Rural District Council, who had formerly employed the plaintiff as its road contractor, ceased to do so.

The plaintiff claims damages.

[See Precedent No. 78.]

---

[11] See County Courts Act, 1959, ss. 104–106.

No. 47

TRESPASS AND CONVERSION

1. On December 26, 1969, the defendant broke and entered a close of the plaintiff's, known as The —— Ironworks, Sheffield, and wrongfully removed and converted to his own use certain machinery of the plaintiff's, namely, a lathe and planing machine.

2. The defendant detains the said machinery and refuses to give up the same to the plaintiff.

The plaintiff claims:—

    (1) Damages for the said trespass;

    (2) The return of the said machinery or £300, its value and damages for its detention.

No. 48

WASTE

1. From Lady Day, 1947, to Lady Day, 1969, the defendant was tenant to the plaintiff of an old-established tavern, known as "The Goat and Compasses," Offley Street, in the City of Norwich.

2. During such tenancy the defendant committed waste to the said premises by wrongfully taking down and removing the ancient signboard belonging to the said premises, which for very many years was fixed over the front door thereof. The defendant wrongfully carried the same away and converted it to his own use, and detained, and still detains, the same from the plaintiff.

And the plaintiff claims:—

    (i) That the defendant may be ordered to restore the said signboard forthwith, and refix the same in its former position; or

    (ii) In the alternative, the return of the said signboard or £——, its value, and damages for its removal and detention.

IN ACTIONS FOR THE POSSESSION OF LAND

No. 49

BY A LANDLORD

1. By an agreement in writing, dated September 22, 1966, the plaintiff let to the defendant a house, No. 52 Broad Street,

Bristol, for the term of three years from September 29, 1966, at the yearly rent of £800, payable quarterly.

2. By the said agreement, the defendant promised to pay the said rent in equal quarterly instalments on the usual quarter days. The said agreement also contained a clause entitling the plaintiff to re-enter in case the said rent, whether lawfully demanded or not, was more than twenty-one days in arrear.

3. The defendant took possession of the said house under the said agreement, and is still in possession thereof. He paid the plaintiff rent up to Lady Day, 1969; he has paid no rent which has accrued since that day.

4. The Rent and Mortgage Interest (Restrictions) Acts do not apply to the said house, the rateable value whereof was at all material times £210.

And the plaintiff claims:—

   (i) Possession of the said house;

   (ii) £400, being two quarters' arrears of rent;

   (iii) Mesne profits from September 29, 1969, till possession of the said house is delivered to the plaintiff.

[For other precedents in similar cases, see Nos. 15–17.]

No. 50

By a Freeholder Never in Possession

1. On January 1, 1965, A B was seised in fee simple in possession of the house known as No. 7 Rotten Row, London.

2. On September 3, 1965, the defendant wrongfully took and still wrongfully retains possession of the said house.

3. By a conveyance dated October 10, 1968, the said A B conveyed the said house to the plaintiff in fee simple.

The plaintiff claims:—

   (1) Possession of the said house.

   (2) Mesne profits from October 10, 1968, until possession is given up to the plaintiff.

No. 51

By a Remainderman

1. The Rev. John Roberts died on July 25, 1900; he was on that date seised in fee simple and in possession of the house known as 182 Piccadilly, in the County of London.

2. By his will dated February 3, 1898, he devised the said house to his daughter, Anne Roberts, for life, with remainder to the plaintiff in fee.

3. Probate of his said will was on September 5, 1900, granted out of the Principal Probate Registry to Thomas Brown and William Smith the executors therein named who on March 20, 1901, impliedly assented to the said devise.

4. Anne Roberts died on October 3, 1965, intestate, and letters of administration to her estate were on December 21, 1965, granted out of the Principal Probate Registry to James Fellows and Thomas Low who, on January 7, 1966, assented to the vesting of the said house in the plaintiff in fee simple.

5. The defendant wrongfully entered into possession upon the death of the said Anne Roberts and still remains wrongfully in possession thereof.

The plaintiff claims:—

(1) Possession of the said house.

(2) Mesne profits from October 3, 1965, until possession is given up to the plaintiff.

IN AN ACTION CLAIMING ONLY A DECLARATION

No. 52

LANDLORD *v.* MORTGAGEE OF TENANT

1. The plaintiffs are the executors and trustees of the will of James Harris, deceased, formerly of ——.

2. By a lease, dated September 12, 1966, the said James Harris demised to one Richard King a building, then and now used as a place of public entertainment, called the —— Music Hall, situate in ——, with certain appurtenances, fixtures, chattels and effects (hereinafter called "the said premises") for a term of twenty-one years from September 15, 1966, at the yearly rental of £468, payable by equal weekly instalments, and subject to the several covenants, stipulations and conditions contained in the said lease.

3. By a mortgage deed, dated October 15, 1966, the said Richard King demised the said premises to the defendants for the residue of the said term of twenty-one years, except the last three days thereof, to secure a loan of £1,000 and interest thereon.

4. On May 31, 1968, the defendants entered into possession of the said premises, and under a power reserved to them in the

said mortgage deed have from that day till now occupied the said premises and carried on the business of the said Richard King thereon, and received the profits thereof.

5. In June, 1968, the said Richard King was adjudicated bankrupt in the Bradford County Court and in September, 1968, the duly appointed trustee of his property under the said bankruptcy, by leave of the court, disclaimed the said lease, and gave notice of such disclaimer to the said James Harris.

6. By an indenture, dated July 30, 1968, made between the said James Harris and the defendants, and indorsed upon the said lease, after reciting the said mortgage deed, and that the defendants, as such mortgagees as aforesaid, had applied to the said James Harris to allow them to continue to occupy the said premises and to vary the terms of the said lease in certain respects as thereinafter mentioned, which he had agreed to do, it was witnessed that:—

[*Here set out the terms of the arrangement.*]

7. The said James Harris died on June 21, 1969. By his last will, dated October 3, 1968, he devised the said premises to the plaintiffs, subject to the said lease.

8. The defendants have regularly paid to the plaintiffs the rent reserved by the said lease. But they deny that they are liable to perform or observe any of the covenants of the said Richard King contained in the said lease. They deny that they are or ever have been in possession of the said premises as tenants thereof either to the said James Harris, or to the plaintiffs. Or, if tenants at all, they assert that they are only weekly tenants of the said premises.

And the plaintiffs, as such executors and trustees as aforesaid, claim:—

(i) A declaration that the defendants are tenants to the plaintiffs of the said premises for the residue of the said term of twenty-one years, and upon all the other terms of the said lease;

(ii) Or, in the alternative, a declaration that the defendants are liable to perform and observe the covenants of the said Richard King contained in the said lease (a) till the expiration of the said term of twenty-one years, or (b) so long as the defendants continue in occupation of the said premises.

Statements of Claim

IN THE CHANCERY DIVISION

No. 53

PRIORITY OF MORTGAGEES

1. By a legal charge dated December 21, 1956, the property situate and known as No. 7 Paradise Alley, Hoxton, was mortgaged by the defendant A B to one J S to secure the repayment of £1,000 and interest at 4 per cent. per annum. The said J S obtained the custody of the title deeds of the said house and has at all material times had such custody.

2. By a legal charge dated January 1, 1957, the said property was mortgaged by the defendant A B to the plaintiff to secure the repayment of £800 and interest at 5 per cent. per annum. The said legal charge was registered under the Land Charges Act, 1925, as a puisne mortgage on January 7, 1957.

3. By a legal charge dated January 5, 1957, the said property was mortgaged by the defendant A B to the defendant E F to secure the repayment of £500 and interest at 6 per cent. per annum. The said legal charge was registered under the Land Charges Act, 1925, as a puisne mortgage on January 11, 1957.

4. By a legal charge dated January 9, 1957, the said property was mortgaged by the defendant A B to the defendant G H to secure the repayment of £300 and interest at 8 per cent. per annum. The said legal charge was registered under the Land Charges Act, 1925, as a puisne mortgage on January 12, 1957.

The plaintiff claims:—

    (i) A declaration that the legal charge of January 1, 1957, ranks in priority to the legal charges of January 5 and January 9, 1957.

    (ii) Foreclosure or sale of the said property.

    (iii) If necessary, a receiver.

    (iv) Further or other relief.

No. 54

SPECIFIC PERFORMANCE

1. By an agreement in writing, dated January 5, 1969, the defendant agreed to sell to the plaintiff the freehold messuage and premises known as Low Gill, Bredbury, near Stockport, in the County of Cheshire, at the price of £4,850. The sale was to be completed on March 1, 1969.

2. Notwithstanding repeated requests by the plaintiff and the plaintiff's solicitors by letter dated ——, the defendant has refused and continues to refuse to take any steps towards completion of the said agreement.

3. The plaintiff has at all material times been and is now ready and willing to perform all his obligations under the said agreement.

The plaintiff claims:—

(1) Specific performance of the said agreement.
(2) Further or alternatively, damages for breach of the said agreement.
(3) A declaration that he is entitled to a lien on the said property in respect of any damages and costs.
(4) Costs.
(5) Further or other relief.

IV.—DEFENCES

(The heading and title of the Defence is the same as that for a Statement of Claim (see Precedent No. 23) but omitting the words " writ issued, etc.")

IN ACTIONS FOR BREACH OF CONTRACT

No. 55

ACCORD AND SATISFACTION

1. The defendant admits that he agreed to sell a Steinway piano to the plaintiff for the sum of 200 guineas, and to deliver the same to him by March 30, 1969, as alleged in the statement of claim.

2. The defendant was unable to procure a Steinway piano by March 30, 1969, in accordance with his said agreement. Thereupon the plaintiff and defendant by letters interchanged between them on April 18, 1969, agreed that the defendant should deliver to the plaintiff and the plaintiff should accept a certain Brinsmead piano, in full satisfaction and discharge of the plaintiff's cause of action set out in the statement of claim, and of all damages and costs, if any, sustained by him in respect thereof.

3. The defendant, in pursuance of the agreement in the preceding paragraph mentioned, on April 30, 1969, delivered the said piano to the plaintiff, and the plaintiff accepted the same in satisfaction and discharge of the said cause of action.

No. 56

COMMISSION

1. The plaintiff did not do any of the work alleged in the statement of claim or earn any of the commission therein claimed.

2. The plaintiff has not effected a sale of, or found a purchaser for, any of the ground rents in the statement of claim mentioned. He never introduced to the defendants any person able and willing to purchase the said ground rents at the price mentioned in the letter set out in the statement of claim.

3. By the express terms of the said letter, it was a condition precedent to the plaintiff's right to recover any commission that he should, on or before January 17, 1970, forward to the defendants the name and address of some person able and willing to purchase the said ground rents at the price mentioned in the said letter. The plaintiff did not forward to the defendants the name or address of any such person on or before the said date, or at all.

4. By the express terms of the said letter the plaintiff was only to be paid the commission, if any, due to him out of the purchase-money paid to the defendants by a purchaser introduced to them by the plaintiff. No purchaser introduced by the plaintiff has ever yet paid any purchase-money to the defendants.

No. 57

" EXTRAS " TO A BUILDING CONTRACT

1. By a contract under seal, dated June 19, 1969, and made between the plaintiffs and the defendants, the plaintiffs agreed to do the work and labour, and to supply the materials therein specified for the defendants for the sum of £2,790.

2. The plaintiffs did the work and labour, and supplied the materials therein specified, and the defendants have paid the plaintiffs the said sum of £2,790. They have also paid to the plaintiffs the sum of £739 for " extras." They thus before action satisfied the plaintiffs' whole claim under the said contract.

3. As to all work, labour and materials other than those for which the defendants so paid the plaintiffs before action, the defendants never ordered the same, or any part thereof. No such work and labour has been done, and no such materials have

497

been supplied by the plaintiffs for or to the defendants at their request or at all.

4. The defendants never agreed to pay the plaintiffs the prices which they have charged for the said work, labour and materials. Such prices are excessive and unreasonable.

5. If, however, the plaintiffs are claiming the sum of £4,169 0s. 8d. (£4,169 · 3½) under the said contract of June 19, 1969, for "extras" within the meaning of the said contract, then the defendants say that the same are not "extras," but formed part of the contract work, and were included and paid for in the said fixed sum of £2,790. The following clauses of the said contract are in that case also material:—

[*Set out the clauses on which the defendants rely.*]

6. No instructions were ever given in writing by the engineer or any other person duly authorised on behalf of the defendants for any of the work, labour or materials, the price of which is sought to be recovered in this action. No such instructions in writing stated that any such matter was to be the subject of an extra or varied charge. No claim was made in writing by the plaintiffs in respect of any such work within one week from the execution thereof, or before the same became out of view or beyond check or admeasurement.

7. The plaintiffs did not deliver from time to time within one week after the expiration of the month in which the work then claimed for was done a true or proper or any claim in a form prescribed by the engineer, or in any other form. The engineer has not certified or recommended the amount claimed in this action or any other amount to be paid to the plaintiffs by the defendants. No dispute has yet been referred to or settled by the engineer, nor has he ever given any decision thereon.

No. 58

FRAUD

(*Defence to No. 4*)

The defendant admits that he accepted a bill mentioned in the indorsement on the writ herein. But he was induced to accept the said bill by the fraud of the plaintiff, of which the following are the particulars:—

[*Here add particulars of the alleged fraud.*]

Defences

No. 59

GOODS SOLD AND DELIVERED
(*Separate Defence of one of two Defendants*)
DEFENCE OF THE DEFENDANT C D

1. This defendant never bought any goods from the plaintiff.

2. No goods were ever delivered by the plaintiff to this defendant at his request, or at all.

3. This defendant never agreed to pay the plaintiff any of the prices charged in the particulars or any other prices.

4. The prices charged by the plaintiff for the said goods are unreasonable and exorbitant.

No. 60

GOODS SOLD AND DELIVERED—INFERIOR QUALITY

1. The plaintiffs never delivered to the defendant any hides of the quality and substance ordered.

2. The plaintiffs tendered to the defendant other hides of a much lighter and inferior quality; these the defendant refused to accept, and he returned the same to the plaintiffs.

No. 61

GOODS SOLD AND DELIVERED—ACCOUNT STATED—SET-OFF

1. The defendant admits that the goods mentioned in the plaintiff's particulars were sold and delivered to him, and that on April 4, 1970, he owed the plaintiff the full amount claimed on the writ (£69 4s. 8d.) (£69·23½) in respect of them.

2. Before that date, the defendant had sold and delivered to the plaintiff certain goods (of which the following are the particulars) and the plaintiff owed the defendant the sum of £37 18s. 3d. (£37·91) in respect of these goods.

Particulars

	£	s.	d.	
1969—March 31—15 loaves	1	2	6	(£1·12½)
,, —April 30—7 cakes	1	8	0	(£1·40)
etc. etc.				
	£37	18	3	(£37·91)

3. On April 4, 1970, the plaintiff and defendant met at the plaintiff's house and agreed the figures on either side, and stated

an account between them. And it was then found that there was a balance of £31 6s. 5d. (£31·32) due from the defendant to the plaintiff, which amount the defendant then and there paid to the plaintiff, and the plaintiff accepted the payment of such balance in satisfaction and discharge of his present claim.

4. In the alternative, as to £31 6s. 5d. (£31·32), part of the plaintiff's claim in this action, the defendant says that before action, to wit, on April 4, 1970, he satisfied and discharged the plaintiff's claim by payment.

5. As to £37 18s. 3d. (£37·91), the residue of the plaintiff's claim in this action, the defendant says that the plaintiff at the commencement of this action was and still is indebted to the defendant to the amount of £37 18s. 3d. (£37·91) for goods sold and delivered, full particulars of which are stated in paragraph 2 above, which amount the defendant is willing to set off against so much of the plaintiff's claim as is herein pleaded to.

No. 62

GOODS SOLD AND DELIVERED—NOT EQUAL TO SAMPLE

(Defence and Counterclaim to No. 30)

1. As to £132 part of the moneys claimed in this action, being the price of forty-four sacks of the barley mentioned in paragraph 3 of the statement of claim, the defendants have since action paid £132 to the plaintiff's solicitors under an order made in this action on February 22, 1970.

2. As to the residue of the plaintiff's claim in this action, the defendants say the said barley was sold to them by sample and the plaintiff warranted and undertook that the same was equal to sample, and was and should be properly screened and well managed.

3. The said barley was not equal to sample, and was not properly screened or well managed, and thereby was and is of less value to the defendants.

4. And by way of set-off and counterclaim, the defendants repeat the allegations contained in paragraphs 2 and 3, above, and claim alternatively damages for the plaintiff's breaches of warranty.

[See Precedent No. 82.]

Defences

No. 63

Minority

At the date of the alleged contract [*or* promise] the defendant was a minor under the age of 18 years. He was born at —— in the County of —— on the —— day of ——, 19—.[12]

No. 64

Policy of Life Assurance

1. In the month of July, 1968, Joseph Brown (mentioned in the statement of claim, and hereinafter called " the assured "), desiring to effect an insurance with the defendant company, signed and delivered to them a declaration in writing, dated the 5th day of July, 1968, which he agreed should be the basis of the contract of assurance which he desired to effect with the defendant company. And on the faith of the statements contained in the said declaration the defendant company granted him the policy sued on, No. 24,942. In the said declaration the assured stated that his age next birthday was 69 years.

2. By the said policy, after reciting the facts in the last paragraph mentioned, and that satisfactory evidence of the statement as to age had to be furnished to the directors, the defendant company covenanted to pay £1,000 to the executors, administrators or assigns of the assured, within one calendar month next after satisfactory proof of title and of the age and death of the assured should have been duly furnished to the directors of the defendant company.

3. No satisfactory proof of the title of the plaintiff or of the age of the assured has ever been furnished to the directors of the defendant company.

4. The defendant company does not admit that the plaintiff is the legal personal representative of the assured.

5. It was a condition of the said policy that all persons making claims thereunder must give satisfactory proof of the time of birth of the assured and of their title to receive any sum due under the said policy, and such further information on each point as the directors should think reasonable. The plaintiff has given no satisfactory proof of the time of birth of the assured, or of her title.

6. It was a condition of the said policy that the declaration, referred to in paragraph 1 above, should form the basis of the

---

[12] As to the precise time at which an infant attains his majority, see Family Reform Act, 1969, s. 9.

contract between the assured and the defendant company, and that if the said declaration was not in all respects true, the said policy should be void. The said declaration was not in all respects true. The age of the assured, on his next birthday, was then 74, and not 69 as therein stated; and the said policy is therefore void.

7. The said policy was made on the life of the assured, for the use and benefit of one David Dawson, and not of the assured. But the name of the said David Dawson was not inserted in the said policy, as is required by section 2 of the Life Assurance Act, 1774, and the defendant company will therefore object that the said policy is illegal and void.

8. The plaintiff is not the holder of the said policy. She is not entitled to receive the moneys, if any, which the defendant company may be liable to pay under the said policy.

No. 65

Rectification of an Agreement
defence and counterclaim

DEFENCE

1. The defendant admits that on May 22, 1969, he signed a written agreement with the plaintiffs. But the substance of such agreement is not correctly stated in paragraph 3 of the statement of claim. The defendant never agreed as in that paragraph alleged.

2. The defendant contends that on the true construction of the said written agreement the plaintiffs are not entitled to be paid any moneys until the defendant has received from abroad the proceeds of the mines, either on sale or from workings, sufficient for such payment. The defendant has never yet received any such proceeds.

COUNTERCLAIM

3. If, however, it should be held that the plaintiffs are entitled under the said agreement as written to be paid any moneys by the defendant before he had received from abroad proceeds of the said mines sufficient for such payment, the defendant counterclaims to have the said agreement rectified, and says that the verbal agreement between the plaintiffs and the defendant was that no moneys should be payable by the defendant to the plaintiffs until he had received proceeds of the mines sufficient for payment of the same.

4. The plaintiffs acted as solicitors for both parties in the matter, and prepared the said written agreement as a record of the said verbal agreement; and the defendant signed the said agreement in the belief, and on the faith of a representation made by the plaintiffs, that it contained the terms of the said verbal agreement, and that no money would become payable by him to the plaintiffs thereunder until he had received proceeds of the mines sufficient for such payment.

The defendant counterclaims to have the said agreement rectified.

[See Precedent No. 87.]

No. 66

RESCISSION OF A CONTRACT

1. The defendant admits that he entered into a contract with the plaintiffs on June 11, 1970, and that the purport thereof is correctly stated in paragraph 1 of the statement of claim. But prior to August 20, 1970, and before any breach by the defendant of the said contract, the plaintiffs and defendant mutually agreed to rescind the said contract, and to substitute a fresh agreement therefor.

2. The terms of the said substituted agreement were reduced into writing on August 20, 1970, and signed by the defendant; and the defendant thereby agreed to pay to the plaintiffs £300 in cash, and also to give them four promissory notes for the remainder of the said purchase-money, and the plaintiffs agreed to accept the said cash and notes in full satisfaction and discharge of their rights under the said contract.

3. On August 27, 1970, the defendant paid the plaintiffs the sum of £300, and handed to them the said notes, and the said cash and notes respectively were accepted by the plaintiffs as the due performance and in full satisfaction and discharge of the said agreement of August 20. The said notes are still outstanding.

4. The defendant admits that he paid the sum of £300 to the plaintiffs, but denies that he did so in pursuance of the said contract of June 11. Such payment was made in performance of the said agreement of August 20.

No. 67

WORK AND LABOUR DONE AND MATERIALS PROVIDED

1. The plaintiff never did any of the work or labour, or provided any of the materials, specified in the statement of claim.

2. None of the said work or labour was done, nor were any of the said materials provided, for the defendant or at his request.

3. The defendant never agreed to pay the plaintiff the prices charged for the said work, labour and materials, or any other prices. The prices charged by the plaintiff are unreasonable and exorbitant.

No. 68

Points of Defence in a Commercial Case

(*Defence to No. 36*)

The lay days did not begin till June 10, 1969, when the ship entered a loading berth in the Avonmouth Docks. The lay days expired on June 20.

In Actions of Tort

No. 69

Fraudulent Misrepresentation

1. Neither defendant ever made any of the representations alleged in the statement of claim.

2. No one of the said alleged representations was false in fact; no one of them was false to the knowledge of either of the defendants; no one of them was made fraudulently or recklessly or without caring whether the same was true or false.

3. The plaintiff was not induced by any of the alleged representations to buy the goodwill, tenancy and licence of the Duke of York Tavern. The plaintiff ascertained for himself the value and extent of the business done at the said tavern, and the class of customers using the same. He himself examined the books and visited the said tavern before he agreed to purchase the same, and he made the said purchase in reliance upon his own judgment and the result of his own inquiries and investigations, and not upon any statement or representation made by the defendants or either of them.

4. The plaintiff has not suffered the alleged or any damage by reason of any act or default of either of the defendants. The defendants will object that the damage claimed is too remote.

No. 70

Infringement of Copyright

1. The document referred to in paragraph 1 of Statement of Claim as a " Chart of the May Races " is not an original work of the plaintiff; he is not the author of it. Similar charts

showing the results of the May races have been published in Cambridge every May Term since 1853.

2. The so-called chart is not the subject of copyright. It is not a literary work; it is merely a pictorial method of stating certain items of news about the boat-races which were already common property.

3. The defendant has not infringed the plaintiff's copyright, if any.

No. 71

LIABILITY OF A LIGHTERMAN

(*Defence to No.* 40)

1. The defendants at all dates mentioned in the statement of claim were and now are warehousemen and wharfingers, but they were not and are not lightermen as alleged, and did not enter into any contract as such.

2. The defendants never agreed to tranship or carry, or to land or warehouse, any of the goods mentioned in the statement of claim upon the terms therein alleged, or for reward, or at all.

3. The defendants deny each and every allegation contained in paragraphs 3, 4 and 6 of the statement of claim.

4. The defendants did not, nor did their servants or agents, negligently or carelessly navigate, moor or keep the said lighter, or do any act, or omit anything, which caused damage to the plaintiff.

5. If the said goods were shipped on board the said lighter, she was at such time tight, staunch and strong, and in every way suitable and reasonably fit for the loading and carriage of the said goods. But the defendants never warranted as alleged in paragraph 5 of the statement of claim or at all. No damage was caused to any of the said goods by reason of the breach of any warranty.

6. Alternatively, the defendants say that if they agreed to tranship and carry the said goods for reward or at all, or if they shipped any of the plaintiff's goods on board the said lighter, they did so upon the terms that they should not be liable for any loss or damage to the said goods, except loss or damage arising from the negligence or wilful acts of themselves or their servants, and that the alleged loss or damage was not so caused.

No. 72

LIBEL

1. The defendants are the proprietors of a weekly newspaper called the "Stock Exchange."

2. The defendants admit that they printed and published in their said newspaper the words set out in paragraph 3 of the statement of claim, but deny that they did so with any of the meanings in the said paragraph alleged. The said words are incapable of the said alleged meanings or any other defamatory or actionable meaning.

3. The said words without the said alleged meanings are no libel.

4. The said words without the said alleged meanings and according to their natural and ordinary signification are true in substance and in fact.

5. The said words are part of a fair and accurate report of a judicial proceeding, *viz.*, an action tried before Mr. Justice —— on ——, in which A B was plaintiff and C D defendant, and were published by the defendants bona fide for the information of the public, and in the usual course of their business as public journalists, and without any malice towards the plaintiff, and are therefore privileged.

6. The said words are fair and bona fide comment on matters of public interest, namely, the said judicial proceeding and the promotion and registration of the J. B. E. Co., and were published by the defendants bona fide for the benefit of the public and without any malice towards the plaintiff.

No. 73

LIBEL

1. The defendant admits that he printed and published in his newspaper the words set out in paragraph 2 of the statement of claim, but he denies that he published them with any of the meanings in paragraph 3 thereof alleged, or with any defamatory meaning.

2. In so far as the said words consist of allegations of fact, they are true in substance and in fact; in so far as they consist of expressions of opinion, they are fair comments made in good faith and without malice upon the said facts, which are matters of public interest.

Particulars
[See Order 82, r. 3, and *ante*, pp. 163–164.]

No. 74

LIBEL—APOLOGY [14]

The defendant admits that she wrote and published the words set out in paragraph 2 of the statement of claim. She denies that they bear the meaning alleged in the said paragraph, but she admits that they are libellous in their natural signification, and that they refer to the plaintiff. She has, since action brought, tendered to the plaintiff a full apology for her publication of the said words, and she now unreservedly withdraws all imputation on the plaintiff's character, and expresses her sincere regret for such publication.

No. 75

LIBEL—NOTICE IN MITIGATION OF DAMAGES

Particulars
(Served pursuant to Order 82, r. 7)

Take notice, that at the trial of this action the defendant intends to give the following matters in evidence with a view to mitigation of damages:—

1. On August 10, 1969, before the publication of the letter set out in paragraph 4 of the statement of claim, the plaintiff wrote and caused to be printed and published in the —— *County Gazette* an anonymous letter with regard to the matters mentioned in paragraph 2 of the statement of claim, in which he commended his own conduct, and then referred to the defendant in the following words:—

[*Set out so much of the anonymous letter as attacked the defendant.*]

2. It was in reply to the attack made on the defendant by this anonymous letter that the defendant wrote the words set out in paragraph 4 of the statement of claim, which the plaintiff alleges to be a libel upon him.

Dated the —— day of ——, 1970.

Yours, etc.,

A B, of ——
Defendant's Solicitor.

To the Plaintiff, and
Messrs. C and D,
his Solicitors.

---

[14] As this is not a plea of tender and apology under the Libel Acts, 1843 and 1845, the fact that money has been paid into court must not be mentioned in the Defence. (Order 22, r. 7.)

Precedents

No. 76

Replevin—Rent in Arrear

The plaintiff held, and still holds, the said premises as tenant to one J S, at the yearly rent of £300, payable quarterly. On August 7, 1970, £150 of the said rent was and still is due and in arrear from the plaintiff to the said J S who thereupon appointed the defendant his bailiff to distrain on the goods upon the said premises for the said arrears of rent. And the defendant accordingly took the goods mentioned in the plaintiff's particulars as a distress for the said rent.

No. 77

Replevin—Cattle Damage Feasant

On July 8, 1970, the defendant was in occupation of a certain field as tenant to Sir J. H.; and the plaintiff's cattle mentioned in the statement of claim were wrongfully straying in the same field, and doing damage there; wherefore the defendant distrained them in the said field.

No. 78

Slander

(Defence to No. 46)

1. The defendant never spoke or published any of the words set out in paragraph 3 of the statement of claim.

2. The defendant did not mean and was not understood to mean what is alleged in paragraph 5 of the statement of claim. The said words are incapable of any of the alleged meanings or of any other defamatory or actionable meaning.

3. The said words without the said alleged meanings are true in substance and in fact.

Particulars

(a) Arlington Road.
   No concrete under channelling.
   No hard core under the road opposite Nos. 13 to 24 inclusive.

(b) Manvers Road.
   [Set out the details]

4. The defendant is a member of the W. Urban District Council. At the meeting of the said district council, held on July 12, 1969, the chairman of the highways committee moved that the plaintiff be paid the balance of the moneys claimed by

him under his contract with the said district council. The defendant made a speech in opposition to this motion. If in the course of such speech the defendant spoke any of the words set out in paragraph 3 of the statement of claim, he did so in the bona fide discharge of his duty as a district councillor and without malice towards the plaintiff, and in the honest belief that what he said was true; and the said words were published only to the members of the said district council, who had a corresponding interest and duty in the matter. The occasion is therefore privileged.

5. The said words are a fair and bona fide comment on matters of public interest in the said district, *viz.*: the condition of the roads in the said district, and the claim of the plaintiff to be paid by the said district council for making the said roads.

6. The defendant will object that the said words are not actionable without proof of special damage, and that the special damage alleged in paragraph 6 of the statement of claim is too remote and not sufficient in law to sustain the action.

No. 79

SLANDER—VULGAR ABUSE

1. The defendant admits that he spoke and published the words set out in paragraphs 2 and 3 of the statement of claim, but he denies that he spoke or published them with the meanings in the said paragraphs alleged.

2. The said words are merely vulgar abuse, and were uttered by the defendant in anger, as all who heard the words were well aware; they were not intended or understood to convey any specific charge or imputation against the plaintiff.

3. The said words are incapable of any of the said meanings, or of any other actionable or defamatory meaning.

4. The defendant will object that the said words (taken either by themselves or with any innuendo of which they were capable) are not actionable without proof of special damage, and that none is alleged.

IN AN ACTION FOR THE POSSESSION OF LAND

No. 80

EJECTMENT OF A TENANT

(Defence and Counterclaim to No. 16)

1. The defendant denies that he was ever tenant at will to the plaintiff of the said premises.

2. Before the determination of such tenancy, if any, the plaintiff, by writing dated October 3, 1969, agreed to grant [15] to the defendant a lease of the said premises at the yearly rent of £120 for the term of twenty-one years, commencing December 25, 1969; and on that date the defendant's tenancy at will, if any, determined, and he has since that date been and still is in possession of the said premises under the said agreement.

And the defendant counterclaims to have the said agreement specifically performed, and to have a lease granted to him in accordance therewith.

[See Precedent No. 84.]

No. 81

ESTOPPEL BY RECORD [16]

The defendant avers that the plaintiff ought not to be admitted to say that the field mentioned in the statement of claim is his close, because of the following facts. On June 7, 1961, the plaintiff brought an action against the defendant in the Queen's Bench Division of the High Court of Justice (1961. B. No. 725), claiming damages for an alleged trespass by the defendant on the said field. The defendant pleaded in his defence in the said action that the said field was his close, and not the close of the plaintiff. The said action was tried on October 3, 1961, before the Honourable Mr. Justice Mee, at Bristol, and upon the said trial the learned judge found that the said field was the close of the defendant, and judgment was accordingly entered in the said action for the defendant, and the said judgment still remains in full force and effect.

V.—REPLIES, ETC.

No. 82

GOODS SOLD AND DELIVERED—NOT EQUAL TO SAMPLE

(Reply and Defence to Counterclaim No. 62)

REPLY

1. The plaintiff admits that the defendants have paid £132 to the plaintiff's solicitors. Save as aforesaid, he joins issue with the defendants upon their defence.

---

[15] This must be specially pleaded although the defendant is in possession. See *ante*, p. 115.

[16] See also the form of reply commended by Davies J. in *Hill* v. *Hill* [1954] P. 291.

DEFENCE TO COUNTERCLAIM

2. The plaintiff denies that the said barley was sold by sample as alleged. All the said barley was bought by the defendants in bulk after inspecting the same upon the plaintiff's premises. The plaintiff never warranted or undertook that it was equal to any sample or was or should be properly screened or well managed.

3. If the said sale was by sample, which the plaintiff denies, the said barley was equal to the sample, and was properly screened and well managed.

No. 83

RECTIFICATION OF AN AGREEMENT

(*Defence to Counterclaim No. 65*)

1. As to the counterclaim, the plaintiffs will object that on the facts therein alleged the defendant is not entitled to have the said agreement rectified.

2. The plaintiffs never agreed as alleged in paragraph 3 of the counterclaim. The said written agreement truly represents, and contains, and is, the only agreement made between the plaintiffs and the defendant, as the defendant always well knew.

3. The plaintiffs never represented as alleged in paragraph 4 of the counterclaim. They made no representation at all with regard to the terms of the said written agreement, nor was the said written agreement prepared as a record of any verbal agreement. The defendant read over the said written agreement, assented to it, and signed it of his own free will, and not in the belief or on the faith of any representation by the plaintiffs or either of them.

4. The plaintiffs will object that parol evidence is inadmissible to vary the said written agreement.

No. 84

EJECTMENT OF A TENANT

(*Defence to Counterclaim No. 80*)

1. And as to the counterclaim, the plaintiff denies that he ever agreed as therein alleged.

2. There is no memorandum of any such agreement sufficient to satisfy the Law of Property Act, 1925, section 40.

3. If the plaintiff ever agreed to grant the defendant a lease of the said premises, which he denies, such agreement provides that the lease should contain a condition by which it would

determine if the defendant became bankrupt. The defendant was adjudicated a bankrupt on December 23, 1969.[17]

No. 85

REJOINDER

1. The defendant joins issue with the plaintiff on paragraphs 2, 3 and 4 of his defence to the counterclaim.

2. And in further answer to paragraph 3 thereof, the defendant says that the plaintiff on the —— day of ——, 19—, within six years before the counterclaim herein acknowledged in writing that he owed to the defendant the sum counterclaimed.

VI.—PETITION

No. 86

WINDING-UP PETITION

In the High Court of Justice,   No.   of 19 .
Chancery Division,
    Companies Court
In the matter of Abie Seedee Limited
        and
In the matter of the Companies Act, 1948.
To Her Majesty's High Court of Justice.

        The humble petition of Effie Geeaich of 7 Paradise Alley, Hoxton, in the County of London, Spinster, sheweth as follows:—

1. Abie Seedee Limited (hereinafter called " the Company ") was incorporated in the month of July, 1951, under the provisions of the Companies Act, 1948, as a company limited by shares.

2. The registered office of the Company is situated at Doemall House, The Spivveries, in the City of London.

3. The nominal capital of the Company is £100 divided into one hundred shares of £1 each. The amount of the capital paid up or credited as paid up is £2.

4. The objects for which the Company was established are to carry on business as general merchants and other objects set forth in the Memorandum of Association thereof.

---

[17] The defendant's bankruptcy affords a good defence to the counterclaim, because a court of equity will not decree specific performance of an agreement to grant a lease in cases where it would be useless to do so. Hence, if the court ordered a lease to be granted, the plaintiff might be able to re-enter at once by reason of the bankruptcy. (See s. 146 (9) and (10) of the Law of Property Act, 1925.)

5. The Company is indebted to your Petitioner in the sum of £100 the price of goods sold and delivered by her to the Company on the 1st day of February, 1965.

6. Your Petitioner has made repeated application to the Company for payment, but the Company has failed and neglected to pay or satisfy the same or any part thereof.

7. The Company is insolvent and unable to pay its debts.

8. In the circumstances it is just and equitable that the Company should be wound up.

Your petitioner therefore humbly prays as follows:—

1. That Abie Seedee Limited may be wound up by the Court under the provisions of the Companies Act, 1948; or

2. That such other Order may be made in the premises as to the Court shall seem just.

And your petitioner will ever pray etc.

Note:—It is intended to serve this petition on Abie Seedee Limited.

VII.—SUMMONSES, ORDERS AND NOTICES

No. 87

ORIGINATING SUMMONS (Q.B.D.) APPEARANCE REQUIRED

(Order 7, r. 2 (1); Form No. 8, Appendix A)

In the High Court of Justice,   1970.—B.—No. 267.
Queen's Bench Division,
    Between A B .   .   .   .   .   Plaintiff
               and
      C D .   .   .   .   .   Defendant.

To C D of —— in the county of ——.

Let the defendant within 8 days after service of this summons on him, inclusive of the day of service, cause an appearance to be entered to this summons which is issued on the application of the plaintiff, A B, of ——, in the county of ——.

By this summons the plaintiff claims against the defendant compound interest under a promissory note made by the defendant in the following words:—[*here set out a full copy of the note*]. And the plaintiff seeks the determination of the Court on the following question, namely, whether the said note carries simple or compound interest?

If the defendant does not enter an appearance, such judgment may be given or order made against or in relation to him as the Court may think just and expedient.

Dated the —— day of ——, 1970.

O.P.—17

Note:—This summons may not be served later than 12 calendar months beginning with the above date unless renewed by order of the Court.

This summons was taken out by —— of —— solicitor for the said plaintiff whose address is ——.

DIRECTIONS FOR ENTERING APPEARANCE
[as in Precedent No. 3.]

No. 88

SUMMONS UNDER ORDER 14
[Heading as in Precedent No. 87.]

Let all parties concerned attend the Master in Chambers in Room No.——, Central Office, Royal Courts of Justice, Strand, London, on Wednesday, the 16th day of February, 1970, at 1.30 o'clock in the afternoon, on the hearing of an application on the part of the plaintiff, for final judgment in this action against the defendant for the amount claimed in the statement of claim, with interest, if any [*or* for possession of the land mentioned in the indorsement on the writ and the arrears of rent and mesne profits therein claimed] and costs.

Take notice that a party intending to oppose this application or to apply for a stay of execution should send to the opposite party, or his solicitor, to reach him not less than three days before the date above-mentioned, a copy of any affidavit intended to be used.

This summons will be attended by counsel.

Dated the 6th day of February, 1970.

This summons was taken out by E F, of ——, solicitor for the above-named plaintiff.

To the above-named defendant and to G H, his solicitor.

No. 89

ORDERS UNDER ORDER 14

[Heading as in Precedent No. 87.]

Upon hearing counsel for plaintiff and defendant, and upon reading the affidavits of A B and C D, both filed the 16th day of February, 1970—

It is Ordered that unless the defendant pays into Court £200 within 7 days from the date of this order the plaintiff may enter final

514

judgment against him for the amount indorsed on the writ with interest, if any,[18] and costs.

And it is ordered that if that sum is so paid the defendant may defend the action and the defendant shall have 14 days in which to serve his defence.

And it is ordered that [*insert directions*] and that the costs of this application be costs in the cause. Fit for counsel.

Or,

It is Ordered that the defendant may defend this action, and that it be transferred to the Westminster County Court under section 45 of the County Courts Act, 1959.

And that the costs of this application be in the discretion of the County Court. Fit for counsel.

Dated the 16th day of February, 1970.

[For other forms of Order see R.S.C.]

No. 90

SUMMONS FOR DIRECTIONS UNDER ORDER 25

[Heading as in Precedent No. 87.]

[N.B.—Applicants to complete the text of any matter required and to strike out the number opposite any matter not required but *not to strike out the text*, which must be left for the Master.]

Let all parties concerned attend the Master in Chambers, Royal Courts of Justice, Strand, London, on ——day the —— day of ——, 19—, at —— o'clock in the ——noon on the hearing of an application for directions in this action, that:

1. This action be consolidated with action(s) 19—, ——, No. — and 19—, ——, No. —.

2. The action be referred to an Official Referee [a Master] and that the costs of this application be costs in the cause.

3. The action be [by consent] transferred to —— County Court, and that the costs of this application be in the discretion of the County Court.

4. Unless the plaintiff within —— days gives security for the defendant's costs in the sum of £—— to the satisfaction of

---

18 The amount of interest, if properly claimed on the writ stating the rate and period (see *ante*, p. 46), will be a matter of mere calculation. The judgment actually entered in pursuance of the master's order will therefore be for a single sum of money and costs. After reciting that the defendant has appeared and the terms of the order as drawn up, it will run as follows: " It is this day adjudged that the defendant do pay the plaintiff £—— and £—— costs [*or* costs to be taxed]." Unless otherwise directed, the judgment will be dated as of the day on which the master's order was made, even though it was not actually entered until later. (Order 42, r. 3.)

the Master, the action be transferred to the —— County Court with stay meanwhile, and that the costs of this application be in the discretion of the County Court [and that if the security be so paid the directions be as follows:—]

5. The plaintiff have leave to amend the writ by —— and that the service of the writ and the defendant's appearance stand, and that the costs incurred and thrown away by the amendment be the defendant's in any event.

6. The plaintiff have leave to amend the statement of claim as shown in the document served herewith and to re-serve the amended statement of claim in —— days, with leave to the defendant to serve an amended defence (if so advised) in —— days thereafter and with leave to the plaintiff to re-serve an amended reply (if so advised) in —— days thereafter and that the costs incurred and thrown away by the amendments be the defendant's in any event.

7. The defendant have leave to amend the defence as shown in [the document served with the defendant's notice under this summons] and to re-serve the amended defence in —— days [with leave to the plaintiff to re-serve an amended reply (if so advised) in —— days thereafter] and that the costs of and the costs thrown away as a result of the amendments be the plaintiff's in any event.

8. The plaintiff serve upon the defendant within —— days the further and better particulars of the statement of claim specified in [the document served with] the defendant's notice under this summons.

9. The defendant serve upon the plaintiff within —— days the further and better particulars of the defence specified in the document served herewith.

10. The plaintiff serve on the defendant within —— days the further and better particulars of the reply specified in [the document served with] the defendant's notice under this summons.

11. The plaintiff give security for the defendant's costs to the satisfaction of the Master in the sum of —— on the ground —— and that in the meantime all further proceedings be stayed.

12. The plaintiff within —— days serve the defendant with a list of documents [and file an affidavit verifying such list] [limited to the documents relating to the—

[special damage claimed]

[plaintiff's industrial injury, industrial disablement, or sickness benefit rights]

[period from —— to ——]

[issues raised in paras. —— of the statement of claim and
paras. —— of the defence]
[issues of ——]]
13. The defendant within —— days serve the plaintiff with a
list of documents [and file an affidavit verifying such list] [limited
to documents relating to the—
[period from —— to ——]
[issues raised in paras. —— of the statement of claim
and paras. —— of the defence]
[issues of ——]]
14. There be inspection of documents within —— days of the
service of the lists [filing of the affidavits].
15. The plaintiff have leave to serve upon the defendant the
interrogatories shown in the document served herewith, and that
the defendant answer the interrogatories on affidavit within
—— days.
16. The defendant have leave to serve upon the plaintiff the
interrogatories shown in the document served with the defendant's notice under this summons, and that the plaintiff answer
the interrogatories on affidavit within —— days.
17. The [plaintiff] [defendant] [retain and preserve pending
the trial of the action] [upon —— days' notice give inspection
of the subject matter of the action, to the [defendant] [plaintiff]
and to his legal advisors [and experts].
18. The statements in —— be admissible in evidence at the
trial without calling as a witness the maker of the statements
[and, if a copy of that document certified by —— to be a true
copy is produced, without production of the original document].
19. An affidavit of —— [in the form of the draft affidavit
[served herewith] [with the defendant's notice under this summons]]
[to be served within —— days] be admissible in evidence at the
trial.
20. Evidence of the following fact(s), namely, —— be
received at the trial by statement on oath of information and
belief [by the production of the following documents or entries
in books or copy documents or copy entries in books, namely,
——].
21. It be recorded that the parties [[plaintiff] [defendant]
refuses to] admit for the purposes of this action that [——] [the
truth of the statements in the document served [herewith] [with
the defendant's notice under this summons]].
22. ——, a witness on behalf of the [plaintiff] [defendant]
may, upon —— days' notice, be examined before [one of the

examiners of the court] [a Master] [a special examiner to be agreed upon by the parties or appointed by the Master] and that the said witness need not attend at the trial.

23. A medical report be agreed, if possible, and that, if not, the medical evidence be limited to —— witnesses for each party.

24. A report by [engineers] [surveyors] [expert ——] be agreed if possible, and that, if not, the expert evidence be limited to —— witnesses for each party.

25. A plan of the *locus in quo* other than a sketch plan be receivable in evidence at the trial.

26. Photographs and a plan of the *locus in quo* be agreed, if possible.

27. By consent [the right of appeal be excluded] [any appeal be limited to the Court of Appeal] [any appeal be limited to questions of law only].

28. [*Space for any other directions*]

29. Trial. Place:—   Mode:—
[Estimated length:—   To be set down within
—— days [and to be tried immediately after the action 19—, ——, No. ——].]

30. The costs of this application be costs in the cause.

Dated the —— day of ——, 19—.

To the Defendant(s) and to his (their) Solicitor(s)

This summons was taken out by —— of —— Solicitors for the Plaintiff.

No. 91

SUMMONS FOR DIRECTIONS IN A COMMERCIAL CASE

[Heading as in Precedent No. 87.]

Counsel [If no counsel, insert " None "].

Nature of Action (*e.g.*, " Breach of Contract," *or* " Constructive Total Loss," *or as may be*).

Let all parties concerned attend the Commercial Judge sitting in Court ——, Royal Courts of Justice, Strand, London, on —— day, the —— day of ——, 19—, at —— of the clock in the forenoon on the hearing of an application on the part of the —— for an order for directions, as follows:—

That the action be transferred to the Commercial list [*if the action is proceeding in a district registry add here:* " and be removed from the district registry of —— to London "].

That points of claim be delivered by the plaintiff in [——] days.

That points of defence be delivered by the defendant in [——] days afterwards.

That after defence lists of documents be exchanged between the parties in seven days and inspection be given within three days afterwards.

[*Further directions as necessary. See previous precedent.*]

That the venue be the City of London.

That the action be tried with [or without] a [special] jury.

That the date of trial be fixed for ——.

That the costs of this application be costs in the cause.

Dated the —— day of ——, 19—.

This summons was taken out by —— of ——, solicitor for ——.

No. 92

NOTICE OF PAYMENT INTO COURT (ORDER 22, rr. 1, 2)

[Heading as in Precedent No. 87.]

Take notice that—

The defendant [C D] has paid £—— into court.

The said £—— is in satisfaction of [the cause of action] [all the causes of action] in respect of which the plaintiff claims [and after taking into account and satisfying the above-named defendant's cause of action for —— in respect of which he counterclaims].

or

The said £—— is in satisfaction of the following causes of action in respect of which the plaintiff claims, namely, —— [and after taking into account *as above*].

or

Of the said £——, £—— is in satisfaction of the plaintiff's cause[s] of action for —— [and after taking into account *as above*] and £—— is in satisfaction of the plaintiff's cause[s] of action for —— [and after taking into account *as above*].

Dated the —— day of ——, 19—.

P Q

Solicitor for the defendant C D

To Mr. X Y, the plaintiff's solicitor.

[and to Mr. R S, Solicitor for the defendant E F.]

[*To be filled in by the Bank of England*]

Received the above sum of —— pounds and —— pence into court in this action.

£——.

Dated the —— day of ——, 19—.

No. 93
ACCEPTANCE OF SUM PAID INTO COURT (ORDER 22, r. 3)
[Heading as in Precedent No. 87.]

Take notice that the plaintiff accepts the sum of £—— paid in by the defendant [C D] in satisfaction of the cause[s] of action in respect of which it was paid in and in respect of which the plaintiff claims [against the defendant] [and abandons the other causes of action in respect of which he claims in this action].
Dated the —— day of ——, 19—.

X Y,
Plaintiff's Solicitor.

To Mr. P Q, Solicitor for the defendant C D, and to Mr. R S, Solicitor for the defendant E F.

No. 94
THIRD PARTY NOTICE CLAIMING INDEMNITY OR CONTRIBUTION *
(ORDER 16)

In the High Court of Justice,   1970.—B.—No.——.
Division.
[——————— DISTRICT REGISTRY]

Between A B	. . . .	Plaintiff,
and		
C D	. . . .	Defendant,
and		
T P	. . . .	Third party.

THIRD PARTY NOTICE

[Issued pursuant to the Order of [Master] —— dated the —— day of ——, 1966.]

To T P of —— in the —— of ——.

Take notice that this action has been brought by the plaintiff against the defendant. In it the plaintiff claims against the defendant [*here state the nature of the plaintiff's claim*] as appears from the writ of summons [*or* originating summons] a copy whereof is served herewith [together with a copy of the statement of claim]

The defendant claims against you [*here state the nature of the claim against the third party as for instance* to be indemnified against the plaintiff's claim and the costs of this action or contribution to the extent of [*one-half*] of the plaintiff's claim *or* the

---

* And see R.S.C. Appendix A, Form No. 21, for Third Party Notice where there is a question or issue to be determined.

520

following relief or remedy namely —— on the grounds that (*state the grounds of the claim*)].

And take notice that if you wish to dispute the plaintiff's claim against the defendant, or the defendant's claim against you, an appearance must be entered on your behalf within 8 days after the service of this notice on you, inclusive of the day of service, otherwise you will be deemed to admit the plaintiff's claim against the defendant and the defendant's claim against you and your liability to [indemnify the defendant *or* to contribute to the extent claimed *or* to —— *stating the relief or remedy sought*] and will be bound by any judgment or decision given in the action, and the judgment may be enforced against you in accordance with Order 16 of the Rules of the Supreme Court 1965.

Dated the —— day of ——, 1970.

(Signed) ——

Solicitors for the Defendant.

DIRECTIONS FOR ENTERING APPEARANCE

The person served with this notice may enter an appearance in person or by a solicitor either (1) by handing in the appropriate forms, duly completed, at the [*here insert the name and address of the appropriate office specified in O.* 16, *r.* 3 (3)], or (2) by sending them to that office by post. The appropriate forms may be obtained by sending a postal order for 1s. (5p) with an addressed envelope, foolscap size, to the [Controller of Stamps, Royal Courts of Justice, Strand, London, W.C.2] [District Registrar, High Court of Justice, ——].

VIII.—DISCOVERY OF DOCUMENTS

No. 95

LIST OF DOCUMENTS

(Order 24, r. 5)

[Heading as in Precedent No. 87.]

DEFENDANT'S LIST OF DOCUMENTS

The following is a list of the documents relating to the matters in question in this action which are or have been in the possession, custody or power of the above-named defendant C D and which is served in compliance with Order 24, rule 2.

1. The defendant has in his possession, custody or power the documents relating to the matters in question in this action, enumerated in schedule 1 hereto.

2. The defendant objects to produce the documents enumerated in part 2 of the said schedule 1 on the following grounds:—

(a) the analysis and report on the ground that it was made and came into existence for the use of his solicitor in this action, and as evidence and information as to how evidence could be obtained, and otherwise for the use of the said solicitor to enable him to conduct the defence in this action, and to advise the defendant in reference thereto. It was prepared by the direction of the said solicitor for his own use in anticipation of litigation and in the conduct of this action, and for no other purpose whatever [20];

(b) twenty-eight documents tied up in the bundle marked A and all the other documents on the ground that they are privileged. They consist of professional communications of a confidential character made to the defendant by his legal advisers for the purpose of giving him legal advice, cases for the opinion of counsel, opinions of counsel, and instructions to counsel prepared and given in anticipation of and during the progress of this action, letters and copies of letters passing between the defendant and his solicitor and third persons either in anticipation of or during this action, and drafts and memoranda made by the defendant's counsel and solicitor for the purpose of this action.

3. The defendant has had, but has not now, in his possession, custody or power the documents relating to the matters in question in this action enumerated in schedule 2 hereto.

4. The documents in the said schedule 2 were last in the defendant's possession, custody or power in the month of October 1963, when he forwarded the document numbered 38 to the plaintiff and the remainder to the Editor of *The —— Observer*.

5. Neither the defendant, nor his solicitor nor any other person on his behalf, has now, or ever had, in his possession, custody or power any document of any description whatever relating to any matter in question in this action, other than the documents enumerated in schedules 1 and 2 hereto.[21]

SCHEDULE 1

PART 1

ORIGINALS

1. Letter from plaintiff to defendant, dated January 21, 1968.
2. Letter from plaintiff's solicitor to defendant, dated June 6, 1968.

---

[20] This was held sufficient in *Collins* v. *London General Omnibus Co.* (1893) 63 L.J.Q.B. 428.

[21] As a general rule, this clause, when verified by affidavit, should be conclusive against a party seeking further discovery; but see *British Association, etc., Ltd.* v. *Nettlefold* [1912] A.C. 709 (*ante*, p. 239).

3. Letter from plaintiff to defendant, dated October 6, 1968.
4. *The —— Observer*; issue for October 13, 1968.

COPIES

5. Letter from defendant to plaintiff, dated October 4, 1968.
6. Inventory and valuation made by John Smith, on October 30, 1968.
7.
8.

PART 2

9. An analysis and report made by Professor —— on or about November 23, 1968, and forwarded by him to the defendant's solicitor on November 24, 1968, for his use in this action.
10-37. Documents numbered 10 to 37 inclusive which are tied up in a bundle marked A being letters, drafts and memoranda. Cases for the opinion of counsel, opinions of counsel and instructions to counsel prepared and given in anticipation of and during the progress of this action.

SCHEDULE 2

38. Letter written and sent by the defendant to the plaintiff on October 4, 1968.
39. Copy of same.
40. Copy of reply of the plaintiff to that letter dated October 6, 1968.
41. Letter written and sent by the defendant to the Editor of *The —— Observer* on October 8, 1968, with the two copies just mentioned, all three of which were inserted by the editor in the issue of that paper for October 13, 1968.

Dated the 17th day of March, 1971.

NOTICE TO INSPECT

Take notice that the documents in the above list, other than those listed in part 2 of schedule 1, [and schedule 2] may be inspected at the office of the solicitor for the above-named defendant at 1 Clement's Inn, Strand, in the County of Middlesex, on the 24th day of March, 1971, between the hours of 9 a.m. and 5 p.m.

To the defendant C D and his solicitor.
Served the 18th day of March, 1971, by W A S of Park Dene, Ilsworth, in the County of Barton, solicitor for the defendant.

No. 96

AFFIDAVIT VERIFYING LIST OF DOCUMENTS

(Order 24, r. 5)

[Heading as in Precedent No. 87.]
I, the above-named defendant C D, make oath and say as follows:—

523

1. The statements made by me in paragraphs 1, 3 and 4 of the list of documents now produced and shown to me marked " — " are true.
2. The statements of fact made by me in paragraph 2 of the said list are true.
3. The statements made by me in paragraph 5 of the said list are true to the best of my knowledge, information and belief.

Sworn, etc.

This affidavit is filed on behalf of the defendant.

IX.—INTERROGATORIES

No. 97

INTERROGATORIES IN AN ACTION FOR DILAPIDATIONS

1. Look at the particulars which the plaintiff has served in this action of the defects of repair which he alleges now exist on the demised premises, and state as to each defect therein alleged whether you admit or deny that it now exists. Do you allege that any and which of such defects existed at the date of the demise of the said premises to you?

2. Is not Mr. A sanitary inspector for the borough of T? Did he not visit and inspect the demised premises, and when? Did he not report thereon? Did he not deliver to you a copy of his report on February 27, 19—, or on some other and what day? Is not every statement of fact contained in that report true? If nay, specify every statement therein contained of which you dispute the accuracy, and state what you allege were the true facts in that behalf.

No. 98

INTERROGATORIES IN AN ACTION FOR GOODS SOLD AND DELIVERED TO A FARMER

1. Is not Mr. J. B. Falding your farm bailiff? Is he not your agent for the management of —— Farm? Is he not authorised to purchase goods, and to order work and labour to be done when the same are necessary for the said farm? If nay, state what his authority and position are.

2. Were not all or some, and which, of the goods mentioned in the particulars delivered herein ordered of the plaintiffs by the said J. B. Falding in the month of September, 19—, or at some

other and what date? If nay, were they not ordered on your behalf by some other and what person?

3. Were not the said goods delivered at the said farm? If nay, state which of the said goods you say were not delivered there. Have you not seen all the said goods, or some and which of them, on your said farm? Have not all the said goods, or some and which of them, been used and consumed on the said farm? If nay, state to the best of your knowledge, information and belief, where each of the said goods now is.

4. Are not the prices charged by the plaintiffs for the said goods fair and reasonable? If nay, state which of the said prices you allege to be exorbitant. Specify in each case what sum you would deem a proper and reasonable price.

5. Do you allege that any price was agreed for any and which of the said goods? Which of the prices charged by the plaintiffs do you allege to be in excess of the agreed price? If any, state precisely what price was agreed for each item, and when and where and between whom such agreement was made, and whether verbally or in writing. If verbally, state the substance of it; if in writing, identify the document.

No. 99

INTERROGATORIES SETTING UP THAT THE GOODS WERE SUPPLIED
TO DEFENDANT AS AGENT ONLY FOR OTHERS

1. Were not the goods, the subject-matter of this action, bought of you by X, Y, and Z, or some one or more and which of them? Were not the said goods supplied by you entirely for their use and benefit, and not at all for the use and benefit of the defendant?

2. Were not the said goods supplied for use in or upon certain brick-making works at Swindon? Who was then the owner of the said works, and who was then the occupier? Were you not then aware that the defendant was neither owner nor occupier of the said brick-making works?

3. Were you not requested to deliver the said goods at the said brick-making works by the said X, Y, and Z, or some one or more and which of them, or by some one, and by whom, for the use and on the account of some and which of them? If nay, who gave you the said orders, and who requested you to supply the said goods, and when?

4. If you say the defendant gave the said orders and made the said request, did he not then expressly tell you that he was

the servant or agent of the said X, Y, and Z, or some one or more of them, and that he was acting in that capacity in giving the said orders and making the said request, and not otherwise? If nay, did he not tell you that he was not acting on his own behalf, but as an agent for some principal?

5. Did you not know, at the time you received the said orders, that the defendant was then the servant or agent of the said X, Y, and Z, or some one or more of them? Did you not know that he was not then acting in his own behalf, but on behalf of some principal?

6. Did you not charge the price of the said goods to the said X, Y, and Z, or to some one or more and which of them? Did you not give them, or some one or more and which of them, credit for the same?

7. Have you not applied to the said X, Y, and Z, or to some one or more and which of them, for payment for the same? Did you not prove against the estate of X for the amount of your claim in this action? Did you not attend and vote at a meeting of his creditors held on July 2, 19—, or some other and what day?

8. Did not the said Y give you a bill of exchange for £60, or some other and what amount, as part payment for the said goods for which you are now suing the defendant? Did not the said Z give you a bill of exchange for the full amount which you now claim from the defendant? Did you not accept the same in full satisfaction and discharge of your present claim? If nay, what was the consideration therefor?

No. 100

INTERROGATORIES IN AN ACTION BROUGHT AGAINST THE EDITOR OF A NEWSPAPER WHO HAS PUBLISHED AN ANONYMOUS LETTER SIGNED " A RATEPAYER "

1. On what day did you receive the letter signed " A Ratepayer," which is the subject of this action? How long was it after the receipt of the said letter that you published the same in your paper?

2. Was the said letter sent to you anonymously? Or was there anything, and what, sent with the said letter to show you who wrote it, or from whom it came?

3. Who delivered the said letter at your office? Who received it? Did you yourself see the person who brought it? If nay, who did? How long had the said letter been in your office when you first saw it?

4. Was the said letter delivered at your premises in any envelope or wrapper? Was it still in such envelope or wrapper when you first saw it? If nay, who had opened such envelope or wrapper? Where is such envelope or wrapper now? How was it addressed? What has become of it, and when did you last see it?

5. Was the said letter sent to you by hand, by rail, by post, and which, or how otherwise? Were there any other and what documents or papers with it? If yea, identify the same and state where the same now are, and what has become of each of them. From what place did the said letter come? Was there any and what postmark on it?

6. Was the said letter accompanied by any request from any and what person that you would insert it in your paper? Were you ever asked to print the said letter? If yea, state when and by whom, and, if such request was in writing, identify the document. Did you consent or refuse to print it? What reply did you make to such request, if any, and when and to whom, and whether verbally or in writing? If verbally, state what you said. If in writing, identify the document.

7.[23] Did you know from whom the said letter had come when you first saw it? Do you know now? If yea, state from whom and how and why you knew this. Is it the fact that you published the said letter without knowing who sent it? Did you recognise the handwriting of the said letter or of the address? If yea, state to the best of your knowledge who the writer is and whether he is, or has at any and what time been, a ratepayer of St. Saviour's parish.

8. Did you before you published the said letter make any and what inquiries as to whether the writer thereof was a ratepayer of St. Saviour's parish, or as to who the writer was? If yea, what was the nature and result of such inquiries, and when and how and of whom did you make them?

9.[24] *Did you, before you published the said letter, make any and what inquiries or investigation as to the truth of the statements contained in it, or any and which of them? Have you ever made any such inquiries or investigation? If so, when and with*

---

[23] This interrogatory is only admissible where the identity of such writer is a fact material to some issue raised in the case. (*Hennessy* v. *Wright* (*No.* 2) (1888) 24 Q.B.D. 445 n.; *Gibson* v. *Evans* (1889) 23 Q.B.D. 384.)

[24] Interrogatory 9 used to be common form where the defendant had pleaded fair comment or privilege. It is now prohibited in such cases by Order 82, r. 6, following the recommendations of the Porter Committee on the Law of Defamation.

what result? What steps, if any, did you take to ascertain whether the words were true?

10. Did you at the time that you published the said letter believe that the allegations contained therein, or some and which of them, were true?

11. Was the said letter, after you received it, altered in any way before insertion in your paper? If yea, specify exactly each such alteration, and state by whom it was made.

X.—ADVICE ON EVIDENCE

No. 101

ADVICE ON EVIDENCE IN AN ACTION BY THE ASSIGNEE OF
A DEBT

This is an action brought by the plaintiffs as assignees of a debt against the executor of the deceased debtor. The defendant refuses to admit either the assignment or notice of the assignment. This is, I presume, only a formal traverse. But, as both facts are denied, they must be strictly proved; otherwise the present plaintiffs cannot recover. It is unnecessary to give the defendant notice to admit the indenture of July 15, 1963, or our copy of the notice of assignment, as these documents are included in our list of documents; but he should be given notice to produce the original notice of assignment served on him on August 2, 1963, as he has not included this in his list. If, as seems likely, he intends to deny service of this notice, it must be proved by the person who posted it, if it went by post, or who served it on him personally, if it was served by hand, unless on the adjourned hearing of the summons for directions the master will make an order under Order 38, r. 3, that evidence of posting or service may be given in some other manner—*e.g.* by production of the posting book or by an affidavit. This he should be asked to do. The execution of the indenture of July 15, 1963, can be proved either by the assignor, Curtis, himself, or by anybody acquainted with his handwriting.

Then comes the main question in the action:—Did the testator at the date of his death owe Curtis £189, the amount assigned by Curtis to the plaintiffs [*etc., deal with the facts and difficulties of this part of the case*]. Curtis himself will be our best witness as to the original transaction; he will prove that the testator ordered him to do the work. He can refresh his memory by referring to the pocket-book in which he took down the testator's order and this pocket-book must be available at court.

The plaintiff's witnesses then will be: Mr. Curtis and his partner, the foreman, etc. [*name them all*]. Mr. B. must be served with a *subpoena duces tecum* to attend with a copy of his letter to the testator and the original reply. Who is " C. Morgan " who witnessed the testator's signature to his last letter to Curtis? He should be in attendance at the trial, and a proof of his evidence should be taken and inserted in the brief, as it may be necessary to call him if any attack is made on the genuineness of the letter.

The following documents must be available at the hearing:—[*name them*].

Instructing solicitors should have a copy made of all the more important documents and of the correspondence for the use of the judge. The letters must be in strict order of date and each on a separate page. The bundle and the page numbering should be agreed with the defendant's solicitors.

No. 102

COMMENCEMENT OF AN ADVICE ON EVIDENCE IN AN ACTION FOR FRAUDULENT MISREPRESENTATION

In this case the onus of proving all the issues lies on the plaintiff; but the defendant must be prepared with evidence to rebut any prima facie case which the plaintiff may establish.

The plaintiff cannot succeed, unless he prove:—

1. That the defendant, or some agent of his duly authorised in that behalf, made representations to the plaintiff as to some existing fact;

2. That those representations were intended to induce the plaintiff to purchase the defendant's brewery and to enter into the agreement of November 12, 1968;

3. That such representations were false in fact;

4. That they were false to the knowledge of the defendant or of his authorised agent, or were made recklessly, without caring whether they were true or false;

5. That such representations induced the plaintiff to buy the defendant's brewery and to enter into the said agreement;

6. That the plaintiff has thereby suffered damage. . . .

No. 103

ADVICE ON EVIDENCE IN AN ACTION OF SLANDER

The burden lies on the plaintiff to establish that the defendant spoke the words complained of, and also to prove the special damage alleged. If Messrs. X and Y give the evidence set out in their proofs, and are not shaken in cross-examination, the plaintiff will succeed in making out a prima facie case.

It will then be for the defendant, if he can, to prove one or other of the two defences which he has pleaded—privilege and truth. In my opinion the occasion was not privileged. But, even if it was, in this case the words complained of relate solely to matters which are within the defendant's own knowledge. He must therefore have known, when he spoke, whether what he said was true or false. He could not have honestly believed his statement to be true, unless it was in fact true. In other words, the defence of privilege merges in the justification.

The main dispute at the trial must, therefore, be as to the truth of the defendant's statement. Now, one portion of what he said *is* true, *viz.*, that the plaintiff did receive the cheque. And a falsehood that is partly true is always the most difficult to meet. The plaintiff must go into the box: he should be our first witness. He must explain to the jury all the circumstances which led him to interfere in this matter.

In particular, the plaintiff must explain why [*here deal with the difficulties seriatim*]. Can the plaintiff's story be corroborated by anyone? Has he any document with which to refresh his memory? Has the defendant made any admission or half admission which helps?

*   *   *   *   *

Our witnesses, then, will be [*name them*].

Have in court the following documents [*specify them*].

Give notice to the defendant to produce [*name any special documents not included in his list*].

XI.—JUDGMENT

No. 104

JUDGMENT AFTER TRIAL BEFORE JUDGE WITHOUT JURY

(Order 42, r. 1)

[Heading as in Precedent No. 87.]

Dated and entered the —— day of ——, 19—.

This action having been tried before the Honourable Mr. Justice —— without a jury, at the Royal Courts of Justice [*or as may be*], and the said Mr. Justice —— having on the —— day of —— 19— ordered that judgment as hereinafter provided be entered for the plaintiff [*or* defendant] [and directed that execution be stayed for the period and on the terms hereinafter provided].

It is adjudged that the defendant do pay the plaintiff £—— and his costs of action to be taxed [*or* that the plaintiff do pay the defendant his costs of defence to be taxed *or as may be according to the judge's order*].

[It is further adjudged that execution be stayed for —— days and if within that time the —— gives notice of appeal and sets down the appeal, execution be further stayed until the determination of the appeal [*or as may be according to the judge's direction.*]

[The above costs have been taxed and allowed at £—— as appears by a taxing officer's certificate dated the —— day of —— 19—.]

XII.—IN THE COURT OF APPEAL

No. 105

NOTICE OF APPEAL IN AN ACTION FOR MALICIOUS PROSECUTION

In the Court of Appeal   19—B.——No ——
On appeal from the High Court of Justice, Queen's Bench Division.

Between A B   .   .   .   .   Plaintiff
                                and
            C D   .   .   .   .   .   Defendant.

NOTICE OF APPEAL

Take Notice that the Court of Appeal will be moved so soon as counsel can be heard on behalf of the defendant

On appeal from [the whole of] [25] the judgment herein of the Honourable Mr. Justice —— given at the trial of this action [with a jury] on the —— day of ——, 19—, whereby it was adjudged that the defendant do pay to the plaintiff £—— and his costs of action to be taxed

For an order that [the verdict of the jury and] the said judgment be set aside and that judgment be entered for the defendant with costs and that the plaintiff do pay to the defendant the costs of this appeal to be taxed

Or, in the alternative,

For an order that [the verdict of the jury and] the said judgment be set aside and that a new trial be had between the parties and that the costs of the action be reserved to the judge upon the new trial

[25] If part only is complained of, substitute " so much of . . . as adjudged that . . . '"

thereof and that the plaintiff do pay to the defendant the costs of this appeal to be taxed.

And further Take Notice that the grounds of this appeal are:—

1. That there was no evidence fit to be submitted to the jury upon the plaintiff's case.
2. That the verdict was against the weight of evidence.
3. That the judge misdirected the jury—
    (a) in not directing them that the action could not be maintained without evidence of malice and that there was no such evidence;
    (b) in not sufficiently explaining to them that the burden lay upon the plaintiff of proving that the defendant acted maliciously;
    (c) in leaving to them the question whether there was or was not an absence of reasonable and probable cause.
4. That the damages were excessive.

And further Take Notice that the defendant proposes to apply to set down this appeal in the Queen's Bench Division Final and New Trial List.

Dated the —— day of —— 19—.

(Signature) ———————————
(Address) ———————————

Defendant's solicitor.

To the plaintiff and
to —— his solicitors.

No notice as to the date on which this appeal will be in the list for hearing will be given; it is the duty of solicitors to keep themselves informed as to the state of the lists. A respondent intending to appear in person should inform the Appeal Clerk, Room 136, Royal Courts of Justice, W.C.2. of that fact and give his address; if he does so, he will be notified by telegram to the address he has given of the date when the appeal is expected to be heard.

INDEX

References in heavy type are to the numbers of the Precedents which appear on pp. **461-532**

Index

Index

Index

Costs—*cont.*

of personal representatives, *see* Personal Representatives.
of petition, 361
of proving documents, 297, 331
of separate causes of action, 30n., 175, 410–411, 413–414
of separate issues, 410–412
of separate statement of claim, 45
of set-off, 225, 227, 408
of several plaintiffs or defendants, 19, 30, 32, 212, 413–415
of shorthand notes, 331, 372, 417
of summons at Chambers, 71, 260, 358, 415–416
of unnecessary copying, 372
of unnecessary traverses, 127, 137, 270
of unsuccessful claim for special damage, 182, 401
on discontinuing action, 174, 252, 399
Order 14 Procedure, 427
party-and-party basis, 403
power to order, 398–399
reserved to trial, 331
security for, 65, 224, 266–267, 373
severance, of, 212
slip rule, 331
solicitor and own client basis, 398, 402, 405–406
special, 331–332, 399
summons for directions, of, 276
taxation of, 226, 256, 398, 399, 402–406
review of, 406
under legal aid, 252, 331, 405, 410
time to deal with, 457
to be paid forthwith, 71, 399, 416
trustees' basis, 358, 399n., 402, 404–405
under County Courts Act, 69–71, 227, 406–409, 412
under Rent Restrictions Acts, 406
under Slander of Women Act, 406
when defence arose after action brought, 210
when discretionary relief claimed, 58, 402,
when money paid into court, 254, 256, 331, 412–413
without order, 399

Counsel,

adjournment for convenience of, 308
advice of, privileged, 242, 317
authority of, to compromise, 327
certificate of, 344
citing authorities, 312
duties of,
after judgment, 330–332
where settlement, etc., likely, 308–309
See also Settlement.
examining witnesses, 311, 313–319

Counsel—*cont.*

indorsement on brief, not privileged, 242
inviting jury to stop case, 313
pleading fraud or justification, 206, 207
signature of, 45, 83, 383
speeches of, 309–313, 325

Counterclaim, 11, 210, 214–216, 219–225, **62, 65**

against assignee, 225
against Crown, 215
against foreign sovereign, 225
against foreigner, 219–220
amendment of, 171
costs of, 225–227
counterclaim to, 223, 234
defence to, 75, 223, 228, 229, 233–234, 431, 436–437, **82–84**
defendant to, 222, 223
distinguished from cross-action, 224–225
distinguished from set-off, 214–216
history of, 214–215, 219
improper or inconvenient, 221–222
interim payment, 55
joinder of issue upon, not permissible, 229
judgment upon, 223, 224–225
must claim some relief, 222
payment into court in satisfaction of, 234
pleading, rules as to, 221–223, 436–437, 442
reply, 229, **82–84**
service of, 223
staying execution where, 67–68
summary judgment on, 425–426
third-party procedure in, 222–223
title of, 223
under Order 14. . . 223

County Court,

appeal from, 363, 367, 368n., 369, 382
exclusion of, by agreement, 271, 366
costs, when action within jurisdiction of, 69–71, 227, 406–409, 412
declaratory judgment in, 187
execution in, 384, 395
transfer to, 69–70, 192, 264–266
costs if opposed, 407
of counterclaim, 224, 265
under Order 14. . . 69–70, 71

"Court Expert," 271–272

Court of Appeal, 1, 13–14, 363–383, **402**

constitution of, 368
costs, 416–418
jurisdiction of, 363–367, 372, 377–378, 380
powers of, 372–373
See also Appeal.

538

Index

Index

Index

Estate, *see* Equity *and* Title.
  costs out of, 349, 403, 404–405
Estoppel, 202–204
  by conduct, 203–204
  by deed, 202–203
  by record, 202, **81**
  title by, 119
Evidence, 453–458
  advice on, 290–305, **101–103**
  affidavit, by, 268, 355, 357, 359, 453–544
  as to character, 303, 316–317
  as to damages, 303–304
  directions as to, 267–270, 301
  documentary, 268, 269, 296–303, 316, 319–323
  examination before trial, 269, 295–296
    costs of, 296, 297, 331
  expert, 269, 271–272, 305, 320, 454
  for foreign tribunal, 295
  fresh, 348, 373, 374, 375–376, 417
  hearsay, 301–302, 455–456
  in commercial cases, 276
  interrogatories as to, 281–284
  material facts, not, 101–105
  may include answers to interrogatories, 278, 311
  medical, 269
  misreception of, 374
  none to go to jury, 325, 374, 375
  not privileged from discovery, 242
  objections to, 313–314
  of convictions, 299, 317, 433
  of entry in banker's book, 269, 300
  of particular fact, mode of giving, 268, 293, 300–301, 454
  on commission, 269
    costs of, 295, 330
  on motion for interlocutory relief, 342
  on originating notice of motion, 359
  on originating summons, 355, 357
  plans, etc., 454
  privileged, *see* Privilege.
  rebutting, 323–324
  recording apparatus, 301
  secondary, 301–303, 322–323, 455–456
  statement, 317
    Civil Evidence Act, 1968, under, 301
    hostile witness, of, 315
    previous proceedings, made in, 456–457
  under letters of request, 269, 295
  verdict against, weight of, 374, 375
  when unnecessary, 58, 293
  See also Affidavit, Copies, Witness *and* Documents.
Examination,
  of judgment debtor, 389, 396
  of witness, at trial, *see* Witness
  before trial, *see* Witness.

Ex parte applications,
  for execution, 387, 389
  for interlocutory relief, 57–59, 185, 340, 342
  for service out of jurisdiction, 38–39
  for substituted service, 52
  generally, 4, 5
  originating notice of motion, by, 359
  originating summons, by, 353, 355
  to join causes of action, 28
Exception,
  to promise, when must be set out in statement of claim, 179
  to rule of law, when must be pleaded, 97
Execution, 13, 384–397
  abroad, 396
  attachment of debts, 389–390
  bankruptcy notice, 384, 390
  Chancery Division, in, 356
  charging order,
    on land, 387–388
    on stocks and shares, 388
  chattels, upon, 385–387, 391, 392
    exempted, 386
  committal, 384, 393–394
  costs of, 385, 390
  county court, in, 384, 395
  Crown, not against, 17
  delivery, writ of, 56, 391–392
  elegit, writ of, abolished, 387
  equitable, 388–389
  fieri facias, writ of, 385–387, 391, 396
  garnishee order, 389–390
  joint tortfeasors, against, 200
  judgment summons, 384, 395–396
  leave to issue, 394–395
  money judgments, 384–390
  partners, against, 389, 394
  possession, writ of, 391
  receiver, 388, 389
  sequestration, writ of, 392–393
  sheriff, duties of, in, 13, 385–386
  stay of,
    at trial, 332, 396–397
    by Court of Appeal, 332, 373, 397
    generally, 396–397
    under Order 14, 68–69, 397
  time for, 394
Executor, *see* Personal Representatives.
Exhibits,
  at trial, 322
  to affidavit, 64
Expert, 269, 271–272, 305, 320, 454

False Imprisonment, 177
  right to trial by jury in action for, 274
Fee, *see* Title.
Fieri Facias, 385–387, 391, 396

542

Index

Firm, *see* Partners.
Fixture List, 273n., 307
Foreign Judgments, 201–202, 299, 396
Foreign Sovereign, 17, 220, 225
Foreigner, *see* Counterclaim *and* Jurisdiction.
Forfeiture,
  by denying landlord's title, 119n.
  relief from, 69
Former Proceedings,
  affecting group in Ch.D., 336, 354
  costs of, unpaid, 201, 272
  defence of, 199–201
    res judicata, 149–150, 201
Fraud, **4, 37, 38, 58, 69, 102**
  action based on, commenced by writ,
    6, 419
  indorsement of writ in, **4**
  appeal where party acquitted of, 378
  as ground for reopening account, 187,
    209
  cross-examination suggesting, 146
  judgment obtained by, 373
  may destroy privilege from discovery,
    242
  particulars of, 112, 123, 206
  pleading, 104, 112, 123, 146, 197, 206,
    209, 230, **37, 38**
  proving, in action on bill of exchange,
    146, 292
  right to trial by jury in action for, 275
Frivolous action, 152, 153–156, 192, 222,
  272
  application, 150

Gaming Acts, 133–134, 188, 198
Garnishee Order, 380, 389–390
  appeal in issue, 364, 370, 382
Goods Sold and Delivered,
  indorsement of writ, **10**
Groups,
  in Chancery Division,
    assignment to, 82, 334–335, 351,
      354, 361
    organisation of, 333–334, 351–352
Guaranty,
  action upon, 128
Guardian *Ad Litem*, 23, 55

Habeas Corpus,
  ad subjiciendum, 1, 382
  ad testificandum, 294
Handwriting,
  proof of, 320

Hire Purchase Action, 60–61
  indorsement of writ in, 43, 60–61, 160
  judgment in default in, 56, 60–61, 228n.
  particulars in, 43, 160
Home Counties Towns, 306n.
House of Lords, 14, 383
Husband and Wife,
  disputes as to property, 6
  staying proceedings between, 372

Illegality,
  court may object to, 198, 379
  must be specially pleaded, 87, 145, 197–
    198
  on face of contract, 198
Indorsement,
  fictitious, 154
  interest, claim for, 46–48
  of writ, 8, 42–49, 83, 175, 420–421
    defective, amendment of, 43, 68,
      168–169, 170, 320
    for account, **20–22**, 48–50
    general, 43, 44, 45, 168, **4–8**
    in action on bond, 189
    in hire-purchase action, 43, 60–61,
      160
    in moneylender's action, 43, 59–60,
      160
    special, 42, 45–46, **9–19**
  on brief, not privileged, 242
  service, of, 52
  striking out, 437
Inducement,
  matters of, 118n., 133, 141, 176
Inevitable accident, pleading, 146, 159
Infant, *See* MINOR
Inferior courts, appeal from, 363, 382
Injunction, **7**
  appeal from grant or refusal, 368
  claim for, 38–39, 57–58, 92, 184–185
  costs where claimed, 58, 404
  interim, 184–185, 340–341
  interlocutory, 184–185, 340–341
Inquiry, 333, 346–348
Insanity,
  pleading, 92
Inspection,
  of documents, 240, 246–249, 267, 301,
    443–448
  of property, 267, 290
Intention,
  pleading, 91, 123
Interest,
  award of, 47–48
  claim for, 46–48
  on bond, 190
  on judgment, 330, 332, 373
Interim payment, 54–55
Interlocutory Judgment, 10, 57, 70, 228

543

Index

Index

Index

Set-off—*cont.*
distinguished from counterclaim, 214–216
distinguished from cross-action, 225
equitable, 67, 217
history of, 214–215, 217
judgment upon, 216, 224n., 225

Setting down,
action for trial, 12, 275, 306–307, 344
in London, 306
afresh, 308
for further consideration, 348–349
appeal, 371–372
point of law, 148, 149–150, 273n.

Settlement,
of action, 23, 251–252, 308–309, 326–327, 343
in defamation actions, 256
when involves minor or patient, 22, 23, 251, 256, 327

Sheriff,
execution by, 13, 385–387
interpleader by, 387

Short Cause, 70, 273, 275

Shorthand Notes, 331, 372, 417

Slander,
action of, defence to, **78, 79, 103**
interrogatories in, 284
mitigating damages in, 101, 207, 282, 303–304
right to trial by jury in, 274
express malice, 229
justification, plea of, 104–105, 124, 164, 207
pleading, 88, **46**
privilege, plea of, 88, 207, 282
publication of, particulars of, 113, 163
statement of claim for, 177
with reference to trade, pleading, 93, 139, 177

Solicitor,
accepting service, 52
action by, for costs, 100, 198, 220
advice privileged, 241–242, 317
duty to inform court,
of settlement, etc., 252, 308–309
issuing writ without authority, 54
name and address,
on writ, 42
negligence of, **42**
signature of, 46, 83

Special Damage,
affecting choice of parties, 21
for continuing cause of action, 330n.
in former proceedings, 200
objection that none alleged, 88, 150
particulars of, 113, 159, 161, 182

Special Damage—*cont.*
pleading, in statement of claim, 161, 182, **41**
costs of, if unsubstantiated, 182

Specific Performance,
as alternative to damages, 186
claim for, 185–186, 334, 336, **54**
summary judgment for, 336

Speeches,
of counsel, order of, 310–311

Speedy Trial, 70, 275

Stamp Objection, 321, 375

Statement of Claim, 11, 43–44, 45–46, 60, 61, 173–191, 436, **23–55**
account stated, 187–189
amendment of, 58, 68, 168, 169, 193, 232, 261, 266, 324
bond, 189–191
claim for relief, 183–187
damages, 181–183
dispensing with, 80–82
equitable relief, 183–184
for declaration of right or title, 186–187
for injunction, 184–185
for specific performance, 185–186
form of, 173–180
in contract, 177–179
in tort, **177**
joinder of causes of action, 175–177
leaping before stile, 95–98
matters of inducement, 118n., 133, 176
modifying writ, 44, 174–175, 183
particulars of, *see* Particulars.
parties, 174–175. *See also* Parties.
receiver, appointment of, 184
replevin, 174, 191
service of, 11, 430
special indorsement is, 45–46
time for, 73

Statute,
construction of, 7
as question at issue, 420
need not be pleaded, 86, 109
particulars prescribed by, 159–160
public, need not be proved, 293
when alters common law, pleading material facts, 97
when regulates common law rights, pleading, 121

Statute of Frauds, 199. *And see references in* Table of Statutes.

Statute of Limitations,
affecting account stated, 187, 188
bar to action, 41, 129
burden of proof under, 292
defeating by amendment or renewal, 16, 52–53, 170
defence of, must be pleaded, 86, 113, 124, 129, 145, 197, 199
under Order 14...67